# McQUAIL'S MEDIA&MASS COMMUNICATION THEORY

Sara Miller McCune founded SAGE Publishing in 1965 to support the dissemination of usable knowledge and educate a global community. SAGE publishes more than 1000 journals and over 800 new books each year, spanning a wide range of subject areas. Our growing selection of library products includes archives, data, case studies and video. SAGE remains majority owned by our founder and after her lifetime will become owned by a charitable trust that secures the company's continued independence.

Los Angeles | London | New Delhi | Singapore | Washington DC | Melbourne

# MCQUAIL'S MEDIA&MASS COMMUNICATION THEORY

## SEVENTH EDITION

## DENIS MCQUAIL & MARK DEUZE

Los Angeles | London | New Delhi
Singapore | Washington DC | Melbourne

Los Angeles | London | New Delhi
Singapore | Washington DC | Melbourne

SAGE Publications Ltd
1 Oliver's Yard
55 City Road
London EC1Y 1SP

SAGE Publications Inc.
2455 Teller Road
Thousand Oaks, California 91320

SAGE Publications India Pvt Ltd
B 1/I 1 Mohan Cooperative Industrial Area
Mathura Road
New Delhi 110 044

SAGE Publications Asia-Pacific Pte Ltd
3 Church Street
#10-04 Samsung Hub
Singapore 049483

Editor: Michael Ainsley
Editorial assistant: Amber Turner-Flanders
Production editor: Imogen Roome
Copyeditor: Sarah Bury
Proofreader: Leigh C. Smithson
Indexer: Adam Pozner
Marketing manager: Susheel Gokarakonda
Cover design: Lisa Harper-Wells
Typeset by: C&M Digitals (P) Ltd, Chennai, India

First edition published 1983
Second edition published 1987
Third edition published 1994
Fourth edition published 2000. Reprinted 2001, 2002,
    2003 and 2005
Fifth edition published in 2005. Reprinted 2006, 2007,
    2008 and 2009
Sixth edition published in 2010. Reprinted 2011, 2012,
    2014, 2015, 2016, 2017, 2018 three times and 2019
This seventh edition published 2020

**Library of Congress Control Number: 2019955634**

**British Library Cataloguing in Publication data**

A catalogue record for this book is available
from the British Library

ISBN 978-1-4739-0250-3
ISBN 978-1-4739-0251-0 (pbk)

# CONTENTS

# PREFACE

Early in 2009, Denis and I had coffee outside a little café in Padua, Italy. We were attending a symposium organized by the *European Journal of Communication* on the consequences of media change. A significant discussion among the participants emerged around the notion of the 'value' of media and mass communication theory and research (see McQuail, 2009). What is our contribution? What story can we, as a field, tell the world? How do we prevent our message being co-opted and colonized by other, older disciplines, such as sociology, psychology, and others? As we chatted, I asked about the new edition of his seminal handbook of the field, and wondered how this book could help structure and give direction to such existential questions. He smiled, and said that the sixth edition would be coming out soon – and that this would be his last one. I immediately felt the weight of this statement – in terms of the formidable role his book has played in shaping and defining the field of mass communication, of the immense impact his work has on articulating what our knowledge contribution is (or could be), and, in a personal sense, the fundamental role this book has played in my career and understanding of what it is that I am doing.

In subsequent years, an idea started brewing. It was perhaps much more of an emotion than an idea: I felt something needed to be done – with the book, with Denis's legacy, with all the students at all the schools and universities around the world who worked their way through *McQuail's Mass Communication Theory* – from 1983 until 2010 and beyond. With the enthusiastic support of Mila Steele at Sage I started developing a proposal for a new, seventh edition of the book. The original plan was pitched in 2013 – it was ridiculously ambitious, based on the expectation that I could somehow find a way to take one or two years off teaching to focus completely on the monumental work that this book would be. Although Denis did his best to support and encourage me over the years that followed, life happened. I moved back to The Netherlands after ten tremendous years working and living in the United States, started a demanding new job at the University of Amsterdam, and reformed the band – Skinflower – that I used to play with back in the 1990s.

Then 2017 came, and the devastating news arrived about Denis's passing, on June 25. I remember meeting Denis at the University of Amsterdam in 1997, when the Amsterdam School of Communications Research (ASCoR) was founded, and I was one of the first PhD students. A fond memory is a session ASCoR organized, where Denis would sit down with the first group of PhD students to give feedback on their proposals. When we met, he laughed heartily and said: 'I just hope you will manage to find the time and money somewhere to do all the things you are planning to do!'

In the following years I had the privilege to work with Piet Bakker to teach *McQuail's Mass Communication Theory* to first-year students in Amsterdam, an experience that subsequently informed my approach and love for teaching such large undergraduate review courses at Münster University, Indiana University, and back at the University of Amsterdam (and this time at the Department of Media Studies).

In short, I always had many reasons to engage with and embrace his 'book of books', personal as well as professional. After his passing, there were no more excuses: the work had to start. Thanks to the continued support and guidance from Mila and Michael Ainsley at Sage, the invaluable help from my friend and colleague Pauline van Romondt Vis in working through the manuscript and making a first assessment of what needed to be done, and the critical reading eye of a small team of dear friends and experts – Peter Neijens, Terry Flew, Kaarle Nordenstreng, Peter Golding, Claes De Vreese, Cristina Archetti, and Sonia Livingstone – who were willing to take a look at chapter drafts, I kept working on the seventh edition throughout 2017, 2018 and 2019, taking breaks to either teach, finish other projects, play music, and grill.

The new edition of *McQuail's Media and Mass Communication Theory* is, first and foremost, a homage to the work and influence of Denis. This is expressed both in keeping true to his structuring of the book (and the field), and by following his narrative through into the world of pervasive, ubiquitous, mobile, social and always-online media we live in today. At the same time, I have taken the liberty to take the first steps in slightly changing things. You will notice that we added 'Media' to the title of the book in order to do justice to the intellectual strides that have been made in media theory, and to signal our intent to bring scholarly traditions of theory and research on media and society from the humanities and social sciences into conversation. In this book you will not find neat separations between these areas of investigation, inspired by both my own background and, more importantly, by consistent calls across the field for more integrated theoretical frameworks, mixed methods and triangulation, in order to do justice to the complexities and nuance of our mass media environment and the mass communication process.

A second intervention has come in the form of the references used to keep the argument moving forward into the twenty-first century. A project that Denis started and I tried to continue as best as I could has been to significantly diversify the range of voices and sources referenced in the narrative of our field. This means less emphasis on scholars from the US and the UK, more intersectional diversity, and also more attention for open access journals and books from around the world.

Given my own background as a scholar of media work, I have tried to sensitize the chapters about production, content and audiences to the changing world of making media. At the same time, we have endeavoured to add more nuance to claims made about audiences of media throughout the book – in large part thanks to the insights and comments of Sonia Livingstone.

In order to keep the narrative moving, I decided to collapse Denis's arguments about the need to be explicit about normative theory into the other chapters of (t)his book. One of the many ways in which he anchored the field has been to make students and scholars alike take responsibility for what they *want* and *expect* of media in society, and the way he articulated normative concerns makes us aware of the idealist, even hopeful assumptions and perspectives that guide our studies in media and mass communication. By integrating the various sections of what used to be a separate chapter on normative theory, I hope to have done justice to what was so important to Denis.

The same goes for the formerly separate discussion of 'social-cultural' media effects, and the influence and effects of media on news, public opinion and political communication. Instead, I followed an approach suggested in various publications by my Amsterdam colleagues Patti Valkenburg and Jochen Peter, by looking at canonical foci of (mass) media effects rather than summarizing and separating various specific theories.

Looking back on the process, I see I spent most time on the Preliminaries (Chapters 1 and 2) and Epilogue (Chapter 18) to explore, investigate and ultimately passionately argue for the continued relevance of conceptualizing 'mass' media and communication, as well as media theory, in an age of big data, algorithmic culture, artificial intelligence, global platform governance, streaming media, and mass self-communication – all of which are processes we cannot adequately understand without the benefit of mass communication and mass media theory.

As I have argued in several instances in this book, what set media and mass communication theory and research as a field apart from other disciplines are two fundamental assumptions about our reality and the world in which we live: first, that media are a pervasive and ubiquitous part of everyday lived experience around the world, and second, that all this mediated communication makes a difference. Although this may seem obvious, most researchers from around the university (and beyond) treat these core observations either as an afterthought, a sideshow, or a problematic aspect influencing whatever phenomenon they are investigating. We assume that any phenomenon 'in the world' is also, to some extent, mediated. This is not an argument for a technological-determinist or media-centric way of thinking. It is a simple recognition of what is at the heart of our field and of the way we make sense of the twin processes of globalization and individualization, of the post-national constellation as much as its nationalist-populist counterpart, of the ongoing automation and technological appropriation of everything as well as a return to emotions and authenticity as the core values that guide human society, and of the truly global challenges we face: climate change, humanitarian crises, and sustainable development. All of these issues to a significant extent are understood through media, in terms of media, and require a response in part via media. I sincerely hope this updated edition contributes to inspiring old and new generations of students and scholars of media and mass communication. It certainly has been a tremendous honour for me to be part of this work.

Mark Deuze – Amsterdam and Seaton Sluice, 2020.

# HOW TO USE THIS BOOK

The text serves two purposes and can therefore be best used on two levels. First, it is a narrative – a 'grand narrative' even – of the field of media and mass communication theory and research: where it comes from, what traditions of thinking and studying have shaped it, how we come to observe and interpret media and the mass communication process today. Secondly, it can be used by readers as a resource for learning about a particular topic. There are several ways this can be approached. The table of contents provides an initial orientation, or map, to the book, and each chapter begins with a list of the main headings to help you orient yourself. The subject index at the end of the book includes all key words and topics and can also be used for an initial search. Each chapter contains boxes to help you explore the background to, relevance of and research on the themes and theories discussed in the book. At the end of every chapter you will find a curated list of further readings, intended to provide a guide to follow-up study of the particular issues outlined in that particular chapter. The extensive Reference list at the end of the book can be seen as your initial library, from where you can chart your own path through the literature.

# PART 1
## PRELIMINARIES

# 1

## INTRODUCTION TO THE BOOK

# OUR OBJECT OF STUDY

At the heart of media and mass communication in society lies the realization that there is nothing 'outside' media anymore. In some way, all the experiences in everyday life are connected to media. Some of this refers to the professionally produced media at our disposal: from the smartphone to the television, from newspapers and books to motion pictures, digital games and recorded music. Yet much of the media that play such a profound role in people's daily lives consist of data, content and experiences that are produced by us – via logins and uploads to social media and platforms, voluntary (and involuntary) participation in all kinds of digital surveillance mechanisms, and by making our own media. Although 'mass' audiences for the most part may be a thing of the past, the potentials of 'mass' media and 'mass' communication are still part of almost all our engagements with media.

Sonia Livingstone (2011: 1472) considers that the significance of media and mass communication theory lies in the fact that 'everything is mediated—from childhood to war, politics to sex, science to religion—and more so than ever before […] Nothing remains unmediated'. Her analysis of the human condition in the context of a media environment that is both ubiquitous and pervasive underscores our decision to expand the coverage in this book from mass communication theory to include the media more explicitly than before. As Livingstone suggests, (mass) communication has always been constitutive of society, fundamental to all human action. However, what is particular about the last few decades is how a whole range of rapidly expanding media technologies have amplified and accelerated human communication on an unprecedented scale. In the process of this 'mediation of everything' (Livingstone, 2009), media have permeated not only the world but also, and perhaps more importantly, the ways in which we (as humans) have access to, act in, and make sense of that world. The study of media and mass communication can therefore be seen as contributing to understanding their role in 'the ordering of social life more generally' (Couldry, 2004: 128).

Media and mass communication theory is crucial to consider, given the fundamental challenges of our time regarding big data, the role of algorithms and the dissolution of individuals into endless databanks, samples, targets and markets, the 'Internet of things' and a renewed scholarly as well as public interest in the political economy of digital culture, and the many efforts in the field (especially since the 2000s) to rethink and re-theorize the profound role media and mass communication play in everyday life, in politics, and in the construction of reality itself (Couldry and Hepp, 2016). The (continued and growing) significance of media and mass communication theory and research in part follows from its status as a 'practical discipline' (Craig, 2018), in that the field primarily concerns itself with what people and social institutions actually do with media – and is generally committed to answering societal communication problems with research of real-world relevance. Additionally, Jensen (2019: 144) considers the role media and communication research play as 'a strategically important (secondary) institution-to-think-with about the performance of media as (primary) institutions-to-think-with'. This is a 'double hermeneutics' typical of the field – as media scholars interpret a reality (such as a media text, a production process or audience behaviour) that has already been interpreted by the senders and receivers of media. In the process, both theory and practice – scholarly analysis and lived reality – (can) change.

The study of media and mass communication follows a few fundamental assumptions (paraphrasing Lang, 2013):

- First, media and mass communication are pervasive and ubiquitous.
- Secondly, media and mass communication act upon (and are acted upon by) people and their social environments.
- Thirdly, media and mass communication change both the environment and the person.
- Fourthly, the primary goals and questions of media and mass communication researchers are to demonstrate the various elements (production – content – reception), roles, influences and effects of media and mass communication, and, if possible, explain how they come about.

The foundational assumptions of the disciplined study of media and mass communication are grounded in a set of basic definitions. Mass communication, first and foremost, refers to messages transmitted to a large audience via one or more media. Media are the (technological and formally organized) means of transmission of such messages. Media theory considers how these messages mean different things to different people as determined by the different channels used to communicate them. Given the proliferation of media in people's everyday lives, it becomes crucial not only to understand and explain how mediated (mass) communication works, but also to appreciate the role specific media play in bringing about certain meanings and impact.

The term 'mass communication' was coined, along with that of 'mass media', early in the twentieth century to describe what was then a new social phenomenon and a key feature of the emerging modern world that was being built on the foundations of industrialism and democracy. To some extent similar to the early twenty-first century, this was an age of mass migration into cities and across frontiers and also of struggle between forces of change and repression and of conflict. Mass media were born into the context and conflicts of this age of transition and have continued to be deeply implicated in the trends and changes of society and culture, as experienced at the personal level as well as that of society.

The early mass media (newspapers, magazines, phonogram, cinema and radio) developed rapidly to reach formats that are still largely recognizable today, with changes mainly of scale and diversification as well as the addition of television and the Internet in the

MCQUAIL'S MEDIA AND MASS COMMUNICATION THEORY
PRELIMINARIES

twentieth century. What were regarded as the key features of mass communication a century ago are still foremost in our minds today: their capacity to reach large swaths of the population rapidly; the universal fascination they hold; their stimulation of hopes and fears in equal measure; the presumed relation to sources of power in society; the assumption of great impact and influence.

Since the late twentieth century new technologies have been developed and taken up – most notably the Internet and mobile hardware and software – that constitute an alternative network of communication. Mass communication, in the sense of a large-scale, one-way flow of public content, continues unabated, and exists next to different types of content and flow that are also carried on a mass scale online. Next to mass communication there has emerged a new kind of system of information and communication on a global scale: **mass self-communication**. According to Castells (2007: 248), it is mass communication because it reaches potentially a global audience online, and it is simultaneously self-communication 'because it is self-directed in the elaboration and sending of the message, self-selected in the reception of the message, and self-defined in terms of the formation of the communication space'.

Much has been made in the literature about the collapse, convergence and continued significance of mass communication theory. Whatever changes are underway there is no doubting the continuing significance of mass media in contemporary society, in the spheres of politics, culture, everyday social life and economics. In respect of politics, the media provide an arena of debate and a set of channels for making policies, candidates, relevant facts and ideas more widely known as well as providing politicians, corporations and brands, interest groups and agents of government with a means of publicity and influence. Through mass self-communication, the political realm becomes accessible to a variety of actors – both individuals sending and forwarding information, and all kinds of more or less transparent organizations seeking to influence elections and the political process through micro-targeted campaigns online.

In the realm of culture, the media are for most people the main channel of cultural representation and expression, and the primary source of images of social reality and materials for forming and maintaining social identity. At the same time, the media have become a playground (if not a battleground) of representations and symbolic struggles over meaning, as original sources compete with the parody and remix culture of the Web, disinformation spreads faster than fact-checked information can keep up with, and anyone can find confirmation of their personal biases and beliefs online. Everyday social life is strongly patterned by the routines of media use and infused by its contents through the way leisure time is spent, lifestyles are influenced, conversation is given its topics and models of behaviour are offered for all contingencies. Particularly through the widespread use of advanced mobile devices, people today have an instantly accessible and highly personalized world of information, culture and entertainment in the palm of their hand, and at their fingertips. In the process, the media have grown in economic value, with ever larger and more international media corporations dominating the media market, with influence extending through sport, travel, leisure, food and clothing industries, and with interconnections with all information-based economic sectors – especially technology and telecommunications companies.

Our focus on mass communication is not confined to the mass media, but relates to all types and processes of communication that are extensive, public and technically mediated. In contrast with earlier editions of this book, and as we will outline below and in subsequent chapters, it would be an increasingly artificial manoeuvre to distinguish mass communication from other types of communication – especially interpersonal communication. Here the word 'public' not only means open to all receivers and to a recognized set of senders, but also relates to matters of information and culture that are of wide interest and concern in a society, without being addressed to any particular individual. There is no absolute line between what is private and what is public, and a key observation about our current media environment must be that 'It used to take effort to be public. Today, it often takes effort to be private' (boyd, 2010: n.p.). This book is designed to contribute to public scrutiny and understanding of media and mass communication in all its forms, and to provide an overview of ideas and research, guided by the themes and issues summarized below.

## THEMES AND ISSUES IN MEDIA AND MASS COMMUNICATION

The contents of the book are cross-cut by a number of general themes that recur in discussions of the social origins, significance and effects of communication, whether at the personal level or that of a whole society. While acknowledging that many more are possible, and that the different matters cross-cut and overlap in various ways, we identify the main themes as follows:

- *Time*. Communication takes place in time and it matters when it occurs and how long it takes. Communication technology has steadily increased the speed at which a given volume of information can be transmitted from point to point. It also stores information for recovery at a later point in historic time. Mass media content in particular serves as a store of memory for a society and for groups within it, and this can be selectively recovered or lost. The way personal data are recorded, stored and used online is a matter of great public concern, involving individual consumers, policymakers, the legal system and a range of companies and corporations.

- *Place*. Communication is produced in a given location and reflects features of that context. It serves to define a place for its inhabitants and to establish an identity.

It connects places, reducing the distance that separates individuals, countries and cultures. Major trends in mass communication are said to have a delocalizing effect, or to establish a new global 'place', which people may not only recognize as familiar, but at times they may even come to prefer the 'placeless place' of a mediated reality (as can be the case for certain online communities).

- *Power.* Social relationships are structured and driven by power, where the will of one party is imposed on another, whether legitimately or not, or by influence, where the wishes of another are sought out or followed. Communication as such has no power of compulsion but it is an invariable component and a frequent means of the exercise of power, whether effectively or not. Despite the generally voluntary character of attention to (and participation in) mass media, the question of their power over people is never far away, as are related concerns regarding the power of media to bridge social differences as well as reinforce them, and to both combat and enhance existing social inequalities.

*Social reality.* The assumption behind classical theory of media and mass communication is that we inhabit a 'real' world of material circumstances and events that can be known. In this view, the media provide us with reports or reflections of this reality, with varying degrees of accuracy, completeness or dependability. The notion of 'truth' is often applied as a standard to the contents of news and non-fiction, however difficult to define and assess – especially in a time of 'fake news' and the rapid spread of disinformation online. With the rise of the Internet has come a growing body of work that considers the contemporary 'mediation of everything' as collapsing the boundaries between online and offline life, between public and private communication, and between mediated and non-mediated lived experience (introducing a 'mixed' reality).

*Meaning.* A related theme that continually arises concerns the interpretation of the 'message', or content, of mass media. Most theories of mass media depend on some assumption being made about the meaning of what they carry, whether viewed from the point of view of the sender, the receiver or the neutral observer. As noted above, there is no unique source of meaning and no way of saying for certain what is meant, providing an endless potential for dispute and uncertainty.

- *Causation and determinism.* It is in the nature of theory to try to solve questions of cause and effect, whether by proposing some overall explanation that links observations or by directing inquiry to determine whether one factor caused another. Questions of cause arise not only in relation to the consequences of media messages on individuals, but also in relation to historical questions of the rise of media institutions in the first place and the reasons why they have certain typical characteristics of production process, content and appeal. Do the media cause effects in society, or are they themselves more the outcome and reflection of prior and deeper social forces?

- *Mediation.* As an alternative to the idea of cause and effect, we can consider the media to provide occasions, links, channels, arenas and platforms for information and ideas to circulate. By way of the media, meanings are formed and social and cultural forces operate freely according to various logics and with no predictable outcome. The process of mediation inevitably influences or changes the meaning received and there is an increasing tendency for 'reality' to be adapted to the demands of media presentation rather than vice versa.

*Identity*. This refers to both an individual sense of wholeness ('self-identity') and to a shared sense of belonging to a culture, society, place or social grouping ('social identity') and involves many factors, including nationality, language, work, ethnicity, religion, belief, lifestyle, etc. The mass media are associated with many different aspects of self- and social identity formation, maintenance and dissolution. They can drive as well as reflect social change and lead to either more or less integration.

*Cultural difference*. At almost every turn, the study of media-related issues reminds us how much the workings of mass communication and media institutions, despite their apparent similarities across the globe, are affected by differences in culture at the level of individual, subgroup, nation, and so on. The production and use of mass media are cultural practices that can both reinforce and resist the universalizing tendencies of the technologies involved, and of much mass-produced content.

*Governance*. This refers to all the means by which the various media are regulated and controlled by laws, rules, customs and codes, as well as by market management. There is a continuing evolution in these matters in response to changes in technology and society.

When we speak of the issues that will be dealt with in this book, we are referring to more specific matters that are problematic or in dispute in the public arena. They relate to questions on which public opinion often forms, on which governments may be expected to have policies for prevention or improvement, or on which the media themselves might have some responsibility. Not all issues are problematic in the negative sense, but they involve questions of current and future trends that are significant for good or ill. No list of issues can be complete, but the following comprise the main headings that come to mind when studying the literature of the field as represented in this book. They serve as a reminder of the significance of the topic of media in society and the potential relevance of theory to handling such questions. The issues are divided according to the terrain they occupy.

- Relations with politics and the state
  - Political campaigns and propaganda.
  - Citizen participation and democracy.
  - Media role in relation to war and terrorism.
  - Influence on the making of foreign policy.
  - Serving or resisting sources of power.

- Cultural issues
  - Globalization of content and flow.
  - Promoting the quality of cultural life and cultural production.
  - Effects on cultural and social identity.
- Social concerns
  - The definition of reality and mediation of social experience.
  - Links to aggression, crime and violence.
  - Relation to social order and disorder.
  - Promotion of an information and media literate society.
  - The use and quality of leisure time.
  - Social and cultural inequality.
- Normative questions
  - Freedom of speech and expression.
  - Social and cultural inequality: class, ethnicity, gender and sexuality.
  - Media norms, ethics and professionalism.
  - Media accountability and social responsibility.
- Economic concerns
  - Degree of concentration.
  - Commercialization of content.
  - Privacy and surveillance capitalism.
  - Global imperialism and dependency.

## MANNER OF TREATMENT

The book has been written as a continuous narrative, following a certain logic. It begins with a brief history of the different media, followed by a general overview of the main concepts and theories that deal with the relation between media and mass communication on the one hand and (individuals and groups in) society and culture on the other. Subsequently, the sequence of content follows a line from the 'source', in the form of mass media organizations, to the content they produce and disseminate, to reception by audiences and to a range of possible effects. This does seem to imply in advance a view of how we should approach the subject, although that is not the intention.

Because of the wide-ranging character of the issues outlined above and the complexity of many of them, it is only possible to give quite brief accounts. Each chapter begins with an introduction giving an overview of the main topics to be covered. Within chapters, the substance of the book is dealt with in headed sections. The topics are not defined according to the themes and issues just outlined, but they reflect the varying focus of theory and the research that has been carried out to test theories. In general, the reader will find a definition of relevant concepts, an explanation of the topic, a short review of relevant evidence from research and an overall assessment of matters of dispute. Each chapter ends with a brief overview of what has been concluded. Key points are summarized in the text in 'boxes' to provide a focus and to aid recall.

## LIMITATIONS OF COVERAGE AND PERSPECTIVE

Although the book is wide-ranging in its coverage and is intended to have an application to the mass communication phenomenon in general, rather than to any particular country, the viability of this aim is limited in various ways. First, the authors have a location, a nationality, a subjective position and a cultural background that shape their experience, knowledge and outlook. There is much scope for personal judgement and it is impossible to avoid it, even when trying to be fair to the various approaches and positions found in the literature. Secondly, the 'mass communication phenomenon' is itself not independent of the cultural context in which it is observed, despite similarities of technology and tendencies to uniformity of media organizational form and conduct as well as content. Although some histories of the mass media institution consider it more or less exclusively as part of a process of 'modernization' from America and Europe to the rest of the world, there are different histories and the diffusion is far from a one-way or deterministic process. In short, this account of theory has an inevitable 'western' bias. Its body of theory derives to a large extent from institutionally dominant white sources, mainly located in Europe, Australia and North America and written in English, and the research reported to test the ideas is overwhelmingly from the same locations. This does not mean it is invalid for other settings, but it means that conclusions are provisional and that a much greater variety of ideas need to be formulated and tested.

We have endeavoured to include a wider range of voices and to nuance our perspective to suit for regional histories of media and mass communication. At the same time we acknowledge the under-representation of many voices in the scholarly debate, in part due to the uneven way research funding works and gets distributed, and also due to the nature of publication and citation practices in the key scholarly media and communication journals, which continue to privilege established white (Chakravartty, Kuo, Grubbs and McIlwain, 2018) and male (Knobloch-Westerwick, Glynn and Huge, 2013) voices. We are committed to heed the call from the field to disseminate diversity widely (Mayer, Press, Verhoeven and Sterne, 2017), even though we are bound to make numerous mistakes and omissions.

The nature of the relation between media and society depends on circumstances of time and place. As noted above, this book largely deals with mass media and mass communication in modern, 'developed' nation states, mainly elective democracies with free-market (or mixed) economies which are integrated into a wider international set of economic and political relations of exchange, competition and also domination or conflict. It is most probable that mass media are experienced differently in societies with 'non-western' characteristics, especially those that are less individualistic and more communal in character, or less secular and more religious. The differences are not just a matter of more or less economic development, since profound differences of culture and long historical experience are involved. The problem goes deeper than an inevitable element of authorial ethnocentrism, since it also lies in the mainstream scholarly tradition that has its roots in western thought.

Although the aim is to provide as 'objective' an account as possible of theory and evidence, the study of media and mass communication cannot avoid dealing with questions of values and of political and social conflict. All societies have latent or open tensions and contradictions that often extend to the international arena. The media are inevitably involved in these disputed areas as producers and disseminators of meaning about the events and contexts of social life, private as well as public. It follows from these remarks that we cannot expect the study of media and mass communication to provide theoretically neutral, scientifically verified information about the 'effects' or the significance of something that is an immensely complex as well as intersubjective set of processes. For the same reasons, it is often difficult to formulate theories about mass communication in ways that are open to empirical testing, or that escape the conclusion that contextual, situational and environmental aspects have greater explanatory value than broad theories of media influence and effects. At the same time, it is clear to all who study media and mass communication that (mediated) communication is 'fundamentally powerful and adaptive' (Lang, 2013: 19). The solution, as many in the field would argue, is to consider theories in context, to develop research designs that are sensitive to individual, communal and cultural specificities, and overall to integrate perspectives and methods from the humanities and the social sciences.

Not surprisingly, the field of media theory is also characterized by widely divergent perspectives. A difference of approach between progressive and conservative tendencies can sometimes be discerned. Progressive theory is, for instance, critical of the power exercised by media in the hands of a dominant class in society (such as the state or large global corporations), while conservative theorists point to the 'liberal bias' of the news or the damage done by media to traditional values, and the perceived power of media to corrupt the minds, attitudes and behaviours of the young. There has also been a difference between a critical and a more applied approach to theory that does not necessarily correspond to the political axis. Lazarsfeld (1941) referred to this as a critical versus administrative orientation. Critical theory seeks to expose underlying problems and faults of media practice and to relate them in a comprehensive way to social issues, guided by certain values. Applied theory aims to harness an understanding of communication processes to solving practical problems of using media and mass communication more effectively (Windahl, Signitzer and Olson, 2007). Given the intense nature of competition for students and research funding that the contemporary university faces, some suggest that this has privileged more applied, 'administrative' and quantitative types of research. On the other hand, we would like to signal an overall expansion of media and mass communication scholarship in all theoretical and empirical directions, as for example expressed in the growing output of research in countless journals, volumes, conferences, and other venues for the dissemination of academic work.

We can also distinguish two other axes of theoretical variation. One of these separates 'media-centric' from 'society-centric' (or 'socio-centric') approaches. The former approach attributes much more autonomy and influence to communication and concentrates on the media's own sphere of activity, as well as its materiality. Media-centric theory sees mass media as a primary mover in social change, driven forward by irresistible developments in information and communication technology. It also pays much more attention to the specific content of media and the potential consequences of the different kinds of media (print, audiovisual, mobile, etc.). Furthermore, media theory emphasizes the importance of the material properties of media, highlighting how elements of particular media as artefacts and infrastructures shape and influence people's experience.

Socio-centric theory mainly views the media as a reflection of larger social, political and economic forces. Theory for the media is a special application of broader social theory (Golding and Murdock, 1978). Theory about (mass) media from a socio-centric perspective uses social theory to historicize trends and developments regarding media and mass communication, emphasizing continuity over novelty. The role of (critical) social theory also puts media and mass communication in a broader context of social transformation and change, encouraging 'reflexivity about the position from which researchers research' when looking beyond media to find answers about what counts as good, just and desirable about the role and performance of media in society (Hesmondhalgh and Toynbee, 2008: 10). Whether or not society is driven by the media, it is certainly true that media and mass communication theory itself is so driven, tending to respond to each major shift of media technology and structure.

The second, horizontal, dividing line is between those theorists whose interest (and conviction) lies in the realm of culture, representation and ideas and those who emphasize material forces and factors. This divide corresponds approximately with certain other dimensions: humanistic versus social scientific; qualitative versus quantitative; and subjective versus objective. While these differences partly reflect the necessity for some division of labour in a wide territory and the multidisciplinary character of media study, they also often involve competing and contradictory ideas about how to pose questions, conduct research and provide explanations. These two alternatives are independent of each other, and between them they identify four different perspectives on media and society (Figure 1.1).

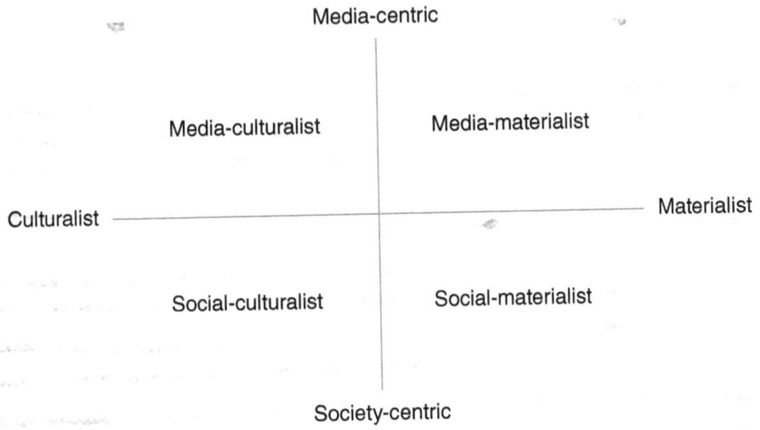

```
                    Media-centric
                         │
                         │
    Media-culturalist    │    Media-materialist
                         │
                         │
Culturalist ─────────────┼───────────────── Materialist
                         │
                         │
    Social-culturalist   │    Social-materialist
                         │
                         │
                    Society-centric
```

Figure 1.1  Dimensions and types of media theory. Four main approaches can be identified according to two dimensions: media-centric versus society-centric and culturalist versus materialist

The four types of perspective can be summarized as follows:

1.  *A media-culturalist perspective.* This approach takes the perspective of the audience member in relation to some specific genre or example of media culture (e.g. reality TV, violent video games or online social networking) and explores the subjective meaning of the experience in a given context.

2.  *A media-materialist approach.* Research in this tradition emphasizes the shaping of media content and therefore of potential effects, by the nature of the medium in respect of the technology and the social relations of reception and production that are implicated by this. It also attributes influence to the specific organizational contexts and dynamics or production.

3.  *A social-culturalist perspective.* Essentially, this view subordinates media and media experience to deeper and more powerful forces affecting society and individuals. Social and cultural issues also predominate over political and economic ones.

4.  *A social-materialist perspective.* This approach has usually been linked to a critical view of media ownership and control, which ultimately are held to shape the dominant ideology transmitted or endorsed by the media. Calls for more stringent regulation of technology and telecommunications industries – such as platforms and social media – tend to be informed by this perspective.

While these differences of approach can still be discerned in the structure of the field of enquiry, there has been a trend towards convergence between the different schools, and integration regarding theory and methods. Even so, the various topics and approaches outlined involve important differences of philosophy and theory that need careful articulation.

# DIFFERENT KINDS OF THEORY

If theory is understood not only as a system of law-like propositions, but as any systematic set of ideas that can help make sense of a phenomenon, guide action or predict a consequence, then one can distinguish at least five kinds of theory which are relevant to media and mass communication. These can be described as: social scientific, cultural, normative, operational and everyday theory.

Social scientific theory offers general statements about the nature, working and effects of media and mass communication, based on systematic and objective observation of media and other relevant sources, which can in turn be put to the test and validated or rejected by similar methods. There is a large body of such theory and it provides much of the content of this book. It covers a very wide spectrum, from broad questions of society to detailed aspects of individual information sending and receiving. Some social scientific theory is concerned with understanding what is going on, some with developing a critique and some with practical applications in processes of public information or persuasion.

Cultural theory is much more diverse in character. In some forms it is evaluative, seeking to differentiate cultural artefacts according to some criteria of quality. Sometimes its goal is almost the opposite, seeking to challenge hierarchical classification as irrelevant to the true significance of culture. Different spheres of cultural production have generated their own corpus of cultural theory, sometimes along aesthetic or ethical lines, sometimes with a social-critical purpose. This applies to film, literature, television, graphic art, digital media, and any other media forms. While cultural theory demands clear argument and articulation, coherence and consistency, its core component is often itself imaginative and ideational. It resists the demand for testing or validation by observation, confident in its solid grounding in (normative) philosophy. Nevertheless, there are opportunities for combined cultural and scientific approaches, and the many problematics of the media call for both.

A third kind of theory can be described as normative since it is concerned with examining or prescribing how media ought to operate if certain social and public values are to be observed or attained. Such theory usually stems from the broader social philosophy or ideology of a given society. This kind of theory is important because it plays a part in shaping and legitimating media institutions and has considerable influence on the expectations concerning the media that are held by other social institutions and by the media's own audiences. A good deal of research into mass media has been stimulated by the wish to apply norms of social and cultural performance. A society's normative theories concerning its own media are usually to be found in laws, regulations, media policies, codes of ethics and the substance of public debate. While normative media theory is not in itself 'objective', it can be studied by the 'objective' methods of the social sciences (McQuail, 1992), just as much as its insistence on public values as the primary drivers of debate and policy regarding the (converging) media, technology and telecommunications sector can be effectively grounded in humanistic enquiry (Van Dijck, Poell and De Waal, 2018).

A fourth kind of knowledge about the media can best be described as praxeological or operational theory since it refers to the practical ideas assembled and applied by both professional and amateur media practitioners in the conduct of their own media work (Deuze, 2007; Hesmondhalgh and Baker, 2011; Duffy, 2017). Similar bodies of accumulated practical wisdom are to be found in most organizational and professional settings. In the case of the media, operational theory serves to guide solutions to fundamental tasks, including how to select news, please audiences, self-promote, design effective advertising, keep within the limits of what platforms and regulations permit, and relate effectively to sources and society. At some points it may overlap with normative theory, for instance in matters of journalistic ethics and codes of conduct, the call for greater social responsibility in public relations practice, and the game industry's accountability for its representation of women. Such knowledge merits the name of theory because it is usually patterned and persistent, even if rarely codified, and it is influential in respect of behaviour. It comes to light in the study of communicators and their organizations (for comprehensive reviews see Banks, Taylor and Gill, 2013; Paterson, Lee, Saha and Zoellner, 2016; Deuze and Prenger, 2019). Katz (1977) compared the role of the researcher in relation to media production to that of the theorist of music or philosopher of science who can see regularities which a musician or scientist does not even need to be aware of.

Finally, there is everyday or common-sense theory of media use, referring to the knowledge we all have from our own personal experience with media. This enables us to make sense of what is going on, and allows us to fit a range of media into our daily lives, to understand how its content is intended to be 'read' as well as how we like to use it, to know what the differences are between different media and media genres, and much more. On the basis of such 'theory' is grounded the ability to make consistent choices, develop patterns of taste, and construct lifestyles and identities as media users, producers and consumers. It also supports the ability to make critical judgements. All this, in turn, shapes what the media actually offer and sets both directions and limits to media influence. For instance, it enables us to distinguish between 'reality' and 'fiction', to 'read between the lines' or to see through the persuasive aims and techniques of advertising and other kinds of propaganda, to resist many of the potentially harmful impulses that the media are said to provoke. The working of common-sense theory can be seen in the norms for use of media which many people recognize and follow. The social definitions that mass media acquire are not established by media theorists or legislators, or even professional media makers themselves, but emerge from the experience and practices of people as media users over time. Such common sense can often be discredited based on scholarly research — a particular example would be the widespread public, political and scientific concern about 'screen time' for children and teenagers, even though the research generally offers 'little evidence for substantial negative associations between digital-screen engagement and adolescent well-being' (Orben and Przybylski, 2019: 1). Common sense, assumptions based on lived experience, and all the biases and prejudices that come with such 'praxeological' theorizing are part and parcel of doing research about media and mass communication, both frustrating and enriching the field.

## THE STUDY OF MEDIA AND MASS COMMUNICATION

Media and mass communication are topics among many for the humanities and social sciences, and only one part of a wider field of enquiry into human communication, including interpersonal and computer-mediated communication (CMC). Under the name 'communication science' (within the social sciences) and 'media studies' (in the humanities), the field has traditionally focused on media ownership and control, content and audiences (Miller, 2009). In the social sciences, the study of media and mass communication has been defined by Berger and Chaffee (1987: 17) as a field that 'seeks to understand the production, processing and effects of symbol and signal systems by developing testable theories, containing lawful generalizations, that explain phenomena associated with production, processing and effects'. While this was presented as a 'mainstream' definition to apply to most research, in fact it is very much biased towards one model of enquiry – the 'objective' quantitative study of communicative behaviour and its causes and effects. It tends to be less successful in dealing with the nature of 'symbol systems' and signification, the process by which meaning is given and made in varied social and cultural contexts, and often bypasses the 'why' of communication. It also leaves something to be considered when it comes to questions of power and normative notions of what can be considered to be 'good' and 'just' when it comes to the relations between people, media and society. Likewise, the more qualitative and interpretative traditions more often found within the umbrella term 'media studies' are generally not based on replicable methods for the gathering and analysis of data – also because scholars in this tradition tend to advocate greater awareness of the influence of the researcher in the research encounter. However, in recent decades the oftentimes sharp divisions between these two fields have blurred (Brannen, 2005), leading to students being trained in both quantitative and qualitative methods, to the rise of more multimethod and triangulated approaches to research, as well as to the emergence of 'hybrid' fields such as digital methods (Rogers, 2013) and digital humanities (Terras, Nyhan and Vanhoutte, 2013).

Difficulties in defining the field have also arisen because of developments of technology, which have blurred the line between public and private communication and between mass, interpersonal and computer-mediated communication. It is now impossible to find any single agreed definition of a science or study of communication, for a number of circumstantial reasons, but most fundamentally because there has never been an agreed definition of the central concept of 'communication' (while such uniform definitions for media have become equally complicated given the often digital, convergent and always-on properties of contemporary media). The term can refer to very diverse things, especially the act or process of information transmission; the giving or making of meaning; the sharing of information, ideas, impressions or emotions; the process of reception, perception and response; the exertion of influence; any form of interaction. To complicate matters further, communication can be either intentional or involuntary and the variety of potential channels and content is unlimited.

No 'science of communication' or 'study of media' can be independent and self-sufficient, given the origins of the study of media and (mass) communication in many disciplines and the wide-ranging nature of the issues that arise, including matters of economics, law, politics and ethics as well as culture. The study of communication has to be interdisciplinary and must adopt varied approaches and methods (see McQuail, 2003b). The range of theory, methods and (operational) definitions in the field of media and mass communication research is neither coherent nor consensual. Like any other academic field or discipline, communication science and media studies comprise a wide-ranging, heterogeneous and not necessarily consistent body of work. Given the 'diversity and creative chaos' (Calhoun, 2011: 1482) or rather 'extraordinary pluralism' (Fuchs and Qui, 2018: 220) in the field, our book does not aim to provide an overarching, all-encompassing theory of media and mass communication that would neatly 'tie the room together' (paraphrasing the character Jeffrey Lebowski in the 1998 movie *The Big Lebowski*). Instead, following Livingstone (2011), we highlight the ways in which the various parts that make up our field are connected, in the process identifying where the expertise and specific knowledges and arguments of the discipline lie. On the other hand, we do suggest that the field of media and mass communication theory has its own 'grand narrative' (Lyotard, [1979]1984), providing connections between the various themes, issues and approaches that are brought into conversation with each other in this book. We will return to this meta-narrative in the concluding chapter, but it is safe to say that it is grounded in a convergence of the concepts and categories we have traditionally used to study the seemingly stable processes of production, distribution and reception of media and mass communication, which in turn necessitates an interdisciplinary integration of theories and methods.

A useful way of locating the topic of media and mass communication in a wider field of communication enquiry is according to the different levels of social organization at which communication takes place. According to this criterion, mass communication can then be seen as one of several society-wide communication processes, at the apex of a pyramidal distribution of other communication networks according to this criterion (Figure 1.2). A communication network refers to any set of interconnected points (persons or places) that enable the transmission and exchange of information between them. Mass communication is a network that connects very many receivers to one source, while recognizing how the ongoing digitalization and convergence of media can serve to conflate mass communication with other networks of communication – simply with a click or a swipe.

At each descending level of the pyramid indicated there is an increasing number of cases to be found, and each level presents its own particular set of problems for research and theorizing. In modern society there will often be one large public communication network, usually depending on the mass media, which can reach and involve all citizens to varying degrees, although the media system is also itself often fragmented according to regional and other social or demographic factors.

Mass media are not the only possible basis for an effective communication network that extends throughout a society. Alternative (non-mass media) technologies for supporting society-wide networks do also exist (especially the network of physical transportation, the telecommunications infrastructure and the postal system), but these usually lack the society-wide social elements and public roles which mass communication has. In the past (and in some places still today), society-wide public networks were provided by the church or state or by political organizations, based on shared beliefs and usually a hierarchical chain of contact. This extended from the 'top' to the 'base' and employed diverse means of communication – from broadcast channels to newspapers, via dedicated online communities and government-controlled telecommunications providers – ranging from formal publications all the way to personal contacts.

Alternative communication networks can be activated under unusual circumstances to replace mass media, for instance in the case of a natural disaster, major accident or outbreak of war, or another emergency. In the past, direct word of mouth was the only possibility, while today mobile telephones and the Internet can be effectively employed for interconnecting a large population. In fact, the original motive for designing the Internet in the USA (through both joint and separate efforts of academics and the military) in the 1970s was precisely to provide an alternative communication system in the event of a nuclear attack.

At a level below that of the whole society, there are several different kinds of communication network. One type duplicates the social relations of larger society at the level of region, city or town and may have a corresponding media system of its own (local press, radio, etc.). Another is represented by the company, work organization or profession, which may not have a single location but is usually very integrated within its own organizational boundaries, within which much communication flow takes place. A third type is that represented by the 'institution' – for instance, that of government, or education, or justice, or religion, or social security. The activities of a social institution are always diverse and also require correlation and much communication, following patterned routes and forms. The networks involved in this case are limited to achieving certain limited ends (e.g. education, maintaining order, circulating economic information, etc.) and they are not open to participation by all.

Below this level, there are even more and more varied types of communication network, based on some shared feature of daily life: an environment (such as a neighbourhood), an interest (such as music), a need (such as the care of small children) or an activity (such as sport). At this level, the key questions concern attachment and identity, co-operation and norm formation. At the intragroup (e.g. family) and interpersonal levels, attention has usually been given to forms of conversation and patterns of interaction, influence, affiliation (degrees of attachment) and normative control. At the intrapersonal level, communication research concentrates on the processing of information (e.g. attention, perception, attitude formation, comprehension, recall and learning), the giving of meaning and possible effects (e.g. on knowledge, opinion, self-identity and attitude).

This seemingly neat pattern has been complicated by the growing 'globalization' of social life, in which media and mass communication play an important part, mainly regarding their role in offering a window on (and a way for universal comparison of) news, information and culture from all over the world into the comforts of our homes (and, in the case of mobile media, our hands). This introduces a yet higher level of communication and exchange to consider – that of crossing and even ignoring national frontiers, in relation to an increasing range of activities (economic, political, scientific, publicity, sport, lifestyle, entertainment, etc.). Organizations and institutions are less confined within national frontiers, and individuals can also satisfy communication needs outside their own society and their immediate social environments. The once strong correspondence between patterns of personal social interaction in shared space and time on the one hand, and systems of communication on the other, have been much weakened, and our cultural and informational choices have become much wider – which of course does not mean people are all making use of this.

This is one reason why notions of 'networked communication' (Cardoso, 2008) governing a 'network society' (Castells, 1996; Van Dijk, 2005), and a 'networked self' in the context of media (Papacharissi, 2010, 2018a, 2018b, 2018c, 2018d), have taken hold, suggesting that the logic of networks – grounded in the rapid rise of new information technologies and spurred on by the decline of nation states and other traditional forms of institutional organization in society – has become the most important causal power in explaining how people experience, participate and make sense of themselves and the world. Such developments also mean that networks are to an increasing degree not confined to any one 'level' of society or communication, as implied by Figure 1.2. New hybrid (both public and private, both individual and collective) means of communication allow networks to form more easily without the usual 'cement' of shared space or personal acquaintance.

In the past, it was possible to match a particular communication technology approximately with a given 'level' of social organization as described, with television at the highest level, the press and radio at the regional or city level, internal systems, telephone and mail at the institutional level, and so forth. Advances in communication technology and their widespread adoption mean that this is no longer possible. The Internet, for instance, supports communication at virtually all levels – and as it moves gradually into all other channels and applications, it potentially transforms every level of communication into any other level. It also sustains chains or networks that connect the social 'top' with the 'base' and are vertical (in both directions) or diagonal, not just horizontal. For instance, a political social media account can provide access to political leaders and elites as well as to citizens at the grass-roots level, allowing a wide range of patterns of flow. The society-wide communicative function of the 'traditional' core mass media of newspapers, television and radio has not greatly changed or disappeared, but their near monopoly of public communication increasingly runs parallel to the power of a variety of networks and platforms to publish and circulate information with great impact.

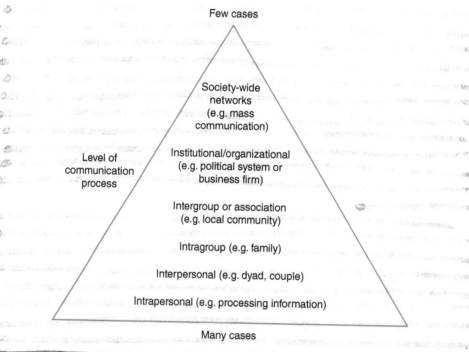

Figure 1.2   The pyramid of communication networks: mass communication is one among several processes of social communication

Despite the complexity of modern society and the contemporary media environment, each level indicates a range of similar questions for communication theory and research. These are posed in Box 1.1.

MCQUAIL'S MEDIA AND MASS COMMUNICATION THEORY
PRELIMINARIES

## TRADITIONS OF ANALYSIS: STRUCTURAL, BEHAVIOURAL AND CULTURAL

While the questions raised at different levels are similar in very general terms, in practice very different concepts are involved, and the reality of communication differs greatly from level to level. For instance, a conversation between two family members takes place according to different 'rules' from those governing a news broadcast to a large audience, a television quiz show or a chain of command in a work organization. For this reason, among others, the scholarly pursuit of media and (mass) communication has, necessarily, to be constructed from several different bodies of theory and evidence, drawn from several disciplines and academic traditions (especially sociology and psychology in the earlier days, but now also economics, history and literary and film studies and more besides), as well as unique approaches developed from within. What cut across all of this are three main alternative approaches to what we are primarily interested in when we study media and mass communication: the structural, the behavioural and the cultural.

The *structural* approach derives mainly from sociology, history, politics, law and economics. Its starting point is 'socio-centric' rather than 'media-centric' (as shown in Figure 1.1), and its primary object of attention is likely to be media systems and organizations and their relationship to the wider society. In so far as questions of media content arise, the focus is likely to be on the effect of social structure and media systems on the patterns and circulation of news, (dis-)information and entertainment. This includes, for instance, the influence of micro-targeted advertising on the outcome of elections, or the role of news management and PR in government policy and business performance. The fundamental dynamics of media phenomena are located in the exercise and abuse of power, in the economy and the socially organized application of technology. The structural approach to media analysis is more linked to the needs of media policy formation, of articulating media with public values, and concerns over human (and equal) rights in a digital context.

The *behavioural* approach has its principal roots in psychology and social psychology but it also has a sociological variant. In general, the primary object of interest is individual human behaviour, especially in matters to do with choosing, processing and responding to communication messages over time. Mass media use is generally treated as a form of motivated (yet also automatic and reflexive) action that has a certain function or use for the individual and also some objective consequences. Psychological approaches are more likely to use experimental methods of research based on individual subjects. The sociological variant focuses on the behaviour of members of socially defined populations and favours the multivariate analysis of representative survey data collected in natural conditions. Individuals are classified according to relevant variables of social position, disposition and behaviour, and the variables can be statistically manipulated. In the study of organizations, (participant) observation is commonly adopted. This approach is often found in relation to the study of persuasion, propaganda and advertising. Communication is primarily understood in the sense of transmission.

The *cultural* approach has its roots in the humanities, in anthropology and in linguistics. While very broad in potential, it has been mainly applied to questions of power, meaning, language and discourse, to the minutiae of particular contexts and experiences. The study of media is part of a wider field of cultural studies. It is more likely to be 'media-centric' (although this is an object of intense debate), sensitive to differences between media and settings of media transmission and reception, most interested in the in-depth understanding of particular contents and situations. Its methods favour the qualitative and in-depth analysis of social and human signifying practices and the analysis and interpretation of 'texts' (which can be the content of media, but also their materiality, the way people make sense of them, and the formulaic, protocol-based and routinized nature of the media production process). The cultural approach draws on a much wider range of theory, including feminist, philosophical, semiotic, psychoanalytic, film and literary theories.

It is important to note that these three traditions, much like the different types of theory and perspectives discussed earlier, have as much overlap as they can be considered to be distinct. It is our contention that a full understanding of media and mass communication in society needs insights from all these traditions, and may particularly benefit from integrated approaches.

# THE STRUCTURE OF THE BOOK

The contents are divided into eighteen chapters, grouped according to eight headings. The first substantive part, 'Preliminaries', articulates the need for an overview of media and mass communication theory in the context of the profound changes and transformations in information and communication technologies in the decade since the previous edition of our book was published. It offers a brief history of the key mass media, articulating media specificity with regard to regulation and control, affordances and adoption. This overview concludes with an appreciation of the various ways in which these different media (and related industry sectors) are converging, and how this impacts our understanding of the role media and mass communication play. The second part, 'Theories', provides a grounding in the most basic and also the most general ideas about media and mass communication, with particular reference to the many relations that exist between media and social and cultural life. It starts with a brief historical review of the rise of mass media and follows with an explanation of the richly diverse ways of studying and theorizing mass media and society. The differences stem from varying perspectives on the media, the diversity of topics addressed, and the different ways of defining the issues and problems depending on the values of the observer. There is not a single set of methods specific to the study of media and mass communication, and it can be argued that the field is becoming increasingly diverse when it comes to approaches to research and theory.

There are different kinds of theory, ranging from strictly scientific (and therefore grounded in empirical research) to normative and everyday theories that people refer to when discussing media among each other. Most basically, a theory is a general proposition, itself based on observation and logical argument, that states the relationship between observed phenomena and seeks either to explain, critique or to predict the relationship, in so far as this is possible. The main purpose of theory is to make sense of an observed reality and guide the collection and evaluation of evidence. A concept is a core term in a theory that summarizes an important aspect of the problem under study and can be used in collecting and interpreting evidence. It requires careful definition. When making sense of some aspect of the dynamic process in media and mass communication, it sometimes helps to use a model to represent the phenomenon under investigation. A model is a selective representation of a phenomenon in verbal or diagrammatic form. It can also describe the relationship between elements in a process – for example, how the process develops over time, where different concepts or actors are located in the process, and how power flows across the process.

The 'Theories' part deals separately with 'society' and 'culture', although the separation is artificial since one cannot exist without the other. But by convention, 'society' refers primarily to social relationships within and across social institutions of all kinds, ranging from those of power and authority (government) to friendship and family relations as well as all material aspects of life. 'Culture' refers to ideas, beliefs, identity and symbolic expression of all kinds, including language, visuals, art, information and entertainment, plus customs and rituals. There are two other components. One relates to the norms and values that apply to the conduct of media organizations. Here theory deals with what media ought to be doing or not doing, rather than simply with why they do what they do. Not surprisingly, there are divergent views on this matter, especially given the strong claims that media make to freedom from regulation and control in the name of free speech and artistic expression and the strong public feelings that also exist about their responsibilities. Normative discussions about the role of media as a social institution are further complicated by the fact that many new and powerful companies have entered the media system – most notably telecommunication providers, platforms (such as Facebook and Google), and other so-called 'Net native' companies that increasingly offer media products and services (consider, for example, Apple, Amazon and Netflix) while insisting they are not media companies in order to prevent falling under the same regulatory regime as broadcast organizations and publishers.

A second component of the 'Theories' section deals with the consequences of media change for theory. Given the ongoing digitalization and convergence of all sectors of the telecommunications, information and media industries, the issue faced is whether such constant transformations require a new and different theory from that applying to 'mass communication' and whether mass communication is in decline. The approach in this book is that 'old' and 'new' media are not as distinct as they seem to be, and that processes of mass communication, interpersonal communication and mass self-communication exist side by side (and often overlap). Media and mass communication research can therefore benefit from classical theories as well as articulate what is different, innovative and possibly new.

The third part, entitled 'Structures', deals with three main topics. First, it deals with the overall media system and the way it is typically organized at a national as well as an international level. The central concept is that of a media 'institution', which applies to media both as a branch of industry subject to economic laws, and as a social institution meeting needs in society and subject to some requirements of law and regulation, guided in some degree by public policy. The media are unusual in being a business 'invested with a public interest' and yet free, for the most part, from any positive obligations (the exception being public broadcasting in most countries). We will consider developments of media (de-)concentration, digitization, and the increasingly global structure of the media industry.

The second topic dealt with is a detailed enquiry into the normative expectations from media on the part of the public, government and audiences, with particular references to the principles and standards of their performance. What are the standards that should apply, how can media performance be assessed, and by what means can the media be made accountable? Thirdly, this part looks at the growing phenomenon of global media and the 'world system' of media that has its origins both in the new computer-based technologies and online modes of production, transmission and (providing) connection and in larger globalizing trends of society.

Part 4, headed 'Organizations', focuses on the locus of media production, whether a firm or a department within a larger firm, or local, regional and global production networks of firms and media professionals, and deals with the numerous influences that shape the production process and the entire product cycle of media. These include pressures and demands from outside the boundaries of the organization, the requirements of routine 'mass production' of news and culture, and the personal and professional tendencies of the 'mass communicators'. There are several theories and models that seek to explain observed regularities in the process of the selection and internal shaping of 'content' before it is transmitted. The most pressing issues in these fields of research are the increased integration of various businesses and modes of production in media and mass communication industries, and the growing role the audience plays in the production process.

The 'Content' part (Part 5) is divided into two chapters, the first of which deals primarily with approaches to, and methods for, the analysis of content. Aside from the simple description of media output according to internally given labels, it is not at all easy to describe content in a more illuminating manner, since there is no agreement on where the 'true meaning' is to be found, as between its producers, its recipients and the text of the 'message' itself. Secondly, theory and evidence are assembled to account for some of the observed regularities in content, with particular reference to the news genre, and to the emergence of new storytelling traditions and formats that seek to engage audiences across multiple media channels, devices and platforms.

In Part 6, 'Audiences', the 'audience' refers to all the many sets of people using media. These are the targets of mass media messages or those who engage in some kind of mediated self-communication. Without the audience there would be no media and mass communication, and it plays a dynamic role in shaping the flow and effects of media. Audience analysis has numerous tasks and can be carried out for many different purposes. It is far more than audience 'measurement' on behalf of the media industry and it has evolved along several theoretically distinct paths. Audience theory deals not only with the 'why' of media use, but also with its determinants and correlates in social and cultural life. Media 'use' has become so intertwined with other activities that we can no longer treat it in isolation from other factors of our experience, nor can we appreciate it solely in 'individual' terms. A key issue to be considered is the evolution of media beyond the stage of mass communication, making a concept based on the image of 'just' a recipient of media inadequate.

Questions of media 'Effects' (Part 7) stand at the start and at the conclusion of the book and are at the centre of social and cultural concern about mass media. They continue to give rise to different theories and much disagreement. Alternative paths towards the goal of assessing effects are outlined. Differences of type of effect are explained, especially the differences between intended and unintended effect and between short-term impact on individuals, groups and communities and longer-term influence on culture and society. The main areas of media effects theory and research still tend to focus, on the one hand, on the potentially harmful social and cultural effects of the most popular forms of content, especially those that involve representations of violence, and on the other hand, on media influence on public knowledge and opinion. Given the contemporary context of a profoundly mediated lifeworld, theorizing media influence and effects faces unique challenges. As Neuman (2016) outlines, there are more sources of authoritative knowledge to choose from, more ways in which people and companies can disseminate and influence public opinion, and more ways of reinforcing beliefs by ignoring unwanted information and remaining within niches of ideological seclusion.

Additionally, it has become crucial to not just consider the reception effects of mediated messages (on people and institutions), but in an age of mass self-communication one also has to appreciate the 'self-effects' of creating or sending messages for the purpose of communicating to others (Valkenburg, 2017). In fact, a review of the emerging research in this area suggests that self-effects may be stronger than reception effects, and that self-effects may reinforce reception effects. As Patti Valkenburg concludes, these and other developments call for integrative research that crosses different communication subdisciplines. This book correspondingly ends with Part 8, an 'Epilogue', discussing possible futures of media and mass communication theory as its themes and issues increasingly feature in the research questions of disciplines across the university.

## CONCLUSION

This chapter has been intended to provide a brief sketch of the overall field of enquiry within which the humanistic and social scientific study of media and mass communication is located. It should be clear that the boundaries around the various topics are not clearly fixed, but change according to shifts of technology and society. Nevertheless, there is a distinct community of scholarship that shares a set of concerns, concepts and tools of analysis that will be explored in the chapters that follow.

## FURTHER READING

Aouragh, M. and Chakravartty, P. (2016) 'Infrastructures of empire: towards a critical geopolitics of media and information studies', *Media, Culture & Society*, 38(4): 559–575.

Lang, A. (2013) 'Discipline in crisis? The shifting paradigm of mass communication research', *Communication Theory*, 23: 10–24.

Livingstone, S. (2011) 'If everything is mediated, what is distinctive about the field of communication?', *International Journal of Communication*, 5: 1472–1475.

Silverstone, R. (1999) *Why Study the Media?* London: Sage.

Wasserman, H. (2018) 'Power, meaning and geopolitics: ethics as an entry point for global communication studies', *Journal of Communication*, 68: 441–451.

# 2

# THE RISE, DECLINE AND RETURN OF MASS MEDIA

The aim of this chapter is to set out the approximate sequence of development of the present-day set of mass media. It is also to indicate major turning points and to tell briefly something of the circumstances of time and place in which different media acquired their public definitions in the sense of their institutional establishment as technologies and industries of mass appeal and production, perceived utility for audiences, and their role in society. These definitions have tended to form early in the history of any given medium and to have been subsequently adapted in the light of newer media and changed conditions. This is a continuing process. The chapter concludes with some reflections about the continued significance of mass media and mass communication in the context of ubiquitous digital, converging, and always online devices and processes.

## FROM BEGINNINGS TO MASS MEDIA

In the opening chapter we distinguished between a *process* of mass communication and the actual *media* that make it possible. The occurrence of human communication over time and at a distance is much older than the mass media now in use. This process was integral to the organization of early societies, which persisted for long periods and extended over large areas. Even the element of large-scale (mass) dissemination of ideas was present at an early point in time, in the propagation of political and religious awareness and obligations. The first mass media as a vehicle for disseminating culture and transmitting messages from a ruling elite to the people and vice versa have been labelled as 'oramedia' in an African context (Ugboajah, 1986). **Oramedia** consist of various forms of indigenous media, including opera, music, dance, drama, poetry and folktales. Similarly, the production of poetry has historically been a key source of mass communication in the Arab world – in particular for state propaganda and religious decrees (Armbrust, 2012). It is important to note that some of the earliest theories of media and mass communication – and in particular those outside the western world – were developed to account for the various ways in which social groups, local communities and indigenous storytelling traditions resisted, subverted or provided a significant alternative to mass communication processes and mass-mediated messages. Next to Ugboajah's concept of oramedia, Luiz Beltrão (1971) developed a theory of '**folkcommunication**' in the 1960s, articulating a process of interpersonal and group forms of cultural expression (mainly identified among marginalized groups and lower classes) existing independently of those by mass and industrialized forms of communication, often developing in contestation of such mass media, and at times being incorporated by the media industry (Woitowicz and Gadini, 2018). The emergence and existence of mass media always exists next to already established mass communication traditions, and develop in conjunction with such forms of expression.

The earliest forms of mass media were printed. Printed mass media got their start in China in approximately 600 BC, as the forerunner of today's newspaper was printed as a daily gazette of government proclamations and edicts – followed some 500 years later by a similar printed version in ancient Rome. By the early Middle Ages, the church in Europe had elaborate and effective means in place to ensure transmission to everyone without exception. This could be called mass communication, although it was largely independent of any 'media' in the contemporary sense, aside from the sacred texts. When independent media arrived in the form of printing, authorities of church and state across all continents reacted with alarm at the potential loss of control that this represented and at the opportunities that opened up for disseminating new and deviant ideas. In much of the Asia-Pacific region this led to tight control over media and direct **censorship** – a practice more or less invented in China with publication ordinances forbidding certain types of private printing decreed as far back as 835 AD (Green, 2003: 3). Other regions of the world share similar histories of tight state, religious or military control over the (earliest types of) mass media, either through direct ownership or censorship. In Europe, the bitter propaganda struggles of the religious wars during the sixteenth century are evidence enough of the power attributed to mass media. It was a historical moment when a technology for mass communication – the printing press – irrevocably acquired a particular social and cultural definition.

In telling the history of mass media, we deal with four main elements that are of significance in the wider life of society. These are:

- certain communicative purposes, needs or uses;
- technologies for communicating publicly to many at a distance;
- forms of social organization that provide the skills and frameworks for organizing production and distribution;
- forms of regulation and control.

These elements do not have a fixed relationship to each other and depend very much on the circumstances of time and place. Sometimes a technology of communication is applied to a pre-existing need or use, as when printing replaced copying by hand or the telegraph replaced the physical transport of key messages. But sometimes a technology, such as film or broadcast radio, precedes any clear evidence of need.

The combinations of the above elements that actually occur are usually dependent both on material factors and on features of the social and cultural climate that are not easy to pin down. Even so, it seems probable that a certain degree of freedom of thought, expression and action has been the single most necessary condition for the development of print and other media, although not for the initial invention. In general, the more open the society, the more inclination there has been to develop communication technology to its fullest potential, especially in the sense of being universally available and widely used.

MCQUAIL'S MEDIA AND MASS COMMUNICATION THEORY
PRELIMINARIES

More closed or repressive regimes either limit development of or set strict boundaries to the ways in which technology can be used. Printing was not introduced into Russia until the early seventeenth century and not in the Ottoman Empire until 1726.

In the following summary of the history and characteristics of different media, a predominantly 'western' perspective and set of values are being applied, since the institutional frameworks of mass media were initially mainly western (European or North American). Even so, cultural differences in part trump technological imperatives and vice versa, and we endeavour to acknowledge key divergences across the various continents (without claiming to offer a complete account for regional diversity). The history of media shows up certain important differences between societies, for instance the large variation in the readership of books and newspapers, the significance of particular media for specific regions, such as community radio in Africa or the genre of **telenovela** throughout Latin America (starting on the radio in the 1930s, then developed for television since the 1950s), or in the rates and pace of Internet diffusion or broadband connectivity.

In the following pages, each of the main mass media is identified in respect of its technology and material form, typical formats and genres, perceived uses and institutional setting.

## PRINT MEDIA: THE BOOK

The history of modern media begins with the printed book – certainly a kind of revolution, yet initially only a technical device for reproducing a range of texts the same as, or similar to, what was already being extensively copied by hand. Only gradually does printing lead to a change in content – more secular, practical and popular works (especially in the vernacular languages) as well as political and religious pamphlets and tracts – which played a part in the transformation of the medieval world. At an early date, laws and proclamations were also printed by royal and other authorities. Thus, there occurred a revolution of society in which printing played an inseparable part (Eisenstein, 1978).

The antecedents of the book lie in classical times when there were numerous established authors and when works of many kinds, both fictional and non-fictional, were copied and circulated for reading or verbal transmission. The printing press greatly accelerated the process of cultural exchange between European, Arab and Eastern ideas, materials and discoveries. However, this was also a cause of great concern of the ruling elites, particularly among religious authorities. In the Arab world book printing became forbidden and, in the West, the culture of the book largely disappeared after the end of the Roman Empire until it was revived by monastic activities, although some key texts were preserved for reasons of learning or religion.

In the early medieval period, the book was not regarded primarily as a means of communication. Rather, it was a store or repository of wisdom, and especially of sacred writings and religious texts that had to be kept in uncorrupted form. Around the central core of religious and philosophical texts there accumulated also works of science and practical information. The main material form of the book at this time was of bound volumes of separate pages within strong covers (known as the *codex*), reflecting the requirements for safe storage and reading aloud from a lectern, plus the demands of travel and transportation. Books were meant both to last and to be disseminated within limited circles. The modern book is a direct descendant of this model, and similar uses are embedded within it. The alternative form of rolls of paper or parchment was discontinued, especially when the printing press replaced writing by hand and required the pressing of flat sheets. This ensured the triumph of the medieval manuscript book format, even when miniaturized.

Another important element of continuity between writing and printing is the library, a store or collection of books (and later on many other media). Libraries, first designed and developed across the Middle East, were initially seen as prestigious status symbols for many empires, and were generally part of temples and palaces, only accessible to a handful of people (often also the only ones who were literate). This remained similar in concept and physical arrangement, at least until the advent of digital libraries. It also reflected and confirmed the idea of a book as a powerful record or permanent work of reference. The character of the library did not change much with printing, although printing stimulated the acquisition of private libraries. The later development of the library has given it some claim to be considered not only as a medium but as a mass medium. It is certainly often organized as a means of public information and was envisaged from the mid-nineteenth century onwards as an important tool of mass enlightenment, coinciding with rapidly rising levels of literacy. It is interesting to note that literacy in these times was considered to be the ability to accurately reproduce a text – not so much the development of a (critical) understanding of it.

The successful application of print technology to the reproduction of texts in place of handwriting was only the first step in the emergence of what we now call a 'media institution' – an organized set of interrelated activities and roles, directed towards goals related to the production and dissemination of media, as governed by a set of rules and procedures. Printing gradually became a new craft and a significant branch of commerce (Febvre and Martin, 1984). Printers were later transformed from tradespeople into publishers, and the two functions gradually became distinct. Equally important was the emergence of the idea and role of the 'author' since earlier manuscript texts were not typically authored by living individuals, or were co-authored by many (often unnamed) authors.

A natural further development was the role of professional author, as early as the late sixteenth century, typically supported by wealthy patrons. Each of these developments reflects the emergence of a market and the transformation of the book into a commodity. Although print runs were small by modern standards, cumulative sales over time could be large. Although printing was invented and pioneered in East Asia, a printing industry developed in the West. There was a thriving book trade across Europe, with much export and import between those countries with printing industries, especially France, England,

MCQUAIL'S MEDIA AND MASS COMMUNICATION THEORY
PRELIMINARIES

the German states and Italy. After European sailors, conquistadors, missionaries, travellers, merchants and functionaries brought European books into Latin America, printing presses were established (starting in Mexico and Peru) in the sixteenth and seventeenth centuries, leading to a market where the role of the Spanish language, thought and culture was both celebrated and contested. Africa followed later, in the nineteenth century, with missionaries acting as intermediaries for the diffusion of Bibles and the early establishment of printing presses (mainly in what is now South Africa).

Many of the basic features of modern media were already embodied in book publishing by the end of the sixteenth century, including the earliest form of a reading public. There was the beginning of **copyright** in the form of privileges granted to printers in respect of certain texts. Various forms of monopoly practice were appearing, which was convenient for the purposes of censorship, but also offered some protection to authors and maintained standards.

The later history of the book is one of steady expansion in volume and range of content and also of struggle for freedom of the press and the rights of authors. Nearly everywhere from the early sixteenth century onwards, government and church authorities applied advance censorship to printed matter (or even claimed outright ownership over printing presses and industries), even if not always with the effectiveness of a modern totalitarian state. A famous early claim for freedom from government licensing was made by the English poet John Milton in a tract published in 1644 (*Areopagitica*). Freedom of the press went hand in hand with democratic political freedoms and the former was only achieved where democracy had triumphed. This close association remains.

The key features of the book both as a medium and as an institution are summarized in Box 2.1. These typical features are interrelated in the idea of the book as it has been known since the sixteenth century. The 'medium' features relate to technology, form and manner of use, and the wider institution of production and distribution.

## 2.1

## The book as a medium and institution: key features

### Medium aspects

- Technology of movable type
- Bound pages, codex form
- Multiple copies
- For personal reading

*(Continued)*

- Individual authorship
- Developing beyond the print form (e-books)

## Institutional aspects

- Commodity form
- Market distribution
- Diversity of content and form
- Claim to freedom of publication
- Subject to some legal limits

# PRINT MEDIA: THE NEWSPAPER

It was almost two hundred years after the invention of printing before what we now recognize as a prototypical newspaper could be distinguished from the handbills, pamphlets and newsletters of the late sixteenth and early seventeenth centuries. Its chief precursor seems, in fact, to have been the letter rather than the book – newsletters circulating via the rudimentary postal service, concerned especially with transmitting news of events relevant to international trade and commerce (Raymond, 1999). It was thus an extension into the public domain of an activity that had long taken place for governmental, diplomatic or commercial as well as for private purposes. The early newspaper was marked by its regular appearance, commercial basis (openly for sale) and public character. Thus, it was used for information, records, advertising, diversion and gossip.

The seventeenth-century commercial newspaper was not identified with any single source but was a compilation made by a printer-publisher. The official variety (as published by Crown or government) showed some of the same characteristics but was also a voice of authority and an instrument of state. The commercial newspaper was the form that has given most shape to the newspaper institution, and its development can be seen in retrospect as a major turning point in communication history – offering first of all a service to its anonymous readers rather than an instrument to propagandists or authorities.

In a sense the newspaper was more of an innovation than the printed book – the invention of a new literary, social and cultural form – even if it might not have been perceived as such at the time. Its distinctiveness, compared with other forms of cultural communication, lies in its orientation to the individual reader and to reality, its utility and disposability, and its secularity and suitability for the needs of a new class: literate town-based business and professional people. Its novelty consisted not in its technology or manner of distribution, but in its functions for a distinct class in a changing and in some cases more liberal social-political climate.

The later history of the newspaper can be told either as a series of struggles, advances and reverses in the cause of liberty, or as a more continuous history of economic and technological progress. The most important phases in press history that enter into the modern definition of the newspaper are described in the following paragraphs. While separate national histories differ too much to tell a single story, the elements mentioned, often intermingling and interacting, have all played a part in the development of the press institution. The principal features of the newspaper are summarized in Box 2.2.

---

**2.2**

## The newspaper as medium and institution: key features

### Medium aspects

- Technology: print (and Internet)
- Periodicity: regular and frequent appearance
- Topicality (and currency) of contents and reference
- Individual or group reading

### Institutional aspects

- Urban, secular audience
- Relative freedom, but self-censored
- In public domain
- Commodity form
- Commercial basis

---

From its early days, the newspaper was an extension of either the state (through ownership, censorship or self-regulation) or religious authority, yet also could become an actual or potential adversary of established power, especially in its own self-perception. Potent images in press history refer to violence done to printers, editors and journalists around the world. The struggle for freedom to publish, often within a broader struggle for freedom and human and communication rights, is emphasized in journalism's own mythology. The part played by alternative media (for example in Latin America) and underground presses under foreign occupation or dictatorial rule (across Europe and the Indian subcontinent) has also been celebrated. Established authority has often confirmed this self-perception of the press by finding it irritating and inconvenient (although also often malleable and, in the last resort, very vulnerable to power). However, early newspapers did not generally seek to offend authorities and were oftentimes produced on their behalf. Then, as now, the newspaper was likely to identify most with its intended readers, as well as with its benefactors – whether private enterprise or state-owned or controlled industry.

There has been a steady progression towards more press freedom, despite major set-backs from time to time. This progress has sometimes taken the form of greater sophistication in the means of control applied to the press. Legal restraint replaced violence, then fiscal burdens were imposed (and later reversed). Now institutionalization of the press within a market system serves as a form of control, and the modern newspaper, as a large business enterprise, is vulnerable to more kinds of pressure or intervention than its simpler forerunners were. The newspaper did not really become a true 'mass' medium until the twentieth century, in the sense of directly reaching a majority of the population on a regular basis, and there are still quite large inter-country differences in the extent of newspaper reading. There has been a gradual worldwide decline in newspaper reading – starting slowly but surely in the late twentieth century and accelerating in the 2010s (with some exceptions in Latin America, Asia and the Middle East). Print revenue went up until the early 2000s and has since plateaued or dropped, despite the growth in online publishing. With social media and the Web becoming the main source of (free) news for young people in particular, the newspaper industry has responded with reducing overheads, reorganizing workflows and cutting jobs. Especially on the local level, many newspapers are struggling or have disappeared.

It has been customary and it is still useful to distinguish between certain types or genres of newspaper (and of journalism), although there is no single typology to suit all epochs and countries. The following passages describe the main variants.

## THE PARTY-POLITICAL PRESS

One common early form of the newspaper was the party-political paper dedicated to the task of activation, information and organization. The party newspaper (published by or for the party or the state) has lost ground to commercial press forms, both as an idea and as a viable business enterprise. The idea of a party press, even so, still has its place as a component in different forms of political governance. Where it does survive in Europe (and there are examples elsewhere), it is typically independent from the state (though possibly subsidized), professionally produced, serious and opinion-forming in purpose. Its uniqueness lies in the attachment of its readers by way of shared party allegiance, its sectionalism and its mobilizing function for party objectives. Examples include the 'vanguard press' of the Russian revolutionary movement, the party-political newspapers (especially social democratic) of several Scandinavian countries, and the official party press of former communist regimes. Some form of state ownership of newspapers exists in some African and Asian countries, Cuba and the Middle East.

## THE PRESTIGE PRESS

The late-nineteenth-century bourgeois newspaper was a focal point in press history and contributed much to our modern understanding of what a newspaper is or should be. The 'high-bourgeois' phase of press history – from about 1850 to the turn of the century in Europe, a bit later on in Latin America (especially regarding the role of community newspapers) and across Africa and Asia – was the product of several events and circumstances. In Europe, the part of the world where the press as a formidable industry took hold, these included the triumph of liberalism and the absence or ending of direct censorship or fiscal constraint, the forging of a business-professional establishment, plus many social and technological changes favouring the rise of a national or regional press of high information quality.

The new prestige or 'elite' press was independent from the state and from vested interests and was often recognized as a major institution of political and social life (especially as a self-appointed former of opinion and voice of the 'national interest'). It tended to show a highly developed sense of social and ethical responsibility (in practice fundamentally conformist) and it fostered the rise of a journalistic profession dedicated to the objective reporting of events. Many countries still have one or more newspapers that try to maintain this tradition. By wide consensus, the newspapers still recognized as having an 'elite' status are likely to include *The New York Times* (United States), *The Guardian* (London), *Le Monde* (France), *El País* (Spain), *NRC Handelsblad* (The Netherlands), *Times of India* (India), *The Sydney Morning Herald* (Australia), *Asahi Shimbun* (Japan), *Daily Nation* (Kenya) and *La Nación* (Argentina). Current expectations about what is a 'quality' newspaper still reflect the professional ideals of the prestige press and provide the basis for criticisms of newspapers that deviate from the ideal by being either too partisan or too 'sensational', or just too 'commercial'. The (national) prestige press currently seems better placed than most to survive the current pressure on newspapers, by virtue of their importance to a political and economic elite, and to do so these newspapers are diversifying their offerings, shifting to a 'digital first' publishing process, and innovating their business model (beyond advertising, subscriptions and sales).

## THE POPULAR PRESS

The last main type of newspaper has been with us for a century or so without much change of essential character. This is the truly 'mass' newspaper that was created for sale to the urban industrial masses and designed to be read by almost everyone. It was a fundamentally commercial enterprise (rather than a political or professional project) and was made possible by advances in technologies of scale, concentrations of population, the spread of literacy, low cost to the reader and large amounts of advertising revenue. In general, the popular press has always specialized in 'human interest' stories (Hughes, 1940), in dramatic and sensational styles of reporting and presentation, in the coverage of crime, disasters, crises, scandals, war and celebrities. Although not primarily interested in politics, it has often played a political role at key moments in national societies. Because of its typical smaller page format, the term 'tabloid' has been widely applied to this type of newspaper and its contents, as in the term 'tabloidization' (Connell, 1998). This means a process of becoming more sensational, trivial and irresponsible.

## THE LOCAL AND REGIONAL PRESS

In many countries, the most important newspaper sectors have been and remain the local and regional press. The forms are too varied to be described as a single type. They can be serious or popular, daily or weekly, urban or rural, with large as well as small circulations. The main features they have in common are a set of news values relevant to a local readership, a typically consensual and bipartisan approach (although there are exceptions), and a dependence on support from local advertisers and sponsors. Some local papers are free, others are paid for and they have generally been most threatened by online news, social media and (loss of) advertising. Local free newspapers or 'freesheets', such as *Metro* (appearing in Asia, Europe and across the Americas; not to be confused with the free *Metro* newspaper in London), *20 minutes* (appearing in Switzerland, Spain and France), and many others around the world earn their revenue almost exclusively from advertising, as advertisers covet the generally younger (and steady) readership these papers provide. Since rapid market expansion in the early 2000s, several of these freesheets have closed down again. Given the global shift to digital and online publication – where freesheets tend to have a minimal presence – the future of these papers is uncertain.

## OTHER PRINT MEDIA

The printing press gave rise to other forms of publication than book and newspaper. These include plays, songs, tracts, serial stories, poems, pamphlets, comics, reports, prospectuses, maps, posters, music, handbills, wall newspapers and much more. The single most significant is probably the periodical (weekly or monthly) magazine that appeared in great diversity and with wide circulations from the early eighteenth century onwards. Initially aimed at the domestic and cultural interests of the gentry, it eventually developed into a mass market of high commercial value and enormous breadth of coverage. The periodical magazine still belongs largely to the domestic and personal sphere and supports a wide range of interests, activities and markets. In the early twentieth century it was more like a mass medium than it is today, and its diffuseness and uncertain impact have led to a general neglect by media and communication research.

These comments apply to the commercial periodical. In many countries there has been and remains a significant opinion-forming or political periodical press, often with an influence beyond its generally modest circulation size. At key moments in some societies particular magazines have played important social, cultural or political roles. In conditions of political oppression or commercial domination, the 'alternative' periodical has often been an essential instrument of resistance and expression for minority movements (see Downing, 2000; Huesca, 2003; Gumucio-Dagron, 2004).

## FILM AS A MASS MEDIUM

Film began at the end of the nineteenth century almost simultaneously in different parts of the world – notably Europe, East Asia, the United States and Latin America – as a technological novelty, but what it offered was scarcely new in content or function. It transferred to a new means of presentation and distribution of an older tradition of entertainment, offering stories, spectacles, music, drama, humour and technical tricks for popular consumption. It was also almost instantly a true mass medium in the sense that it quite quickly reached a very large proportion of populations, even in rural areas. As a mass medium, film was partly a response to the 'invention' of leisure – time out of work – and an answer to the demand for affordable and (usually) respectable ways of enjoying free time for the whole family. Thus, it provided for the working class some of the cultural benefits already enjoyed by their social 'betters'. To judge from its phenomenal growth, the latent demand met by film was enormous. Of the main formative elements named above, it would not be the technology or the social climate but the needs met by the film for individuals that mattered most. The most apparent are those for escape from humdrum reality into a more glamorous world, the wish for strong narratives to be caught up in, the search for role models and heroes, and the need to fill leisure time in safe, affordable and sociable ways. In these respects, not much has changed.

The characterization of the film as 'show business' in a new form for an expanded market is not the whole story. There have been three other significant strands in film history. First, the use of film for propaganda is noteworthy, especially when applied to national or societal purposes, based on its great reach, supposed realism, emotional impact and popularity. The two other strands in film history were the emergence of several schools of film art (Huaco, 1963) and the rise of the social documentary film movement. These were different from the mainstream in having a minority appeal, a strong element of realism, and in containing social critique (or a combination thereof). Both have a link, partly fortuitous, with film as propaganda in that both tended to develop at times of *social crisis*.

There continue to be thinly concealed ideological and implicitly propagandist elements in many popular entertainment films, even in politically 'free' societies. This reflects a mixture of forces: deliberate attempts at social control; an unthinking adoption of populist or conservative values; various marketing and PR infiltrations into entertainment; and the pursuit of mass appeal. Despite the dominance of the entertainment function in film history, films have often displayed didactic, propagandistic tendencies. Film is certainly more vulnerable than other media to outside interference and may be more subject to conformist pressures because so much capital is at risk. It is a reflection of this situation that, in the aftermath of the 9/11 attack on the Twin Towers, US government leaders sought a meeting with leaders of the film industry to discuss ways in which film could make a contribution to the newly announced 'war on terror'. Similarly, in 2018, the Chinese government created special units for film, press and publication, directly under Communist Party control, whose responsibilities include overseeing film production, distribution, exhibition and censorship in a recognition of the powerful role of cinema. It subsequently stimulated the production of (commercially very successful) action movies with patriotic messages.

The main turning points in film history have been: the 'Americanization' of the film industry and film culture in the years after the First World War (Tunstall, 1977); the rise and global success of large commercial film industries in India ('Bollywood' from the 1970s) and Nigeria (sometimes labelled 'Nollywood', emerging in the 1970s and 1980s, although the term does not do justice to the production of successful films in over 300 Nigerian languages); the rise of Latin American filmmaking, partly inspired by the establishment of a Foundation of the New Latin American Cinema in 1985 as an emancipation project for the production, preservation and development of the region (and exemplified by the enormous success and Oscar wins of Mexican directors Alfonso Cuarón, Guillermo del Toro and Alejandro González Iñárritu in the 2010s); and globally the coming of television and the separation of film from the cinema. Although 'Americanization' is not so much on the research agenda anymore, the growing globalization of the film (and television) industry and the rise of international co-productions (Baltruschat, 2010) have led to concerns about the worldwide dominance of the English language, as well as a possible homogenization of narrative development and genre conventions.

After the Second World War, the US film industry quickly established itself as a dominant model for filmmaking around the world, which contributed to a homogenization of film culture and a convergence of ideas about the definition of film as a medium. Television took away a large part of the film-viewing public, especially the general family audience, leaving a much smaller and younger film audience. It also took away or diverted the social documentary stream of film development and gave it a more congenial home in television, where it appeared in journalistic magazines, special reports and 'public affairs' programming. However, it did not have similar effects on the art film or for film aesthetics, although the art film may have benefited from the 'demassification' and greater specialization of the film/cinema medium. For the first two generations of filmgoers, the film experience was inseparable from having an evening out, usually with friends and usually in venues that were far grander than the home. In addition, the darkened cinema offered a mixture of privacy and sociability that gave another dimension to the experience. Just as with television later, 'going to the pictures' was as important as seeing any particular film.

The 'separation of film and cinema' refers to the many ways in which films can be seen, after initial showing in a film theatre. These include television broadcasting, cable transmission, videotape and disc sale or hire, satellite TV, digital broadband Internet and mobile streaming. These developments have several potential consequences. They make film less typically a shared public experience and more a private one. They reduce the initial 'impact' of mass exposure to a given film. They shift control of selection in the direction of the audience and allow new patterns of repeat viewing and collection. They make it possible to serve many specialist markets and easier to cater for the demand for any kind of content, including violent, horrific or pornographic content. They also prolong the life of films. Despite the liberation entailed in becoming a less 'mass' medium, the film has not been able to claim full rights to political and artistic self-expression, and most countries retain an apparatus of licensing, censorship and powers of control.

Although the film/cinema medium has been subordinated to television in many respects, it has also become more integrated with other media, especially book publishing, popular music and television itself. In terms of the Internet, the emergence and global popularity of streaming services has injected film production and distribution with new emphasis. Overall, film has acquired a greater centrality (Jowett and Linton, 1980), despite the reduction of its immediate audience, as a showcase for other media and as a cultural source, out of which come books, strip cartoons, songs and television 'stars' and series. Thus, film is as much as ever a mass culture creator. Even the decline of the cinema audience has been more than compensated by a new domestic film audience reached by television, digital recordings, platforms and streaming services. Key features are summarized in Box 2.3.

## 2.3

## The film medium and institution: key features

### Medium aspects

- Audiovisual channels of reception
- Private experience of public content
- Extensive (universal) appeal
- Predominantly narrative fiction
- International in genre and format

*(Continued)*

## BROADCASTING

Radio and television have, collectively, a hundred-plus-year history as mass media, and both grew out of pre-existing technologies – telephone, telegraph, moving and still photography, and sound recording. Despite their obvious differences in content and use, radio and television can be treated together in terms of their history. Radio seems to have been a technology looking for a use, rather than a response to a demand for a new kind of service or content, and much the same is true of television. According to Williams (1975: 25), 'Unlike all previous communications technologies, radio and television were systems primarily designed for transmission and reception as abstract processes, with little or no definition of preceding content'. As with all newer media, radio and television came to borrow from existing media, and most of the popular content forms of both are derivative from film, music, stories, theatre, news and sport.

A distinctive feature of radio and television has been their high degree of regulation, control or licensing by public authority – initially out of technical necessity, later from a mixture of democratic choice, state self-interest, economic convenience and sheer institutional custom. A second and related feature of radio and television media has been their centralized pattern of distribution, with supply radiating out from metropolitan centres, with little or no return flow. Perhaps because of their closeness to power, radio and television have hardly anywhere acquired, as of right, the same freedom that the press enjoys, to express views and act with political independence. Broadcasting was thought too powerful as an influence to fall into the hands of any single interest without clear limitations to protect the public from potential harm or manipulation. A major exception is the history of community radio across the African continent (except the Arab north and South Africa), where it is the dominant mass medium up to this day, largely because of its flexibility, low cost and oral character.

Television has been continuously evolving, and it would be risky to try to summarize its features in terms of communicative purposes and effects. Initially, the main genre innovation of television stemmed from its capacity to transmit many pictures and sound live, and thus act as a 'window on the world' in real time. Even studio productions were live broadcasts before the days of efficient video recording. This capacity of simultaneity has been retained for some kinds of content, including sporting events, some newscasting and certain kinds of entertainment show. What Dayan and Katz (1992) characterize as 'media events' (such as state visits, the Olympic Games, coronations, large political demonstrations) are often likely to have significant live coverage. Most TV content is not live, although it often aims to create an illusion of ongoing reality. A second important feature of television is the sense of intimacy and personal involvement that it seems able to cultivate between the spectator and presenter or the actors and participants on screen.

The status of television as the most 'massive' of the media in terms of reach, time spent and popularity has barely changed and it adds all the time to its global audience. However, live television consumption is on the decline around the world as streaming on-demand video takes hold.

Despite the fact that television has been largely denied an autonomous political role and is primarily considered a medium of entertainment, it plays a vital role in modern politics. It is considered to be the main source of news and information for most people, the mass medium people across all walks of life find easiest to understand, and the main channel of communication between politicians and citizens at election times (Grabe and Bucy, 2009). In this informally allocated role of public informer, television has generally remained a force to be reckoned with. Television broadcasting in most countries follows one of two trajectories: resembling the American model of national, regional and local outlets (such as in China, Japan and the Philippines), and the British model of national public service broadcasting (which can be found all over the former British colonies in Asia and Africa). Latin America knows a television landscape dominated by a small number of big corporations (often with strong current or former ties with governments and former dictatorships in the region; see Sparks, 2011).

Beyond providing public information, television plays the role of educator – for children at school and adults at home. For many decades it was largest single channel of advertising in nearly all countries, and this has helped to confirm its mass entertainment functions. This role is increasingly being usurped by online advertising, as the Internet consumes most of people's 'media time' in many countries around the world. In terms of its distribution, broadcast television has fragmented in most countries into many separate channels. Even so, the typical pattern that remains is one in which a few (national) channels are very dominant in audience and financial terms. An enduring feature of the appeal of television seems to lie in the very fact that it is a medium that brings people together to share the same experiences in an otherwise fragmented and individuated society, and not only in the circle of the family.

The main features of broadcast television and radio are summarized in Box 2.4.

---

**2.4**

## Television as medium and institution: key features

### Medium aspects

- Very diverse types of content
- Audiovisual channels
- Close, personal and domestic association
- Varied intensity and involvement experience

### Institutional aspects

- Complex technology and organization
- Subject to legal and social control
- National *and* international character
- High public visibility

---

Radio notably refused to die in the face of the rise of television and it has prospered on the basis of several distinctive features. Competition with television led to a degree of deliberate differentiation. The close supervision of national radio systems relaxed after the rise of television and, given the relative flexibility and cost-efficient nature of the technology, there was an alternative, oppositional or 'pirate' phase, in which amateurs, community organizations and independent entrepreneurs set up competing stations. Radio ceased to be a highly regulated national 'voice' and became freer to experiment and to express new, minority and even deviant sounds in voice and music. As a medium, it has much more channel capacity and therefore much greater and more diverse access. It is much cheaper and more flexible in production than television and also cheap and flexible in use for its audience. There are no longer limitations on the place where radio can be listened to or the time of reception, since listening can be combined with other routine activities. It has possibilities for interaction with its audience by way of the telephone and can accommodate many different genres. In fact, radio has flourished since the coming of television and the Internet, even if it can no longer claim the mass audience of its glory days. With the advent of streaming audio and podcasting, and the consistently significant role of the mass medium in various regions of the world (in particular as it supports small-scale broadcasting in indigenous languages), the future of radio looks bright. The main features discussed are outlined in Box 2.5.

## 2.5
## Radio as medium and institution: key features

### Medium aspects

- Sound appeal only
- Portable and flexible in use
- Multiple types of content, but more music
- Participative (two-way) potential
- Individual and intimate in use

### Institutional aspects

- Relative freedom
- Local and decentralized
- Economical to produce

## RECORDED MUSIC

Until recently, relatively little attention has been given to music as a mass medium in theory and research, perhaps because the implications for society have never been clear and, until the late 1990s era of filesharing online – which so-called 'Napster effect' accelerated digital developments throughout the industry (see Waldfogel, 2012) – there have not been sharp discontinuities in the possibilities offered by successive technologies of recording, reproduction and distribution. Recorded and replayed music has not even enjoyed a convenient label to describe its numerous media manifestations, although the generic term 'phonogram' has been suggested (Burnett, 1996) to cover music accessed via record players, tape players, compact disc players, VCRs (video cassette recorders), broadcasting and cable. With the emergence of digital audio, peer-to-peer filesharing and streaming music in the 1990s and early 2000s, the music industry was forced to transform – the first of all the other media industries to do so with regard to the challenge of surviving the digital age.

The recording and replaying of music began around 1880 and records were quite rapidly diffused, on the basis of the wide appeal of popular songs and melodies. The first record stores opened their doors in Wales (1894) and the USA (1930s). Their popularity and diffusion were closely related to the already established place of the piano (and other instruments) in the home. Much radio content since the early days has consisted of music, even more so since the rise of television. While there may have been a gradual tendency for the 'phonogram' to replace private music-making, there has never been a large gap between mass-mediated music and personal and direct audience enjoyment of musical performance (concerts, choirs, bands, dances, etc.). The phonogram makes music of all kinds more accessible at all times in more places to more people, but it is hard to discern a fundamental discontinuity in the general character of popular musical experience, despite changes of genre and fashion.

Even so, there have been big changes in the broad character of the phonogram since its beginnings. The first change was the addition of radio broadcast music to phonogram records, which greatly increased the range and amount of music available and extended it to many more people than had access to gramophones or jukeboxes. The transition of radio from a family to an individual medium in the post-war 'transistor' revolution was a second major change, which opened up a relatively new market of young people for what became a burgeoning record industry. Each development since then – portable tape players, the Sony Walkman (1979), the compact disc and music video (accelerated with the launch of MTV in 1981), the iPod (2001), and streaming music platforms such as Swedish company Spotify (premiering in 2008) – has given the spiral another twist, still based on a predominantly young audience. The result has been a mass media industry which is very interrelated, concentrated in ownership and internationalized (Negus, 1992). Despite this, music media have significant radical and creative strands, which have developed despite increased commercialization (Frith, 1981).

The growth of music downloading and sharing via the Internet has added to the distribution traffic and seriously challenged the power of music rights holders. Through the establishment of (or participation in) ad-supported and subscription streaming services, which pay artists or labels a tiny portion of each song streamed, the global music industry, after decades of decline, from 2014 started to recoup its revenue lost from the decline of physical sales. Another significant development for recorded music has been its expansion into other media, most notably advertising, film and digital games. Music licensed or composed specifically for inclusion in campaigns, independent and major motion pictures and 'triple A' games (a reference to big budget console video games) earns a significant return on investment, whereas sales of CDs (and other physical carriers) fall.

While the cultural significance of music has received sporadic attention, its relationship to social and political events has been recognized and occasionally celebrated or feared. Since the rise of the youth-based industry in the 1960s, mass-mediated popular music has been linked to youthful idealism and political concern, to supposed degeneration and hedonism, to drug-taking, violence and anti-social attitudes. Music has also played a part in various nationalist independence movements. For instance, songs of self-empowerment and protest were a potent element in the pursuit of civil rights in the United States and independence of Ireland from Britain, in the fight against apartheid in South Africa, and more generally in the emancipation of women (and other minorities) in many parts of the world. The end of Soviet control of Estonia was described as the 'singing revolution' (from 1987 to the establishment of independence in 1991) because music enabled people to come together and express their aspirations for restoration of autonomy and the suppressed national culture.

While the content of music has never been easy to regulate, its distribution has predominantly been in the hands of established institutions, and its perceived deviant tendencies have been subject to some sanctions. In any case, most popular music expresses and responds to rather enduring conventional values and personal needs, with no subversive aim or potential. These points about music are summarized in Box 2.6.

## 2.6
## Recorded music (phonogram) as medium and institution: key features

### Medium aspects

- Sound experience only
- Personal and emotional satisfactions
- Main appeal to youth
- Mobile, flexible individual in use
- Increasingly distributed via streaming services

### Institutional aspects

- Low degree of regulation
- High degree of internationalization
- Multiple technologies and platforms
- Links to major media industry
- Organizational fragmentation
- Central to youth culture

# DIGITAL GAMES

As with recorded music, the digital games industry and its enormously popular products have yet to receive much mainstream attention in media and mass communication research. However, the field of digital games studies is growing rapidly, led by prominent scholars who either focus on the aesthetic of game narratives and gameplay, or seek to understand the rather unique features of production and game work

(Raessens and Goldstein, 2011). A key debate early in the history of the computer game industry and the field of game studies was whether games should be examined in the same way as films, books and television programmes, or whether games are an entirely different medium (Juul, 2005). It has become quite clear that understanding the role and impact of digital games needs both perspectives. Digital games have a rich heritage in multiple fields, including the personal computing industry, software programming, cartoons and animated films, and toy manufacturing and design (Izushi and Aoyama, 2006).

From relatively modest beginnings, when games were developed as ways to test computers, to impress visitors and sponsors of computer labs (at universities and corporate research and development divisions), or were made just for fun in the 1950s and 1960s, the 1970s saw the emergence of digital games as a fully fledged commercial mass media industry. As computers were still too expensive for the home, digital games became popular and commercially viable as arcade games – especially from 1972 with the release of *Pong* (now part of the permanent collection of the Smithsonian Institution in Washington, DC due to its cultural impact). After an early crash of the (North American) games industry, Japanese companies came to dominate the global market, starting in 1983 with the release of the Nintendo Entertainment System (NES), bringing successful arcade games such as *Donkey Kong* into the home. Around the same time, personal computers became more affordable and user-friendly, and machines running games next to home office software, such as the Commodore (Commodore Business Machines, 1982), MSX (Microsoft Japan and Sanyo, 1983) and Macintosh (Apple, 1984), entered the general consumer market. In the 1990s and 2000s, digital games made numerous advances (in terms of graphics, sound, complexity of gameplay, the introduction of motion sensing hardware, and increased interaction with 'gamers'), accelerated by the introduction of dedicated game consoles that doubled as multimedia and multi-purpose entertainment units, such as the PlayStation (Sony, 1994) and the Xbox (Microsoft, 2001). Since the introduction of smartphones and tablet computers, mobile gaming has added a third global market for digital games (next to personal computers and consoles).

The majority of digital games are produced and sold in Japan, the United States and the United Kingdom. The games industry has become so commercially successful (and culturally influential) that numerous governments (such as in Singapore, South Korea, and Ireland) have developed policies to stimulate these industries in their countries – similar to efforts made by governments to lure film and television productions, for example through tax credits, subsidies for training and studio facilities, and the provision of resources. Despite this kind of support, the global success of digital games is also a cause for concern for governments, parents, teachers and scholars alike. Consistent among such concerns are:

- Production
  - The often less-than-ideal working conditions that exist throughout the industry.
  - A lack of diversity among those making games (Kerr, 2016).

- Content
  - Their graphic and increasingly realistic nature.
  - The addictive qualities of certain games and game features (Bean, Nielsen, van Rooij and Ferguson, 2017).
- Reception
  - The potential effects of (violent, addictive) games (Kowert and Quandt, 2015).
  - The overly sexualized representation of female characters (Lynch, Tompkins, van Driel and Fritz, 2016).

With the growing popularity of mobile games and a shift towards cloud-computing-based gaming applications, new competitors (from the Internet and telecommunications sectors) have entered the global market. Additionally, with the success of digital games comes more regulation, for example, regarding intellectual property rights and licences, consumer protection, age ratings and classification, data protection and privacy, and gambling legislation. It is safe to say that digital games are not just a mass media industry in their own right, but that elements from the production, content and reception of games are now present in all other industries, and that tie-ins of games with other media offerings are increasingly common. Key features about digital games today are summarized in Box 2.7.

## 2.7
## Digital games as medium and institution: key features

### Medium aspects

- Comprehensive multimedia experience
- Personal and emotional satisfactions
- Mass appeal (different game types appeal to different generations)
- High involvement

### Institutional aspects

- High degree of regulation
- High degree of internationalization
- Multiple technologies and platforms
- Global media industry
- Increasingly central to popular culture

# THE COMMUNICATIONS REVOLUTION: NEW MEDIA VERSUS OLD

The expression 'new media' has been in use since the 1960s and has had to encompass an expanding and diversifying set of applied communication technologies. The editors of *The Handbook of New Media* (Lievrouw and Livingstone, 2006) point to the difficulties of saying just what the 'new media' comprise. They choose to define them in a composite way, linking information communication technologies (ICT) with their associated social contexts, bringing together three elements: technological artefacts and devices; activities, practices and uses; and social arrangements and organizations that form around the devices and practices. As noted above, much the same definition applies to 'old media', although the artefacts, uses and arrangements are different. As far as the essential features of 'new media' are concerned, the main ones seem to be their interconnectedness, their accessibility to individual users as senders and/or receivers, their interactivity, their multiplicity of use and open-ended character, and their ubiquity. Another key marker for these newer media is their convergent nature, in that they increasingly mix different media – in hardware, software, in form and content, as in everyday use. This is part of the reason that the distinction 'old' versus 'new' media is difficult to uphold.

Our primary concern in this book is with media and mass communication, which is closely related to the old media and seems thus to be rendered obsolete by new media. However, as noted already, mass communication is not a process that is limited to mass media, nor has it necessarily declined. The new media technologies also carry mass communication activities, and in many ways heighten concerns about the role and impact of mass media and communication in society. The key to the immense power of the computer as a communication machine – and computation as a communication technique – lies in the process of digitalization that allows information of all kinds in all formats to be carried with the same efficiency and without hierarchy. In principle, there is no longer any need for the various different media that have been described, since they can all be subsumed in the same computerized communication network and reception centre (in the home or on a smartphone, for instance). Alongside computer-based technologies there are other innovations that have in some degree changed some aspects of mass communication (Carey, 2003). While mostly supporting mass self-communication, the many new possibilities for private 'media-making' (camcorders, PCs, printers, cameras, mobile phones, etc.) have expanded the world of media and forged bridges between public and private communication and between the spheres of the professional and the amateur.

The implications of all this for mass media are still far from clear, although it is certain that the 'traditional' media have simultaneously benefited greatly from new media innovations and have experienced profound challenges to their business models and production practices by new technologies and competitors. Secondly, we can conclude that the communications revolution has generally shifted the 'balance of power' from the media into two directions. First, to the audience in so far as there are more options to choose from and more active uses of media available. Traditional mass communication was essentially one-directional, while the new forms of communication are essentially *interactive*. Mass communication has in several respects become less massive and less centralized. Secondly, power has shifted from those who control the means of production and distribution – traditionally the key source of revenue for mass media industries – to those who have successfully monetized the place and moment of (digital) consumption: hardware and software manufacturers such as Microsoft and Apple, Internet giants such as Alphabet (parent company of Google) and Tencent, and online platforms such as Facebook and WeChat.

## THE INTERNET

Beyond that, it is useful to distinguish between the implications of enhanced transmission and the emergence of any new medium as such. The former means more speed, capacity and efficiency, while the latter opens up new possibilities for content, use, influence and effects. The foremost claim to status as a new medium and a mass medium is the Internet. Even so, 'mass' features are not its primary characteristic. The Internet began primarily as a non-commercial means of intercommunication and data exchange between professionals operating at the behest of the US military, but its more recent rapid advance has been fuelled by its potential as a purveyor of goods and many profitable services and as an alternative to other means of personal and interpersonal communication (Castells, 2001). The 'killer application' of the Internet is social media, which dominates the use of the Internet around the world. Initially, diffusion proceeded most rapidly in North America and Northern Europe. A little over half of the world's population uses the Internet today, with Africa, the Middle East and Latin America being the fastest-growing markets (Arora, 2019). Some applications of the Internet, such as online news, are clearly extensions of newspaper journalism, although online news itself is also evolving in new directions, with new capabilities of content and new forms (such as where a member of the public adopts the role of journalist). As the Internet moves into other sectors and industries, it becomes increasingly difficult to separate its status as a medium from other media.

The Internet's claim to full medium status is based in part on it having a distinctive technology, manner of use, range of content and services, and a distinct image of its own. However, the Internet has no clear institutional status and is not owned, controlled or organized by any single body, but is simply a network of internationally interconnected computers operating according to agreed protocols. Numerous organizations, but especially service providers and telecommunication bodies, contribute to its operation (Braman and Roberts, 2003). The Internet as such does not exist anywhere as a legal entity and is not subject to any single set of national laws or regulations (Lessig, 1999). On the other hand, many international organizations as well as national governments are seeking more legal control over the Internet, and specifically the dominant role social media companies and search engines (such as Facebook and Google) have come to play in everyday life. Those who use the Internet can be accountable to the laws and regulations of the country in which they reside as well as to international law. We return to the question of the Internet throughout this book, but for the moment we can record its chief characteristics as a (mass) medium. Essential features of the Internet are summarized in Box 2.8, without distinguishing between 'medium' and 'institutional' aspects.

## 2.8
## The Internet as a medium: key features

- Computer-based technologies
- Hybrid, non-dedicated, flexible character
- Interactive potential
- Private and public functions
- Growing degree of regulation
- Interconnectedness
- Ubiquity and de-locatedness
- Accessible to individuals as communicators
- A medium of both mass and interpersonal communication

## DIFFERENCES BETWEEN MEDIA

It is much less easy to distinguish these various media from each other than it used to be. This is partly because some media forms are now distributed across different types of transmission channel, reducing the original uniqueness of form and experience in use. Secondly, the increasing convergence of technology, based on digitalization, can only reinforce this tendency. The clear lines of regulatory regime between the various media are already blurred, both recognizing and encouraging greater similarity between different media. Thirdly, globalizing tendencies are reducing the distinctiveness of any particular national variant of media content and institution. Fourthly, the continuing trends towards integration of national and global media corporations have led to the housing of different media under the same roof, encouraging convergence by another route.

Nevertheless, on certain dimensions, clear differences do remain. There are some obvious differences in terms of typical content. There is also evidence that media are perceived differently in terms of physical and psychosocial characteristics (see Box 6.4, Chapter 6). Media vary a good deal in terms of perceived trust and credibility, although findings vary from country to country. Here we look only at two enduring questions. First, how *free* is a medium in relation to the wider society? Secondly, what is a medium good for and what are its perceived *uses*, from the point of view of an individual audience member?

## DIMENSION OF FREEDOM VERSUS CONTROL

Relations between media and society have a material, a political and a normative or social-cultural dimension. Central to the political dimension is the question of freedom and control. The main normative issue concerns how media ought to use the freedom they have. As noted above, near-total freedom was claimed and eventually gained for the *book*, for a mixture of reasons, in which the claims of politics, religion, science and art all played some part. This situation remains unchallenged in free societies, although the book has lost some of its once subversive potential as a result of its relative marginalization (book reading is a minority or minor form of media use). The influence of books remains considerable, but has to a large extent to be mediated through other more popular media or other institutions (education, politics, etc.).

The *newspaper* press bases its historical claim to freedom of operation much more directly on its political functions of expressing opinion and circulating political and economic information. But the newspaper is also a significant business enterprise for which freedom to produce and supply its primary product (information) is a necessary condition of successful operation in the marketplace. Broadcast television and radio are still generally licensed and have limited political freedom in practice, partly because of their privileged access to scarce spectrum space (despite the proclaimed 'end of scarcity') and partly because of their believed impact and power to persuade. But they are also often expected to use their informative capacity to support the democratic process and serve the public good in other ways. Even so, the current trend is for market forces to have a greater influence on the conduct of broadcasting than either political control or voluntary social responsibility.

The various *newer media*, using cable, satellite or telecommunications networks for distribution, have often successfully staved off more regulation regarding their appropriate degree of political freedom, but this situation is changing. Freedom from control may be claimed on the grounds of privacy or the fact that these are not media of indiscriminate mass distribution but are directed to specific users. They are so-called 'common carriers' that generally escape control over their content because they are open to all on equal terms and primarily for personal or business rather than public matters.

They also increasingly share the same communicative tasks as media with established editorial autonomy. The 'underdetermined' status of most digital and online media in respect of freedom is a matter of dispute, since they are *de facto* very free, but also give rise to widespread fears of misuse, and have become indispensable to the lives of so many people around the world.

The intermedia differences relating to *political* control (freedom means few regulations and little supervisory apparatus) follow a general pattern. In practice, this means that the nearer any medium gets to operating as a *mass medium*, the more it can expect the attention of governments and politicians, since it affects the exercise of power (and the maintenance of social order). In general, activities in the sphere of art, fiction, fantasy or entertainment are more likely to escape attention than are activities that touch directly on the ongoing reality of events and circumstances.

Virtually all media of public communication have a radical potential, in the sense of being potentially subversive of reigning systems of social control. They can provide access for new voices and perspectives on the existing order; new forms of organization and protest are made available for the subordinate or disenchanted. The role of social (and mobile) media in the mobilization and organization of new (mass) social movements, such as the Arab Spring, the Indignados in Spain, the globally dispersed Occupy movement, and the Black Lives Matter and #MeToo movements, is crucial to consider in this context. Even so, the institutional development of successful media has usually resulted in the elimination of the early radical potential, partly as a side-effect of commercialization, partly because authorities fear disturbance to society (Winston, 1986). According to Beniger (1986), the driving logic of new communication technology has always been towards increased control. This generalization is now being tested with reference to the Internet and looks like being validated.

The *normative* dimension of control operates according to the same general principles, although sometimes with different consequences for particular media. For instance, film, which has generally escaped direct political control, has often been subject to self-censorship and to monitoring of its content, on grounds of its potential moral impact on the young and impressionable (especially in matters of violence, crime or sex). The widespread restrictions applied to television in matters of culture and morals stem from the same tacit assumptions. More recently, digital games have come to the forefront of normative concerns. These are all media that are very popular and have a potentially strong emotional impact on many people, and thus need to be supervised in 'the public interest'.

However, the more communication activities can be defined as either educational or 'serious' in purpose or, alternatively, as artistic and creative, the more freedom from normative restrictions can usually be claimed. There are complex reasons for this, but it is also a fact that 'art' and content of higher moral seriousness do not usually reach large numbers and are seen as marginal to power relations.

The degree of control of media by state or society depends partly on the feasibility of applying it. The most regulated media have typically been those whose distribution is most easily supervised, such as centralized national radio or television broadcasting or local cinema distribution. Books and print media generally are much less easy to monitor or to suppress. The same applies to local radio, while desktop publishing and photocopying and all manner of ways of reproducing sound and images have made direct censorship a very blunt and ineffective instrument.

The difficulty of policing national frontiers to keep out unwanted foreign communication is another consequence of new technology that promotes more freedom. While new technology in general seems to increase the promise of freedom of expression, the continued strength of institutional controls, including those of the market, over actual flow and reception should not be underestimated. It is also becoming clearer that the Internet is not impossible to control, as once believed, since all traffic can be monitored and traced and some countries have effectively blocked certain websites, applications and content they dislike and can punish users. There is also extensive self-censorship by service providers and platform companies in the face of threats or legal uncertainty.

The main issues raised in this section are summarized in Box 2.9, dealing with social control, with particular reference to two aspects: means or types of control and motives.

## 2.9
## Social control of media

### Types of control

- Censorship of content
- Legal restrictions
- Control of infrastructures
- Economic means
- Self-regulation or self-censorship

### Motives for control

- Fear of political subversion
- For moral or cultural reasons
- Combat cyber-crime
- National security

## DIMENSIONS OF USE AND RECEPTION

The increasing difficulty of typifying or distinguishing media channels in terms of content and function has undermined once stable social definitions of media. The newspaper, for instance, may now be as much an entertainment medium, or a consumers' guide, as it is a source of information about political and social events. Cable and satellite television systems are no longer confined to offering general programming for all. Streaming services (for music, film, television and games) blur the boundaries between all kinds of media. Even so, a few dominant images and definitions of what media 'are best for' do appear to survive, the outcome of tradition, social forces and the 'bias' of certain technologies.

For instance, television, despite the many changes and extensions relating to production, transmission and reception, remains primarily a medium of family entertainment, even if the family is less likely to be viewing together (see Chapter 15). It is still a focus of public interest and a shared experience in most societies – whether people are 'binge-watching' a series via a streaming service or tuning in to a regular scheduled programme. It has both a domestic and a collective character that seem to endure. The traditional conditions of family living (shared space, time and conditions) may account for this, despite the technological trend to individuation of use and specialization of content. Even those who watch on their own often participate through what the industry calls 'second screen' activities, as people increasingly share their viewing experience online via social media.

---

**2.10**

**Dimensions of media use: questions arising**

Inside or outside the home?

Individual or shared experience?

Public or private in use?

Interactive or not?

---

The questions about media use in Box 2.10 indicate three dimensions of media reception that mainly apply to traditional media: whether it is within or outside the home; whether it is an individual or a shared experience; and whether it is more public or more private. Television is typically shared, domestic and public. The newspaper, despite its changing content, conforms to a different type. It is certainly public in character, but is less purely domestic and is individual in use. Radio is now many things but often rather private, not exclusively domestic and more individual in use than television. The book, the music phonogram and digital games also largely follow this pattern. In general, the distinctions indicated have become less sharp as a result of the changes of technology in the direction of proliferation and convergence of reception possibilities.

Digital and online media have added to the uncertainty about which medium is good for what purpose, but they have also added a fourth dimension by which media can be distinguished: that of degree of interactivity. The more interactive media are those that allow continual motivated choice and response by users. While the video game, Internet and social media platform are clear examples where interaction is the norm, it is also the case that multi-channel cable or satellite television has an increased interactive potential, as do the recording and replay facilities of analogue and digital video recorders and applications. Interactivity has developed from a simple reaction possibility to the creation and supply of content across all media industries.

## THE CONTINUED SIGNIFICANCE OF MASS MEDIA AND COMMUNICATION

Throughout the history of (the study of) media and mass communication, claims have been made that 'mass media' as well as 'mass communication' are concepts that perhaps do not fit the contemporary media environment (anymore). Especially following the rapid developments in new information and communication technologies, scholars postulated as far back as the 1980s that 'technological change may facilitate a long-needed paradigm shift in communication science' (Reardon and Rogers, 1988: 297). The introduction of GSM (Global System for Mobile communications) phones and the World Wide Web as the graphic user interface of the Internet – both in the early 1990s – amplified predictions about the end of mass media and communication, as 'the [portable and decentralized] characteristics of the new media are cracking the foundations of our conception of mass communication' (Chaffee and Metzger, 2001: 369). However, after studying 'old' and 'new' media as well as offline and online communication practices over several decades, and considering the various ways in which media devices, institutions and (networks of) people adapt to this constantly changing context, we have to conclude that mass communication has remained (or returned as) a significant way to make sense of our media environment. Similarly, the former mass media organizations (such as publishers, broadcast and cable television firms) are in many ways bigger and more influential than ever before, increasingly operating on a global scale. With this we do not wish to claim that existing theories, models and approaches to media and mass communication can be seamlessly deployed to describe and explain the current state of affairs. It is clear that many, if not most of media and mass communication theories 'need to be readjusted to some degree to reflect changes brought about by the patterns of flow, structure, access, and ownership of new media' (Weimann et al., 2014: 821).

To some extent it is possible to argue that online, social and mobile media bring a return to the 'mass' concept in media and communication. Whereas mass media and communication can be typified with the characteristics of generally less-than-interactive, one-to-many types of transmission, new media add elements of multiple-way interaction and many-to-many communication, blurring the boundaries between formerly distinct media and communication types. As defined in the first chapter, mass communication refers to messages transmitted to a large audience via one or more media, whereas mass media are the (technological and formally organized) means of transmission of such messages. In a new media context, the distinctions between one or more senders and a 'mass' of receivers versus the perceived intimacy of personal communication, between the formal and informal organization of communication, and between different (yet converging) technologies seem to be difficult to maintain.

It is important to note that the distinctions between mass and (inter-)personal media and communication were never that clear to begin with – as the concept of 'mass' media and communication emerged in the 1930s – and always had a normative bent. At that time, 'mass communication' was set aside as one-way, impersonal and distant communication – related to the realm of politics, propaganda, advertising and public relations – whereas 'interpersonal communication' was considered to be the holy grail of direct, immediate, face-to-face and body-to-body contact (Fortunati, 2005b). John Durham Peters (1994) has argued that the privileging of interpersonal communication as a 'warmer' form of communication may in fact be quite incorrect, in that the opportunities for highly individual experience and sensemaking that mass media and mass communication afford (in other words: how people fill the gap between sending and receiving messages) can in fact be found in any form of conversation. To Peters, mass communication is the most basic form of communication, whereas '[i]nterpersonal communication could be seen as a series of interlocked acts of mass communication' (ibid.: 132). In a contemporary context, it can certainly be argued that interactive communication technologies simply multiply opportunities for all forms of conversation, and '[w]hat has evolved is mass communication, and as a result, the joint effects of mass and interpersonal communication differ from those which they formerly rendered' (Walther and Valkenburg, 2017: 421).

Collapsing mass communication and interpersonal communication along dimensions of personalization into a model of 'masspersonal' communication (O'Sullivan and Carr, 2018) in fact reaffirms their age-old separation, highlighting the significance of Peters' (1994) observation that people can serve as mass media (think about door-to-door election campaigners, salespeople and teachers) and mass media can simulate interpersonal communication (especially in the age of social bots, 'smart' speakers, adaptive web design, etc.). In today's digital, online and interconnected media environment, 'the three forms of communication (interpersonal, mass communication, and mass self-communication) coexist, interact, and complement each other rather than substituting for one another' (Castells, 2009: 55). As the presupposed warmth and authenticity of interpersonal contact converges with the distant and public nature of mass communication in the context of our comprehensively mediated lifeworld, new and pressing questions of import, impact and efficacy emerge.

The study of mass media and communication is still at the heart of this book and our field – in part, because the contemporary 'media manifold' (Couldry, 2016) reinvigorates concerns about the role and influence of mass media and mass communication practices, and in part due to the nature of mass communication as underlying all forms of communication, in turn amplified by processes particular to mass media. We observe how all of this gets exemplified by a preponderance of research topics covered in contemporary scholarship signalling a prevalence of 'mass' concepts (often mixed or integrated with other levels of communication) including, but not limited to, the following:

- Big data as a primary driver of the digital economy, and as an increasingly powerful tool in political communication (for example, regarding the micro-targeting of individuals on a massive scale with customized messages as a staple of contemporary election campaigns).
- The Internet of things as the rise of a 'non-human' mass communication network (linking things such as home appliances, health monitoring systems and all kinds of sensors to the Internet), affecting our lives in numerous ways.
- A political economy of digital capitalism, inspired by the enormous global (market) power of telecommunications, information and media corporations, such as Microsoft, Apple, Amazon, Alphabet (including Google), Facebook, Tencent and the Alibaba Group.
- The recurring public concern with 'balkanization' (Sunstein, 2001), 'telecocoons' (Habuchi, 2005), 'echo chambers' (Jamieson and Cappella, 2008), 'filter bubbles' (Pariser, 2012) and other forms of highly personalized information spaces within which people spend significant time when using media, suggesting an ongoing conflation of 'mass' communication and interpersonal (and even intrapersonal) communication (Walther and Valkenburg, 2017). The empirical work to date tends to find that people's media habits are a complex mix between self-selected and pre-selected personalization that generally does not lead to polarization, and that there are many factors mitigating the role of personal preferences, algorithms and recommender systems (Moller, Trilling, Helberger & Van Es, 2018; Dutton and Fernandez, 2019).
- The rise of all kinds of (more or less) new social movements and forms of collective action primarily facilitated and organized through online and mobile communication networks, which are playing a key role in influencing sentiments around matters of public interest.

- A growing recognition by teachers, scholars, policymakers and politicians regarding the need to invest in digital literacy and making citizens 'mediawise', while at the same time developing new policies to effectively govern the Internet (and curtail people's Internet use) with regard to areas such as privacy, online harm and copyrights.

- A renewed interest in the influence and impact of media, featuring multivariate, mixed method and multi-step flow communication research designs to accommodate the 'double bind' of media effects: on the one hand, scholars in the field do not assume – as was common in much of the twentieth century – that media are all-powerful and have direct effects on people, instead acknowledging how the impact of media is indirect, conditional and transactional (Valkenburg, Peter and Walther, 2016). On the other hand, it is beyond any doubt that we live in a time of 'deep mediatization' (Couldry and Hepp, 2016), where media can be considered to be at the centre of today's institutions and activities, fuelling social and political transformations through an interplay of people's use and consumption practices and the media's own internal logic.

## CONCLUSION

This chapter has offered a commentary on the evolution of mass media from the early days of printing to the present age of information communication technology and the global information society. It has told the story not as neat genealogy, but mostly in terms of brief sketches of the mass media and their main forms, with examples and cases in various regions around the world. It has highlighted their main characteristics in terms of capacity to communicate, uses for an audience and regard by the larger society. Although the primary distinction used to be according to a type of technology, equal importance attaches to social, cultural and political factors. Certain technologies survived the evolutionary struggle, so to speak, and few others (not described here) did not make it. All the different media can be considered to be converging subsequent to the rise of the Internet. The same applies to the various uses to which the media have been put.

There is no overall determining logic at work and it must be noted that the evolution of media is much more complex and messier than represented here. As Dourish and Bell (2011) suggest, one has to recognize both the 'myth' and the 'mess' of media and communication technologies when trying to understand them. Notable is the fact that all the media described are still with us and, in different ways in different parts of the world, flourishing, despite predictions to the contrary. They have all found a means of adapting to changed conditions and new competitors. This does not provide a happy new equilibrium, however. Briggs and Burke (2010) conclude, upon reviewing the social history of media from the early days of the printing press up to the contemporary convergent media ecosystem: all of this can best be understood as being in continuous flux.

# FURTHER READING

Briggs, A., Burke, P. and Ytreberg, E. (2020) *A Social History of the Media*, 4th edition. Cambridge: Polity Press.

Lehman-Wilzig, S. and Cohen-Avigdor, N. (2004) 'The natural life cycle of new media evolution', *New Media and Society*, 6(6): 707–730.

McLuhan, M. (1962) *The Gutenberg Galaxy*. Toronto: University of Toronto Press.

Peters, J.D. (1994) 'The gap of which communication is made', *Critical Studies in Mass Communication*, 11(2): 117–140.

Van Dijck, J.A.G.M. (2013) *The Culture of Connectivity: A Critical History of Social Media*. Oxford University Press.

Weimann, G., Weiss-Blatt, N., Mengistu, G., Mazor Tregerman, M. and Oren, R. (2014) 'Reevaluating "The End of Mass Communication?"', *Mass Communication and Society*, 17(6): 803–829.

# PART 2
## THEORIES

# 3

# CONCEPTS AND MODELS FOR MASS COMMUNICATION

This chapter is concerned with defining basic concepts for the study of *media and mass communication* and explaining their origins in terms of the way the relationship between mass media and society has developed over the last century. Although new media have arisen and social and economic circumstances are very different, there are many continuities and many of the issues that faced the early media theorists and researchers are still with us, sometimes in more acute form. This overview of concepts provides a framework that can be applied to the themes and issues listed in Chapter 1. In the second part of the chapter attention focuses on the main perspectives and methods that have been adopted, with particular reference to the difference between critical and applied research, and between quantitative, cause-and-effect methods and qualitative, cultural approaches. Lastly, the chapter outlines four models that have been developed for framing and studying the mass communication process, each with its own bias, but also with distinctive advantages. They are not so much alternative as complementary. In conclusion, an attempt is made to integrate the various approaches to the study of media and mass communication along the lines of the kind of media involved, and the kind of communication process identified as the object of study. With this overview we do not want to ignore or 'solve the problem' of the rich diversity and – according to some – fragmentation of the field. Instead, we seek to provide a conceptual framework that will help the student and scholar chart their own path.

## EARLY PERSPECTIVES ON MEDIA AND SOCIETY

The twentieth century can plausibly be described as the 'first age of mass media' in the institutional sense of the concept – as earlier forms of mass media and communication existed in many parts of the world (see Chapter 2). However, the kind of industrial organization, institutional arrangement and networked infrastructure available marked the twentieth century as a turning point. This period also inspired both wonder and alarm at the real or perceived influence of the mass media. Despite the enormous changes in media institutions and technology, and in society itself, and also the rise of media studies and communication science as an academic discipline, the terms of public debate about the potential social significance of 'the media' seem to have changed remarkably little.

A description of the issues that emerged during the first two or three decades of the twentieth century is of more than just historical interest, as early thinking provides a point of reference for understanding the present. Four sets of ideas were of particular importance from the outset, and continue to shape crucial questions of research and policy to this day. One concerned the question of the *power* of the new means of communication; a second, the question of social *integration* or disintegration that they might cause; and the third, the question of public *enlightenment*, which they might either promote or diminish. Fourth, there is a recurring concern about the role of new technologies in making it possible and easy to store our memories and access all the information we want, while our media culture also seems to become more ephemeral and 'despatialized' (that is, we can engage with media anytime, anyplace, anywhere). In short, our media environment simultaneously can place us anywhere – connecting with others, with content and experiences all over the world – and virtually nowhere, as our engagement with all of this often happens without any context (other than our own frame of reference). These themes are dealt with in depth in subsequent chapters; here, we will briefly address their history in thinking about (mass) media and society.

## THE POWER OF MASS MEDIA

A belief in the **power** of mass media was initially based on the observation of their great reach and apparent impact, especially in relation to the new popular **newspaper** press – and this belief spans continents and cultures. According to DeFleur and Ball-Rokeach (1989), newspaper circulation in the USA peaked in 1910, although it happened a good deal later in Europe and in other parts of the world. The popular press was mainly funded by commercial **advertising**, its content was characterized by sensational **news** stories, and its control was often concentrated in the hands of powerful press 'barons' and wealthy families, such as across Latin America. The First World War saw the mobilization of press and film in most of Europe and the United States for the national war aims of contending states. The results seemed to leave little doubt of the potency of media influence on the 'masses', when effectively managed and directed.

This impression was yet further reinforced by what happened in the Soviet Union and later in Nazi Germany, as well as throughout much of Asia and Africa, where the media were pressed into the service of **propaganda** on behalf of ruling party elites and state governments. History shows that governments, regardless of national or cultural context, have always been concerned with the power of the media, especially whenever a medium would reach truly 'mass' status (such as radio and newspapers early in the twentieth century, television in the 1970s and 1980s, and the Internet in the 2010s). The co-option of news and **entertainment** media by the allies in the Second World War removed any doubts about their perceived propagandist value. Before the century was half way on its course, there was already a strongly held and soundly based view that mass publicity was effective in shaping opinion and influencing behaviour. It could also have effects on international relations and alliances. More recent events, including the fall of communism, the Balkan wars, two Gulf wars, the Arab Spring and the ongoing 'war on terror', have confirmed the media as an essential and volatile component in any international power struggle, where **public opinion** is also a factor. The conditions for effective media power have generally included a national media industry capable of reaching most of the population, a degree of consensus in the message disseminated (whatever its direction) and some measure of credibility and trust in the media on the part of audiences.

While, by now, there is much more knowledge and also scepticism about the direct 'power' of media and mass communication, there is still much reliance on mass media in the spheres of advertising, **public relations** and political **campaigning**, and increased investments in targeting people (as groups or even as individuals) via social media. Politics tends to be routinely conducted and also reported on the assumption that skilful media presentation is absolutely vital to success in all normal circumstances, while some (generally more populist) politicians and parties turn to the Internet and social media in particular to bypass or 'disintermediate' (Katz, 1988) traditional news media in order to engage the electorate directly, which is seen as part of the explanation for their success (Kruikemeier, Gattermann and Vliegenthart, 2018).

## COMMUNICATION AND SOCIAL INTEGRATION

Social theorists in the late nineteenth and early twentieth centuries were very conscious of the 'great transformation' that was taking place, as slower, traditional and communal methods gave way to fast-paced, secular, urban living and to a great expansion in the scale of social activities. Many of the themes of European and North American sociology at this time reflect this collective self-consciousness of the problems of change from small-scale to large-scale and from rural to urban societies. The social theory of the time posited a need for new forms of integration in the face of the problems caused by industrialization and urbanization. Crime, prostitution, poverty and dependency were associated with the increasing anonymity, isolation and uncertainty of modern life.

While the fundamental changes were social and economic, it was possible to point to newspapers, film and other forms of popular **culture** (music, books, magazines, comics) as potential contributors to both individual crime and declining morality and also to rootlessness, impersonality and a lack of attachment or **community**. In the United States, large-scale immigration from Europe in the first two decades of the twentieth century highlighted questions of social cohesion and integration, just as much as migration to these parts of the world is a similar issue of concern roughly one hundred years later. This was exemplified at the time in the work of the Chicago School of Sociology and the writings of Robert Park, G.H. Mead, Thomas Dewey and others (Rogers, 1993). Hanno Hardt (1979, 1991) has reconstructed the main lines of early theory concerning communication and social integration, both in Europe and in North America. Much of the follow-up work attributed to the 'founding fathers' of media and communication research, such as Paul Lazarsfeld, Robert K. Merton and Elihu Katz, was in fact made possible by the work and research of a significant group of women, including Herta Herzog, Thelma Ehrlich Anderson, Hazel Gaudet Erskine and Rose K. Goldsen, working at universities and research units across Europe and North America – reminding us of the gendered history of knowledge production in our field (Rowland and Simonson, 2014; see also the website outofthequestion.org). Whereas social cohesion and integration are common themes in African, Asian and Latin American media and communication scholarship as well, this has been generally framed more in terms of nation-building, regional and national development, and public education in an emancipatory sense regarding former colonial or dictatorial rule (Willems, 2014).

The links between popular mass media and social integration were easy to perceive in terms both negative (more crime and immorality) and individualistic (loneliness and loss of collective beliefs), but a positive contribution to cohesion and community was also expected from modern communications. Mass media were a potential force for a new kind of cohesion, able to connect scattered individuals in a shared national, regional and local experience. They could also be supportive of the new democratic politics and of social reform movements. Not least in importance was the contribution of mass media, especially the cinema and emerging entertainment formats on television (such as the telenovela and soap opera), to making hard lives more bearable.

How the influence of media came to be interpreted was often a matter of an observer's personal **attitude** to modern society, their assessment of the relationship between state (or colonial) power and the media, and the degree of optimism or pessimism in their social outlook. The early part of the twentieth century, as well as (or perhaps because of) being a high point of nationalism, revolution and social conflict, was also a time of hopeful thinking, democratic advance, and scientific and technological progress.

In our time, circumstances have changed, although the underlying theme remains the same. There is still concern about the weakness of the ties that bind individuals together and to their society, the lack of shared values, the lack of social and civic participation, and the decline in 'public values' governing the new media environment (as strictly commercial and utilitarian considerations seem to prevail; see Van Dijck et al., 2018). The ties of trade unions, politics, religion and family have all changed, although these relationships are not necessarily weaker than before. The structure of social organization – of the 'ties that bind' – tends to have a more networked rather than linear or monolithic form, especially in urbanized regions (Hannerz, 1980). Problems of integration arise in relation to new ethnic groups and migrants who have arrived in (or kept at arm's length away from) industrialized countries, from the rapid spread of disinformation online and offline, and especially from the exploitation of such historical developments for political and electoral gain. There are new demands for communications media to provide for the **identity** and expressive needs of old and new minorities within larger societies as well as to contribute to social harmony and people's sense of belonging. It remains of crucial importance for the study of media and mass communication to question all-too-easy conclusions regarding the direction of media effects either way.

## MASS COMMUNICATION AS MASS EDUCATOR

The spirit of the early twentieth century (modern and hopeful) supported a third set of ideas about mass communication – that the media could be a potent force for public enlightenment, supplementing and continuing the new institutions of universal schooling, public libraries and popular education. Political and social reformers saw a positive potential in the media, taken as a whole, and the media often also saw themselves as, on balance, making a contribution to progress by spreading **information** and ideas, exposing political corruption and also providing much harmless enjoyment for ordinary people. In many countries, journalists were becoming more professional, organizing themselves in unions and trade associations, as well as adopting **codes** of ethics and good practice.

The democratic task of the press in informing the newly enfranchised (and increasingly literate) masses was widely recognized. The newly established radio institutions of the 1920s and 1930s in Europe were often given a public cultural, educational and informative mission as well as the task of promoting national identity and unity. Elsewhere in the world, radio and later television broadcasting remained either firmly in the hands of the state, or acted as direct or indirect mouthpieces for government while in private ownership. Exceptions to this rule are local and community media – predominantly (shortwave) radio in, for example, Africa and Latin America. However, as this began to change, stakeholders involved in the process passionately advocated the powerful role of the media to inform and educate the masses.

Each new mass medium has been hailed for its educational and cultural benefits and has been feared for its disturbing influence. The potential for communication technology to promote enlightenment has been invoked once again in respect of the latest communication technologies – those based on the computer and telecommunications. More fears than hopes are now being voiced about the enlightenment role of the major mass media, as they increasingly seek to make profits in a highly competitive marketplace where entertainment and individual profiling through the data gathered via online consumer behaviours have more market value than education or art. Public **broadcasting** is again being defended against market forces on the grounds of its contribution to public knowledge and societal solidarity. Arguments are heard for a similar public service presence in **cyberspace**.

## THE MEDIA AS PROBLEM OR SCAPEGOAT

Despite hopeful as well as fearful scenarios, the passing of decades does not seem to have changed the tendency of public opinion both to blame the media and to demand that they do more to solve society's ills. There are successive instances of alarm relating to the media, whenever an insoluble or inexplicable social problem arises. The most constant element has been a negative perception of the media, especially the inclination to link media portrayals of crime, sex and violence with the seeming increase in social and moral disorder. These waves of alarm have been called '**moral panics**', partly because they are based on little evidence either of media cause or actual effect (Drotner, 1992).

A related structural concern is that of media addiction, especially with regard to the young and the time children and teenagers spend with (their) media. In their review of trends and data about young people and new media, Palfrey and Gasser (2008) depict those they call 'digital natives' as an alien species who live in a completely mediated environment estranged from their parents, other adults and professionals. Various observers claim that today's youth is different from previous generations in that they do not view technology as technology, but rather as air because they grew up with it – as just another part of the environment. Rather than appreciating the fact that such claims have been made about 'the young' throughout history – remember those kids and their evil rock and roll music – or recognizing the lack of evidence supporting such claims, in the context of the ongoing **mediatization** of society numerous influential books have been published suggesting that all this 'mediatime' makes us dumb (Bauerlein, 2008), lonely (Turkle, 2011), or just a combination of fat, dumb, aggressive, lonely, sick, narcissistic, miserable and unhappy (Spitzer, 2012; Twenge, 2017).

New ills have also been found to lay at the door of the media, especially such phenomena as populist political protest and electoral success, xenophobia, misogyny, and even the supposed decline of democracy and rise of political apathy and cynicism. Individual harms now include references to depression, acquisitiveness, obesity (or its opposite) and lassitude. A popular object of such waves of alarm has been the Internet, suspected of encouraging paedophilia, (extreme) **pornography**, violence and hate as well as aiding terrorist organizations and international crime. Paradoxically or not, it has usually been the media themselves that have highlighted and amplified many of these alarmist views, perhaps because they seem to confirm the power of the media or because older media like to report on the perceived failings and dangers of their newer competitors, and most likely because they are already popularly believed and also newsworthy.

# THE 'MASS' CONCEPT

This mixture of popular **prejudice** and social theorizing about the media has formed the background against which funding for research has been allocated, studies have been commissioned, hypotheses have been formulated and tested, and more precise theories about media and mass communication have been developed. And while the interpretations of the direction (positive or negative) of mass media influence show much divergence, the most persistent element in public estimation of the media has been a simple agreement on their strong influence. In turn, this perception owes much to various meanings of the term 'mass'. Although the concept of '**mass society**' was not fully developed until after the Second World War, the essential ideas were circulating before the end of the nineteenth century. The key term 'mass' in fact unites a number of concepts which are important for understanding how the process of mass communication has usually been understood, right up to the present.

Early uses of the term usually carried negative associations. It referred initially to the multitude or the 'common people', usually seen as uneducated, ignorant and potentially irrational, unruly and even violent (as when the mass turned into a mob of rioters) (Bramson, 1961). It could also be used in a positive sense, however, especially in the socialist tradition, where it connoted the strength and solidarity of ordinary working people when organized for collective purposes or when having to bear oppression. The terms 'mass support', 'mass movement' and 'mass action' are examples whereby large numbers of people acting together can be seen in a positive light. As Raymond Williams (1961: 289) commented: 'There are no masses, only ways of seeing people as masses.'

Aside from its political references, the word 'mass', when applied to a set of people, has unflattering implications. It suggests an amorphous collection of individuals without much individuality. This is close to the meaning which early sociologists sometimes gave to the media **audience**. It was the large and seemingly undifferentiated audiences for the popular media that provided the clearest examples of the concept. The main features attributed to the mass are given in Box 3.1. These include both objective and subjective or perceived features.

## 3.1

### The concept of mass: theoretical features

- Composed of a large aggregate of people
- Undifferentiated composition
- Mainly negative perception
- Lacking internal order or structure
- Reflective of a wider mass society

## THE MASS COMMUNICATION PROCESS

The term 'mass communication' came into use in the late 1930s, but its essential features were already well known and have not really changed since, even if the media themselves have in some ways become less massive. Early mass media were quite diverse in their scale and conditions of operation. For instance, popular films could be seen in village tents as well as metropolitan picture palaces. The newspaper press ranged from popular city dailies to small local weeklies. Even so, we can discern the typical form of mass communication according to certain general characteristics, which have already been introduced in Chapter 1.

The most obvious feature of the mass media is that they are designed to reach the *many*. Potential audiences are viewed as large aggregates of more or less anonymous consumers, and the relationship between sender and receiver is affected accordingly. It is important to note that such large aggregates of people as audiences for the messages of mass media do not preclude social or otherwise meaningful connections and experiences (Freidson, 1953). The 'sender' is often the organization itself or a professional communicator (journalist, presenter, producer, entertainer, etc.) whom it employs. If not this, it is another voice of society given or sold access to media channels (advertiser, politician, preacher, advocate of a cause, etc.). A fascinating feature of the contemporary media environment is how the term 'mass' can refer both to the senders and receivers of information, as people massively engage in minor or major forms of one-to-many communication through (video) weblogs, posts to photosharing platforms, edits to wiki-based webpages, and any and all uploads, likes and tags to one of the countless social media platforms available. Finally, in the digital context, a sender can also mean some kind of automated software that pushes content to someone based on their browsing, clicking, or programme selection behaviour.

The relationship is inevitably one-directional, one-sided and impersonal, and there is a social as well as a physical distance between sender and receiver. The former usually has more authority, prestige or expertise than the latter. One should not mistake all this mass self-communication, by which the receiver becomes the sender, to mean that control has shifted towards the audience. Indeed, as Terranova (2000) noted early on, the contributions people make to social (and other online) media primarily amount to 'free labour' in the service of the corporations that run such platforms. The relationship is not only asymmetrical, it is often calculative or manipulative in intention. It is essentially non-moral, based on a service promised or asked for in some unwritten contract with no mutual obligation. Online, such contracts take the form of End-User Licensing Agreements that we all have to electronically sign (sometimes over and over again) when using any kind of online service, software or platform.

The symbolic content or message of mass communication is typically 'manufactured' in standardized ways (mass production) and is reused and repeated in identical forms. Its flow is overwhelmingly one-directional. It has generally lost its uniqueness and originality through reproduction and overuse. The media message is a product of work with an exchange value in the media market and a use value for its receiver, the media consumer. It is essentially a commodity and differs in this respect from the symbolic content of other types of human communication. Even the wide variety of contributions through mass self-communication quite often follows some kind of industrial conventions, albeit modified by a general lack of formal and informal rules, standards and codes of practices to which media professionals tend to adhere.

One early definition (Janowitz, 1968) of the mass communication process reads as follows: 'Mass communications comprise the institutions and techniques by which specialized groups employ technological devices (press, radio, films, etc.) to disseminate

MCQUAIL'S MEDIA AND MASS COMMUNICATION THEORY
THEORIES

symbolic content to large, heterogeneous and widely dispersed audiences.' In this and similar definitions, the word 'communication' is really equated with 'transmission', as viewed by the sender, rather than the fuller meaning of the term, which includes the notions of response, sharing and interaction. This definition is also limited by its equating the *process* of mass communication with the *means* of transmission. However, the two are not synonymous. In particular, new media can (sometimes simultaneously) serve both for mass communication and for personalized, individual communication.

Mass media also had uses that cannot be strictly counted as mass communication (for example, as a means of passing time, seeking companionship, etc.). There are other common uses of the same technologies and other kinds of relationships mediated through the same **networks**. For instance, the basic forms and technologies of 'mass' communication are the same as those used for very local newspapers or radio and they might also be used in education. Mass media can also be used for individual, private or organizational purposes. The same media that carry public messages to large publics for public purposes can also carry personal notices, advocacy messages, charitable appeals, situations-vacant advertisements and many varied kinds of information and culture. This point is especially relevant at a time of **convergence** of communication technologies, when the boundaries between public and private and large-scale and individual communication networks are increasingly blurred.

Mass communication was, from the beginning, more of an idea than a reality. The term stands for a condition and a process that is theoretically possible, intrinsically dynamic, and therefore rarely found in any pure form. Where it does seem to occur, it often turns out to be less massive, and less technologically determined, than it appears on the surface. The defining characteristics of the concept are set out in Box 3.2. All of these have an objective basis, but the concept as a whole is often used in a subjective and imprecise way.

---

## 3.2

## The mass communication process: theoretical features

- Large-scale distribution and reception of content
- One-directional flow
- Asymmetrical relation between sender and receiver
- Impersonal and anonymous relationship with audience
- Calculative or market relationship with audience
- Standardization and commodification of content

---

# THE MASS AUDIENCE

Herbert Blumer (1939) was the first to define the mass formally as a new type of social formation in modern society, by contrasting it with other formations, especially the *group, crowd* and *public*. In a small group, all its members know each other, are aware of their common membership, share the same values, have a certain structure of relationships which is stable over time, and interact to achieve some purpose. The crowd is larger but still restricted within observable boundaries in a particular space. It is, however, temporary and rarely re-forms with the same composition. It may possess a high degree of identity and share the same 'mood', but there is usually no structure or order to its moral and social composition. It can act, but its actions are often seen to have an affective and emotional, often irrational, character.

The third collectivity named by Blumer, the public, is likely to be relatively large, widely dispersed and enduring. It tends to form around an issue or cause in public life, and its primary purpose is to advance an interest or opinion and to achieve political change. It is an essential element in democratic politics, based on the ideal of rational discourse within an open political system and often comprising the better-informed section of the population. The rise of the public is characteristic of modern liberal democracies and related to the rise of the 'bourgeois' or party newspapers described earlier.

The term 'mass' captured several features of the new audiences for cinema and radio (and to some extent the popular press) that were not covered by any of these three concepts. The new audience was typically much larger than any group, crowd or public. It was very widely dispersed, and its members were usually unknown to each other or to whoever brought the audience into existence. It lacked self-awareness and self-identity and was incapable of acting together in an organized way to secure objectives. It was marked by a shifting composition within changing boundaries. It did not act for itself but was, rather, 'acted upon' (and thus an object of manipulation). It was heterogeneous in consisting of large numbers from all social strata and demographic groups, but also homogeneous in its choice of some particular object of interest and according to the perception of those who would like to manipulate it. The main features attributed to the mass audience are summarized in Box 3.3, reflecting changes in the features of mass audiences to account for the formation of a mass audience when, through their own contributions to the sending and receiving of messages, certain issues go 'viral' via online (social) media.

The audience for mass media is not the only social formation that can be characterized in this way, since the word 'mass' is sometimes applied to consumers in the expression 'mass market' or to large bodies of voters (the 'mass electorate'). It is significant, however, that such entities also often correspond with media audiences and that mass media are used to direct or control both consumer and political behaviour. A similar process works the other way around in the contemporary context, as masses of what Zizi Papacharissi (2014) calls 'affective publics' can influence political and economic processes in profound ways (for example, through online activism).

MCQUAIL'S MEDIA AND MASS COMMUNICATION THEORY
THEORIES

Within the conceptual framework sketched, media use was represented as a form of 'mass behaviour', which in turn encouraged the application of methods of 'mass research' – especially large-scale surveys and other methods for recording the reach and response of audiences to what was offered. A commercial and organizational logic for 'audience research' was furnished with theoretical underpinnings. It seemed to make sense, as well as being practical, to discuss media audiences in purely *quantitative* terms. In fact, the methods of research tended only to reinforce a **biased** conceptual perspective (treating the audience as a mass market). Research into ratings and the reach of press and broadcasting reinforced a view of the audience as a mass market of consumers.

## THE MASS MEDIA AS AN INSTITUTION OF SOCIETY

Despite changing technology, mass communication persists within the whole framework of the mass media institution. This refers broadly to the set of media organizations and activities, together with their own formal or informal rules of operation and sometimes legal and policy requirements set by the society. These reflect the expectations of the public as a whole and of other social institutions (such as politics, governments, law, religion and the economy). Media institutions have gradually developed around the key activities of **publication** and dissemination. They also overlap with other institutions, especially as these expand their public communication activities – to find a political party, company or business without an active media presence is a rarity today. In doing so, mass media become powerful in society in two ways: first, they are an institution with a certain internal logic (see Part 4 of this book) and prominent sphere of (economic, social, cultural and political) influence, and secondly, because 'media simultaneously become an integrated part of other institutions like politics, work, family, and religion as more and more of these institutional activities are performed through both interactive and mass media' (Hjarvard,

2008a: 105). This 'mediatization' of society, whereby society to an increasing degree is submitted to, or becomes dependent on, the media and their logic, provides a fruitful topic of theoretical discussion in the field, as it is an attempt to recognize the prominent role of mass media and the process of mass communication in society without reverting to early twentieth-century misgivings about the all-powerful nature of media (see Chapter 4).

Mass media traditionally have been internally segmented according to type of technology (print, film, television, etc.) and often within each type (such as national versus local press or broadcasting). They also change over time and differ from one country to another. The key trend over the last few decades has been an increased convergence and integration of different technologies, types and forms of mass media. Even so, there are several typical defining features, in addition to the central activity of producing and distributing 'knowledge' (information, ideas, culture) on behalf of those who want to communicate, and in response to individual and collective demand.

While it is quite common to find the entire set of mass media referred to as an institution in such expressions as the 'effects of the media' or 'responsibilities of media in society', in free societies there is no formal institution of the media in the way that there is in respect of health, education, justice or the military. Nevertheless, the media separately or together do tend to develop institutional forms that are embedded in and recognized by the wider society. The 'press' is a good example of this. There are no formal definitions or boundaries, but it typically describes all newspapers and magazines, journalists, editors and media owners. In many countries there is no formal external regulation, but there are voluntary codes of conduct and ethics. The press accepts some public responsibilities and receives some rights and privileges in return, especially a guarantee of freedom. Other media, such as broadcasting, develop their own institutional identity. There is enough in common between all media to justify a reference to a single 'media institution', the main conceptual features of which are shown in Box 3.4.

## 3.4

## The mass media institution: main theoretical features

- The core activity is the production and distribution of information and culture
- Media acquire functions and responsibilities in the 'public sphere' that are overseen by the institution
- Control is mainly by self-regulation, with limits set by society
- Boundaries of membership are porous
- The freedom and relative independence of media are governed by the state

# MASS CULTURE AND POPULAR CULTURE

The typical *content* that flowed through the newly created channels to the new mass audience was from the start a very diverse mixture of stories, images, information, ideas, sports, entertainment and spectacles. Even so, the single concept of '**mass culture**' was commonly used to refer to all this (see Rosenberg and White, 1957). Mass culture had a wider reference to the tastes, preferences, manners and styles of the mass (or just the majority) of people. It also once had a generally negative connotation, mainly because of its associations with the assumed cultural preferences of 'uncultivated', non-discriminating or just lower-class audiences.

The term is quite dated, partly because class differences are less sharply drawn or clearly acknowledged and they no longer separate an educated professional minority from a large, poor and ill-educated working-class majority. It is also the case that the former hierarchy of 'cultural taste' is no longer widely accepted. Even when in fashion, the idea of mass culture as an exclusively 'lower-class' phenomenon was not empirically justified, since it referred to the normal cultural experience of almost everyone to some degree (Wilensky, 1964). The expression 'popular culture' is now generally preferred because it simply denotes what many or even most people like. It may also have some connotation of what is popular with the young in particular. More recent developments in media and **cultural studies** (as well as in society) have led to a positive valuation of popular culture. For some media scholars (Fiske, 1987; Costera Meijer, 2001), the very fact of popularity is a token of value in political as well as cultural terms, and can be deployed as a marker of quality as much as any other form of expression.

## DEFINITIONS AND CONTRASTS

Attempts to define mass culture often contrasted it (unfavourably) with more traditional forms of (symbolic) culture. Wilensky, for instance, compared it with the notion of 'high culture', which would refer to two characteristics of the product:

> (1) it is created by, or under the supervision of, a cultural elite operating within some aesthetic, literary, or scientific tradition ... (2) critical standards independent of the consumer of their product are systematically applied to it. ... 'Mass culture' will refer to cultural *products manufactured solely for the mass market.* Associated characteristics, not intrinsic to the definition, are *standardization* of product and *mass behaviour* in its use. (Wilenski, 1964: 176, original emphasis)

Mass culture was also differentiated from an earlier cultural form – that of folk culture, indigenous culture or a traditional culture which more evidently comes from the people and usually predates (or is independent of) mass media and the mass production of culture (see Beltrão, 1971). Original folk culture (especially expressed in dress, customs, song, stories, dance, etc.) was being widely rediscovered in Europe during the nineteenth century and throughout Latin America in the first half of the twentieth century. Often, this was for reasons connected with the rise of nationalism, otherwise as part of the 'arts and crafts' movement and the romantic reaction against industrialism. The rediscovery (by the middle classes) was taking place at the very time that it was rapidly disappearing among worker and peasant classes because of social change. After the end of the colonial era (throughout Africa and parts of Asia), the removal of dictatorships and military regimes (across Latin America) and the rise of emancipatory social movements such as among the Aboriginals in Australia and Native Americans in the United States, more attention was paid, investments made and scholarly work done on indigenous and minority media, in recognition of 'the longstanding contribution that media makes to fulfilling of social justice goals' (Podkalicka and Rennie, 2018: 3).

Folk culture was originally made unselfconsciously, using traditional forms, themes, materials and means of expression, and had usually been incorporated into everyday life. Critics of mass culture often regretted the loss of the integrity and simplicity of folk art, and the issue is still alive around the world (Woitowicz and Gadini, 2018). The new urban industrial working class of Western Europe and North America were the first consumers of the new mass culture. No doubt the mass media drew on some popular cultural streams and adapted others to the conditions of urban life to fill the cultural void created by industrialization, but intellectual critics could usually see only a cultural loss. In recent decades, observations have been made that highlight the mixing of mass, popular and folk or indigenous cultures in media genres, paying attention to the different ways of appropriation and re-appropriation of themes and symbols across cultures – in part inspired by globalization. The main features of mass culture are summarized in Box 3.5.

## 3.5

## The idea of mass culture: main features

- Non-traditional form and content
- Intended for mass consumption
- Mass produced and formulaic
- Pejorative image
- Commercial
- Homogenized

MCQUAIL'S MEDIA AND MASS COMMUNICATION THEORY
THEORIES

## OTHER VIEWS OF MASS CULTURE

The rise of mass culture was open to more than one interpretation. Bauman (1972), for instance, took issue with the idea that mass communication media *caused* mass culture, arguing that they were more a tool to shape something that was happening in any case as a result of the increasing cultural homogeneity of national societies. In his view, what is often referred to as 'mass culture' is more properly just a more universal or standardized culture. Several features of mass communication have contributed to the process of standardization, especially dependence on the market, the supremacy of large-scale (often multinational) organization and the application of new technology to cultural production. This more objective approach helps to defuse some of the conflict that has characterized the debate about mass culture. In some measure, the 'problem of mass culture' reflected the need to come to terms with new technological possibilities for symbolic reproduction (Benjamin, 1977) which challenged established notions of art. The issue of mass culture was fought out in social and political terms, without being resolved in aesthetic terms.

Despite the search for a seemingly value-free conception of mass culture, the issue remains conceptually and ideologically troublesome. As Bourdieu (1986) and others have clearly demonstrated, different conceptions of cultural merit are strongly connected with social class differences. Possession of economic capital has usually gone hand in hand with possession of 'cultural capital' (cf. the accumulation of knowledge, behaviours and skills that one can tap into to demonstrate one's cultural competence, and thus one's social status or standing in society), which can sometimes also be used for material advantages. Class-based value systems once strongly maintained the superiority of 'high' and traditional culture against much of the typical popular culture of the mass media. The support for such value systems (though maybe not for the class system) has weakened, although the issue of differential cultural quality remains alive as an aspect of a continuing cultural and media policy debate.

Lastly, we can keep in mind that, as noted above, 'popular culture' has been widely 'revalued' by social and cultural theorists. It is no longer viewed as lacking in originality, creativity or merit and is often celebrated for its meanings, cultural significance and expressive value. If anything, the collapse of categories such as 'mass' and 'popular' culture (and a subsequent highly personalized reassembly of culture) can be seen as a central feature of media and mass communication today.

## REASSESSING THE CONCEPT OF MASS

The idea of a mass or a mass society was always an abstract notion, expressing a critical view of contemporary cultural trends. Nevertheless, some of the ills and discontents that it once referred to are still with us, sometimes under new names. These include: experience of loneliness and feelings of isolation; feelings of powerlessness in the face of economic, political and environmental forces outside our control; the sense of impersonality in much of modern life, sometimes made worse by information technology; a decline in togetherness; and a loss of security.

A particular instance of the continued relevance of the 'mass' concept in a contemporary context is the rise in popularity of the zombie, as a figure from popular culture (in an endless array of books, movies and video games) as well as a metaphor for the lived experience of many people. The relatability of the zombie seems to be grounded in people's feelings of powerlessness in the face of contemporary global threats, such as stock fluctuations and crashes, terrorism and climate change. Zombies can perhaps be considered to be the 'monster of the moment', putting a particular kind of human face on a widespread sense of crisis (Deuze, 2015).

What is probably clearer now is that mass media can be as much a part of the solution as of the problem. Depending on who and where we are, they offer ways of coping with the difficulties of large-scale society, making sense of our predicament and mediating our relations with larger forces. The media are now probably less 'massive', one-directional and distant, and more responsive and participative. But they are not always benign in their workings. They can exert power without accountability and destroy individual lives by aggressive intrusion into privacy, by **stereotyping** and stigmatizing, and by systematic misinformation. When they agree on some issue there is little tolerance of deviance, and when they decide to support the authorities there is no court of appeal. They can undermine as well as support the democratic political process. They have in fact some of the characteristics of benevolent despots – by turn endearing, capricious, ferocious or irrational. For these reasons, it is necessary to keep a long memory even for what seem to be old-fashioned notions.

# THE RISE OF A DOMINANT PARADIGM FOR THEORY AND RESEARCH

The ideas about media and society, and the various sub-concepts of 'mass' that have been described, have helped to shape a framework of research into mass communication which has been described as 'dominant' in more than one sense. The 'dominant paradigm' combines a view of powerful mass media in a mass society with the typical research practices of the emerging social sciences, especially social surveys, social-psychological experiments and statistical analyses. The underlying view of society in the dominant paradigm is essentially normative. It presumes a certain kind of normally functioning 'good society', which would be democratic (elections, universal suffrage, representation), liberal (secular, free-market conditions, individualistic, freedom of speech), pluralistic (institutionalized competition between various parties and interests), consensual and orderly (peaceful, socially integrated, fair, legitimate), and also well informed. The liberal-pluralist perspective does not view social inequality as essentially problematic or even unjust, as long as tensions and conflicts can be resolved by existing institutional means.

The potential or actual good or harm to be expected from mass media has largely been judged according to this model, which coincides with an idealized view of western society. The contradictions within this view of society and its distance from social reality are often ignored. Most early research concerning media in developing or Third World countries was guided by the assumption that these societies would gradually converge on the same (more advanced and progressive) western model. The literature increasingly not just calls for 'dewesternizing' and internationalizing media and mass communication research (Curran and Park, 2000; Thussu, 2009b), but actively includes voices, experiences and research published outside the western world (Willems, 2014; Wasserman, 2018). Furthermore, as Waisbord and Mellado (2014: 362) show, 'dewesternization' often has a different meaning and longer history outside the United States and Europe, as it tends to be seen as 'a necessary shift to reorient intellectual work against academic Eurocentrism', rather than just to broaden perspectives, 'shake up certainties grounded in a narrow set of cases and analytical perspectives, and to break away from the provincialism of scholarly research'. Gunaratne (2010), in turn, argues for universalizing media and mass communication scholarship by way of integrating the worldviews, intellectual histories and trajectories from different parts of the world next to the dominant western way of conceptualizing and theorizing. Many scholars, in particular those working in non-western countries, advocate theories and methods that do not just react to the dominant approaches from the West, but build on indigenous or otherwise 'native' communication and media traditions (M'Bayo, Sunday and Amobi, 2012; Murthy, 2016; Jia, 2017).

Although progress is slow, it is clear from these fields of research that as much as there are similarities in theorizing about mass media and society, there are countless unique divergences – and the role of mass media is never neatly linear, nor necessarily progressive. Expectations about the role media would play in various (non-western) societies and communities around the world certainly shared the at once hopeful and frightful, and more often than not developed as a critique of western models of 'development' rather than simply embracing a progressive narrative.

Early communication research was also influenced by the notion that the model of a liberal, pluralist and just society was threatened by an alternative, totalitarian form (communism), where the mass media were distorted into tools for suppressing democracy. The awareness of this alternative helped to identify and even reinforce the norm described. The media often saw themselves as playing a key role in supporting and expressing the values of the 'western way of life'. Since the virtual extinction of communism (and its subsequent merger with capitalism), other enemies have emerged, notably international terrorism, sometimes linked (by the media and authorities) with religious fundamentalism or other 'extremist', populist or revolutionary movements.

## ORIGINS IN FUNCTIONALISM AND INFORMATION SCIENCE

The theoretical elements of the dominant paradigm were not invented for the case of the mass media, but were largely taken over from sociology, psychology and an applied version of information science. This took place especially in the decade after the Second World War, when there was a largely unchallenged North American **hegemony** over both the social sciences and the mass media (Tunstall, 1977). Sociology, as it matured theoretically, offered a functionalist framework of analysis for the media as for other institutions. Lasswell (1948) was the first to formulate a clear statement of the 'functions' of communication in society – meaning essential tasks performed for its maintenance (see Chapter 4). The general assumption is that communication works towards the integration, continuity and order of society, although mass communication also has potentially dysfunctional (disruptive or harmful) consequences. Despite a much-reduced intellectual appeal, the language of functions has proved difficult to escape from in discussions of media and society.

The second theoretical element influential in the dominant paradigm guiding media research stemmed from information theory, as developed by Shannon and Weaver (1949), which was concerned with the technical efficiency of communication channels for carrying information. They developed a model for analysing information transmission that visualized communication as a sequential process. This process begins with a *source* that selects a *message*, which is then *transmitted*, in the form of a *signal*, over a *communication channel*, to a *receiver*, who transforms the signal back into a message for a *destination*. The model was designed to account for differences between messages as sent and messages as received, these differences being considered to result from *noise* or *interference* affecting the channels. This 'transmission' model was not directly concerned with *mass* communication, but it was popularized as a versatile way of conceiving many human communication processes, with particular reference to the effects of message transmission.

A third pillar of the paradigm is to be found in the methodological developments of the mid-century period. A combination of advances in 'mental measurement' (especially applied to individual attitudes and other attributes) and in statistical analysis appeared to offer new and powerful tools for achieving generalized and reliable knowledge of previously hidden processes and states. The methods seemed able to answer questions about the influence of mass media and about their effectiveness in persuasion and attitude change. An additional contribution to the paradigm was the high status of 'behaviourism' in psychology and of the experimental method in particular, often based on one version or another of **stimulus–response** theory. These developments were very much in line with the requirements of the transmission model.

## BIAS OF THE PARADIGM TOWARDS STUDYING MEDIA EFFECTS AND SOCIAL PROBLEMS

According to Rogers (1986: 7), the transmission model 'was the single most important turning point in the history of communication science' and it 'led communication scientists into a linear, effects-oriented approach to human communication in the decades following 1949'. Rogers also notes that the result was to lead communication scientists into 'the intellectual cul-de-sac of focusing mainly upon the *effects* of communication, especially mass communication' (ibid.: 88). Rogers and others have long recognized the blind spot in this model, and more recent thinking about communication research is much more nuanced in its approach. Even so, the linear causal approach was what many wanted, and still do want, from communication research, especially those who see communication primarily as an efficient device for getting a message to many people, whether as advertising, political propaganda or public information.

The fact that communication neither usually appears that way from the point of view of receivers, nor works as envisaged, and that generally the effects or efficiency of the transmission model are not supported by the evidence of over 60 years of communication research (Rains, Levine and Weber, 2018), has taken a long time to register. The theoretical materials for a very different model of (mass) communication were actually in place relatively early – based on previous thinking by several (North American) social scientists, especially G.H. Mead, C.H. Cooley and Robert Park. Such a 'model' would have represented communication as essentially social and interactive, concerned with the sharing of meaning, not impact (see Hardt, 1991).

Against this background, the path taken by 'mainstream' mass media research is clear enough. Research has mostly been concerned with the measurement of the effects of mass media, whether intended or unintended. The main aims of research in the dominant paradigm have been the improvement of the effectiveness of communication for legitimate ends (such as advertising or public information) or the assessment of whether mass media are a cause of social problems (such as crime, violence or other kinds of delinquency, but also social unrest). Traces of the linear causal model are widely found in research, and even the findings that have accumulated around its 'failure' have been paradoxically supportive. The main reasons for only finding a number of small effects in all these decades of dedicated research is generally thought to be the mediating role of social group and personal relationships, as well as a host of other variables, including historical and cultural context (Miller, 2009) and frequency of exposure (Lang, 2013). Overall, there is a recognition that 'communication is multi-determined and highly 'contingent' (Rains et al., 2018: 14), substantiating the call for more integrated (theoretical and methodological) approaches.

Box 3.6 summarizes the ideas presented in the preceding section. The elements of the paradigm bring together several features of the case: the kind of society in which it might apply, some ideas about the typical purposes and character of mass communication, assumptions about media effects, plus a justification of the role of research.

---

**3.6**

## The dominant paradigm of communication research: main assumptions

- A liberal-pluralist ideal of society
- The media have certain functions in society
- Media effects on audiences are direct and linear
- Group relations and individual differences modify effects of media
- Quantitative research and variable analysis
- Media viewed either as a potential social problem or a means of persuasion
- Behaviourist and quantitative methods have primacy

---

## AN ALTERNATIVE, CRITICAL PARADIGM

The critique of the dominant paradigm also has several elements, and what follows is a composite picture woven from different voices that are not always in accord. In particular, there is a theoretical and methodological line of criticism that is distinct from normative objections. From a pragmatic point of view, the simple transmission model does not work for a number of reasons: it assumes communication to be 'perfect' from the outset; signals simply do not reach receivers or not those intended; messages are not understood as they are sent; there is always much 'noise' in the channels that further distorts the message; and in its focus on what communication *is* it excludes a consideration of what communication *means*. Moreover, little communication is actually unmediated; what evades the mass media is typically filtered through other channels or by way of personal contacts. All this undermines the notion of powerful media. Early notions of the media as a hypodermic syringe or 'magic bullet' that would always have the intended effect were swiftly shown to be quite inadequate (Chaffee and Hochheimer, 1982; DeFleur and Ball-Rokeach, 1989). It has been clear for several decades that mass media simply do not have the direct effects once attributed to them (Klapper, 1960). In fact, it has always been difficult to prove any substantial effect.

## A DIFFERENT VIEW OF SOCIETY AND THE MEDIA

Most broadly, the 'alternative paradigm' rests on a different view of society, one which does not accept the prevailing liberal-capitalist order as just or inevitable or the best one can hope for in the fallen state of humankind. Nor does it accept the rational-calculative, utilitarian model of social life as at all adequate or desirable, or the commercial model as the only or best way to run media. There is an alternative, idealist and sometimes utopian **ideology**, but not necessarily a worked-out model of an ideal social system. Nevertheless, there is a sufficient common basis for rejecting the hidden ideology of pluralism and of conservative functionalism.

There has been no shortage of vocal critics of the media themselves, from the early years of the twentieth century, especially in relation to their commercialism, low standards of truth and decency, control by unscrupulous monopolists and much more. The original ideological inspiration for a well-grounded alternative has been socialism or **Marxism** in one variant or another. The first significant impulse was given by the *émigrés* from the **Frankfurt School** who went to the USA in the 1930s and helped to promote an alternative view of the dominant commercial mass culture (Jay, 1973; Hardt, 1991; see Chapter 5). Their contribution was to provide a strong intellectual base for seeing the process of mass communication as manipulative and ultimately oppressive (see Chapter 5). Their critique was both political and cultural. The influential ideas of C. Wright Mills (1956) concerning a mass society where a ruling elite benefited from a mass society (partly established through mass media governed by the same private interests that constitute political institutions) rather than one constituted out of active publics articulated a clear alternative view of the media, and eloquently exposed the liberal fallacy of pluralist control.

It was during the 1960s and 1970s that the alternative paradigm really took shape, under the influence of the 'ideas of 1968', combining anti-war and liberation movements of various kinds as well as neo-Marxism. The causes at issue included student democracy, feminism and anti-imperialism. What is important to note here is that the kind of theories and research projects developed from this model – generally considered to be the basis for the discipline of media studies – also worked from an assumption that the media are all-powerful and (especially in the case of television) possibly 'turn people away from artistic and social traces of authentic intersubjectivity and towards control of individual consciousness' (Miller, 2009: 39). Much later media studies would come to embrace popular culture, and gradually came to study all parts of the communication process (including the producers and industries of the media), following a trajectory not that dissimilar from communication science.

The main components of, and supports for, an alternative paradigm are as follows. The first is a much more sophisticated notion of ideology in media content which has allowed researchers to 'decode' the ideological messages of mass-mediated entertainment and news (which tend towards legitimating established power structures and defusing opposition). The notion of fixed meanings embedded in media content and leading to predictable and measurable impact was rejected. Instead, we have to view meaning as constructed and messages as decoded according to the social situation and the interests of those in the receiving audience. This does not suggest that the powerful role of mass media is successfully 'broken down' by a critical audience, however – it just recognizes the multiple and often contradictory ways people make sense of mediated messages.

Secondly, the economic and political character of mass media organizations and structures nationally and internationally has been re-examined. These institutions are no longer taken at face value but can be assessed in terms of their operational strategies, which are far from neutral or non-ideological. The key focus of research in this area has been the notion of power: where it lies, how it is wielded, who it benefits and who gets excluded. As the critical paradigm has developed, it has moved from an exclusive concern with working-class subordination to a wider view of other kinds of domination, especially in relation to youth, identity, gender and ethnicity.

Thirdly, these changes have been matched by a turn to more 'qualitative' research, whether into culture, discourse or the ethnography of mass media use. This is sometimes referred to as a 'linguistic' turn since it reflected the renewed interest in studying the relation between language and society (sociolinguistics) and a conviction that the symbolic mediation of reality is actually more influential and open to study than reality itself. It is linked to the interest in exposing concealed ideological meanings, as noted above. This has provided alternative routes to knowledge and forged a link back to the neglected pathways of the sociological theories of symbolic interactionism and phenomenology that emphasized the role of individuals in expressing and constructing their own personal environment (see Jensen and Jankowski, 1991). This is part of a more general development of cultural studies, within which mass communication can be viewed in a new light. According to Dahlgren (1995), the cultural studies tradition 'confronts the scientistic self-delusion' of the dominant paradigm, but there is an inevitable tension between textual and socio-institutional analysis.

The communication relations between the First World and the Third World, especially in the light of changing technology, have also encouraged new ways of thinking about mass communication. For instance, the relationship is no longer seen as a matter of the enlightened transfer of development and democracy to 'backward' lands. It is at least as plausibly seen as economic and cultural domination. Lastly, although theory does not necessarily lead in a *critical* direction, the 'new media' have forced a re-evaluation of earlier thinking about media effects, if only because the model of one-directional mass communication can no longer be sustained. The main points of the perspective are summarized in Box 3.7.

MCQUAIL'S MEDIA AND MASS COMMUNICATION THEORY
THEORIES

## 3.7

### The alternative paradigm: main features

- Critical view of society and rejection of value neutrality
- Rejection of the transmission model of communication
- Non-deterministic view of media technology and messages
- Adoption of an interpretative and constructionist perspective
- Qualitative methodology
- Preference for cultural or political-economic theories
- Wide concern with inequality and sources of opposition in society

## PARADIGMS COMPARED

The alternative perspective is not just a mirror image of the dominant paradigm or a statement of opposition to the mechanistic and applied view of communication. It is based on a more complete view of communication as sharing and ritual rather than as just 'transmission'. It is complementary as well as being an alternative. It offers its own viable avenues of enquiry, but following a different agenda. The paradigm has been especially valuable in extending the range of methods and approaches to mass media in the broadest possible sense, including the articulation of minority or otherwise disenfranchised voices. The interaction and engagement between media experiences and social-cultural experiences are central to all this.

While this discussion has presented two main versions, it is arguable that both the 'alternative' and the 'dominant' approach each bring together two distinct elements – one 'critical' (motivated by strong value judgements of the media), the other 'interpretative' or 'qualitative' (more concerned with understanding). Potter, Cooper and Dupagne (1993) proposed a threefold division of the main paradigms for communication science: a 'social science' approach in which empirical questions about media were investigated by means of quantitative methods; an interpretative approach, employing qualitative methods and emphasizing the meaning-giving potential of media; and a 'critical analysis' approach based on critical social theory, especially from a leftist or political economic perspective. Fink and Gantz (1996) found this scheme to work well in a **content analysis** of published communication research. Meyrowitz (2008) has suggested that there are root narratives in the various research approaches to the effects and influence of media. He names these root narratives as, respectively, narratives of 'power and resistance' (often specific to the cultural/media studies approach), 'purposes and pleasures' (generally informing the social scientific approach), and 'structures and patterns' (derived from **medium theory**, itself a subset of the more generic 'media theory', investigating the characteristics of the medium rather than its content, senders or receivers of messages). Lang (2013) in turn suggests that the paradigms align in their assumption that media and mass communication are (or can be) powerful agents of change in society, where the dominant perspective seeks to find evidence (and explanations) for such effects, and the alternative perspective simply takes this powerful role for granted, instead opting to explore avenues for critique of the way media operate in society.

Leaving aside these issues of classification, it is clear that the alternative paradigm continues to evolve under the dual influence of changing theory (and fashion) and also the changing concerns of society in relation to the media. Original critical concerns about ideological manipulation, commercialism and social problems remain in focus as new issues have arisen. These relate, among others, to the environment, personal and collective identity, health and risk, trust and authenticity. Meanwhile, older issues, such as racism, war propaganda and inequality, have refused to go away, gaining new currency in a time of populist politics, new social movements and terrorism.

The differences of approach between dominant and alternative paradigms are deep-rooted, and their existence underlines the difficulty of having any unified 'science of communication'. The differences stem also from the very nature of (mass) communication, which has to deal in symbolic representation, values and ideas and cannot escape from being interpreted within ideological frameworks. While the reader of this book is not obliged to make a choice between the two main paradigms, knowing about them will help to make sense of the **diversity** of theories and of disagreements about the supposed 'facts' concerning mass media. Furthermore, as is emphasized throughout the book, calls are made across the field for mixed methods, triangulation of research approaches, and paradigmatic integration in order to address the complexity of the contemporary media and (mass) communication landscape.

## FOUR MODELS OF COMMUNICATION

The original definition of mass communication as a process depended on objective features of mass production, reproduction and distribution which were shared by several different media. It was very much a technologically and organizationally based definition, subordinating human considerations. Its validity has long been called into question, especially as a result of the conflicting views just discussed and, more recently, by the fact that the original mass production technology and the factory-like forms of organization have themselves been made obsolescent by social and technological change. We have to consider alternative, though not necessarily inconsistent, models (representations) of the process of public communication. At least four such models can be distinguished in the history of media and mass communication theory and research.

# A TRANSMISSION MODEL

At the core of the dominant paradigm can be found a particular view of communication as a process of *transmission* of a fixed quantity of information – the *message* as determined by the sender or source. Simple definitions of mass communication often follow Lasswell's (1948) observation that the study of mass communication is an attempt to answer the question, 'Who says what to whom, through what channel and with what effect?'. This represents the linear sequence already mentioned, which is largely built into standard definitions of the nature of predominant forms of mass communication. A good deal of early theorizing about mass communication (see, for example, McQuail and Windahl, 1993) was an attempt to extend and improve on this simplistic version of the process.

Perhaps the most complete early version of a model of mass communication, in line with the defining features noted above and consistent with the dominant paradigm, was offered by Westley and MacLean (1957). Their achievement was to recognize that mass communication involves the interpolation of a new 'communicator role' (such as that of the professional journalist in a formal media organization) between 'society' and 'audience'. The sequence is thus not simply (1) sender, (2) message, (3) channel, (4) many potential receivers, but rather (1) events and 'voices' in society, (2) channel/communicator role, (3) messages, (4) receiver. This revised version takes account of the fact that mass communicators do not usually originate 'messages' or communication. Rather they *relay* to a potential audience their own account (news) of a selection of the events occurring in the environment, or they give **access** to the views and voices of some of those (such as advocates of opinions, politicians, advertisers, performers and writers) who want to reach a wider public. There are three important features of the complete model as drawn by Westley and MacLean: one is the emphasis on the *selecting* role of mass communicators; the second is the fact that selection is undertaken according to an assessment of what the audience will find interesting; and the third is that communication is not purposive, beyond this last goal. The media themselves typically do not aim to persuade or educate or even to inform – they primarily seek to publish (and have an audience pay attention to) their work.

According to this model, mass communication is a self-regulating process that is guided by the interests and demands of an audience that is known only by its selections and responses to what is offered. Such a process can no longer be viewed as linear, since it is strongly shaped by 'feedback' from the audience both to the media and to the advocates and original communicators. This view of the mass media sees them as relatively open and neutral service organizations in a secular society, contributing to the work of other social institutions. It also substitutes the satisfaction of the audience as a measure of efficient performance for that of information transfer. It is not accidental that this model was based on the American system of free-market media. It would not very accurately fit a state-run media system or even a public broadcasting institution. It is also innocent of the idea that the free market might not necessarily reflect the interests of audiences or might also conduct its own form of purposeful propaganda.

## A RITUAL OR EXPRESSIVE MODEL

The transmission model remains a useful representation of the rationale and general operation of some media in some of their functions (especially general news media and advertising) – if only because professional communicators and institutions tend to think primarily in such terms about the process of (mass) communication. It is, however, incomplete and misleading as a representation of most media activities and of the diversity of communication processes that are at work. One reason for its weakness is the limitation of communication to the matter of 'transmission'. This version of communication, according to James Carey (1975: 3),

> is the commonest in our culture and is defined by terms such as sending, transmitting or giving information to others. It is formed off a metaphor of geography or transportation. . . . The centre of this idea of communication is the transmission of signals or messages over time for the purpose of control.

It implies instrumentality, cause-and-effect relations and one-directional flow. Carey pointed to the alternative view of communication as 'ritual', according to which

> communication is linked to such terms as sharing, participation, association, fellowship and the possession of a common faith. . . . A ritual view is not directed towards the extension of messages in space, but the maintenance of society in time; not the act of imparting information but the representation of shared beliefs. (ibid.: 8)

This alternative can equally be called an 'expressive' model of communication, since its emphasis is also on the intrinsic satisfaction of the sender (or receiver) rather than on some instrumental purpose (such as selling a product, advertising a service or persuading a prospective voter). Ritual or expressive communication depends on shared understandings and emotions. It is celebratory, consummatory (an end in itself) and decorative rather than utilitarian in aim and it often requires some element of 'performance' for communication to be realized. Communication is engaged in for the pleasures of expression and reception as much as for any useful purpose. The message of ritual communication is usually latent and ambiguous, depending on associations and symbols that are not chosen by the participants but made available in the culture. Medium and message are usually hard to separate. Ritual communication is also relatively timeless and unchanging.

Although, in natural conditions, ritual communication is not instrumental, it can be said to have consequences for society (such as more integration) or for social relationships.

From a ritual perspective, the endless status updates, shout-outs, blurbs, tweets, texts, clips, and other tiny snippets of information people continuously exchange online – elements of our 'phatic' media culture (based on small communicative gestures that are distinctly social, but are not intended to transmit substantial information) – are not about the message we send, but about the process of communication itself (Donath, 2007). This type of communication is not meaningless, as it implies 'the recognition, intimacy and sociability in which a strong sense of community is founded' (Miller, 2008: 395).

In some planned communication campaigns – for instance, in politics or advertising – the principles of ritual communication are merged with the expectations of transmission, through the use of potent symbols, latent appeals to cultural values, togetherness, myths and tradition. Ritual plays a part in unifying and in mobilizing affect and action in both the online and offline worlds, as much as it can serve to support 'imagined' communities, or even a completely 'virtual' sense of belonging (for example, being part of online communities of 'otherkin': people who identify as partially or completely non-human).

## COMMUNICATION AS DISPLAY AND ATTENTION: A PUBLICITY MODEL

Besides the transmission and ritual models, there is a third perspective that captures another important aspect of mass communication. This can be summarily labelled a *publicity model*. Often the primary aim of mass media is neither to transmit particular information nor to unite a public in some expression of culture, belief or values, but simply to catch and hold visual or aural attention. In doing so, the media attain one direct economic goal, which is to gain audience revenue (since attention equals consumption, for most practical purposes), and an indirect one, which is to sell (the probability of) audience attention to advertisers. As Elliott (1972: 164) has pointed out (implicitly adopting the transmission model as the norm), 'mass communication is liable not to be communication at all', in the sense of the 'ordered transfer of meaning'. It is more likely to be 'spectatorship', and the media audience is more often a set of spectators rather than participants or information receivers. The *fact* of attention often matters more than the *quality* of attention (which can rarely be adequately measured).

While those who use mass media for their own purposes do hope for some effect (such as persuasion or selling) beyond attention and publicity, gaining the latter remains the immediate goal and is often treated as a measure of success or failure. The publicity strategies of multimedia conglomerates are typically directed at getting maximum attention for their current products in as many media as possible and in multiple forms (interviews, news events, photos, guest appearances, social media sites, etc.). The goal is described as seeking to 'achieve a good share of mind' (Turow, 2009: 201). A good deal of research into media effect has been concerned with questions of image and awareness.

The fact of being known is often more important than the content of what is known and is the only necessary condition for **celebrity**. Similarly, the supposed power of the media to set political and other 'agendas' is an example of the attention-gaining process. Much effort in media production is devoted to devices for gaining and keeping attention by catching the eye, arousing emotion, stimulating interest. This is one aspect of what has been described as '**media logic**' (see p. 356), with the *substance* of a message often subordinated to the devices for presentation (Altheide and Snow, 1979, 1991). In a contemporary context, one could speak of an emerging dominant '**platform logic**' (Plantin et al., 2018), whereby digital platform-based services (such as those offered by Facebook and Google) increasingly determine access to (and attention for) any kind of information and services, while other institutions build or reorganize infrastructures to accommodate the logic of such platforms. The primary purpose of these platforms is attention, defined as 'time spent' using the platform interface.

The attention-seeking goal also corresponds with one important perception of the media by their audiences, who use the mass media for diversion and passing time. They seek to spend time 'with the media', both to escape and to supplement everyday reality, for example by reading a (free) newspaper on the train or browsing through various apps on a smartphone when waiting for a friend. The relationship between sender and receiver according to the display–attention model is not necessarily passive or uninvolved, but it is morally neutral and does not, in itself, imply a transfer or creation of meaning.

Going with the notion of communication as a process of display and attention are several additional features that do not apply to the transmission or ritual models:

- *Attention-gaining is a zero-sum process.* The time spent attending to one media display by one person cannot be given to another, and available audience time is finite, although time can be stretched and attention diluted. By contrast, there is no quantifiable limit to the amount of 'meaning' that can be sent and acquired or to the satisfaction that can be gained from participating in ritual communication processes.

- *Communication in the display–attention model exists only in the present.* There is no past that matters, and the future matters only as a continuation or amplification of the present. Questions of cause and effect relating to the receiver do not arise.

- *Attention-gaining is an end in itself and in the short term is value-neutral and essentially empty of meaning.* Form and technique take precedence over message content.

These three features can be seen as underlying, respectively, the *competitiveness*, the *actuality/transience* and the *objectivity/detachment* which are pronounced features of mass communication, especially within commercial media institutions.

# ENCODING AND DECODING OF MEDIA DISCOURSE: A RECEPTION MODEL

There is yet another version of the mass communication process, which involves an even more radical departure from the transmission model than the two variants just discussed. This depends very much on the adoption of the critical perspective described above, but it can also be understood as the view of mass communication from the position of many different receivers who do not perceive or understand the message 'as sent' or 'as expressed'. This model has its origins in **critical theory**, **semiology** and **discourse analysis**. It is located more in the domain of the cultural rather than the social sciences. It is strongly linked to the rise of '**reception analysis**' (see Holub, 1984; Jensen and Rosengren, 1990). It challenges the predominant methodologies of empirical social scientific audience research and also the humanistic studies of content because both fail to take account of the 'power of the audience' in giving meaning to messages.

The essence of the 'reception approach' is to locate the attribution and construction of meaning (derived from media) with the receiver. Media messages are always open and 'polysemic' (having multiple meanings) and are interpreted according to the context and the culture of receivers. Among the forerunners of reception analysis was a persuasive variant of critical theory, formulated by Stuart Hall (1974/1980), which emphasized the stages of transformation through which any media message passes on the way from its origins to its reception and interpretation. Hall accepted the premise that intended meaning is built into (encoded) symbolic content in both open and concealed ways that are hard to resist, but recognized the possibilities for rejecting or re-interpreting the intended message.

It is true that communicators choose to encode messages for ideological and institutional purposes and to manipulate language and media for those ends (media messages are given a 'preferred reading', or what might now be called 'spin'). Secondly, receivers ('decoders') are not obliged to accept messages as sent but can and do resist ideological influence by applying variant or oppositional readings, according to their own experience and outlook. This is described as 'differential decoding'. Thirdly, the devices and interfaces of different kinds of media – a television set, a smartphone, the website of a newspaper or community **portal** – influence and shape how a message looks and how it ends up with a receiver.

In Hall's model of the process of **encoding** and decoding (see also Chapter 13), he portrays the television programme (or any equivalent media text) as a *meaningful discourse*. This is encoded according to the *meaning structure* of the mass media production organization and its main supports, but decoded according to the different meaning structures and frameworks of knowledge of differently situated audiences. The path followed through the stages of the model is simple in principle. Communication originates within media institutions whose typical frameworks of meaning are likely to conform to dominant power structures. Specific messages are 'encoded', often in the form of established content **genres** (such as 'news', 'pop music', 'sport reports', '**soap operas**', 'police/ detective series') which have a face-value meaning and inbuilt guidelines for interpretation by an audience. The media are approached by their audiences in terms of 'meaning structures', which have their origin in the ideas and experience of the audience.

While the general implication is that meaning as decoded does not necessarily (or often) correspond with meaning as encoded (despite the mediation of conventional genres and shared language systems), the most significant point is that decoding can take a different course from that intended. Receivers can read between the lines and even reverse the intended direction of the message, and different media technologies shape messages in different ways. It is clear that this model and the associated theory embody several key principles: the multiplicity of meanings of media content; the existence of varied 'interpretative' communities; and the primacy of the receiver in determining meaning. While early effect research recognized the fact of selective perception, this was seen as a limitation on, or a condition of, the transmission model, rather than part of a quite different perspective. Contemporary concerns tend to include more awareness of the audience, as well as the materiality of the media, when exploring the ways in which mediated messages are received and understood.

## COMPARISONS

The discussion of these different models shows the inadequacy of any single concept or definition of mass communication that relies too heavily on what seem to be intrinsic characteristics or biases of the *technology* of multiple reproduction and dissemination. The human uses of technology are much more diverse and more determinant than was once assumed, and the technologies themselves are equally varied and complex. Of the four models summarized in comparative terms in Table 3.1, the transmission model is largely taken from older institutional contexts – education, religion, government – and is really appropriate only to media activities that are instructional, strictly (one-way) informational or propagandist in purpose.

Table 3.1  Four models of the mass communication process compared: each model involves differences of orientation on the part of the sender and receiver

| Model | Orientation of | |
|---|---|---|
| | Sender | Receiver |
| Transmission model | Transfer of meaning | Cognitive processing |
| Expressive or ritual model | Performance | Consummation/shared experience |
| Publicity model | Competitive display | Attention-giving spectatorship |
| Reception model | Preferential encoding | Differential decoding/construction of meaning |

The expressive or ritual model, while originating in the study of art, drama and entertainment and the many symbolic uses of communication, is particularly useful when interpreting the phatic communication culture of the Internet. It also applies to the many new audience participant and 'reality' media formats. The publicity or display–attention model reflects the central media goals of attracting audiences (high ratings and wide reach) for purposes of prestige or income. It covers that large sector of media activity that is engaged in advertising or public relations, directly or indirectly. It also applies to activities of news management and media 'spin' carried out by governments and other political actors in their own self-interest. The reception model reminds us that the seeming power of the media to mould, express or capture is partly illusory since the audience in the end disposes. The publicity and reception models can be seen as specifications of the transmission and ritual models of communication, in that they acknowledge some key dynamics of the media industry and the way institutions use (and think about) mass media.

## TOWARDS AN INTEGRATED MODEL FOR MEDIA AND MASS COMMUNICATION RESEARCH

As mentioned elsewhere throughout this book, the general trend (and recommendation) in the literature in recent years points towards increasing integration and cross-fertilization of models, methods and paradigms in media and mass communication theory and research. However, this is easier said than done. Academic units tend to be organized along either social scientific or humanistic disciplinary boundaries, scholarly journals are equally singular in their preferred approaches, and combining perspectives can be time-consuming and costly (for example, when it comes to mixed-method research designs).

In an attempt to show how the most common approaches and themes in media and mass communication research align according to the four main models, Figure 3.1 offers a rough guide with the understanding that many if not most of these themes map across the various models of communication. The new media environment, shifting our time and attention towards personal (and customizable) media, contributes to a collapsing of categories, while at the same time remaining mindful of the boundaries between concepts and models is helpful in order to formulate coherent and meaningful research questions.

Research in media and mass communication can be mapped along four key areas of investigation, each with its own prevailing perspectives about the nature of our relationship with (our) media. In quadrant 1, studies that focus on how mass media messages influence and shape public opinion and sentiment can be grouped, generally consisting of media effects, agenda-setting and **framing** research. Studies in quadrant 2, while similarly interested in the workings of mass media, focus more on the historical and long-term mutual shaping of media, communication, culture and society. Approaches in this

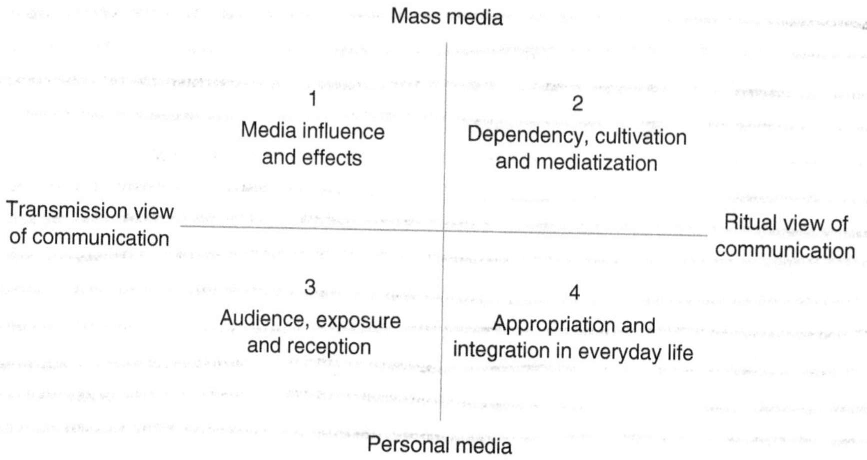

Mass media

|  | Mass media |  |
|---|---|---|
| 1<br>Media influence<br>and effects | | 2<br>Dependency, cultivation<br>and mediatization |

Transmission view                                                                Ritual view of
of communication                                                                 communication

|  |  |  |
|---|---|---|
| 3<br>Audience, exposure<br>and reception | | 4<br>Appropriation and<br>integration in everyday life |

Personal media

Figure 3.1  Integration of the transmission and ritual models of the mass communication process set against the most common themes of media and mass communication research and the emerging new media ecosystem

area were originally informed by media dependency theory (Ball-Rokeach and DeFleur, 1976), and more recently became rearticulated in terms of (deep) mediatization research – in a conceptual attempt to move away from media effects while maintaining a mass media-centred focus (Hepp, Hjarvard and Lundby, 2015).

Quandrant 3 turns our attention towards the various ways in which people use media, specifically when it comes to our personal and customizable media environment. Research in this area zooms in on people's motivations and uses of media (generally informed by uses and gratifications theory), encapsulating most audience and reception studies. Quadrant 4 extends this work by articulating the various media people use with the ways in which we organize and arrange our lives and lifestyles. Although such an approach to media as an ensemble of devices and activities collectively constituting how people understand and co-ordinate their everyday life has been advocated in the literature for many decades (Bausinger, 1984), only quite recently has such work started to become more common, often informed by comparable considerations of 'media life' (Deuze, 2012), 'polymedia' (Madianou and Miller, 2013), media repertoires (Haddon, 2016), transmedia use (Fast and Jansson, 2019), mediatization and 'communicative figurations' (Hepp, Breiter and Hasebrink, 2018).

# CONCLUSION

The basic concepts and models for the study of mass communication that have been outlined in this chapter were developed on the basis of the special features indicated (scale, simultaneity, one-directionality, etc.) and under conditions of transition to the highly organized and centralized industrial society of the twentieth century. Not everything has changed, but we are now faced with new technological possibilities for communication that are not massive or one-directional, and there is a shift away from the earlier massification and centralization of society. These matters are taken up again in Chapter 6.

These changes are widely recognized in media and mass communication theory, and numerous exciting approaches, models and perspectives have emerged correspondingly. We still have mass politics, mass markets and mass consumption. The media have extended their scale on a global dimension. The beliefs vested in the power of publicity, public relations and propaganda by other names are still widely held by those with economic and political power. The 'dominant paradigm' that emerged in early communication research is still with us because it fits many of the conditions of contemporary media operation and meets the needs of media industries, advertisers and publicists. Media propagandists remain convinced of the manipulative capacity of the media and the malleability of the 'masses'. The notion of information transfer or transportation is still alive and well.

As far as a choice of model is concerned, we cannot simply choose one and ignore the others. They are relevant for different purposes. The transmission and attention models are still the preferred perspectives of media industries and would-be persuaders, while the ritual and decoding models are deployed as part of the resistance to media domination as well as shedding light on the underlying process. Neither party to this underlying conflict of purpose and outlook can afford to discount the way mass communication appears to the other side since all models reflect some aspects of the communication process.

The four models are compared in Table 3.1, which summarizes points made in the text and highlights the fact that each model posits a distinctive type of relationship between sender and receiver which involves a mutually agreed perception of its central character and purpose. In Figure 3.1 we bring the various models into conversation with each other regarding how the most common approaches in media and mass communication research map onto the changing media environment where mass and interpersonal media co-exist, and where the communication process can be understood in terms of both ritual and transmission.

## FURTHER READING

Hepp, A., Breiter, A. and Hasebrink, U. (eds) (2018) *Communicative Figurations: Transforming Communications in Times of Deep Mediatization*. Cham, Switzerland: Springer.

Meyrowitz, J. (2008) 'Power, pleasure and patterns: intersecting narratives of media influence', *Journal of Communication*, 58(4): 641–663.

Rowland, A.L. and Simonson, P. (2014) 'The founding mothers of communication research: toward a history of a gendered assemblage', *Critical Studies in Media Communication*, 31(1): 3–26.

Van Dijck, J., Poell, T. and De Waal, M. (2018) *The Platform Society*. Oxford: Oxford University Press.

Waisbord, S. (2019) *Communication: A Post-discipline*. Cambridge: Polity Press.

MCQUAIL'S MEDIA AND MASS COMMUNICATION THEORY
THEORIES

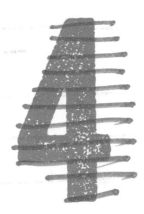

# THEORIES OF MEDIA AND SOCIETY

In this chapter, we look more closely at ideas about the relation between (mass) media and society, reserving the cultural implications for Chapter 5, even though society and culture are inseparable and the one cannot exist without the other. Treating society first also implies a primacy for society that is questionable, since the media can also be considered as a constitutive part of 'culture'. In fact, most media theory relates to both 'society' and 'culture' together and has to be explained in relation to both. For present purposes, the domain of 'society' refers to the material base (economic and political resources and power), to social relationships (in national societies, communities, families, etc.), and to social roles and occupations that are socially regulated (formally or informally). The domain of 'culture' refers primarily to other essential aspects of social life, especially to *symbolic expression* (and the way people create *shared narratives*), *values*, *meanings* and *practices* (social customs and routines, institutional ways of doing things and personal habits).

Most of the chapter is concerned with explaining the main theories or theoretical perspectives that have been developed for understanding the way media work in society. Such theories generally take material and social circumstances as a primary determinant for explaining the role of mass media and communication in society. However, and particularly in more contemporary approaches to theory development, there is also scope for recognizing the influence that ideas and culture can have on material conditions. Before theories of media and society are considered, the main issues or broad themes that have framed enquiry into media and mass communication are described. A general frame of reference for looking at the connections between media and society is also proposed. First, we return in more detail to the conundrum of the relation between culture and society.

## MEDIA, SOCIETY AND CULTURE: CONNECTIONS AND CONFLICTS

Mass media and communication can be considered as both a 'societal' and a 'cultural' phenomenon, and they are also a range of technologies. The media institution is part of the structure of society, and its technological infrastructure is part of the economic and power base, while the ideas, images and information disseminated by the media are evidently an important aspect of our culture (in the sense defined above). In an age of mass self-communication, media become important in a third way, as the primary vehicles through which people establish their identities and shared narratives online and in turn how these mediated relationships manifest in everyday offline life.

In discussing the problem of *direction* in the relationships between media, society and culture, Rosengren (1981) offered a simple typology which cross-tabulates two opposed propositions: 'social structure influences culture'; and its reverse, 'culture influences social structure'. This yields four main options that are available for describing the relation between mass media and society, as shown in Figure 4.1.

Social structure
influences culture

|  | Yes | No |
|---|---|---|
| **Culture influences social structure** — Yes | *Interdependence* (two-way influence) | *Idealism* (strong media influence) |
| **Culture influences social structure** — No | *Materialism* (media are dependent) | *Autonomy* (no causal connection) |

Figure 4.1    Four types of relation between culture and society

If we consider mass media as an aspect of society (base or structure), then the option of *materialism* is presented. There is a considerable body of theory that views culture as dependent on the economic and power structure of a society. It is assumed that whoever owns or controls the media can choose, or set limits to, what they do. Studies that consider media as institutions that are powerful in their own right depend on this proposition, such as work on the consequences of increased concentration of media ownership, and on the interplay between business, political and media power.

If we consider the media primarily in the light of their content (thus more as culture), then the option of *idealism* is indicated. The media are assumed to have a potential for significant influence, but it is the particular ideas and values conveyed by the media (in their content) which are seen as the primary causes of social change, irrespective of who owns and controls the media as an industry. The influence is thought to work through individual motivations and actions. This view leads to a strong belief in various potential media effects for good or ill. Examples include the promotion by the media of peace and international understanding (or having the opposite effect), of pro- or anti-social values and behaviour, and of enlightenment or the secularization and modernization of traditional societies. A form of idealism concerning media also lies behind the view that changes in the materiality of media – their forms and technology – can change our way of looking at the world, and even shape our relations with others (as in the foundational theories of McLuhan, 1962, 1964).

The two options remaining – of interdependence and of autonomy – traditionally found less distinctive theoretical development, although there is a good deal of support in common sense and in evidence for both. In recent years, as more sophisticated methods (both quantitative and qualitative) are developed, more integrated, mixed and multivariate approaches can be found. *Interdependence* implies that mass media and society are continually interacting and influencing each other (as are society and culture). The media (as cultural industries) respond to the demand from society for information and entertainment and, at the same time, stimulate innovation and contribute to a changing social-cultural climate, which sets off new demands for communication. Gabriel Tarde, writing in about 1900, envisaged a constant interweaving of influences: 'technological developments made newspapers possible, newspapers promote the formation of broader publics, and they, by broadening the loyalties of their members, create an extensive network of overlapping and shifting groupings' (in Clark, 1969). Today, the various influences are so bound together that neither media and mass communication nor modern society is conceivable without the other, and each is a necessary, though not a sufficient, condition for the other. From this point of view, we have to conclude that the media may equally be considered to mould and to mirror society and social changes.

The option of *autonomy* in the relations between culture and society is not necessarily inconsistent with this view, unless interpreted very literally. It is at least very likely that society and mass media can be independent of each other up to a point. Societies that are culturally very similar can sometimes have very different media systems. The autonomy position also supports those who are sceptical about the power of the media to influence ideas, values and behaviour – for instance, in allegedly promoting conformity, stimulating 'modernity' or damaging the cultural identity of poorer or less powerful countries. There are different views about how much autonomy in relation to society the media can have. The debate is especially relevant to the central thesis of 'internationalization' or '**globalization**', which implies a convergence and homogenization of a worldwide culture, as a result of the media. The autonomy position would suggest that imported media culture is superficial and need not significantly touch the local culture. It follows that **cultural imperialism** (as a result of western-dominated global media) is not likely to happen simply by chance or against the will of the culturally 'colonized' (see Chapter 9).

## AN INCONCLUSIVE OUTCOME

As with many of the issues to be discussed, there are more theories than there is solid evidence, and the questions raised by this discussion are much too broad to be settled by empirical research. According to Rosengren (1981: 254), surveying what scattered evidence he could find, research gives only 'inconclusive, partly even contradictory, evidence about the relationship between social structure, societal values as mediated by the media, and opinions among the public'. This assessment is just as valid today, suggesting that no single theory holds under all circumstances. Based on an extensive review of media and communication scholarship published between 1951 and 2015, Mihelj and Stanyer (2019) developed a distinction between two main approaches that cut across the literature: media/communication as an *agent* of social change, and media/communication as an *environment* for social change. The authors conclude that publications bridging the two approaches are still quite rare, and advocate an integrated approach, suggesting research with an emphasis on *processes* as opposed to *outcomes* of media and mass communication, as this would be specifically suited to 'investigating the contingent, unpredictable, and multidirectional nature of contemporary change' (Mihelj and Stanyer, 2019: 496).

It certainly seems that the media can serve to repress as well as to liberate, to unite as well as to fragment society, to promote as well as to hold back change – just not in equal ways, and always determined by context and circumstance. What is also striking in the theories to be discussed is the ambiguity of the role assigned to the media. They are as often presented in a 'progressive' as in a 'reactionary' light, according to whether the dominant (pluralist) or alternative (critical, radical) perspective is adopted. Despite the uncertainty, there can be little doubt that the media, whether moulders or mirrors of society, are the main messengers *about* society, and it is around this observation that the various theoretical perspectives can best be organized.

## MASS COMMUNICATION AS A SOCIETY-WIDE PROCESS: THE MEDIATION OF SOCIAL RELATIONS AND EXPERIENCE

A central presupposition, relating to questions both of society and of culture, is that the media institution is essentially concerned with the production and distribution of *knowledge* in the widest sense of the word. Such knowledge enables us to make some sense of our experience of the social world, even if our 'making of meaning' occurs in relatively autonomous and varied ways. The information, images and ideas made available by the media may, for most people, be the main source of an awareness of a shared past time (history) and of a present social location. They are also a store of memories and a map of where we are and who we are (identity), and may also provide the materials for orientation to the future. As noted at the outset, the media to a large extent serve to constitute our perceptions and definitions of social reality and normality for the purposes of a public, shared social life, and are a key source of standards, models and norms.

The main thing to emphasize is the degree to which the different media have come to be interposed between ourselves and any experience of the world beyond our immediate

MCQUAIL'S MEDIA AND MASS COMMUNICATION THEORY
THEORIES

personal environment and our direct sensory observation. They also provide most of us with the main point of contact with the institutions of the society in which we live. In a secular society, in matters of values and ideas, media tend to 'take over' from the early influences of school, parents, religion, siblings and companions. We are consequently very dependent on media for a large part of our wider 'symbolic environment' (the 'pictures in our heads'), however much we may be able to shape our own personal version (often through the very media that expose us to countless alternatives of such environments). It is the media which are likely to forge the elements that are held in common with others, since we now tend to share much the same media sources and 'media culture'. Without some degree of shared perception of reality, whatever its origin, there cannot really be an organized social life. Hjarvard (2008a) sketches a theory of social and cultural change in which the media gradually develop historically until they emerge in the nineteenth century as an independent social institution. More recently, this has developed further to become a means of integrating other social institutions (Couldry and Hepp, 2016). Given people's highly varied and individually specific way of using multiple media (television, mobile devices, print media, and so on), we consume, make sense of as well as participate in the production and spreading of shared media culture (Jenkins, Ford and Green, 2013). People, as 'pathfinders within mediascapes' (Hill, 2018), therefore experience a shared (and public) space in media as much as they collaborate in the maintenance of it.

## THE MEDIATION CONCEPT

These comments can be summed up in terms of the concept of mediation of contact with social reality. Mediation involves several different processes. As noted already, it refers to the relaying of second-hand (or third-party) versions of events and conditions that we cannot directly observe for ourselves. These messages come to us not just via the filters (or 'gates') of professional media, but also through the algorithm- and network-based platforms of social media. Secondly, it refers to the efforts of other actors and institutions in society to contact us for their own purposes (or our own supposed good). This applies to politicians and governments, advertisers, educators, experts and authorities of all kinds. It refers to the indirect way in which we form our perceptions of the groups and cultures to which we do not belong. An essential element in mediation, as defined here, is the involvement of some technological device between our senses and things external to us.

Mediation also implies some form of *relationship*. Relationships that are mediated through (mass) media are likely to be more distant, more impersonal, and are generally (yet certainly not always) weaker than direct personal ties. The mass media do not monopolize the flow of information we receive, nor do they intervene in all our wider social relations, but their presence is inevitably very pervasive. Early versions of the idea of 'mediation of reality' were inclined to assume a division between a public terrain in which a widely shared view of reality was constructed by way of mass media messages, and a personal sphere where individuals could communicate freely and directly. In our digital media environment, this simple division is difficult to uphold, since a much larger share of communication, and thus of our contact with others and our environmental reality, is mediated via technology (telephone, computer, email, apps, etc.), although on an individual and a private basis. Furthermore, through the increasing manipulation of our personal data, as gathered through our countless online interactions, much of the mediation between us and our social reality is taken over by technologies, as algorithms order and offer messages for us in ways that are anything but transparent. The implications of this change are still unclear and subject to diverse interpretations from a growing body of scholarship in (digital) media and mass communication research.

Thompson (1993, 1995) has suggested a typology of interaction to clarify the consequences of the new communication technologies that have detached social interaction and symbolic exchange from the sharing of a common locale. He notes (1993: 35) that 'it has become possible for more and more individuals to acquire information and symbolic content through mediated forms of interaction'. He distinguished two types of interaction alongside face-to-face interaction. One of these, which he calls 'mediated interaction', involves some technical medium, such as paper, electrical wires, and so on, which enables information or symbolic content to be transmitted between individuals who are distant in space or time or both. The partners in mediated interaction need to find contextual information as well having fewer interactions than in face-to-face contact.

The other type is called 'mediated quasi-interaction' and refers to relations established by the media of mass communication. There are two main distinguishing features. First, in this case, participants are not oriented towards other specific individuals (whether as sender or receiver), and symbolic forms (media content) are produced for an indefinite range of potential recipients, such as a post on Facebook or an uploaded video to YouTube. Secondly, mediated quasi-interaction is monological (rather than dialogical), in the sense that the flow of communication is one-way rather than two-way. There is also no direct or immediate response expected from the receiver. Thompson (ibid.: 42) argues that the 'media have created a new kind of **public sphere** which is despatialized and non-dialogical in character', and is potentially global in scope. Digital media have evolved to include all kinds of interaction that mimics direct personal (and even face-to-face) contact, from messages left in online chatrooms or via applications on one's smartphone to real-time interaction via video-conferencing software, sometimes using additional technologies like headsets, including interactions with non-human actors (such as chatbots and other software agents). All of this contributes to the realization of a 'mediation of everything' (Livingstone, 2009), whereby any and all experiences of ourselves in the world are, to some extent, mediated.

## MEDIATION METAPHORS

In general, the notion of mediation in the sense of media intervening between ourselves and 'reality' is no more than a metaphor, although it does point to several of the roles played by the media in connecting us to the realm of experience. The terms that are often used to describe this role reflect different attributions of purposefulness, **interactivity** and effectiveness. Mediation can mean different things, ranging from neutrally informing, through negotiation, to attempts at manipulation and control. The variations can be captured by a number of communication images, which express different ideas about how the media may connect us with reality. These are presented in Box 4.1.

---

### 4.1

### Metaphors for media roles

As a *window* on events and experience, which extends our vision, enabling us to see for ourselves what is going on, to compare and contrast with our own views and experience.

As a *mirror* of events in society and the world, implying a reflection, although the angle and direction of the mirror are decided by others, and we are less free to see what we want.

As a *filter, gatekeeper* or *portal*, acting to select parts of experience for special attention and closing off other views and voices, whether deliberately or not.

As a *signpost, guide* or *interpreter*, pointing the way and making sense of what is otherwise puzzling or fragmentary.

As a *forum* or *platform* for the presentation of information and ideas to an audience, often with possibilities for response and feedback.

As a *disseminator* who passes on and makes information not available to all.

As an *interlocutor* or informed partner in conversation who responds to questions in a quasi-interactive way.

As an *interloper* that becomes involved in a place or situation where they are generally considered not to belong.

---

Some of these images are to be found in the media's own self-definition – especially in the more positive implications of extending our view of the world, providing integration and continuity and connecting people with each other. Even the notion of filtering can be embraced in its positive sense of selecting and interpreting what would otherwise be an unmanageable and chaotic supply of information and impressions. At the same time, the ongoing mediation of everything (as well as rising levels of media awareness and literacy) also causes people to actively question the role of media as a filter, becoming wary of bias, manipulation, and the media's motivations and goals. These versions of the mediating process reflect differences of interpretation of the role of the media in social processes. The media can extend our view of the world in an open-ended way as well as limit or control our impressions. Secondly, they may choose between a neutral, passive role and one that is active, participant or even activist. They can vary on two main dimensions: one of openness versus control, another of neutrality versus being actively participant.

## A FRAME OF REFERENCE FOR CONNECTING MEDIA WITH SOCIETY

The general notion that media and mass communication interpose in some way between 'reality' and our perceptions and knowledge of it refers to a number of specific processes at different levels of analysis. The Westley and MacLean (1957) model (see p. 93) indicates some of the additional elements needed for a more detailed frame of reference. Most significant is the idea that the media are sought out by institutional advocates as channels for reaching the general public (or chosen groups and even micro-targeting individuals), and for conveying their chosen perspective on events and conditions. This is broadly true of competing politicians and governments, businesses and advertisers, religious leaders, some thinkers, writers and artists, and so on. We are reminded that experience has always been mediated by the institutions of society (including the family), and what has happened is that a new mediator (mass communication) has been added which can extend, compete with, replace or even run counter to the efforts of other social institutions.

The simple picture of a 'two-step' (or multiple) process of mediated contact with reality is complicated by the fact that mass media are not completely free agents in relation to the rest of society. They are subject to formal and informal control by the very institutions that have an interest in shaping public perceptions of reality. Their objectives do not necessarily coincide with the aim of relaying some objective 'truth' about reality. An abstract view of the 'mediation of reality', based on Westley and MacLean but also reflecting these points, is sketched in Figure 4.2. The media provide their audience with a supply of information, images, stories and impressions, sometimes according to anticipated needs, sometimes guided by their own purposes (for example, gaining revenue or influence), and sometimes following the motives of other social institutions (for instance, advertising, making propaganda, projecting favourable images or sending information). Given this diversity of underlying motivation in the *selection* and *flow* of the 'images of reality', we can see that mediation is unlikely to be a purely neutral process. The 'reality' will always be to some extent selected and constructed and there will be certain biases. These will reflect especially the differential opportunities available for gaining media access and also the influence of 'media logic' in constituting reality (see p. 356).

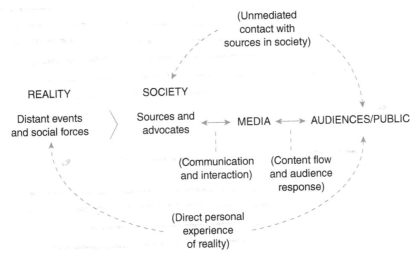

**Figure 4.2** A frame of reference for theory formation about media and society: media interpose between personal experience and more distant events and social forces (based on Westley and MacLean, 1957)

Figure 4.2 also represents the fact that experience is neither completely nor always mediated by the mass media. There are still certain direct channels of contact with social institutions (for example, political parties, community organizations, work associations, places of worship, in-store customer service). There is also some possibility of direct personal experience of some of the more distant events reported in media (for example, crime, poverty, illness, war and conflict). In an age of mass self-communication, these direct personal experiences of reality often become the subject of intense mediation because we – when we witness or participate in certain events (such as a wedding, a concert or an accident) – regularly choose to share this experience online. For any given event, there are often multiple versions of it circulating through social media and mass media alike, interacting in various ways (for example, when news media incorporate people's tweets and other social media status updates in their reporting of events). The potentially diverse sources of information (including personal contact with others, online and offline) are never completely independent from each other, and can provide some checks on the adequacy and reliability of 'quasi-mediated interaction' (as much as they introduce an element of doubt and suspicion regarding whatever we hear and see from others or the media).

## MAIN THEMES OF MEDIA–SOCIETY THEORY

The main themes and issues to be dealt with in this book have already been introduced in the opening chapters (notably Chapters 1 and 3). Here we return in more depth to these matters. The theories available to us are fragmentary and selective, sometimes overlapping or inconsistent, often guided by conflicting ideologies and assumptions about society. Theory formation does not follow a systematic and logical pattern but responds to real-life problems and historical circumstances, and it often builds on earlier, established assumptions. Before describing some of the theories that have been formulated, it is useful to look at the main themes that have shaped the debate during the 'first age of mass communication', especially relating to power, integration, social change and space/time.

## THEME I: POWER AND INEQUALITY

The media are invariably related in some way to the prevailing structure of political and economic power. It is evident, first, that media have an economic cost and value and are an object of competition for control and access. Secondly, they are subject to political, economic and legal regulation. Thirdly, mass media are very commonly regarded as effective instruments of power, with the potential capacity to exert influence in various ways. Fourthly, the power of mass media is not equally available to all groups or interests. Box 4.2 introduces the theme of media power by naming the main kinds of effects, whether intended or not, that have been attributed to the mass media.

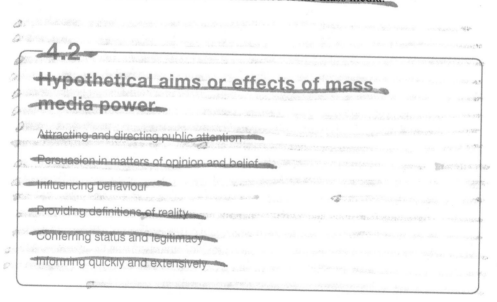

### 4.2

### Hypothetical aims or effects of mass media power

Attracting and directing public attention

Persuasion in matters of opinion and belief

Influencing behaviour

Providing definitions of reality

Conferring status and legitimacy

Informing quickly and extensively

In discussions of media power, two models are usually opposed to each other: one a model of dominant media, the other of pluralist media (see Table 4.1). The first of these sees media as exercising power on behalf of other powerful institutions. Media organizations, in this view, are likely to be owned or controlled by a small number of powerful interests and to be similar in type and purpose. They disseminate a limited and undifferentiated view of the world shaped by the perspectives of ruling interests. Audiences are constrained or conditioned to accept the view of the world offered, with little critical response. The result is to reinforce and legitimate the prevailing structure of power and to head off change by filtering out alternative voices.

Table 4.1 Two opposing models of media power (mixed versions are more likely to be encountered)

|  | Dominance | Pluralism |
|---|---|---|
| Societal source | Ruling class or dominant elite | Competing political, social, cultural interests and groups |
| Media | Under concentrated ownership and of uniform type | Many and independent of each other |
| Production | Standardized, routinized | Creative, free, original |
| Content and world view | Selective and decided from 'above' | Diverse and competing views, responsive to audience demand |
| Audience | Dependent, passive, organized on a large scale | Fragmented, selective, reactive and active |
| Effects | Strong and confirmative of established social order | Numerous, without consistency or predictability of direction, but often no effect |

The pluralist model is, in nearly every respect, the opposite, allowing for much diversity and unpredictability. There is no unified and dominant elite, and change and democratic control are both possible. Differentiated audiences initiate demand and are able to resist persuasion and react to what the media offer. In general, the 'dominance' model corresponds to the outlook both of conservatives pessimistic about the 'rise of the masses' and of critics of the capitalist system disappointed by the failure of a revolution to happen. It is consistent with a view of the media as an instrument of 'cultural imperialism' or a tool of political propaganda. The pluralist view is an idealized version of what liberalism and the free market will lead to. While the models are described as total opposites, it is possible to envisage mixed versions, in which tendencies towards mass domination or economic monopoly are subject to limits and counter-forces and are 'resisted' by their audiences. In any free society, minorities and opposition groups should be able to develop and maintain their own alternative media, and there would exist a reflective discourse in mainstream media about their own biases and presumptions.

The question is whether media exercise power in their own right and interest. However, this possibility exists and is to be found in fictional as well as factual portrayals of media moguls and empires. There are cases of media owners using their position to advance some political or financial goal or to enhance their own status. There is prima facie evidence of effects on public opinion and actions. More often, the independent power of the media is said to cause unintended harmful effects. These relate, for example, to the undermining of democratic politics, cultural and moral debasement, and the causing of personal harm and distress, mainly in the pursuit of profit. Essentially, they are said to exert power without responsibility and – in free societies – use the shield of laws governing **freedom of expression** and **freedom of the press** to avoid accountability. This longstanding discussion of media effects gives rise to a number of questions, which are posed in Box 4.3.

---

**4.3**

**The power of mass media: questions arising**

Are the media under top-down control?

If so, who controls the media and in whose interest?

Whose version of the world (social reality) is presented?

How effective are the media in achieving chosen ends?

Do mass media promote more or less equality in society?

How is access to media allocated or obtained?

How do the media use their power to influence?

Do the media have power of their own?

How are the media being held accountable?

---

# THEME II: SOCIAL INTEGRATION AND IDENTITY

## A DUAL PERSPECTIVE ON MEDIA

Theorists of media and mass communication have often shared with scholars in related disciplines (such as psychology, sociology, anthropology and social and cultural studies) an interest in how social order is organized and maintained, and in the attachment of people to various kinds of social unit. The media were early associated with the problems of rapid urbanization, social mobility and the decline of traditional communities. They have continued to be linked with individualization, social dislocation and a supposed increase in individual immorality, crime and disorder. A good deal of early media theory and research focused on questions of integration. For instance, Hardt (2003) has described the concerns of nineteenth- and early-twentieth-century German theorists with the integrative role of the press in society. The principal functions of the press he discerned are set out in Box 4.4. Many of the contemporary concerns with the decline of journalism (in terms of audiences, industry revenue and employment) and the rise of misinformation and disinformation online can be traced back to these perceived functions of media in general, and the news industry in particular.

---

### 4.4
## The perceived social functions of the early press

- Binding society together
- Giving leadership to the public
- Helping to establish the 'public sphere'
- Providing for the exchange of ideas between leaders and masses
- Satisfying needs for information
- Providing society with a mirror of itself
- Acting as the conscience of society

---

Mass communication as a process has often been typified as predominantly impersonal and isolating, and thus leading to lower levels of social solidarity and sense of community. Addiction to television has been linked to non-participation and declining 'social capital' in the sense of participating in social activities and having a sense of belonging (Putnam, 2000). The media have brought messages of what is new and fashionable in terms of goods, ideas, techniques and values from city to country and from the social top to the base. They have also portrayed alternative value systems, potentially weakening the hold of traditional values. These concerns have amplified in the digital age, with claims about social media and smartphone addiction regularly making headlines around the world (see Chapter 17: 568–569). Similarly, the role of the Internet can perhaps be considered as the medium perfectly fitting our age of 'universal comparison' (Bauman, 2000: 7), where people constantly compare themselves with the lifestyles, values and ideas of countless others, which in turn can lead to continuous (and often conspicuous) consumption.

An alternative view of the relation between mass media and social integration has also been in circulation, based on other features of mass communication. It has a capacity to unite scattered individuals within a more or less unified large audience, or to integrate newcomers into urban communities and immigrants into a new country by providing a common set of values, ideas and information and helping to form identities (Janowitz, 1952; Clark, 1969; Stamm, 1985; Rogers, 1993). This process can help to bind together a large-scale, differentiated modern society more effectively than would have been possible through older mechanisms of religious, family or group control. In other words, mass media seem in principle capable of both supporting and subverting social cohesion. The positions seem far apart, one stressing centrifugal and the other centripetal tendencies, although in fact in complex and changing societies both forces are normally at work at the same time, one compensating to some extent for the other.

## AMBIVALENCE ABOUT SOCIAL INTEGRATION

The main questions that arise for theory and research can thus (much as in the case of power) be mapped out on two criss-crossing dimensions. One refers to the direction of effect: either *centrifugal* or *centripetal*. The first refers to the stimulus towards social change, freedom, individualism and **fragmentation**. The second refers to effects in the form of more social unity, order, cohesion and integration. Both social integration and dispersal can be valued differently, depending on preference and perspective. One person's desirable social control is another person's limitation of freedom; one person's individualism is another person's non-conformity or isolation. So the second dimension can be described as normative, especially in the assessment of these two opposite tendencies of the working of mass media. The question it represents is whether the effect at issue should be viewed with *optimism* or *pessimism* (McCormack, 1961; Carey, 1969). While early critics of mass communication (for example, C. Wright Mills) emphasized the dangers of over-integration and social conformity, the individualizing effects of newer media have consistently been viewed by social critics as socially corrosive – that is, until these 'new' media settled in and became a regular part of people's everyday lives (and another newly popular technology warranted concern).

In order to make sense of this complicated situation, it helps to think of the two versions of media theory – centrifugal and centripetal – each with its own position on a dimension of evaluation, so that there are, in effect, four different theoretical positions relating to social integration (see Figure 4.3). These can be named as follows:

1.  *Freedom, diversity*. This is the optimistic version of the tendency for media to have a fragmenting effect on society that can also be liberating. The media spread new ideas and information and encourage mobility, change and social progress.

MCQUAIL'S MEDIA AND MASS COMMUNICATION THEORY
THEORIES

2. *Integration, solidarity.* This optimistic version of the reverse effect of mass communication as a unifier of society stresses the need for a shared sense of identity, belonging
   and citizenship, especially under conditions of social change.

3. *Normlessness, loss of identity.* The pessimistic alternative view of greater freedom points
   to detachment, loss of belief, rootlessness and a society lacking in social cohesion.

4. *Dominance, uniformity.* Society can be over-integrated and over-regulated, leading to central control and conformity, with the (mass) media as instruments of discipline and control.

Optimistic vision

| 1 | 2 |
| Freedom, diversity | Integration, solidarity |

Centrifugal effect — Centripetal effect

| 3 | 4 |
| Normlessness, loss of identity | Dominance, uniformity |

Pessimistic vision

**Figure 4.3** Four versions of the consequences of mass communication for social integration

This version of the integrating effects of mass communication leaves us with a number of
questions (see Box 4.5) that have to be answered for different societies at different points
in time, and no general answer is possible.

---

**4.5**

**Questions about media and integration**

- Do mass media increase or decrease the level of social control and conformity?
- Do media strengthen or weaken intervening social institutions, such as family,
  political party, local community, church, trade union?
- Do media help or hinder the formation of diverse groups and identities based
  on subculture, opinion, social experience, social action, and so on?
- Do mass media promote individual freedom and choice of identity?
- Do online media have bridging or bonding effects with different social groups?

# THEME III: SOCIAL CHANGE AND DEVELOPMENT

A key question that follows on from the preceding discussion is whether or not mass communication should be viewed primarily as a cause or as an effect of social change. Wherever the media exert influence they also cause change; the options of centralization or fragmentation are two main kinds of social change that have been discussed. As we have seen, no simple answer can be expected, and different theories offer alternative versions of the relationship. At issue are the different ways of relating three basic elements in the investigation of media and social change: (1) the technology of communication and the form and content of media; (2) changes in society (social structure and institutional arrangements); and (3) the distribution among a population of opinions, beliefs, values and practices. All consequences of mass media are potentially questions about social change, but most relevant for theory have been the twin issues of 'technological determinism' and 'media centrism', and the potential to apply the workings of mass media to the process of development. The first refers to the effect on society of changing media. The second refers to the more practical question of whether or not (and how) mass media might be applied to economic and social development (for example, as an 'engine of change' or 'multiplier of modernity'). Questions about change and development are set out in Box 4.6.

---

## 4.6

### Questions about change and development

- What part do or can media play in major social change?
- Are the media typically progressive or conservative in their working?
- Can media be applied as an 'engine of change' in the context of development?
- How much of media-induced change is due to technology rather than to typical content?
- What (and who) do media include or exclude in communicating change?

---

The story of the rise of the media, as told in Chapter 2, tends to depict media as a generally progressive force, especially because of the link between democracy and freedom of expression, and between media and the opening of markets and liberalization of trade. However, there are other narratives to consider. For instance, critical theory has typically viewed the media in modern times as conformist and even reactionary. In the early twentieth century, as in Nazi Germany and Soviet Russia, the media were employed as a tool of change, even if with mixed success. In the twenty-first century, governments and social movements alike continue to rely on media – both 'old' and 'new' – either to instill conservatism or to accelerate processes of transformation.

The case of 'modernization' and development in Third World countries received much attention in the early post-Second World Word War years, when mass communication was seen, especially in the USA, as a powerful means of spreading American ideals throughout the world and at the same time helping to resist communism. But it was also promoted as an effective instrument of social and economic development, consistent with the spirit of free enterprise. Several effects were predicted to follow on from the voluntary import of US mass media content. These included consumer aspirations, values and practices of democracy, ideas of liberty, and literacy (see Lerner, 1958). Subsequently, there was a large investment in communication projects designed to diffuse many technical and social innovations (Rogers and Shoemaker, 1973). The results were hard to evaluate and the efforts described gradually became redundant or impossible to pursue in a changed world.

Later in the twentieth century, the biggest change associated with mass media has probably been the transition from communism in Europe after 1985. The process of *glasnost* gave the media a part to play in internal change within the Soviet Union, and once started they seemed to amplify it. A source of significant contemporary research interest in media and mass communication scholarship in the context of social change and development is the role newer mass (self-communication) media, such as social and mobile media, play in the mobilization of new social movements, including, for example, the use of independent media networks during protests against the World Trade Organization in Seattle in 1999, the 'orange' revolution in the Ukraine of 2004–2005 (where demonstrators bypassed traditional state media for online sources of information), mass protests in Iran during 2009 (predominantly using Twitter to self-organize), the so-called 'Arab Spring' across North Africa and the Middle East in 2010, as well as networked anti-austerity protests such as the Occupy movement around the world in 2011 and beyond (Castells, 2012; Papacharissi, 2014; Zayani, 2015; Robinson, 2017).

In January 2015, these and other developments inspired the International Panel on Social Progress (IPSP), an academic initiative aimed to provide options for social justice in what was generally seen as an increasingly unequal process of change as a consequence of deregulation and the opening-up of the global market after the collapse of the Soviet Union. Part of this initiative was a specific charter on the role of media in social change in an attempt to address the role of media and information infrastructures that make social progress and global justice possible. Comprising a committee of prominent media and communication scholars from around the world, the panel put forward the argument that:

Social progress is contingent on accessible, affordable and inclusive media infrastructures – including traditional media, digital platforms, social media and the Internet. Any intervention that works for social progress must also consider the need for a parallel struggle to democratize media infrastructures and demand better, more transparent media policies and governance. (Couldry et al., 2018: 180)

The group identified three factors complicating media and social change: (1) unequal distribution of media resources (especially between the wealthy and the poor); (2) uneven relations between the corporations (and state-run agencies) providing access to the new spaces of connection and the rights and interests of diverse people, groups and communities using such platforms; and (3) the facilitation of media and digital literacy, so that when people do engage in 'an online infrastructure that *mediates* social life' (ibid.: 177; italics in original), they can do it to further open dialogue, free speech, and 'respectful cultural exchange and action for social progress' (ibid.: 181). The IPSP report keenly noted how similar initiatives in the past, such as UNESCO's MacBride Report of 1980 and the World Summit on the Information Society in 2003, had achieved only limited success (Vincent and Nordenstreng, 2016).

## THEME IV: SPACE AND TIME

Communication has often been said to have space and time dimensions and also to 'build bridges' over discontinuities in our experience created by distance and time. Jansson and Falkheimer (2006) argue for a 'spatial turn' in media studies, seeing how contemporary communication technologies always occur in space (for example, the place where we log on or switch on), also seemingly collapsing spatial categories by instantaneously connecting people and devices from disparate places around the world, while configuring new spaces within which people interact, form communities and develop meaningful relationships. There are numerous aspects to such propositions. Communication makes possible an extension of human activity and perception across distance in several ways. Most obviously, in the form of transportation, we are taken from place to place and our contacts, experiences and horizons are extended. Symbolic communication can achieve something of the same effect without our having to move physically, just as media relationships can develop without having to be physically co-present. We are also provided with maps and guides to places and routes to points in real space. The location of our activity is defined by webs of communication, by shared forms of discourse and by much that is expressed in language and other forms of expression. Virtually all forms of symbolic communication (books, art, music, newspapers, cinema, etc.) are identified with a particular location and have a varying 'transmission' range that can be specified geographically. Processes of mass communication are typically described and registered in spatial terms, with reference to particular media markets, circulation or reception areas, audience 'reach', and so on. At the same time, the end of cost and capacity constraints on electronic transmission means that communication is no longer tied to any one territory and is, in principle, delocalized.

Political and social units are generally territorial and use communications of many kinds to signal this fact. Businesses that operate globally often attempt to localize their communications to signal allegiance to a particular place. Communication is always initiated at one point and received at one or many other points. Bridges are built and physical distance seems to be reduced by the ease of communication and reception. The Internet has created various kinds of 'virtual space' and new maps to go with it, especially those that show the web of interconnections. New technologies have made it possible for messages sent to materialize at distant points. The theme of space has gained new currency in the newer media environment that can be seen as both 'uprooting' and 'repotting' existing notions of place and space.

Much the same can be said in relation to time. The multiplication and acceleration of channels for transmission and exchange of communication have made instantaneous contact with other sources and destinations an everyday possibility. We no longer have to wait for news or wait to send it, from whatever place. There is effectively no time restriction on the amount of information that can be sent. There is increasingly no time restriction on when we can receive what we want to receive. Technologies of storage and access allow us to disregard the constraint of time on much communication behaviour. All that is lacking is more time to do all this (and to make sense of it all). Paradoxically, although new technologies make it possible and easy to store our memories and all the information we want, information and culture seem to be subject to faster obsolescence and decay. The limits are set by the human capacity to process any more any faster. The long-heralded problem of information overload has arrived in daily experience. Whatever the costs and benefits, it is hard to deny the revolutionary character of the shift to digital, online media. For the key propositions, see Box 4.7.

---

## 4.7
## Media effects relating to space and time: key propositions

- Media abolish distance
- Virtual space is an extension of real space
- Media serve as collective memory
- The gap between technical transmission and human reception capacity widens exponentially
- Media lead to delocalization and detemporalization

---

# MEDIA–SOCIETY THEORY I: THE MASS SOCIETY

In this and the following sections, several distinctive theoretical approaches to these themes are discussed. They are presented more or less in chronological order of their formulation and they span the range from optimistic to pessimistic, from critical to neutral.

The first to be dealt with, mass society theory, is built around the concept of 'mass' which has already been discussed in Chapter 3. The theory emphasizes the interdependence of institutions that exercise power and thus the integration of the media into the sources of social power and authority. Content is likely to serve the interests of political and economic power holders. The media cannot be expected to offer a critical or an alternative definition of the world, and their tendency will be to assist in the accommodation of the dependent public to their fate.

The 'dominant media' model sketched above reflects the mass society view. Mass society theory gives a primacy to the media as a causal factor. It rests very much on the idea that the media offer a view of the world, a substitute or pseudo-environment, which is a potent means of manipulation of people but also an aid to their psychic survival under difficult conditions. According to C. Wright Mills (1951: 333), 'Between consciousness and existence stand communications, which influence such consciousness as men have of their existence'.

Mass society is, paradoxically, both 'atomized' and centrally controlled. The media are seen as significantly contributing to this control in societies characterized by largeness of scale, remoteness of institutions, isolation of individuals and lack of strong local or group integration. Mills (1951, 1956) also pointed to the decline of the genuine public of classic democratic theory and its replacement by shifting aggregates of people who cannot formulate or realize their own aims in political action. This regret has been echoed by arguments about the decline of a 'public sphere' of democratic debate and politics, in which large-scale, commercialized mass media have been implicated (Dahlgren, 2005). More recently, the public sphere, under the influence of newer mass media, has been re-imagined in media and communication scholarship in terms of the rise of a more affective arena inspired by people's mass self-communication (Papacharissi, 2016), indicating 'a more nuanced appraisal of the role of subjectivity and personal stories in the articulation of the common good' (Wahl-Jorgensen, 2019: 1).

Although the expression 'mass society' is no longer much in vogue, the idea that we live in a mass society persists in a variety of loosely related components. These include a nostalgia (or hope) for a more 'communitarian' alternative to the present individualistic age as well as a critical attitude towards the supposed emptiness, loneliness, stress and consumerism of life in a contemporary free-market society. The seemingly widespread public indifference towards democratic politics and lack of participation in it are also often attributed to the cynical and manipulative use of mass media by politicians and parties. The rise of populist politics, on the other hand, tends to be seen as fuelled by a 'disintermediation' of traditional media by politicians as well as publics, as they meet each other online to create new forms of 'mass' society and community.

The actual abundance and diversity of many old and new forms of media seem, however, to undermine the validity of mass society theory in its portrayal of the media as one of the foundation stones of the mass society. In particular, online and mobile media have given rise to equally optimistic and pessimistic visions of what society can become that runs counter to the central mass society thesis. The relative monopoly control typical of the rise of the original mass media is now challenged by the rise of online media that are much more accessible to many groups, movements and also individuals. This challenges not just the economic power of old media, but also their guaranteed access to large national audiences at the time of their own choosing. The much darker side to this vision suggests that the Internet also opens up new means of control and **surveillance** of the online population and points out that media conglomerates are increasingly seeking to control the Internet (Zuboff, 2019). Furthermore, many (especially outside the media and mass communication research community) have suggested that people's freedom to link and communicate with anything and anyone primarily online stimulates social polarization and makes people blind to co-existence. The central enduring ideas about the mass society theory of media are stated in Box 4.8.

## 4.8

### Mass society theory of media: main propositions

- Society is organized centrally and on a large scale
- The public becomes atomized
- Media are centralized, with one-way transmission
- People come to depend on media for their identity
- Media are used for manipulation and control

# MEDIA–SOCIETY THEORY II: POLITICAL ECONOMY

Political-economic theory is a socially critical approach that focuses primarily on the relation between the economic structure and dynamics of media industries and the ideological content of media. From this point of view, the media institution has to be considered as part of the economic system, with close links to the political system. As media industries accumulate wealth, their status and close relation to vested interests grows. The consequences are to be observed in the reduction of independent media sources and marginalizing of alternative voices, concentration on the largest markets and products aimed at the lowest common denominator to attract a mass audience, avoidance of risks, and reduced investment in less profitable media tasks (such as investigative reporting and documentary filmmaking). We also find neglect of smaller and poorer sectors of the potential audience and often a politically unbalanced range of news media.

The main strength of the approach lies in its capacity for making empirically testable propositions about market determinations, although the latter are so numerous and complex that empirical demonstration is not easy. While the approach centres on media activity as an economic process leading to the commodity (the media product or content), there is a variant of the political-economic approach that suggests that the primary product of the media is really *audience*. This refers to the fact that they deliver audience attention to advertisers and shape the behaviour of media publics in certain distinctive ways (Smythe, 1977). What commercial media sell to their clients is a certain more or less guaranteed number of potential customers according to a market-relevant profile. As in today's market, where 'pay-per' and subscription models have become the main source of revenue in the media economy and advertising-supported media are on the decline, the primary focus of contemporary analyses of the **political economy** of the media has shifted towards the global reach and power of Internet platforms, as well as the rise of corporate ventures that integrate or combine information, telecommunications and technology services (examples are Alibaba, Alphabet, Apple and Samsung), compared to which media industries are relatively small. In this context, 'media industries run the risk of becoming poorly paid providers of the technology and telecommunication industries' (Miège, 2019: 82).

The political-economic approach has been heavily influenced by the work of (and subsequent scholarship on) Karl Marx. There have been several variants of Marxist-inspired analysis of modern media (Meehan and Wasko, 2013; Fuchs and Mosco, 2016). The question of power is central to Marxist interpretations of mass media. While varied, Marxist-inspired approaches to a critical political economy have always emphasized the fact that, ultimately, they are instruments of control by and for a ruling class. Marxist theory posits a direct link between economic structure, ownership and the dissemination of messages that affirm the legitimacy and the value of a class society. These views have been supported in modern times by evidence of tendencies towards the great concentration of media ownership by capitalist entrepreneurs (for example, Bagdikian, 1988; McChesney, 2000) and by much correlative evidence of conservative tendencies in the content of media so organized (for example, Herman and Chomsky, 1988).

Revisionist versions of Marxist media theory in the twentieth century concentrated more on ideas than on material structures. They emphasized the ideological **effects of media** in the interests of a ruling class, in 'reproducing' the essentially exploitative relationships and manipulation, and in legitimating the dominance of capitalism and the subordination of the working class. Louis Althusser (1971) conceived this process to work by way of what he called 'ideological state apparatuses' (all means of **socialization**, in effect), which, by comparison with 'repressive state apparatuses' (such as the army and police), enable the capitalist state to survive without recourse to direct violence. Gramsci's (1971) concept of *hegemony* relates to this tendency. Marcuse (1964) interpreted the media, along with other elements of mass production systems, as engaged in 'selling' or imposing a whole social system which is at the same time both desirable and repressive.

Analyses of media and mass communication infrastructures and the consequences of their concentration precede Marx, as Winseck (2016) shows, referring to late-nineteenth- and early-twentieth-century works of sociologists and social theorists. Instead of assuming a direct relation between media ownership, content, messages and social order, this strand of the political economy of the media is less concerned with the specific content of media messages and their presumed effects on public opinion, instead focusing on issues of structural power – where those who finance and control media, telecommunication and technology companies get to define the (narrow) parameters within which these businesses operate. This explains the industry's shift from 'production and vertical integration of the entire supply chain to a focus on the control of distribution, finance, and copyright' (Winseck, 2016: 93; see also Wasko, 2004). Fuchs (2009) uses a political-economic approach to argue that the key to the Internet economy lies especially in the **commodification** of the users of free-access platforms which deliver targets for advertisers and publicists as well as often providing content at no cost to network providers and site-owners. In the case of very popular platforms such as Facebook and YouTube, the distinction from mass communication is not very clear.

Important questions remain. How might the power of the media be countered or resisted? What is the position of forms of media that are not clearly in capitalist ownership or in the power of the state (such as independent newspapers or public broadcasting)? Critics of mass media in the political-economic tradition either rely on the weapon of exposure of propaganda, pin their hopes on some form of collective ownership or alternative media as a counter to the media power of the capitalist class, or advocate different business models for media companies less reliant on advertising or commercial sponsorship.

The relevance of political-economic theory has been greatly increased by several trends in media business and technology. First, there has been a growth in **media concentration** worldwide, with more and more power of ownership being concentrated in fewer hands and with tendencies for mergers between electronic hardware and software industries (Murdock, 1990; McChesney, 2000; Miège, 2019). Secondly, there has been a growing global 'information economy' (Melody, 1990; Sussman, 1997), involving an increasing convergence between telecommunication and broadcasting. Thirdly, there has been a decline in the public sector of mass media and in direct public control of telecommunication under the banner of 'deregulation', 'privatization' or 'liberalization' (McQuail and Siune, 1998; van Cuilenburg and McQuail, 2003). Fourthly, there is a growing rather than diminishing problem of information inequality. The expression '**digital divide**' refers to the inequality in access to and use of advanced communication facilities (Norris, 2002), but there are also differences in the quality of potential use. The essential propositions of political-economic theory (see Box 4.9) have not changed since earlier times, but the scope for application is much wider (Mansell, 2004; Mosco, 2009).

## MEDIA–SOCIETY THEORY III: FUNCTIONALISM

Functionalist theory explains social practices and institutions in terms of the 'needs' of the society and of individuals (Merton, 1957). Grounded in the work of Emile Durkheim, society is viewed as an organic system of linked working parts or subsystems, each making an essential contribution to continuity and order. The media can be seen as one of these systems. Organized social life is said to require the continued maintenance of a more or less accurate, consistent, supportive and complete picture of the working of society and of the social environment. It is by responding to the demands of individuals and institutions in consistent ways that the media achieve unintended benefits for the society as a whole.

The theory depicts media as essentially self-directing and self-correcting. While apolitical in formulation, it suits pluralist and voluntarist conceptions of the fundamental mechanisms of social life and has a conservative bias to the extent that the media are more likely to be seen as a means of maintaining society as it is rather than as a source of major change.

Although functionalism in its early versions has been largely discarded in sociology, it survives as an approach to the media in new forms (for example, Luhmann, 2000), and it still plays a part in framing and answering research questions about the media. It remains useful for some purposes of description and it offers a language for discussing the relations between mass media and society and a set of concepts that have proved hard to replace. This terminology has the advantage of being to a large extent shared by mass communicators themselves and by their audiences and of being widely understood.

# SPECIFYING THE SOCIAL FUNCTIONS OF MEDIA

The main functions of communication in society, according to Lasswell (1948), were surveillance of the environment, correlation of the parts of the society in responding to its environment, and the transmission of the cultural heritage. Wright (1960) developed this basic scheme to describe many of the effects of the media and added entertainment as a fourth key media function. This may be part of the transmitted culture but it has another aspect – that of providing individual reward, relaxation and reduction of tension, which makes it easier for people to cope with real-life problems and for societies to avoid breakdown (Mendelsohn, 1966). With the addition of a fifth item, mobilization – designed to reflect the widespread application of mass communication to political and commercial propaganda, we can name the following set of basic ideas about media tasks (functions) in society:

- Information
  - Providing information about events and conditions in society and the world.
  - Indicating relations of power.
  - Facilitating innovation, adaptation and progress.

- Correlation
  - Explaining, interpreting and commenting on the meaning of events and information.
  - Providing support for established authority and norms.
  - Socializing.
  - Co-ordinating separate activities.
  - Consensus building.
  - Setting orders of priority and signalling relative status.

- Continuity
  - Expressing the dominant culture and recognizing subcultures and new cultural developments.
  - Forging and maintaining commonality of values.

- Entertainment
  - Providing amusement, diversion and the means of relaxation.
  - Reducing social tension.

- Mobilization
  - Campaigning for societal objectives in the sphere of politics, war, economic development, work and sometimes religion.

We cannot give any general rank order to these items, or say anything about their relative frequency of occurrence. The correspondence between function (or purpose) and precise content of media is not exact, since one function overlaps with another and the same content can serve different functions. The set of statements refers to functions for society and needs to be reformulated in order to take account of the perspectives either of the media themselves (their own view of their tasks) or of the individual user of mass media, as in '**uses and gratifications**' theory and research (see Chapter 15). Media function can thus refer both to more or less objective tasks of the media (such as news or editorializing) and to motives or benefits as perceived by a media user (such as being informed or entertained).

Among the general 'functions for society', most agreement seems to have been achieved on the idea of the media as a force for social integration (as noted already). Studies of media content have also often found that mainstream mass media tend to be conformist and supportive rather than critical of dominant values. This support takes several forms, including the avoidance of fundamental criticism of key institutions, such as business, the justice system and democratic politics; giving differential access to the 'social top'; and symbolically rewarding those who succeed according to the approved paths of virtue and hard work, while symbolically punishing those who fail or deviate. Dayan and Katz (1992) argue that major social occasions portrayed on television (public or state ceremonies, major sporting events), and often drawing huge audiences worldwide, help to provide otherwise missing social cement. One of the effects of what they call '**media events**' is to confer status on leading figures and issues in society. Another is on social relations: 'With almost every event, we have seen *communitas and camaraderie* emerge from normally atomized – and sometimes deeply divided – societies' (Dayan and Katz, 1992: 214). A key example would be the terrorist attacks on the World Trade Center complex in New York of September 11, 2001.

In the light of these observations, it is not so surprising that research on effects has failed to lend much support to the proposition that mass media, for all their attention to crime, sensation, violence and deviant happenings, are a significant cause of social, or even individual, crime and disorganization. On the other hand, the way crime features in (television) news can be seen to contribute to a functionalist theory of media ritualizing such events to remind audiences about society's morality – much as Durkheim originally suggested (Grabe, 1999). However, what is functional or not is nearly always disputable on subjective grounds. For instance, media critical of authorities are performing a useful watchdog role, but from another point of view they are undermining authority and national unity. This, together with its failure to account for (ethnic, gender and social) diversity and (individual) agency, is a fundamental weakness of functionalism. The key propositions of the theory are found in Box 4.10.

## 4.10

### Functionalist theory of media: main propositions

- Media are an institution of society
- They perform the necessary tasks of order, control and cohesion
- They are also necessary for adaptation and change
- Functions are recognizable in the effects of the media
- Management of tension
- There are also unintended harmful effects which can be classified as dysfunctions

# MEDIA—SOCIETY THEORY IV: SOCIAL CONSTRUCTIONISM

Social **constructionism** is an abstract term for a very broad and influential tendency in the social sciences, sparked off especially by the publication of Berger and Luckman's book *The Social Construction of Reality* (1967), which was updated to account specifically for the role of media and mass communication in Couldry and Hepp's book *The Mediated Construction of Reality* (2016). In fact, the intellectual roots are a good deal deeper, and can be found in the symbolic interactionism of Blumer (1969) and the phenomenological sociology of Alfred Schutz (1972). In this work, the notion of society as an objective reality pressing on individuals is countered with the alternative (and more liberating) view that the structures, forces and ideas of society are created by human beings, continually recreated or reproduced and also open to challenge and change. In Couldry and Hepp's account, these continuous challenges and changes are considered as inseparable from the structuring role media play in all aspects of life, and particularly in the dependence of society's institutions on media to perform their functions. There is a general emphasis on the possibilities for action and also for choices in the understanding of 'reality'. Social reality has to be made and given meaning (interpreted) by human actors (in media). These general ideas have been formulated in many different ways, according to other theoretical ideas, and represent a major paradigm change in the human sciences in the later twentieth century, with renewed interest and analyses in the twenty-first century, inspired by the pervasive and ubiquitous nature of media in society.

Berger and Luckman's work in many ways is at the centre of thinking about processes of media influence as well as being a matter of debate. The general idea that mass media influence what most people believe to be reality is of course an old one, and is embedded in theories of propaganda and ideology (for instance, the role of the media as producing a 'false consciousness'). The unthinking, but unceasing, promotion by media of nationalism, patriotism, social conformity and belief systems could all be interpreted as examples of social construction. Later critical theory argued for the possibility of such ideological impositions being contested and resisted, emphasizing the possibilities for reinterpreting the hegemonic message. Even so, the emphasis in critical theory is on the media as a very effective *reproducer* of a selective and biased view of reality.

Aside from the question of ideology, there has been much attention to social construction at work in relation to mass media news, entertainment and popular culture and in the formation of public opinion. In respect of news, there is now more or less a consensus among media scholars that the picture of 'reality' that news claims to provide cannot help but be a selective construct made up of fragments of factual information and observation that are bound together and given meaning by a particular frame, angle of vision or perspective. The genre requirements of news and the routines of news processing are also at work. Social construction refers to the processes by which events, persons, values and ideas are first defined or interpreted in a certain way and given value and priority, largely by mass media, leading to the (personal) construction of larger pictures of reality. In contemporary versions of social constructionism and media theory, this process gets re-articulated with today's media for mass self-communication – giving people a co-creative (albeit far from equal) role to play in the construction of reality. The central propositions are set out in Box 4.11.

---

**4.11**

**Social constructionism: main propositions**

- Society is a construct rather than a fixed reality
- Media provide the materials for reality construction
- Meanings are offered by media, but can be negotiated or rejected
- Media selectively reproduce certain meanings
- Media cannot give an objective account of social reality (all facts are interpretations)
- Media both stimulate and complicate the formation of shared narratives and meanings

---

# MEDIA—SOCIETY THEORY V: COMMUNICATION TECHNOLOGY DETERMINISM

There is a long and still active tradition of searching for links between the dominant communication technology of an age and key features of society, bearing on all the themes outlined above. To label this body of thinking 'determinist' does not do justice to the many differences and nuances, but there is a common element of 'media-centrism' (see Chapter 1) as opposed to the 'media-centred' approach in, for example, Couldry and Hepp's (2016) update on social constructionism and media. While a *media-centric* approach would assume contemporary media to be a categorical cause of changes in society, public opinion and people's behaviour, a *media-centred* perspective would place media at the centre of society's institutions and activities, through which any and all social and political transformations are shaped and structured. In a deterministic frame of reference regarding media and communication technology, there is a tendency to concentrate on this potential for (or bias towards) social change as brought about by a particular communication technology and to subordinate other variables: smartphones turn (young) people into zombies, rather than the pressures of everyday life, the stresses of navigating today's sprawling urban environments or simply 'making it work' at home, in school and on the job in a complex, globalizing world.

Any history of communication (as of other) technologies testifies to the accelerating pace of invention and of material and other consequences, and some theorists are inclined to identify distinct phases. Rogers (1986), for instance, locates turning points at the invention of writing, the beginning of printing in the fifteenth century, the mid-nineteenth-century start to the telecommunication era, and the age of interactive communication beginning in 1946 with the invention of the mainframe computer. Schement and Curtis (1995) provide us with a detailed timeline, extending from prehistory to modern times, of communication technology inventions, which they classify according to their being either 'conceptual/institutional' (such as writing) or 'devices for acquisition and storage' (such as paper and printing) or being related to processing and distribution (such as computers and satellites). History shows several apparent trends but especially a shift over time in the direction of more speed, greater dispersion, wider reach and greater flexibility. Overall, the history of communication technology underlines the capacity for communication more readily to cross barriers of time and space. These matters are discussed in more detail in Chapter 5 with reference to the cultural and social factors shaping the evolution of media technologies.

## THE TORONTO SCHOOL

One of the early prominent theorists in this tradition was the Canadian economic historian Harold Innis, who founded the '**Toronto School**' of thinking about the media in the period after the Second World War. Innis (1950, 1951) attributed the characteristic features of successive ancient civilizations to the prevailing and dominant modes of communication, each of which will have its own 'bias' in terms of societal form. For example, he regarded the change from stone to papyrus as causing a shift from royal to priestly power. In ancient Greece, an oral tradition and a flexible alphabet favoured inventiveness and diversity and prevented the emergence of a priesthood with a monopoly over education. The foundation and endurance of the Roman Empire was assisted by a culture of writing and documents on which legal-bureaucratic institutions, capable of administering distant provinces, could be based. Printing, in its turn, challenged the bureaucratic monopoly of power and encouraged both individualism and nationalism.

There are two main organizing principles in Innis's work. First, as in the economic sphere, communication leads over time to monopolization by a group or a class of the means of production and distribution of knowledge. In turn, this produces a disequilibrium that either impedes changes or leads to the competitive emergence of other forms of communication, which tend to restore equilibrium. This can also be taken to mean that new communication technologies undermine old bases of social power. Secondly, the most important dimensions of empire are *space* and *time*, and some means of communication are more suitable for one than for the other (this is the main so-called bias of communication). Thus, empires can persist either through time (such as ancient Egypt) or extensively in space (such as Rome), depending on the dominant form of communication.

McLuhan's (1962) developments of the theory offered new insights into the consequences of the rise of print media (see also Eisenstein, 1978), although his main purpose of explaining the significance of electronic media for human experience has not really been fulfilled (McLuhan, 1964) (see also Chapter 5). Of printing, McLuhan wrote: 'the typographic extension of man brought in nationalism, industrialism and mass markets, and universal literacy and education'.

Gouldner (1976) interpreted key changes in modern political history in terms of communication technology. He connects the rise of 'ideology', defined as a special form of rational discourse, to printing and the newspaper, on the grounds that (in the eighteenth and nineteenth centuries) these stimulated a supply of interpretation and ideas (ideology). He then portrays the later media of radio, film and television as having led to a decline of ideology because of the shift from 'conceptual to iconic symbolism', revealing a split between the 'cultural apparatus' (the intelligentsia), which produces ideology, and the 'consciousness industry', which controls the new mass public. This anticipates a continuing 'decline in ideology' as a result of the new computer-based networks of information. Gouldner's work is mirrored in recent claims, made by several prominent news organizations around the world, that new social movements such as the 'Arab Spring' (taking place in 2010 and beyond) could be considered to be 'social media revolutions' given the profound role such technologies played in the various countries (for example, Facebook in Tunisia, Twitter in Egypt and YouTube in Syria).

In recent years, theoretical advances in the realm of 'hard' or 'soft' media determinism have been made regarding media in general, and television in particular (Scannell, 2014), and with specific consideration of the Internet as a technology that can be seen as an extension of life and the human condition (Briggs and Burke, 2010: 286). Both Katherine Hayles (2012) and John Durham Peters (2016) offer perhaps the most comprehensive contemporary articulation of the theory, arguing how the ongoing digitalization and datafication of the world – a historical process running parallel to the rise in human evolution (something Hayles calls 'technogenesis') – fundamentally affects our understanding of nature and culture, motivating an understanding of media as ontological as well as semiotic. In other words, to Hayles and Durham Peters, media are not only *about* the world, media *are* the world. The main propositions of media technological determinism are presented in Box 4.12.

## 4.12

## Media technological determinism: main propositions

- Communication technology is fundamental to society
- Each technology has a bias to particular communication forms, contents and uses
- The sequence of invention and application of communication technology influences the direction and pace of social change
- Communication revolutions lead to social revolutions

## MOVING AWAY FROM MEDIA DETERMINISM

Most scholarly observers are wary of single-factor explanations of social change and do not really believe in direct mechanistic effects from new technology. Effects occur only when inventions are taken up, developed and applied, usually to existing uses at first, then with a great extension and change of use according to the capacity of the technology and the needs of a society. Development is always shaped by social and cultural context (Lehman-Wilzig and Cohen-Avigdor, 2004; Stober, 2004).

It no longer makes sense to think in terms of a single dominant medium with some unique properties. Instead, as Bausinger argued in 1984, we should think of media as an 'ensemble' with various technologies and uses featuring more or less simultaneously. At present, very many different new media forms co-exist with many of the 'old' media, none of which have disappeared. At the same time, the argument that media are converging and linking to comprise an all-encompassing network has considerable force and implications (Neuman, 1991). Furthermore, social historians Briggs and Burke (2010) remind us not just of a movement towards increasing convergence (of media and our uses thereof), but perhaps more importantly of continuous flux as the key driving force in the history of communication technology. It may also be true that newer media forms can have a particular technological, social or cultural 'bias' (see Chapter 6), which makes certain effects more likely. These possibilities are discussed in the following section.

## MEDIA–SOCIETY THEORY VI: THE INFORMATION SOCIETY

The assumption of a revolutionary social transition as a result of new communication technology has been with us for quite some time, although it is not without its critics (for example, Leiss, 1989; Ferguson, 1992; Webster, 1995, 2002). Ferguson (1986) treated this 'neo-technological determinism' as a *belief system* which was tending to operate as a self-fulfilling prophecy. The term 'communications revolution', along with the term '**information society**', has now almost come to be accepted as an objective description of our time, of the type of society that is emerging and of the massive social events occurring.

The term 'information society' seems to have originated in Japan in the 1960s (Ito, 1981), although its genealogy is usually traced to the concept of the 'post-industrial' society first proposed by the sociologist Daniel Bell (1973). Another source was the idea of an 'information economy' developed by the economists Machlup (1962) and Porat (1977). Bell's work belonged to the tradition that relates types of society to succeeding stages of economic and social development. The main characteristics of the post-industrial society were found in the rise in the service sector of the economy relative to manufacture or agriculture, and thus the predominance of 'information-based' work. Theoretical knowledge (scientific, expert, data-based) was becoming the key factor in the economy, outstripping physical plant and land as bases of wealth. Correlatively, a 'new class' was emerging based on the possession of knowledge and personal relations skills. Most of the observed post-industrial trends were seen to accelerate in the last quarter of the twentieth century. The production and distribution of information of all kinds, especially using computer-based network technology, have themselves become a major sector of the economy.

Aside from the accumulating evidence of the significance of information in contemporary economy and society, there has not been much agreement or clarity about the *concept* of 'information society'. Melody (1990: 26–27) describes information societies simply as those that have become 'dependent upon complex electronic information networks and which allocate a major portion of their resources to information and communication activities'. Van Cuilenburg (1987) put the chief characteristic as the exponential increase in production and flow of information of all kinds, largely as a consequence of reduced costs following miniaturization and computerization. However, he also called attention to our relative incapacity to process, use or even receive much more of the increasing supply of information. Since then, this imbalance has become much greater. Reductions in costs of transmission have continued to fuel the process of exponential growth. There is a continually decreasing sensitivity to distance as well as to cost and a continually increasing speed, volume and interactivity of possibilities for communication.

Despite the importance of the trends under way, it has not really been established that any revolutionary transformation in society has yet occurred, as opposed to a further step in the development of capitalism (Schement and Curtis, 1995: 26). What is still missing is evidence of a transformation in social relationships (Webster, 1995). Several commentators have emphasized the increased 'interconnectedness' of society as a result of 'information society' trends extending to a global level. According to Neuman (1991: 12), this is the underlying 'logic behind the cascade of new technologies'.

Some writers (for example, Van Dijk, 1992; Castells, 1996) choose to use the term 'network society' instead of 'information society'. Van Dijk (2005: 240) suggests that modern society is in a process of becoming a network society: 'a form of society increasingly organizing its relationships in media networks which are gradually replacing or complementing the social networks of face to face communication'. A network structure of society is contrasted with a centre–periphery and hierarchical mass society, or one that largely conforms to the traditional bureaucratic model of organization that was typical of industrial society in the nineteenth and twentieth centuries. It exhibits numerous overlapping circles of communication that can have both a vertical and a horizontal range, contributing to an increasing degree of complexity and unpredictability of information and communication processes. Such networks can serve to exclude as well as connect.

The idea of interconnectedness relates to another aspect of contemporary society that has attracted comment, and that is the high degree of *dependence* on others. This is hardly a new idea since it was the basis of Durkheim's century-old social theory concerning the division of labour. But there is arguably a qualitative change in our era, resulting from the continued excursions of information technology into every aspect of life, especially where intelligent machines (that is, machine learning and artificial intelligence) augment or even replace human agency. One aspect that has been emphasized by Giddens (1991) is the degree to which we have to put our trust in expert systems of all kinds for maintaining normal conditions of life. We live with increased awareness of risks of many kinds (health, environmental, economic, military) that are both derived from the public circulation of information and managed by reference to information. Elsewhere Giddens (1999: 2) refers to the globalized world as one 'out of control – a runaway world'. In addition, it would seem that the 'culture' of contemporary society, in the traditional sense of mental and symbolic pursuits and customary ways of passing time free from essential obligations, is largely dominated by a vast array of informational services in addition to the mass media, while all of these services, processes and networks have become digital.

The contemporary iteration of theorizing the information society and network society is that of a 'data society', where all our actions in life have become 'datafied' – that is, turned into data that can be processed by computers – and these data now fuel the global information economy. The companies that perhaps did not invent, but most certainly have been most successful in monetizing this particular articulation of the information and network society are so-called platforms: digital places where people come together to shop, learn, play, work and exchange products and services of any kind. Generally speaking, such platforms offer their services for free – consider Uber, Airbnb, Facebook, Twitter, Instagram, Tinder, Amazon, Google, and many more specialized sites and applications – as their primary source of revenue is the data generated from people's interactions on their platform. As more and more of our everyday life takes place in media, the economic (and corresponding political) power of these platforms is immense, especially given their relatively short existence (Helmond, 2015). Growing concerns about this 'platform society' focus on their general lack of transparency and the absence of public values governing their actions, despite their significant influence and impact on public affairs (Van Dijck et al., 2018).

The information society concept (as the network society and platform society concepts) has been dominated by economic, sociological, geographical and technological considerations. This fits in a historical pattern of how each new advance in communications technology has predominantly been treated as an opportunity for politics and economics, according to James Carey (2009: 27), while such developments have been rarely seen 'as opportunities to expand people's powers to learn and exchange ideas and experience'. While the *cultural* dimension tends to be relatively neglected, it may be easier to demonstrate the rise of a 'digital culture' that extends into all aspects of everyday life than the reality of an information society (Deuze, 2006).

It is clear that the 'information economy' is much larger than the mass media on their own, and the primary information technologies involved are not those of mass production and distribution of print material for the general public or mass dissemination by broadcasting or electronic recordings. It can be argued that the birth of the 'information age', while presaged by mass communication, marks a new and separate historical path. Certainly, the mass media were well established before the supposed information 'revolution', and may be better considered as part of the industrial age rather than of its successor. There were early voices that foretold the death of mass media precisely because of the rise of new information technologies that are said to render them obsolete (for example, Maisel, 1973).

The information society concept has not been universally accepted as helpful for analysis, for reasons that have in part been explained. A central problem is the lack of an overt political dimension, since it seems to have no core of political purpose, simply an (attributed) inevitable technocratic logic of its own (Van Dijk, 2005). In this it may at least match the predominant spirit of the times in both popular and intellectual 'western' circles. It is quite clear that in several contexts, the information society idea has been harnessed for public policies with technocratic goals for nation states or regions (Mattelart, 2003). The general consensus about the significance of changes occurring in communication technology is not accompanied by unanimity about the social consequences. Hassan (2008) believes that the information society idea is essentially ideological and supportive of the neo-liberal economic project that benefits most from global interconnectivity. Some of these issues are returned to in Chapter 6, which deals with new media developments. However, certain main theoretical points are summarized in Box 4.13.

---

## 4.13
### Information society theory: main propositions

- Information work replaces industrial work
- Production and flow of information accelerates
- Society is characterized by increasing interconnectivity
- Disparate activities converge and integrate
- There is increasing dependency on complex systems
- Trends to globalization accelerate
- Constraints on time and space are much reduced
- Consequences are open to alternative interpretations, both positive and negative
- There are increased risks of loss of control
- Information society theory is an ideology more than a theory

---

## MEDIA–SOCIETY THEORY VII: MEDIATIZATION

As media become ever more pervasive and ubiquitous, access to media in general and use of the Internet in particular have come to be considered by many as a principal (some would say banal) part of everyday life around the world. The very fact that it has become commonplace and rather self-evident to state that media play a profound role in all aspects of society and everyday life signifies an important shift from media as having 'effects' on people and society, to media as being part and parcel of any process governing societal affairs.

At the start of the twenty-first century, it has become clear that media and mass communication are not just acting upon established processes in society, but are also creating routines within and across society's institutions on their own. Whereas earlier 'grand theories' of media–society relationships were grounded in paradigms from established humanities and social scientific disciplines, the field of media studies and (mass) communication research turned to its own concepts and research traditions (including media systems dependency, cultivation and framing theories, medium theory and media ecology theory). Emerging from interdisciplinary theorizing and empirical research on the various ways in which different media emerge and find a place in everyday life, within and across different cultures, and the inner workings of society's institutions in Europe (Silverstone, 1999, 2007) and Latin America (Martín-Barbero, 1993; Canclini, 1995[1989]), scholars proposed 'mediatization' as a sensitizing concept (see also Asp, 1990; Mazzoleni and Schulz, 1999; Krotz, 2007). As Stig Hjarvard, in an early attempt to define the concept, suggests, the 'mediatization' of society refers to a phase or process 'whereby society to an increasing degree is submitted to, or becomes dependent on, the media and their logic. This process is characterized by a duality in that the media have become *integrated* into the operations of other social institutions, while they also have acquired the status of social institutions *in their own right*. As a consequence, social interaction – within the respective institutions, between institutions, and in society at large – take place via the media' (Hjarvard, 2008a: 113; italics in original).

Hjarvard contends that, over time, the media have to some extent taken over the role of society's key institutions (such as the state, church and family) as providers of information and moral orientation, while 'at the same time as the media have become society's most important storyteller about society itself' (Hjarvard, 2008b: 13). Mediatization has since been taken up far and wide in media and mass communication research, as it applies to work both within social science-oriented approaches and to broader cultural studies approaches to the study of media–society relationships and transformations. In their review of the emerging field, Couldry and Hepp (2016) identify three factors and research streams inspiring this development:

- the growing importance of media to people in general;

- the increasing interdisciplinary and diverse research approaches to media (beyond the classical sender–message–receiver model of communication); and

- the rapid uptake of media and (mass) communication as objects of study across a variety of disciplines, including but not limited to anthropology, science and technology studies, philosophy, pedagogy, political science and sociology.

Mediatization theory has produced studies in two directions, given its double-sided definition: an 'institutionalist' and a 'constructionist' tradition (Hepp, 2013). In institutionalist accounts, mediatization is seen as a process in which non-media social actors have to adapt to 'media's rules, aims, production logics, and constraints' (Mazzoleni and Schulz, 1999: 249).

In social constructionist accounts, it is seen as a process in which changes in media, information and communication technologies influence and shape the way culture and society function over time. This broad appeal of the concept has led to numerous critical discussions in the field, with Deacon and Stanyer (2014) and Corner (2018) in particular expressing concern over its rather loose and all-encompassing definition and application, and the fact that mediatization as a research framework to date lacks an independent identity next to existing work in media and mass communication research that treats its object of study with careful attention to its social, cultural, political and technological contexts.

While critical, Lunt and Livingstone (2016) point out that mediatization, as a general framework, inspires cross-disciplinary work that would integrate media and (mass) communication research with other fields of study. They point out how mediatization theory sensitizes media researchers to a heightened historical awareness, to be mindful of links between media changes and social transformations, as well as to the intersections among 'metaprocesses' such as globalization, individualization, commercialization and urbanization with mediatization. The key theoretical points regarding mediatization as a theory are highlighted in Box 4.14.

## 4.14

### Mediatization theory: main propositions

- Media have come to play a profound role in society
- Media are an accepted part of everyday life
- Media, as institutions, take up a powerful role in culture, politics and the economy
- Non-media social actors have to adapt to the media in order to perform their role
- This duality is a historical phase or process
- Mediatization is a sensitizing concept more than a theory

## CONCLUSION

These theoretical perspectives on the relation between media and society are diverse in several respects, emphasizing different causes and types of change and pointing to different paths into the future. They cannot all be reconciled, since they represent alternative philosophical positions and diverse methodological preferences. Nevertheless, we can make some sense of them in terms of the main dimensions of approach, each of which offers a choice of perspective and method. First, there is a contrast between a critical and a more or less positive view of the developments at issue. Although scientific enquiry seeks a degree of **objectivity** and neutrality, this does not prevent one from either approving or disapproving of a tendency indicated by a theory. In respect of Marxism, political-economic theory and mass society theory, there is an inbuilt critical component. In contrast, functionalism leans in a positive direction as far as the working of media is concerned. Information society and mediatization theory are open to critical and positive views, while social constructionism and technology determinism are open-ended regarding the source (rather than the direction) of change.

Secondly, there is a difference between a more socio-centric and a more media-centric view. We can view media either as dependent on society and mirroring its contours or as primary movers and moulders. The main media-centric theories are those relating to communication technology and the information society, whereas authors in the mediatization tradition opt for a 'media-centred' rather than a 'media-centric' perspective.

This account is incomplete without the theory relating to media and culture that will be discussed in Chapter 5, but it gives some idea of the general structure of thinking about mass media and society, leading to contemporary considerations of increased significance regarding the role media (as technologies and institutions next to as industries, texts and audiences) play in societal affairs.

# FURTHER READING

Bausinger, H. (1984) 'Media, technology and daily life', *Media, Culture & Society*, 6: 343–351.

Couldry, N., Rodriquez, C., Bolin, G., Cohen, J., Volkmer, I., Goggin, G., Kraidy, M., Iwabuchi, K. and Linchuan Qiu, J. (2018) 'Media, communication and the struggle for social progress', *Global Media and Communication*, 14(2): 173–191.

Curran, J. and Hesmondhalgh, D. (2019) *Media and Society*, 6th edition. London: Bloomsbury Academic.

Mihelj, S. and Stanyer, J. (2019) 'Theorizing media, communication and social change: towards a processual approach', *Media, Culture & Society*, 41(4): 482–501.

Silverstone, R. (2007) *Media and Morality: On the Rise of the Mediapolis*. Cambridge: Polity Press.

Thompson, J.B. (1995) *The Media and Modernity*. Cambridge: Polity Press.

# MEDIA, MASS COMMUNICATION AND CULTURE

This chapter sets out to explore the more 'cultural' dimensions of the theories already discussed in Chapter 4 and to introduce some additional perspectives. The general framework of 'mediation' remains relevant, but here the emphasis shifts to *what* is mediated (the particular meanings) and to the process by which meaning is given and made (sometimes referred to as 'signification'). Since the earlier days of media and mass communication research, a distinctive 'culturalist' perspective on mass media has developed, especially under the influence of the humanities (literature, linguistics, philosophy, cultural studies), as distinct from the more social scientific emphasis of communication research. At some points, or on some issues, the two traditions have merged, although there remain substantial differences of thinking and method. This book – and this chapter – was in its first editions written primarily from a social scientific perspective, but increasingly follows the field of media and mass communication research in its calls for more integrated, mixed and interdisciplinary approaches, theories and methods in order to adequately address the complexities of today's media environment.

The distinctly culturalist approach takes in all aspects of the production, forms and reception of texts in this sense and the discourses that surround them. While mass media necessarily fall within the range of cultural studies, the latter has a much wider range of reference, and there is only a limited overlap of issues and theory. As will be shown, a culture cannot only be defined in terms of texts, but relates just as much to patterns of life and thought, and potentially to all human activity. To put it briefly, 'media-cultural' theory is concerned not only with the content of mass media, but also with the context of production and reception and with all the surrounding discourses and practices, with a specific eye towards how people experience and understand themselves, each other and the world they live in through the media – and how this understanding interconnects with social forces (Grossberg, 1986).

## COMMUNICATION AND CULTURE

James Carey (1975) proposed an alternative to the dominant view of communication as *transmission* in the form of a 'ritual' model (see p. 94), and he has also advocated an approach to communication and society in which culture is allotted a more central place. 'Social life is more than power and trade … it also includes the sharing of aesthetic experience, religious ideas, personal values and sentiments, and intellectual notions – a ritual order' (Carey, 1988: 34). Accordingly, he defined communication as 'a symbolic process whereby reality is produced, maintained, repaired and transformed' (ibid.: 23).

In order to take further the question of the relation between media, *mass* communication and culture in this sense, we need to be more precise about what presents itself as an object of study. This is made difficult by the many senses in which the term 'culture' is used, itself a reflection of the complexity of the phenomenon. Culture is defined by Carey as a *process*, but it can also refer to some *shared attribute* of a human group (such as their physical environment, tools, religion, values, customs and practices, or their whole way of life). Culture also can refer to *texts* and *symbolic artefacts* (for example, works of art and architecture, also including tattoos or graffiti) that are encoded with particular meanings by and for people with particular cultural identifications.

## TOWARDS DEFINING CULTURE

It is not possible to give a precise definition of culture because the term covers so many things and is variously used, but if we extract essential points from these different usages, it seems that culture must have all of the following attributes. It is something collective and shared with others (there is no purely individual culture, it is always relational in some way). It must have some symbolic form of expression, whether intended as such or not. It has some pattern, order or regularity, and therefore some evaluative dimensions (if only a degree of conformity to a culturally prescribed pattern). There is (or has been) a dynamic continuity over time (culture lives and changes, has a history and potentially a future). Perhaps the most general and essential attribute of culture is communication, since cultures cannot develop, survive, extend and generally succeed without communication. Finally, in order to study culture, we need to be able to recognize it and locate it, and essentially there are three places to look: in people, in things (texts, artefacts) and in human practices (socially patterned behaviours). These main features are summarized in Box 5.1.

There are some obvious implications for the study of media and mass communication, since every aspect of the production and use of mass media has a cultural dimension. We can focus on *people* as producers of culturally meaningful media texts, or as 'readers of texts' from which they take cultural meanings, with implications for the rest of social life.

## 5.1

### The main properties of culture

- Collectively formed and held
- Open to symbolic expression
- Ordered and differentially valued
- Systematically patterned
- Dynamic and changing
- Spatially located
- Communicable over time and space

We can focus on the *texts* and *artefacts* themselves (films, books, newspaper articles) and on their symbolic forms and possible meanings. We may want to study the *practices* of *makers* of media products or of *users* of the media. Media audience composition and behaviour (practices around the choice and use of media) are always culturally patterned, before, after and during the media experience.

## THEMES OF MEDIA-CULTURAL THEORY

This broad terrain can be narrowed down by identifying the main questions and theoretical issues, as outlined in the following paragraphs.

1. *The quality of mass culture.* The first 'cultural' question on the agenda of media theory was that of the quality of the new mass culture made possible by mass communication. This topic has already been discussed (pp. 81–83) and, as we saw, the initial tendency was to view mass culture in a negative light. It nearly always involved a view of people as a mass – the new form of social collectivity, which was otherwise often perceived as without any other culture of its own.

2. *The nature of popular culture.* The rise of a distinctive 'media culture' has also stimulated a rethinking about the nature of 'popular culture', which has now to be seen not just as a cheap alternative, mass produced for mass consumption, but as a vital new branch of cultural creativity and enjoyment (Schudson, 1991; McGuigan, 1992). The issue of mass culture also stimulated the rise of critical cultural theory, which, among other things, has been extended to consider issues of gender, ethnicity, sexuality, and of subculture in relation to mass communication.

3. *The impact of technology.* A third key theme relates to the potential consequences of the new technologies themselves for lived experience and meaning-making and of human rights (such as privacy) in the emerging modern world. Communication technology has many implications for the way we may come to know our own social world and our place in it. Before the invention of audiovisual media, cultural experience was mediated by personal contact, religious ceremonies, public performance or printed texts (for a small minority). Mediated cultural experience is accessible to virtually all in a great variety of forms that may alter its meaning and salience.

4. *Political economy and culture.* There are political-economic aspects of the organized production of culture represented by mass media industries, as well as in the emerging platform economy. We have come to think of the media as a 'consciousness industry', driven by economic logic as well as by cultural changes. An important aspect is the 'commodification' of culture in the form of the 'software' produced by and for the communication 'hardware', both of which are sold and exchanged in enlarging markets.

5. *Globalization.* Along with technological change and 'marketization' has come a steady increase in the internationalization of cultural production and distribution (this has sometimes been referred to as 'Americanization'). The theme of 'globalization' captures a range of debates about the costs and benefits, or just the consequences, for pre-existing cultural content and forms. Does globalization lead to homogenization, diversification or **hybridization**? Can minority forms survive and new ones develop? How does the global production network of media industries influence what stories get told, who gets heard and seen, and what about its impact on the creative process of media making?

6. *Identity.* This is linked to another theme of media-cultural theory, relating to cultural identity and class, which can be defined at various levels, from the national or ethnic to the local and linguistic, including issues related to gender and ethnicity. The typical culture (in the sense of media texts) produced by the major media industries is often globalized in form, even when it appears in local or national variants and languages. Communication is necessary for identity, and mass media (including the Internet) can be both harmful and beneficial for identity. In some parts of the world there has been a search for some means through public policy to secure valued forms of cultural diversity. More recently, research on identity and the media has focused on the intersectional querying of identity and subjectivity (Hermes, Kooijman, Littler and Wood, 2017).

7. *Ideology.* Last but not least is the question of how ideology of many different kinds is embodied in cultural production and how it can be 'read' in media texts and find some effect on an audience. Particular attention is paid to covert or unconscious meanings that stem from the cultural context or the language or coding system employed. These points are summarized in Box 5.2.

---

## 5.2

## Themes of media-cultural theory

- Mass culture quality and basis for popular appeal
- Communication technology effects
- Commodification and marketization of culture
- Globalization
- Cultural diversity and identity
- Cultural identity and class
- Gender, ethnicity, sexuality and subculture
- Ideology and hegemony embedded in cultural forms

---

# THE BEGINNINGS: THE FRANKFURT SCHOOL AND CRITICAL CULTURAL THEORY

A socially based critical concern with the rise of mass culture goes back at least to the mid-nineteenth century, and in the mid-twentieth century was represented in England by the rise of more radical (and populist) critical theory as expressed in the work of Richard Hoggart, Raymond Williams and Stuart Hall. The initial thrust of these critics was to attack the commercial roots of cultural 'debasement' and to speak up for the working-class consumer of mass culture as the victim (and not only that) rather than the villain of the story. The aim was to redeem the people on whose supposedly 'low tastes' the presumed low quality of mass culture was often blamed. In North America at about the same time or earlier, a similar debate was raging (see Rosenberg and White, 1957), with an eloquent denunciation of the banality of mass culture. Since then, 'mass culture' itself has largely been rescued from the stigma of low quality, although in the course of this the original concept of mass culture has been largely abandoned.

For the wider development of ideas about mass communication and the character of 'media culture', within an international framework, the various national debates about cultural quality have probably been less influential than a set of ideas, owing much to neo-Marxist thinking, which developed and diffused in the post-war years. The term 'critical theory' refers to this long and diverse tradition, which owes its origins to the work of a group of post-1933 *émigré* scholars from the Marxist School of Applied Social Research in Frankfurt. The most important members of the group were Max Horkheimer and Theodor Adorno, but others, including Leo Lowenthal, Herbert Marcuse and Walter Benjamin, played an important role (see Jay, 1973; Hardt, 1991).

The School had been established originally to examine the apparent failure of revolutionary social change as predicted by Marx. In explanation of this failure, they looked to the capacity of the 'superstructure' (especially ideas and ideology represented in the mass media) to subvert the material and historical forces of economic change (and also the promise of the Enlightenment). History (as interpreted by Marx) seemed to have 'gone wrong' because ideologies of the dominant class had come to condition the economic base, especially by promoting a 'false consciousness' among the working masses. The *commodity* is the main instrument of this process. The theory of commodification originates in Marx's *Grundrisse*, in which he noted that objects are commodified by acquiring an exchange value, instead of having merely an intrinsic use value. In the same way, cultural products (in the form of images, ideas and symbols) are produced and sold in media markets as commodities. These can be exchanged by consumers for emotional satisfaction, amusement and illusory notions of our place in the world, often resulting in the obscuration of the real structure of society and our subordination in it (false consciousness).

Marcuse (1964) gave the description 'one-dimensional' to the mass consumption society founded on commerce, advertising and spurious egalitarianism. The media and the 'culture industry' as a whole were deeply implicated in this critique. Many of these ideas were launched during the 1940s by Adorno and Horkheimer (1972, in translation), which contained a sharp and pessimistic attack on mass culture. This was criticized for its uniformity, worship of technique, monotony, escapism and production of false needs, its reduction of individuals to customers and its removal of all ideological choice (see Hardt, 1991: 140).

In several respects, the critique of mass culture outlined is very close to that found in different versions of the then contemporary mass society theory. The intellectual tradition outlined by Marx, the different generations of the Frankfurt School and subsequent thinkers, such as the more pragmatist Chicago School of Sociology (Wahl-Jorgensen, 2006), inspired a critical cultural theory that, according to Fuchs (2016), combines universal ethics based on people's positive capacities (such as striving for freedom, sociality, co-operation), a critique of domination, exploitation and alienation, the principle of dialectical reason (whereby every concept always also embodies its own negation, offering an opportunity for transcendence), a critique of ideology in favour of how people and things appear in reality, and an orientation towards (and support of) 'social struggles for a better world' (Fuchs, 2016: 8).

## IDEOLOGY AND RESISTANCE

Critical cultural theory has now extended well beyond its early concerns with ideological domination, although in one way or another the study of ideology in media culture remains central. So does the significance of media culture for the experience of particular groups in society, such as youth, the working class, ethnic minorities and other marginal categories. Research and theory on these topics were pioneered at the Centre for Contemporary Cultural Studies at the University of Birmingham during the 1970s. Stuart Hall is the person most associated with the work of this school. His key definition of the cultural studies approach is presented in Box 5.3.

### 5.3

### Stuart Hall on the cultural studies approach

[The cultural studies approach] is opposed to the base–superstructure way of formulating the relationship between ideal and material forces, especially where the base is defined by the determination by the 'economic' in any simple sense. . .

It defines 'culture' as both the means and values which arise amongst distinctive social groups and classes, on the basis of their given historical conditions and relationship, through which they 'handle' and respond to the conditions of existence. (Quoted in Gurevitch, Bennet, Curran and Woollacott, 1982: 267)

The critical approach associated with the **Birmingham School** (which was suddenly closed due to university restructuring in 2002) was also responsible for an important shift from the question of ideology embedded in media texts to the question of how this ideology might be 'read' by its audience. Stuart Hall (1974/1980) proposed a model of *encoding–decoding* media discourse, which represented the media text as located between its producers, who framed meaning in a certain way, and its audience, who 'decoded' the meaning according to their rather different social situations and frames of interpretation (see p. 97).

These ideas proved a considerable stimulus to rethinking the theory of ideology and of false consciousness. They led to research on the potential for 'differential decoding' (for example, Morley, 1980), with a view, especially, to finding evidence of working-class resistance to dominant media messages. The direct results were meagre in this respect, but indirectly the theory was very effective in 're-empowering' the audience and returning some optimism to the study of media and culture. It also led to a wider view of the social and cultural influences which mediate the experience of the media, especially ethnicity, gender and 'everyday life' (Morley, 1986, 1992). The main tenets of critical cultural theory are listed in Box 5.4.

## 5.4

### Critical cultural theory points: main propositions

- Mass culture is a debased form in capitalist society
- Mass culture produces false consciousness
- Commodification is the central process
- Mass culture embodies a hegemonic ideology
- Ideology can be decoded differentially, resisted and even reversed

# THE REDEMPTION OF THE POPULAR

The mass media are largely responsible for what we call either 'mass culture' or 'popular culture', and they have 'colonized' other cultural forms in the process. The most widely disseminated and enjoyed symbolic culture of our time (if it makes any sense to refer to it in the singular) is what flows in abundance by way of the media of films, television, magazines, music, digital games, and so on. It makes little sense to suppose that this flood can in some way be dammed, turned back or purified, or to view the predominant culture of our time simply as a deformed offspring of commerce from a once pure stock.

There is even less possibility of distinguishing an elite from a mass taste, since everyone is attracted to some of the diverse elements of popular media culture, and separation between different production and taste cultures is the exception rather than the rule. Tastes will always differ, and varying criteria of assessment can be applied, but the media culture of our time is an accomplished (if constantly changing and highly diverse) fact and can therefore be treated on its own terms. The term 'mass culture' is likely to remain in circulation, but the alternative form 'popular culture' (meaning essentially 'culture which is popular' – much enjoyed by many people) seems preferable and should no longer carry a pejorative association. Popular culture in this sense is a hybrid product of numerous and never-ending efforts for expression in a contemporary idiom aimed at reaching people and capturing a market, and an equally active demand by people for what Fiske (1987) would call 'meanings and pleasures'. In addition, popular culture has come to be recognized by media scholars as playing a role in the way especially young people appropriate and remix media through social media platforms, spreadable videos and memes – not just for recognition and fun, but also to raise awareness and to bring about political change (Jenkins et al., 2016).

# THE (SEMIOTIC) POWER OF THE PEOPLE

The so-called 'redemption of the popular' depends a good deal on the decoding theory of Hall outlined above (pp. 97–98). According to this, the same cultural product can be 'read' in different ways, even if a certain dominant meaning may seem to be built in. Fiske (1987) defines a media text as the *outcome* of its reading and enjoyment by an audience. He defines the plurality of meanings of a text as its 'polysemy'. The associated term '**intertextuality**' refers partly to the interconnectedness of meanings across different media contents (blurring any line between elite and popular culture), but also to the interconnectedness of meanings across media and other cultural experiences. An example of both terms is provided by the fact that a cultural phenomenon, like a pop singer or a movie franchise, can appeal to, yet have quite different meanings for, different groups using different media.

There are entirely different readings of much popular media content in different sub-cultures, opening a way of escape from potential social control. Fiske (1987: 126) writes:

> The preferred meanings in television are generally those that serve the interests of the dominant classes; other meanings are structured in relations of dominance–subordination ... the semiotic power of the subordinate to make their own meanings is the equivalent of their ability to evade, oppose, or negotiate with this social power.

For Fiske, the primary virtue of popular culture is precisely that it is popular, both literally 'of the people' and dependent on 'people power'. He writes: 'Popularity is here a measure of a cultural form's ability to serve the desires of its customers. . . . For a cultural commodity to become popular it must be able to meet the various interests of the people amongst whom it is popular as well as the interests of its producers' (ibid.: 310). Popular culture must be relevant and responsive to needs or it will fail, and success (in the market) may be the best test that culture is both (in practice the criterion of success supersedes any notion of intrinsic quality). Fiske rejects the argument that lines of division of cultural capital follow the lines of division of economic capital (Bourdieu, 1986). Instead he argues that there are two economies, with relative autonomy: one cultural and the other social. Even if most people in a class society are subordinated, they have a degree of *semiotic power* in the cultural economy – that is, the power to shape meanings to their own desires. Beyond this focus on what audiences 'do' with media and popular culture, it is increasingly important to consider what people 'make' with media, as their roles as consumers in the digital environment often coincide what those of producers (Jenkins, 2004). Herein also lies critical potential for people to transform, to subvert or simply to forward and thereby promote certain media messages over others.

## UNANSWERED QUESTIONS

Despite the re-evaluation of popular culture that has occurred, and the rise of postmodern (or 'liquid' modern) culture, as discussed below, several charges of the kind made by Frankfurt School critics remain on the table. Much of the content offered by media that is both popular and commercially successful is still open to much the same objections as in more elitist and less enlightened times. Market-oriented media culture often displays one or more of the following limitations. It can be, variously, repetitive, undemanding, thematically limited and conformist. Many examples can be found of popular content that is ideologically tendentious, nasty and positively anti-intellectual. Its production is governed by a predominantly commercial logic since most popular culture is financed and brought to market by large corporations with an overriding concern for their own profits, rather than for enriching the cultural lives of the people. Audiences are viewed as consumer markets to be manipulated and managed. Popular formulas and products tend to be used until threadbare, then discarded when they cease to be profitable, whatever the audience might demand in the 'cultural economy' (even though audiences at times push back, launching campaigns via social media, and sometimes succeed in breathing new life into certain shows and franchises). Even when corporate media producers include progressive messages in their content – such as addressing the sexualized representation of women in video games, making mainstream 'tentpole' movies with black (or otherwise minority) lead actors, and journalists sharing their sources and process when investigating an important story – an argument can be made that this is done, at least in part, because it is profitable to do so.

The new 'cultural populism' has, not surprisingly, produced its own backlash (McGuigan, 1992; Ferguson and Golding, 1997). Gitlin (1997) sees the new cultural studies as a populist project that has simply inverted the old hierarchy of cultural values, without overthrowing it. In his view it has become anti-political, which was not its avowed intention. Instead of being against capitalism, it has come to 'echo the logic of capitalism' (ibid.: 32).

The 'redemption' arguments largely ignore the continuing semiotic inequality whereby a more educated and better-off minority has access both to popular culture *and* to 'unpopular' culture (such as classical music, great literature and modern and avant-garde art). The majority is still limited to popular forms alone and totally dependent on the commercial media market (Gripsrud, 1989).

There is a risk in the backlash against polemical and overstated claims for popular culture. One way out of the impasse, without going back to the past, is to make use of the concept of **lifestyle**, in recognition of the flux and diversity of contemporary social life, especially as cultural capital is more widely and evenly distributed by way of the educational system (Andersson and Jansson, 1998). The contemporary lifestyle is identified both by preferences and by styles of media use. It is eclectic, fragmented and relaxed in style, and the contemporary 'hybrid' media culture tends to amplify and accelerate such a mediated life.

The idea of 'quality' of mass media cultural provision nevertheless remains on the agenda of applied media theory, even if its meaning has shifted, because there are still relevant policy issues and also public concerns about quality. Quality no longer refers exclusively to the degree of conformity to a traditional cultural canon, but may be defined in terms of creativity, originality, diversity of cultural identity and various ethical or moral principles (Schrøder, 1992), depending on whose perspective is chosen. Of course, as advocates of popular culture also argue, quality has also to be measured by the pleasures and satisfactions it provides, and these can be indicated, albeit crudely, by success in the market. It can certainly no longer be assumed that what has most appeal has less 'quality', but the material economic dynamic of cultural production cannot be so easily distinguished from the 'semiotic' cultural economy. It is also clear from enquiries into the meaning and measurement of 'cultural quality' that there is no single source of objective definition and that quite different criteria are applied by, for instance, professional media producers, audiences, social or cultural critics and media managers (Ishikawa, 1996) (see Chapter 10). There is no agreed theory of popular culture but relevant points of debate are listed as propositions in Box 5.5.

---

**5.5**

## The debate about popular culture: main points of debate

- Popular culture represents the power of the people
- Popularity is a quality in itself
- Popular culture has universal appeal
- Popular culture is important to many subgroup identities
- Popular culture is commodified culture

---

# GENDER AND THE MASS MEDIA

Hermes (2007: 191) argues that we need to understand how the media represent gender because 'constructions of femininity and masculinity are part of a dominant ideology'. Beyond this, she points out that the media still offer guides and examples of general behaviour and we need to be able to decode these messages. One area where the theory of differential cultural reading of media texts has made important advances, in collaboration with feminist research, is in relation to gender. While communication studies, even of the radical critical tendency, have long seemed to be largely 'gender-blind' (perhaps more a matter of unwillingness to see), in the 1990s and early 2000s one could justifiably speak of a 'cultural feminist media studies project' (van Zoonen, 1994; Gallagher, 2003). This went far deeper and wider than the original limited agenda of matters such as the under-representation of women in the media and the stereotyping and sex-role socialization which was and still is a feature of much media content. Concerns also went beyond issues of pornographic media content which matter to feminists (and others) in part because they are offensive and symbolically degrading, and because they might be a stimulus to rape and violence – but also (in the dialectical spirit of critical cultural theory) have led to an appreciation of porn as a playground for diverse sexual identities, as a form of self-expression, and embraced by feminism as a right to control one's own fantasy (Jacobs, Janssen and Pasquinelli, 2007).

The amount of gender-related media research is now very large and, although in part it follows lines of theory pioneered with reference to social class and ethnicity, it has several other dimensions. These include attention to Freudian psychoanalytic theory following the ideas of Jacques Lacan and Nancy Chodorow. Their focus was primarily on the role of gender in 'positioning' the spectator in relation to images (film, television, photographic) of male and female. Another line of research focused on the part played by the media in transmitting a patriarchal ideology concerning the place of women in society. There are now many connections with the wider field of feminist studies (Long, 1991; Kaplan, 1992) and gender, sex and media (Ross, 2012).

According to van Zoonen (1994), most of the earlier gender-relevant media research, including psychoanalytic theory, implicitly at least, followed the transmission model of effect, based on the direct reaction of a receiver to a message stimulus. She suggests that an alternative paradigm, essentially culturalist in character, offers a better way of understanding how the media are related to gender. At the core of the approach is the idea of 'gender as discourse, a set of overlapping and sometimes contradictory cultural descriptions and prescriptions referring to sexual difference' (van Zoonen, 1994: 40). The second key basis is an emphasis on the active *construction* of meanings and identities by 'readers' of media texts. In general, this kind of media research addresses the following main questions: How are discourses of gender encoded in media texts? How do audiences use and interpret gendered media texts? How does audience reception contribute to the construction of gender at the level of individual identity?

The question of gender touches almost every aspect of the media–culture relationship. Most central is probably the question of gender definition. Van Zoonen (1991: 45) writes that the meaning of gender 'is never given but varies according to specific cultural and historical settings … and is subject to ongoing discursive struggle and negotiation'. Partly at issue is how gender differences and distinctiveness are signified (see Goffman, 1976; Hermes, 2007). Another general aspect of the struggle is over the differential value in society attaching to masculinity and to femininity.

The gendering of content may also be studied at the point of production since much of the media selection and production work is carried out by men, or by men and women working within a highly gendered industrial context. In this matter, attention has also been directed to 'the news', which was for long largely a male preserve and in its dominant forms and contents (politics, economics, sport) has been oriented more to male audiences. A continuing theme of feminist media critique has been the relative invisibility of women in news (as sources and experts), or their ghettoization to certain topics and their role as younger sidekicks to generally older male anchors. This has been changing, not least because the news media, offline as well as online, are actively seeking to interest female audiences and are also engaging in extreme competition. Gender in media work continues to be an important focus of production studies given the overall lack of diversity among media professionals (see Chapter 10).

Studies of media audiences and the reception of media content have shown that there are relatively large differences according to gender in the manner of use of media and the meanings attached to the activity. Certain genres are clearly gendered in both production values and their appeal (Grabe and Bucy, 2009). A good deal of the evidence can be accounted for by patterned differences in social roles, by the typical everyday experience and concerns of men and women, and by the way gender shapes the availability and use of time. It also relates to power roles within the family and the general nature of the relationships between women and male partners or of women in the wider family (Morley, 1986).

Different kinds of media content (and their production and use) are also associated with expressions of common identity based on gender (Ferguson, 1983; Radway, 1984) and with the different pleasures and meanings acquired (Ang, 1985). In considering these matters, however, it is especially important to take note of van Zoonen's warning that the context is continually changing and that 'the codes that confer meaning onto the signs of femininity are culturally and historically specific and will never be completely unambiguous or consistent' (1994: 149).

A gender-based approach also raises the question of whether media choice and interpretation can provide some lever of change or element of resistance for all kinds of marginalized groups in a social situation still generally structured by inequality. The potential for oppositional reading and resistance has been invoked both to explain why women seem attracted to media content with overtly patriarchal messages (such as romance fiction) and to help re-evaluate the surface meaning of this attraction (Radway, 1984).

Feminism is a political as well as cultural project and feminist media studies have inevitably been caught up in wider debate within cultural (media) studies about the political significance or not of popular culture. This stems in part from the great attention that has been paid to popular genres like soap operas and talk shows that are oriented to female audiences. Things have changed in the media, with much more content by women, with women, and for women, with no inhibitions about female sexuality (for example, McRobbie, 1996). Sex and sexuality to some extent have been taken out of the rather limited conventions and controls of the porn industry and now include interesting new offerings within the genre of 'real sex films' (Tulloch and Middleweek, 2017). Even the digital games industry – the least diverse when it comes to gender representation in the workforce and on the screen – experiments with more diverse characters and their sexual identities.

One of the key contributions of gender-based scholarship in media and mass communication is that it has laid the groundwork for a contemporary recognition of the significant role of the body and emotions in the way people process and give meaning to media. Hermes (1997), in this context, has argued for a concept of 'cultural citizenship'. She writes (1997: 86):

The lynch-pin of theories of the public sphere is reason … popular culture research (guided by postmodernist and feminist theory) has argued that emotion and feeling are just as important to our everyday lives. If democracy can be said to be about deliberation among the many about how to attain the best life possible for as many as possible, then it makes no sense to set such exclusive store by reasoned argument in our theorization of it. We need to rethink citizenship as cultural citizenship and accept that those who inhabit mass democracies use many different logics to shape their lives.

In recent years, the increasingly complex nature of digital media culture and the growing participation of people from all walks of life (and corners of the world) online has brought concerns about gender and the media under the umbrella of intersectionality, as issues of gender, ethnicity, class, age, and a variety of other concepts are seen as linked, and gender tends to be seen as too dichotomous a variable to consider (Collins, 2000). The various points discussed are reviewed in Box 5.6 in terms of a set of propositions about media and gender.

---

## 5.6

## Gender and media: propositions

- Media have marginalized women in the public sphere
- Media purvey stereotypes of femininity and masculinity
- Production and content of media are gendered
- Reception of media is gendered
- The female perspective offers alternative criteria of quality
- The personal is political
- Media offer positive and supportive as well as negative role models
- Gender-based research appreciates the role of the body and emotions
- Gender is increasingly caught up in debates on intersectionality

---

# COMMERCIALIZATION

Embedded in the early critique of mass culture, and still alive in much of the discussion on the future of the Internet (certainly in the context of media policy), is the notion of 'commercialism' (the condition) or **commercialization** (the process). The concern about the dominance of commercial values and market logic dominating debates and policies regarding people's media access and use incorporates ideas that are relevant to current media industry dynamics and to media-cultural change, and it is closely related to the critique of commodification. The critique of commercialization is to some extent difficult to reconcile with the redemption of the popular, since popularity is usually a necessary condition of commercial success and to dislike one implies a dislike of the other. On the other hand, what makes something popular is not necessarily aligned with commercial appeal or success. It is not so much the market success (or failure) that is at stake here – the key issues of concern in the critique of commercialization are the ongoing efforts of media industries to reconcile (and in the process infuse) popular appeal with strictly commercial values.

While at one level the term 'commercialism' may refer objectively to particular free-market arrangements, it has also come to imply consequences for the type of media content that is mass produced and 'marketed' as a commodity, and for the relations between the suppliers and the consumers of media. The term 'commercial', applied as an adjective to some types of media provision, identifies correlates of the competitive pursuit of large markets (Bogart, 1995). Aside from an abundance of advertising matter (commercial propaganda), commercial content is likely, from this perspective, to be more oriented to amusement and entertainment, more superficial, undemanding and conformist, more derivative and standardized. Although most newspapers and broadcast news organizations operate under some kind of commercial imperative, when the balance tips towards commercialization this can lead to a decline in quality (see Box 5.7). Evidence in support of his view can be found in McManus (1994), while Esser (1999) shows that a shift towards sensation, emotion and scandal may indeed have some negative effects on democracy. On the other hand, cross-national comparative research by Boczkowski and Mitchelstein (2013) shows a distinct 'news gap' between the story preferences of consumers and journalists at quality newspapers in seven countries in North and South America and Western Europe, suggesting that news organizations are clearly not operating with 'saleability' as their primary concern.

---

**5.7**

## Newspaper commercialization

The primary content of newspapers today is commercialized news and designed to appeal to broad audiences, to entertain, to be cost effective and whose attention can be sold to advertisers. The result is that stories that may offend are ignored in favor of those more acceptable and entertaining to a larger number of readers, that stories that are costly to cover are downplayed or ignored and that stories creating financial risks are ignored. This leads to the homogenization of newspaper content, to coverage of safe issues and to a diminution of the range of opinion and ideas expressed. (Picard, 2004: 61)

There has been much comment on the '**tabloidization**' of newspapers as they compete for readers. The equivalent process in television has led to many new forms of 'reality' television, which deal in all kinds of '**human interest**' and dramatic topics in a variety of formats. The term 'tabloidization' comes from the smaller format of the more popular (or boulevard) newspapers in some countries. Generally, as Langer (2003) shows, it is a question of access (who gets in the news) and of representation (how they are depicted). Connell (1998) discusses the British variants, taking the term to mean that 'sensationalist' news discourses have displaced 'rationalist' discourses, with a strong emphasis on narrative. Bird (1998) looked at the 'tabloidization' of American television news and concludes from her audience study that there has been a real trend towards *personalization* and *dramatization*, which does make news more accessible to the many, but has also led to a trivialization of what people actually learn from news. The term '**infotainment**' has been widely used in this connection (Brants, 1998).

Parallel to the rise of the Internet as the dominant (mass) medium on the planet is a growing concern about its lack of public governance and oversight, as corporations profit from such regulatory lack to develop revenue models almost exclusively based on extracting, manipulating and selling people's personal data – a commercial system Shoshana Zuboff (2019) critiques as 'surveillance capitalism'. Although several governments and international bodies, such as the European Union, have introduced legislation in recent years to counter some of the unbridled corporate appropriation of the online space, the trend towards commercialization continues.

While it is true that essentially the same market arrangements can just as easily support the supply and consumption of greatly varied and high-quality cultural products and services, the critique of commerce has another dimension. It can be argued that commercial relationships in communication are intrinsically distancing and potentially exploitative. The commercial variant of a communicative relationship does not support the formation of ties of mutual attachment or lead to shared identity or community. It is calculative and utilitarian on both sides, reflecting essential features of the 'transmission' or 'publicity' rather than the 'ritual' model of communication in society (see pp. 93–96). The fundamental problem is that profit becomes the overwhelming motive, reducing the agency and choice of people using media.

It makes little sense to argue that the free-market arrangements that have sustained print media for five hundred years, audiovisual cultural production for one hundred years, and online production for a couple of decades are intrinsically 'harmful' to culture. A narrower concept of 'commercial' as a critical expression is called for and the components of this have been indicated. The key components of the crucial yet contested concept of commercialization are reviewed in Box 5.8 in the form of a set of propositions advanced by critics.

## Critique of commercialization: propositions

- Leads to trivialization and tabloidization
- Causes content and service decisions to be market-driven
- Involves exploitation of 'weaker' consumers
- Promotes consumerist attitudes to culture and life
- Commodifies culture and relations with the audience
- Reduces cultural integrity of media content
- Leads to over-reliance on advertising and loss of independence
- Limits options, choice and agency of media users

# COMMUNICATION TECHNOLOGY AND CULTURE

McLuhan's (1964) advance on Innis (see p. 134) was to look at the process by which we experience the world through different media of communication and not just at the relation between communication and social power structures. He proclaimed that all media (by which he meant anything that embodies cultural meaning and can be 'read' as such) are 'extensions of man', thus extensions of our senses. Like others, he drew attention to the implications of a shift from a purely *oral* communication to one based on a written language (by about 5000 BC), followed by a predominance of visual language and communication in the (late) twentieth century (see also Ong, 1982). Much of cultural experience remained predominantly oral until comparatively recent times. McLuhan also focused on *how* we experience the world through media, not on *what* we experience of it in media. Each new medium transcends the boundaries of experience reached by earlier media and contributes to further change. McLuhan correctly saw different media working together.

Meyrowitz (1985) proposed a theory of mass media and social change that owes something to Marshall McLuhan (with help from Irving Goffman). Meyrowitz's (1985) thesis is that the all-pervasiveness of electronic media has fundamentally changed social experience by breaking down the compartmentalization between social spaces that was typical of earlier times. Human experience, in his view, has traditionally been segmented by role and social situation and sharply divided between private ('backstage') and public ('onstage') domains. **Segmentation** was by age, gender and social status, and the 'walls' between zones of experience were high. Television appears to put all aspects of social experience on show to all, without distinction. There are no longer any secrets, for instance, about adulthood, sex, death or power.

Contemporary iterations of such theories that take the technology (and technological infrastructure of media) as a starting point for explanations for our relationship with each other and the world in media focus on how newer media (such as the Internet) usher in an age of universal comparison, where the private lives of countless strangers are on permanent display – both to every Internet user and to the companies providing access, products and services online. In the process, argue Bolter and Grusin in their theory of 'remediation' (1999), newer media adopt and remix features of older media while becoming increasingly intuitive to operate and use. This relative 'invisibility' of media makes them all the more influential in shaping people's experience and sensemaking of reality, as more and more of our lives play out in media, one way or another. All such theories owe a debt to McLuhan's initial theorizing of media as extensions of our senses.

A general proposition of McLuhan about mass media was that, as more of our senses are engaged in the process of taking meaning (as media become increasingly 'cool', or frictionless and intuitive to use, as against single-sense or 'hot' media), the more involving and participatory the experience is. According to this view, experiencing the world by reading printed text is isolating and non-involving (encouraging the rational, individual attitude). Television viewing is involving, although not very informing, and also conducive to a less rational and calculative attitude. No proof (or disproof) has ever been offered, and the ideas were described by McLuhan himself only as perceptions or 'probes'. As he wished, they stimulated much speculation in an era in which audiovisual media have seemed in many respects to take over from print media, and both forms of media are subsumed in online media.

The Toronto School (see Chapter 4) was the primary impulse towards a new branch of theory described as 'medium theory'. In this context, a medium is any vehicle for carrying meaning, with some distinctive characteristics in respect of technology, form, manner of use, means of encoding or social definition. This covers a wide range, starting with drawing and continuing through printing to all the current electronic media. There is a 'soft' form of determination at work, in which a medium is attributed a certain bias towards particular kinds of content, uses and effects. This approach has proved more fruitful than 'hard' determination in identifying the more subtle influences of the ways in which media are used, for instance in political communication and in seeing the differences between new and old media.

Most other relevant theory of communication technology has focused on possible influences on the form or content of given media messages and thus on the meanings they make available. Even so, no causal nor direct technology–culture effect can be established because the technologies themselves are also cultural artefacts, and there is no way of breaking into the circle. Such theory as we have is little more than a description of observable patterns in the cultural meanings offered via mass media, which may be influenced by various characteristics, not only technological, of a given medium. A general view of the process by which changing technology can influence media culture is given in Figure 5.1. Perhaps the most important point that it illustrates is that technologies are unlikely to have a direct impact on cultural practices; their effects are mediated through a relevant institution, in this case the mass media.

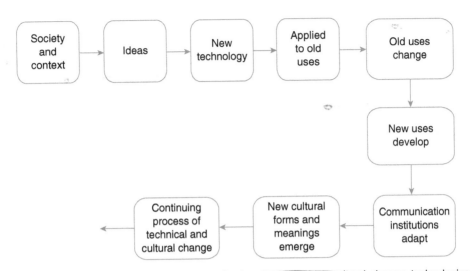

Figure 5.1   Interactive sequence of communication, technological, cultural change: technologies arise from society and have effects on society depending on the form of application

In trying to account for technological influence on (media) culture, we may extend the notion of *bias* introduced by Innis and recognize several tendencies that follow from the characteristics of a particular media technology (and its institutional development). We can name five types of media bias as follows, without exhausting the possibilities. There is a bias of *sense experience*, following McLuhan, so that we may experience the world in more or less visual imagery (see Hartley, 1992) or in more or less of an involving and participant way. Secondly, there is a bias of *form* and representation, with 'messages' strongly coded (as in print) or essentially uncoded, as in photographs (Barthes, 1967). Thirdly, there is the bias of message *content*, for instance in terms of more or less realism or polysemy, more open or closed formats (other dimensions are possible). Fourthly, there is a bias of *context of use*, with some media lending themselves to private and individualized reception, others being more collective and shared. Fifthly, there is a bias of *relationship*, contrasting one-way with interactive media.

Bias does not mean determinism, but it contains a predilection towards certain kinds of experience and ways of mediation. Ellis's (1982) comparison of broadcast television with cinema film provides an instructive illustration of how the (unintended) bias of a medium can work in subtle but systematic and multiple ways, affecting content and probable ways of perception and reception. The comparison is shown in summary terms in Box 5.9. The differences shown are not only or even primarily due to technology, but to many other factors. While many things have changed in the succeeding decades, the comparison is still largely valid, and can serve as inspiration to explore contemporary biases of media and communication technologies.

## Example of media bias: comparison of certain typical features of television and cinema (Ellis, 1982)

| BROADCAST TELEVISION | CINEMA FILM |
|---|---|
| **Content and form** | |
| Identifies narrator | No narrator |
| Distinguishes fact from fiction | Only fiction or blurred |
| Realistic | Dreamlike |
| Domestic, familiar | Exotic |
| Open-ended | Logical, sequential |
| Impression of being live | Not live, historic present |
| Neutral attitude | Takes sides |
| Tone of normality and safety | Tension and anxiety |
| **Audience aspects** | |
| Permanent audience | Occasional one-off audience |
| Low engagement | Rapt attention, self-loss |
| Intimacy | Detachment, voyeurism |

One of the few effects of new communication technology on which there is wide agreement is the trend towards the internationalization of mass communication. The question of potential cultural effects flowing from this trend has been much debated. The movement towards a global media culture has several sources, most notably the greatly increased capacity to transmit sounds and (moving) images at low cost across frontiers and around the world, overcoming limits of time and space. Equally potent as a cause is the rise of global media businesses (and global markets for media products), which provides the organizational framework and driving force for globalization. Neither of these conditions has arrived suddenly, nor is the idea of transnational culture itself novel (it long predates the very idea of the national), but what may be new is the increased transcultural communicative potential of pictures and music, and the rising complexity of national and international media policy (for example, regarding the governance of online platforms, the privacy of Internet users and the protection of copyrights of professional media makers).

The relevant changes in the structure of media industries and global media flow have been extensively studied, but the cultural consequences are much less open to observation and have led to great speculation. The process of cultural 'transnationalization' that is assumed to be taking place has a variety of meanings and is discussed in more detail in Chapter 9.

## MASS MEDIA AND POSTMODERN CULTURE

The notion of a 'postmodern condition' (Harvey, 1989) captured the imagination of many social and cultural theorists, and it seemed very much a theory for the information society (see Chapter 4). Despite its wide currency, and its more nuanced iterations of a 'late' (Giddens, 1991) or 'liquid' (Bauman, 2000) modernity, it is a complex and obscure concept that involves several ideas that are relevant to media and mass communication theory. Its political implication is that the 'Enlightenment project' has reached its historic conclusion, especially the emphasis on material progress, egalitarianism, social reform and the application of bureaucratic means to achieving socially planned objectives. It is also now commonplace to refer to our era as 'postmodern' or 'late modern' in the literal sense of being a late stage of the 'modern' period that was characterized by rapid social change, industrialization and the factory system, capitalism, bureaucratic forms of organization and mass political movements. Contemporary articulations of these theories note how different versions of modernity are at work more or less simultaneously, requiring great care on the part of the scholar regarding how to use social theory when doing media research (Hesmondhalgh and Toynbee, 2008).

Postmodernity and its associated theories of our late modern times imply a clear chronological and conceptual distinction from 'modernism'. As Morley (1996) points out, this in itself raises some difficulties since the term 'modern' originated in the fifth century AD (in its Latin form) and has taken on different meanings in different epochs since then. In its current meaning it usually refers to typical features of society and culture of the nineteenth and early twentieth centuries, without any clear indication of any dividing line. The principal theorist of 'modernization' (without explicitly making the claim), writing a century ago, can probably be considered to be the German sociologist Max Weber, whose key concept in the analysis of social change was 'rationalization'. In this respect, we can also plausibly regard modernism as originally a specifically western (European) notion.

As a social-cultural philosophy, **postmodernism** undermines the traditional notion of culture as something fixed and hierarchical. It favours forms and an understanding of culture (and associated concepts, such as identity) that is transient, of the moment, affective and emotional. Many features of (commercial) popular media culture reflect postmodernist or late modern elements, contributing to disembedding social interactions from local contexts (by moving them online), and to a new, 'networked' way in which groups and communities self-organize via media (such as online support groups, hashtag activism and encrypted messaging systems) rather than via traditional institutions. Postmodern and late modern concerns about the role of media and mass communication also include content, especially the ways in which elements of popular culture from all over the world are taken up, remixed and redistributed by people online. Music video on television was hailed as the first postmodern television service (Kaplan, 1987; Grossberg, 1989; Lewis, 1992), and in the YouTube era such proliferation of (re)mixed messages gets further amplified and accelerated (Burgess and Green, 2018).

This is a potent set of ideas that goes much further than providing a defence for the once much maligned and patronized 'culture of the masses'. It is an entirely new representation of the situation that has turned some of the weapons of cultural critics against themselves (for instance, their claim to speak on behalf of the masses). The idea of postmodernism has been easier to characterize in cultural than in social terms since the features of 'modern' society mentioned are still in evidence, maybe even reinforced if one thinks of how much the world is ruled by global financial markets that operate with inexorable and uniform logic. This inspired the critical response of late or liquid modernism, where traditional institutions remain, but suffer from ongoing crises of legitimacy and become increasingly 'disintermediated' by processes online.

Arguably, one of the most powerful contributions of postmodernism comes from a widely cited characterization of postmodernism by Lyotard ([1979]1984), claiming that there is no longer any *grand narrative*, no organizing or explanatory framework or central project for humanity (see also Chapter 18). The cultural aesthetics of postmodernism involve a rejection of tradition and a search for novelty, invention, momentary enjoyment, nostalgia, playfulness, pastiche and inconsistency. Jameson (1984) refers to postmodernism as the 'cultural logic of late capitalism', even though this logic is claimed to be profoundly disorganized and inherently unstable. Gitlin (1989) goes as far as to suggest that postmodernism is specifically North American, capturing many features of American culture – and particularly its media. Grossberg, Wartella and Whitney (1998) associate it especially with the process of the commercialization of everything. In one of the most compelling criticisms of postmodernity and its theorists, Ziauddin Sardar (1999) argues that postmodernism operates to further marginalize or even erase the non-West, considering no role for them to survive or in any other way give meaning to their own histories, identities and cultures *vis-à-vis* the onslaught of western culture, consumerism and capitalism.

Certainly, the postmodern ethos is much more favourable to commerce than were earlier cultural perspectives, since opposition to capitalism is undermined and commerce can be seen as responding to consumer wants or as actively promoting changes in fashion, style and products. However, there is scope for social and cultural optimism as well as pessimism within the range of postmodern thought. Ien Ang has also underlined the need to distinguish between conservative and critical postmodernism as intellectual attitudes. She writes: 'the former does indeed succumb to an "anything goes" attitude … [but] the latter, critical postmodernism is motivated by a deep understanding of the limits and failures of what Habermas calls the "unfinished project of modernity"' (Ang, 1998: 78; also Habermas, 1997).

Postmodern, late modern or liquid modern thinking can greatly benefit from the analysis of contemporary media, from the many forms of advertising, new storytelling genres emerging that cut across different media (for example, 'transmedia' – see Chapter 13), to the often disjointed and confusing experience we have of living in different realities – online and offline – simultaneously. Castells (2009) coins this lived experience as a culture of 'real virtuality', expressing the hope that people will use these networks to engage in co-operative and non-profit work, as McRobbie (2016) also documents among cultural workers in different parts of the world trying to make a living beyond a strictly capitalist or commercial framework, as have Deuze and Witschge (2020) among journalists starting their own news organizations around the world. Poster (2006: 138) cautions that we should use concepts of postmodernity (and attendant concepts) for the cultural study of new media 'in a manner that makes it suitable for analysis without either a celebratory fanfare or sarcastic smiles'.

The appeal of the postmodern and liquid modern concept is based on its helping to link many perceived tendencies in the media (including new media) and in its summing up of the essence of the media's own logic. It also seems useful as a word to connect diverse social changes (for instance, the fragmentation of the class structure and the continued relevance of class as a category for social analysis, the decline and resurrection of political ideology, the twin processes of globalization and localization). Some key propositions of such social theory in terms of their relevance to media and mass communication research are shown in Box 5.10.

## 5.10
## Post-, late and liquid modernism: propositions

- The rational-linear modern era is passing
- There are no longer any reliable large organizing ideas about culture and society
- There are no fixed cultural values or identities
- There is increasing currency in affect and emotions as criteria for understanding the world and experience
- Online and offline reality are co-existent
- The key qualities in culture are satire and sarcasm, novelty, pastiche, humour and shock
- Commercial culture is the dominant feature of contemporary modern culture

# CONCLUSION

This chapter has summarized a broad range of cultural issues in which the mass media are implicated. Indeed, it is impossible now to distinguish between a sphere of 'culture' and that of media, as perhaps once could have been done. This applies to all the senses in which the term 'culture' has been used, including symbolic reproduction, the artefacts we employ, everyday social life and all the rituals of society. Media are the centre of the whole complex and the central task for theory has had to be redefined. In the earliest period of self-consciousness about the media (the first half of the twentieth century) it was possible to debate the 'effects' of radio, television, film, and so on, on something that was called 'culture', usually referring to a valued set of objects, practices, relations and ideas. This formulation is now largely outmoded, although there is some opportunity for observing cultural shifts at moments of development in technology. The elimination of the 'causal model' does not, however, lessen the number of questions that can be addressed, or prevent answers being provided by alternative routes and methods and from new perspectives. There is still an axis of critical thinking that can be applied to what we observe. There are still many new problematic (as well as positive) features of culture in the media age to be studied and debated.

# FURTHER READING

Fiske, J. (1987) *Television Culture*. Abingdon: Routledge.

Fuchs, C. and Qiu, J.L. (2018) 'Ferments in the field: introductory reflections on the past, present and future of communication studies', *Journal of Communication*, 68(2): 219–232.

Hermes, J. (2005) *Re-reading Popular Culture: Rethinking Gender, Television, and Popular Media Audiences*. Malden, MA: Wiley-Blackwell.

Hesmondhalgh, D. and Toynbee, J. (eds) (2008) *The Media and Social Theory*. Abingdon: Routledge.

McRobbie, A. (2016) *Be Creative: Making a Living in the New Culture Industries*. Cambridge: Polity Press.

Morley, D. (2015) 'Cultural studies, common sense and communications', *Cultural Studies*, 29(1): 23–31.

# NEW MEDIA THEORY

Theory relating to media and mass communication has to be continually reassessed in the light of new technologies and their applications. Throughout this edition we recognized the arrival of new types of media that extend and change the entire spectrum of socio-technological possibilities for public and private communication. To speak of a complete transformation would be premature, but it is clear that the digital age ushers in a process of profound change for quite some time to come. The underlying assumption in this chapter is that a medium is not just an applied technology for transmitting certain symbolic content or linking participants in some exchange. It also embodies a set of social relations that interact with features of the new technology. New theory is only likely to be required if there is a fundamental change in the forms of social organization of media technologies, in the social relations that are promoted, or in what Carey (1998) terms the 'dominant structures of taste and feeling'. At the same time, we try to stay mindful of Scannell's (2017: 5) warning about the trap of 'presentism' in media research 'that fails to engage with earlier traditions of communication theory and should undertake some unforgetting'.

## NEW MEDIA AND MASS COMMUNICATION

The mass media have changed very much, certainly from the early-twentieth-century days of one-way, one-directional and undifferentiated flow to an undifferentiated mass. There are social and economic as well as technological reasons for this shift, but it is real enough. Secondly, information society and network theory, as outlined in Chapter 4, also indicates the rise of a new kind of society, quite distinct from mass society, one characterized by complex interactive networks of communication. In the circumstances, we need to reassess the main thrust of media social-cultural theory.

The 'new media' discussed here are in fact a disparate set of communication technologies that share certain features, apart from being relatively new, made possible by **digitalization** and being widely available for personal use as communication devices and infrastructures. From the outset we recognize with Nancy Baym that 'newness is a state of time rather than of technology' (quoted in Baym et al., 2012: 258), which should orient us to identifying concrete attributes or affordances of particular technologies instead of focusing on their novelty.

As we have seen (p. 52), 'new media' are very diverse and not easy to define, but we are particularly interested in those media and applications that on various grounds enter the sphere of mass communication or directly or indirectly have consequences for the 'traditional' mass media. Attention focuses mainly on the collective ensemble of activities that fall under the heading 'Internet', especially on the more public uses, including online news, advertising, broadcasting applications (including the downloading of music and the uploading of video, etc.), forums and discussion activities, the World

Wide Web (WWW), information searches, certain community-forming potentials – all of which and more tend to be subsumed by online platforms and are offered through a wide array of information and communication technologies (ICTs).

Generally, new media have been greeted (not least by the old media) with intense interest, positive and even euphoric expectations and predictions, and a general over-estimation of their significance (Rössler, 2001). At the same time, journalists, pundits and scholars are equally likely to respond with great concern and dystopian analyses about their supposedly disruptive or even destructive impact. With all these technolo-gies competing and evolving, it is important to note that – from a historical perspective – newer media and their uses do not replace but rather tend to act as accelerators and amplifiers of long-term trends in the socio-technical history of other media. In this development there is no necessary end-point, and different media are usually trans-formed through a complex interplay of real and perceived needs, competitive and political pressures, and continuous social and technological changes – a development Fidler (1997) describes as the 'mediamorphic process'. In general, it seems prudent to heed Fidler's warning against 'technomyopia': the tendency of people to overestimate the short-term impact of technology, while simultaneously underestimating its long-term potential. The main aim of this chapter is to offer a preliminary review of the impact of the evolution of the Internet and online media on other mass media and on the nature of mass communication itself.

As a basic orientation to the topic, it is helpful to look at the relationship between per-sonal media and mass media, as conceptualized by Marika Lüders (2008) and displayed in Figure 6.1. The underlying assumption is that the distinction between mass and personal communication is no longer clear since the same technologies can be and are used for both purposes (see Chapter 2). The differences can only be understood by introducing a social dimension, relating to the type of activity and social relations involved. Instead of the concept 'medium', Lüders prefers the term 'media forms', which refers to specific applications of the technology of the Internet, such as online news, social networking, etc. She writes (2008: 691):

> Distinctions between personal media and mass media may be outlined as differ-ences in the type of involvement required from users. Personal media are more symmetrical and require users to perform actively as both receivers and producers of messages.

The second main relevant dimension is that of the presence or not of an institutional or professional context that is typical of mass media production. Between them, the two dimensions of symmetricality and institutionalism locate the different types of relation between personal and mass media. An additional element is the distinction made by Thompson (1993) between (technically) mediated and quasi-mediated communication.

MCQUAIL'S MEDIA AND MASS COMMUNICATION THEORY
THEORIES

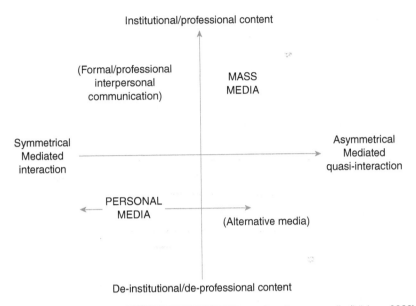

Institutional/professional content

(Formal/professional
interpersonal
communication)

MASS
MEDIA

Symmetrical
Mediated
interaction

Asymmetrical
Mediated
quasi-interaction

PERSONAL
MEDIA

(Alternative media)

De-institutional/de-professional content

Figure 6.1   Two-axes model of relationship between personal and mass media (Lüders, 2008)

# WHAT IS NEW ABOUT THE NEW MEDIA?

To determine the level of 'newness' of any medium, one has to first decide what approach to take: the technological characteristics and affordances of the technology involved, the perspective of the user and the particular social context within which the medium gets used, or the content and services being offered through a particular device, platform or interface. In terms of technological characteristics, the Internet can be defined by its digital, networked, interactive, virtual, customizable and generally open (as in anyone can produce as well as consume content and services online) nature.

The most fundamental aspect of information and communication technology (ICT) is probably the fact of digitalization, the process by which all texts (symbolic meaning in all encoded and recorded forms) can be reduced to a binary code and can share the same process of production, distribution and storage. The most widely noted potential consequence for the media institution is the convergence between all existing media forms in terms of their organization, distribution, reception and regulation. Many different forms of mass media have so far survived, retained their separate identity and even flourished, even though in terms of market value these institutions lag far behind Internet platforms and services that also – and increasingly – offer content and services traditionally the exclusive domain of mass media. For now, the general institution of mass media survives as a distinct element of public social life. The 'new electronic media' do not necessarily replace the existing spectrum. On the other hand, we have to consider that digitalization and convergence might have much more revolutionary consequences, especially in the long term.

If we consider the main features of the media institution, as outlined in Box 3.4 (p. 80), it seems that the Internet in particular already deviates from that typification on three of the six points named. First, the Internet is not only or even mainly concerned with the production and distribution of messages, but is at least equally concerned with processing, exchange and storage. Secondly, the new media are as much an institution of private as of public communication and are regulated (or not) accordingly. Thirdly, their operation is not typically professional or bureaucratically organized to the same degree as mass media. These are quite significant differences that underscore the fact that the new media correspond with mass media primarily in being widely diffused, in principle available to all for communication, and to some extent free from direct control (with exceptions in parts of the world where Internet access is in fact offered through state-run organizations).

Attempts to characterize the new media, especially as embodied in the Internet, have been hindered by their very diversity of uses and governance as well as by uncertainty about their future development. The computer, as applied to communication, has produced many variant possibilities, not one of which is dominant. Postmes, Spears and Lea (1998) describe the computer as a 'uniquely undedicated' communication technology. In a similar vein, Poster (1999) describes the essence of the Internet as its very underdetermination, not only because of its diversity and uncertainty in the future, but also because of its essentially postmodernist character. He also points to key differences with broadcasting and print, as shown in Box 6.1.

## 6.1

## New media differences from old

The Internet incorporates radio, film and television and distributes them through 'push' technology:

It transgresses the limits of the print and broadcasting models by (1) enabling many-to-many conversations; (2) enabling the simultaneous reception, alteration and redistribution of cultural objects; (3) dislocating communicative action from the posts of the nation, from the territorialized spatial relations of modernity; (4) providing instantaneous global contact; and (5) inserting the modern/late modern subject into a machine apparatus that is networked. (Poster, 1999: 15)

More succinctly, Livingstone (1999: 65) writes: 'What's new about the internet may be the combination of interactivity with those features which were innovative for mass communication – the unlimited range of content, the scope of audience reach, the global nature of communication.' This view suggests extension rather than replacement. An assessment made five years after this by Lievrouw (2004) underlines a general view that the 'new media' have gradually been 'mainstreamed', routinized and even 'banalized'. Research on political communication speaks of the 'normalization' of the Internet, meaning its adaptation to the needs of the established forms of campaigning (Vaccari, 2008b). Contemporary research on the Internet and all its related phenomena indeed takes its cue from the banal, everyday and altogether mundane nature of online media in people's daily lives, as it is exactly in their unremarkable aspect that new media can play a profound role in shaping our experience of each other and the world.

In general, differences between new and old media can be appreciated in more detail if we consider the main roles and relationships that are found within the traditional media institutions, especially those concerned with authorship (and performance), publication, production and distribution, and reception. In brief, the main implications are as follows.

For authors, there are increased opportunities through posting on the Internet, desktop publishing, **blogging**, vlogging and similar autonomous acts. However, the status and rewards of the author, as understood until now, have depended on the significance and location of publication and on the degree and kind of public attention received. Writing a private letter or a poem, or taking photographs, is not true authorship. The conditions of public recognition and esteem have not really changed with the new technology, and the condition of having a large audience and widespread fame may even have become more difficult to achieve. It is not easy to become famous on the Internet without the co-operation of either the traditional mass media or the platforms that provide much of the publication space online. There are also increasing difficulties in maintaining copyright as well as some reliable source of revenue arising from competition with the supply of free user-generated content.

For publishers, the role continues but has become more ambiguous for the same reasons that apply to authors. Until now, a publisher was typically a business firm or a non-profit public institution. The new media open up alternative forms of publication and present opportunities and challenges for traditional publishing. The traditional publication functions of **gatekeeping**, editorial intervention and validation of authorship will be found in some types of Internet publication, but not in others. Platform companies increasingly replace publishers as the key agencies for getting published works – whether written words, audio, video, graphics, or a combination thereof – to a mass audience, and these businesses operate quite differently, not the least because their publication and distribution management is generally determined by constantly changing algorithms.

As to the audience role, there are possibilities for change, especially in the direction of greater autonomy and equality in relation to sources and suppliers. The audience member is no longer really part of a mass, but is either a member of a self-chosen network or special public or an individual. In addition, the balance of audience activity shifts from reception to searching, consulting and interacting more personally, as well as contributing their own 'work' to publication. This shift coincides with media industries increasingly converging their operations and production processes in order to capture the illusive audience – a twin process that Jenkins (2006) calls convergence culture. As a result, the term 'audience' is in need of supplementation with the overlapping term of 'user', with quite different connotations (see pp. 498–499).

Despite this, there is evidence of continuity in the mass audience (see Chapter 14) and there is still a demand by the audience for gatekeeping, curation and editorial guidance – even if such functions are to some extent taken over online by software and algorithms. Rice (1999: 29) remarks on the paradox of the extended range of choices facing the audience:

> Now individuals must make more choices, must have more prior knowledge, and must put forth more effort to integrate and make sense of the communication. Inter-activity and choice are not universal benefits; many people do not have the energy, desire, need or training to engage in such processes.

Into this gap between audience agency and audience effort the platform companies have sprung, offering to automate algorithmically much of user choice. These comments are incomplete without reference to the changed roles in relation to the economics of media. For the most part, mass media were financed by selling their products to audiences and being paid by client advertisers for the chance of audience attention to their messages. The Internet introduces many complications and changes, with new types of relation and forms of commodification, new competitors and new rules.

As far as the relations between different roles are concerned, we can posit a general loosening and more independence, especially affecting authors and audiences. Rice (1999: 29) has noted that 'the boundaries between publisher, producer, distributor, consumer and reviewer of content are blurring', even though this does not mean all have the same (legal, economical) status. This casts doubt on the continued appropriateness of the idea of the media as an institution in the sense of some more or less unified social organization with some core practices and shared norms. In the general meltdown, it is likely that we will recognize the emergence of separate, more specialized institutional complexes and networks of media activity. These will be based either on technologies or on certain uses and content (for example, relating to news journalism, entertainment franchises (in film, television and video games), business, sport, pornography, tourism, education, professions, etc.), with at times a limited or absent institutional identity. In that sense, the twentieth-century mass media have withered away. At the same time, through converging operations, solidifying business operations across many different areas, collaboration with

Internet platforms and fostering relationships with audiences as 'fans', many mass media companies are seeking to retain their institutional status.

On a concluding note, we have to signal the increasing importance of artificial intelligence in the study of media and mass communication (Guzman and Lewis, 2019). With the rise of 'big data' as a fundamental driver of the global economy, the significance of powerful computer hardware and software to process all of this information – and to translate it into actionable intelligence, such as business opportunities, electoral gains and reputation boosts – is of profound interest to researchers. Collaborations with experts in computer engineering and data science, digital methods, digital humanities, information studies and so on, abound. Key issues in this emerging field of study are the evolving relations and boundaries between humans and machines, the role of ethics in computer-based decision-making processes, and a host of regulatory issues involving so-called 'predictive analytics' that govern the business models of so many Internet companies.

Box 6.2 lists the main changes brought about with the rise of new media.

## 6.2

## Main changes linked to the rise of new media

- Digitalization and convergence of all aspects of media
- Increased interactivity and network connectivity
- Mobility and delocation of sending and receiving
- Adaptation of publication and audience roles
- Appearance of diverse new forms of media 'gateway'
- Fragmentation and blurring of the boundaried 'media institution'
- Emergence of platforms as powerful online intermediaries
- Rise of artificial intelligence and predictive analytics

# POLITICAL PARTICIPATION, NEW MEDIA AND DEMOCRACY

The earlier mass media of press and broadcasting were widely seen as beneficial (even necessary) for the conduct of democratic politics, as much as for effective state control. The benefit stemmed from the flow of information about public events to all citizens and the exposure of politicians and governments to the public gaze. However, negative effects were also perceived because of the dominance of channels by a few voices, the predominance of a 'vertical flow', and the heightened commercialism of the media market, leading to the neglect of democratic communication roles. The typical organization and forms of mass communication limit access and discourage active participation and dialogue.

The new electronic media have been widely hailed as a potential way of escape from the oppressive 'top-down' politics of mass democracies in which tightly organized political parties make policy unilaterally and mobilize support behind them with minimal negotiation and grass-roots input. They provide the means for highly differentiated provision of political information and ideas, almost unlimited access in theory for all voices, and much feedback and negotiation between leaders and followers. They promise new forums for the development of interest groups and formation of opinion. They allow dialogue to take place between politicians and active citizens, without the inevitable intervention of a party machine. Not least important, as Coleman (1999: 73) points out, is the 'role of new media in the subversive service of free expression under conditions of authoritarian control of the means of communication'. It is certainly not easy for governments to control access to and the use of the Internet by dissident citizens, but neither is it impossible.

Even 'old politics', it is said, might work better (and more democratically) with the aid of instant electronic polling and new tools of campaigning. The ideas concerning the public sphere and civil society, discussed elsewhere, have stimulated the notion that new media are ideally suited to occupy the space of **civil society** between the private domain and that of state activity. The ideal of an open arena for public conversation, debate and exchange of ideas seems open to fulfilment by way of forms of communication (the Internet, in particular) that allow citizens to express their views and communicate with each other and their political leaders from the comfort of their own home, place of work or mobile device.

The arguments for welcoming a 'new politics' based on new media are quite diverse and different perspectives are involved. Dahlberg (2001) describes three basic camps or models. First, there is the model of 'cyber-libertarianism' that wants an approach to politics based on the model of the consumer market. Surveys, plebiscites and televoting fit this outlook, replacing older processes. Secondly, there is a 'communitarian' view that expects the benefits to come from greater grass-roots participation and input and the strengthening of local political communities. Thirdly, there is a perceived benefit to 'deliberative democracy' made possible by improved technology for interaction and for exchange of ideas in the public arena.

Bentivegna (2002) has summarized the potential benefits of the Internet to politics in terms of six main attributes, as shown in Box 6.3. She also describes the main limitations and the obstacles which have so far prevented any democratic transformation. In her view, 'the gap between the political realm and citizens has apparently not been reduced, participation in political life has remained … stable' (Bentivegna, 2002: 56). The reasons cited include the 'glut of information' that limits the effective use that can be made of it; the fact that the Internet creates private 'lifestyle' alternatives to public and political life in the form of the virtual communities discussed above; the cacophony of voices that impedes serious discussion; and the difficulties for many in using the Internet. In addition, there is the now much demonstrated fact that the new media tend to be used mainly by the small minority that is already politically interested and involved (Davis, 1999; Norris, 2000). If anything, new media possibilities may widen the gap between active participants and the rest.

## 6.3

## Theoretical benefits of the Internet for democratic politics

- Scope for interactivity as well as one-way flow
- Co-presence of vertical and horizontal communication, promoting equality
- Disintermediation, meaning a reduced role for journalism to mediate the relationship between citizen and politicians
- Low costs for senders and receivers
- Immediacy of contact on both sides
- Absence of boundaries and limits to contacts

Political participation online, as a distinct mediated democratic process, tends to involve two main role-players: globally dominant media corporations (providing much of the access and infrastructure through which people can participate online) and transnational social movements (which can be little more than people temporarily joined in shared engagement using a hashtag on social networking sites). This process exists next to a more traditional orientation of nation-based mass media institutions and the politics and politicians of the nation state. Chadwick (2017) suggests that political communication today is increasingly shaped by interactions among older and newer media logics, constituting a 'hybrid' media system. Chadwick argues that power is exercised by those who create, tap and steer information flows to suit their goals, and in ways that modify, enable and disable the agency of others across and between a range of older and newer media settings.

Early expectations of the Internet as making a big difference in the way people experience and participate in the political process have since been downplayed in favour of more nuanced perspectives. Scheufele and Nisbet's (2002: 65) enquiry into the Internet and citizenship concluded that there was a 'very limited role for the Internet in promoting feelings of efficacy, knowledge and participation'. A meta-analysis of 38 studies on the effects of Internet use on political engagement concludes quite convincingly that new media do not have a negative effect, albeit that positive effects are specifically related to the use of Internet for news (Boulianne, 2009). More recent studies similarly point to the fact that the link between Internet use and political participation does not make people act all that differently from previous media eras – those who use the Internet to find information about politics and political parties are more likely to vote than those who tend only to use the Internet to express themselves about politics and political issues now and then (Feezell, Conroy and Guerrero, 2016).

There is also evidence that the existing political party organizations have generally failed to make use of the potential of the Internet, but rather turned it into yet another branch of the propaganda machine. Vaccari (2008a) speaks of a process of 'normalization', after high expectations. This does not necessarily mean that such 'traditional' use of a new medium is unsuccessful, as the political campaigns of more 'populist' politicians such as Donald Trump (elected as President of the United States in 2016) and Jair Bolsonaro (elected as President of Brazil in 2018) show. These campaigns featured the effective use of social media channels such as WhatsApp, Twitter and Facebook to target specifically tailored messages to particular groups of voters.

## THE MAIN THEMES OF NEW MEDIA THEORY

In Chapter 4, mass media were looked at in the light of four very broad concerns: to do with power and inequality, social integration and identity, social change and development, and space and time. Up to a point, theoretical perspectives on the new media can still be discussed in relation to the same themes. However, it also soon becomes clear that on certain issues the terms of earlier theory do not fit the new media situation very well. In respect of power, for instance, it is much more difficult to locate the new media in relation to the possession and exercise of power. They are not as clearly identified in terms of ownership, nor is access monopolized in such a way that the content and flow of information can be easily controlled.

Communication does not flow in a predominantly vertical or centralized pattern from the 'top' or the 'centre' of society. Government and law do not control or regulate the Internet in a hierarchical way as they do the 'old media' (Collins, 2008). As the Internet has become the dominant medium around the world, governments and large media conglomerates, as well as 'Net native' corporations, step in to negate some of its earlier freedoms (Dahlberg, 2004). As the data gathered through the (voluntary and involuntary) surveillance of Internet users becomes ever more comprehensive and profitable, new media can be seen as contributing to the controlling power of central authority, both in business and in state affairs.

There is now greater equality of access available as sender, receiver, spectator or participant in some exchange or network. It is no longer possible to characterize the dominant 'direction' or bias of influence of information flows (as with press and television news and comment), although the issue of the degree of freedom available to the new 'channels' is far from settled. From its open and democratic early phase, the Internet is increasingly becoming more regulated and dominated by telecommunications companies and corporations that operate on a global scale. Debates about 'Net neutrality' and other issues related to Internet governance have been fierce, and are not likely to be settled anytime soon. Of key importance is the question of consumer protection in the age of big data and 'dataveillance' as the main source of revenue online. Legislation, such as the 2016 General Data Protection Regulation (GDPR) of the European Union, intends to safeguard data protection and privacy, even though its introduction (as that of similar laws elsewhere in the world) comes with much discussion and controversy.

In relation to integration and identity, the conceptual terrain is much the same as that dealt with earlier. The same broad issue is still whether the new media are a force for fragmentation or cohesion in society. However, early critics suggested that the basic configuration of the Internet and the nature of its use point to predominantly fragmenting social effects (Sunstein, 2006; Pariser, 2012). On the other hand, it opens up the way for new and diverse vicarious relationships and networks that are integrating in different ways and may be more binding (Slevin, 2000). The 'bridging' and 'bonding' effects (Putnam, 2000; Norris, 2002) of the Internet show how the new media environment can contribute to respectively social integration and polarization at the same time. Older concerns about mass media took as their basis the central case of the nation state, usually coinciding with the territory served by a mass medium. Alternatively, it might be a region, city or other political-administrative zone. Identity and cohesion were largely defined in geographical terms. The key questions are no longer confined to pre-existing social relationships and identities. Wellman (2002) has suggested that social integration in the context of new media primarily works through 'networked individualism', which would indicate a societal shift from group-based interaction in a single, local family and community to multiple, sparsely knit networks stretched across space and time. Research suggests that, while people of all ages appreciate the use of ICTs in maintaining ties and relationships with family, friends and networks online, most still prefer to spend quality time in person (Quan-Haase, Wang, Wellman and Zhang, 2018). The key is to appreciate how such processes of traditional affiliation and mediated interactions exist side by side, can overlap and also contradict one another as they constitute our sense of identity and belonging online.

Rasmussen (2000) argued that new media have qualitatively different effects on social integration in a modern network society, drawing on Giddens' (1991) theories of modernization. The essential contribution is to consider media as contributing to both bridging and widening the gap that is said to be opening up between the private and public worlds, the 'lifeworld' and the world of systems and organizations. In contrast to television, the new media can play a direct role in individual life projects. They also promote a diversity of uses and wider participation. In short, the new media help to re-embed the individual after the 'disembedding' effects of modernization, with consequences only rarely uniform or one-directional.

In respect of potential for social change, the potential for new communications as an agent of planned economic or social change requires reassessment. At first sight, there is a big difference between mass media that can be systematically applied to goals of planned development by way of mass information and persuasion (as in health, population and technical innovation campaigns) and the open-ended, non-purposive uses that are typical of new technology. The loss of direction and control over content by the sender seems to be crucial.

However, it may be that more participatory media are equally or better suited to producing change because they are more involving as well as more flexible and richer in information. This would be consistent with the more advanced models of the change process. As the Internet matures and more data about people's use of the various Internet-related products and services becomes available, producing social change by micro-targeting individuals online with customized (commercial or political) messages becomes quite possible. On the other hand, such methods – used by advertising and marketing firms – are rarely very effective, and the information we receive online still has to compete with a wide array of other sources of information and communication that make up the average user's media diet.

Much has been written about the new media overcoming barriers of space and time. In fact, 'old media' were good at bridging space, although perhaps less good in relation to cultural divisions. They were much faster than the physical travel and transportation that preceded them. But their capacity was limited and transmission technology required fixed structures and great expense to overcome distance. Sending and receiving were both very much physically located (in production plants, offices, homes, etc.). New technology has freed us from many constraints, although there are other continuing social and cultural reasons why much communication activity still has a fixed location. The Internet, despite its apparent lack of frontiers, is still largely structured according to territory, especially national and linguistic boundaries (Halavais, 2000), although there are also new factors in its geography (Castells, 2001). Communication used to be concentrated in the USA and Europe, and cross-border traffic originally was dominated by English. Today, the dominant geography of the Internet is Asian (specifically China and India), and although English is still the most used language online, other languages have become quite prominent, especially Chinese, Spanish, Arabic and Portuguese.

How far time has been conquered is more uncertain, except in respect of greater speed of transmission, the escape from fixed time schedules, and the ability to send a message to anyone anywhere at any time (but without guarantee of reception or response). We still have no better access to the past or the future, or more time for communication, and the time saved by new flexibility is quickly spent on new demands of technology and inter-communication.

## APPLYING MEDIUM THEORY TO THE NEW MEDIA

As Rice et al. (1983: 18) observed some time ago, the 'notion that the channel of communication might be as important a variable in the communication process as source, message, receiver and feedback, may have been overlooked'. Referring to the work of the Toronto School (see Chapter 4, p. 133), they add that 'One need not be a technological determinist to agree that the medium may be a fundamental variable in the communication process'. Nevertheless, it is still very difficult to pin down the 'essential' characteristics of any given medium, and the ground for distinguishing between 'new' and 'old' media is not very solid.

The main problem lies in the fact that in actual experience it is hard to distinguish the channel or medium from the typical content that it carries or the typical use that is made of it or the context of use (for instance, home, work or public place). Precisely the same problem has bedeviled earlier research into the relative advantages and capacities of different 'traditional' media as channels of communication. However, this does not mean that there is no important difference or emerging discontinuity between old and new. At the moment we can do little more than make plausible suggestions.

Rice (1999) has argued that it is not very profitable to try to characterize each medium according to its specific attributes. Instead, we should study the attributes of media in general and see how new media 'perform' in these terms. Baym (2015) offers a helpful checklist of questions to be asked of each new medium in order to compare it to other media:

- What kinds of interactivity are available?
- What is/are the temporal structure/s possible (synchronous, asynchronous)?
- How available are social cues, including the physical, non-verbal and social/identity cues?
- Is the medium stored?
- Is it replicable?
- How many people can messages reach using that medium?
- What kinds of mobile engagement does that medium afford?

Contrasts and comparisons of media tend to 'idealize' certain features of a medium (for example, face-to-face communication or the virtues of the traditional book), ignoring the paradoxes of positive and negative consequences. The diversity of the category 'new 'media' and their continually changing nature set an obvious limit to theory forming about their 'consequences'. The technological forms are multiplying but are also often temporary. We can identify five main categories of 'new media' which share certain channel similarities and are approximately differentiated by types of use, content and context, as follows:

- *Interpersonal communication media.* These include the telephone (now predominantly mobile), email and messenger applications (such as Whatsapp and Telegram). In general, content is private and perishable, and the relationship established and reinforced may be more important than the information conveyed.
- *Interactive play media.* These are mainly computer-based and video games, plus virtual reality devices. The main innovation lies in the interactivity and perhaps the dominance of 'process' over 'use' gratifications.
- *Information search media.* This is a wide category, but the Internet (and its interface, the World Wide Web) is the most significant example, viewed as a library and data source of unprecedented size, actuality and accessibility. The search engine has risen to a commanding position as a tool for users as well as a source of income for the Internet. Besides the computer used for Internet access, mobile devices such as the smartphone and tablet (and also the laptop) are important channels for information retrieval.
- *Collective participatory media.* This category includes especially the uses of the Internet for sharing and exchanging information, ideas and experience and developing active (computer-mediated) personal relationships. Social networking sites belong under this heading. Uses range from the purely instrumental to the affective and emotional. The commercial aspect of these media is embodied by online platforms, both commodifying and virtualizing all aspects of people's lives (from Uber to Deliveroo and Tinder to AirBnB).
- *Substitution of broadcast media.* The main reference is to uses of media to receive or download content that in the past was typically broadcast or distributed by other similar methods. Watching films and television programmes and listening to the radio and music, etc., are the main activities.

The diversity indicated by this typology makes it hard to draw up any useful summary of medium characteristics that are unique to the new media or applicable to all five categories. Fortunati (2005a) emphasized the parallel tendencies of 'mediatization' of the Internet and 'Internetization' of the mass media as a way of understanding the process of mutual convergence. In terms of affordances, certain characteristics stand out when it comes to new media: their (1) interactivity and (capacity for) virtuality, (2) on-demand and real-time access, (3) creation, distribution and consumption of content by (almost) everyone, and (4) their hybrid character (converging different types of media forms and mediated communication, offering platforms for both mass and interpersonal communication) (Baym et al., 2012).

The subjective perception of new media characteristics shows wide variations between people. A different set of criteria are relevant for comparison with mass communication. Box 6.4 indicates certain dimensions or variables that have been thought to help in differentiating new from old media, as seen from the perspective of an individual 'user'.

---

## 6.4

## Key characteristics differentiating new from old media, from the user perspective

- *Interactivity*: as indicated by the ratio of response or initiative on the part of the user to the 'offer' of the source/sender
- *Virtuality*: the extent to which the medium can produce an alternative reality, community or 'world' within which the user can roam freely
- *Social presence* (or sociability): experienced by the user, meaning the sense of personal contact with others that can be engendered by using a medium
- *Media richness*: the extent to which media can bridge different frames of reference, reduce ambiguity, provide more cues, involve more senses and be more personal (including multimedia, crossmedia or transmedia options)
- *Autonomy*: the degree to which a user feels in control of content and use, independent of the source, including opportunities to create (and remix and share) their own content
- *Privacy*: associated with the use of a medium and/or its typical or chosen content
- *Personalization* (or customizability): the degree to which content and uses are personalized and unique

---

## THE MEANING AND MEASUREMENT OF INTERACTIVITY

Although interactivity is most frequently mentioned as the defining feature of new media, it can mean different things and there is already an extensive literature on the topic. Kiousis (2002) arrived at an early 'operational definition' of interactivity by reference to four indicators: proximity (social nearness to others), sensory activation, perceived speed and telepresence. In this definition, more depends on the perception of the user than on any intrinsic or objective medium quality. Downes and McMillan (2000) name five dimensions of interactivity, as follows:

- the direction of communication;
- flexibility about time and roles in the exchange;
- having a sense of place in the communication environment;
- level of control (of the communication environment);
- perceived purpose (oriented to exchange or persuasion).

It is clear from this that conditions of interactivity depend on much more than just the technology employed. Although we can characterize new media according to their potential, this is not the same as empirical verification. A case in point is the potential for sociability and interactivity. While it is true that the computer machine does connect people with other people, at the point of use it involves solitary behaviour, individualistic choices and responses, and frequent anonymity. The relationships established or mediated by the new communicating machines can be transient, shallow and without commitment, as much as they are meaningful, enriching and a powerful source of social support. They are regarded as an antidote to the individualism, rootlessness and loneliness associated with modern life, as well as a logical development towards forms of commodified social interaction that can be achieved to order. Overall, to most people social interaction online does not substitute or replace other kinds of personal relationships, suggesting that research should deliberately include the mixing of online–offline practices and sensemaking processes.

## NEW PATTERNS OF INFORMATION TRAFFIC

Another useful way of considering the implications of the changes under discussion is to think in terms of alternative types of information traffic and the balance between them. Two Dutch telecommunication experts Bordewijk and van Kaam (1986) have developed a model that helps to make clear and to investigate the changes under way. They describe four basic communication patterns and show how they are related to each other. The patterns are labelled 'allocution', 'conversation', 'consultation' and 'registration'.

### ALLOCUTION

With allocution (a word derived from the Latin for the address by a Roman general to assembled troops), information is distributed from a centre simultaneously to many peripheral receivers, with limited opportunity for feedback. This pattern applies to several familiar communication situations, ranging from a lecture, church service or concert (where listeners or spectators are physically present in an auditorium) to the situation of broadcasting, where radio or television messages are received at the same moment by large numbers of scattered individuals. Another characteristic is that time and place of communication are determined by the sender or at the 'centre'. Although the concept is useful for comparing alternative models, the gap between a personal address to many and impersonal mass communication is a very large one and is not really bridgeable by a single concept. The case of an 'assembled audience' is quite different from that of a 'dispersed audience'.

## CONVERSATION AND EXCHANGE

With conversation, individuals (in a potential communication network) interact directly with each other, bypassing a centre or intermediary and choosing their own partners as well as the time, place and topic of communication. This pattern applies in a wide range of situations where interactivity is possible, including the exchange of personal letters or electronic mail. The electronically mediated conversation does, however, usually require a centre or intermediary (such as the telephone exchange or service provider), even if this plays no active or initiatory role in the communication event. There is also the matter of the communication interface (such as the particular software environment of a messaging app) influencing the exchange. Characteristic of the conversational pattern is the fact that parties are equal in the exchange. In principle, more than two can take part (for example, a small meeting, a telephone conference or a computer-mediated discussion group). However, at some point, increased scale of participation leads to a merger with the allocutive situation.

## CONSULTATION

Consultation refers to a range of different communication situations in which an individual (at the periphery) looks for information at a central store of information – data bank, library, reference work, computer file system, and so on. Such possibilities are increasing in volume and diversifying in type. In principle, this pattern can also apply to the use of a traditional print-based newspaper (otherwise considered an allocutive mass medium), since the time and place of consultation and also the topic are determined by the receiver at the periphery and not by the centre.

## REGISTRATION

The pattern of information traffic termed 'registration' is, in effect, the consultation pattern in reverse, in that a centre 'requests' and receives information from a participant at the periphery. This applies wherever central records are kept of individuals in a system and to all systems of surveillance. It relates, for instance, to the automatic recording at a central exchange of telephone calls, to electronic alarm systems and to automatic registration of television set usage in 'people-meter' audience research or for purposes of charging consumers. It also refers to the collation of personal particulars of e-commerce customers, for the purposes of advertising and targeting. The accumulation of information at a centre often takes place without reference to, or knowledge of, the individual. While the pattern is not historically new, the possibilities for registration have increased enormously because of computerization and extended telecommunication connections. Typically, in this pattern, the centre has more control than the individual at the periphery to determine the content and occurrence of communication traffic.

## AN INTEGRATED TYPOLOGY

These four patterns complement and border upon (or overlap with) each other. The authors of the model have shown how they can be related in terms of two main variables: of central versus individual control of information; and of central versus individual control of time and choice of subject (see Figure 6.2). The allocution pattern stands here for the typical 'old media' of mass communication and conforms largely to the transmission model – especially broadcasting, where a limited supply of content is made available to a mass audience. The consultation pattern has been able to grow, not only because of the telephone and new telematic media, but because of the diffusion of video- and sound-recording equipment and the sheer increase in the number of channels as a result of cable and satellite. The new media have also differentially increased the potential for all these different modes of communication. As noted, 'registration' becomes both more practicable and more likely to occur. It can be viewed as extending the powers of surveillance in the electronic age.

The arrows inserted in Figure 6.2 reflect the redistribution of information traffic from allocutory to conversational and consultative patterns. In general, this implies a broad shift of balance of communicative power from sender to receiver, although this may be counterbalanced by the growth of registration and a further development of the reach and appeal of mass media. Allocutory patterns have not necessarily diminished in volume, but they have taken new forms, with more small-scale provision for segmented audiences based on interest or information need ('narrowcasting'). Finally, we can conclude from this figure that patterns of information flow are not as sharply differentiated as they might appear, but are subject to overlap and convergence, for technological as well as social reasons, and perhaps increasingly so. The same technology (for example, the telecommunications infrastructure) can provide a household with facilities for each of the four patterns described.

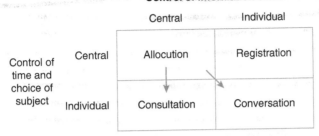

**Control of information store**

| | | Central | Individual |
|---|---|---|---|
| Control of time and choice of subject | Central | Allocution | Registration |
| | Individual | Consultation | Conversation |

**Figure 6.2** A typology of information traffic. Communication relationships are differentiated according to the capacity to control the supply and the choice of content; the trend is from allocutory to consultative or conversational modes (Bordewijk and van Kaam, 1986)

This way of portraying the changes under way invites us to consider again the relevance of the current body of media theory concerning 'effects'. It seems that much of this only applies to the allocutory mode, where a transmission model may still be valid. For other situations, we need an interactive, ritual or user-determined model. It seems evident that in the new media environment different modes, models and media of communication exist side by side and exhibit a mutual shaping effect (see Chapters 16 and 17).

# COMPUTER-MEDIATED COMMUNITY FORMATION

The idea of 'community' has long held an important position in social theory, especially as a tool for assessing the impact of social change and as a counterpoise to the idea of a mass. In earlier thinking, a community referred to a set of people sharing a place (or some other bounded space), an identity and certain norms, values and cultural practices, and usually small enough to know or interact with each other. A community of this kind usually shows some features of differentiation by status among its members and thus an informal hierarchy and form of organization. We should not overly romanticize notions of community, Doreen Massey (2005, 2007) warns, with reference to historical work on the formation of communities, as the boundaries of what constitutes spatial community tend to be relational, temporal and symbolic, rather than existing on a grid of absolute space. Any more or less stable notion of community must be seen as fundamentally contingent. This helps us to qualify normative claims about the more or less stable or ephemeral nature of communities online.

The traditional mass media were viewed ambivalently in their relation to the typical (local) community. On the one hand, their largeness of scale and importation of outside values and culture were viewed as undermining local communities based on personal interaction. On the other hand, the media in adapted localized forms could serve and reinforce community, potentially providing a social glue or cement. Although it is another use of the term 'community', it was also observed that mass-distributed, small-scale media (specialist publications or local radio) could help sustain 'communities of interest' – as is still very much the case in large parts of the world (most notably on the African continent). The general estimation was that the larger the scale of distribution, the more inimical to community and local social life, but even this judgement was challenged by evidence of continued localized interpersonal behaviour. Not least relevant was the fact that mass media often provide topics of conversation for discussion and thus help to lubricate social life in families, workplaces and even among strangers.

Against this background, there has been a continuing debate about the consequences of each succeeding media innovation. In the 1960s and 1970s, the introduction of cable television was hailed not only as a way of escaping from the limitations and drawbacks of mass broadcast television, but as a positive means of community creation. Local cable systems could link up homes in a neighbourhood to each other and to a local centre. Programming could be chosen and made by local residents (Jankowski, 2002). Many extra services of information and help could be added on at low cost. In particular, access could be given to a wide variety of groups and even individual voices, with limited expense. The restricted bandwidth of broadcast television ceased to be a major practical constraint, and television by cable promised to approach the abundance of print media, at least in theory.

The notions of a 'wired community' and a 'wired city' became popular (see Dutton, Blumler and Kraemar, 1986) and experiments were conducted in many countries to test the potential of cable television. This was the first 'new medium' to be treated seriously as an alternative to 'old-style' mass media. In the end, the experiments were largely discontinued and failed to live up to expectations. The more utopian hopes were based on false foundations, especially the assumption that such community-based miniature versions of large-scale professional media were really wanted enough by the people they were meant to serve. Problems of financing and organization were often unsurmountable. Cable distribution became not an alternative to mass media, but predominantly just another means of mass distribution, albeit with some space for local access in some places. What was distinctive about these cable visions was the fact that a physical 'community' already existed but with unfulfilled potential that better intercommunication was supposed to realize. Similar claims and expectations are made about the potential of digital or 'smart' cities – a fuzzy concept first used in the 1990s, and that contains the following as its key characteristics (Albino, Berardi and Dangelico, 2015: 13):

- a city's networked infrastructure that enables efficiency and development;
- an emphasis on business-led urban development and creative activities for the promotion of urban growth;

- social inclusion of various urban residents and social capital in urban development;
- the natural environment as a strategic component for the future.

## VIRTUAL COMMUNITY

A new set of expectations concerning community has developed around **computer-mediated communication (CMC)**. The core idea is that of a '**virtual community**' that can be formed by any number of individuals by way of the Internet of their own choice or in response to some stimulus (Rheingold, 1994).

Some features of real communities can be attained, including interaction, a common purpose, a sense of identity and belonging, various norms and unwritten rules ('netiquette', for instance), with possibilities for exclusion or rejection. There are also rites, rituals and forms of expression. Such online communities have the added advantage of being, in principle, open and accessible, while real communities are often hard to enter. The traditional notion of community is useful as a starting point for theory about the consequences of new media, as the forms of association in both local and virtual communities can exhibit uncertain, fluid and cosmopolitan properties (Slevin, 2000).

There have been numerous empirical studies of online 'communities', usually based on some common interest, for instance fandom for a music group, or on some shared characteristic, such as sexual orientation or a particular social or health situation (see Jones, 1997, 1998; Lindlof and Schatzer, 1998). The typical conditions for the formation of a virtual community seem to include social status (often perceived as minority-based), physical dispersal of members and a degree of intensity of interest. It can be appreciated that CMC offers possibilities for motivated and interactive communication that are not available from mass media or from the immediate physical environment. Most studies of online communities indicate that face-to-face and online contacts are not exclusive and have a mutual interaction.

The claim to the term 'community' in its established meaning is undermined by the lack of transparency and authenticity of the group formed by way of computer-mediated communication. Not least important is the lack of commitment of 'members'. Postman (1993) has criticized the adoption of the community metaphor because there is a lack of the essential element of accountability and mutual obligation. Likewise, Bauman (2000: 201) laments that such groups are examples of 'cloakroom communities', where people temporarily gather 'to ward off the condensation of genuine (that is comprehensive and lasting) communities which they mime and (misleadingly) promise to replicate or generate from scratch'. On the other hand, researchers of online communities – in recent years especially those emerging for (and populated by) refugees and migrants as they make their precarious way in the world – suggest that such concerns fail to appreciate how virtual communities serve all kinds of meaningful functions for their participants, and indeed have real consequences beyond the online environment (Paz Aléncar, Kondova & Ribbens, 2018; Leurs, 2019). Although computer-mediated communication does offer new opportunities to cross social and cultural boundaries, it can also indirectly reinforce the same boundaries. Those who want to belong to a community in cyberspace have to conform to its norms and rules in order to be recognized and accepted. At the heart of the community concept in the context of new media is the notion of 'affective publics', as Zizi Papacharissi (2014) articulates. People can be drawn to virtual communities as much as local ones, driven as they are by personal sentiment. In doing so, the private and the public nature of communication get mixed in our contemporary 'networked life', as Sherry Turkle (2011: 157) notes, 'which is always on and always with us'.

## TECHNOLOGIES OF FREEDOM?

The heading to this section forms the title of a seminal work by Ithiel de Sola Pool (1983) that celebrated electronic means of communication because of the escape they offered from what he regarded as the illegitimate imposition of censorship and regulation on broadcast radio and television. The essence of his argument was that the only logical (though disputed) case for state control of media was spectrum shortage and the need to allocate access opportunity in semi-monopoly conditions. The emerging new era could grant the freedom enjoyed by print media and common carriers (telephone, mails, cable) to all public media. Distribution by cable, telephone line, new radio waves and satellite was rapidly removing the claim for regulation arising out of scarcity. Moreover, the growing 'convergence of modes' of communication made it increasingly impossible as well as illogical to regulate one type of medium and not others.

The freedom that has been claimed as a feature of the new media (especially the Internet) is not precisely the same freedom as Pool was claiming for media in general. Essentially, Pool wanted the freedom of the market and the 'negative freedom' (no government intervention) of the US **First Amendment** to apply to all media. The image of freedom attached to the Internet has had more to do with its vast capacity, its 'network-of-networks' technological infrastructure, and with the lack of formal organization, governance and management that characterized its early history when it was a more or less freely accessible playground for all comers, with much use subsidized by academic institutions or other public bodies. Castells (2001: 200) writes that 'the kind of communication that thrives on the Internet is that related to free expression in all its forms. . . . It is open source, free-posting, decentralized broadcasting, serendipitous interaction . . . that find their expression on the Internet'. This view is in line with the aspirations of its founders. The system was there for all to use, even if the original motives for its creation were strategic and military, while the motives for its subsequent promotion and expansion were mainly economic and in the interests of telecommunication operators.

The system had and retains an inbuilt resistance to attempts to control or manage it. It appeared not to be owned or managed by anyone in particular, to belong to no territory or jurisdiction. In practice, its 'content' and the uses made of it were not easy to control or sanction, even where jurisdiction could be established. In this it shared many features of common carrier media, such as mail and telephone.

The relative free and unregulated beginnings of the Internet have been changing as the medium matures – in this it resembles the histories of other mass media. As it has become more like a mass medium, with high penetration and a potential for reaching an important segment of the consumer market, there is a higher stake in forms of regulation and management. As Lessig (1999: 19) has pointed out: 'The architecture of cyberspace makes regulating behavior difficult, because those you're trying to control could be located in any place . . . on the Net.' However, the means are available by way of control of the architecture and of the code that governs the architecture. It is increasingly a medium for commerce (selling goods as well as information services), so that financial security has to be achieved. It has also become big business. Hamelink (2000: 141) remarks that although no one owns the Net and there is no central regulatory body, 'it is possible for some industrial players to own all the technical means that are required to access and use the Net'. He anticipates a near future when 'governance and access to cyberspace will be in the hands of a few gatekeepers . . . controlled by a small group of market leaders' (ibid.: 153). Twenty years later, this prediction seems to be confirmed.

As the Internet penetrates more homes and becomes a banal part of people's everyday lives, the demands for applying criteria of 'decency' (among other issues) and also for means of enforcement have grown, despite jurisdictional difficulties. As with earlier media, once a claim to great social impact is made, the demand for control grows and the practical obstacles to control turn out not to be so insurmountable. More and more of the normal legitimate accountability claims against public media are arising (for example, about intellectual property, libel, privacy). The seeming anarchy of many service providers and content organizers is giving way to a more structured market situation. Pressure is being put on service providers and platform companies to take some responsibility for what appears on their services, even if the control is haphazard, non-transparent and can have a 'chilling' effect. Influential contemporary calls for regulation and media policy regarding the Internet in general and social media in particular primarily make the argument for a revitalization of public values (Van Dijck et al., 2018), the public interest (Napoli, 2019), and 'radical democratic pluralism' (Cammaerts & Mansell, 2020) as the guiding principles to which new media should be held accountable.

## A NEW MEANS OF CONTROL?

Police and intelligence services are paying more attention to the need for surveillance and control, especially in respect of potential transborder crime, child pornography, terrorism, domestic disaffection, plus many new kinds of cyber-crime. Twenty years into the twenty-first century, there is an ever-growing list of exceptions to the freedoms of the Internet, varying from one national jurisdiction to another and correlated with the general level of freedom (or its absence) in each state. The situation after the western declaration of a 'war on terror' since 2001 has made it easier for governments and authorities to implement restrictions on the liberty of the Net, as in most other spheres (Braman, 2004). Taken together, the tendencies described lead to a severe modification of the Internet's anarchic and open image, although this may simply reflect the onset of 'normalization' that has been exhibited before in respect of other media. The situation is too early and too unsettled to make an assessment, but not too early to say that even the freest means of communication cannot escape the operation of various 'laws' of social life. These include those of communication itself (which bind participants together in some mutual obligations or expectations), and especially those of economics and social pressure.

The more apocalyptic visions of the future indicate a potential for social control through electronic means which far outstrips those available in the industrial age, except where brute force could be used. The monitoring and tracking of informational traffic and interpersonal contacts are increasing, based essentially on the 'registration' pattern of computerized information traffic indicated above (Jansen, 1988). In a contemporary iteration of such an analysis, observers note how 'surveillance capitalism' has become the dominant economic (and political) model in the digital age, offering new ways of manipulating and perhaps even controlling consumers and citizens alike (Zuboff, 2019).

From a historical perspective, Beniger's (1986) interpretative history of communication innovations since the early nineteenth century is insightful, in that they fit within a pattern not of increasing liberation, but of increasing possibilities for management and control. Beniger uses the term 'control revolution' to describe the communications revolution. Whatever the potential, the needs of commerce, industry, military and bureaucracy have done most to promote development and determine how innovations are actually applied. Another chronicler of communication innovation (Winston, 1986) recognized that most new technologies have innovative potential, but the actual implementation always depends on two factors. One is the operation of 'supervening social necessity', which dictates the degree and form of development of inventions. The second is the 'law of the suppression of radical potential', which acts as a brake on innovation to protect the social or corporate status quo. In general, Winston argues for theories of 'cultural' rather than technological determination. Carey (1998: 294) took a similar position about the 'new media', arguing that 'globalization, the Internet and computer communications are all underdetermined by technology and history. The final determination of these new forms is one prepared by politics'.

Of crucial importance when studying these developments is a nuanced understanding of what 'freedom' means in this context (Chalaby, 2001). The freedom from surveillance and 'right to privacy' is a different kind of freedom, protecting anonymity, not publication. Both of these (and other) kinds of freedom are important, but the potential and actual uses of the Internet are too diverse for all forms of freedom to be claimed. Freedom of speech and expression, as established for other media, recognizes some limits on the rights of others, the necessities of society and the realities of social pressure. It is unrealistic to expect the Internet to enjoy freedoms that have been restricted for other media on grounds accepted as legitimate.

## NEW EQUALIZER OR DIVIDER?

The rhetoric surrounding new media throughout history has often embodied a claim that the new medium – whether it was the printed newspaper, broadcast radio or television, or the Internet – helps to produce a more equal, better informed and more liberated society. From a historical point of view, such high expectations have tended to fall flat against developments in social reality, even though literacy rates regarding both media and citizenship have been rising steadily throughout the world during the twentieth century. Critics of overly optimistic readings of the 'new' point out that new media are generally no different from the old media in terms of the social stratification of ownership and access. It is the better-off that first acquire and then upgrade the technology and are always ahead of the poor. They are differentially empowered and, if anything, move further ahead. Social and information gaps widen rather than narrow and there emerges an 'information underclass' as well as a social underclass.

Much is made of the 'digital divide' as a successor to the 'information gap' that was once predicted as a result of the coming of television (Norris, 2000; Hargittai, 2004). Historic conditions play a part in shaping the impact of new technology, not only in the developing world but in former communist countries such as Russia (Rantanen, 2001; Vartanova, 2002). As Selwyn (2004) points out, access to channels is not the same as actual use. Even use is structured according to the availability of skills and other resources, which are not evenly distributed, leading to a second-level 'digital divide' that cannot be overcome by technology. Furthermore, a third-level 'digital divide' can be identified in terms of who benefits most from being online (Helsper, 2012), showing how the Internet remains more beneficial for those with higher social status. Findings from research in this area suggest that 'access to and use of the Internet might amplify existing inequalities above and beyond the intensity of internet use' (Van Deursen and Helsper, 2015: 45).

It is true that the networks, circles and connections between users of new technology based on telecommunications and computers do not have to follow the lines of national frontiers in the same way as old mass media almost invariably have done. It may therefore be less appropriate to apply the centre–periphery model of mass communication, which reflects the varying degrees of dependency in poorer and smaller countries and regions on a few 'primary producers' of news and entertainment. The possession of the right technology does open doorways to new possibilities for information and intercommunication, irrespective of the 'level of development' of one's own home place. Some of the gaps and obstacles to development may be leapfrogged. Other constructions of distinction or difference between new media users in the West and those in the Global South or between those in developed and developing nations are also subject to revision, as the work of Payal Arora (2019) among Internet users in China, India, Brazil and across the Middle East shows: cat videos are universal, and people regardless of social status or location love to have fun and make connections online.

A particular poignant area for critical consideration in media and mass communication research is the environmental impact of the technologies under investigation. In part, this relates to the sourcing of precious metals that are needed for batteries, computer chips and other hardware necessary for our media to work. All too often these materials are mined in developing countries with little or no oversight regarding working conditions. These materials are then put together in factories – mostly located in China – where workers, some as young as 16 years old, work nights and overtime to produce the hugely popular devices, in breach of labour laws. Regular reports of inhumane working conditions in such production facilities have prompted companies like Samsung, Apple and Amazon to develop and enact strict supplier codes of conduct, although the enforcement of such contracts is far from universal.

There are equally problematic issues at the end of a media device's life, considering the enormous global impact of electronic waste, or 'e-waste'. Given the fast-paced rate of upgrades and replacements in consumer electronics such as the smartphone, tablet and television – as the obsolescence of media is generally planned – hundreds of millions of electronic devices are discarded annually, most of which are still working. Correspondingly, a profitable global market for collecting and deposing of electronic waste is growing rapidly, with little oversight. Most of the materials and components in our media end up in illegal dumpsites in Africa (Nigeria and Ghana are the world's leading destinations for electronic waste, according to the United Nations). Recognizing the severity of this issue, in 2007 the United Nations, together with a host of other organizations, started the Solving The E-waste Problem (STEP) initiative. The tracking, management and disposal of electronic waste is a global (and not a municipal or otherwise local) problem because of the complexity and cost involved in safely disposing of the many hazardous yet also valuable, often precious materials that make up media artefacts. The value of e-waste is partly determined by the fact that many of the parts are still working or can be made to work, and thriving local economies for recycling e-waste are also emerging. At the same time, those who work on electronic scrapyards regularly expose themselves to toxins that cause respiratory and dermatological problems, eye infections, neurodevelopmental issues, and ultimately, shorter lives. Maxwell and Miller (2012) are among those media scholars advocating a 'greening' of the media.

In the early days of mass media, there was also a belief that the communicative reach and power of radio and television could help bridge the gaps in social and economic

MCQUAIL'S MEDIA AND MASS COMMUNICATION THEORY
THEORIES

development. The reality proved to be different, and mass media, in their transnational forms at least, were likely to do more for their originating societies and cultures than for their supposed beneficiaries in the 'Third World'. The same tendency to see technology as a changer of the world is still present (Waisbord, 1998). It is hard to see how the situation is different, despite the greater potential for the 'users' and receivers of new media to claim access and to take over the means of cultural oppression. As always, it takes deliberate effort to counter the tendency of technologies and new media to reinforce and amplify existing power relationships and inequalities in culture, society and the economy.

# CONCLUSION

This excursion into theory for new media has been somewhat inconclusive, although recognizes a strong case for revision of theory. Even so, public communication continues much as before. The central values of liberalism, democracy, work, human rights and even communication ethics are evolving rather than collapsing in the twenty-first century. Even the old problems addressed by such values are still in place, including unbridled consumerism, injustice, inequality, crime, terrorism and war. The more specific and central question addressed by this chapter is whether or not the ideas and frameworks that were developed to pose and test questions about media and mass communication are still serviceable.

There are some reasons for supposing that they might not be. There is a definite trend towards the 'demassification' of old media as the proliferation of channels and platforms for transmission eats into the 'mass audience' and replaces it with innumerable small and more 'specialized' audiences. The more this happens, and it can apply to radio and television as well, the less the mass media will provide a common basis in knowledge and outlook or serve as the 'cement of society'. This has been widely regretted as a loss to the larger enterprise of a democratic and socially just society. With regard to people's role as citizens in democracy, some evidence suggests that new media have contributed to the rise of a new style of populist politics, propelling parties and leaders to popularity largely fuelled by data-driven campaigns using social media (while bypassing the 'traditional' route of the mainstream news media). This would counter claims that the decline in engagement in politics can be attributed to the new media. However, they are also not an antidote, as the political attachment to such people and ideas tends to be fickle.

It is arguable that there is no 'media institution' any more, but many different loosely connected elements operating in a global network of media production. There are new forces at work and new trends that may not be open to capture by familiar concepts and formulas. Nevertheless, the basic features of the role of media in public and private life seem to persist. The new media have gradually come to be accepted as mass media for the good reason that their uses exhibit many of the features of old media, especially when treated by their owners as mass advertisers and as distribution centres for media content, such as music and films. As numerous studies show, there are striking regularities in Web-use behaviour that conform to familiar mass media patterns, such as concentration on a small number of very popular sites by very large numbers of users.

What does seem to be clear is an ongoing hybridization and convergence of different modes and models of communication, of different institutional arrangements, and of different practices in and uses of producing and consuming media. In this process, powerful new players emerge, particularly due to the dominance of Web-based platforms and the convergence of the technology, media and telecommunications sectors (Faustino and Noam, 2019).

The evidence so far does not support the view that new technology is having a strongly deterministic effect towards change in the medium term; it is neither producing any very reliable explosion of freedom nor (as yet) seriously diminishing what freedom of expression exists already. Nevertheless, there are areas with potential for change that require monitoring. One is the redrawing of social (and cultural) boundaries, which the formation of new networks of interconnected individuals encourages. Another is the potential transformation of political communication (really of politics) in the widest sense as the old 'allocutive' means seem to perform less well. Finally, there remains the issue of potentially increasing divisions in the benefits of new media as a result of underlying social and economic inequalities.

## FURTHER READING

Arora, P. (2019) *The Next Billion Users*. Cambridge, MA: Harvard University Press.

Baym, N.K. (2015) *Personal Connections in the Digital Age*, 2nd edition. Cambridge: Polity Press.

Fortunati, L. (2005a) 'Mediatizing the net and intermediatizing the media', *International Communication Gazette*, 67(6): 29–44.

Lüders, M. (2008) 'Conceptualizing personal media', *New Media and Society*, 10(5): 683–702.

Morris, M. and Ogan, C. (1996) 'The Internet as mass medium', *Journal of Communication*, 46(1): 39–50.

Quan-Haase, A. (2020) *Technology and Society: Social Networks, Power, and Inequality*, 3rd edition. Oxford: Oxford University Press.

MCQUAIL'S MEDIA AND MASS COMMUNICATION THEORY
THEORIES

# PART 3
## STRUCTURES

# MEDIA STRUCTURE AND PERFORMANCE: PRINCIPLES AND ACCOUNTABILITY

This chapter is about the standards and criteria of quality that can be applied to the operation of the mass media, for the most part from the point of view of the outside society and the 'public interest'. Expectations about the functioning of the media have developed over time and in different places and their application depends on time, place and circumstances. There is no unique set of criteria for serving the public interest – even the notion of a 'public interest' is quite contested. This chapter therefore starts with a historical appreciation of the role of the media in the public interest. The criteria for evaluating the performance of media that follow such conceptualizations can overlap with market criteria, especially those to do with value for money, consumer choice and profitability, and they often overlap with social-normative criteria; for instance the audience for news typically values alternative sources and reliable, unbiased information, and most people tend to agree that some matters are of 'social importance' for media to cover.

Despite the diversity of expectations, criteria and interests, there are a small number of basic values that are usually highly regarded where public communication is concerned, and these values provide the framework for the presentation in this chapter. These can be summarized under the following headings: *freedom, equality, diversity, truth and information quality* and *social order and solidarity*.

The main aim here is to say briefly why each of these values is important and what each means in terms of what the media typically do. We need to be able to define the values in terms of more or less concrete or observable 'outputs' if we are to assess media quality and hold media accountable for their actions. The task is complicated by the fact that the values apply at different levels of media operation. For present purposes, we can distinguish between three levels: structure, conduct and performance. *Structure* refers to all matters relating to the media system, including its form of organization and finance, ownership, form of regulation, infrastructure, distribution facilities, and so on. *Conduct* refers to the manner of operation at the organizational level, including the methods of selecting and producing content, editorial decision-making, market policy, relations established with other agencies, procedures for accountability, and so on. *Performance* essentially refers to content: to what is actually transmitted to an audience. The main values outlined have a different reference at each level, and for the most part we concentrate on structure and performance rather than conduct.

# THE MEDIA AND THE PUBLIC INTEREST

One way of summarizing the situation arising from the many pressures on media to deliver certain benefits to society is to say that there is a 'public interest' in how the media conduct themselves. This concept is both simple and also very contested in social and political theory. The idea of a public interest has deep historical roots in identifying those matters that needed some collective public control and direction for the good of the society or nation, for instance the building and maintenance of roads and waterways, the regulation of weights, measures and currency, the provision of policing and defence.

In more modern times, the phrase was used to apply to the management and ownership of public utilities, such as water, gas, electricity and telephones. These were matters that could not easily be left to private individuals or the working of the market (Held, 1970; Napoli, 2001).

As applied to the mass media, its simple meaning is that the media carry out a number of important, even essential, tasks in a contemporary society and it is in the general interest that these are performed and performed well. It also implies that we should have a media system that is operated according to the same basic principles governing the rest of society, especially in relation to justice, fairness, democracy and reigning notions of desirable social and cultural values. It is clearly in the public interest that the media do not cause social problems or extreme offence. But the idea of a public interest also involves positive expectations, as in the original fields of application.

This simple notion does not take us very far in practice. The first problem encountered is that public control, even in the supposed public interest, of all media is inconsistent with freedom of expression, as usually understood. Moreover, media are usually established not to serve the public interest as such, but to follow some goal of their own choosing. The goal is sometimes defined in cultural, professional or political terms, but more often it is the goal of making profit as a business. Sometimes it is both at the same time. This points to the key problem of determining just what the public interest might be and of who should decide it. There are always diverse and conflicting versions of what is good for a society as a whole, and there is even support for the view that it is better for the media not to pursue any normative goal at all. Rather, the many different media should be left free to do what they want, within the limits of the law. Where media are run on a commercial basis, as they mainly are, the media's view of what is the public interest tends to equate it with what interests the public. This shifts the responsibility for norms, ethics and values to society.

Held (1970) has described two of the main versions of what constitutes the public interest and how its content might be established. One is a 'majoritarian' view, according to which the issue should be settled by reference to the popular vote. In the case of media, this would tend to equate the public interest with 'giving the public what it wants', pleasing the majority of consumers in the media market. Another way of interpreting the majoritarian position is to consider some kind of social solidarity among the public about which matters are of 'social importance' for media to cover. The opposing view is called 'unitarian' or 'absolutist' since the public interest would be decided by reference to some single dominant value or ideology. This would lead at best to a paternalistic system in which decisions about what is good are decided by guardians or experts. Between the free-market version of the public interest and the paternalistic model, there are alternatives, but none offers clear guidance. The other main way is an approach that involves debate and democratic decision-making on the one hand and, on the other, *ad hoc* judicial determinations of what is or is not in the public interest

MCQUAIL'S MEDIA AND MASS COMMUNICATION THEORY
STRUCTURES

in a given case. As we will see later, there are a number of different ways in which the accountability of media to society in terms of the public good can be achieved or at least pursued (see pp. 226–230).

Whatever the arguments about the concept of public interest, it is quite obvious that the mass media have everywhere been subject to extensive control and regulation by law and other formal or informal means with a view to getting them to do what 'society' wants, or to prevent them from doing what it doesn't. The actual means and content of control vary a good deal from one national media 'system' to another, influenced by the usual political, cultural and economic determinants. They vary also from one medium to another and are rarely internally coherent or consistent.

Leaving theory aside, in the practice of media politics, law and regulation, there seems to have been quite a lot of agreement on the main components of the public interest in respect of mass media, going well beyond the minimum requirement of causing no harm. To judge from many cases where public interest has had to be specified, the main requirements from the media are as listed in Box 7.1. These points summarize the main normative expectations relating, respectively, to the structure and content of media in western-type democracies.

## 7.1

## Main public interest criteria for media

### Structure

- Freedom of publication
- Plurality of ownership
- Extensive reach
- Diversity of channels and forms

### Content

- Supportive of the democratic political system
- Supportive of public order and the law
- Diversity of information, opinion and culture
- High quality of information and culture
- Respectful of international obligations and human rights
- Avoiding harm to society and individuals

# MEDIA FREEDOM AS A PRINCIPLE

The pursuit of freedom of expression and publication has been a central theme in the history of the press and is intimately connected with democracy. As Colin Sparks (1995: 45) notes, 'It is not possible to advance even the most limited and formal definitions of democracy which do not recognise the integral role of the media to the actual functioning of all its elements'. In her comparative study on patterns of media performance in forty-seven established democracies worldwide for the period 1990 to 2008, Lisa Müller (2014: 219) concludes 'there is no doubt that media performance is a major determinant for the well-functioning of different dimensions of a democratic regime'. This includes countries beyond well-established western democracies. As Müller points out, in many former non-democratic regimes slowly liberalizing mass media helped to develop pluralism in political attitudes, preferences and alternatives, and to socialize both masses and elites to the new democratic rules of the game (see also Gunther and Mughan, 2000).

Nevertheless, there are different versions and aspects of freedom, and the word does not speak for itself. Freedom is a condition, rather than a criterion, of performance, and thus applies primarily to media structure. Once a right to freedom exists, we cannot easily distinguish between one freely chosen use of freedom of expression and another, within limits set by law, although we evaluate these uses according to other values.

We have to make a distinction between freedom of the media and freedom of expression, although sometimes the same thing is meant. Freedom of expression is a much wider right. It refers to the substance or content of what is communicated (opinion, ideas, information, art, etc.), while freedom of the press refers to one main 'container', vehicle or means for enabling publication. Zeno-Zencovich (2008) compares this to the difference between wine (the contents) and the bottle. The important point is that in law and regulation, the safeguarding of freedom tends to have been transferred from the substance to the means. According to Zeno-Zencovich (2008: 7), 'the sense of freedom of expression as a political freedom enjoyed by individuals and the groups in which they associate has been lost and has become attached to persons who can at best be considered marginal to the diffusion of thought'. This is an implicit attack on the right of owners of media to claim all rights of freedom on the grounds of possession of the means of publication.

The various potential benefits to individuals and society that freedom can provide, in addition to the intrinsic value of the right to free expression, help to indicate other relevant criteria of assessment that can be applied. These benefits are outlined in Box 7.2.

# FREEDOM AT THE LEVEL OF STRUCTURE

Freedom of expression has a dual aspect: offering a wide range of voices and responding to a wide-ranging demand or need. For the benefits of freedom of expression and publication to be realized, certain conditions are called for. There must be access to channels of expression and also opportunities to receive diverse kinds of information. The main structural conditions for effective media freedom are as follows:

- absence of censorship, licensing or other controls by government so that there is an unhindered right to publish and disseminate news and opinions and no obligation to publish what one does not wish to;
- real independence from excessive control and interference by owners and outside political or economic interests;
- the equal right and possibility for citizens to have access to channels of expression and publication as well as access as receivers ('right to communicate');
- competitiveness of the system, with limits to media concentration and cross-ownership;
- freedom for news media to obtain information from relevant sources;

These conditions of structure leave many issues unresolved. There are several potential conflicts and inconsistencies embedded in these requirements. First, freedom of public communication can never be absolute but has to recognize limits sometimes set by the private interests of others or by the higher collective good of a society. In practice, a 'higher good' is usually defined by the state or other power holders, especially in time of war or crisis. Secondly, there is a potential conflict of interest between owners or controllers of media channels and those who might want access to the channels but have no power (or legal right) to secure it (either as senders or as receivers). Thirdly, the conditions as stated place control of freedom in the hands of those who own the media of publication and do not recognize the rights to freedom of publication of those who work in the media (for example, journalists, producers, etc.). Fourthly, there may be an imbalance between what communicators want to say and what others want to hear: the freedom of one to send may not coincide with the freedom of another to choose. Finally, it may be necessary for government or public power to intervene in the media structure to secure some freedoms that are not, in practice, delivered by the unfettered system (for instance, by setting up public broadcasting or regulating ownership). A number of the problems indicated are dealt with by adopting rules of conduct and conventions that are not matters of obligation or right.

## FREEDOM AT THE LEVEL OF PERFORMANCE

As noted, it is not easy to assess the freedom of the content of media since freedom of expression can be used in many different ways, or even misused, as long as it does not actually do harm. Nevertheless, the expected benefits of freedom of publication, as summarized in Box 7.2, do give some indication of additional criteria and expectations. For instance, in respect of news and information (journalism), the media are expected to make use of their freedom to follow an active and critical editorial policy and to provide reliable and relevant information. Free media should not be unduly conformist and should be marked by diversity of opinion and information. They should carry out an investigative and watchdog role on behalf of the public (see Waisbord, 2000). A free media system is characterized by innovation and independence. Similar criteria apply in the area of culture and entertainment. Conditions of freedom should lead to originality, creativity and great diversity. Free media will be prepared, when necessary, to offend the powerful, express controversial views and deviate from convention and from the commonplace. The more that the qualities of content mentioned are missing, the more we may suspect that the structural conditions of media freedom are not being met or that the media are not making use of their freedom.

In order to adequately assess media performance across countries and over time, Müller (2014) developed a two-dimensional concept of mass media's democratic requirements: the vertical and the horizontal media function (see also McQuail, 1992; Voltmer, 2000). The vertical media function relates to the requirement for media to 'disseminate information about the activities and decisions of political office-holders, especially about official misconduct, to as many citizens as possible' (Müller, 2014: 207). A horizontal media function can be assessed in terms of how the media succeed in constituting an open public sphere that reflects the diversity of the society. These functions can be measured at the level of both media *structure* (how widely the access to information from print, broadcast and online news sources is distributed across a country's population) and media *content* (the extent to which the news media in a given country cover political affairs, the three constitutional branches and the public administration in a critical way – for example, by exposing corruption, malpractice and fraud).

The main elements discussed can now be expressed as logically related components, as summarized in Figure 7.1. Some of the elements appear again in respect of other values, especially that of diversity.

**Freedom principle**

*Structural conditions:*

| Independence of channels | Access to channels | Diversity of contents |

*Leading to performance values of:*

| Reliability, critical stance, originality | Choice, change, relevance |

Figure 7.1 Criteria of freedom in media structure and performance

# MEDIA EQUALITY AS A PRINCIPLE

The principle of equality is valued in democratic societies, although it has to be translated into more specific meanings when it is applied to the mass media. As a principle, it underlies several of the normative expectations that have already been referred to.

## EQUALITY AT THE LEVEL OF STRUCTURE

In relation to communication and political power, equality at the level of structure should lead to different or opposed interests in society having more or less the same mass media access opportunities to send and receive. In practice, this is most unlikely to be realized, although steps may be taken by public policy to put right some of the inequalities. The institution of public broadcasting is one means in this direction. Public policy can also limit media monopoly and provide some support for competing media. Equality supports policies of universal provision in broadcasting and telecommunication and of sharing out the costs of basic services. Equality also implies that the normal principles of the free market should operate freely, fairly and transparently.

## EQUALITY AT THE LEVEL OF PERFORMANCE

Equality requires that no special favour be given by the media to power holders and that access to media should be given to contenders for office and, in general, to oppositional or deviant opinions, perspectives or claims as well as established positions. In relation to business clients of the media, equality requires that all legitimate advertisers be treated on the same basis (the same rates and conditions). Equality will support the expectation of fair access, on equivalent terms, for alternative voices (the diversity principle in another form) that meet relevant criteria. In short, equality calls for an absence of discrimination or bias in the amount and kind of access available to senders or receivers, as far as is practicable. Considerations of equality take us into the area of objectivity, discussed in more detail below, as well as into the topic of diversity (to follow). The real chances of media equality are likely to depend on the level of social and economic development of a society and the capacity of its media system. There will have to be enough space on different and mutually independent channels for any degree of equality to be realized in practice. Even so, neither high economic welfare nor an extensive system is a sufficient condition of equality. The United States, for instance, meets both conditions, but does not seem to have communication equality of actual media use or of outcomes in an equally informed society (Entman, 2005; Curran, Iyengar, Lund and Salovaara-Moring, 2009). The reason may lie in the fact that the society values freedom of opportunity over both actual economic and social equality. The main sub-principles related to the value of equality can be expressed as in Figure 7.2.

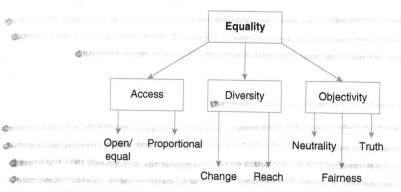

Figure 7.2 Equality as a media performance principle, together with related concepts

## MEDIA DIVERSITY AS A PRINCIPLE

The principle of diversity (also identified as a major benefit of freedom and linked with the concepts of access and equality) is especially important because it underpins the normal processes of progressive change in society. This includes the periodic replacement of ruling elites, the circulation of power and office, and the countervailing power of different interests which pluralistic forms of democracy are supposed to deliver. Diversity stands very close to freedom as a key concept in any discussion of media theory (Glasser, 1984). It presupposes, most generally, that the more, and more different, channels of public communication there are, carrying the maximum variety of (changing) content to the greatest variety of audiences, the better. Put like this, diversity seems rather empty of any value direction or prescription about *what* should actually be communicated. Indeed, this is a correct interpretation since diversity, like freedom, is neutral as to content. It is a valuation of variety, choice and change in themselves. Even so, it is up to society to decide which values should be upheld by a media system, for example ethnicity, or political or religious values, etc. Diversity in what the media have to offer is also clearly a direct benefit to audiences and can be a reflection of a wide range of access to channels of publication. Despite the general valuation of diversity, there can be too much of a good thing, leading to a fragmented and divided society – a widely shared concern given the plethora of possible sources of information and entertainment at anyone's disposal online.

The main expected benefits of diversity for society are outlined in Box 7.3.

---

### 7.3

### Main public benefits expected from diversity

- Opening the way for social and cultural change, especially where it takes the form of giving access to new, powerless or marginal voices
- Providing a check on the misuse of freedom (for instance, where the free market leads to a concentration of ownership)
- Enabling minorities to maintain their separate existence in a larger society
- Limiting social conflicts by increasing the chances of understanding between potentially opposed groups and interests
- Adding generally to the richness and variety of cultural and social life
- Maximizing the benefits of the 'free marketplace of ideas'

---

## DIVERSITY AT THE LEVEL OF STRUCTURE

The main structural requirements for the diversity of a media system are much the same as for equality. There should be many (or sufficiently) different and independent media firms or producers to match the requirements of the society. In accounting for diversity of *provision*, the extent to which real alternatives are on offer can be registered according to several alternative yardsticks. The media system should consist of different types of media (such as press, radio or television). It should reflect geographical diversity, with media for national, regional or local populations. Media should also reflect the structure of the society, where relevant, according to language, ethnic or cultural identity, politics, religion or belief. There is evidence, however, that enlarging the number of channels and choices (as happened in Europe after the deregulation of television) does not necessarily enlarge the diversity of content; rather, there is simply much more of the same mixture (van der Wurf, 2004).

Two basic variants of the 'diversity as equal treatment' principle have been identified. According to one version, a literal equality should be on offer: everyone receives the same level of provision and has the same chances for access as the senders. This applies, for instance, where contending parties receive equal time in an election, or in those countries (such as Canada, Switzerland or Belgium) where separate language groups receive an equivalent separate media service. An alternative and more usual version means only a 'fair', or appropriate, allocation of access and treatment. Fairness is generally assessed according to the principle of proportional representation. Media provision thus should proportionately reflect the actual distribution of whatever is relevant (social groups, political beliefs, etc.) in the society, or reflect the varying distribution of audience demand or interest. Another basic variable of structure is whether diversity is achieved by having separate channels (for example, newspaper titles) for different interests (so-called external diversity) or having different voices represented within the same channel (internal diversity).

The inadequacy of formal structural provision in fully commercial media systems has been demonstrated by comparative studies of media ownership (Noam and The International Media Concentration Collaboration, 2016). Throughout history, media industries have been converging and companies are increasingly conglomerated – whether this concerned the integration of broadcasting, cable and telephony in the twentieth century, or as a response to the growing competition with digital and Internet-based firms and online streaming services. In fact, multinational media corporations primarily tend to make their money through acquisition and mergers, rather than through the production of specific media content (Knee, Greenwald and Seave, 2009). There is a contrast between the diversity supported by a liberal pluralist view of freedom – which would call for media to be effectively in the hands of the more powerless and disadvantaged, with an equalization of chances to communicate on their own behalf – and a market-driven notion of freedom – which would emphasize rights of priority of ownership over regulation, allowing a handful of powerful companies to control most of the world's media. There is a delicate balance between a strictly commercial interpretation of freedom and one that takes the public value of diversity and plurality as a point of departure.

## DIVERSITY AT THE LEVEL OF PERFORMANCE

The differentiation of media provision (content) should approximately correspond to the differences at source or to those at the receiving end. Essentially, the content provided by the media system should match overall the information, communication and cultural needs of the society. In fact, diversity of performance is most likely to be assessed in terms of the output of particular media organizations – newspaper titles, television stations, and so on. The question of diversity of media content can be assessed according to numerous dimensions. These include genre, taste, style or format in culture and entertainment; news and informational topics covered; political viewpoints, and so on. The possibilities for assessment are unlimited, but most questions of diversity turn on one or more of the following criteria: reflection of social and cultural differences; equal access to all voices; and a wide choice for consumers. The main criteria for measuring diversity are summarized in Box 7.4.

## 7.4

## Main requirements of the diversity norm for structure and performance

- Media should reflect in their structure and content the various social, economic and cultural realities of the societies (and communities) in which they operate, in a more or less proportional way
- Media should offer more or less equal chances of access to the voices of various social and cultural minorities that make up the society
- Media should serve as a platform for different interests and points of view in a society or community
- Media should offer relevant choices of content at one point in time and also variety over time of a kind that corresponds to the needs and interests of their audiences

As with freedom of expression, complete diversity is an unattainable ideal. There are also certain inconsistencies and problems in these normative requirements. The degree of diversity that is possible is limited by media channel capacity and by editorial selections that have to be made. The more that media are *proportionally* reflective of society, the more likely it is that small, or even quite large, minorities will be effectively excluded from mass media since a small proportion of access will be divided between many claimants, with unequal social and economic resources. Similarly, catering properly for dominant groups and for consistent expectations and tastes in mass media limits the chance to offer a very wide choice or much change. However, the full range of many different minority media in a society can help to compensate for the limitations of 'traditional' mass media. Thus, diversity of structure can compensate for a lack of diversity in dominant channels. It is important to keep in mind that diversity in itself is not necessarily of value, unless it relates to some criterion or dimension that is significant. Karppingen (2007) criticizes 'naïve pluralism' in media politics relating to diversity. Too much diversity can even be dysfunctional for the public arena, when it leads to social fragmentation, such as can be the case given both the way the Internet caters to every specific taste and subgroup, and the media industry's tendency to divide the public up in target markets – two processes greatly accelerated by the use of data science (and specifically algorithms such as those that drive recommendations on Netflix and playlists on YouTube).

# TRUTH AND INFORMATION QUALITY

The historic claims for freedom of expression were strongly related to the value of *truth* in one or other of its senses. Most important in the early days of public communication (by print) were religious truth as guarded by the established church; personal religious truth according to the individual conscience; scientific truth; legal truth; and historical truth (social and economic reality), especially as it affected government and business. Although the meaning of truth and its value vary according to the context and topic mentioned, there was and remains a broadly shared interest (sometimes a necessity) in having access to 'knowledge' (information) that can be depended on (reliability) from trusted sources, that matches the reality of experience, and that is relevant and useful in various applications. While the expectation that media should provide information of acceptable quality has a more practical than philosophical or normative foundation, it is hardly less important in modern thinking about media standards than the principles of freedom, equality or diversity.

The benefits stemming from a supply of trustworthy knowledge hardly need stating, especially when one considers what the opposite would be: lies, misinformation, propaganda, slander, superstition or ignorance. But it is worth noting the main arguments for having media structures that will help to produce high information quality (and truth), as in Box 7.5.

## 7.5

## The benefits of information quality (media truth)

- Contributing to an informed society and a skilled workforce
- Providing the basis for democratic decision-making (an informed and critical electorate)
- Guarding against propaganda and irrational appeals
- Warning against risks
- Meeting everyday needs of the public for information

# THE OBJECTIVITY CONCEPT

The most central concept in media theory relating to information quality has probably been that of objectivity, especially as applied to news information. Objectivity is a particular form of media *practice* (as described below) and also a particular attitude to the task of information collection, processing and dissemination. It should not be confused with the broader notion of truth, although it is one version of it. One main feature is the adoption of a position of detachment and neutrality towards the object of reporting. Secondly, there is an effort to avoid partisanship: not taking sides in matters of dispute or showing bias. Thirdly, objectivity requires strict attachment to accuracy and other truth criteria (such as relevance and completeness). It also presumes a lack of ulterior motive or service to a third party. The process of observing and reporting should thus not be contaminated by subjectivity, nor should it interfere with the reality being reported on. In some respects, it has an affinity with the ideal of rational, 'undistorted' communication advocated by Habermas (1962/1989).

This version of an ideal standard of reporting practice has become a dominant ideal for the role of the professional journalist (Willnat, Weaver and Choi, 2013). It has links with the principle of *freedom* since independence is a necessary condition of detachment and truthfulness. Under some conditions (such as political oppression, crisis, war and police action), the freedom to report can only be obtained in return for a guarantee of objectivity. On the other hand, freedom also includes the right to be biased or partisan. The link with *equality* is also strong: objectivity requires a fair and non-discriminatory attitude to sources and to objects of news reporting, all of which should be treated on equal terms. Additionally, different points of view on matters where the facts are in dispute should be treated as of equal standing and relevance, other things being equal.

In the relationships that develop in the operating environments of media, objectivity may be crucial. Agencies of the state and advocates of various interests are able to speak directly to their chosen audiences by way of the media, without undue distortion or intervention by the gatekeepers and without compromising the independence of channels. Because of the established conventions of objectivity, media channels can distance their editorial content from the advertising matter that they carry, and advertisers can do likewise in respect of editorial content. Editorial opinion can also be distinguished from news.

In general, media audiences appear to understand the principle of objective performance well enough, and its practice helps to increase public credence and trust both in the information and in the opinions which the media offer. Finally, because the objectivity standard has such a wide currency, it is often invoked in claims and settlements concerning bias or unequal treatment. Policies for broadcasting in many countries impose, by various means, a requirement of objectivity on their public broadcasting systems, sometimes as a condition of their independence from government. Most modern news media set a lot of store by their claim to objectivity in its several meanings. In recent years, partly under the influence of increased visibility and scrutiny by audiences, journalists and certain news organizations have adopted transparency as their definition of objectivity, that is 'making visible and transparent the limitations inherent in their own processes of truth and meaning-making' (McNair, 2017: 1331). In the history of objectivity and the various meanings this concept has had in different news cultures and organizations, a general trend has been that the media themselves find that objectivity gives their own news product a higher and wider market value (Schudson, 1978). Although Vos and Craft (2017: 12) find that journalists and news organizations now routinely appeal to transparency as a standard by which to judge journalistic practice, they also warn against an uncritical acceptance of this contemporary iteration of objectivity, as 'it is an overbearing, disordered force. It is overboard, its advocates are overwrought, and the public is left overwhelmed. It provides the opposite of what it promises – instead of clarity we are left with obfuscation. Worst of all, it is naïve; and it is soft'.

## A FRAMEWORK FOR OBJECTIVITY RESEARCH AND THEORY

One version of its components has been set out by Westerstahl (1983) in the context of research into the degree of objectivity shown by the Swedish broadcasting system. This version (Figure 7.3) recognizes that objectivity has to deal with *values* as well as with facts, and that facts also have evaluative implications.

In this scheme 'factuality' refers, first, to a form of reporting that deals in events and statements that can be checked against sources and are presented free from comment, or at least clearly separated from any comment. Factuality involves several other 'truth criteria': completeness of an account, accuracy, and an intention not to mislead or suppress what is relevant (good faith). The second main aspect of factuality is 'relevance'. This is more difficult both to define and to achieve in an objective way. It relates to the process of *selection* rather than to the form of presentation and requires that selection takes place according to clear and coherent principles of what is significant for the intended receiver and/or the society (Nordenstreng, 1974). In general, what affects most people most immediately and most strongly is likely to be considered most relevant (although there may be a gap between what the public perceives as of interest and what experts say is significant).

According to Westerstahl's scheme, impartiality presupposes a 'neutral attitude' and has to be achieved through a combination of balance (equal or proportional time/space/emphasis) as between opposing interpretations, points of view or versions of events, and neutrality in presentation.

The scheme in Figure 7.3 has been given an extra element, that of 'informativeness', which is important to the fuller meaning of objectivity. The reference is to qualities of informational content which are likely to improve the chances of actually getting information across to an audience: being noticed, understood, remembered, and so on. This is the pragmatic side of information, which is often undervalued or neglected in **normative theory** but is essential to the fuller notion of good informational performance.

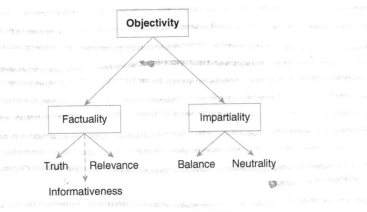

Figure 7.3  Component criteria of objectivity (Westerstahl, 1983)

The main information quality requirements are as follows:

- Mass media should provide a comprehensive supply of relevant news and background information about events in the society and the world around.
- Information should be objective in the sense of being factual in form, accurate, honest, sufficiently complete and true to reality, and reliable in the sense of being checkable and separating fact from opinion.
- Information should be balanced and fair (impartial), reporting alternative perspectives and interpretations in a non-sensational, unbiased way, as far as possible.

## LIMITS OF OBJECTIVITY

Several potential difficulties are embedded in these norms, especially because of uncertainty about what constitutes an adequate or relevant supply of information and about the very nature of 'objectivity' (Hemánus, 1976; Westerstahl, 1983; Hackett, 1984; Ryan, 2001). On a fundamental level, Muñoz-Torres (2012) argues how claims about objectivity, especially in journalism, are misguided in that they assume that by excluding values and opinions from facts and neutral observation, reporting somehow will be better. In doing so, values emerge in the basic presumptions about objectivity. Furthermore, a journalist strictly adhering to 'facts' still has to make value judgements about which facts to omit – as the world offers us infinite facts. Muñoz-Torres makes a similar case against the opposite of objectivity, relativism, showing how these positions are part of the same conceptual framework. With Ward (2005), Muñoz-Torres (2012: 581) proposes a 'major rethinking of the conception of truth, understood as correspondence between mind and reality, in which both experience and reason play jointly a key role'.

Beyond such fundamental issues, it has often been argued that following the rules of objectivity leads to new and less obvious forms of bias. It can give advantages to well-organized and well-financed or otherwise dominant parties to matters of dispute, regardless of the intrinsic value of the position taken. Few would argue for impartiality towards evil deeds, but the concept does not help to find any line to draw. There are also possible inconsistencies with claims of media freedom (which does not distinguish between 'true' and 'false' expression) and of diversity (which emphasizes the multiplicity and inconsistency of reality). We can also note that such criteria are more appropriate to the *totality* of media information in a society, rather than to any particular channel or sector. Not all media are equally expected by their own audiences to provide full and objective information on 'serious' topics.

The debate about appropriate standards of information has given rise to a divide between those who press for maximum information quality (the 'full news standard') and those who argue in favour of a more realistic minimum standard (the 'burglar alarm' version, essentially headlines and short items). This last would alert citizens only to essential matters and relevant issues and dangers of the moment. An upholder of the full news standard, Bennett (2003) has criticized the minimal view on the grounds that it is an alarm that often does not ring. An alternative view is that the amount and weight of news is less important than its diversity, giving citizens a real chance of understanding events and evaluating alternative courses of action (Porto, 2007).

## SOCIAL ORDER AND SOLIDARITY

The normative criteria that belong under this heading are those that relate to the integration and harmony of society, as viewed from different (even opposed) perspectives. On the one hand, there is a rather consistent tendency on the part of those in authority to look to public communication media for at least tacit support in the task of maintaining order. On the other hand, pluralistic societies cannot be conceived as having one single dominant order which has to be maintained, and mass media have mixed and divided responsibilities, especially with reference to alternative social groups and subcultures and to the expression of the conflicts and inequalities of most societies. Problems also arise over how far the media can go in their support for opposition or potential subversion (as it may seem from 'the top'). The relevant principles concerning the media are mixed and not mutually compatible, but can be expressed in something like the following way.

The concept of order is used here in a rather elastic way, to apply to symbolic (cultural) systems such as religion, art and customs, as well as to forms of social order (community, society and established structures of relations). This broad distinction is also cut across by a distinction of perspective – from 'above' and 'below', as it were. This distinction is essentially that between established authority of society on the one hand, and individuals and minority groups on the other. It also corresponds approximately to the distinction between order in the sense of control and order in the sense of solidarity and cohesion – the one 'imposed', the other voluntary and self-chosen. These ideas about order can be arranged as shown in Figure 7.4.

|  |  | Perspective | |
|---|---|---|---|
|  |  | From 'above' | From 'below' |
|  | Social | Control/ compliances | Solidarity/ attachment |
| Domain |  |  |  |
|  | Cultural | Conformity/ hierarchy | Autonomy/ identity |

Figure 7.4 Ideas concerning mass media and order depend on whose order and what kind of order is involved

Any complex and viable social system will exhibit all the sub-aspects of order shown here. There will be mechanisms of social control as well as voluntary attachments, often by way of membership of component groups in society. There will be a sharing of common meanings and definitions of experience as well as much divergence of identity and actual experience. Shared culture and solidaristic experience tend to be mutually reinforcing. The relationship between mass communication and these different concepts has been handled in theories of media and society in divergent, though not logically inconsistent, ways (see Chapter 4). Functionalist theory attributes to mass media a latent purpose of securing the continuity and integration of a social order (Wright, 1960) by promoting co-operation and a consensus of social and cultural values.

Critical theory has usually interpreted mass media as agents of a dominant, controlling class of power holders who seek to impose their own definitions of situations and their values and to marginalize or delegitimize dissent. The media are often seen as serving conflicting goals and interests and as offering alternative versions of an actual or desirable social order. The question '*Whose* order?' has first to be settled. Relevant normative theory cannot be concerned only with the disruption of order (such as with conflict, crime or deviance), but should also relate to the failings of the established order as perceived by more marginal, or minority, social and cultural groups.

## EXPECTATIONS AND NORMS RELATING TO ORDER

From the perspective of social control, the relevant norms are often applied to condemn positive portrayals of violence, disorder and deviance or to support privileged access and positive symbolic support for established 'order' institutions and authorities – the law, church, school, police, military, and so on. The second sub-principle (that of solidarity) involves the recognition that society is composed of many subgroups, different bases of identity and different interests. From this perspective, a viable normative expectation from mass media is that they should sympathetically recognize the alternatives and provide access and symbolic support for relevant minority groups and views. In general, this (normative) theoretical position will encompass an outward-looking and empathic orientation to social groups and situations that are marginal, distant or deviant from the point of view of a dominant national society.

To summarize a very mixed set of normative perspectives concerning social order:

- In respect of the relevant public which they serve (at national or local level, or as defined by group and interest), the media should provide channels of intercommunication and support.

- The media may contribute to social integration by paying concerned attention to socially disadvantaged or injured individuals and groups.

- The media should not undermine the forces of law and order by encouraging or symbolically rewarding crime or social disorder.

- In matters of national security (such as war, threat of war, foreign subversion or terrorism), the freedom of action of media may be limited by considerations of national interest.

- On questions of morals, decency and taste (especially in matters of the portrayal of sex and violence and the use of bad language), the media should to some degree observe the reigning norms of what is broadly publicly acceptable and avoid causing grave public offence.

## CULTURAL ORDER

The domain of the 'cultural' is not easy to keep separate from that of the 'social' or to define, but here it mainly refers to the symbolic content transmitted. Normative media theory has typically been concerned either with matters of cultural 'quality' (of media content) or with 'authenticity' in respect of real-life experience. The subdivision of the sphere of the cultural for the present purposes of representation in a normative framework follows a similar line to that applied in the social domain: between a 'dominant', official or established culture and a set of possible alternatives or subcultures. In practice, the former implies a hierarchical view of culture, according to which cultural values and artefacts that have been 'certified' by established cultural institutions will be relatively privileged compared with 'alternative' cultural values and forms.

## CULTURAL QUALITY NORMS

Normative theory, often expressed in wider cultural policies, can support different kinds of cultural quality in the mass media. First, it often protects the 'official' cultural heritage of a nation or society, especially in education and science, art and literature. Secondly, it supports distinctive regional, local or minority group variants of cultural expression, on the grounds of authenticity and identity and for political reasons. Thirdly, some theory recognizes the equal rights of all cultural expressions and tastes, including 'popular culture', however commercialized.

Although there have been many heated discussions about the possible cultural responsibilities of mass media, there is little agreement on what to do about them, and less action. Principles of cultural quality are likely to be advanced as desirable but are rarely enforceable. There is rarely enough consensus on what criteria of cultural quality mean for action to be taken. Even so, we can identify the most commonly invoked principles as follows:

- Media content should reflect and express the language and contemporary culture (artefacts and way of life) of the people whom the media serve (nationally, regionally and locally); it should be relevant to current and typical social experience.
- Some priority should be given to the educational role of the media and to the expression and continuity of the best in the cultural heritage of a country.
- Media should encourage cultural creativity and originality and the production of work of high quality (according to aesthetic, moral, intellectual and occupational criteria).
- Cultural provision should be diverse, reflecting demand, including demand for 'popular culture' and entertainment.

## THE MEANING OF ACCOUNTABILITY

Having established the basic values and principles that are involved in assessing the quality of public communication generally, and the performance of media in particular, the question remains of how to hold media institutions accountable for their actions. The concept of accountability is built on the concepts of freedom and responsibility. Accordingly, freedom in this context is not an independent force but an element based on the human right of freedom of expression, which 'carries with it special duties and responsibilities' as determined by Article 19 of the International Covenant on Civil and Political

Rights (Nordenstreng, 2010: 423). Often the term 'accountability' is used interchangeably with 'answerability', especially where the latter means to have to explain or justify one's actions. There are several different ways in which this can take place. Pritchard (2000: 3) writes that the essence of accountability lies in a process of naming, blaming and claiming. Essentially this means to identify a problem, name the media outlet responsible and claim some apology or compensation.

The core reference with regard to accountability is to a process of public scrutiny whereby the public activities of the media (acts of publication) are confronted with the legitimate expectations of society. The latter can be expressed in terms of the criteria that have just been outlined. We define **media accountability** in a provisional way here as follows:

> Media accountability is all the voluntary or involuntary processes by which the media answer directly or indirectly to the society and those immediately affected for the quality and/or consequences of publication.

Because of the complexity and sensitivity of the issues that arise, it is clear that we are not dealing with a simple or single mechanism of social control or regulation. The various elements that contribute to accountability are part of the normal operation of the media in any open society. In keeping with central tenets of normative theory – referring to ideas of how the media *ought* or *are* expected to be organized and to behave in the wider public interest or for the good of society as a whole – media accountability processes should meet four general criteria:

- They should respect rights to free publication.
- They should prevent or limit harm arising from publication to individuals as well as to society.
- They should promote positive aspects of publication rather than merely being restrictive.
- They should be public and transparent.

The first of these four criteria reflects the primacy of the requirement of free expression in democracies. The second implies that obligations to 'society' are in the first instance obligations to individual human beings with rights, needs and interests. The third puts the emphasis on dialogue and interaction between media and other institutions of society. The fourth implies that internal control by the media is not sufficient. The fundamental difficulty of meeting these four criteria lies in the inescapable tension between freedom and accountability, since total freedom recognizes no obligations to answer for the actions of others, within the normal limits of the law. Typically, constitutional law in democracies rules out any constraint on the 'freedom of the press', so the legitimate scope for avoiding accountability is very wide (see Dennis, Gilmor and Glasser, 1989). Given that many countries do not meet the criteria for liberal democracies in general, or have widely diverging views on what constitutes either 'freedom' or the 'public interest', it must be clear that media accountability means different things in different contexts.

This presentation of the case here is based on the assumption that there is such a thing as a 'public interest', as discussed above. Secondly, it assumes that the media are important enough to society to justify holding them to account and that effective accountability is not necessarily inconsistent with basic freedom. Freedom involves some elements of responsibility to others and is limited according to the rights of others. We understand freedom here in terms of autonomy of media institutions and professionals regarding control or oversight from non-media actors.

It is useful here to make a distinction between the concepts of accountability and responsibility. The latter refers to the obligations and expectations that are directed at the media. Accountability, on the other hand, refers primarily to the processes by which media are called to account. As Hodges (2004: 173) puts it:

The issue of responsibility is: To what social needs should we expect journalists to respond ably? The issue of accountability is: How might society call on journalists to explain and justify the ways they perform the responsibilities given to them? Responsibility has to do with defining proper conduct, accountability with compelling it.

In considering processes of accountability, it is useful to distinguish between responsibilities in terms of the degree of compulsion involved. Some are entirely voluntary and self-chosen, some are contracted between media and audiences or clients, and others are required by law. The pressure to be accountable can thus be moral or social rather than legal. In general, the more voluntary, the softer or more optional are the mechanisms of accountability, the less conflict with freedom is involved. A softer mode of accountability is one that does not involve a financial or other penalty, but instead usually involves a verbal process of enquiry, explanation or apology. The media prefer to avoid external adjudication and penalties, for obvious reasons: hence the prevalence of self-regulatory mechanisms of accountability. These may also be more appropriate to issues of communication, where there is usually no physical or material damage.

Although responsibility should precede accountability, media industries and professionals generally do not distinguish between the two in practice. Maras (2014) shows how such 'responsibility gaps' between expectations and standards, and differences in the ways in which roles are understood, are quite common, thereby threatening the whole idea of accountability. With Maras, we would argue for greater reflection on the nature and requirements of accountability.

# TWO ALTERNATIVE MODELS OF ACCOUNTABILITY

For accountability to take place there has to be some response to what the media do (publication), and the media have to listen. Accountability means answering to *someone* for *something* according to some *criterion* and with varying degrees of obligation on the part of the media. Combining some of these ideas, it becomes possible to sketch two alternative models of accountability: one that can be called a liability mode and another that can be termed an answerability mode.

The *liability model* puts the emphasis on potential harm and danger that might arise from media publication, whether harm to individuals or to society (for instance, danger to morals or public order). The measures taken in line with this model will involve material penalties imposed by private or public law.

In contrast, the *answerability model* (or mode) is non-confrontational and emphasizes debate, negotiation, voluntariness and dialogue as the best means to bridge differences that arise between media and their critics or those affected. The means of accounting will be predominantly verbal rather than formal adjudications, and any penalties will also be verbal (for example, publication of apologies, corrections or replies) rather than material.

It is always difficult to weigh up the balance between private (individual) harm (for instance, to the reputation of a public figure) and possible public benefit (such as exposure of some scandal or abuse). In practice, there are also likely to be 'chilling' effects on publication where severe material penalties might follow after the event of publication. The greatest danger is to small publishers, giving greater advantage to rich media corporations who can afford to risk financial losses in the pursuit of audiences. The 'answerability' model is generally most consistent with ideas of participant democracy and most likely to encourage diversity, independence and creativity of expression. The main features of the two 'modes' are summarized in Table 7.1.

Table 7.1  Two accountability models compared (McQuail, 2003a: 205)

| Answerability | | Liability |
|---|---|---|
| Moral/social basis | v | Legal basis |
| Voluntary | v | Imposed |
| Verbal forms | v | Formal adjudication |
| Co-operative | v | Adversarial |
| Non-material penalty | v | Material penalty |
| Reference to quality | v | Reference to harm |

# LINES AND RELATIONS OF ACCOUNTABILITY

By definition, accountability involves a relationship between media and some other parties. We can recognize two separate stages of accountability: one *internal* and the other *external*. The former involves a chain of control within the media, such that specific acts of publication (for example, news items or television programmes) can be made the responsibility of the media organization and its owners. Important issues do arise in this respect concerning the degree of autonomy or freedom of expression of those who work in the media (for example, journalists, writers, editors, producers). There is a tension between freedom and responsibility 'within the walls' of the media, so to speak, which is too often resolved in favour of media owners. In any case, we cannot rely on internal control or management to satisfy the wider social need for accountability. Internal control may either be too strict (protecting the organization from claims) and thus a form of self-censorship, or too much directed at serving the interests of the media organization rather than society.

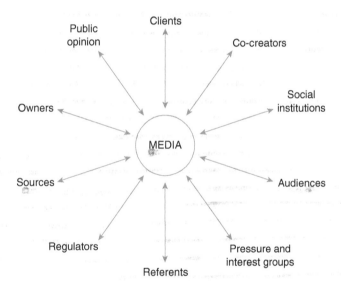

Figure 7.5  Lines of accountability between media and external agents in relation to publication

Here we are concerned with the 'external' relationships between media and those affected by, or with an interest in, publication. These are varied and overlapping, as we can appreciate from a simple enumeration of the main potential partners, as shown in Figure 7.5. Accountability relations routinely arise between media and:

- their own (consuming and co-creating) audiences;
- their clients, such as advertisers, sponsors or backers;

- those who supply content, including news sources and producers of entertainment, sports and cultural production;
- those who are the subject of reporting, whether as individuals or as groups (here called 'referents');
- owners and shareholders of media firms;
- government regulators and law-makers as guardians of the public interest;
- social institutions that are affected by media or depend on media for their normal operation;
- public opinion, standing here for 'society as a whole';
- various pressure and interest groups that are affected by publication.

## FRAMES OF ACCOUNTABILITY

Given the variety of issues and potential claimants, it is not surprising that there are numerous types of process. In addition, different media are subject to different 'regimes', or even none at all. The entire mass production process involves a routine and continuous accounting, both internally in anticipation of problems and externally after publication, by many interested parties – including the audience online. Most of this activity falls within the scope of the 'answerability' model outlined above. However, more problematic issues and stronger claims do arise and media are likely to resist them. In this case, more coercive procedures may become involved. Typically, an accountability process in such cases requires some formal procedures and a machinery of external third-party adjudication. Here too there is much room for diversity since forms of adjudication can range from the justice system, where legal offence is alleged (for example, libel), to voluntary systems instituted by the media themselves.

Because of this diversity, it is useful to think in terms of a small number of basic 'frames of accountability', each representing an alternative, although not mutually exclusive, approach to accountability, and each having its own typical discourse, logic, forms and procedures. A frame in this sense involves several common elements: there must be a relationship between a media 'agent' and some external 'claimant', often with a third party as an adjudicator; there are some criteria or principles of good conduct; and there are rules, procedures and forms of account. We can define a frame of accountability as follows:

A frame of accountability is a frame of reference within which expectations concerning conduct and responsibility arise and claims are expressed. A frame also indicates or governs the ways in which such claims should be handled.

Following, in part, the example of Dennis et al. (1989), the four most generally prevalent accountability frames in this sense can be identified respectively under the headings:

*law and regulation, financial/market, public responsibility* and *professional responsibility*. We can briefly describe them by reference to the typical instruments and procedures; the issues they are most suited to dealing with; the degree of compulsion involved; and the relative advantages and disadvantages they have.

## THE FRAME OF LAW AND REGULATION

The first of these frames refers to all public policies, laws and regulations that affect media structure and operation. The main purpose should be to create and maintain the conditions for free and extensive intercommunication in society and to advance the public good as well as to limit potential harm to legitimate private and public interests.

The main *mechanisms and procedures* normally comprise regulatory documents concerning what media may and may not do, together with formal rules and procedures for implementing the provisions of any regulation. The main issues dealt with under this heading relate either to alleged harm to individuals or to other matters on which media (especially electronic media) can be regulated and called to account.

As to the *advantages* of this approach to accountability, the first is that there is ultimately some power to enforce claims. There is also democratic control, by way of the political system, over ends and means as a check on abuse of powers of compulsion. Any limits to freedom, as well as to the scope of any regulation, are clearly established. The *disadvantages* and limitations are quite severe, most importantly because of the potential conflict between the aim of protecting freedom of publication and making the media accountable. The fear of penalties can work in much the same way as (pre-publication) censorship, even where this is not legitimate. Law and regulation are easier to apply to structures (for example, questions of ownership) than to content, where freedom of expression arises and where definitions are difficult. In general, law and regulation give more advantage to those with power and money, even when the intention is to protect the interests of all. Having evaluated systems of media accountability across the African continent, Tettey (2006) notes that state-controlled mechanisms are not always conducive to democracy, because they can be subject to abuse and tend to be fraught with political tension.

Finally, it has been observed that laws and regulations are often ineffective, hard to enforce, unpredictable in their wider and long-term effects and hard to change or remove when they become out of date. They can also become part of a system of vested interests (for instance, in matters of subsidy or licensing).

## THE MARKET FRAME

The market has not always been seen as a significant mechanism of public accountability, but in practice it is an important means for balancing the interests of media organizations and producers and those of their clients and audiences (consumers). The *mechanisms* are the normal processes of demand and supply in a free (and therefore competitive) market that should in theory encourage 'good' and discourage 'bad' performance. Various kinds of audience and market research provide evidence, additional to sales, about the public response to what is offered by the media.

In principle, a wide range of issues is covered by market accountability, although the main focus is on aspects of communication 'quality' as seen by the consumer. Quality relates not only to content, but also to technical quality. The market should encourage improvement by way of competition. There is no *compulsion* involved in control through market forces, which is one of the *advantages* of the approach. The laws of supply and demand should ensure that the interests of producers and consumers are kept in balance. The system is self-regulating and self-correcting, with no need for outside regulation or control.

The *limitations* of the market have probably received more attention than have the advantages. From one critical perspective, the main problem of the media is that they are too 'commercialized', meaning organized for ends of profit rather than communication and lacking any true standard of quality. From this point of view, the market cannot serve as a check on itself. Without taking this principled standpoint, there are other arguments against the market as a means of accounting. One is the fact that markets are rarely perfect and the theoretical advantages of competition are not realized. Where private monopoly develops, there is no effective counterweight to media practices that seek only to maximize short-term gain. Market thinking tends to define freedom and quality of media in terms of freedom and welfare of media owners.

## THE FRAME OF PUBLIC RESPONSIBILITY

This refers to the fact that the media organizations are also social institutions that fulfil, with varying degrees of voluntariness and explicit commitment, certain important public tasks that go beyond their immediate goals of making profits and giving employment. Dennis et al. (1989) use the term 'fiduciary' model to refer to a similar idea of media being held in trust on behalf of the public. Others have written of a 'trustee model' of media, based on a similar notion, but usually with reference to public broadcasting (Hoffmann-Riem, 1996; Feintuck, 1999). Whether they acknowledge this or not, public opinion in open societies generally expects the media (taken as a whole) to serve the public interest in matters of information, publicity and culture. Where media are seen to be failing, they may be called to account by public opinion or other guardians of the public interest, including politicians.

The *mechanisms and procedures* mainly consist of the activities of pressure groups, including media consumer organizations and the public opinion surveys by which general public opinion is expressed. In a number of countries, there are various forms of press or broadcasting councils and procedures for public complaint that are adopted voluntarily by the media industry as a means of meeting claims from society. Governments have sometimes instituted commissions and inquiries to assess performance. Some media are operated as public trusts on a non-profit basis to serve some public informational or social purpose. The very large volume of public debate, review and criticism, often carried by the media (or some of them), is an important means of informal control.

The main *advantages* of a developed public responsibility frame include the fact that the needs of society can be expressed in a direct way – by claims made, on the media, to provide for these needs. In addition, intrinsic to this frame is the idea of a continuous interactive relationship between media and society. The public can answer back to the media in their roles as citizens or members of some interest group or minority (not just as consumers or as individuals with legal rights), and the media are under pressure to respond and have the means to do so. This mode of accountability is very open and democratic by definition as well as being voluntary and therefore protective of freedom.

There are also *limitations*. An obvious weakness is the very voluntary character mentioned. Some media reject the trustee status and will use their freedom not to be responsible. There is not necessarily any real 'system' of accountability here, except in relation to public broadcasting, and it works better in some countries and traditions than in others. Trends towards globalization (multinational control of media) and media concentration undermine this model.

## THE FRAME OF PROFESSIONAL RESPONSIBILITY

This refers to accountability that arises out of the self-respect and ethical development of professionals working in the media (for example, journalists, advertisers, public relations), who set their own standards of good performance. It can also apply to associations of owners, editors, producers, and so on, that aim to protect the interests of the industry by self-regulation.

The *mechanisms and procedures* generally consist of a published set of principles or code of conduct that is adopted by members of a media professional group, together with some procedures for hearing and judging complaints and claims against particular media actions. The *issues* can be any matter dealt with in the code of ethics or conduct, but normally relating to some harm or offence caused to an individual or group. The development of professionalism in the media is often supported by government and other public institutions and assisted by improved education and training.

The *advantages* are that the system of accountability (in so far as there is one) is generally likely to work because it is both voluntary and in the self-interest of the media and professionals. It has the benefit of being non-coercive and it encourages voluntary self-improvement as well as self-control. In practice, there are also considerable *limitations*. It is narrow in its application and does not usually exert strong pressure on powerful media.

It is not sufficiently independent of the media themselves and is also very fragmentary in its coverage (Fengler, 2003). In general, professionalism is not very strongly developed within the media and employees have relatively little autonomy in relation to management and owners. Furthermore, as Wasserman (2010) notes, there is no clear consensus about what media freedom and responsibility means to various role-players in the media system – for example, in the context of new African democracies.

## COMPARATIVE ASSESSMENT

It is clear that in an open society there are likely to be many overlapping processes of accountability but no complete system, and no single one of the 'frames' described is sufficient for the task on its own or uniquely superior to the others. There are many gaps (performance issues are not dealt with adequately), and some media accept no responsibility except what is imposed by market forces.

The diversity of forms and means of accountability can be considered a positive feature in itself, even if the overall result is not satisfactory. In general, according to the principle of openness, we should prefer forms of accountability that are transparent, voluntary, and based on active relationships and dialogue and debate. The alternatives of external control, legal compulsion and threats of punishment may be more effective in the short term, and sometimes the only way to achieve some goals, but in the long term they run counter to the spirit of the open society.

## CONCLUSION

In this chapter, the main normative principles that apply to the working of media, the standards they are widely expected to adhere to, have been described. The processes of accountability that have been briefly outlined, although they improve the chances of implementation of the standards outlined, are not to be confused with means of control by government or anyone else. They are not incompatible with media freedom, but are inescapable components of the normal operating environment of media in an open society.

The continuing changes in the media have not yet fundamentally altered the *content* of the norms described, but they have affected their relative force and the priorities among them. The increasing number of alternative media channels, in particular, has reduced the pressure on seemingly 'dominant' media (for instance, the national newspaper press or broadcast television) to fulfil some perceived public roles. There is probably less fear of media monopoly, despite concentration tendencies towards oligopolies, because the potential for competition is greater – particularly on a global scale. More media channels also seem to promise more diversity, although the quality of that diversity is far from assured.

With the Internet, new claims for (and rules about) the responsibility and accountability of media operating online are emerging, specifically when it comes to concerns about the market dominance and privacy-related features of platforms such as Facebook and Google. Beyond specific regulations and expectations regarding the press, other media professions are also confronted with accountability systems, for example regarding gender stereotypes in advertising or the percentage of national content on international streaming services such as Netflix. Although the Internet has often been claimed to be 'ungovernable' (Lessig, 1999), it is hard to imagine that it would be able to escape accountability indefinitely. Apart from this, of course, too much systematic accountability would run counter to the promise of freedom and diversity that is a main benefit of the contemporary media environment.

## FURTHER READING

Bertrand, C.-J. (2003) *An Arsenal for Democracy: Media Accountancy Systems*. Creskill, NJ: Hampton Press.

Everwein, T., Fengler, S. and Karmasin, M. (2019) *Media Accountability in the Era of Post-truth Politics: European Challenges and Perspectives*. Boca Raton, FL: CRC Press.

Kreiss, D. and McGregor, S.C. (2019) 'The "arbiters of what our voters see": Facebook and Google's struggle with policy, process, and enforcement around political advertising', *Political Communication*, 36(4): 499–522.

Lauk, E. and Kus, L. (2012) 'Media accountability – between tradition and innovation', *Central European Journal of Communication*, 2: 168–174.

McQuail, D. (1992) *Media Performance: Mass Communication and the Public Interest*. London: Sage.

Müller, L. (2014) *Comparing Mass Media in Established Democracies: Patterns of Media Performance*. Basingstoke: Palgrave Macmillan.

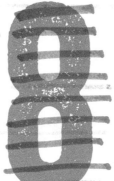

# 8

# MEDIA ECONOMICS AND GOVERNANCE

So far, mass media have been discussed as if they were an institution *of* society rather than an industry *in* society. They have become increasingly more of the latter without necessarily becoming less of the former, and an understanding of the main principles of the structure and dynamics of the media calls for an economic as well as a political and a social-cultural analysis. Although the media have grown up in response to the social and cultural needs of individuals and societies, they are largely run as business enterprises. A trend in this direction has accelerated in recent decades for several reasons, especially because of the increasing industrial and economic significance of the entire information and communication sector. Associated with this is the widespread privatization of state telecommunication enterprises and an extension of their activities nationally and internationally. The shift to free-market economies in former communist or more or less dictatorial states has been an additional factor. Even where media are run as public bodies, they are more subject to financial discipline and operate in competitive environments.

A book about media and mass communication theory is not the place for a thorough treatment of these matters, but it is impossible to understand the social and cultural implications of mass media without at least a sketch of the wider political and economic forces at work shaping (the behaviour of) media institutions. The public regulation, control, and economics of media embody certain general principles that belong to the sphere of theory, and the decisions media institutions make play an important role in shaping both the public arena and the private sphere. The aim of this chapter is to explain these principles, avoiding detail of local and temporary circumstances.

---

## MEDIA 'NOT JUST ANY OTHER BUSINESS'

The key to the unusual character of the media institution is that its activities are inextricably both economic and political as well as being very dependent on continually changing technologies. These activities involve the production of goods and services which are often both private (consumption for individual personal satisfaction) and public (viewed as necessary for the working of society as a whole and also in the public domain). The public character of the media derives mainly from the political function of the media in a democracy, but also from the fact that information, culture and ideas are considered as the collective property of all. Nor, as with other public goods, such as air and daylight, does their use diminish their availability for others.

More specifically, mass media have grown up historically with a strong and widely shared image as having an important part to play in public life and being essentially within the public domain. What media do or do not do has mattered to societies, and this has been reflected in complex systems of ideas about what they should or should not be doing (see Chapter 7). It is also reflected in varied mechanisms to encourage, influence, protect or limit them on behalf of a supposed 'public interest'. Despite this, the media generally have to operate wholly or partly according to the dictates of market economics. Even in this aspect, they may attract the attention of governments for the same reasons that other private businesses are subject to various forms of legal and economic regulation.

## ALTERNATIVE THEORETICAL PERSPECTIVES

Not surprisingly, there is no agreed objective description of the media institution that can be separated from the varying national/societal circumstances in which media operate. One option is to apply an *economic/industrial* perspective (see Tunstall, 1991), looking at the distinctive and varying characteristics of the media as economic enterprises, as between different media and different contexts. An alternative perspective is that offered by critical *political-economic* theory (as introduced on p. 125). This provides concepts derived especially from the critique of capitalism, with reference to processes of concentration of ownership and commercialization. A third main possibility is to examine media structures according to a *public interest* or policy perspective in the light of normative criteria of conduct and performance that have been discussed in the previous chapter. There is a fourth possibility: to look at the media institution from an *internal* or *media professional* point of view. Each of these perspectives will be drawn on for some purposes in the following pages.

We can represent the unique position of media as being at the centre of three main forces – political, economic and technological – and thereby requiring alternative modes of analysis (Figure 8.1).

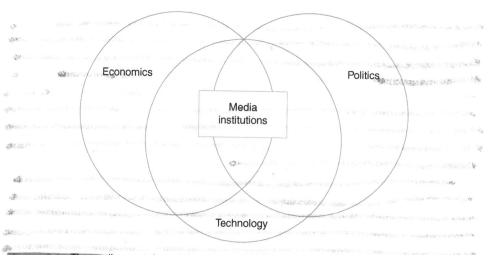

Figure 8.1   The media are at the centre of three overlapping kinds of influence

A theoretical analysis is only possible if certain general issues or problems are first identified. At a descriptive level, we focus mainly on the question of *differences*. How do media differ from each other in economic and policy terms? How and why are the economics and regulation of media untypical both of normal business and of normal public services? How and why do national media institutions vary in structure and control? This last aspect of the comparison is important precisely because media are not only businesses, responding to economic forces, but are also deeply rooted (usually nationally based) social and cultural institutions.

There is also relevant theory concerning the current *dynamics* of media industries, especially the trends towards expansion, diversification and convergence of media, mainly on the basis of new technology and new economic opportunities, enabled by trends towards deregulation (for example, regarding restrictions on media ownership). There are trends towards the concentration, integration and internationalization of media activity. Of particular significance is the gradual convergence of the technology, media and telecommunications sectors of the economy as a response to the challenges and opportunities of the Internet as a mass medium (Faustino and Noam, 2019). Four main questions arise here. First, what are the likely consequences of media concentration and can the trends indicated be managed on behalf of the public interest? Secondly, what are the consequences of media internationalization for media and society? Thirdly, how far is media change being driven by technology and how far by economics or politics and social forces? Fourthly, the expansion and convergence of media-based communication by way of telecommunications and ICTs, especially mobile phones and the Internet, have raised new regulatory issues as well as creating pressure for regulation that did not exist before. In particular, the telecommunications system is increasingly a vehicle for distributing content that was originally broadcast, such as films, music and television. This is one example of the convergence of technology, with all media digitalized and, in principle, interconnected.

The main questions for theory are posed in Box 8.1.

## 8.1

### Questions for theory arising from economy and governance

- How do particular media differ in economic and political terms?
- How and why do national media systems differ in structure and control?
- How and why are the economics of media different from those of other industries?

*(Continued)*

- What are the causes and consequences of media concentration?
- What are the causes and consequences of internationalization?
- What is the relative weight of technological developments as a force for media change?
- How is the performance of media affected by the source of finance?

# THE BASICS OF MEDIA STRUCTURE AND LEVELS OF ANALYSIS

The scene can be set by a reminder of the main features of economically developed media systems. The term 'media system' refers to the actual set of mass media in a given national society, despite the fact that there may be no formal connection between the elements. Most media systems, in this sense, are the chance result of historical growth, with one new technology after another being developed and leading to the adaptation of existing media. Sometimes a media system is linked by a shared political-economic logic, as with the free-enterprise media of the USA or the state-run media of China. Many countries have 'mixed' systems, with private and public elements, and these may well be organized according to a set of national media policy principles, leading to a degree of integration. Occasionally, there may be a single ministry of communications, or communications regulatory body, which has some responsibilities across a range of different media, private or public, which adds another 'systemic' component (Robillard, 1995). The media may also be treated as a coherent system by their audiences or by advertisers, and certainly the term 'the media' is often used in this collective sense.

Within the media system, specific different types are to be found based on different medium technologies: print, television, radio, recorded music, the Internet, telecommunications, and so on. However, these are often subdivided into different 'media forms', for instance print media into books, magazines, newspapers. The resulting groupings may also be described as media 'sectors', especially in policy discourse or for purposes of economic analysis, but the divisions are often arbitrary and *ad hoc*, so the unity of such 'sectors' is often as illusory as is that of the whole system. There are many differentiating as well as integrating factors (especially through separate or shared distribution systems, as well as through franchising and transmedia productions). For instance, the medium of film can refer to the cinema, video and disc hire or sale, broadcast, subscription or streaming television, and so on. These are different means of distribution, often different businesses and organizations, although there is usually some form of vertical integration. Film can also refer to just one element of a broader franchise (such as the Marvel Cinematic Universe or Pokémon) that can include digital games, television series, (comic) books and magazines, mobile applications, websites, and online communities. Such franchises and **transmedia** properties (where various media forms are part of a broader storyworld) have become the primary focus of the bigger media corporations, as they allow tie-ins across a range of different media.

We need to distinguish another unit of analysis: that of the firm or enterprise, which may constitute a significant part of a sector or have holdings which cut across boundaries of media type or geography (the multimedia, and often multinational, firm). Some media products can be regarded as belonging to specific 'genres' (for example, international news, romantic fiction, etc.) and finally as particular products (as a film, book title, song, etc.) for purposes of analysis, independent of the medium or sector. The main (approximate) media system components are shown in Box 8.2. A new and somewhat different element has been added in the form of the Internet platform. Generally, these firms did not start as media companies, but gradually evolved to acquire and include media offerings, such as streaming audio and video, digital games and online news, as part of their portfolio in order to generate more traffic to their platforms. Major examples include Google, Apple, Facebook, Amazon and Microsoft in the West, and Tencent, Reliance and Rakuten in the East. As the term implies, platforms are places where producers and consumers of media products and services meet. Their economic power is derived from network effects, whereby a platform gains additional value as more people use it, and as a platform becomes a prominent interface where businesses and consumers meet it reduces the likelihood of new platforms entering the market. Although these platforms are the

---

## 8.2

## Media structure and levels of analysis

- International media
- Media system (all national media)
- Multimedia firm (with major holdings in several media)
- Media sector (newspapers, books, television, film, music, etc.)
- Circulation/distribution area (nation, region, city, locality)
- Unit medium channel (newspaper title, television station, etc.)
- Particular genre
- Unit media product (book, film, song, etc.)
- Internet platforms

---

properties of firms that are based on specific countries, they operate on a global scale and through countless intermediaries, introducing a somewhat separate level of analyses when it comes to understanding the contemporary media institution.

# SOME ECONOMIC PRINCIPLES OF MEDIA STRUCTURE

## DIFFERENT MEDIA MARKETS AND SOURCES OF INCOME

According to Picard (1989: 17), 'A market consists of sellers that provide the same good or service, or closely substitutable goods or services, to the same group of consumers'. In general, markets can be defined according to place, people, type of revenue and the nature of the product or service. At the heart of the inner workings of media firms big and small is their business model – how a company creates value at all levels of the business value chain: ideation, creation, production, packaging, promotion and marketing, distributing and consumption.

The mainstream media of newspapers, radio and television can be classified according to a fundamental line of economic division between the *consumer market* for media products and services and the *advertising market*, in which a product or service is sold to advertisers in the form of access to the audience. Often there is no distinction between the two, since newspapers, for example, provide both types of market at the same time. One can note that within the consumer market there is another division: between transactions for 'one-off' products like books, games, videos and newspapers sold directly to consumers, and those for subscriptions to continuous media services like cable or broadcast television or streaming media. In fact, there are other sources of income besides the two mentioned, and as revenue from advertising and sales is declining in the face of global competition and rising costs involved with maintaining media productions and firms, such alternative income sources are increasingly important. They include sponsorship, merchandising, product placement and public relations, as well as public money and support from private backers, non-profit trusts, and not forgetting direct support from an audience (for example, through gifts, membership or crowdfunding).

The Internet has added further complication since companies and creators have to find new sources of revenue while covering more costs, including the expense of being online, payments for websites, coding and programming, data management and analytics. It has also undermined the economics of older media by making most content available without charge or open to piracy. The first victim of advertising on the Internet seems to be the newspaper in both local and national variants. This impact seems irreversible as far as the 'mass audience' for news is concerned. The share of all advertising taken by online media has grown steadily since the turn of the century, and within that category are several different types, especially display, search and classified advertising. This has presented several practical and theoretical problems.

The most pressing practical problem has been to obtain some measure of value of 'audience' use in order to charge advertisers. Bermejo (2009) has charted the story of different efforts to measure the audience, ending up with the concept of a 'visit' or 'click' as an indicator of frequency of use. However, this gives no indication of the time spent on a particular site, and other means of pricing have to be found to charge those who want to place advertisements or messages in other locations, especially platforms and search engines, that are a focus of interest because of their high popularity and profitability (Machill, Beiler and Zenker, 2008). As audiences for media content are increasingly aggregated by Internet platforms, rather than the media industries involved with the production and marketing of the content, such platforms pose significant challenges for media firms to earn a return on their investment. On the other hand, through a platform media makers and firms can access vast (new) audiences and build relationships with them (more on this in Chapters 10 and 11). The theoretical problems mentioned relate especially to the implications for the 'commodification' of content and relations with the audience.

## ADVERTISING, CONSUMER AND FLEXIBLE REVENUE: IMPLICATIONS

The difference between the three main sources of revenue for media industries – direct product sales, advertising, and alternative or flexible income streams derived from a variety of sources – is still a useful tool for comparative analysis and for explaining media features and trends. The distinction cuts across the difference between media types, although some media are rather unsuitable for advertising, while others can operate equally in different markets (especially television, radio, newspapers, magazines and the Internet). There are some 'advertising revenue only' media, with little or no consumer revenue – for instance, free newspapers, promotional magazines, quite a lot of television, and Internet platforms.

The distinction also has a non-economic significance. In particular, it is usually thought (from the critical or public interest and professional perspectives) that the higher the dependence on advertising as a source of revenue, the less independent the content from the interests of the advertisers and business generally. This does not necessarily mean less independence, but it may imply less credibility as an information source, if the content of news relates to what is advertised, and less creative autonomy. In the extreme case of media that are totally financed or sponsored by advertising, the ostensible content is hard if not impossible to distinguish from advertising itself, propaganda or public relations. This is particularly the case for 'native' advertising: productions that appear in a news medium that resemble the publication's editorial content, but are paid for by an advertiser and intended to promote the advertiser's product or brand.

Native advertising is described as a new way for advertisers to reach audiences, and as an additional source of revenue for news organizations. There is significant potential to deceive audiences, as journalists, advertising and public relations professionals agree (Schauster, Ferrucci and Neill, 2016). Research among audiences suggests that consumers, if they recognize such editorial content as advertising, they would evaluate the material more negatively (Wojdynski and Evans, 2016). Similar strategies abound in non-news media, with advertisers providing or participating in scriptwriting for television series and motion pictures next to more established strategies, such as product placement (including in digital games).

The question of advertiser influence on media organizations is discussed again in Chapter 10. There is little doubt about certain general kinds of influence, such as the bias towards youth and higher-income groups and the preference for neutral rather than politicized media (Tunstall and Machin, 1999).

From the economic perspective, operation in the different markets raises other considerations. One is the question of financing, since the costs of advertising-supported media are usually covered in advance of production, while in the consumer market the income has to follow the production and publication of content. When multiple or flexible sources of revenue are involved, a delicate balance has to be struck between investments in the various stages of the value chain of media. A direct consequence of the decline of advertising as a main source of revenue has been a shift of investment in major media firms from production to distribution, marketing and promotion. Bilton (2017) theorizes a 'disappearing product' in this context, as media products are no longer the primary source of value in the media industries.

Secondly, there are different criteria and methods for assessing market performance. Advertising-based media are assessed according to the number and type of consumers (who they are, where they live) reached by particular messages (for example, circulation, readership and reach/ratings), and the extent to which this reach translates into what the industry calls 'engagement': a measure of consumer activity – including some kind of interactive connection, attachment and emotional involvement – around a particular brand, product or service (Brodie, Hollebeek, Jurić and Ilić, 2011). These measures are necessary for attracting would-be advertising clients and for establishing the rates that can be charged. The market performance of media content that is paid for directly by consumers is assessed by the income received from sales and subscriptions. Ratings of (qualitative and quantitative) satisfaction and popularity are relevant to both markets, and are increasingly datafied as information from engagement and sales are measured and translated – often instantaneously – into data that are used to modify media products and services. In a review of how media production changes under the influence of 'platformization' and the real-time measurement of market performance, Nieborg and Poell (2019: 85) conclude that media products and services accessible via digital platforms become 'contingent commodities': malleable, modular in design, informed by datafied user feedback, and open to constant revision and recirculation.

Performance in one market can affect performance in another, where a medium operates in both. For instance, an increase in newspaper sales (producing more consumer revenue) can lead to higher advertising rates, provided that the increase does not lead to a lower than average level of socio-economic composition, with a reverse effect on unit advertising rates. It is also clear that the difference of revenue base can lead to different kinds of opportunity or vulnerability to wider economic circumstances. Media that are heavily dependent on advertising are likely to be more sensitive to the negative impact of general economic downturns than media that sell (usually low-cost) products to individual consumers. The latter may also be in a better position to cut costs in the face of falls in demand (but this depends on the cost structure of production).

Most media companies, whether traditional or digital, are in the process of changing business models to subscription-based ones or a mixed model of subscription, advertising and other sources of revenue. According to Chan-Olmsted and Wang (2019), the success of such subscription-based models signals a rise of consumer sovereignty in the media sector. The empowerment of media consumers here translates to advertising avoidance and consumer willingness to pay for high-quality content and a good consumption experience.

## MEDIA MARKET REACH AND DIVERSITY

The difference between the key revenue markets interacts with other features of the media market. As noted above, the social composition of the audience reached (and 'sold' to advertisers) is important because of differences in purchasing power and in the type of goods advertised. There is a logic in the advertising-based mass media which favours a convergence of media tastes and consumption patterns (less diversity). This is because homogeneous audiences are often more cost-effective for advertisers than heterogeneous and dispersed markets (unless they are very large mass markets for mass products). This is one reason for the viability of the free newspaper that provides complete coverage of a particular area with relatively high homogeneity (Bakker, 2002). However, in a digital economy there can be a premium on diversity, when a medium can accurately deliver small but profitable niche markets. This is one of the potentials of the Internet – at times called a 'long tail' economy consisting of many niches rather than a mass market, although both types of market structures are common online.

The relationship between the pursuit of mass markets and homogeneity of audience is much less clear in the case of the Internet, since the enormous capacity of the latter enables it to reach a great variety of audiences with a great variety of content – even within the same platform or service. This does not necessarily mean the start of a new era of diverse and unstratified media provision, since the economic model of online media tends to respond mostly to network effects, favouring the largest websites, platforms and streaming services. A major innovation of the Internet as an advertising medium is its capacity to target and reach many dispersed markets for particular products and services, based on data obtained from online clicks, time spent and other sources of our 'digital shadow' (including surveillance through 'smart' speakers, transcriptions of voice-over-Internet calls and chat logs).

## COMPETITION FOR REVENUE

It has been argued more generally that 'competition for a single revenue source results in imitative uniformity' (Tunstall, 1991: 182). Tunstall suggests that this is the reason for the perceived 'low-taste' quality (or just 'imitative uniformity') of North American network television, which is financed almost entirely from mass *consumer* advertising (see DeFleur and Ball-Rokeach, 1989). The same applies to the alleged low standards of the British tabloid newspapers, which compete for much the same mass (down-)market. Certainly, one of the benefits argued for a public sector television has been that it avoids the situation where all broadcasting competes for the same audience revenue sources (for example, Peacock, 1986). However, it is also the case that advertising itself is increasingly diversified, allowing support for a wide range of media content. The competition of different media for the same advertising income can encourage diversity. The degree and kind of competition are important modifying variables. Reliance on advertising as such need not lead to uniformity of provision.

There has been a rapid growth in the use of the Internet for advertising. Network and public television are increasingly taking a back seat to surfing the Web, digital games and streaming video services, which all have more diversified sources of revenue next to advertising. Traditional media companies, such as newspaper publishers and broadcasting organizations, are in particularly precarious positions *vis-à-vis* other media businesses competing for the attention of the audience.

## MEDIA COST STRUCTURE

The issue of media cost structure was noted earlier as a variable in the economic fortunes of media. One of the peculiarities of traditional mass media as compared with some other economic enterprises is the potential imbalance between the 'fixed costs' and the 'variable costs' of production. The former refers to such things as land, physical plant, equipment and distribution network. The variable costs refer to materials, 'software' and (sometimes) labour. The higher the ratio of fixed to variable costs, the more vulnerable a business is to a changing market environment, and traditional mass media typically have a high ratio, with heavy capital investments (such as printing presses, studios and other costly infrastructure) which have to be recouped later by subscription, sales and advertising revenue.

It is in the nature of the typical media product that it has a very high 'first-copy' cost. A single daily newspaper or the first print of a film carries all the burden of the fixed costs, while the marginal cost of additional copies rapidly declines. This makes traditional media, such as newspapers, vulnerable to fluctuations in demand and in advertising revenue, puts a premium on economies of scale and exerts a pressure towards agglomeration. It also exerts pressure towards the separation of production from distribution since the latter often involves high fixed costs (for instance, cinemas, cable networks, satellites and transmitters). High fixed costs also erect a high barrier to would-be new entrants into the media business. Under authoritarian regimes, the economic vulnerability of newspapers as well as broadcasting services has made it easier for governments to threaten them with very costly interruptions of supply or distribution.

In this matter also, digital media opened up new uncertainties for the established media. Fixed costs can be much lower than with traditional media, with much lower entry costs and therefore greater ease of entering the market. Nevertheless, the production costs of high value content that competes for high popularity in international markets such as films and games will continue to be under upward pressure. New factors have also been introduced into the media market with the appearance of new formats and websites, such as social networking or online marketplaces and platforms, and the general appearance of user-produced content. The division between fixed and variable costs is less relevant to new developments. In response, many traditional media companies are in the process of reorganizing their cost structures and workflows to accommodate the new media context, for example by newspapers becoming 'digital first' publications. This process frequently involves cutting fixed costs in all phases of the value chain, including labour. In summary, Box 8.3 lists the main conclusions that have been drawn from the study of media markets.

---

8.3

## Economic principles of media markets

- Media still differ according to whether they have fixed or variable cost structures
- Media markets have an increasingly multiple-income character, especially online
- Media based on advertising revenue are more vulnerable to unwanted external influence on content
- Media based on consumer revenue are vulnerable to shortage of finance
- Different sources of revenue require different measures of market performance

*(Continued)*

- Where a multiple market applies, performance in one market can affect performance in another
- Advertising in specialist media can promote diversity of supply
- Certain kinds of advertising benefit from concentration of the audience market
- Competition for the same revenue sources leads to uniformity
- Market performance is increasingly determined by consumer engagement

# OWNERSHIP AND CONTROL

Fundamental to an understanding of media structure is the question of ownership and how the powers of ownership are exercised. The belief that ownership ultimately determines the nature of media is not just a question of political economy, but virtually a common-sense axiom summed up in Altschull's (1984: 254) 'second law of journalism': 'the contents of the media always reflect the interests of those who finance them'. Not surprisingly, there are several different forms of ownership of different media, and the powers of ownership can be exercised in different ways.

As implied by Altschull's remark, it is not just ownership that counts; it is a wider question of who actually pays for the media product. Although there are media whose owners do personally pay for the privilege of influencing content, most owners just want profit (and some prestige), and most media are financed from different sources. These include a range of private investors (among them other media companies), advertisers, consumers, various public or private subsidy givers, and governments. It follows that the line of influence from ownership is often indirect and complex – and it is rarely the only line of influence.

Most media belong to one of three categories of ownership: commercial companies, private non-profit bodies and the public sector. However, within each of these there are significant divisions. For media ownership it will be relevant whether a company is public or private, a large media chain or conglomerate or a small independent. It may also matter whether or not a media enterprise is owned by a so-called 'media tycoon' or 'mogul', typified as wanting to take a personal interest in editorial policy (Tunstall and Palmer, 1991). Non-profit bodies can be neutral trusts, designed to safeguard independence of operations (as with the *Guardian* newspaper), or bodies with a special cultural or social task, such as political parties, churches, and so on. Public ownership also comes in many different forms, ranging from direct state administration to elaborate and diversified constructions designed to maximize the independence of decision-making about content.

The structure of ownership and organization in the media sector has a 'polarized' structure and tends to look like an hourglass, with a handful of large multinational organizations at one end of the hourglass, few medium-sized companies in the middle, and a large number of small-sized enterprises at the other end. Furthermore, the larger companies are interconnected in multiple ways, often not through formal ownership but rather through business partnerships, collaborations and financial arrangements. Increasingly, the large corporations from one part of the industry, such as advertising, film or games, are also engaged in other media, seeking to converge operations or diversify their assets (Hesmondhalgh, 2018). A more normal industrial size distribution would have fewer large organizations and more middle-sized organizations creating a pyramid in place of the hourglass. As stated in a report from the European Commission on the media and cultural sector, this particular structure creates a corresponding 'hourglass effect' in the distribution of employment, 'with concentrations of people working in either the small number of larger companies, or the growing multitude of small and micro-businesses. Most workers in the sector – apart from a few executives – experience job mobility, seasonal variations, discontinuous career development, short-term contracts, part-time working, extended working hours, a vocational ethos and multiple jobs (leading to an accumulation of work and expertise both inside and outside the media)' (Hackett, Ramsden, Sattar and Guene, 2000: 4).

## THE EFFECTS OF OWNERSHIP

For mass communication theory, it is nearly always the ultimate publication decision that matters most. Liberal theory rests on the assumption that ownership can be effectively separated from control of editorial decisions. Larger (allocative) decisions about resources, business strategy, and the like, are taken by owners or boards of owners, while producers, editors and other decision-makers are left free to take the professional decisions about content which is their special expertise. Regarding journalism, in some situations and countries there are intermediary institutional arrangements (such as editorial statutes) designed to safeguard the integrity of editorial policy and the freedom of journalists. Otherwise, professionalism, codes of conduct, public reputation (since media are always in the public eye) and common (business) sense are supposed to take care of the seeming problem of undue owner influence (this is discussed in Chapter 10). In the digital age, consumers are also becoming a force to be reckoned with for media companies and owners. For example, if an owner threatens to end a television series, consumers can take to social media to informally organize a campaign to protest against the decision, sometimes forcing a reversal.

The existence of checks and balances cannot, however, obscure several facts of life for everyday media management. One is that, ultimately, commercial media have to make profits to survive, and this often involves taking decisions that directly influence content (such as cutting costs, closing down, shedding staff, investing or not, and merging operations; see Doyle, 2013). Publicly owned media do not escape an equivalent market logic, especially now that the public sector is under pressure by many governments around the world. It is also a fact that most private media have a vested interest in the capitalist system and are inclined to give support to its most obvious defenders – mainstream political parties, especially those on the more conservative end of the ideological spectrum. There are many less obvious ways in which a similar tendency operates, not least potential pressure from large advertisers.

Public ownership is thought to neutralize or balance these particular pressures, although that too means following a certain editorial line (albeit one of neutrality). The conventional wisdom of liberal theory suggests that the best or only solution to such problems lies in multiplicity of private ownership. The ideal situation would be one in which many small or medium-sized companies compete with each other for the interest of the public by offering a wide range of ideas, information and types of culture. The power that goes with ownership is not necessarily bad in itself but only becomes so when concentrated or used selectively to limit or deny access. This position underestimates the fundamental tension between market criteria of size and profit and social-cultural criteria of quality and influence. They may simply not be reconcilable (Baker, 2007), or at the very least operate in constant tension. The issue of concentration lies at the heart of the theoretical debate. The key propositions about ownership and control are presented in Box 8.4.

## 8.4
### Media ownership and control

- Freedom of the press supports the rights of owners to decide on content
- Form of ownership inevitably has an influence on content
- Multiplicity of ownership and free competition are the best defence against misuse of powers of ownership
- There are usually checks and balances in the system to limit undesirable owner influence, including consumer power online

## COMPETITION AND CONCENTRATION

In the theory of media structure, much attention has been paid to the question of uniformity and diversity. Most social theory concerned with the 'public interest' places a value

MCQUAIL'S MEDIA AND MASS COMMUNICATION THEORY
STRUCTURES

on diversity, and there is also an economic dimension involved: that of monopoly versus competition. Free competition, as noted, should lead to variety and to a change of media structure, although critics point to a reverse effect: that it leads to monopoly, or at least oligopoly (undesirable on economic as well as social grounds) (Lacy and Martin, 2004). As far as media economics are concerned, there are three main aspects to the question: *intermedia* competition, *intramedium* competition and *interfirm* competition. Intermedia competition depends chiefly on whether products can be substituted for one another (such as news on the Internet for news on television or in the newspaper), and on whether advertising can be substituted from one medium to another. Both substitutions are possible but they occur only up to a certain point. There always appears to be some 'niche' in which a particular medium has an advantage (Dimmick and Rothenbuhler, 1984). All media types also seem to be able to offer some distinctive advantages to advertisers: of form of message, timing, type of audience, context of reception, and so on (Picard, 1989). The rise of the Internet is challenging all media on several points at once (see Küng, Picard and Towse, 2008).

## HORIZONTAL VERSUS VERTICAL CONCENTRATION

In general, because units of the *same* medium sector are more readily substitutable than those *between* media, the focus of attention is often directed at intramedium competition (such as of one newspaper with another in the same market, geographically or otherwise defined). This is where concentration has most tended to develop – within the same medium sector (this may also in part be the result of public policies to limit crossmedia monopoly). In general, media concentration has been distinguished according to whether it is 'horizontal' or 'vertical'. Vertical concentration refers to a pattern of ownership that extends through different stages of production and distribution (for instance, a film studio owning a cinema chain) or geographically (a national concern buying city or local newspapers, say).

Large media corporations tend to go through phases of increased concentration and deconcentration, often making large profits in the process of acquiring or selling off businesses, properties and assets. In the process, non-media companies come to own media assets for a variety of reasons. As Noam (2018) shows in a comparison of such trends across twenty-six countries, such acquisitions follow three distinct rationales: first, to seek influence for personal or business interests; secondly, to pursue business collaborations and synergies across the conglomerate; and thirdly, as a way to diversify the portfolio of firms, products and services. Although such cross-ownership of media and non-media companies was popular in the twentieth century and continues to be a rising presence in Latin America, the Arab world and India, overall Noam concludes that 'conglomerates with media dimensions have not done well in highly developed countries with a relatively competitive business structure' (ibid.: 1105). Reasons for this lack of success over time have to do with the (real or perceived) complexity of managing such conglomerates, a lack of flexibility in moving with changing market demands, cultural incompatibilities, and a preference among investors for more focused companies. In recent years more indirect forms of cross-ownership have emerged, largely through finance and investment firms.

While the overall tendency toward convergence and concentration is a structural feature of the global media industry (Flew, 2018), there is also a trend towards 'disaggregation' of media activities, especially the separation of production activity from promotion, marketing and distribution. This has been accelerated by the Internet because there are many competing providers of content and there is an over-abundance of media content and production. The old-style hierarchy of control of large media firms over the production process has given way to a more unstructured network model in which market arrangements drive the relations between parts of the organization rather than direct 'command and control' (Collins, 2008).

Horizontal concentration refers to mergers within the same market (for example, of two competing city or national newspaper organizations, or of a telephone and a cable network). Both of these processes have happened on a large scale in a number of countries, although the effects may have been modified by continuing intermedia choice and the rise of new media. Diversity is often protected by public policies against 'crossmedia ownership' (different media being owned and operated by the same firm, especially in the same geographical market). The media can also become involved in horizontal concentration through the merging of firms in different industries, so that a newspaper or television channel can be owned by a non-media business (see Murdock, 1990). This does not directly reduce media diversity but can add to the power of mass media, and has greatly contributed to the rise of media corporations as a significant force in economic as well as cultural and political life.

Strictly in terms of ownership of multiple properties, Noam (2018) finds that the media in the USA are less concentrated than many other countries. The most concentrated national media systems are China, Egypt, South Africa, Russia, Turkey and Mexico. Beyond the number of media outlets and assets a company owns, Benson (2019) argues for media and mass communication scholarship to take a closer look at forms of ownership. He identifies five forms of media ownership:

- stock market traded firms, where most, if not all, business decisions are subsequent to the pressure to maximize shareholder profits;
- dominant shareholder ownership, where one owner, group or family of owners may counterbalance the need to turn a profit;
- private ownership, including individual or family ownership as well as private investors, such as hedge funds;

- public or state ownership, such as public broadcast operations;
- civil society ownership, which includes churches and other religious groups, labour unions, political parties, arts societies and other types of association or non-profit organization.

## OTHER TYPES OF CONCENTRATION EFFECT

Another relevant set of distinctions by type of concentration (de Ridder, 1984) relates to the *level* at which it occurs. De Ridder distinguished between publisher/concern (ownership) and editorial and audience levels. The first refers to increased powers of owners (for instance, the growth of large chains of separate newspapers, television stations or the conglomeration of motion picture studios). The units making up such media enterprises *can* remain editorially independent (as far as content decisions are concerned), although rationalization, co-ordination and streamlining of business and organization often leads to the sharing of certain services and reduces the difference between them. In any case, there is a separate question as to whether editorial concentration, as measured by the number of independent titles, rises or falls in line with publisher concentration. The degree of editorial independence is often hard to assess. The impact of the Internet on these two types of concentration cannot yet be adequately assessed. There is clearly a *de facto* increase in the number of services, platforms and owners, but there are also evident tendencies for empire-building by large and successful operators such as Google and Tencent.

The third issue – that of audience concentration – refers to the concentration of audience market share, which also needs to be separately assessed. A relatively minor change of ownership can greatly increase audience concentration (in terms of the proportion 'controlled' by a publishing group). A large number of independent newspaper titles does not in itself set limits to media power or ensure much real choice if most of the audience is concentrated on one or two titles, or is served by one or two firms. The condition of the system is certainly not very diverse in that case. The reasons for concern about concentration turn on these two points.

Audience concentration can be achieved without ownership. Large media conglomerates seek outlets for products across boundaries of media and ownership. The aim is to maximize the reach among defined target groups. All forms of exposure count towards this goal, including informal mentions or appearances on social media sites such as YouTube, often in return for payments. In recent years, the media industry (among other industries) have turned to hugely popular vloggers to act as 'influencers' on their generally global audience, by using and promoting their products in their content. As blogging and vlogging (and other forms of Internet publishing) tend to escape the strict regulation governing advertising and sponsorship in newspapers and broadcast media, this can be quite a lucrative deal for some.

## DEGREES OF CONCENTRATION

The degree of media concentration is usually measured by the extent to which the largest companies control production, employment, distribution and audience. Although there is no ceiling beyond which one can say that the degree is undesirable, according to Picard (1989: 334), a rule of thumb threshold of acceptability is one where the top four firms in an industry control more than 50 per cent, or the top eight firms more than 70 per cent. Given the hourglass structure of the media industry, most media sectors have crossed these limits of acceptable concentration.

The situation of concentration can vary from one of perfect competition to one of complete monopoly, with varying degrees in between. Different media occupy different places on this continuum, for a variety of reasons. Perfect competition is rare, but a relatively high level of competition is shown in many countries by book and magazine publishing. Film, television and national newspapers are generally oligopolistic markets, while true monopoly is now very rare. It was once to be found in the unusual case of 'natural' monopoly – for instance, in cable and telecommunication. A 'natural monopoly' is one where the consumer is best served, on grounds of cost and efficiency, by there being a single supplier (it is usually accompanied by measures to protect the consumer). Most of such monopolies have been abolished in a wave of privatization and deregulation of telecommunications.

The reasons for increasing media concentration and integration of activities are the same as for other branches of business, especially the search for economies of scale and greater market power. In the case of the media, it has something to do with the advantages of a vertically integrated operation since larger profits may be made from distribution than from production. There is also an incentive for media companies to acquire media with a stable cash flow of the kind that used to be provided by conventional television channels and daily newspapers (Tunstall, 1991), and today are more likely to come from franchising and licensing of content across multiple media properties (such as in the case of *Star Wars* or the Marvel Cinematic Universe). Control of software production and distribution can be very helpful for electronic companies and digital game studios, which need to make heavy investments in product development and innovations.

There are also increasing advantages in sharing services and being able to link different distribution systems and different markets. This is generally known as 'synergy'. As Murdock (1990: 8) remarks: 'In a cultural system built around "synergy" more does not mean different; it means the same basic commodity appearing in different markets and in a variety of packages.' In this kind of environment, an upward spiral to concentration is continually being applied because the only way to survive is by growth. The unification of the Single European Market since 1993 has played a part in this spiralling effect. Often, national restrictions on growth within a single country (because of anti-monopoly or crossmedia ownership regulations) have stimulated cross-national monopoly forming

(Tunstall, 1991). The setting up of the World Trade Organization (WTO) in 1994 to implement the General Agreement on Tariffs and Trade (GATT) has marked a new phase in media transnationalization. The trend towards international deregulation has contributed to media corporations increasingly operating on a global scale, in terms of both global production and distribution networks. In general, it is clear that globalization and the drive for 'free markets' have been mutually reinforcing, primarily driven by economic and commercial motives, further accelerated by the rise of the Internet and the corresponding need (or desire) by media companies to diversify their portfolio, increasingly including a variety of online assets.

## POLICY ISSUES ARISING

Policy is a crucial area for mass media industries and organizations, as governments around the world through legislation, regulation and subsidies set and define the parameters within which they can effectively operate. As media, telecommunications and ICT businesses converge, one should not forget that this is not just because of technological affordances or economic opportunism, but also largely due to government policies (such as the influential Telecommunications Act of 1996 in the United States; see Aufderheide, 1999) and an ongoing process of deregulation that 'helped pave the way for a wave of mega-mergers in the cultural industries in the late 1990s' (Hesmondhalgh, 2018: 161).

For the media companies to survive in the contemporary digital context, they have generally resorted to lobbying governments and international policy agencies (such as the World Trade Organization and the European Union) to harmonize copyright law and practice towards 'longer and stronger' copyrights (ibid.: 166) at the expense of both consumers and media makers. A recent example is the EU Copyright Directive of 2019, implemented to ensure the rights of newspapers, publishers and media groups regarding digital and cross-border uses of protected content. Media industries lobbied heavily to get this directive passed, which included provisions that would make companies such as Google and Facebook liable for the content that users share on their platforms. Some have argued this will inevitably lead to upload filters, stifling free speech. Opposition to the directive has come from major tech companies and Internet users, as well as human rights organizations and advocates.

The trend towards greater media convergence and concentration is a consequence of media policies in that it gives rise to a range of more or less new public policy issues. One such issue relates to pricing, another to the product and a third to the position of competitors. The main pricing issue has to do with consumer protection: the more monopoly there is, the greater the power of the provider to set prices. The main product issue has to do with the content of a monopoly-supplied media service, especially questions of adequate quality and choice, both for the consumer and for would-be providers of content. The third issue, concerning competitors, refers to the driving out of competitors as a result of economies of scale or advantages in the market (for advertising, sponsorships and other forms of financial support) of a high density of coverage or the use of financial power to engage in 'ruinous competition'.

For all the reasons given, there has been much research directed at the consequences of concentration (whether good or bad). The results of research have been generally inconclusive, partly because of the complexity, whereby the fact of concentration is usually only one aspect of a dynamic market situation. Baker (2007) has warned of the limited value and relevance of many empirical studies of the effects of concentration, especially the statistical studies common in the late 1980s. Typically, the time frame is too short to be revealing and the key events that reveal misuse of power are too sporadic to be captured. In addition, the risk of abuse cannot be measured precisely, but requires an evaluative assessment. Most attention has focused on the consequences for content, with particular reference to the adequacy of *local news and information*, the performance of the *political and opinion-forming* functions of media, the degree of *access* to different voices, and the degree and kind of *choice and diversity*. While, by definition, media concentration always reduces choice in some respects, it is possible that the profits of monopoly can be returned to the consumer or community in the form of better media, however defined (which is also a value judgement) (Lacy and Martin, 2004). More likely is that the profits from concentration will be channelled to shareholders, which is a primary purpose behind concentration (Squires, 1992; McManus, 1994).

This signals a second area of research around concentration and convergence – marketization – which refers to 'the permeation of market exchange as a social principle' (Slater and Tonkiss, 2001: 25). In a critical assessment of the history of pervasive marketization of media and mass communication since the 1980s, David Hesmondhalgh (2018: 164) concludes that 'the pressures towards globalisation and convergence are proving extremely difficult for policymakers to resist'. This difficulty is amplified through the complexity of adapting media policies and regulations to the convergent media environment of today (Flew, 2016). A key example is the hotly debated issue of whether companies such as Google, Facebook, Apple and Tencent are media businesses, which would make them responsible for the content we share and use on their platforms. Another issue is the role of China, as it advocates a global Internet governance framework that would enshrine 'national cyber-sovereignty', possibly leading to a much more fractured Internet experience for users, depending on where they access the network of networks (Flew, Martin and Suzor, 2019). Protecting the public domain, user rights and fair use remains a constant struggle in the context of a powerful market logic dominating the global policy debate.

The main points made about media competition and concentration in this section are summarized in Box 8.5.

## 8.5

## Concentration and competition

- Concentration can be found at three levels: intermedia, intramedium (within a sector) and interfirm
- Concentration can be either horizontal or vertical
- Concentration can be observed within an organization at three levels: publisher/owner, editorial and audience
- Degree of concentration can be measured in terms of market value share, audience share and share of channels
- The effects of concentration are difficult to assess beyond an increase in market power and reduction of diversity
- Concentration is reckoned to be excessive where three or four firms control more than 50 per cent of the market
- Concentration is driven by excessive competition, the search for synergy and very high profit
- Some kinds and degree of concentration can benefit consumers
- Undesirable effects of excessive concentration are loss of diversity, higher prices and restricted access to media
- Concentration can be combated by regulation and by encouraging new entrants to the market

# MASS MEDIA GOVERNANCE

The manner in which the media are controlled in democratic societies reflects both their indispensability (taken as a whole) for business, politics and everyday social and cultural life, and their relative immunity to government regulation. Some controls, limitations and prescriptions are necessary, but principles of freedom (of speech and markets) require a cautious, even minimal, approach to regulatory control. It makes sense to use the term 'governance' in this context to describe the overall set of laws, regulations, rules and conventions which serve the purposes of support and control in the general interest, including that of media industries. Governance refers to a process in which a range of different actors co-operate for different purposes, with actors drawn from market and civil society institutions as well as from government. It thus refers not only to formal and binding rules, but also to numerous informal mechanisms, internal and external to the media, by which they are 'steered' towards multiple (and often inconsistent) objectives.

Despite the 'bias against control', there is an extensive array of actual or potential forms of control on media. Because of the diversity and global complexity of the terrain covered, it is inappropriate to speak of a 'system' of governance, although there are some general principles and regularities to be found in much the same form in many countries. Essentially, governance entails some set of standards or goals, coupled with some procedures of varying strictness for enforcing or policing them. Generally speaking, governance implies a less hierarchical approach, usually with strong elements of self-regulation. According to Collins (2006), the drift away from hierarchy is driven largely by the increasing complexity of the systems in question. It applies particularly to the Internet because of the general absence of direct state control, an unclear (and to some extent boundaryless) legal framework and the mixture of private and public uses.

## PURPOSES AND FORMS OF GOVERNANCE

The variety of forms of governance that apply to the mass media reflects the diversity of purposes of control for different actors. These include:

- the protection of the essential interests of the state and of public order, including the prevention of public harm;
- the safeguarding of individual rights and interests;
- meeting the needs of the media industry for a stable and supportive operating environment;
- the promotion of freedom and other communication and cultural values;
- the encouragement of technological innovation and economic enterprise;
- the setting of technical and infrastructural standards;
- the meeting of international obligations, including observance of human rights;
- the encouragement of media accountability.

It is clear that such wide-ranging goals call for a diverse set of mechanisms and procedures, given the limited scope for direct governmental action. The outline in Chapter 7 of four frameworks for media accountability (by law, through the market, as public responsibility, and professionalism) has already given an overview of the main alternatives available. The complex terrain can be mapped out according to two main dimensions: *external* versus *internal*, and *formal* versus *informal*, as sketched out in Figure 8.2. The main forms of governance are classified in this way into four types, each with appropriate mechanisms for implementation.

|  | Formal | Informal |
|---|---|---|
| **External** | Law and regulation applied via courts and public regulatory bodies | Market forces Lobby groups Public opinion Review and criticism |
| **Internal** | Management Self-regulation by firm or industry Professionalism Codes of ethics and conduct | Organizational culture Reflection |

Figure 8.2   The main forms of media governance

Governance applies at various levels. First, we can distinguish between the international, national, regional and local levels, according to the way a media system is organized. In practice, international regulation has traditionally been limited mainly to technical and organizational matters, but the scope of control is growing, especially as media are becoming more international and global Internet platforms become powerful players (see Chapter 9). Matters of human rights, privacy protection and potential public harm claim increasing attention. The potential of media propaganda – at times amplified by the algorithms of online social networks – for fomenting inter-ethnic and international hatred has been forced on world attention by calamitous events in the Balkans, the Arab world, Southeast Asia and elsewhere as well as the difficult task of reconstructing media after conflict (see Price and Thompson, 2002). Most forms of governance operate at the national level, but some countries with a federalized or regional structure devolve responsibility for media matters from the centre. International policy agencies are becoming increasingly important as mass media, telecommunications and ICT industries converge and operate across national boundaries.

More relevant to note here is the distinction between *structure*, *conduct* and *performance* that has already been introduced (p. 203), and where regulation can apply respectively to a media system, a particular firm or organization, or some aspect of content. As a general rule, control can be applied more readily the further away the point of application is from content because there is less chance of infringing essential freedoms of expression. Here structure relates mainly to conditions of ownership, competition, infrastructure, universal service or other carriage obligations. It includes the major matter of public broadcasting. Conduct relates to such matters as editorial independence, relations with sources and government, matters to do with the justice system, formal self-regulation and accountability.

The level of performance covers all matters to do with content and services to audiences, often with particular reference to alleged harm or offence. The main propositions relating to media governance in relatively free media systems are given in Box 8.6.

---

**8.6**

**Media governance: main propositions**

- Different media need different forms of governance
- Control is more justifiable for mass media than for small-scale media because of the scale of possible effects
- Control can be applied more legitimately to structure than to content
- Neither pre-publication censorship nor punishment for publication alone are consistent with freedom and democracy
- Self-regulation is generally preferable to external or hierarchical control
- Governance increasingly occurs on an international level

---

# THE REGULATION OF MASS MEDIA: ALTERNATIVE MODELS

For historical and other reasons, different media have been subject to different types and degrees of regulation. The differences are related to four main factors: first, the strength of a medium's claim to freedom, especially in the light of its typical content and uses; secondly, the degree to which a potential harm to society is perceived; thirdly, for reasons of equitable allocation; and fourthly, the relative practicability of effective regulation. Three models in particular have been identified (Pool, 1983) and are outlined below. These still help to explain the main differences in the degree to which governments can intervene, although they are becoming less distinct, especially because of deregulation and technological convergence. The essential features of each model are compared in Table 8.1.

Table 8.1  Three regulatory models compared

|  | Print | Broadcasting | Common carrier |
|---|---|---|---|
| Regulation of infrastructure | None | High | High |
| Regulation of content | None | High | None |
| Sender access | Open | Restricted | Open |
| Receiver access | Open | Open | Restricted |

## THE FREE PRESS MODEL

The basic model for the press is one of freedom from any government regulation and control that would imply censorship or limits on freedom of publication. Press freedom is often enshrined as a principle in national constitutions and in international charters, such as the European Convention on Human Rights (ECHR, Article 10) or the United Nations Charter (Article 19). However, the press freedom model is often modified or extended by public policy in order to guarantee the expected public interest benefits of a free and independent press. Prominent among the reasons for public policy attention to journalism in general and newspapers in particular has been the trend towards concentration and convergence with television and online channels which, despite the result of free economic competition, effectively reduces access to press channels and choice for citizens.

Because of this, media often receive some legal protection as well as some economic benefits. National cinema production tends to be supported to some extent by state governance, as well as press freedom. Both imply some element of public scrutiny and supervision, however benevolent. Economic benefits can range from postal and tax concessions to loan and subsidy arrangements. There may also be anti-concentration laws and rules against foreign ownership. The press freedom model applies in much the same way to book publishing (where it originates) and to most other print media. By default, it also applies to music, although without any special privileges. Legal action can still be taken against the press for certain offences, such as defamation.

## THE BROADCASTING MODEL

By contrast, radio and television broadcasting and, less directly, many newer means of audiovisual delivery have been subject from their beginning to high levels of restriction and direction, often involving direct public ownership. The initial reasons for regulation of broadcasting were mainly technical or to ensure the fair allocation of scarce spectrum and control of monopoly. However, regulation became deeply institutionalized, at least until the 1980s when new technologies and a new climate of opinion reversed the trend.

The general concept of public service lies at the core of the broadcasting model, although there are several variants as well as weaker forms (as in the USA, and almost non-existent forms, such as throughout Africa), in-between forms (such as the fragmented landscape in Latin America) or somewhat stronger forms (as in parts of Europe), even though marketization has had a profound impact on the position of public broadcasting around the world. Public service broadcasting in a fully developed form (such as in Britain) generally has several main features, supported by policy and regulation. The broadcasting model can involve many different kinds of regulation. Usually, there are specific media laws to regulate the industry and often some form of public service bureaucracy to implement the law. Quite often, the services of production and distribution may be undertaken by private enterprise concerns, operating concessions from the government and following some legally enforceable supervisory guidelines.

The decline in strength of the broadcasting model has been marked by increasing tendencies towards the 'privatization' and 'commercialization' of broadcasting (see McQuail and Siune, 1998; Steemers, 2001; Bardoel and d'Haenens, 2008; Enli, 2008). This has involved, most notably, the transfer of media channels and operations from public to private ownership, increased levels of financing from advertising, and the franchising of new commercial competitors for public broadcasting channels. New restrictions on activities (for example, online) have been imposed for reasons of protecting other media from unfair competition from subsidized media. A test of public interest has to be met for any such extension. Despite its relative decline, the broadcasting model shows no sign of being abandoned, and generally mixed systems of public and commercial broadcasting operate around the world. It has generally performed well in the audience market (aided by its financial security), but its value to civil society is recognized as much as it has come under pressure by marketization. Not least in its advantages is its guarantee of adequate and fair access to all political parties in the democratic process and its tendency to privilege access for issues of 'national' interest.

## THE COMMON CARRIER MODEL

The third main model of regulation predates broadcasting and is usually called the common carrier model because it relates primarily to communication services such as mail, telephone and telegraph, which are purely for distribution and intended to be open to all as universal services. The main motive for regulation has been for efficient implementation and management of what are (or were) 'natural monopolies' in the interests of efficiency and the consumer. In general, common carrier media have involved heavy regulation of the infrastructure and of economic exploitation, but only very marginal regulation of content. This is in sharp contrast to broadcasting, which is characterized by a high degree of content regulation, even where infrastructure is increasingly in private hands.

While the three models are still useful for describing and making sense of the different patterns of media regulation, the retention of these separate regimes is increasingly called into question. The main challenge comes from the technological 'convergence' between modes of communication, which makes the regulatory separation between print, broadcasting and telecommunication increasingly artificial and arbitrary (Iosifides, 2002). The same means of distribution, especially satellites and telecommunication, deliver all three kinds of media (and others). Cable systems are now often legally permitted to offer telephone services, broadcasting can deliver newspapers, and the telephone network can provide television and other media services.

MCQUAIL'S MEDIA AND MASS COMMUNICATION THEORY
STRUCTURES

# THE HYBRID STATUS OF THE INTERNET

The Internet has developed in a spirit of *de facto* freedom from any control (Castells, 2001) and in its early days was considered as a 'common carrier' medium, using the telecommunications system for the transmission and exchange of messages and information. It is still relatively free in practice, more so even than the press since it offers open access to all would-be senders. Even so, its freedom lacks formal protection in law and can be quite vulnerable, both to state intervention and to unchecked marketization. This follows from its growing commercial functions, fears about its uses and effects as well as its adaptation to other functions, including broadcasting. Its status in relation to the three models outlined is mixed, with both national and international regulatory bodies introducing and developing governance structures as the medium becomes the dominant way for citizens and consumers to access (and make) media.

One of the distinctive features of the Internet is that it tends not to be regulated specifically at the national level and does not fall neatly into any jurisdictional zone. It is also especially hard to regulate because of its transnational character, diversity of functions and unsubstantial character. There is a variety of international and national self-regulatory and steering bodies, but their responsibilities and powers are limited (Hamelink, 2000). Much of the burden of what control there is falls on the shoulders of Internet service providers, whose rights and legal obligations have traditionally been poorly defined (Braman and Roberts, 2003). Uncertainty can sometimes protect freedom, but it also holds back development and opens the way for outside corporate or state control.

There is an increasing likelihood that the Internet is simply too important to be left in its semi-regulated condition. Collins (2008) argues against three myths of Internet governance: first, that the market can take care of most decisions; secondly, that self-governance is pervasive and effective; and thirdly, that its governance is essentially different from that of older media. He points to many examples of emerging elements of external control nationally and internationally, in particular that the Internet is not a single medium and will not call for a single regulatory regime. In the context of the Internet's status as the dominant medium of our time, there is an argument to be made for a move from national media policies towards global media policy (Mansell and Raboy, 2011), grounded in the concept of the public interest (Napoli, 2019).

Figure 8.3 summarizes the key differences between media on two key dimensions – mass versus interpersonal (I/P) pattern and instant versus delayed or mediated contact – that are of significance for public regulatory policy. The principles of structure and policy summarized under each of the four media types are those that have applied in the United States, but they are also now widely the same in other parts of the world as a result of privatization and deregulation. The main exception relates to broadcasting, which often has an element of public ownership and control. A most important point to note is that the Internet can appear in all four quadrants, depending on the use in question and how it is classified. It can be a broadcasting, exchange, consultation or personal medium. Since it has no fixed classification, no single regime will serve the purposes of regulation, and policy has to take the goals of communication into account, regardless of the technology. The difference between public and private uses remains of primary importance.

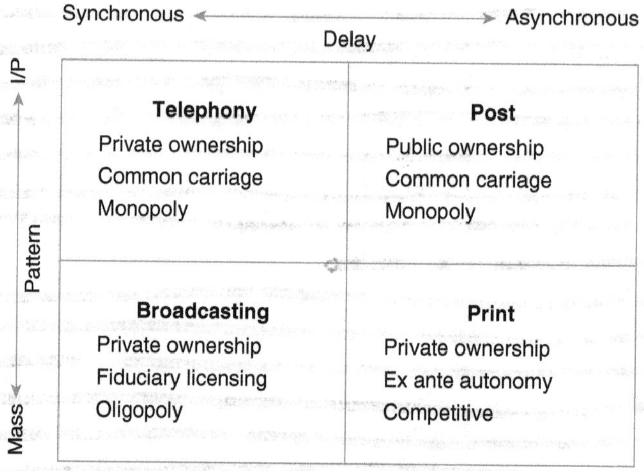

Synchronous ←————————————→ Asynchronous

Delay

|  | **Telephony** | **Post** |
| --- | --- | --- |
| I/P | Private ownership | Public ownership |
| | Common carriage | Common carriage |
| | Monopoly | Monopoly |
| **Pattern** | **Broadcasting** | **Print** |
| | Private ownership | Private ownership |
| | Fiduciary licensing | Ex ante autonomy |
| Mass | Oligopoly | Competitive |

Figure 8.3   Policy regimes governing past communication platforms

*Source*: Bar and Sandvig (2008: 535)

# MEDIA POLICY PARADIGM SHIFTS

The trend towards convergence of regulatory models for different media is part of a larger pattern of change in approaches to media policy. Some elements of this have already been noted, including the early attempts to make the mass media more accountable to society and, more recently, the influence of globalization and the trends towards 'deregulation' and privatization of media. Following van Cuilenburg and McQuail (2003), over the longer term of a century of communication development, we can detect three main phases of communication policy in different parts of the world.

The first can be described as a phase of *emerging communication industry policy* lasting from the later nineteenth century until the Second World War. There was no coherent policy goal beyond those of protecting the strategic interests of governments and nations and promoting the industrial and economic development of new communication systems (telephony, cable, wireless telegraphy, radio, etc.).

The second main phase can be described as one of *public service*. It begins with the recognition of a need to legislate for broadcasting, but this time with a new awareness of the social significance of the medium for political, social and cultural life. Communications were seen as much more than technologies. New ideas of 'communication welfare' were introduced which went much further than the requirement of controlled allocation of scarce frequencies. Policy was positive in promoting certain cultural and social goals as well as negative in the sense of forbidding certain kinds of harm to 'society'. For the first time, the press came within the scope of public policy in order to limit the power of monopoly owners and maintain 'standards' in the face of commercial pressures. This phase reached its apex in Europe in the 1970s and has been in relative decline ever since, although important elements remain.

A third phase of policy has developed as a result of many of the trends that have already been discussed, but especially the trends of marketization, internationalization, digitalization and convergence. The key event has been the move to centre stage of telecommunications (Winseck, 2002). The period into which we have moved is one of intense innovation, growth and competition on a global scale. The policy challenge is to deal with our current age of abundant but unevenly distributed information (Winseck, 2019). Policy is still guided ultimately by political, social and economic goals, but they have been reinterpreted and reordered. Economic goals take precedence over the social and political. The current policy paradigm seems to be that of consumer rights and 'light touch' regulation as determined by international policy agencies rather than more or less strict notions of quality and control based on public values. On the other hand, national interests both in democratic states as well as more dictatorial regimes continue to inform policy responses to new media. This will prove to be a fascinating area for media and mass communication research for the years to come.

## MEDIA SYSTEMS AND POLITICAL SYSTEMS

Much of the foregoing discussion of media policy and regulation, including in previous chapters about the role and expectations of media in national contexts, leaves little doubt about the complex and powerful links between mass media and the national political system (and even the state itself), even where there is formally little or no connection. This is not to argue that the media are necessarily subordinate to politicians or government. The links between the two are as often characterized by conflict and suspicion as they are by mutual dependence, or producing a certain 'media logic' whereby political and media systems seem to be primarily oriented towards each other rather than to consumers or citizens.

The links between political and media systems do show large intercultural differences (Gunther and Mughan, 2000). Nevertheless, in each case the connections are related to structure, conduct and performance. First, there is a body of law, regulation and policy in every country, which has been negotiated through the political system, and which guarantees rights and freedoms and sets obligations and limits even to the freest of media in the public sphere. In many countries there is a public sector of the media (usually broadcasting) over which governments have ultimate control, and there are diverse ways in which the management of these organizations is penetrated by political interests, even where they have some autonomy.

Owners of private media generally have financial and strategic interests that lead to efforts to influence political decision-making. Not infrequently they have open ideological positions and even political ambitions of their own. The endorsement of political parties by newspapers is more common than not and sometimes political parties control newspapers. For electoral reasons, politicians are often obliged to court the favour of powerful media so that the flow of influence can be two-way.

At the level of performance, the content of most daily news media is still often dominated by politics, but not usually because it is so fascinating and newsworthy for the public. While citizens do need to be informed and advised in the longer term, they do not really need what they are offered every day. The reasons lie partly in the advantages for news media in terms of a free staple commodity and partly in the enormous efforts made by political interests (in the widest sense) to gain access to the public for their diverse ends. It also stems from long-standing links between media and political institutions, which cannot easily be broken. Politics cannot do without the media, and the kind of (news) media we have would struggle without politics.

There have been numerous attempts to analyse the relationship. Siebert, Peterson and Schramm's classic book *Four Theories of the Press* (1956) still offers a founding principle that has guided most attempts. This is given in the form of a quotation in Box 8.7.

---

**8.7**

**The basic principle of media–society relationships**

The press always takes on the form and coloration of the social and political structures within which it operates. Especially, it reflects the system of social control where the relations of individuals and institutions are adjusted (Siebert et al., 1956: 1)

---

Hallin and Mancini (2004) distilled three ideal-typical models of the relationship between national media systems and political systems, based on a study of seventeen western democracies. The first model is labelled as 'liberal' or 'North Atlantic'; the second as 'democratic corporatist' or 'Northern European'; and the third as 'polarized pluralist' or 'Mediterranean'. The labels indicate the geographical setting of the models, which in turn reflects the influence of a number of important cultural and economic factors with deep historical roots. In Box 8.8, a summary comparison is provided of some key aspects of each model, derived from some of the main variables studied. In this presentation, the term 'parallelism' means that media tend to be structured and aligned according to competing parties and ideologies in the country concerned. 'Clientelism' means that media are penetrated by outside interests and serve their ends voluntarily or for money, thus departing from legal-rational norms of conduct (Roudikova, 2008).

---

## 8.8

### Three models of the media–political system relationship (Hallin and Mancini, 2004)

| | Liberal | Democratic corporatist | Polarized pluralist |
|---|---|---|---|
| **Role of state in media** | Weak | Strong (welfare) | Strong |
| **Consensus or polarization of politics** | Mixed | More consensus | More Polarized |
| **Professionalization of journalism** | Low | High | Medium |
| **Press–politics parallelism** | Low | Medium | High |
| **Presence of clientelism** | Low | Low | High |

---

A limitation of this proposal is the rather narrow base of also similar democratic systems on which it rests, although it has since been applied in research in many other countries and is open to adaptation and extension. It is also rather biased towards the press. Typically, any given case tends to deviate from any single one of the types to a greater or lesser degree, reducing the value of the typology. Even so, it has proved its value as an entry point for analysis. Applications of Hallin and Mancini's study to the 'new democracies' added to Europe after the fall of communism around 1990 (Jakubowicz, 2007), the media systems of Israel, Brazil, South Africa, Russia, China and the Arab world (Hallin and Mancini, 2012), and across Central and Eastern Europe (Herrero et al., 2017) have proven useful, even though no single model adequately captures the differences between and sometimes within countries. Although Hallin and Mancini originally concluded that the most likely outcome of developments in the media sector would be an ongoing convergence of models, this has been challenged in subsequent studies, showing a more complex 'hybridized' media system with elements of each system present in the same national or regional context.

The issue of media–state relations cannot be settled only by reference to general models, nor by limiting oneself to the press (and not all other media and cultural industries) or just to the political context of governance. The question arises as to why in modern times the mainstream media in free democracies seem so inclined to reflect rather than challenge the policy directions of the government of the day. Why do they so readily carry out the role of 'social controller', signalled many decades ago, rather than the role of watchdog and critic celebrated, for example, in journalistic ideology? There are several kinds of answer. Bennett (1990) has put forward a well-supported theory of relations between the state and government power on the one hand, and the press on the other, as things are in the USA. It holds that responsible journalists generally limit their understanding of their critical role in relation to the state, where issues of conflict arise, to representing or 'indexing' the range of views of government and other major institutional actors. They do not have an obligation to introduce minority or 'extreme' viewpoints, or to reflect an independent voice of 'public opinion'. The theory was supported by a study of the coverage by *The New York Times* of the US funding of the *contras* in Nicaragua. Subsequently, other cases have been studied, notably the Iraq war that started in 2003 (Bennett, Lawrence and Livingstone, 2007). A vivid illustration of the effects of indexation is given by Bennett et al. (2007) in the case of the publication of the Abu Ghraib torture photographs in 2004. The administration refused to use the word 'torture', preferring 'abuse' or 'mistreatment', and were overwhelmingly followed in this by the mainstream US media. 'Indexing' theory offers a convincing explanation of this phenomenon, as expressed by Bennett et al. in Box 8.9.

## 8.9

### The central idea of indexing theory

The core principle of the mainstream press system in the United States appears to be this: the mainstream news generally stays within the sphere of official consensus and conflict displayed in the public statements of the key government officials who manage the policy areas and decision-making process that make the news. Journalists calibrate the news based on this dynamic power principle. ... This ongoing, implicit calibration process conducted by the press corps creates a weighting system for what gets into the news, what prominence it receives, how long it gets covered, and who gets the voice on stories. (Bennett et al., 2007: 49)

Although the rationale described in Box 8.9 is consistent with democratic principle, since journalists primarily reflect the perspective of elected representatives, it also allows the latter much power to define their own view of public opinion and act accordingly without much restraint from the press. What is missing seems to be a role for the media in speaking for the public or informing independently. The process described as 'indexing' is clearly present in other countries, partly because it is in some respects a consequence of the addiction of journalists to the practice of objectivity, which requires both 'balance' and easy access to credible sources that leads generally to the authorities and established 'experts'. In countries with well-established public broadcasting systems, these tend to follow a version of the 'indexing' logic, although with scope for diversity. However, the precise situation depends on the prevailing political culture. In Japan, for instance, the public broadcaster takes care of impartial information, but the mainstream newspaper press, despite political diversity, operates a form of news cartel (the *kasha* press clubs) that maintains a cosy relationship with power and generally acts as a conduit for the information provided by government and other institutions (Gamble and Watanabe, 2004). In Russia, there is much evidence that the media are very dependent on government and commercial support, with an almost institutionalized clientelism infecting journalism (Dimitrova and Strömbäck, 2005; Roudikova, 2008). There is clearly much national and international variation in the various ways in which mass media and the state both collaborate and are in conflict with each other – quite often at the same time.

## CONCLUSION

This chapter has provided an overview of the main features of media economics and of the typical system of regulation (governance). Both show distinctive features compared with other industry sectors and other institutional areas. The key to differences in both cases is the dual character of media, being both a commercial enterprise and a key element in the political, cultural and social life of society. They cannot be left entirely to the marketplace or be closely regulated. Neither media firms nor governments have a free hand to implement policy. Although the trend is towards greater freedom, there will be limits to action, especially given the rise of the Internet and the entry into the media market by powerful new global actors from the telecommunications and ICT sectors.

As far as governance is concerned, the most typical and distinguishing features are as follows. Mass media can only be regulated in marginal or indirect ways by governments. The forms of governance are extremely varied, including internal as well as external and informal as well as formal means. The internal and informal are probably the more important. Different forms of regulation are applied to different technologies of distribution. Forms of governance are rooted in the history and political cultures of each national society, and are increasingly in negotiation and tension with international regulatory agencies. The key debate lies between commercial values and marketization on the one hand and public values and the public interest on the other.

# FURTHER READING

Cammaerts, B. and Mansell, R. (2020) 'Digital platform policy and regulation: Toward a radical democratic turn'. *International Journal of Communication* 12, 135–154.

Chadwick, A. (2017) *The Hybrid Media System*, 2nd edition. Oxford: Oxford University Press.

Flew, T., Martin, F. and Suzor, N. (2019) 'Internet regulation as media policy: rethinking the question of digital communication platform governance', *Journal of Digital Media & Policy*, 10(1): 33–50.

Hallin, D.C. and Mancini, P. (eds) (2012) *Comparing Media Systems beyond the Western World*. Cambridge: Cambridge University Press.

Küng, L., Picard, G. and Towse, R. (eds) (2008) *The Internet and the Mass Media*. London: Sage.

Noam, E. (2018) 'Beyond the mogul: from media conglomerates to portfolio media', *Journalism*, 19(8): 1096–1130.

# 9

## GLOBAL MASS COMMUNICATION

The pace of internationalization has accelerated because of what David Held (2010: 149–150) calls the 'deep drivers' of globalization: the development of global markets and a complex global economy, the pressure of worldwide migration and the movements of refugees, the ongoing diffusion of democratic and consumer values around the world, all of which are supercharged by the interconnected infrastructure and culture of global communications and media. The mass media are in a special position as both an object and an agent of the globalizing process. They are also the means by which we become aware of it. Changes in distribution technology have been the most evident and immediate cause of change, but economics has also played a decisive part. We look at the internationalization of media ownership and of the content that flows through media channels.

There are several reasons for devoting a separate chapter to this aspect of media and mass communication. One is history, specifically the fact that the global character of mass media became increasingly problematized after the Second World War. Problems arose from ideological struggles between the free-market West and communist East, economic and social imbalance between the developed and the developing world, plus the growth of global media concentration threatening freedom of expression. The issue of cultural and economic domination by the media of the developed world and the consequences for minority cultures everywhere is of considerable significance, as is its counterpart: that of continuing social fragmentation on a global scale. We have reached a point where qualitative change might lead to more genuinely global media, involving independent media serving audiences across national frontiers. This means the emergence of international media as such, with their own audiences, and not just the internationalization of content and organization of media. The Internet takes a central position in scenarios for the future of international communication and also brings questions of governance of global media into sharper focus.

# ORIGINS OF GLOBALIZATION

Histories of globalization can be written from a variety of perspectives; we will follow that of media and mass communication here, considering their role as instrumental to the globalizing process.

Books and printing were international in their origins since they predated the era of nation states and served cultural, political and commercial worlds that extended throughout Europe and beyond. Many early printed books were in Latin or were translated from another language, and the earliest newspapers were often compiled from newsletters that circulated widely throughout Europe. The early-twentieth-century newspaper, film or radio station were recognizably the same from New York to New South Wales and Vladivostok to Valparaiso. Nevertheless, the newspaper as it developed became very much a national institution, and national boundaries largely delineated the circulation of print media in general. The national character of early mass media was reinforced by the exclusiveness of language as well as by cultural and political factors. When film was invented, it too was largely confined within national frontiers, at least until after the First World War. Its subsequent diffusion, especially in the form of the Hollywood film, is the first real example of a transnational *mass* medium (Olson, 1999). When radio was widely introduced during the 1920s, it was once more an essentially national medium, not only because of the spoken word in different languages, but also because transmission was generally only intended to serve the national territory.

By comparison, we are now being constantly reminded of how international the media have become and how the flow of news and culture encompasses the globe and draws us into a single 'global village', to use the words of McLuhan (1964). The major newspapers from the mid-nineteenth century onwards were well served by powerful and well-organized news agencies that made use of the international telegraph system, and foreign news was a staple commodity of many newspapers across the world. The predominant features of the geopolitical scene, especially nationalism itself and also imperialism, encouraged an interest in international events, especially where war and conflict provided good news copy (this predates the nineteenth century; for example, Wilke, 1995). In the early part of the twentieth century, governments began to discover the advantages of the media for international as well as domestic propaganda purposes. Since the Second World War many countries have used radio to provide a worldwide service of information and culture designed to foster a positive national image, promote the national culture and maintain contact with expatriates.

Early recorded music also had a quasi-international character, first, because of the classical repertoire, and secondly, because of the increasing diffusion of American popular songs, sometimes associated with musical films. There has always been a real or potential tension between the desire to maintain a national, cultural and political hegemony and the wish to share in cultural and technological innovations from elsewhere. National minorities have also sought to assert a cultural identity in the face of imperialist cultural domination in the literal sense (for instance, within the British, Austrian and Russian empires). The United States was a latecomer to the imperialist role. After the Second World War in particular, it pursued a policy of advancing US media penetration around the world, not least in the form of a belief system about the desirable structure of media in society – a combination of free markets, free expression and ostensible political neutrality, with inevitable contradictions.

Television has been the most potent influence in the accelerating media globalization process, partly because, as with the cinema film, its visual character helps it to pass barriers of language. In its early days, the range of terrestrial transmission was limited to national frontiers in most countries. Now, cable, satellite and other means of transmission have largely overcome these limitations. The Internet is a further accelerant for internationalization, which does not have to observe national boundaries at all, even if language, legislation and regulation, culture and social relations do ensure that frontiers still structure the flow of content.

Whether we can consider the media as global depends on whether one considers media devices, content and social arrangements in terms of their technological and industrial infrastructure, or in terms of how people use them. The globalization of media, Flew (2018) argues, is a matter of reach rather than presence. Media certainly have a global reach, and their operations are often internationally networked. However, how people use and experience them, how media adapt to local proclivities and circumstances, and how competition as well as collaboration between global and local media inspires new types of products and services, all contributing to a distinctly particular and situated understanding of media.

## DRIVING FORCES: TECHNOLOGY AND MONEY

Technology certainly gives a powerful push to globalization. The arrival of television satellites in the late 1970s broke the principle of national sovereignty of broadcasting space and made it difficult and ultimately impossible to offer effective resistance to television transmission and reception from outside the national territory. But the extent to which satellites reach global audiences directly with content from abroad is often exaggerated and is still relatively small, even in regions such as Europe. There are other means of diffusion that work in the same direction – for instance, by connecting cable systems and simply by physically transporting discs. The main route has been by exports of content channelled through nationally based media. As streaming media are quickly becoming the medium of choice for people around the world, the Internet has become the dominant way in which television reaches audiences, even though what is available in each country varies, and international streaming platforms strive to include local content in an attempt to cater for particular tastes and regional markets.

While technology has been a necessary condition of extensive globalization, and the truly global medium of the Internet illustrates this most clearly, the most immediate and enduring driving forces behind globalization have been economic (and the brakes have been cultural). Television was established on the model of radio broadcasting, as a continuous service at least during the evening, then later during the day and ultimately on a 24-hour basis. The cost of filling broadcasting time with original or domestic material has always exceeded the capacity of production organizations, even in wealthy countries. It is virtually impossible to fill schedules without great repetition or extensive importing.

The expansion of television since the 1980s, made possible by new, efficient and low-cost transmission technologies, has been driven by commercial motives and has fuelled demand for imports. It has also stimulated new audiovisual production industries in many countries that look, in their turn, for new markets. The main beneficiary, and the main exporter, has traditionally been the United States, which has a large and surplus production of popular entertainment and an entrée into many markets secured by the cultural familiarity of its products, mainly as a result of decades of American films. The English language is an added advantage but is not decisive, since most TV exports have always been dubbed or subtitled when transmitted. In recent decades this has changed, as international co-productions have become a significant market force, as global distribution of local content has taken off, and considering the rise of (economically and culturally) powerful media industries in countries such as India, China, Brazil and Nigeria.

An important component of international mass communication is advertising, linked to the globalization of many product markets and reflecting the international character of many advertising agencies and the dominance of the market by a small number of firms. The same advertising messages appear in different countries, and there is also an indirect internationalizing effect on the media that carry the advertising. Last but not least of the forces promoting globalization has been the vast expansion and the privatization of telecommunications infrastructure and business (Hills, 2002). The main causes of media globalization are given in Box 9.1.

---

## 9.1
## Causes of media globalization

- More powerful technologies for long-distance transmission
- Commercial enterprise
- Follow-on from trade and diplomatic relations
- Colonization and imperialism, past and present
- Economic dependency
- Geopolitical imbalances
- Advertising
- Expansion of telecommunications

---

# GLOBAL MEDIA STRUCTURE

As a background to this discussion, it is useful to have an overview of the 'global media system', in so far as this can be done, since there is no formal arrangement beyond national frontiers. The simplest way to begin is with the many separate sovereign states that interact and communicate with each other. The pathways of flow and exchange between nations follow some regular and predictable (although changing) patterns and this helps us to visualize a structure of a kind. The states involved vary a great deal and the factors of variation largely shape the overall 'structure'. The main factors are size (of territory and population), level of economic development, language, political system and culture. The size of a country affects all aspects of media, but population provides either an economic base for domestic production or a large target market for other countries' exports. Language and culture encourage certain flows between countries with a mutual affinity and also set limits to what is possible, as do political and ideological barriers. Economic muscle is the main determinant of dominance in the overall set of relationships. The world of the media is also in some respects stratified by region. Tunstall (2007: 330) points to four levels. Below the global level are located the nation state, the national region and the locality. Given the acceleration of media concentration and convergence in the last two decades, media are increasingly organized either as multinational corporations or as national companies (which often still tend to be linked in a variety of ways with other media companies elsewhere in the world).

Much theory and research has explored the basic structure outlined, but a central organizing idea is that of a centre–peripheral pattern of relations between nations (Mowlana, 1985). Those with a core position have the most developed media, and are wealthier and larger in population. The peripheral nations have the reverse characteristics. There are, of course, intermediary positions. Core nations are likely to have larger flows to other countries, which are not balanced by return flows. Mutual exchanges are likely to be greater between countries that are 'close' in terms of geography, culture or economic relations. Peripheral countries are less likely to export media content, but their capacity to import is also limited by lack of development. This sometimes leads to a different kind of self-sufficiency than that enjoyed by rich core nations.

The underlying circumstances of global media structure set the scene for theorizing, debate and research about the reality and desirability of globalization. At the start, around the 1960s, thinking was dominated by the extreme dominance of the USA, especially in Hollywood entertainment and the global news agencies. The Soviet Union was a core counterplayer, along with China and the rest of the communist world. The Third World provided a large set of peripheral countries, although with much variation. With the near demise of communism and rapid development of much of Asia and Latin America, the world structure looks quite different. The USA does not dominate anymore as a producer of international entertainment, and media industries and sources of investment for media production increasingly come from businesses in the Indian subcontinent, China, and a few other large countries, including Japan, Brazil, Indonesia, Nigeria and Mexico (see Flew, 2018). Of recent concern are the role and status of Internet platform companies (such as Facebook, Google, Baidu and Tencent), which may not want to be seen as 'media' companies, but have become the primary gateways through which most people access media content. These corporations – among the highest valued business ventures in the world – have also started to invest in their own content channels in an effort to diversify their portfolio and get people to increase the amount of time spent on their respective platforms. The reach of these corporations is global, as are their structures, with headquarters in the USA and China, and countless divisions and subsidiaries – including, for example, companies in the Philippines and elsewhere that monitor and curate the content that users upload and share on their platforms – all over the world.

At the heart of questions about global media structure are both cultural and political-economic concerns, addressing issues of diversity and inclusion or exclusion of voices (of users as well as professional media producers), and issues of concentration of owner-ship and lack of transparent governance and oversight (Flew, 2018; Napoli, 2019). The main questions arising from the structure of the global media system are posed in Box 9.2.

---

## 9.2
## Global media structure: main questions arising

- What is the pattern of dominance and imbalance of media flow?
- What are the causes of patterns observed?
- What are the consequences of the structure as observed?
- What are dynamics and directions of change?
- How should we evaluate media globalizing trends?

---

## MULTINATIONAL MEDIA OWNERSHIP AND CONTROL

The recent phase of the 'communications revolution' has been marked by a new phenom-enon of media concentration, both transnational and multimedia, leading to the world media industry being increasingly dominated by a small number of very large media firms (Chalaby, 2003). In some cases, these developments are the achievement of a fairly tra-ditional breed of media 'mogul' (Tunstall and Palmer, 1991), though with new names. Despite the high visibility of larger-than-life media moguls, it is likely that the trend is rather towards more impersonal patterns of ownership and operation, as befits such large global enterprises. Media developments in rapidly growing markets such as Latin America and India have given rise to their own national media moguls and multimedia firms, often with foreign investments (see Chadha and Kavoori, 2005). Rather than world 'domination' by a handful of media conglomerates, there is a relatively moderate internationalization, in part because of national cultures and the private interests of owners, but also because of counter-movements, protests and resistance (Miège, 2019).

Certain types of media content lend themselves to the globalization of ownership and control of production and distribution. These include news, feature films, popular music recordings, television serials and books. Miège (1989) refers to these as 'editorial' media, and Tunstall (1991) considers them as 'one-off' media, by contrast with the 'flow' media of newspapers, radio and television stations, which have generally resisted multinational ownership – and relied much more on advertising rather than sales as their main source of revenue. The 'one-off' product used to be more easily designed for an international market and lends itself to flexible marketing and distribution over a longer time span. As corporations have become more integrated and diversified, the focus has shifted somewhat from 'one-off' products to media properties that can be franchised and serialized across the same and different media, often with tie-ins to other industries (such as toys, consumer electronics and fashion).

'News' was among the first products to be 'commodified' by way of the main international news agencies. These are, in effect, 'wholesale' suppliers of news as a commodity, and it is easy to see why national news media find it much more convenient and economical to 'buy in' news about the rest of the world than to collect it themselves, given the cost and risk of foreign news desks. The rise of the global news agencies of the twentieth century was made possible by technology (telegraph and radio telephony) and stimulated by war, trade, imperialism and industrial expansion (Boyd-Barrett, 1980, 2001; Boyd-Barrett and Rantanen, 1998). Government involvement was quite common. For these reasons, the main press agencies in the era after the Second World War were North American (UPI and Associated Press), British (Reuters), French (AFP) and Russian (Tass). Since then, the US predominance has declined in relative terms with the virtual demise of UPI, while other agencies have grown (such as the German DPA, Chinese Xinhua and the Japanese Kyodo). In 1992, after the fall of the Soviet Union, Tass was replaced by Itar–Tass, which is still a state agency. Tunstall and Machin (1999: 77) refer to a virtual 'world news duopoly' controlled by the US Associated Press and the British Reuters. The French AFP, German DPA and Spanish EFE are also big players. It is clear that predominance is shaped by the domestic strength of the media organizations concerned, in terms of market size, degree of concentration and economic resources. The English language confers an extra advantage.

A good example of internationalization of media ownership, production and distribution leading to a 'hourglass structure' of the media industries (see Chapter 8) is that of the popular music industry, with a high proportion of several major markets being in the hands of three companies. Advertising provides another example of very high concentration and internationalization. About five leading super-agencies have the lion's share of the world's advertising expenditure: the British WPP Group, US-based Omnicom Group and Interpublic Group, the French Publicis Groupe, and Dentsu in Japan. Advertising agencies have increasingly expanded to become 'full-service' agencies or networked firms, also offering and controlling market research, media buying and public relations companies. As Thussu (2009a: 56) comments, 'a Western, and more specifically, Anglo-American stamp is visible on global advertising', with a trend towards global branding. Most attention tends to be paid to the US-based multimedia firms with global operations, but there are now quite a few multimedia conglomerates elsewhere in the world, all diversified entities looking for economies of scale and market power.

Globalization and concentration of large media companies tend also to lead to cartel-forming, and the very large firms co-operate in various ways as well as compete. Companies also co-operate by sharing revenue, co-producing, co-purchasing movies, and dividing up local outlets. Although the story becomes increasingly complicated by the rise of Japanese, Indian, Brazilian as well as European media enterprises, there is little doubt that the USA overall has benefited most from global expansion in media markets. At the same time, the global media market is 'disrupted' in many ways by non-media competitors from the likes of platform companies on the one hand and small high-risk media businesses (or startups) seeking niche audiences and venture capital on the other. This leads to a 'polarized' competitive environment in which prospects for mid-sized mass media companies, such as national newspapers and broadcasting organizations, are less than ideal given their generally more conservative approach to business strategy (see Chapters 8 and 10–11).

## VARIETIES OF GLOBAL MASS MEDIA

Global mass communication is a multifaceted phenomenon that takes a variety of forms. These include the following:

- Direct transmission or distribution of media channels or complete publications from one country to audiences in other countries. This covers foreign sales of newspapers (sometimes in special editions) and books, certain satellite television channels and officially sponsored international radio broadcast services.

- Certain specifically international media, such as Eurosport, CNN International, BBC World, TVCinq, Telesur, Al-Jazeera, Russia Today, Africanews, and so on, plus the international news agencies. This includes difficult-to-classify English-language online media with an international audience, such as European multi-regional digital news publisher *The Local* (Archetti, 2019).

- Content items of many kinds (films, music, TV programmes, journalistic items, etc.) that are imported to make up part of domestic media output.

- Formats and genres of foreign origin that are adapted or remade to suit domestic audiences.

- International news items, whether about a foreign country or made in a foreign country, that appear in domestic media.

- Miscellaneous content such as sporting events, advertising and pictures that have a foreign reference or origin.
- The World Wide Web (last but not least) in many different forms, overlapping with some of the above.

It is clear from this inventory that there is no sharp dividing line between media content that is 'global' and that which is 'national' or local. Mass communication is almost by definition 'global' in potential, although most countries have a mainly domestic media supply. The United States is one such case, but American media culture does have many foreign cultural influences, through trade and immigration. It is also indirectly globalized by the orientation of much of its own production towards world markets, as well as its co-optation of international media genres, products, services and 'stars', and its tendency to outsource a significant portion of its media production to other countries (a process called 'runaway production').

Despite the many manifestations of media globalization, there are few media outlets (channels, publications, etc.) that actually address a significantly large foreign audience directly (even if the potential in terms of households reached is large). At most, certain successful products (for example, a hit film or TV show, a music recording or a sporting event) will receive a worldwide audience in the end. This implies that 'exporting' countries still have a considerable capacity to influence the 'national' media experience of 'receiving' countries. We have to consider how far the 'foreign' content has been subject to 'gatekeeping' controls at the point of import (for instance, edited, screened and selected, dubbed or translated, given a familiar context). The main mechanism of 'control' is not usually policy or law, or even economics (which often encourages imports), but the audience demand for their 'own' media content in their own language. There are natural barriers of language and culture that resist globalization (B011ereyst, 1992). Economics can limit as well as stimulate imports. In general, the wealthier a country, even when small in population, the more chance it has to afford its media autonomy. The forms of globalization are diverse and the meaning of the term, elastic. Some of these meanings are shown in Box 9.3.

## 9.3
## The meanings of media globalization

- Increasing ownership by global media firms
- Increasing similarity of media systems across the world
- The same or very similar news and entertainment products are found globally

*(Continued)*

- Audiences can choose media from other countries
- Trends of cultural homogenization and westernization
- Decontextualization of media experience in respect of location and culture
- Reduction in national communication sovereignty and more free flow of communication

# INTERNATIONAL MEDIA DEPENDENCY

According to dependency theorists, a necessary condition for throwing off the dependent relationship is to have some self-sufficiency in the realm of information, ideas and culture. Mowlana (1985) proposed a model in which two dimensions are the most important determinants of the degree of communication dependence or autonomy. The model represents a now familiar sequence from sender (1) to receiver (4), mediated by a technologically based production (2) and distribution (3) system. In international communication, contrary to the typical national media situation, the four stages of origination, production, distribution and reception can be (and often are) spatially, organizationally and culturally separated from each other. Media products from one country are typically imported and incorporated into a quite different distribution system and reach audiences for which they were not originally intended. Quite commonly, especially in respect of film and television, the entire origination and production of products occurs in one country and the distribution in another.

This typically extended and discontinuous process is dependent on two kinds of expertise (and also of property), one relating to hardware, the other to software. Production hardware includes cameras, studios, printing plants, computers, and so on. Production software includes not only actual content items, but also performance rights, management, professional norms and routine operating practices of media organizations (know-how). Distribution hardware refers to transmitters, satellite links, transportation, home receivers, recorders, and so on. Distribution software includes publicity, management, marketing and research. Both production and distribution stages are affected by extramedia as well as intramedia variables – on the production side by circumstances of ownership and the cultural and social context, and on the distribution side by the economics of the particular media market.

The model thus describes conditions of multiple dependency in the flow of communication from more to less developed countries. The latter are often dependent in respect of all four main types of hardware and software, and each may be controlled by the originating country. Self-sufficiency in media terms is virtually impossible, but there can be

MCQUAIL'S MEDIA AND MASS COMMUNICATION THEORY
STRUCTURES

extreme degrees of insufficiency, and it is never possible to truly 'catch up', especially in a digital context where the largest corporations greatly benefit from network effects. As Golding (1977) first pointed out, the potential influence that goes with media dependency is not confined to cultural or ideological messages in content; it is also embedded in professional standards and practices, including for example journalistic ethics and **news values**. These points can also be explained in terms of the centre–periphery pattern discussed above. It is important to note the not insignificant 'communication power' (Castells, 2009) that local industries, media startups and online networks of media makers and users have in the digital age, offering opportunities for resistance, dissidence and struggle over the design and structure of the global media system.

The global communication situation is one of increasing complexity as a result of new markets, new media and changes in economic fortunes and geopolitical realities, but some forms of dependency will persist, with different patterns for different media. However, overall, the framework explains less than it did formerly. It is more difficult to assign information and culture to a country of origin. Multinational production and marketing in the control of large corporations and multilateral media flows will establish their own patterns of dominance and dependency. At the same time, much is still dependent on and governed by local and national interests, policies, tastes and cultures. As Flew (2018: 26) warns us, when considering contemporary global media, we should 'avoid falling into a determinist trap of assuming that media globalization means the end of nation-states, national cultures and identities, and territorially defined systems of production, distribution and governance'.

## CULTURAL IMPERIALISM AND BEYOND

In the era immediately following the Second World War, when communication research was largely an American monopoly, the mass media were commonly viewed as one of the most promising channels of modernization (that is, westernization) and especially as a potent tool for overcoming traditional attitudes (Lerner, 1958). From this perspective, the flow of mass media from the developed or capitalist West to the less developed world was seen as both good for its recipients and also beneficial in combating the alternative model of modernization based on socialism, planning and government control. The kinds of media flow envisaged were not direct propaganda or instruction, but the ordinary entertainment (plus news and advertising) that was presumed to show a prosperous way of life and the social institutions of liberal democracy at work. The flood of American print, film, music and television provided the main example and testing of the theory.

This was a very ethnocentric way of looking at global communication flow, and it eventually provoked a critical reaction from scholars and political activists and also from those at the receiving end, audiences and consumers. Before long the issue was inescapably caught up in Cold War polemics and resistance movements in semi-colonial situations (especially in Latin America, where the media and communication research agenda became anchored in critical analyses of the domination of US cultural industries, the capitalist structure of media markets, and the links between these phenomena; see Waisbord, 2014). However, unlike the international propaganda efforts of previous times, the new 'media imperialism' seemed to be carried out at the willing request of the mass audience for popular culture and was thus much more likely to 'succeed'. Of course, it was not the audience making a direct choice, but domestic media firms choosing on their behalf, for economic rather than ideological reasons.

Most of the issues surrounding global mass communication have a direct or indirect connection with the thesis of 'cultural imperialism', or the more limited notion of 'media imperialism' (see below). Both concepts imply a deliberate attempt to dominate, invade or subvert the 'cultural space' of others and suggest a degree of coercion in the relationship. It is certainly a very unequal relationship in terms of power. It also implies some kind of overall cultural or ideological pattern in what is transmitted, which has often been interpreted in terms of 'western values', especially those of individualism, secularism and materialism.

It has a political as well as a cultural content, however, in the first case essentially a submission to the global project of American capitalism (Schiller, 1969). In the case of relations with Latin America noted already, the idea of an American 'imperialist' project for the hemisphere, certainly in the 1960s and 1970s, was not fanciful (Dorfman and Mattelart, 1975). Critical theorists have not always agreed on whether it was the economic aims of global market control or the cultural and political aims of 'westernization' and anti-communism that took precedence, although the two aspects are connected. The (critical) political-economic theorists emphasize the economic dynamics of global media markets that work to shape the flows of media commodities. Not surprisingly, such dynamics favour the free-market model and in general promote western capitalism.

The critics of global media imperialism have generally been countered by a mixed set of supporters of the free market, those who celebrate voices of struggle and resistance, or just pragmatists who see the imbalance of flow as a normal feature of the media market. In their view, globalization has benefits for all and is not necessarily problematic (for example, Pool, 1974; Hoskins and Mirus, 1988; Noam, 1991; Wildman, 1991). It may even be temporary or reversed under some circumstances. Biltereyst (1995) has described the situation in terms of two dominant and opposed paradigms under the headings of *dependency* and *free flow*. In his view, both paradigms rest on somewhat weak grounds empirically. The critical dependency model is based very largely on evidence of quantity of flow and some limited interpretation of ideological tendencies of content. There is inconclusive research on the posited effects. The free-flow theorists tend to assume minimal effects on the grounds that the audience is voluntary, and they tend to make assumptions about the cultural neutrality and ideological innocence of the

MCQUAIL'S MEDIA AND MASS COMMUNICATION THEORY
STRUCTURES

globally traded content. It is also quite possible to view the ongoing globalization of media as having no ultimate goal or purpose and no real effect (in line with the 'cultural autonomy' position signalled in Chapter 4, p. 107). It is simply an unplanned outcome of current political, cultural and technological changes.

If the process of global mass communication is framed from the point of view of the national societies at the receiving end, according to the media imperialist thesis there are at least four propositions to consider. These are listed in Box 9.4 and will be discussed later in the chapter. However, there has been a shift in thinking about globalization that has moved on from the overwhelmingly negative perspective of media imperialism. It is not a return to the 'optimism' of the modernization phase, but more a reflection of second, late or 'liquid' modern (Bauman, 2000) ideas and new cultural theory that nuances the normative judgements of earlier theory.

## 9.4

## Media imperialism: main propositions

- Global media promote relations of dependency rather than economic growth
- The imbalance in the flow of mass media content undermines cultural autonomy or holds back its development
- The unequal relationship in the flow of news increases the relative global power of large and wealthy news-producing countries and hinders the growth of an appropriate national identity and self-image
- Global media flows give rise to a state of cultural homogenization or synchronization, leading to a dominant form of culture that has no specific connection with real experience for most people

## GLOBALIZATION RE-EVALUATED

The cultural imperialism thesis has been largely abandoned (Sreberny-Mohammadi, 1996; Golding and Harris, 1998). As we have seen, there has been a strong challenge to the critique of popular mass media and its general cultural pessimism. This has also affected thinking about the effects of global cultural exchange, although perhaps not about the global flow of news. Certainly, we quite often encounter positive views of the global inclusiveness brought about by mass media, in particular the Internet. The shared symbolic space can be extended, and the constraints of place and time that are associated with nationally compartmentalized media systems can be evaded. Globalization of culture can even look good compared with the ethnocentrism, nationalism and xenophobia that characterize some national media systems. The new era of international peace (the 'new world order') that was supposed to have been ushered in by the end of the Cold War was thought to require a significant presence of internationalist media (Ferguson, 1992). The long-term consequences of the ongoing 'war on terror' are myriad, but work such as that done by Parks (2018) and Palmer (2019) on both media entertainment as well as news coverage, and the structure of the global media industry suggests that media companies have worked to further western or specifically US perspectives through uninformed coverage and often xenophobic representations of disparate cultures.

Most of the propositions arising from the media imperialism thesis tend to frame global mass communication as a process of cause and effect, as if the media were 'transmitting' ideas, meaning and cultural forms from place to place, sender to receiver. To that extent, the critics use much the same language as the original 'theorists of development'. There is a general consensus that this 'transportation' model of how media work is not very appropriate outside certain cases of planned communication. If nothing else, we need to take much more account of the active participation of the audience in shaping any 'meaning' that is taken from mass media (Liebes and Katz, 1990).

It is arguable that the media can also help in the process of cultural growth, diffusion, invention and creativity, and are not just undermining existing culture. Much modern theory and evidence supports the view that media-cultural 'invasion' is *resisted* or redefined according to local culture and experience. Often the 'internationalization' involved is self-chosen and not the result of imperialism. Lull and Wallis (1992) use the term 'transculturation' to describe a process of 'mediated cultural interaction' in which Vietnamese music was crossed with North American strains to produce a new cultural *hybrid*. There are many examples of a similar process at work in the world, not least through increasing international co-productions in film and television leading to global media 'ecologies' of production (Baltruschat, 2010). Theorists tend to see globalization as accompanied by a process of 'glocalization', according to which international media adapt to the circumstances of the regions served (Kraidy, 2003). The incorporation of different formats and performance standards into domestic production is another aspect of the process (Wasserman and Rao, 2008), as are requirements for international channels and streaming services such as Netflix to incorporate and promote local content.

The 'problem' of potential cultural damage from transnationalized media may well be exaggerated. Globally, many distinct regional and national (as well as subnational) cultures within Europe and other regions are still strong and resistant – among both media consumers and producers – even though media production and consumption are now more networked than ever. Audiences can probably tolerate several different and inconsistent worlds of cultural experience (such as local, national, subgroup and global) without one having to destroy the others. The media can extend cultural choices in a creative way, and internationalization can work creatively. This relativizing of the problem does not abolish it, and there are circumstances under which cultural loss does occur, such as in the case of indigenous media and media produced in minority languages.

This revised perspective on globalization rests on the observation that the international flow of media generally responds to demand, and has to be understood in terms of the wants and needs of receivers and not just the actual or supposed motives of the suppliers. This fact does not in itself invalidate the media imperialist critique, given the inner workings of the global media market. A vital contemporary component of the media imperialism thesis focuses on the ways in which global media flows (in news and entertainment) primarily reflect and promote the values of a 'transnationalist capitalist class' (Sklair, 2000). Many features of the world media situation attest to the even more powerful grip of the capitalist apparatus and ethos on media nearly everywhere, with no place left to hide.

## THE MEDIA TRANSNATIONALIZATION PROCESS

Under this heading we look at the process by which content and audience experience are in some sense globalized. It is an effect process (if there is one) with two stages: first, the transformation of content; and secondly, the impact on audiences. In his analysis of the international flows of television, Sepstrup (1989) suggested that we differentiate *flows* in the following way:

- *national* – where foreign (not home-produced) content is distributed in the national television system;
- *bilateral* – where content originating in and intended for one country is received directly in a neighbouring country;
- *multilateral* – where content is produced or disseminated without a specific national audience in mind.

In the *national* case, all content is distributed by the home media, but some of the items will be of foreign origin (films, TV shows, news stories, etc.). The *bilateral* case refers mainly to direct cross-border transmission or reception, where audiences in a neighbouring country are reached on a regular basis. This is common, for example, in respect of the USA and Canada, Britain and Ireland, The Netherlands and Belgium. The *multilateral* type covers most examples of overtly international media channels. The first type of internationalization is by far the most important in terms of volume of flow and reach to audiences, yet at the same time, as we have noted, it is potentially open to national control.

The model of transnationalizing effects proposed by Sepstrup (1989) on the basis of this characterization is reproduced in Figure 9.1. This shows the relationship between three notional countries, in which X is a major producer and exporter of media content and Y and Z are importers. There are three main lines of transnationalizing effect: national, bilateral and multilateral. The first of these operates on the basis of imports and is really a process by which a national media system is internationalized by way of borrowing content. The next step in the process, if there is one, is that the national system becomes the agent for influencing its audiences in an 'international' direction, for good or ill. For this to take place, the content not only has to be transmitted, but has to be received and responded to in a positive way. Only if this happens can we speak of a process of internationalization that affects the culture and the society.

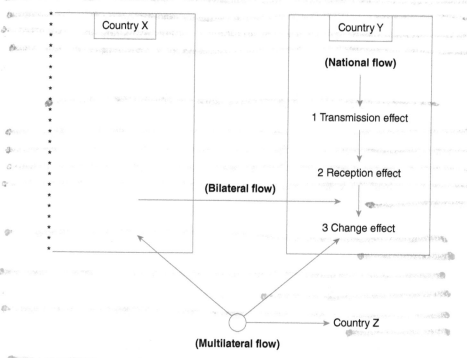

Figure 9.1    Internationalization of television: three types of flow (McQuail and Windahl, 1993: 225, based on theory in Sepstrup, 1989)

Of the other two processes, the case of bilateral flow (direct cross-border transmission) most often occurs when neighbouring countries already have much in common in terms of culture, experience and usually language. The case of multilateral flow from one country direct to many others is growing in importance with the growth of the Internet, which facilitates multiple multilateral flows.

The more that content is filtered through the national media system, the more it is subject to selection and adapted, reframed and recontextualized to fit local tastes, attitudes and expectations. The chance of 'culture clash' is diminished. This transformation is greater where the receiving countries are well developed, culturally and economically.

The transformation process (in the transmission) is likely to be least operative where there is already cultural affinity between the country of origin and the country of reception (and thus less room for cultural change). It is also limited where the receiving country is poor and undeveloped, the cultural distance is high and the opportunity to accept influence (in the form of new ideas or new kinds of behaviour) is low.

The direction of any transnationalizing effect seems very predictable from the structure of the world media system as outlined above, although the degree of effect from mass communication alone is very uncertain. With the Internet, the possibility of access to global information and cultural resources vastly increases, even though there are still countries where access to such media is heavily controlled and censored. In most places, access is now possible without reliance on the various gatekeepers that always restrict and control the flow of content in more traditional media. These gatekeepers operate at both the sending and receiving ends of distribution channels. The Internet (and the World Wide Web) is a genuinely global medium. Early on, Internet 'content' was dominated by 'western' (and English language) originators, however diverse, a situation now brought into balance because of the rise of Internet use, industrial development and innovation in Brazil, Russia, India, China, South Africa (the so-called BRICS countries) and elsewhere in the world. A key concern now is perhaps not so much the US or western dominance in the transnationalization of the media system, but rather the relatively unfettered market logic of capitalist enterprise that pervades the Internet and global media flows.

## INTERNATIONAL NEWS FLOW

The international flow of news warrants particular attention in the context of global media. As noted earlier, the globalization of news really began in earnest with the rise of the international news agencies in the nineteenth century (see Boyd-Barrett and Rantanen, 1998), and news was the first media product to be effectively commodified for international trade. The reasons for this are not altogether clear, although the history of mass media shows the early and perennial importance of a service of current information for attracting audiences. The 'news' has become a more or less standardized and universal genre as a component of print and electronic media, and along with it the 'news story'. The news story can have a value as useful information, can satisfy curiosity and human interest, and is particularly conducive to sharing among friends and networks online, regardless of where it is heard or picked up.

The televising of news accelerated the cross-cultural appeal of news by telling the story in pictures to which can be added words in any language or with any 'angle'. Television news film agencies followed in the footsteps of the print news agencies. Television news film, like print news, has been based on the principle of journalistic 'objectivity', which is designed to guarantee the reliability and credibility of accounts of events. While earlier international 'foreign' news concentrated on politics, war, diplomacy and trade, there has been an enormous expansion of the scope for international news, with particular reference to sport, the world of showbusiness, finance, technology, travel, fashion, sex, and much more.

A debate about the imbalance of news flow as between North and South raged during the 1970s and became highly politicized, caught up in Cold War polemics. An attempt was made by media-dependent countries to use the United Nations Educational, Scientific and Cultural Organization (UNESCO) as a means towards a new world information and communication order (NWICO) that would establish some normative guidelines for international reporting (see Hamelink, 1994; Carlsson, 2003). A claim was also made for some control over reporting on grounds of equity, sovereignty and fairness. These requests were strongly rejected by defenders of the 'free-flow' principle (essentially the free market), mainly western governments and western press interests (see Giffard, 1989). An international inquiry made recommendations for new guidelines (McBride et al., 1980), but it was largely ignored and the path via UNESCO was also closed (see Hamelink, 1998). A new phase of accelerated liberalization of communication, nationally and internationally, and other geopolitical changes largely closed down the debate, even though the underlying circumstances were little changed.

Along the way, however, much light was shed by research and by the public debate on the actual structure of news flow and the underlying dynamics of the global news industry. It was repeatedly confirmed that news (whether press or TV) in more developed countries does not typically give a great deal of space to foreign news (except in specialist or elite publications). Foreign news is largely devoted to events in other countries that are large, nearby and rich, or connected by language and culture. It is also narrowly focused on the interests of the receiving country, and can at times be outright xenophobic in tone. Most foreign news can often be accounted for by attention to a small number of ongoing crises (for example, conflict in the Middle East) of relevance to the developed world, reported on by foreign correspondents who are increasingly operating in a temporary and freelance capacity and are highly dependent on local 'fixers' to do their work (Palmer, 2019). Large areas of the physical world are found to be systematically absent or miniscule on the implied 'map' of the world represented by the universe of news event locations (for example, Gerbner and Marvanyi, 1977; Womack, 1981; Rosengren, 2000). In particular, developing countries are only likely to enter the news frame of developed countries when some events there threaten the economic or strategic interests of the 'great powers'. Alternatively, news is made when problems and disasters reach such a scale that they become of interest to audiences in distant and safer lands. This situation does not seem to be remedied online, as upheaval among Internet users in rich, developed countries additionally steers international news media to the same kind of stories, which are often reported on without the necessary context.

The reasons for the provincial 'bias' of international news selection that still largely persists are not hard to find or to understand. In the first place, they result from the organization of news flow by way of agencies and each news medium's own gatekeeping. The ultimate arbiter is the average news consumer, who is usually thought of as not very interested in distant events. Agencies collect news 'abroad' with a view to what will interest the ultimate 'home' audience, and the foreign news editors of home media apply an even more precise set of criteria of a similar kind. The result is to largely eliminate news of distant places that is not dramatic or directly relevant to the receiving nation.

There has been much research into the factors shaping the structure of foreign news. Most basic is the fact that the flow of news reflects patterns of economic and political relations as well as geographical closeness and cultural affinity (Rosengren, 1974; Ito and Koshevar, 1983; Wu, 2003). The flow of news is positively correlated with other forms of transaction between countries. We need or want to know about those parts of the world with which we trade or with whom we are friendly or unfriendly. The other main factor is power: we need to know about more powerful countries that can affect us. There are more detailed explanations of foreign news selection. Galtung and Ruge (1965) originally proposed that selection was the outcome of three sets of factors: *organizational*, dealing with the availability and distribution of news; *genre related*, dealing with what conventionally counts as of interest to news audiences; and *social-cultural* factors, mainly referring to the values by which topics are chosen.

Other analyses of patterns of attention in foreign news have largely confirmed the validity of these points (for recent cross-national comparative studies, see for example, Segev, 2015; Grasland, 2019). News will tend not to deal with distant and politically unimportant nations (except in some temporary crisis), with non-elites or with ideas, structures and institutions. Long-term processes (such as development or dependency) are not easy to turn into news, as normally understood. However, we should keep in mind that most studies of news have concentrated on 'serious' (that is, political and economic) content and hard news in established 'quality' news outlets. Less attention has been given to areas that may be quantitatively and in other ways more significant, in particular material about sport, music, weather, lifestyle, culture and entertainment, celebrity **gossip** and other human interest matters which may easily become 'news'. The news that most people enjoy is dominated by such topics and they are quite likely to be international in character, reflecting global media culture.

A study of international news relating to the events of 9/11 by Cristina Archetti (2008) shows much nuance regarding some of the tendencies outlined. Her study of four countries (the USA, France, Pakistan and Italy) examined the sources drawn on in news reports of the events. It showed that each media channel had its own distinctive pattern of sources, the majority coming from its own national resources. Secondly, there is little evidence of the media agenda of a foreign country being imported, since news selections were made according to the domestic (own nation) perspective. Thirdly, weaker players in the news system, such as Pakistan, actually had a more diverse source pattern than the American media, making foreign news dominance unlikely. All in all, the study calls into question both globalizing and homogenizing effects.

Early expectations about the Internet were hopeful that it would widen access to and enrich the flow of international news, simply by virtue of the seemingly unlimited capacity and the open availability from sources around the world. Studies on the determinants of news in fifteen countries showed that online journalism followed almost the same patterns as traditional news outlets and the associated factors were the same, especially patterns of trade, news agencies, geographical proximity and cultural proximity (Wu, 2007; Chang, Himelboim and Dong, 2009). In contrast, the UK stands out as having a clear pattern of linkage to nearly all the peripheral countries. British media, especially the BBC, are more inclined to send hyperlinks to websites in the countries reported in the news.

A summary of the factors relevant to news flow is given in Box 9.5.

---

**9.5**

**Factors affecting the selection and flow of international news**

- Occurrence of events abroad with home relevance or interest
- Timing of events and news cycles
- Reporting and transmitting resources available
- Operation of international news agencies
- Journalistic news values
- Patterns of geography, trade and diplomacy
- Cultural affinity between countries

---

## THE GLOBAL TRADE IN MEDIA CULTURE

There has been an enormous expansion of television and film production and transmission outside the United States since the 1970s, leaving the USA relatively less dominant in global media terms than it was during much of the twentieth century. This means that more countries can satisfy more of their own needs from home production. Sreberny-Mohammadi (1996) cited findings that show unexpectedly high levels of local production in, for example, India and Korea. She warned against over-interpretation of the evidence of 'indigenization', since much is produced by large corporations operating under exactly the same logic as the former villains of cultural imperialism. In the background to the European case, there is a long history of grumbling (usually by cultural elites) about the threat of 'Americanization' to cultural values and even civilization. In the aftermath of the Second World War, the dominance of American media was an accomplished fact, but impoverished countries still restricted film imports and supported nascent national film and television industries. In general, television services were developed on the basis of national public service models that gave some priority to promoting and protecting the national cultural identity.

More recent attitudes in western Europe to importing audiovisual content have been shaped by three main factors, aside from expansion and privatization. One has been the political-cultural project of the European Union. The second has been the goal of creating a large internal European market, in which European audiovisual industries should have their place in the sun. Thirdly, there was a wish to reduce the large trade deficit in media products. All goals were perceived to be undermined by the one-directional transatlantic flow of content. According to Tunstall and Machin (1999), the attempts to enlarge the market have mainly benefited American exporters by creating a single market and opening it up to competition.

The mixing of cultural and economic motives and arguments confused the issue considerably, but the EU accepts the principle of open markets. The resulting compromise has allowed principles of free trade and cultural sovereignty to survive, although without much practical effect on the course of events. The European Union retains and has introduced some policies that give some protection to European television and film industries (especially its Directive on Television Without Frontiers, which privileges European production). National media policies also contribute to subsidizing local media production, such as television in Sweden, film in Denmark, games in South Korea and advertising in South Africa.

Although media imports to a domestic market basically arise from the real or perceived attractiveness of the product to the media audience, it is also clear that, in any given country, the most popular television programmes (highest ratings) and motion pictures (ticket sales) are nearly always home produced (even if based on international media formats). The price of US exports is always adjusted to the particular market situation, and there is a 'cultural discount' factor in operation that relates the price to the degree of cultural affinity between exporter and importer (the lower the affinity, the lower the price) (Hoskins and Mirus, 1988). Imported content from the USA falls largely into the category of drama and fiction and reflects the high cost of own production on the part of other countries rather than the overwhelming appeal or superior quality of the product.

The story of one of the earliest and biggest transnational media channels, MTV, as told by Roe and de Meyer (2000), is indicative of what happened more generally over time to the transnational satellite television channels that spearheaded the 'invasion' of Europe and the rest of the world in the 1980s and 1990s. MTV was initially very successful in gaining a new youth audience for mainly Anglo-American pop music. However, competing channels in Germany, The Netherlands and elsewhere forced MTV to respond with a policy of regionalization, employing the 'local' language but not changing the music significantly. This process continued with increasingly limited success, and the lesson does seem to be that audiences ultimately (also) want to see their own stars, language and culture reflected in their media.

Because this book is about mass media it largely ignores other forms of cultural globalization, although these are often connected with the media and vice versa. Rich countries have always appropriated cultural elements from colonies, dependencies and trading partners in the form of ideas, designs, fashions, cuisine, flora and much more. Immigrant groups have also taken their culture with them when they converge on the same rich countries. The diffusion of symbolic cultures now also takes place by way of the media, advertising and marketing, often via the search for new products to feed the lifestyle demands of consumers. This works in both directions (centre and periphery). Moorti (2003) describes the case of the import of Indian motifs into American fashion culture, especially the bindi (vermilion mark) and nose-ring. Such symbols are adopted by American women as a fashion statement and also a signifier of cosmopolitanism and exoticism, without anything changing in the hierarchical relationship between white and Asian women. Moorti calls this 'symbolic cannibalism' and a typical example of commodification rather than real multiculturalism. Many similar examples can be found.

The games industry is a good example of a highly successful global media industry that mixes and disseminates cultural artefacts cross-culturally, such as the Japanese Pokémon and Super Mario franchises, receiving worldwide acclaim while referencing both western and eastern characters and influences. Another example from the games industry which shows how contentious these adaptations can be is the heavily censored German version of the popular shooter game *Wolfenstein*, deleting or replacing its Nazi imagery to comply with local laws. Localization of digital games has become an intricate process whereby specific storylines, characters and design elements of a game are painstakingly adapted to local sensitivities and tastes. The consumer-centric practice of localization, transnationalization and internationalization is now common in the global games industry (Kerr, 2016) as well as for television and film (Esser, Smith and Bernal-Merino, 2018).

## GLOBAL MEDIA CULTURE, GLOBAL MEDIA STUDIES

Two recurring themes of debate and research arising out of media globalization, renewed in the age of 'always on' digital media, concern (cultural) identity and community. First, imported media culture is thought to hinder the development of the native culture of the receiving country, or even many local and regional cultures within a country. Often the perceived problems are associated with a smaller country being located in the shadow of a dominant nation, as in the case of Canada *vis-à-vis* the USA or Ireland and the UK.

Underlying the above issues is a strong 'belief system' holding that cultures are both valuable collective properties of nations and places, and also very vulnerable to alien influences – particularly of those coming from the richest parts of the world. The value attributed to a national culture is rooted in ideas developed during the nineteenth and twentieth centuries, when national independence movements were often intimately connected with the rediscovery of distinctive national cultural traditions. The frequent lack of correlation between newly established national boundaries (often invented) and 'natural' cultural divisions of peoples has done little to modify the rhetoric about the intrinsic value of national culture.

A similar situation arises in the case of national minorities trapped within a larger nation state and with limited autonomy. There is a good deal of confusion about the meaning of national or cultural identity, although in a given case it is usually clear what is involved. Schlesinger (1987) suggests an approach by way of a general concept of 'collective identity'. A collective identity, in this sense, persists in *time* and is resistant to change, although survival also requires that it be consciously expressed, reinforced and transmitted. For this reason, having access to and support from relevant communications media is evidently important. Television can play a significant part in supporting national identity, by way of language and representation. Castello (2007), drawing on Catalan experience, makes a convincing case for the view that a nation needs its own fiction and therefore a cultural policy that helps it to flourish. Furthermore, since international media flows favour rich western nations and the electronic spectrum tends to be unequally distributed, a global media culture inherently is biased towards the values and priorities of the richest nations that also control much of the media and telecommunications infrastructure in the world. Media internationalization to some extent leads to more homogenization or 'cultural synchronization' and various forms of cultural imperialism (Miller and Kraidy, 2016: 28ff). According to Hamelink (1983: 22), this process 'implies that the decisions regarding the cultural development of a given country are made in accordance with the interests and needs of a powerful central nation. They are then imposed with subtle but devastating effectiveness without regard for the adaptive necessities of the dependent nation'. As a result, cultures are less distinctive and cohesive and also less exclusive.

One cultural consequence of media globalization may be overlooked because it is obvious: the rise of a globalized media culture as such (see Tomlinson, 1999). There is no shortage of examples of cultural themes, styles, images and performances that are circulated and consumed on a global basis by way of mass communication (and new media). Global media culture is to some extent typified by its emphasis on novelty, fashion, celebrity in all fields, sports, youth and sex. Often the particular stars of celebrity culture are truly global; sometimes they are local but the phenomenon is otherwise the same. Not by chance, the international media are given some credit (or blame) for promoting this type of culture. The trend is found as much in news as in entertainment. According to Thussu (2009a), the globalization of television along the US market-driven model has led to the worldwide circulation of 'infotainment', with the same standards of newsworthiness and often the same news and the same sources, everywhere. While such a global media culture may appear value-free, in fact it embodies a good many of the values of western capitalism, including individualism and consumerism, hedonism and commercialism. On the other hand, as observers like Henry Jenkins (in Jenkins et al., 2016) among others note, global media culture can also be a playground for international youth activism and what can be called a 'playful' type of citizenship, as people use widely recognizable symbols from popular media culture to raise awareness about a variety of issues of both local and global importance, such as the plight of refugees, climate change, and so on (Glas et al., 2019).

A second key concern regarding our globalized media culture relates to its impact on people's sense and experience of community. Just about everyone – even those not necessarily online or plugged in – is drawn into media at one point or another. In the process, more or less new forms of being together, forming groups and alliances, hanging out with others, or otherwise maintaining some sense of belonging emerge. The various ways in which ever-growing numbers of people, both young and old, engage with each other through media is sometimes taken as a new form of community. The promise of online communities tends to be seen as either bridging existing social divides or bonding people with already similar beliefs. Drawing data from various international research projects, Pippa Norris (2002) asserts that most online groups serve both functions at the same time, and her conclusions have been supported by more recent work. This sense of community may not be different from older, pre-modern types of social networks – as these were also largely based on relations based on kinship, proximity, peer status and interdependency, as defined through the immediate extended family, work or school environment.

Linking emerging forms (and socials norms of) community with new media, Ito (2005) signals an emerging 'hypersociality', as people develop and perform identities in everyday life in relation to customizable, interactive media forms (such as video games and television series in combination with websites). Wittel (2001) proposes a 'network sociality', lamenting the often fleeting, seemingly ephemeral connections and contacts people have online. In a broad take on the issue of community and media, Lash (2002) suggests that previously long-lasting and proximal social bonds – such as exemplified by the neighbourhood community, the extended family, employees and their colleagues – gradually are giving way to distanciated and generally temporary 'communicational' bonds.

Claims about the 'virtualization' of communities as they are more or less exclusively created and maintained on the Internet run the risk of ignoring historical precedent, as earlier studies about community formation and preservation suggest that the boundaries and practices of what constitutes community tend to be as much contingent, relational, temporal, symbolic and exclusive in the world's cities and towns as they are in online social networks, chat groups or massive multiplayer online role-playing games (Castronova, 2005; Massey, 2007). A perspective that combines communities as they form online as well as offline is developed as 'networked individualism', defined as a societal shift from group-based interaction in a single, local, and often solidary, family and community to individuals connected through loosely tied personal networks by means of digital technology (Quan-Haase et al., 2018), which in turn raises significant concerns about digital inequalities and the ways in which networked individualism as experienced and enacted online can help to relieve as well as exacerbate existing inequalities experienced in terms of 'life course, gender, race, and class, as well as health care, politics, economic activity, and social capital' (Robinson et al., 2015: 569).

The main hypothesized effects of globalization are summarized in Box 9.6.

---

## 9.6

### Cultural effects of globalization: potential effects

- Synchronization of culture
- Cultural imperialism: undermining national, regional and local cultures
- Commodification of cultural symbols
- Hybridization and evolution of cultural forms
- Rise of a global 'media culture'
- Deterritorialization of culture
- Integration of online and offline communities
- Rise of digital inequalities

---

Whether we have a truly global media culture relies on what 'media' and 'culture' mean in this context. Flew (2018) suggests that there is considerable evidence to suggest that a global convergence of cultures through media is not happening (see quotation in Box 9.7).

---

## 9.7

### Global media, global culture

If culture is understood in the more structural sense of a shared symbolic order, with the media increasingly at the heart of such systems of communication, then global media may indeed be generating forms of global culture . . . If, however, the concept of culture is understood in the anthropological sense of being a *lived and shared experience*, or 'way of life of a people', then it is hard to maintain that we live in a global culture, or that we are heading towards one. (Flew, 2018: 22, italics in the original)

---

Given the worldwide interconnections enabled by the Internet, the dynamism of international media flows, and concerns about cultural identity and community in the context of a global media culture, Miller and Kraidy (2016) outline the contours of a global approach to media and mass communication research. They suggest a hybrid approach, including, but not limited to, the social sciences and humanities, and focused on how the global production, distribution and reception of media addresses or reinforces the unequal exchange of 'textuality, technology, environment, and labor' (ibid.: 36). This agenda of a global media studies makes us aware of how the global ICT infrastructure, in conjunction with a dominant political economy of major media industries that is primarily supported by advertising and data mining, requires the study of media 'to scale up to the global scope of humanity' (ibid.: 180).

# GLOBAL MEDIA GOVERNANCE

In the absence of global government, international communication is not subject to any central or consistent system of control. The forces of the free market and of national sovereignty combine to keep it this way. Nevertheless, there is quite an extensive set of international controls and regulations that do constrain nationally based media, typically as a result of voluntary co-operation for necessity or mutual advantage (Ó Siochrú and Girard with Mahan, 2003). For the most part, such regulation is designed to facilitate global media in technical and trade matters, but some elements are concerned with normative matters, however non-binding.

The origins of global governance are to be found in agreements designed to facilitate the international postal service, by way of the Universal Postal Union in the mid-nineteenth century. At about the same time (1865), the International Telegraph Union was founded to help co-ordinate interconnections and establish agreement on tariffs, with a subsequent extension to responsibility for the radio spectrum. In both cases, for the moment, governments and state monopolies played a key role. After the Second World War, the United Nations provided an arena for debate on mass media matters, with particular reference to freedom of expression (guaranteed by its charter), the free flow of communication between countries and issues of sovereignty. In 1978 an attempt was made by UNESCO, at the behest of Third World countries, to introduce a media declaration stating a number of principles for the conduct of international media, especially in relation to propaganda for war and hostile reporting. Opposition by western countries and free-market media led to its failure, but it did place a number of new and contentious issues on the agenda of concern and debate and contributed to the recognition of certain communication rights and obligations. There are still international treaties, including South Korea's Personal Information Protection Act of 2011, the 2016 General Data Protection Regulation (GDPR) of the European Union, the 2018 Lei Geral de Proteçao de Dados (LGPD) in Brazil and

Australia's 2018 Privacy Act, that offer some redress to those injured by the misuse of communication and personal information.

The paradigm shift that occurred towards deregulation and privatization, coupled with the new 'communications revolution' based on computers and telecommunications, closed off the path towards greater international normative regulation. But the same shift increased the need for technical, administrative and economic co-operation on a range of issues. The development of the Internet, and particularly the rapid rise of platform companies, has stimulated calls for international regulation.

The following bodies now play a variety of key roles in the emerging system of global governance:

- The International Telecommunication Union (ITU), governed by a council of delegates nominated by national governments, deals with telecommunication technical standards, spectrum allocation, satellite orbits and much besides.

- The World Trade Organization has immense power on economic matters and impinges more and more on the media, as they become bigger business and more commercialized. Central are issues of free trade and protection, with implications for limits to national sovereignty in relation to media policy. The policy of the EU for protecting (public) broadcasting is especially vulnerable. Apart from the EU, other regional trade organizations, such as the North American Free Trade Association (NAFTA), can impinge on media issues.

- The United Nations Educational, Scientific and Cultural Organization (UNESCO), a branch of the UN established in 1945, has wide competence on cultural and educational matters, but little power. It is active on questions of freedom of expression and the Internet, and increasingly invests in media literacy initiatives.

- The World Intellectual Property Organization (WIPO), established in 1893, has a main aim of harmonizing relevant legislation and procedures and resolving disputes between owners of rights, authors and users.

- The International Corporation for Assigned Names and Numbers (ICANN) is the latest addition to the array of governance bodies. It is a non-profit public–private body that aims to represent the community of Internet users. It started in 1994 after the privatization of the World Wide Web and its main function was to allocate addresses and domain names, plus some server management functions. It has little power to deal directly with the emerging social and other problems relating to the Internet. It was answerable to the United States Department of Commerce National Telecommunications and Information Administration (NTIA), but in 2016 the co-ordination and management of ICANN transitioned to a global multi-stakeholder community, which is made up of private-sector representatives, technical experts, academics, civil society, governments and individual Internet end users.

- The Internet Governance Forum (IGF) is a multi-stakeholder forum for policy dialogue on issues of Internet governance, founded in 2006 at the behest of the United Nations.

- There are many other bodies with varying remits for issues relating to international media. Many represent various industry interests, including those of publishers, journalists and producers. There are also many non-governmental organizations (NGOs) speaking for interests in 'civil society'. For the reasons given, effective regulation is still largely confined to technical and economic matters rather than social and cultural issues, with the possible exception of freedom of expression and consumer data protection. Nevertheless, there are many signs of growing internationalism and, arguably, a need for a global frame of analysis next to one that is based on national states and affairs.

# CONCLUSION

Global media and mass communication are a reality, and since the second half of the twentieth century there has almost certainly been a steady strengthening of the conditions of globalization. These are: the existence of a dynamic commercial marketplace for media and ICT industries; the existence of and respect for an effective 'right to information', and thus political freedom and freedom of speech; and the technologies that can offer fast, capacious and low-cost channels of transmission across borders and large distances. Nevertheless, the real chances for global sending or receiving and the probability of it taking place depend on more mundane matters, especially those relating to the national media system and its degree of connectedness to other systems, as well as new and enduring digital inequalities.

Paradoxically, the country endowed with all of the conditions mentioned, the USA, is one of the least likely to be a beneficiary by way of the mass media coming from outside its own frontiers. This does not apply to many sectors where the US imports 'culture' from around the world along with other products. The means are there but the will and motivation seem to be missing. The countries most favoured by a real experience of international media are likely to be small and wealthy enough both to sustain a viable national culture and to enjoy the eclectic fruits of the global information society. There has to be an appreciation of these fruits, or some pressing need, for global mass communication to prosper, and the Internet certainly has laid the groundwork for such a more or less shared media culture.

A condition for global communication to become a more significant component of public communication (as opposed to an important element of media markets) is the ongoing movement towards a global political order and some form of international government, although this is a trend counterbalanced with developments towards strengthening national sovereignty in many parts of the world, including the countries that for the longest time have led the charge towards a global media culture: the UK and the USA.

## FURTHER READING

Archetti, C. (2008) 'News coverage of 9/11 and the demise of the media flows, globalization and localization hypotheses', *International Communication Gazette*, 70(6): 463–485.

Flew, T. (2018) *Understanding Global Media*, 2nd edition. London: Palgrave Macmillan.

Miller, T. and Kraidy, M.M. (2016) *Global Media Studies*. Cambridge: Polity Press.

Robinson, L., Cotten, S.R., Ono, H., Quan-Haase, A., Mesch, G., Chen, W., Schulz, J., Hale, T.M. and Stern, M.J. (2015) 'Digital inequalities and why they matter', *Information, Communication & Society*, 18(5): 569–582.

Sklair, L. (2000) 'The transnational capitalist class and the discourse of globalisation', *Cambridge Review of International Affairs*, 14(1): 67–85.

Tunstall, J. (2007) *The Media Were American*. Oxford: Oxford University Press.

# PART 4
## ORGANIZATIONS

# 10

# THE MEDIA ORGANIZATION: STRUCTURES AND INFLUENCES

Theory about mass communication began with little awareness of the place where media messages originated, except for the vague designation of a 'mass communicator' as source. The originating organization was taken for granted and theory began with the message itself. Research on media production, after beginning with descriptions of media occupations, especially in film and journalism (Rosten, 1937, 1941), gradually widened its focus so as to take account of professional cultures and the occupational context of media work that could affect what was produced.

This chapter looks in turn at each of the main kinds of influence that are brought to bear during the production and processing phase of mass communication. These include external influences from society, technology and the media market as well as from owners, advertisers and the audience. These are looked at primarily from the perspective of the 'communicators' themselves. Attention is also paid to relations internal to the media organization and to the conflict, tensions and problems encountered. The main tensions arise from recurring dilemmas that lie at the heart of making media professionally. These include the potential clash between profit on the one hand and art or social purpose on the other, and the problem of reconciling creative and editorial freedom with the demands of routine and large-scale production, as well as engagement with a demanding and to some extent 'participatory' audience.

The overriding aim of the chapter is to identify and assess the potential influence of various organizational and communicator factors on what is actually produced. Research into media production is important in order to understand this relatively invisible and inaccessible aspect of the media and mass communication process. It uncovers the inner workings of media as industries that have become such a significant part of cultural, economic and political life, and it theoretically engages the question of what mediated messages mean in terms of the exchange between producers and users of content.

Major changes in the structure of media industries, especially the processes of globalization, ownership conglomeration, organizational fragmentation and labour precariousness, provide new theoretical challenges. The Internet has also given rise to new kinds of media organization, as well as amplifying the role of the audience as a co-creator of content.

---

# RESEARCH METHODS AND PERSPECTIVES

A very simple and general framework within which questions can be posed was introduced in Chapter 8. Structural features (for instance, size, forms of ownership and media-industrial functions) can be seen as having direct consequences for the conduct of particular media organizations. Conduct refers to all the systematic activities that in turn affect performance, in the sense of the type and amount of media content and services produced and offered to audiences. According to this model, we need to look not only at internal features of media organizations, but also at their relations with other organizations and with the wider society.

Most of the research and theory discussed in the following pages are 'media-centric' rather than 'society-centric' (see Chapter 1), taking or recording the view from within the media. This may lead to an overestimation of the significance of organizational influences on content. From a 'society-centric' point of view, much of what media organizations do is determined by external social forces, including, of course, the (real or perceived) tastes and demands of media audiences. The history of media production research tends to be informed by this organizational bias, as sociologists (mainly in the French- and English-speaking world) from the late 1960s onwards started to study the production of art and entertainment. Such research tended to be inspired by the increasing economic importance of cultural products and corresponding concerns about the 'commoditization of culture' (Miège, 1979), as well as the rise of cultural policies by national governments to promote, subsidize and protect certain media industries (such as national cinema and public broadcasting). A second strand of early production research was based on more comprehensive political-economic approaches, with a focus on the relation between the production, distribution and consumption of communication in historical and cultural context (Mosco, 1996). As media industries continued to grow in importance as social institutions and as an economic force, scholars in management studies, business studies and policy studies started to take note (Hesmondhalgh, 2010). What all of this scholarship tends to find are structural elements of precariousness and unequal power relations throughout the media industries, often highly patterned, formulaic and routinized activities and processes, and increasingly complex productions that cross and mix multiple media in order to gain the attention of (both consuming and co-creating) audiences (Deuze, 2007).

The predominant method of research has been participant observation of media people at work or in-depth interviewing of involved informants. However, this method requires co-operation from the media organizations under study and this is difficult to obtain. On some points, survey research has provided essential additional information (for instance, on questions of occupational role and social composition). Additionally, research based on market statistics, sales data, publicly available ownership and financial records has been conducted, although mainly by scholars outside media and mass communication.

In general, the theory that has been formulated on the basis of research into media organizations, while fragmentary, has been fairly consistent. It supports the view that content is systematically more influenced by organizational routines, practices and goals than by personal or ideological factors. However, this proposition is itself open to alternative interpretations. It could be taken to mean that ownership and control influence content, thus supporting the social critical view. Or it could reflect the fact that any kind of standardized or mass production process involves some systematic influence on content. From the latter perspective, the 'bias' that has been observed in media content is more likely to be caused by work routines than by hidden ideology.

# THE MAIN ISSUES

The central concerns of research into media industries, organizations and production are summarized by David Hesmondhalgh (2010: 6–7) as:

- Organization: What is the process by which media products come to us? How is their production organized, coordinated and managed?
- Ownership, size and strategy: How important are the size and ownership of the media corporations, and what is the role of smaller companies?
- Work: What is the nature of work in the media industries?

Within these concerns, a key question involves the degree of freedom that a media organization possesses in relation to the wider society. For example, how much freedom is possible within the organization, and, subsequently, what is the relative autonomy (or lack thereof) of those working in a freelance, outsourced, subcontracted or otherwise 'atypical' way for the media industry, while operating outside the media organization. A second recurring theme in media and mass communication research on production relates to the matter of influence on media professionals, producers, organizations and industries. These two questions roughly correspond to the duality of structural effects on organizational conduct and the effects of the latter on the content produced. Reese and Shoemaker (2016) developed five main hypotheses concerning the influence of structural and organizational factors on content, as shown in Box 10.1.

---

## 10.1
### Hypotheses about factors influencing content (Reese and Shoemaker, 2016)

- Content is influenced by media workers' personal characteristics, socialization and attitudes (a communicator-centred, individual-level approach)
- Content is influenced by professional conventions, rituals and routines
- Content is influenced by the culture of a particular media organization
- Content is influenced by the interplay of economic, political and cultural factors (the meso-level environment for media)
- Content is influenced by the larger social system within which media operate (macro considerations including globalization, commodification and ideology)

---

As Reese and Shoemaker (2016) note, the dynamic and converging nature of many of the developments affecting media industries and organizations makes one appreciate how a single issue – for example, the role of technology shaping media production – should be studied at each of these levels of analysis. In general, their hierarchy of influences model presumes that media organizations are not really autonomous, but are penetrated by other sources of power (especially technological, political and economic). The more it appears that outside forces shape the operation of media, the more plausible this hypothesis becomes.

It is difficult to speak of a 'media organization' as if there were a single ideal-typical form. The original term was largely based on the model of an independent company, such as that of the early newspaper, within which all the principal activities of management, financial control, information collecting, editing and processing, the production of content (news), plus printing and distribution, took place under one roof. This model was always untypical of media in general, not applying, for instance, to the film, book publishing or music industries, and applying only variably to radio and television. It is virtually impossible to apply it to most of the so-called new media, which interrelate several separate and disparate organizational functions.

The diversity of organizational forms is matched by the diversity of occupational groups that might qualify as 'mass communicators'. These have been taken as including movie moguls and press tycoons, actors and actresses, television producers, film directors, scriptwriters, book authors, newspaper and broadcast and online journalists, songwriters, disc jockeys, musicians, literary agents, newspaper and magazine editors, website designers, advertising creatives, public relations practitioners, game developers, artist and repertoire ('A&R') managers, and many more. Most of these categories can be subdivided according to the type of medium, size or status of the work organization, employment status, and so on. An increasing amount of media work takes place on a freelance or otherwise entrepreneurial basis, and many media workers belong to no single production organization, even if they may be members of professional or craft associations. As a result, the concepts of 'mass communicator' and of 'media profession' are almost as leaky as that of media organization.

The uncertainty surrounding what counts as a media organization and what counts as a mass communicator is also fuelled by the contemporary notion that the individual professional is their own 'organization' in an increasingly casualized labour market. Production scholars see this uncertainty as the main defining feature of media work in a world that is characterized by 'liquidity', mobility and a lack of compartmentalization (Hesmondhalgh and Baker, 2011; Deuze and Prenger, 2019). Such uncertainty colours every aspect of the media production value chain, including the ways in which stories can be told in a digital, online environment – in effect rendering the distinct boundaries between media channels porous. The same content can appear on many media platforms, either copied-pasted (as in the case of multimedia productions), parsed to meet the requirements of each medium separately (that is, crossmedia work), or as part of a complex narrative or 'storyworld' that spans across multiple media and may include contributions by consumers – a form of transmedia storytelling (Jenkins, 2006; Scolari, 2009). There is no professional or economic monopoly on the potential to reach a large audience by way of the Internet, although the search and recommendation algorithms of platform companies act as new gatekeepers to some extent. Furthermore, social media act as sources, producers, distributors and promoters of media content, partly because of deliberate strategies by media organizations, but generally beyond the control of professional media makers.

Despite this uncertainty and diversity, it still makes sense to try to place questions of media organization within a common framework. One useful step is to think in terms of levels of analysis, so that the different phases of media work and the significant relations between units of organizational activity and between media and the 'outside world' can be identified for study. Dimmick and Coit (1982), for instance, describe a hierarchy with nine different levels at which influence or power may be exercised. The main levels and associated sources of influence, in descending order of 'distance' from the point of production, are supranational, the society, media industry, supra-organizational (for example, media conglomerates), the community, intra-organizational and individual. Weischenberg (1992) deployed a more or less similar 'onion' model to differentiate between media system (societal context, standards and laws, media policy), media institution (political, economic, technological and organizational imperatives), media content (cf. media forms and channels, sources, perspectives and goals), and media actors (the individual level of the professional communicator). The aforementioned hierarchy of influences model by Reese and Shoemaker (first introduced in Shoemaker and Reese, 1991, and updated and modified in Reese and Shoemaker, 2016) is widely used. There is no hierarchy in the sense that the 'higher-order' influence has primacy in terms of strength and direction.

Overall, it is appropriate to consider the relations between media communicators, organizations and their environment as, in principle, interactive and negotiable. It is also appropriate to emphasize that the media organization operates within and maintains its own 'boundaries' (however permeable) and has some degree of autonomy. The models by Dimmick and Coit, Weischenberg, and Reese and Shoemaker all recognize the significance of the individual who carries out media work and is subject to the requirements of the organization, but also has some freedom to define their place in it. Most of the discussion that follows relates to the central area of the 'organizational level', but also takes account of the relations across the boundary between the work organization and other agents and agencies of the wider media institution and society.

It is clear from Chapter 7 that media organizations in their relations with the wider society are formally or informally regulated and influenced by normative expectations on either side. Such matters as the essential freedoms of publication and the ethical guidelines for many professional activities are laid down by the 'rules of the game' of the particular society. This implies, for instance, that the relations between media organizations and their environments are governed not solely by law, market forces or political power, but also by unwritten social and cultural guidelines and obligations.

# THE STRUCTURE AND ORGANIZATION OF THE MEDIA INDUSTRIES

Media companies operating in fields as diverse and interconnected as public relations, marketing, advertising and journalism traditionally have been considered as cultural industries, representing those companies and professions primarily responsible for the industrial production and circulation of culture (Hesmondhalgh, 2018). Cultural industries were originally defined by Adorno and Horkheimer in 1948 as companies and firms involved with the creation, industrial reproduction and mass distribution of cultural works. In the late 1990s, governments in Australia and the United Kingdom broadened this definition in their policies intended to accommodate (and push) a shift in their national economies from an emphasis on manufacturing and agricultural production to a 'creative' economy. The creative industries were defined in the UK as 'those industries which have their origin in individual creativity, skill and talent which have a potential for job and wealth creation through the generation and exploitation of intellectual property' ('Creative Industries Mapping Document', Department for Digital, Culture, Media and Sport, 2001).

The concept of creative industries aimed to reconcile the emergence of increasingly individual and small-scale, project-based or otherwise collaborative forms of commercial and not-for-profit media production with institutionalized notions of cultural production as it exclusively takes place within the cultural industries (Hartley, 2005). In doing so, media industries (advertising, film and video, games, music, publishing, television and radio) were considered together with cultural heritage (museums, natural landscapes), festivals, (art) photography, architecture, the art and antiques market, crafts, (graphic) design, designer fashion and the performing arts.

Two arguments can be made against the conflation of 'cultural' and 'creative' industries. A fundamental critique can be levelled against the proposed merger between individual cultural work and mass cultural production, as it consists of 'the reduction of creativity to the formal indifference of the market' (Neilson and Rossiter, 2005: 8). Specifically related to the structure and key characteristics of the media as cultural industries, Miège (2019) identifies at least four key differences between cultural and creative industries (as summarized in Box 10.2).

## 10.2

### Specificities of media as cultural versus creative industries (Miège, 2019)

- Media industries have many routinized production practices; in creative industries, there is a lot of heterogeneity of practices
- Creative industries have to reserve a much larger part of their resources for fixed assets (such as rehearsal and performance spaces) and physical distribution (such as a shop)
- Media industries have a remarkable diversity of products that can be easily reproduced for mass (even global) audiences
- Working conditions in media industries are based on artisan appeal within a distinctly industrial production context

A fundamental feature of the media which relates to how this industry is structured and organized is the unpredictable character of its products and services – something Caves (2000) describes as the 'nobody knows' principle: uncertainty exists because it is difficult to predict the audience response to a product beforehand, and market success or failure is not easily understood afterwards. Media industries tend to deploy a series of strategies to counter the enormous uncertainty and risk involved in producing their goods and services, such as calculating cost per series or catalogue rather than per product; price fixing with wide margins; not paying wages and instead relying on per-project contracts and various forms of unpaid work; and the distribution of economic risks to smaller subcontractors called on to take artistic risks and innovate (Miège, 2019: 76). This in turn relates to the specific ways in which work is organized across the media industries, as companies and firms tend to operate with a small core of permanent staff, subcontracting and outsourcing most of the actual production work to a large contingent of professionals without a formal status (who are generally paid after the moment of conception via systems such as copyright enforcement and freelance remuneration). As Miège notes, this structural way of doing things 'helps to provide fluid management of strong artistic and intellectual workforces that need to be able to adapt at any time to any number of fresh demands: genres, forms, standards, technologies, markets' (ibid.).

The main mass media industries – advertising (including marketing communications and public relations, as these three professions often operate together in the context of 'full-service' agencies or business networks), film, broadcasting (television and radio and online steaming services), journalism, digital games, and music and recording – share an increasingly similar industry structure, taking on a hourglass shape. The hourglass structure (as discussed in Chapter 8) of the mass media industries is borne out of two simultaneous developments: the number of media outlets and media products has been growing at a rapid rate, while media corporations are getting much larger, often merging or partnering with competitors and including fledgling firms through acquisitions. A diagrammatic overview of organizations and businesses in the media industries therefore reveals an 'hourglass effect' in the distribution of employment, with concentrations of people working in either the small number of larger companies, or the growing multitude of small and micro-businesses, and much smaller or even declining employment in medium-sized businesses (Deuze, 2007: 61). Larger media corporations tend to strive towards some kind of horizontal and vertical integration. Horizontal integration is achieved by extending control over the entire production and distribution process of a single industry, which in the advertising industry, for example, means that the majority of well-known agencies have been bought by large strategic holding groups such as Omnicom, Interpublic, Havas and Publicis. Similar trends can be observed in other media, whereby such groups are often part of even bigger conglomerates, indicating the practice of horizontal integration by combining related or complimentary businesses.

On the other end of the hourglass one finds countless small enterprises, ranging from individual media entrepreneurs to smaller companies and loose networks of collaborating professionals – generally working in part-time, freelance, for-hire, subcontracted and otherwise contingent capacities. The major film, game and music companies, for example, have always operated a deliberate balance with so-called 'independent' production houses, 'boutique' or 'arthouse' development studios and labels to discover, cultivate and promote new talent (and to redistribute risk away from the main business). In the game industry, for example, there is an important role for third-party developers, or 'indie' (short for 'independent') development studios, which develop their own projects and try to sell them to a publisher, or market their games directly to gamers online. The history of the media as an industry shows how both types of media organization need each other – the one for the development and outsourcing of specialized activities (such as innovation and experimentation), the other at times for acting as powerful sponsors or clients.

Overall, media production tends to take place in the offices and work spaces of specific institutions: production houses, development studios, corporate structures. However, much of this work is contingent, freelance and temporary. People are constantly moving in and out of these institutions, continuously reconstituting the creative process. The media industries tend to have a rapid turnover of workers, among both those who are employed and those who are hired or subcontracted. Firms and companies can be understood as 'inhabited' institutions (Hallett and Ventresca, 2006), where constantly changing groups of professionals do their work. This inhabited nature of the industry to a large extent explains the otherwise industrial, highly routinized, and at times strictly formulaic nature of the production process (see Chapter 11).

# THE MEDIA ORGANIZATION IN A FIELD OF SOCIAL FORCES

Any theoretical account of media organizations and occupations has to take note of a number of different relationships within and across the boundaries of the organization. These relationships are often active negotiations and exchanges, and sometimes conflicts, latent or actual. The influential model of mass communication drawn by Westley and MacLean (1957) represents the communicator role as that of a broker between, on the one hand, would-be 'advocates' in society with messages to send and, on the other, the public seeking to satisfy its information and other communication needs and interests.

Gerbner (1969) portrayed mass communicators as operating under pressure from various external 'power roles', including clients (such as advertisers), competitors (other media in the main), authorities (especially legal and political), experts, other institutions and the audience. He wrote (ibid.: 246–247):

> While analytically distinct, obviously neither power roles nor types of leverage are in reality separate or isolated. On the contrary, they often combine, overlap and telescope … the accumulation of power roles and possibilities of leverage gives certain institutions dominant positions in the mass communication of their societies.

Using these ideas and relying on the wide support for such a view in the research literature, we can portray the position of the media organization in general terms as follows. Those within it, however temporarily contracted or employed, have to make decisions at the centre of a field of different constraints, demands or attempted uses of power and influence, as in Figure 10.1. The general hierarchy of influences has been converted into a view of more specific actors and agencies in the environment of a media organization. This representation is primarily derived from research on news media, but the picture would be much the same for many similar 'self-contained' and multipurpose media, including broadcast television (see, for example, Wallis and Baran, 1990).

The pressures and demands illustrated in Figure 10.1 are not all necessarily constraining on media organizations. Some can be sources of liberation, for instance, by way of alternative sources of income, or government policy protection for their task. Some of the forces cancel or balance each other (such as audience support against advertiser pressure, or media institutional prestige against external institutional or source pressure). Lack of external pressure would probably indicate social marginality or insignificance.

A further refinement of this scheme, based on the work of Engwall (1978), involves the internal division of the media organization into three dominant work cultures (management, technical and professional), indicating the main sources of tension and lines of demarcation which have been found to exist within media organizations. This presentation

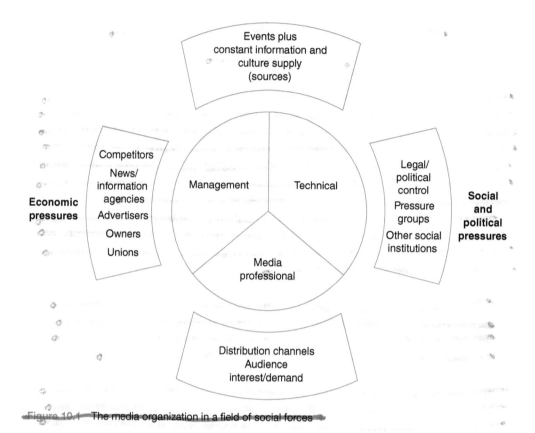

Events plus
constant information and
culture supply
(sources)

Competitors
News/
information
agencies
Advertisers
Owners
Unions

**Economic
pressures**

Management

Technical

Media
professional

Legal/
political
control
Pressure
groups
Other social
institutions

**Social
and
political
pressures**

Distribution channels
Audience
interest/demand

Figure 10.1   The media organization in a field of social forces

allows us to identify five main kinds of relationship – with society, with pressure groups, with owners, clients and sources, with audiences and also internally – which need to be examined in order to gain some understanding of the conditions affecting organizational activity and the mass communicator role. Each of the five types of relationship is discussed in the following pages.

## RELATIONS WITH SOCIETY

A good deal has already been said on this matter, especially in Chapters 7 and 8. The influence of society is ubiquitous and continuous, and arises in virtually all of the media's external relationships. In liberal-democratic societies, the media are free to operate within the limits of the law, but conflicts still occur in relations with government and with powerful social institutions. The media are also continually engaged, sometimes in an antagonistic way, with their main sources and with organized pressure groups. In emerging democracies, media organizations are often expected to act in the interests of nation-building and national coherence, whereas in more dictatorial regimes, media are considered to be mouthpieces of the state. In all types of society, the media are seen as vitally important. How these issues are defined and handled depends in part on the self-defined goals of the media organization.

## THE AMBIGUITY OF MEDIA ORGANIZATIONAL GOALS

Most organizations have mixed goals, and rarely are they all openly stated. Mass media are no exception, and they may even be particularly ambiguous in this respect. In organizational theory, a differentiation is often made between utilitarian and normative organizational goals (for example, Etzioni, 1961). The utilitarian organization aims to produce or provide material goods or services for financial ends, while the normative organization aims to advance some value or achieve a valued condition, based on the voluntary commitment of its participants. Mass media organizations often have a mixture of utilitarian and normative goals and forms of operation. Most media are run as businesses but often with some 'ideal' goals, and some media are run primarily for 'idealistic' social or cultural purposes, without seeking profit – but still have to pay the bills. For instance, public broadcasting organizations (in Europe especially) have generally had a bureaucratic form of organization but with non-profit social and cultural goals. Most major film studios also operate smaller, 'arthouse' studios in order to experiment with smaller budgets, to earn a reputation and credibility as a nurturer of talent, and to diversify their portfolio of (intended) 'tentpole' or 'blockbuster' movies.

The goals of media organizations are complex. Generally speaking, a media company or professional tends to embrace or prefer an 'editorial' logic, meaning that they feel creative decisions should be made based on what the media makers deem worthy to pursue. However, as most media are commercial businesses, a 'market' logic is present, too. In that context, goals are set as determined by target audience tastes and needs, and commercial appeal. Success in this context is measured by audience metrics such as viewing or listening figures, ticket sales, hits and clicks, and time spent. A third logic that has been emerging, especially since the early 2000s in conjunction with the interactive nature of the Internet, considers the active engagement of the audience – in the form of user-generated content and other types of 'co-creative' contributions by the audience – as an important goal to pursue for media organizations. In some cases, especially in countries where the freedom of media organizations is curtailed by state interests or when a company operates in conditions of complete dependence on external clients, a fourth 'external' logic prevails. In such instances, decisions are governed in strict accordance with rules and parameters set elsewhere. In practice, these logics and goals of media organizations often conflict, and at times converge.

Some media organizations (especially public service media and those with an opinion-forming or informational purpose) clearly do seek to play some part in society, but the nature of this role is also open to diverse interpretations. Certain kinds of publication, especially prestige or elite newspapers, have set out deliberately to be influential through the quality of their information or the authority of their opinion (Padioleau, 1985). There are several other options for the exercise of influence, and it is not the exclusive property of an internationally known elite press. Small-scale media can be influential in more restricted spheres, and influence can obviously be exercised by major motion pictures and popular television. There is a significant strand of thinking and work in advertising and public relations that advocates promoting social goals to bring about positive change in society (Dahlen and Rosengren, 2016). Similar ambitions can be found among game developers, for example in areas such as 'newsgames' (using a game to explicate an important news story) and serious games (making a game with goals other than entertainment, for example in areas such as personal health, exercise and education).

The various goals of media organizations are summarized in Box 10.3. These are not mutually exclusive, but typically one or another is given overriding priority.

---

## 10.3
## Main goals of media organizations

- Profit
- Social influence and prestige
- Maximizing an audience
- Sectional goals (political, religious, cultural, educational, etc.)
- Serving the public interest

---

## THE JOURNALIST'S ROLE: ENGAGEMENT OR NEUTRALITY?

Within the broad field of media organizations and production, journalism stands out – as an object of scholarly research, as well as in terms of the expectations that society has of the work that journalists do and the role that the profession of journalism plays in democratic societies. Whereas organizations across the various media industries have been studied in the past, news organizations in general and newsrooms in particular stand out as a historical site of dedicated scholarly interest, starting in the 1950s with newspaper studies (in Germany, the UK and the US) and continuing to this day. What is striking about this long tradition of research into news organizations, argue Westlund and Ekström (2019), is that despite the obvious differences between the mid-twentieth century and today, reporters throughout engage in similar procedures and routines in their pursuit of information from a diverse set of reliable sources, turning this into news that follows certain enduring news values (Harcup and O'Neill, 2017). From the outset to today, this predominance of set practices, factory-style production processes, rituals and routines has been problematized as compromising creativity as a core value of media professionals (Lynch and Swink, 1967; Tuchman, 1971; Bantz, McCorkle and Baade, 1980; Malmelin and Virta, 2016).

Of particular significance is the link, established in the literature, between the values journalists find important in their work and the performances of these roles in the stories they produce. The correlation between professional perception and performance speaks directly to the journalists' views of their roles and responsibilities in society. There is strong evidence to suggest that, despite the diverse personal characteristics of journalists, what mainly explains the way they go about doing newswork is how they define their goals, motivations and roles in society. As Willnat et al. (2013: 11) state, 'How journalists define their desired roles in society is closely related to the professional competencies of journalists. This is because their perceived roles tend to set the boundaries of journalistic skills, knowledge, and abilities'. When it comes to the goals that journalism in general and journalists in particular strive for, a broad choice has to be made between a more active and participant or a more neutral and societal role for the journalist. Cohen (1963: 191) distinguished two separate self-conceptions of the reporter's role as that of 'neutral reporter' or 'participant'. The first refers to ideas of the press as informer, interpreter and instrument of government (lending itself as channel or mirror), the second to the traditional '**fourth estate**' notion, covering ideas of the press as representative of the public, critic of government, advocate of policy and general watchdog.

The weight of evidence is that the neutral, informative role is most preferred by journalists, and it goes with the importance attached by most journalists to objectivity as a core professional value (Janowitz, 1975; Johnstone, Slawski and Bowman, 1976; Schudson, 1978; Tuchman, 1978; Weaver and Wilhoit, 1996). Strong political commitment (and active engagement) is by definition not easy to reconcile with even-handed neutral reporting, and many news organizations have guidelines designed to limit the influence of personal beliefs on reporting. The preference for 'objectivity' also accords with the commercial logic of media businesses, since partisanship tends to narrow the audience appeal. Journalists in popular tabloid media seem to adopt much the same view on this as do more heavyweight journalists for the elite press, even if the results are very different (Deuze, 2005).

In place of the simple 'neutral versus participant' dichotomy, Weaver and Wilhoit (1986, 1996) in subsequent surveys opted for a tripartite division of roles as interpreter, disseminator or adversary, in that order of prominence. The interpreter role was based on the items 'analysing and interpreting complex questions', 'investigating claims made by government' and 'discussing national policy as it happens'. The second type – that of disseminator – mainly relates to 'getting information to the public quickly' and 'concentrating on the largest possible audience'. The third, adversary, role (applying to both government and business) was much weaker but was still recognized to some degree by a majority of journalists. A plurality of role conceptions held by journalists has consistently been stressed by Weaver and Wilhoit (1986: 116), who write: 'only about 2 percent of the respondents are exclusively one-role oriented'. They also remind us that, on such matters as role perception and journalistic ethics, there seem to be large cross-cultural differences. It looks as if role conceptions are both variable and quite strongly related to political culture and the degree to which democracy is firmly established (see Weaver, 1998: 477–478). For instance, in countries where democracy is weaker, there is less emphasis on the watchdog role.

In later studies, and especially in more cross-national comparative work, these roles (each consisting of a set of related statements regarding the goals and motivations of journalists) have been upheld, with the addition of a variety of role perceptions applicable in different countries, cultures and local contexts (Mellado, Hellmueller and Donsbach, 2017). Willnat et al. (2013) concluded in an overview of a twenty-two-nation study of journalists that reporting news to the public quickly, providing analysis of events and being a watchdog are considered important by most, even though there are considerable differences of the relative weight of these goals across countries, and the exact meaning of such roles tends to be defined differently. Reports from the ongoing Worlds of Journalism comparative study, which included surveys among over 27,500 journalists from sixty-seven countries between 2012 and 2016, suggest a rich diversity of journalistic cultures where role perceptions cannot be neatly captured or explained by national boundaries (Hanitzsch, Hanusch, Ramaprasad and De Beer, 2019). When coupled with content analyses of the news, researchers conclude that there is a 'multilayered hybridization of journalistic cultures at the performative level, showing that the presence of professional roles in news reflects heterogeneous, but at the same time, fluid and dynamic journalistic cultures' (Mellado et al., 2017: 962). These contemporary findings suggest an international homogenization of journalistic values, goals and reporting styles, as well as an increasing situational, organizational and even individual heterogenization of 'journalisms' around the world. Although there are certainly national differences and the national news culture of a country to some extent influences much of what journalists do, it has become quite clear that there is much more to journalism than its original definition and understanding as a profession made it out to be.

## JOURNALISM AS A PROFESSION

The study of the journalistic role governing the profession's relations with society has been strongly influenced by the general notion of a profession, derived from the sociology of occupations. The relationship that journalism has with society tends to be governed by its status as a profession, an 'expert system' that society relies on for its supply of reliable, trustworthy information of public value and interest. A profession is typically thought to have several key features, especially a significant public role in society; a core body of expertise requiring long training; self-control of entry and regulation; and clear codes of ethics and conduct. On balance, there seem to be stronger arguments for denying journalism the status of profession than otherwise. Knight, Geuze and Gerlis (2008) provide a catalogue of objections to the claim, especially the low public esteem for and trust in journalists and their susceptibility to influence from powerful sources or commercial interests.

Fengler and Russ-Mohl (2008) add a new dimension to the debate by proposing an 'economic theory of journalism', explaining the profession by the economic motives and calculations on the part of individual journalists or media firms. Support for this view can be found in Bourdieu's 'field theory of journalism', which focuses on the key issue of autonomy. In this theory, the reference is to a 'field of forces' in which many external influences are at work. In the case of journalism, the pressures come mainly from the neighbouring fields of economics or politics, resulting in a lower degree of autonomy. Benson and Neveu (2005: 11) emphasize the degree to which news has become a political institution in its own right. Treating journalism as a loosely interrelated set of activities, with unclear boundaries, does seem to accord with the increasingly diverse reality of 'newswork' (Deuze and Witschge, 2020). In the end, it may not greatly matter to those outside whether or not the occupation is classed as a profession, although the degree to which relevant criteria of professionalism are met does matter. These criteria have to do with the quality of work done, the reliability of information published, the honesty of purpose and the benefits for society that are sought.

Several observers have emphasized the existence of an 'ideology of journalism', although there are different versions of what it contains, depending on the institutional setting and national location. Deuze (2005: 447) has given a fairly consensual view of the main components of journalistic ideology. These are as shown in Box 10.4.

## 10.4

### The occupational ideology of journalists: main elements (Deuze, 2005)

- Public service
- Objectivity
- Autonomy
- Immediacy
- Ethics

The ideal-typical values in the ideology of journalism can be found in the work and self-perception of journalists across countries, cultures and types of journalism. As Deuze notes, some of these elements are inconsistent or contradictory. Furthermore, what 'objectivity' means to a journalist working for a quality newspaper in a western liberal democracy may be very different from a conception of the value among reporters and editors of a community news startup in Uganda or a state broadcaster in mainland China, even though all these journalists would say that objectivity is an important value for their work. The occupational ideology of journalism therefore gets meaning in the particular news culture of a given country or place of work – in the more or less established ways of doing the work, of making news and of making sense of newswork.

For members of most professions, the appropriate wider social role they perform is usually 'taken care of' by the institution – as in medicine or teaching – leaving individuals to concentrate on the practice of their skills. To a certain extent this is true of mass communicators, but full professionalization has been held back by the internal diversity of media and the wide range of goals. There is also continued uncertainty about what is actually the central and unique professional skill of the journalist (and this is even more in question for other media occupations). The sociologist Max Weber (1948) referred to the journalist as belonging to 'a sort of pariah caste' and, like the artist, lacking a fixed social classification. Schudson (1978) aptly characterized journalism as an 'uninsulated profession', because of the lack of clear boundaries. This in turn can be said for many, if not most, media professions.

The question of whether journalism should be considered a profession remains in dispute, both within and without the media world. Windahl et al. (2007) conclude that the knowledge base of journalists does not command the same respect as that of occupational groups that are acknowledged to be professions. Kepplinger and Koecher (1990: 307) maintain that 'journalists cannot really be counted among the professional class', largely on the grounds that they behave very selectively with those they have to deal with and professionals should treat everyone equally. They write that journalists also deny a moral responsibility for unintentionally negative consequences of their reports, while applying a stronger standard to others. However, the same authors also observe that 'this selectivity is a basis for the reputation of journalism and a prerequisite for its success' (ibid.: 307). Olen (1988) makes a similar point by contending that journalism should not become a profession since it involves the exercise of a right to freedom of expression that cannot be monopolized by an institution (that of journalism).

It can also be argued that the critical role of the press may oblige it at times to act in an 'irresponsible' way, as defined by established institutions. Intended here are actions that break rules and conventions but also may serve the public interest. Such actions can range from exposing scandals in high places to revealing alleged national secrets. The publication of the secret 'Pentagon papers' by *The New York Times* in 1971, against strong government pressure, is a favourite example. The documents showed US policy in Vietnam in a very negative light and contributed to further decline in public support for the war, but was also argued to have cost American lives. In the UK, the publication in 2009 of stolen confidential details of expenses claimed by members of parliament was widely held to be justified by its results. Michael Schudson (2005) offers an interesting take on the role of journalism in (democratic) society, suggesting that certain 'unlovable' tendencies of the press – a preoccupation with events, a sports-minded fascination with horse-racing coverage and conflict, a cynical attitude towards politics (and politicians), and a strong alienation of journalists from the sources and communities they cover – may be essential. His argument is that 'the news media are supposed to be institutionalised outsiders even though they have in fact become institutionalised insiders' (Schudson, 2005: 30–31).

## RELATIONS WITH PRESSURE AND INTEREST GROUPS

Relations between media and society are often mediated through a wide range of more or less informal, but often organized, pressure groups that seek to influence directly what the media do – especially by trying to set limits to what they publish. There are many examples of established bodies, such as religious, occupational or political bodies, complaining and lobbying on a range of issues, often to do with matters of morality, perceived political bias or minority representation. In many countries, there is legal and social pressure on the media to be positive towards minorities of all kinds, including ethnic groups, women, gays and lesbians, and more sensitive to the needs of vulnerable groups such as children, the poor, disabled and homeless people, and the mentally ill.

While the media are usually cautious in handling such pressures and are reluctant to yield their autonomy (the pressures often tend to cancel each other out), there is evidence of success by outside agencies in influencing content. Usually access depends on perceived legitimacy of the claim to be heard, but sometimes PR can influence this perception (Yoon, 2005). Access may also be given where a medium's commercial interests might be threatened by bad publicity. Beyond pressure being applied directly, there is widespread influence and access of outside agencies on the production of media content. Examples include non-governmental organizations that provide journalists with materials (and sometimes produce news themselves) in developing nations (Wright, 2018), of scriptwriters collaborating with both commercial and educational partners to write material for series and films, and of foreign correspondents in conflict zones relying heavily on local 'fixers' and other locally based media employees (Palmer, 2019).

It is usually impossible to distinguish unacceptable pressure (or the act of yielding to it) from the general tendency of the media to try to please as many of their audiences (and advertisers) as possible and to avoid hurting minorities or encouraging anti-social activities. The media are also wary of legal reprisal and inclined to avoid unnecessary controversy. Media avoidance behaviour in response to social or legal pressure has to be accepted as legitimate, within the rules of the media-institutional 'game', but the general result is to ensure a differentially more positive treatment for the better-organized and more socially central minorities and causes (Shoemaker, 1984). Weaker and more deviant groups get a worse press and exert little influence. Paletz and Entman (1981: 125) exemplified such marginal groups with little positive access to, or control over, media coverage as 'unofficial strikers, urban rioters, welfare mothers, student militants, radicals and impoverished reactionaries'. The composition of this category will vary, but the general principle remains the same.

Social media are offering an at times powerful and resonating outlet for the grievances of minority groups affected, using the interlinked character of many sites, platforms and services to generate recognition and support – such as through the #BlackLivesMatter and #AllLivesMatter online debates from 2014 onwards (Carney, 2016), the Umbrella movement in Hong Kong (Lee and Chan, 2015), and various anti-austerity movements in Europe (Treré, Jeppesen and Mattoni, 2017). According to Karatzogianni (2015), the different forms that digital protest and activism take have their origins in the 1990s with the Zapatista movement in Mexico and the anti-globalization movement using their own independent media or 'Indymedia', spreading across the world and going global with the Occupy movement (emerging in 2011). Digital media are recognized as a predictor of protest participation and a platform for the co-ordination of connective actions. Kaun and Uldam (2018: 2102) signal how digital activism is often explored in ahistorical ways that foreground a technology-centred perspective, and that many studies reinforce the myth that digital media are used in a universal manner to promote political change. Overall, it seems fruitful to move beyond explanations that either stress local and individual context or privilege the role of technologies and media-specificity, mirroring the age-old distinction between society-centric and media-centric approaches (see Chapter 1).

## RELATIONS WITH OWNERS AND CLIENTS

The central issue that arises under this heading is the extent to which media organizations can claim to exercise autonomy in relation, first, to their owners and, secondly, to other direct economic agencies in their environment, especially those that provide operating funds: investors, advertisers and sponsors. In some countries and contexts, the role of the state as an owner or client has to be recognized, providing powerful impetus for media organizational behaviour. According to Altschull's (1984: 254) dictum that 'The content of the news media always reflects the interests of those who finance the press', the answer is fairly clear – not just for journalism, but all media professions operate in a complex and interdependent relationship with owners, sources of revenue and external actors such as the state.

# PROPRIETOR INFLUENCE

There is no doubt that owners in market-based media have ultimate power over content and can ask for what they want to be included or left out. There is plenty of circumstantial evidence to show that this power is used (Shoemaker and Reese, 1991; Curran and Seaton, 1997; see also Chapter 9). As the last decades have seen increased concentration of media ownership, providing new impetus to the commercialization of media production, such owner pressures are part of the everyday reality of media work. Even so, there are quite strong conventions relating to journalism and other media professions which protect the decision-making autonomy of professional media makers. As Marjoribanks (2011) notes, a full account of the organization, practices and effects of media production, including multinational corporations, should acknowledge both the opportunities and constraints offered by proprietor influence.

Nevertheless, there is an inevitable tendency for media owners to set broad lines of policy, which are to some extent followed by the staff they employ. There may also be informal and indirect pressure on particular issues that matter to owners (for instance, relating to their other business interests) (Turow, 1994). As media organizations engage in varying partnerships, alliances and cross-investments with other industries, including financial, technological and political organizations (Arsenault and Castells, 2008: 730), the global increasingly comes to influence the local in media production, leading to an ongoing transnationalization.

On the other hand, media organizations and professionals push back, either formally through protests (even though union-based activism such as strikes are rare in media work), co-ordinated efforts to seek publicity about limits to press freedom or creative autonomy, and through otherwise 'organized networks' (Rossiter, 2006). The worldwide press condemnation of UNESCO's efforts to improve international reporting, as reported by Giffard (1989), is a convincing example of the media industry protecting its own interests.

The general effect of oligopolistic media ownership on content has proved difficult to pin down (see, for example, Picard, McCombs, Winter and Lacy, 1988), although there is little doubt that a condition of true monopoly would be harmful for freedom of expression and consumer choice. Shoemaker and Reese (1991) conclude that those who work for large chains are likely to have a lower attachment to and involvement in the community in which they work. For them, the (larger) media organization takes precedence over community influence. Correlatively, locally based media may gain strength and independence from ties with the community or city that they serve. The degree of freedom for journalists, producers, writers and entertainers in public broadcasting may be formally less than in market-based media (although this is not necessarily so), but the limits are normally clear and not subject to arbitrary breach or suspension.

Considering case studies of workplace autonomy across the various holdings of News Corporation, there is evidence of a 'Murdochisation of the media' in, for example, China and India (Thussu, 2007) in that commercial interests and market values become more important than public values, while Marjoribanks (2011) emphasizes situational negotiation and at times even resistance of professionals working within the multinational media industry. Such work underscores the significance of considering issues influencing the media organization from different levels of analysis – from the micro-level of the backgrounds and interactions of media producers, the meso-level of organizational cultures, corporate strategies and editorial policies, and the macro-level of regulatory, technological and competitive environments (Cottle, 2003: 24).

## THE INFLUENCE OF ADVERTISERS

The consequences of advertising financing for media content are perennially discussed. On the one hand, it is obvious that the structure of much of the mass media industry in most capitalist countries reflects the interests of advertisers – something that has developed historically along with other social and economic changes. It is no accident that media markets often coincide with other consumer divisions. Most free-market media are finely tuned to jointly maximizing the needs of advertisers and their own interests as a normal condition of operation. The 'normal' influence extends to the matching of media content patterns according to the consumption patterns of targeted audiences. Media content, design, layout, planning and scheduling often reflect advertiser interests. Consider, for example, product placement in motion pictures and digital games, script development with commercial partners, and established news media producing 'native advertising' for commercial clients. What has been less easy to demonstrate is that particular advertisers can directly intervene to influence significant publication decisions in their own interests, beyond what is already provided for in the system.

As with proprietorial intervention in news, there is little doubt that it happens from time to time on a local or specific basis. McManus (1994) describes a systematic pattern of commercial influence on reporting. Scholarship as well as investigative reporting has unearthed evidence of advertisers using their market power to attempt to block particular communications that damage their interests and also of advertiser pressure that influences personnel as well as editorial decisions in the media. But influence comes in diverse forms that are often hard to detect and not necessarily illegitimate (for instance, providing information that has a promotional value, product placement, sponsoring, etc.).

Advertiser influence is generally ethically disapproved of, especially when it affects news (Meyer, 1987), and it may not even be in the interests either of media (especially news media) or of advertisers to be seen to be too close to each other. Both can lose credibility and effectiveness if a form of conspiracy against the media public is suspected. Considering the rise of 'paid-for' rather than 'earned' publicity, especially as branded content and native advertising are becoming profitable sources of revenue for news publications (as they have been for other media), it is important to investigate the link between public trust and commercial enterprise. In general, it seems that economically strong and 'elite' media are in the best position to resist undue pressure (see Gans, 1979). But the same is true of media that are supported by varied balanced sources of revenue. Media organizations most likely to be influenced by advertiser pressure are those whose sole or overwhelming source of revenue is advertising, especially where the competition is heavy (Picard, 2004). Some argue that advertising-supported media are on the way out given the dominance of the advertising market by Internet platforms (Google and Facebook, in particular). However, advertising can be as much a defence against undue influence as it is the source of dependency.

The main pressures and constraints on news arising from the media market have been summarized by McManus (1994) in terms of a 'market model'. This is derived from the principle that market forces require conduct that minimizes cost, protects the interests of owners and clients, and maximizes the income-producing audience. The model is expressed in the statement about news selection contained in Box 10.5.

---

## 10.5
## Main predictions of the market model (McManus, 1994)

The probability of an event/issue becoming news is:

- inversely proportional to the harm the information might cause to investors or sponsors
- inversely proportional to the cost of covering it
- directly proportional to the expected breadth of the appeal to audiences that advertisers are willing to pay for

---

The main difference from a 'journalistic theory of news production' lies in the lack of any reference in such a theory to harm owners or costs and a concentration on the significance of the story and the size of an interested audience. As McManus notes, the two theories do not lead to differences of selection in all cases and, under certain ideal conditions of rationality, perfect knowledge and diversity, the models might even converge.

## RELATIONS WITH THE AUDIENCE

Although the audience is, by conventional wisdom, the most important of the clients and influences in the environment of any media organization, research tends to show the audience as having a low salience for many actual communicators, however closely engagement, clicks, ratings and sales figures are followed by management. Media professionals display a high degree of 'autism' (Burns, 1969), consistent perhaps with the general attitude of professionals, whose very status depends on their knowing better than their clients what is good for them. Although customer interaction and relationships are considered very important in the industry, the internal hierarchies among media professionals are generally made up of those responsible for user-friendliness, audience interaction and development at the bottom of the ladder. In game development, this is exemplified by the job that everyone has to do (especially newcomers) but that nobody likes: quality assurance. In this final phase of development, every aspect of the game is tested for problems, the reporting of which creates tensions between the production team and the testing department (it is sometimes called a 'death march' towards the moment of the release of a game; Deuze, 2007: 221). In journalism, ombudsmen and reader representatives are similarly considered less important than political correspondents and parliamentary reporters – those who are least likely to interact with the audience. However, there are subtle yet important changes afoot in this context, as audience interaction and participation become increasingly important for both creative development and commercial success (Jenkins, 2006; see also Chapter 11).

## HOSTILITY TO THE AUDIENCE?

Altheide (1974: 59) comments that the pursuit of large audiences by the television stations which he studied 'led to a cynical view of the audience as stupid, incompetent and unappreciative'. Elliott (1972), Burns (1977) and Schlesinger (1978) found something of the same to be true of British television. Schlesinger (1978: 111) attributed this partly to the nature of professionalism: 'A tension is set up between the professionalism of the communicator, with its implied autonomy, and the meeting of apparent audience demands and desires, with their implication for limiting autonomy.' Ferguson (1983) also reported a somewhat arrogant attitude to the audience on the part of women's magazine editors. In her study of Australian journalists, Schultz (1998) uncovered some resentment of the need to please the audience, thus limiting autonomy. She associated this with a 'reduced capacity to understand public opinion' (ibid.: 157) and an unwillingness to accept accountability mechanisms. Gans (1979) reported that US TV journalists were appalled by the lack of audience recognition of what they found good.

The situation stems partly from the fact that the dominant criterion applied by the organization is nearly always an audience metric (that is, the volume of sales of the product, the size of the audience sold to the advertiser, the number of hits and clicks, the time spent on a website or app). However, most media professionals, with some justification, do not recognize such metrics as a very reliable measure of intrinsic quality. Interestingly, as research by Boczkowski and Mitchelstein (2013) shows, neither does the audience – in that audience attention as measured by online metrics does not necessarily mean that this is the kind of content audiences want or deem valuable.

It is possible that hostility towards the audience and their aversion to metrics is somewhat exaggerated by media respondents themselves, since there is contrary evidence that some media people have a strong positive attitude to their audience, are genuinely committed to users' positive experience and wellbeing, and metrics are important to media makers who want recognition as much as they seek autonomy in their work. Willnat et al. (2013) found that the single most important factor contributing to work satisfaction of journalists across twenty-one countries is the level of perceived freedom and job autonomy. At the same time, having an impact is at the forefront for media professionals generally, and journalists in particular. The resistance to ratings and other audience statistics, which are largely a management tool with little to say about actual audiences (Ang, 1991), should not necessarily be equated with negative views of the audience. In the sphere of online media, direct feedback from the audience can sometimes be threatening to individual communicators, but there is also a new opportunity to turn contacts into a tool of management. Audience participation has become an influential element in the media industry as media users are increasingly becoming media (co-)producers, redefining the media industry in terms of practices such as reciprocal journalism (Lewis, Holton and Coddington, 2014), upstream marketing, two-way symmetrical public relations and interactive advertising – all indicating an increasingly participatory relationship between media organizations and audiences.

## INSULATION AND UNCERTAINTY

Historically, most mass communicators in established media do not need to be concerned about the immediate response of the audience, making decisions about content in advance of any response. This, coupled with the intrinsic difficulty of 'knowing' a large and very disparate audience, contributes to the relative insulation described above. The traditional institutional device for making contact with the audience, that of audience research, serves an essential management function and relates media to the surrounding financial and political system, conveying little that is meaningful to the individual mass communicator. Attitudes to the audience tend to be guided and differentiated according to the role orientations set out above. This situation has changed, and audience metrics, feedback and participation have become part and parcel of the practice of media production, even though some professionals baulk at the suggestion of sharing their creative process.

## IMAGES OF THE AUDIENCE

There remains a continuing problem of uncertainty for those who do want to communicate, who do want to change or influence the general public and use media for this purpose, or who direct themselves at minorities or minority causes where impact matters (see Hagen, 1999). One readily available solution is the construction of an abstract image of the kind of people they would like to reach (Bauer, 1958; Pool and Shulman, 1959). The audience has never been a given but must be seen in terms of what Ien Ang (1991) has called a socially constituted and institutionally produced category. The audience in this context becomes something imagined. Communicating to a large and amorphous audience 'out there' is bound to remain problematic for those who care about getting a message across, being recognized and appreciated for their work, and having some kind of impact.

In contemporary media organizations the audience generally is not the faceless 'mass' of before. Instead, at times highly detailed information is available, particularly about those who access the media product or service online. There remains a question as to what extent media professionals in fact make active use of such data when making creative decisions, but it has quickly become a fairly conventional matter of fact that the audience of today is fickle, has many other options, needs to be constantly surprised (and entertained), and is reluctant to trust the media organization. Such framing of this 'new' empowered consumer as unpredictable masses is not without problems. Turow (2005: 120) considers the construction of twenty-first-century media users in the marketing and advertising industry as chaotic, self-concerned and unconcerned about sharing their personal data online, as only serving an emerging strategic logic of mainstream media organizations 'to present their activities not as privacy invasion but as two-way customer relationships, not as commercial intrusion but as pinpoint selling help for frenetic consumers in a troubling world'.

Media organizations, as distinct from the individual 'communicators' within or otherwise working with them, are to a large extent in the business of producing spectacles as a way of creating audiences and generating profit and employment. They need some firm basis on which to predict the interests and likely degree of attention of an audience, given the 'nobody knows' dilemma, as outlined earlier. As Pekurny (1982) has pointed out, traditional audience metrics such as feedback from ratings cannot tell you how to improve television programmes, and neither are they often available until long after a programme is made. Pekurny mentioned at the time that the 'real feedback system' is not the home viewing audience, but the writers, producers, cast and network executives themselves. In addition, there is strong reliance on the 'track records' of particular producers and production companies and on reusing successful past formulas. This conclusion is supported by Ryan and Peterson (1982), who tell us that in popular music the most important factor guiding selection in the production process is the search for a good 'product image'. This essentially means trying to match the characteristics of previously successful songs. This model of media production still exists, but generally speaking the role of data analysts and market researchers (using close to real-time statistics on consumer behaviours online) in co-determining decisions about management and production is becoming increasingly important.

# ASPECTS OF INTERNAL STRUCTURE AND DYNAMICS

The analysis made so far, in line with the scheme in Figure 10.1, points to a degree of differentiation and division within the boundaries of the organization. There are several sources of division. One of the most obvious is the diversity of function (such as news, entertainment or advertising) of many media organizations, with different interests competing for status and finance. The personnel of media organizations come from different social backgrounds and vary according to age, gender, ethnicity, social background and other attributes. Beyond diversity of function and staff, we have already noted a duality of purpose of many media (both material and ideal) and the endemic conflict between creative ends (which have no practical limits) and the need to organize, plan, finance and 'sell' media products. Most accounts of media-organizational goals point to differences of orientation and purpose that can be a source of latent conflict, supplemented by emerging studies on the precarity and lack of diversity as causes of significant concern in media work (among media policymakers as well as managers and makers themselves).

## INTERNAL DIVERSITY OF PURPOSE

The fact that mass media organizations have mixed goals is important for locating the media in their social context, understanding some of the pressures under which they operate and helping to differentiate the main occupational choices available to media workers. The media organization is engaged in both making a product and providing a service. It also uses a wide variety of production technology, from the simple to the complex. Within an organization, several different 'work cultures' flourish, each justified according to a different goal or work task. Engwall (1978) considers the media organization as 'hybrid', identifying in the newspaper he studied a news-oriented culture and a politically oriented culture, as well as an economically oriented and a technically oriented culture. The first two tend to go together and signal the typical normative attitude of media workers following an 'editorial' logic, while the second two are more 'utilitarian', having much in common with their counterparts in other business organizations. In so far as this situation can be generalized over time and across different media, media organizations are likely to be as internally divided as to purpose as they are different from each other. That this should happen without excessive conflict suggests some fairly stable forms of accommodation to the attendant problems. Such an accommodation may be essential in what Tunstall (1971) has characterized by the paradoxical term of 'non-routine bureaucracy' and points to a fundamental paradox when understanding media organizations: while the organization of work tends to be governed and informed by quite rigid formulas, conventions, routines and rituals, the attitudes and behaviours of both media organizations and individual professionals are anything but formal.

# THE INFLUENCE OF PERSONAL CHARACTERISTICS OF MASS COMMUNICATORS

Many studies of media organizations or occupations include, as a matter of course, an examination of the social background and outlook on society of the group of respondents under study. This is sometimes because of an assumption that the personal characteristics of those most directly responsible for media production will influence content. It is a hypothesis that accords well with the ideology or mythology of the media themselves, which privileges individual creativity and professional autonomy, and stands opposed to the notion of organizational, commercial or technological determinism. It is also a familiar idea among audiences that the personality and values of the author, for instance of a novel, game or a film, will give the work its primary meaning, despite its being processed in a media industry. The expectation that media will 'reflect society' can be supported on the grounds either that it is what their audiences want or that those who work in the media are a cross-section of society, at least in their values and beliefs. Given the facts that the image of the audience tends to be an industrial construct and the media profession can be considered to be anything but representative of society, this expectation has to be nuanced considerably.

Views regarding the supposed influence of personal characteristics need to be modified to allow for the influence of organizational goals and settings. Most media products are the work not of a single author but of teams, and ideas of personal authorship are not very relevant, despite the tendency of media to promote individual stars and celebrities. Studies of media organizations that tend to be more diverse – for example, in terms of gender, age or ethnicity – show no significant differences in terms of content produced with those who are less diverse, suggesting a continuing prominence of socialization as a powerful determinant of decision-making processes.

The first question to arise is whether there is any distinctive pattern of social experience or personal values to be found among media communicators. Inevitably, there are as many descriptions of social background as there are studies, and even though most concern journalists, there is no single pattern to report. However, there is a good deal of evidence to show that media professionals in many countries come from (or have) well-educated, middle-class socio-economic backgrounds, without being rich. That said, there are evidently big variations between the stars in any given discipline, the ordinary salariat and the vast surplus of contingent labourers across all branches of media business. These characteristics are intersectional, in that differences in cultural background, ethnicity, gender and age tend to be linked throughout the industry. Among newcomers and younger journalists, advertising professionals and those in the film and television industries, one finds many more women and people of colour than among established practitioners. As mentioned, there seems little doubt about the general class position of the average media worker:

it is a middle-class occupation, but less professionalized or well paid than other established professions (law, medicine, accountancy, etc.) and with a small elite of well-paid stars. Peters and Cantor's (1982) account of the movie acting profession is an early example that stresses the extreme gap between the powerless and insecure many and the minority at the top – a gap that arguably has grown considerably as precarious employment is paramount across the media industries.

Other variables playing a powerful role in determining the individual's role in a media organization include personal motivations and beliefs, personality (for example, introvert or extravert), talent and skill development. Given the increasing precarity of employment in the media and the subsequent toll this takes on the professionals involved – often reporting high rates of stress and burnout, frustration about work–life balance and uncertainty about the future – these elements become important to consider when making sense of how media organizations function and perform.

The theoretical significance of such observations is less easy to establish. Johnstone et al. (1976) concluded that 'in any society those in charge of mass communication tend to come from the same social strata as those in control of the economic and political systems'. Gans (1979) also suggested that the middle-class position of the journalistic profession is a guarantee of their ultimate loyalty to the system. Therefore they are free, because they can be trusted to see and interpret the world in much the same way as the real holders of power, holding the same basic ideology and values. Gans found that news journalists generally held what are called 'motherhood' values, including support for the family and a nostalgia for small-town pastoralism. They also tended to be ethnocentric, individualistic and in favour of 'responsible capitalism', moderatism, social order and leadership. Gans' interpretation is persuasive, even more so because it tends to be supported by evidence from other media professions, not just in the USA but also elsewhere.

There is a documented tendency of 'middle-classification' in the media industries, reducing the social mobility within media professions. This is largely caused by a rise in the costs involved in securing a position in the industry (considering the need for specific higher education degrees, relocation to expensive urban centres where media industries tend to be located, and having to do speculative or otherwise underpaid work), limiting the diversity of voices and participants in the professional media organization.

In an attempt to theorize the significance of personal characteristics of media professionals for understanding the overall behaviour and performance of media organizations, Hesmondhalgh and Baker (2015) provide a critical appreciation of the tendency towards 'sexual work segregation' as certain domains of media work are strongly associated with women and some with men. In game development, most of the programming and coding of the gameplay is done by men; in journalism, one finds few women among those reporting on the main political and economic institutions (such as parliament, the state and big business); in advertising, film, television and the music and recording industries, few among those in 'greenlighting' positions (that is, giving the go-ahead on creative projects) are women. Although this is not necessarily the same as gender discrimination, the ramifications of such a sexed division of labour between men and women can be profound. Box 10.6 presents the issues outlined by Hesmondhalgh and Baker relating to the (lack of) equality of men and women in media occupations.

---

## 10.6

## Consequences of sexual work segregation (Hesmondhalgh and Baker, 2015: 25)

- Inequality: jobs and occupations carried out by women rather than men tend to be paid less;
- Limits to autonomy, freedom and recognition: if a certain job is considered 'male', it can prevent women from pursuing it – or from pursuing it based on their own vision and idea(l)s;
- Limits collective flourishing: it is harder for people to match their talents to occupations, inhibiting the ability of all to contribute;
- Contributes to social stereotypes: prevailing and repeated categorizations of people (for example, considering women as 'more caring' and 'friendly' than men) reinforces sexed division of labor.

---

The significance of Hesmondhalgh and Baker's analysis is that it can be extended, through intersectionality, with other personal characteristics of mass communicators, which helps to explain to some extent why the industry and its organizations are structured the way they are. Linda Steiner (2012) reminds us how gender is perhaps too dichotomous a variable to consider when studying the lack of diversity – especially in positions of power – in the media industry workforce. Not only is the division of labour gendered, the subdivisions of experience as a media professional are further stratified along lines of 'race, class, national culture, professional culture, of generation and of historical moment' (ibid.: 219).

Sexual abuse, harassment and assault have been recurring topics of social media exchanges (in different countries and languages around the world). A 2017 post on Twitter by American actress Alyssa Milano using the hashtag #MeToo started a global trend of sharing stories online of workplace sexual harassment. It is perhaps not surprising that this followed the call of a Hollywood actress in response to widely covered accusations of predatory behaviour by well-known film producer Harvey Weinstein. Tens of thousands of people replied, including many from the media industries, and posts were spread and read by millions. The #MeToo phenomenon speaks not just to sexism and misogyny, but also to unequal power relationships in media organizations that affect women disproportionately. Verhoeven, Coate and Zemaityte (2019) additionally find that even when women do assume powerful positions in the industry – such as by becoming film directors – their work does not get the same or even similar distribution as those films directed by men. The authors conclude that 'male-dominated gatekeeping occurs at many points in the life-cycle of films directed by women' (ibid.: 136), arguing that their non-binary and intersectional approach allowed them to move beyond simply acknowledging the rise of women as movie directors to show the continuing processes of exclusion behind the scenes.

There is much more to be said about the role and personal characteristics of media professionals, and how a lack of diversity is a structural problem for the industry. Key to contemporary concerns about this is an appreciation of intersectionality or 'multi-dimensionality' of people's identities that consist of more than group categorizations such as gender, race or class. A second important theme of emerging research in this area links experiences of precarity and a 'culture of uncertainty' (Ekdale, Tully, Harmsen and Singer, 2015) with psychological wellbeing, quality of life and the lack thereof (Reinardy, 2011; O'Donnell, Zion and Sherwood, 2016), which hinders innovation, leaves practitioners fearful and frustrated, and potentially turns people away from the various media professions.

## ROLE CONFLICTS AND DILEMMAS

Not surprisingly, most studies of media organizations reveal many different kinds of latent conflict, based on a variety of factors, although quite often reflecting a tension between the aspirations of 'lower-level' participants and those in control of media. The influence of proprietors has already been discussed. An early newsroom study by Breed (1955) detailed the (mainly informal) socializing mechanisms that helped to ensure the maintenance of policy. Young reporters would be expected to read the newspaper they worked on and to sit in on editorial conferences. Policy was also learned through informal gossip with colleagues. Deviations were discouraged by feelings of obligation to superiors, by the satisfaction of belonging to the in-group and sometimes by management sanctions and rewards in giving assignments. In general, according to Breed's research, what policy actually was remained covert. Research by Bantz (1985), however, led to the conclusion that the organizational culture of news organizations is intrinsically oriented towards conflict.

Conflict is a key aspect of the intense, stressful and pressure-rich working environments of media organizations, as evidenced in cross-national comparative research among advertising teams (Grabher, 2002) and film productions (Cantor, 1971; Miller et al., 2005). Conflicts arise out of the pressure-cooker working environment typical of media production processes, and tend to be related to time (or a lack thereof), governance (of complex projects with a dynamic diversity of participants and stakeholders, often working with conflicting goals) and communication. Professionals and groups least likely to have conflicts with owners and managers tend to be those whose goals and motivations align closely with proprietors.

The lessons of other research on communicators seem to lead to a similar conclusion: that where conflict occurs between media organization and employee, it is likely to be where the political tendency or economic self-interest of the organization gets in the way of individual freedom of expression. Bauman (2005: 55) considers this tension a vicious circle, as 'management's plot against the endemic freedom of culture is a perpetual *casus belli*. On the other hand, culture creators need managers if they wish … to be seen, heard, and listened to, and to stand a chance of seeing their task/project through to completion'. Flegel and Chaffee (1971) support the view that a devotion to the craft and a 'technical orientation' towards a quality product, requiring co-operation, help to reduce conflict and promote a sense of autonomy. According to Sigelman (1973), the potential problem of conflict on grounds of belief is usually avoided by selective recruitment and self-selection by entrants into media organizations with compatible work environments. Perhaps most significant in media is the fact that being able to handle the work according to the reigning policy and goals of the organization becomes a skill and even a value in itself. This in turn leads to a certain homogenization of the media workforce, and requires an extraordinary amount of 'emotional labour' by the professionals involved, denoting 'the process by which workers are expected to manage their feelings in accordance with organizationally defined rules and guidelines' (Wharton, 2009: 147).

Turow (1994) raises the possibility of an increasing potential for internal conflict and even a need for it as a result of more and more concentration of ownership. Turow's evidence shows that role conflicts within such larger media enterprises do happen and that there is a tendency for 'silent bargains' to be made that encourage conformity and co-operation with overall company policy. A covert reward system exists that stresses caution and loyalty. This is perhaps a paradox in media production: on the one hand, media work takes place within and with organizations that depend on informal but fairly stable structures, a shared set of beliefs (mainly established through workplace socialization) and a highly routinized process, while on the other hand, the pervasive need for these industries to be creative and innovative tend to be seen as thriving in settings where conflict and difference of opinion are actively encouraged (Küng, 2017).

The main kinds of role dilemma that have arisen are summarized in Box 10.7. However, there are indications that pressure or opportunity for media professionals to operate as independent workers (or 'free agents') is giving rise to a new dilemma. Loyalties to an established title or channel are divided or much weaker and there are new options for autonomy, especially for those freelancers with a broad portfolio of skills and clients, and for those who have secured a particular niche for themselves.

## CONCLUSION

As we have seen, media occupations are weakly 'institutionalized' when compared, for instance, with law, medicine or accountancy, and professional success will often depend on the unaccountable ups and downs of public taste or on personal and unique qualities that cannot be imitated or transmitted. Apart from certain performance skills, it is hard to pin down an essential or 'core' media accomplishment. It may be that the freedom, creativity and critical approach that many media personnel still cherish, despite both the bureaucratic and precarious setting of their work, are ultimately incompatible with full professionalization in the traditional sense, as well as with the overriding commercial values that govern the decisions of media owners and managers. There are inevitable conflicts at the heart of media work, whether open or latent. Perhaps the most fundamental dilemma is one of autonomy versus constraint in an institution whose own ideology places a value on originality and freedom, yet whose organizational setting requires relatively strict control.

## FURTHER READING

Arsenault, A.H. and Castells, M. (2008) 'The structure and dynamics of global multi-media business networks', *International Journal of Communication*, 1(2): 707–748.

Banks, M., Taylor, S. and Gill, R. (eds) (2013) *Theorizing Cultural Work*. Abingdon: Routledge.

Deuze, M. and Prenger, M. (eds) (2019) *Making Media: Production, Practices and Professions*. Amsterdam: Amsterdam University Press.

Hesmondhalgh, D. and Baker, S. (2011) *Creative Labour: Media Work in Three Cultural Industries*. Abingdon: Routledge.

Mellado, C., Hellmueller, L., Márquez-Ramírez, M., Humanes, M.L., Sparks, C., Stepinska, A., Pasti, S., Schielicke, A., Tandoc, E. and Wang, H. (2017) 'The hybridization of journalistic cultures: a comparative study of journalistic role performance', *Journal of Communication*, 67: 944–967.

Reese, S.D. and Shoemaker, P.J. (2016) 'A media sociology for the networked public sphere: the hierarchy of influences model', *Mass Communication and Society*, 19(4): 389–410.

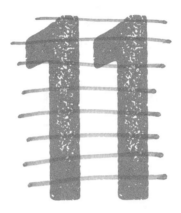

# 11

---

# THE PRODUCTION
# OF MEDIA CULTURE

We have looked up to now at a range of more or less constant factors that shape the work of media organizations. These relate, in particular, to the composition and internal social structure of the media workforce and the relations that are maintained, under a variety of economic and social pressures, with the world outside the organization. The context of the media is never really static, but it may appear stable as a result of a balance achieved between outside forces and organizational goals. There is much change and destabilization. The most significant single cause of change is the process of convergence, and the most significant actual change is the rise of online and mobile **connectivity** and creative (as well as commercial) potential for integrating older and newer channels of mass communication into media products and services.

In respect of production, convergence mainly shows itself in the inter-changeability and inter-operability of media platforms and the blurring of several long-standing boundaries between professional and amateur, public and private, fixed and mobile. Before considering media-organizational activities in greater detail, we consider the main features and trends determining the production of media culture. In subsequent sections we focus mainly on two interrelated aspects of organizational activity, which can be described respectively as 'selecting' and 'processing'. The first refers to the sequence of decisions, which extends from the choice of 'raw material', as it were, to delivering the finished product. The second refers to the application of work routines and organizational criteria (including both professional and business aspects) that affect the nature of this product as it passes through the 'chain' of decision-making.

This way of describing media-organizational work originates primarily from research on news production, but it can apply more or less equally to a range of other media products and media settings (Hirsch, 1977). In the case of news, the chain extends from 'noticing' an event in the world, through writing about or filming it, to preparing a news item for transmission. In the case of a book, a movie, a television show or a piece of popular music, a similar chain extends from an idea in someone's head, through an editorial selection process and many phases of transformation, to the final product (Ryan and Peterson, 1982). In this context, we will also look at the consequences of developments outlined earlier regarding concentration of media ownership (Chapter 8), globalization (Chapter 9), and the generally precarious working conditions for professionals within and outside media organizations (Chapter 10).

All phases of media production involve a large volume of work that becomes routinized as a matter of necessity. The regularities of behaviour and thinking that result from these routines give rise to empirical generalizations and to the possibility of theorizing about what is going on. The routines also reflect the 'operational' theories in the heads of media professionals.

Given the long history of journalism and its privileged position in society, most of the arguments and discussion here will focus on news media and news workers. Where possible, links with other media industries will be made. This is especially relevant given the current overall sense of collapse (rather than the more deliberate sounding 'convergence')

*(Continued)*

across the media industries: a collapse of parts, units, functions, roles, business and revenue models, for example. This includes a collapse of boundaries between journalism and other media professions, as journalists become 'content managers' and engage in 'native advertising' in order to provide their employers with additional revenue, or as they become 'media entrepreneurs' in combining low-paying work for news media with better-paying jobs elsewhere in the media industry, particularly in the field of marketing and public relations.

# FEATURES OF MEDIA PRODUCTION

Media industries are a combination of public service and for-profit companies engaged in the industrial and creative production and circulation of culture. This 'culture' refers not only to the production of spoken and written words, audio, still or moving images, but also (and increasingly) to providing platforms for people to produce and exchange their own content. In contemporary definitions of what production within these industries involves, four elements tend to get mixed up, which to some extent makes an adequate assessment of media work rather difficult: content, connectivity, creativity and commerce – which all translate into the production of culture (see Figure 11.1). Media industries produce content, but also invest in platforms for connectivity – where fans and audiences provide the free labour needed to promote, publicize and spread the messages of media firms and producers (Jenkins et al., 2013). Media production consists of semi-autonomous culture creation, but tends to take place within a distinctly commercial context. These four values and goals – content and connectivity, creativity and commerce – are the subject of constant struggle and negotiation within the media industries.

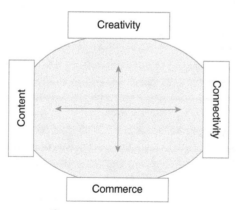

Figure 11.1 Modelling media work

In economic terms, the media generally serve a dual product market: media are sold as newspapers, magazines, movies, games, and so on to audiences, while at the same time the attention of that audience – expressed as ratings, circulation figures, unique site visitors, etc. – is sold to advertisers. This is a fascinating area of tension within the industry, as the wants and needs of audiences, creators and advertisers may not always be the same, and in the current digital and networked media ecosystem the roles played by advertising creatives, media producers and content consumers are increasingly intertwined. This networked character also reveals the often global nature of the media production process (or 'pipeline'), as many industries – such as digital game development, film and television – offshore, subcontract and outsource various elements in the production process to save costs, attract new types of capital (such as state subsidies and tax breaks) and talent, and redistribute risks. Examples are securing international financing for television projects, shooting a movie 'offshore' at several locations around the world, moving an online division or marketing department of a newspaper elsewhere, mixing music recorded in Los Angeles in a studio outside London, localizing game titles set in one regional, cultural or national context in another part of the world, adding local soundtracks and hit songs to generic advertising campaigns generated for global brands, separating out the marketing and distribution of titles, and so on. Such supranational forms of market-based cultural production primarily benefit and in part result from structural trends characterizing the media industries in recent years: growth, integration, globalization and concentration of ownership (see Chapters 9 and 10).

Although it is tempting to see the dominant multinational media corporations as efficient risk-averse monoliths, research on the relationship between international strategic management and firm performance of global media conglomerates shows otherwise. Analysing the product and geographic diversification strategies of these conglomerates, Sylvia Chan-Olmsted and Byeng-Hee Chang (2003), for example, conclude that although these companies initially expanded and diversified to reduce overall risks, the increased complexity of international operations and exposures to uncertainties, coupled with risk regarding consumer tastes, regulations and investment in distribution, in fact leads to performance declines. Furthermore, research on synergy management, global–local relationships and intra-corporate co-operation in media conglomerates such as Bertelsmann (Schulze, Thielmann, Sieprath and Hess, 2005) and News Corporation (Marjoribanks, 2000) suggests that the organization of work in these companies is far from streamlined, uniform or necessarily successful, as much depends on particular values, behaviours and beliefs of individual actors in the production process.

Each field, genre or discipline in the media has its own peculiarities and distinctiveness. Still, the trends towards business integration, technological convergence and the mutually reinforcing developments of localization and globalization ('glocalization') have made working experiences in the media industries increasingly similar. It becomes possible to discuss 'the' media according to a couple of key distinctive features, as summarized in Box 11.1.

## 11.1

## Key features of media production

- Informal networks of collaboration, expertise and influence
- Largely project-based nature of production
- Highly structured, patterned and at times formulaic processes
- High degree of communicative complexity and affective labour

Bilton (2007: 46) typifies the cultural geography of the media industries as consisting of a range of informal networks of collaboration, expertise and influence: 'These networks extend in two dimensions, horizontally, through peer-to-peer relationships with organizations and individuals, and vertically, through supply chain relationships which contribute to different phases of cultural production and distribution.' Bilton emphasizes the informal, collaborative and intangible nature of the production process. At the same time, much of the actual work in media production follows highly structured, patterned and at times formulaic processes – in part to meet deadlines, to conform to production and release schedules, and to effectively manage the risks involved with making a cultural product for the mass market.

A second crucial contextual aspect of media work for the negotiation of commerce, connectivity, content and creativity is the largely project-based nature of production. The organization of work in projects with a limited lifespan occurs both within certain companies – as in temporary teams assembled for particular clients in a full-service advertising or integrated marketing communications firm – and between companies. The way media owners, managers and professionals enact and give meaning to the work in this industry exhibits a certain degree of communicative complexity, which is required in order to address the dynamic, fast-paced, high-pressure and complex nature of media production.

Above all, media work is a form of affective labour: work that elicits an affective investment from its practitioners exceeding conscious deliberation, and that is intended to evoke a similarly pre-cognitive response among audiences. In the contemporary attention economy, engagement is a key aspect of making media: not just getting people to notice and pay attention to your product or service, but to get people engaged, to suspend their disbelief, to keep consumers coming back for more. Insights from consumer psychology and behavioural design are becoming quite popular in the media industries, propelled by the enormous amount of data that media users generate online. At the same time, media professionals are also, to some extent, expected to surrender completely to their work, in part encouraged by comfortable and at times even playful working environments – which, in the case of freelancers, also include the private home, or any one of the countless coffee shops and cafés serving as the urban landscape of media production (Hartmann, 2009).

In short, it is possible to summarize that informal networks among generally short-term (and often freelance) employed professionals who care deeply about their work within a broader industry structure dominated by complex and highly structured project-based work are what epitomize media production.

## KEY TRENDS IN THE PRODUCTION OF MEDIA CULTURE

Working in the media industries, both large and small, means coming to terms with a couple of related and overlapping trends. Focusing on those trends that are somewhat particular to the professional identity of a media professional, we consider the tendency of cultural companies to cluster in specific urban areas, the risky and unpredictable nature of the media business, the complexity of controlling and collaborating with creative individuals in the context of project-based labour and commercial enterprise, and the pervasive nature of technology and information management in all aspects of the creative process (Deuze, 2007: 63–74; Deuze and Prenger, 2019).

Media companies are attracted to the city, and the development of what Scott (2000) calls the cultural economy of cities is bound up with the presence of clusters of cultural firms and media industries, ranging from large vertically integrated corporations to small networks of media entrepreneurs. Clustering is primarily motivated by a strategy to counter the risky nature of the media business. The key risk in media work lies in the paradoxical nature of the media product. In some ways, a cultural commodity – a film, a digital game, an advertising campaign – is just like any other commercial product in that it is made to appeal to a certain audience. On the other hand, the success or failure of the media product relies on its novelty and difference, and on its ability to meet the difficult-to-predict sensitivities and tastes of consumers. The first trend signifies an economically sound strategy of producing the kind of content that has proven itself in the marketplace. This linear differentiation process (Turner, 2003) in the production and development of cultural commodities can be set against a concurrent need for diversifying and differentiating production, as the public's tastes, preferences and attention spans rapidly (and continually) change. Focusing on diversifying ('liquefying') the production portfolio is thus an equally important thing to do for media industries.

Linearity and liquidity are rather different production styles and market strategies. The tension this creates can be seen as typical and indeed fundamental to the creative process of media production. Opting either way always involves taking risks, as the outcome of both strategies is unpredictable. Risk and its counterpart, trust, are constitutive in the organization and management of media work. In media industries, 'risk is managed and trust is negotiated in informal contexts, social networks and social spaces …

new ties of trust, whether they be strong or weak, help break down industry boundaries and themselves become part of the creative process leading to unforeseen collaborations and/or new cultural product' (Banks, Lovatt, O'Connor and Raffo, 2000: 463). It is therefore quite common for professionals to work with different employers in the same industry, whose companies are often physically located in the same block of streets and office buildings, and whose employees frequent the same restaurants, bars and clubs for lunch, after-work activities and networking parties. All the time, these professionals may subsequently or simultaneously work on projects that fit either linear or liquid production styles.

## THE SPECIAL NATURE OF MEDIA MANAGEMENT AND PRODUCTION

Media professionals are somewhat different from their colleagues in other fields of production in that they often care deeply about their work, as mentioned earlier. The difficulty of media management is underscored by the combination of this rather unique element of media workers' sense of professional identity and a structural sense of risk and unpredictability at the heart of the cultural production process. The creative process is sustained by inspiration and informed by talent, vitality and commitment, which makes creative work volatile, dynamic and risk-ridden, shaped by crucial tacit skills that are often vague and remain unspoken (Leadbeater and Oakley, 1999). 'In media organizations, you have a rapidly changing, dynamic atmosphere where people within the organization frequently see themselves more as independent contractors than employees. They see the organization as merely a conduit for their work' (Redmond and Trager, 2004: 59). Caves (2000) adds that as a result of this, there are many more people wanting to work in these industries than there are jobs available, and most of them are willing to accept below-average salaries, contingent wages and temporary contractual arrangements without benefits or any kind of guarantees for future employment. This shifts the power balance in the industry in favour of owners and employers – with the exception of 'stars' and high-profile talent, as well as at certain moments when an industry is dependent on innovation and new ideas to attract audiences (such as when a new generation of consoles is introduced in the global games industry, or when a particular television series or film franchise becomes internationally successful to the extent that new seasons or sequels need to be relatively quickly commissioned and produced).

The management of media industries is, by all accounts, special (Lowe and Brown, 2016). It not only involves the supervision and facilitation of creative individuals in the context of project-based labour and commercial enterprise, it also entails managing contacts and contracts with outsourced and subcontracted labour, as well as with all kinds of auxiliary industries, such as reproduction facilities, licensors, vendors, distributors and retailers. Some of the people in these fields are internal to the media firm, but most of them are not. Often every single project – a digital game, a film, a special section of a magazine or newspaper – is produced by a team of people specifically assembled for that purpose. Interestingly, just as consumers can choose products primarily for their sign-value rather than their use-value, the putting together of a team does not necessarily involve choosing the best people for the project at hand; it also means getting people together who trust each other, who have earned the trust of a manager or client in the past, or who are known to be able to work with each other without too much conflict. In other words, project-based media production, like media consumption, tends to be done within a cultural context of what it means to the people involved, more so than according to rational, scientific, objective or strictly economic principles.

The organization of teamwork in the media centres on meeting a series of deadlines of deliverables and milestones – an installment in a series of stories, a set of photographs for a magazine spread, a specific asset such as the soundtrack of a video game – forcing co-operation among project participants with different skills and perspectives on the project outcome. Team-based labour also tends to be portable, in that workers move from project to project rather than carrying out a continuing set of tasks. This means that employers are continually faced with re-composing a workforce, while workers are always looking and preparing for their next job (Christopherson and van Jaarsveld, 2005).

## THE SPECIAL ROLE OF TECHNOLOGY

Throughout the literature on the structure, management and work in the media, the pervasive and ubiquitous role of technology stands out. The media industries are among the key accelerators of the development and innovation of new information and communication technologies. Print journalism is a media profession that has contributed to increasing demands on the efficiency, cost-effectiveness and quality of printing presses, digital reproduction and distribution methods, and desktop publishing tools. The digital games industry supercharged upgrades to processor speeds, memory compression, three-dimensional ('3D') graphics and screen pixilation technologies for personal computers and game consoles. The film industry contributed to the development of digital surround sound and widescreen projection systems in theatres and, increasingly, at home, whereas the music and recording industries greatly facilitated the introduction and advancement of portable music players and sound editing software.

In the daily work environment and practices in the media, technology plays a crucial part in the creative process. A significant concern regarding this trend is the standardization of work practices implied by an omnipresence of technologies. In order to facilitate technological convergence and the corresponding managerial expectation of a synergy between different practices and processes, media companies increasingly rely on content management systems (CMS), which are sophisticated software packages generally acquired on the commercial market, further developed using open source applications and finally customized in-house. As different media formats – audio, moving and still images, text – become increasingly standardized regarding their translation to the digital, the exchange and re-purposing or 'windowing' of multimedia content becomes more manageable. Yet this lowering of the threshold for technological convergence can at the same time be considered to be problematic for media practitioners, who like to see themselves as creative workers, not as 'slaves' to the relatively limited range of options offered by pre-programmed templates, shells and formats offered by technologies like CMS.

Concerns regarding the efficient ordering, standardizing and streamlining promises and effects of technology can be read next to more 'techno-optimist' notions, celebrating their digital, networked, interactive and easy-to-use potential. Bar and Simard (2006: 360) make the point that control over the configuration and application of technologies in organizations is flexibly separate from ownership of the underlying network infrastructure. This, they argue, creates opportunities for individuals and teams using these technologies to shape them in different ways. However, this expectation of some kind of collaborative social shaping is not given to all, as Aronowitz and DiFazio (1995) warn against the deleterious effects of computerization and signal increased opportunities for exploitative labour practices enabled through such 'cybernetization' of the workplace. In journalism, a related contemporary concern, for example, concerns the automation of news-work and the rise of 'robotic' reporters; that is, software-generated content (Carlson, 2015) associated with an ongoing loss of jobs as well as workplace autonomy.

Although different technologies are used in different contexts throughout the different areas of the media industries, today media professionals are expected to come to terms with numerous technologies in their work. This particular aspect of media production gets increasing attention in media and mass communication research, as scholars consider the material context of production as one among many variables to consider (Lewis and Westlund, 2015). Furthermore, many of the technologies commonly used in media production are converging. Technological convergence refers to the coming together of audio, video, telecommunication and data onto a common platform, enabled by the digitization of all these formerly separate technologies. People increasingly use the same device for multiple functions, making the computer (as a standalone device or as integrated into other hardware, like a cell phone) a truly 'universal machine' that can be used to simultaneously work and play. As these purposes can be served both from home and the office, the boundary between those kinds of places and experiences begins to lose significance. Convergence in media work thus relates to two intertwined processes: the convergence of place – as in the workplace and the home office – and the convergence of technology – as in the digital, networked hardware and software available to set the parameters of the production process, and to further the means for managerial control over media work. Such control takes place through workflow standardization, workplace surveillance, and the decentralization of work through telework and the outsourcing of specific segments (cf. 'deliverables') of a project to external actors and networks. As such, convergence directly affects four key aspects of mass media industries: the content of communication, the relationships between media producers and consumers, the structure of firms, and ultimately how media professionals do their work.

The introduction of all kinds of content management systems, company intranets, and desktop management and publishing software in newsrooms, advertising agencies, film and television (post-)production houses tends to mean two different but important things for the professionals involved: it speeds up as well as standardizes the production process, potentially contributing to a loss of autonomy and a sense of having to do and learn more on top of one's existing competences, skills and talent. New technologies force people to learn new skills and unlearn old ones, while the production process accelerates at the same time. Technologies are also developed and implemented differently across different organizations or even parts of a single organization, leading to a constant reshuffling of adaptation processes and experiences.

Whether real or perceived, there is a prevailing sense and discourse throughout the media industries that traditional ways of doing things do not work (anymore) in the digital age. Particularly when it comes to business models, the relative stability of advertising and sales has collapsed into online (and offline) business models that combine revenue streams from multiple sources, cultivate and commodify relations with consumers, and bypass media producers altogether in order to co-create with media users (as citizen journalists, influencers and productive fans). At the same time, the rapid adoption of digital devices and platforms as the go-to technologies for accessing and experiencing media fundamentally altered the habits of audiences, collapsing the categories of consuming and producing media. Collapse is also present in the distinctly 'making' aspects of media making, as genres, storytelling formats and creative practices collapse in favour of hybrid or hybridized media products and production processes. Everywhere we see an ongoing convergence of different domains, sectors and disciplines within and across the media industries, bringing new challenges for managing media firms and production processes.

## MEDIA-ORGANIZATIONAL ACTIVITIES: GATEKEEPING AND SELECTION

Media-organizational activities are the specific instances where overall trends and features of media production are operationalized and articulated. Here we focus on two fundamental activities, which can be described respectively as 'selecting' and 'processing'. The first refers to the sequence of decisions, which extends from the choice of 'raw material', as it were, to delivering the finished product. The second refers to the application of work routines and organizational criteria (including both professional and business aspects) that affect the nature of this product as it passes through the 'chain' of decision-making.

The term 'gatekeeping' has been widely used as a metaphor to describe the process by which selections are made in media work, especially decisions regarding whether or not to allow a particular news report to pass through the 'gates' of a news medium into the news channels (see White, 1950; Reese and Ballinger, 2001; Shoemaker et al., 2001). However, the idea of gatekeeping has a much wider potential application since it can apply to the work of literary agents and publishers, and to many kinds of editorial and production work. It applies to decisions about the distribution and marketing of existing media products (for example, films, games). In a wider sense, it refers to the power to give or withhold access to different voices in society and is often a locus of conflict. One common tension in democratic societies is between governments (or politicians) and the media over the amount and kind of attention they receive in mass media. Another example relates to the kind of representation and amount of access given to minorities. A contemporary concern relates to the algorithms of Internet businesses such as platforms, streaming services and webshops (that is, Facebook, Netflix, Amazon) that automate what people will see next, adding another gatekeeping layer in the publication and distribution of media.

Despite its appeal and plausibility, the gatekeeping concept has a number of weaknesses and has been continuously revised since its first applications. Weak points are its implication of there being one (initial) gate area and one main set of selection criteria, its simple view of the 'supply' of media products, and its tendency to reduce decision-making to the act of a single individual or organization. In a comprehensive overview of the concept and related research, Shoemaker (1991) has extended the original model to take account of the wider social context and many factors at work. With specific reference to journalism, she draws attention to the role of advertisers, public relations, pressure groups, plus varied sources and 'news managers' in influencing decisions. In her model, gatekeeping usually involves multiple and successive acts of selection over the period of news production. Often group decision-making is involved. Reference is made not only to aspects of content, but also to the kind of audience expected and to questions of cost. The main points of this model have been largely confirmed in case studies of specific news organizations.

More important is the extent to which gatekeeping is an autonomous professional action, rather than a choice mainly forced by economic pressures at the level of the media organization or by political pressures from outside (see Chapter 10 on the various influences on organizational decision-making in the media). Gatekeeping online, often automated, can bypass mass media and make the original concept of gatekeeper obsolete (Bro and Wallberg, 2015). Established journalism is no longer a privileged source of news, nor is it able to selectively control the supply. Nevertheless, there is no reduction in the wish of interested actors to ensure that their particular message gets rapid, extensive and prominent public attention, and for this it is still usually necessary to pass through the gates of the mass media. Alternatively, brand advocates and politicians alike seek to engage with consumers and citizens directly via social media, using their name recognition and reputation to 'disintermediate' the news media (Hermida, 2010). As searching and finding, filtering, curating and selecting valuable information online becomes a challenge to all, professional gatekeeping can possibly be expected to return to prominence as a valued service.

## IDEOLOGICAL VERSUS ORGANIZATIONAL FACTORS

In early studies of news gatekeeping (White, 1950; Gieber, 1956), most interest was focused on the large number of items that failed to gain entry and on the reasons for exclusion. In the nature of the early research, there was a tendency to emphasize the subjective character of news selection decisions and the autonomy of the news editor. Later, more attention was given to systematic influences on selection that can be considered as either 'organizational' or 'ideological'. The former refers primarily to bureaucratic routines and factory-like procedures, the latter to values and cultural influences, which are not purely individual and personal but which stem also from the social (and national) setting of media activity. The necessity for normal processes of news selection to be strongly influenced by routine was recognized long ago by Walter Lippmann (1922: 123), when he wrote: 'without standardization, without stereotypes, without routine judgements, without a fairly ruthless disregard of subtlety, the editor would soon die of excitement'.

Subsequent research demonstrated that the content of news media tends to consistently follow a predictable pattern and that different organizations behave in a similar way when confronted by the same events and under equivalent conditions (Glasgow Media Group, 1976; McQuail, 1977; Shoemaker and Reese, 1991). There appears to be a stable perception on the part of news decision-makers about what is likely to interest an audience and a good deal of consensus within the same social-cultural settings (Hetherington, 1985). A condition for this generalization is one of limited diversity within the media system as a whole. This observation about the news industry extends to some extent across all mass media industries, and points to a paradox in the production of culture: these are industries where flexibility, talent, creativity and innovation are privileged, and that attract larger numbers of workers based on this arguably exciting promise. At the same time, research suggests that the industry overwhelmingly runs on factory-like production processes, relying heavily on quite rigid schedules and procedures, and curtails experimentation and originality in favour of 'exploitative innovation' (March, 1991), referring to the tendency to make more of the same and stick with what works.

An alternative explanation to that of subjective individual judgement steeped in recognition of media production as a patterned procedure is to be found in the concept of news value, which is an attribute of a news event that transforms it into an interesting 'story' for an audience. However, news values are always relative, such that a current event of interest can be rapidly eclipsed by another that is more recent as well as more interesting. While the general idea of news values was already familiar, a study of foreign news in the Norwegian press by Galtung and Ruge (1965) led to the first clear statement of the news values (or 'news factors') that influence selection. They indicated three main types of factor that played a part: organizational, genre-related and social-cultural. The organizational factors are the most universal and least escapable, and they also have some ideological consequences. The collection of news has to be organized, and there is a bias towards events and news stories that fit the time frame and the machinery of selection and retransmission. This favours recent events that occur near the reporting facilities (often in cosmopolitan centres with good communications) and with the availability of creditable sources. Genre-related factors include a preference for news events that fit advance audience expectations (consonance with past news) and that can be readily placed within a familiar interpretative 'frame', for instance, frames of conflict or endemic crisis.

At the same time, these news values are context-dependent and should not be interpreted as neutral practices particular to a more or less detached professional way of doing things. The social-cultural influences on foreign news selection stem from certain western and ideological values that focus on individuals and involve an interest in elite people and also negative, violent or dramatic happenings. As such, news values can be seen as a consensual structure or map that journalists use to help them make sense of the world (Hartley, 1982). Since the influential study of Galtung and Ruge (1965), many follow-up studies have been published, to some extent confirming the way these values work, adding additional values, accounting for extra-media influences, or suggesting methodological and conceptual updates. In a review of fifty years of news value research, Joye, Heinrich and Wöhlert (2016) identified one major shortfall in news coverage found across this entire body of work: established news media tend to report based on what they call 'distorted' worldviews, given the tendency of news organizations to use a fairly stable notion of the nation (or local community) as their primary frame of reference. At the heart of such critique is the expectation that journalism in a globalized world should take responsibility to include a wider variety of voices, offering 'multiperspectival' news (Gans, 2011), and in doing so represent a global plurality of views, especially considering the context of worldwide migration and the contemporary multicultural society. Contemporary journalism is taking up this call to some extent, as examples of 'networked' (Beckett and Mansell, 2008) and cross-border collaborations of journalists from different countries and media (Alfter, 2019) abound, including with people not necessarily self-identifying as journalists (Robinson, 2017). A second observation about the study of news values calls for consideration of news produced by non-traditional outlets, including citizens, (international) non-government organizations, and all kinds of media entrepreneurs emerging all over the world.

The main factors predicted to influence news coverage are listed in Box 11.2, taken from a recent update of several original news value studies (Harcup and O'Neill, 2017).

## 11.2

### News event factors predictive of coverage (Harcup and O'Neill, 2017: 13)

*Exclusivity*: Stories generated by, or available first to, the news organization as a result of interviews, letters, investigations, surveys, polls, and so on.

*Bad news*: Stories with particularly negative overtones, such as death, injury, defeat and loss (of a job, for example).

*Conflict*: Stories concerning conflict, such as controversies, arguments, splits, strikes, fights, insurrections and warfare.

*Surprise*: Stories that have an element of surprise, contrast and/or the unusual about them.

*Audiovisuals*: Stories that have arresting photographs, video, audio and/or which can be illustrated with infographics.

*Shareability*: Stories that are thought likely to generate sharing and comments via Facebook, Twitter and other forms of social media.

*Entertainment*: Soft stories concerning sex, showbusiness, sport, lighter human interest, animals, or offering opportunities for humorous treatment, witty headlines or lists.

*Drama*: Stories concerning an unfolding drama, such as escapes, accidents, searches, sieges, rescues, battles or court cases.

*Follow-up*: Stories about subjects already in the news.

*The power elite*: Stories concerning powerful individuals, organizations, institutions or corporations.

*Relevance*: Stories about groups or nations perceived to be influential with, or culturally or historically familiar to, the audience.

*Magnitude*: Stories perceived as sufficiently significant in the large numbers of people involved or in potential impact, or involving a degree of extreme behaviour or extreme occurrence.

*Celebrity*: Stories concerning people who are already famous.

*(Continued)*

Although the first gatekeeping studies presumed that news selection was guided by an expert assessment of what would interest audiences, there has been mixed support for this view. Cross-national comparative research comparing audience interests in news topics and editorial judgements of the same matter has shown wide mismatching, and a 'news gap' certainly exists (Boczkowski and Mitchelstein, 2013). The study of news values can be extrapolated to other media industries regarding two key observations about the nature of the production process. First, the way decisions about which content to produce and bring to market are made – whether this concerns motion pictures, digital games, television shows or advertising campaigns – still tends to take national boundaries as a touchstone premise. Despite the globalization of media and society, most content is either specifically made for a (presumed) 'national audience' or foreign formats are adapted to suit local tastes (see Chapter 9 on the global trade in media culture). Within nations, audiences are further segmented according to increasingly specific data profiles, parsing people along lines of ethnicity, gender, class, age and other variables, making it less likely for people to 'meet' in the media and recognize themselves in shared narratives. A second observation seems to run counter to this trend, as it concerns the twin developments of (the rise of) global production networks and a new international division of cultural labour.

As social theories about the network society (see Chapter 4) suggest, the networked form of enterprise is quite typical for media work, especially considering the ongoing outsourcing, offshoring and subcontracting of (specialized and flexible) parts of the creative process – from financing to distribution and usage – across the planet. While multinational diversified media corporations remain territorially anchored to their preferred 'home' markets of Japan, the United States and Europe, their networks stretch out across the globe (Arsenault and Castells, 2008). Still, the evidence suggests a 'continuing strong regionality of global corporate media strategies' within a highly uneven worldwide media system (Hoyler and Watson, 2013: 106). The work of scholars in the area of global production networks (Coe et al., 2004; Johns, 2006) shows how these 'extra-local' (that is, connecting people and firms across different locales into a single media production) processes do not exclusively play into the hands of powerful corporations, but at specific times and instances – which can be exploited by media workers – can favour the entrepreneurial individual, the free agent or the smaller (and thus more agile) firm.

MCQUAIL'S MEDIA AND MASS COMMUNICATION THEORY
ORGANIZATIONS

As the production of culture becomes contingent on a global network of companies and talent, the responsibility for preparing, finding and keeping employment (or income/revenue) becomes integrated in a new international division of predominantly flexible, contingent labour (Miller and Leger, 2001). The media have a tendency to cluster in specific (urban) areas, within which regions an ongoing exchange of finance, resources, labour, talent and skills takes place between people and organizations (Scott, 2000). People flock to these areas in search of employment in the cultural industries. However, the migration patterns within the international division of cultural labour tend to be mostly regional or virtual, rather than global. People tend to remain firmly in place as their talent migrates to fulfil part of the production pipeline, such as a location for a film shoot, the development of a particular asset of a digital game, the marketing and customer relationship management services of a news organization. Locational agglomeration and the global networked form of enterprise can thus be seen to reinforce each other, adding to the contingency of media production, while at the same time professionals in these industries and across the value chain are more connected than ever before. The cultural geography of media production is organized as a range of informal networks of collaboration, expertise and influence that can stretch across the globe.

Miller and Leger (2001) argue that all this internationalization of production and work should not be mistaken for a weakening of corporate and, notably, American control. This is a poignant critique to consider in the context of contemporary efforts by companies such as Netflix to expand its services around the world, including setting up local production studios and offices, and sourcing local talent. Just as the selection of news by established firms tends to follow certain predictable patterns, so does the production of media through global production networks.

# THE STRUGGLE OVER ACCESS BETWEEN MEDIA AND SOCIETY

The question of access to the media (and thus to society itself as the audience) by any one institutional element of the society has already been raised at several points. The initial frame of reference in Chapter 4 (Figure 4.2) represents the media as creating (or occupying) channels 'between' the institutions of society and its members. One of the main kinds of pressure on media organization is that for access by social and political interests.

The way the issue has been posed assumes that the mass media effectively control the flow of information between society and its members. However, this is called into question by the appearance of new media that produce not only content but also 'connectivity' of anyone with anyone else. This enables many new and uncontrolled channels to develop and for the roles of sender and receiver to converge (Jenkins, 2006). Although the mediation of power in most societies still seems to be carried out by mass media in new and integrated forms, the rapid rise of Internet platforms disrupts the flow of media and relations of access on a global scale, given the extraordinary number of people connecting, sharing and commenting on media through these online services on a daily basis.

In democratic societies, including those offering a high degree of freedom to their media, there are clear expectations, sometimes backed by considerable pressure, that mass media will make channels available for society-wide communication, especially 'downwards' from leaders or elites to the base of society. This may be achieved by legal provision, by purchase of time/space in a free market, or by the media voluntarily serving as an open means of public communication. It matters a good deal to the media how 'access for society' is achieved, since freedom of the media in general, and journalism in particular, is generally held to include the right not to publish and thus to withhold access. The same rationale applies to contemporary efforts by governments around the world to rein in or otherwise curtail the freedom that Internet platforms and online social media enjoy, gradually implementing policies intended to protect citizens (especially children and teenagers), to demand transparent governance structures, and to return some control back to the societies within which these companies operate.

## A CONTINUUM OF MEDIA AUTONOMY

The situation can be understood in terms of a continuum: at one extreme the media are totally 'penetrated' by, or assimilated to, outside interests, whether state or not; at the other end, the media are totally free to exclude or admit as they see fit. Under normal conditions neither extreme will be found. Pluralistic theory presupposes that the diversity of organizations and possibilities for access will ensure an adequate mix of opportunity for 'official' voices of society and for critical and alternative views.

'Access for society' means more, however, than giving a platform for opinions, information, and the like. It also relates to the manner in which media portray what passes for the reality of society. They may do this in ways that alter, distort or challenge it. In the end, the question of societal access involves a very complex set of conventions over the terms according to which media freedoms and societal claims can be exercised and reconciled. Much depends on the standardized characteristics of formats and genres and on the manner in which they are intended to portray social reality or are understood to do so by their audiences.

This question was illuminated in an early study regarding the case of television production in one country (Britain) by Elliott (1972), and his ideas could be applied to press media and to other national media systems. His typology (Figure 11.2) shows the variability of competence of the media organization over the giving or withholding of access to other would-be communicators. It portrays the inverse relationship between the degree of freedom of access available to society and the degree of extensiveness of control and action by media.

| Scope of production/ media autonomy | Production function | Directness of access by society | Type of access for society | Television example |
|---|---|---|---|---|
| Limited | 1  Technical facilitation | Total | 1  Direct | Party broadcast |
| | 2  Facilitation and selection | | 2  Modified direct | Education |
| | 3  Selection and presentation | | 3  Filtered | News |
| | 4  Selection and compilation | | 4  Remade | Documentary |
| | 5  Realization and creation | | 5  Advisory | Realistic social drama |
| Extensive | 6  Imaginative creation | Zero | 6  No control by society | Original television drama |

Figure 11.2  A typology of production scope and directness of access by society: access by society is inversely related to communicator (editorial) autonomy (Elliott, 1972)

The larger the scope of control by the media themselves (scope of production), the more limited the direct access by the society. There is a varying degree of intervention or mediation by the media as between the 'voice of society' or social reality on the one hand, and the society as audience on the other. This formulation underlines the basic conflict between media autonomy and social control. Access is bound to be a site of struggle.

In the contemporary context, access has become a much more complex concept, as actors intent on getting their message across do not have to pass through the filters and 'gates' of professional media anymore to reach mass audiences. Using personal data widely available for purchase, both companies and individuals can customize information to target specific people with tailor-made messages intended to influence opinions and change behaviours. This kind of 'micro-targeting' of citizens and consumers is cause for great concern, although we should be wary of overwrought claims regarding the effect all of this has on people's attitudes and actions. In their study of the relationship between people's exposure to political personalized advertisements on Facebook and voters' responses towards those ads, Kruikemeier, Sezgin and Boerman (2016), for example, found that users seem to generally understand the persuasive communication techniques that are used on social media and are resistant to such ads. In follow-up research, Metz, Kruikemeir and Lecheler (2019) did find that politicians who share their personal lives online can count on a positive response, suggesting that it can pay off for public figures to bypass or 'disintermediate' professional news media in order to access citizens (as voters or consumers) more directly.

# MEDIA-ORGANIZATIONAL ACTIVITIES: PROCESSING AND PRESENTATION

Media industries, organizations and professionals are all part of a particular media production value chain – from conception, execution (also pre-production), production (including editing, transcription, duplication), marketing (including packaging and promotion), to distribution and consumption (see Hesmondhalgh, 2018: 95–96). Although there are distinct differences between the various industries in how these steps unfold, ultimately all productions follow a particular logic (Deuze, 2007: 110–112).

A helpful tool to chart the way media organizations process and present their work across the key media industries is Dahlgren's concept of *media logic*, as it refers to 'the particular institutionally structured features of a medium, the ensemble of technical and organizational attributes which impact on what gets represented in the medium and how it gets done. In other words, media logic points to specific forms and processes which organize the work done within a particular medium. Yet, media logic also indicates the cultural competence and frames of perception of audiences/users, which in turn reinforces how production within the medium takes place' (Dahlgren, 1996: 63). Media logic can be medium-specific because it primarily relates to production patterns within a given technological and organizational context. Dahlgren's concept, derived from earlier work by Altheide and Snow (1991), is a bit more specific to the inner workings of the media industry in comparison with other models of media organizational activity, such as Peterson and Anand's comprehensive six-facet model of the production of culture (2004), which examines the role of technology, law and regulation, industry structure, organizational structure, occupational careers, and the market. In earlier work, Bernhard Miège (1989) developed the concept of *production logic* in order to understand media industries, based on five characteristics: the economic value chain, the dominant power brokers, the creative workers/professions, the revenue stream and the overall market structure.

Considering the main media professions, each of these can be analysed in terms of its media logic, which means the institutional, technological, organizational and market features of how media production works in, respectively, advertising (including public relations and marketing communications), journalism, television and film, the music and recording industry, and digital games. The focus here will be on the organization of activities of media production, as the main institutional and organizational features of the mass media have been discussed in Chapter 10, and the role of audiences will be discussed at the end of this chapter. In general terms, as suggested before, what typifies media professions today is an increasing complexity and ongoing liquefaction or even collapse of the boundaries between different fields, disciplines, practices and categories.

# THE ORGANIZATION OF MEDIA PRODUCTION: ADVERTISING

Advertising agencies tend to cluster in certain regions around the world. Among the top urban centres where creative talent and potential project partners are concentrated are cities such as Tokyo, New York (home of the 'adland' of Madison Avenue), Frankfurt, Paris, London (where Soho is considered an 'ad village'), Los Angeles, Milan, São Paulo, Amsterdam and Madrid. The organization of work in advertising, PR and marketing firms centres almost exclusively on a project-by-project basis. There are two types of project organization relevant to the advertising industry, one within full-service firms – which offer media buying, planning and creative functions as well as marketing and PR services – constituted by employees from different departments, and one based on temporary co-operative efforts across firm boundaries, generally including numerous external services and professionals. The architecture of the work of large and small agencies can be best understood as one of what Grabher (2002) calls back-to-back (and for some, simultaneous) 'project ecologies' and Cottle (2003: 170) refers to as the 'production ecology', which can be characterized by 'a set of competitive institutional relationships and co-operative dependencies'. The concept of the project ecology comes closest to the lived reality of the daily work in the advertising industry, as it allows for 'interdependencies between projects and as well as other more traditional 'permanent' forms of organization' (Grabher, 2002: 245).

Key to understanding project ecologies in advertising is their heterarchical character: project teams are networks of professionals (temporarily) sharing common goals in which each participant shares more or less the same horizontal position of power and authority. The project ecology of advertising involves:

- one or more marketing managers on the client side;
- account managers, planners and creatives in an advertising agency or media bureau – sometimes with partnerships at one or more other agencies within the same group or holding firm; and
- a group of local or even international creative (such as art and film directors, special-ized photographers, graphic designers) and technical (offering services in audio and video processing, printing, lithography, ICT) professionals who are hired on a project basis through largely personal network ties.

The way agencies secure projects and clients is often through the production of 'spec-work' (short for speculative work), which can be conceptual designs or sometimes entire campaigns produced for free to be presented to prospective clients in the hope that this will lead to a new account. This kind of speculative labour is quite common in the media indus-tries (Fast, Örnebring and Karlsson, 2016), as scriptwriters and 'below-the-line' workers for film and television can attest. Even unpaid or underpaid internships, increasingly to be found in the news industry as well as the other industries discussed here, can be considered to be such a form of speculative labour.

The Internet and the rise of social and mobile media have brought about a significant change in the way the advertising industry goes about its business. The commission system – whereby advertising agencies charge their clients a percentage on top of all the work they do – has been gradually replaced by a performance-based system. Instead of producing advertisements for a specific medium, among which the television ad used to be the gold standard, agencies now tend to work across multiple media. And the success or failure of campaigns is increasingly determined by the extent to which audiences participate in all kinds of ways in co-creating, distributing and promoting the brand message (Nixon, 2011). An interesting contemporary trend is the tendency of companies 'to use advertising to do more than affect customers and sales, for example by being a positive change in society' (Rosengren, 2019: 390).

## THE ORGANIZATION OF MEDIA PRODUCTION: JOURNALISM

In journalism, newspaper, magazine, television, radio and online newsrooms tend to have quite different work practices. As a rule of thumb, news outlets are located near the centre of the city or region where their core audience is located, and competitors tend to cluster together – again, a common trend throughout the cultural industries. The organizational processes involved in the selection of news are typically very hierarchical rather than democratic or collegial, although within particular production units the latter may apply. Most of the work in news organizations is based on a set of routine, standardized activities. Summarizing the ways in which journalists generally report the news, Bennett (2003: 165ff) suggests that they confront three separate sources of incentives to standardize their work habits: routine co-operation with news sources, such as public relations officials, spokespeople for organizations, celebrities and politicians; work routines of specific news organizations that especially newcomers learn about by having to adapt themselves to mostly unwritten rules and conventions about the 'house style' way of doing things; and daily information sharing and working relations with fellow reporters, which in the case of certain beats results in journalists moving as a pack from event to event, encountering their competitor-colleagues at the same places, covering the same issues.

This relatively stable and standardized way of doing things exists side by side with a much more dynamic organization of newswork, in part because of the fact that many, if not most, journalists today do their work in part-time, contingent or freelance capacities. This reality has prompted critical reflection in the field on the source of knowledge about news production, because newsrooms are in many ways 'problematic sites of fieldwork' (Anderson, 2011: 152). This is not simply an operational problem in the current climate of newswork destabilization. As Karin Wahl-Jorgensen (2009: 23) puts it, the newsroom-centricity in journalism studies has meant that scholars have tended to focus on journalists' culture as it emerges within the limited areas of newsrooms and other centralized sites for news production, usually paying scant attention to places, spaces, practices and people at the margins of this spatially delimited news production universe. Such newsroom-centricity has implications beyond the mere privileging of some actors and the exclusion of others; it also privileges an analysis of relatively fixed patterns of newswork. Cottle (2007: 10) notes how such a focus on 'organizational functionalism' privileges routines and patterned ways of producing news over differentiation and divergence. Examples of less formalized ways of making news generally involve journalists working for less institutionalized and more audience-oriented outlets, such as journalism startups, popular magazines, local news stations, human interest and infotainment genres (van Zoonen, 1998).

The processing line in the news industry follows from story assignments made by editors and goes through a sequence of news conference, play decisions (prominence and timing), layout or lineup, final editing, content page makeup or television anchor script, and final lineup. This sequence can be fed up to the penultimate stage just before the deadline, which in the case of the current digital environment tends to include a 'rolling' deadline next to those that are particular to broadcast schedules or print runs. In general, the sequence extends from a phase where a universe of substantive ideas is considered, through a narrowing down according to news judgements and to what is fed from the source channel, to a third phase, where format, design and presentation decisions are taken, governed by the specific technological affordances of the channel(s) where the news is presented.

The model for news processing is compatible with what seems to occur in other situations, where content is also processed, although over a longer time scale and with more scope for production to influence content (see Figure 11.2). For instance, Elliott (1972), in his study of the making of a television documentary series, distinguishes three 'chains': a subject chain concerned with assembling programme ideas for the series, a contact chain connecting producer, director and researcher with their contacts and sources, and a presentation chain in which realities of time slot and budget were related to customary ideas for effective presentation.

## THE ORGANIZATION OF MEDIA PRODUCTION: MUSIC AND RECORDING

The music industry offers a different model, although there is still a sequence from ideas to transmission. Ryan and Peterson (1982) have drawn a model of the 'decision chain' in the popular music industry, which consists of six separate links. These are: (1) from songwriting to publishing; (2) from demo tape to recording (where producer and artist are selected); (3) and (4) from recording to manufacturing and marketing; (5) and (6) from there to consumption via radio, jukebox, live performance or direct sales. In this case, the original ideas of songwriters are filtered through music publishers' ideas concerning presentation (especially artist and style), which then play a part in promoting the product in several different markets.

The Internet and the rise of filesharing (cf. Napster founded in 1999 and Limewire in 2000) and streaming platforms (such as Spotify starting in 2006) have profoundly changed the industry. On the company side, labels have responded by trying to get artists to sign so-called '360' contracts that allow a record label to receive a percentage of the earnings from all the activities of an artist, including music sales, performances and touring, appearances in films and television or advertising campaigns, endorsements and merchandising. This strategy offsets some of the business risk for labels in the context of declining music sales. On the artist side, it becomes theoretically possible to bypass the industry altogether, publishing and publicizing music directly to audiences online, building and sustaining contacts with fans, and setting prices independently. Baym (2018) considers this kind of 'relational labour' as potentially liberating, yet cautions against the extremely labour-intensive nature of such new artist–fan relationships.

## THE ORGANIZATION OF MEDIA PRODUCTION: FILM AND TELEVISION

Companies and services in the film and television industries have 'an overwhelming tendency to locational agglomeration' (Scott, 2000: 83), of which Hollywood in Los Angeles is the best example. The reputation or image of certain places as being conducive to media industries such as film or television has particular clustering effects: talent, services and auxiliary companies gravitate towards these places, transforming them into distinct areas where everybody seems to be involved in the industry in one way or another. This clustering allows the different media industries quick and relatively cheap access to services, talent and skills.

Although the labour markets for film and television have different histories around the world, the situation is becoming increasingly similar. Employment relations in these industries have been transformed from the structured and clearly bounded state of European public broadcasters' internal labour markets into 'boundaryless' external labour markets, where a growing group of skilled professionals and experts flexibly supplies an industry of a few big companies and many small producers. Film and television professionals develop various strategies to counter such precarity, especially by organizing into groups or teams that tend to move from project to project together for a certain period of time. These networks of interdependence or 'semi-permanent work groups' (Blair, 2003) benefit employer and employee, as the first can outsource the hiring and firing of team members to those in charge of specific aspects of the production process (such as team leads in game development, magazine editors, or assistant directors in film and television), whereas the employees can secure future employment through their personal networks. These networks are not without power, as the creative talent of their – again, often informal – leaders can be an essential element in the production process, which allows them to make certain demands.

Because of the dynamic nature of the production process and the flexible working arrangements, the organization of production in film and television is in fact quite hierarchical and governed by strict divisions of labour separating conception and execution, 'with the former derived from creative, high skill, high value-added workers and the latter undertaken by routine, low skill, low value-added workers' (Warhurst, Thompson and Lockyer, 2005: 15). Although many professionals and small production houses continuously pitch shows, submit scripts, and do all kinds of speculative work on concepts and projects, only few actually get 'greenlighted', which is a reference to the process of formally approving the financing in order to move a project from the development phase to pre-production and principal photography. Such decisions used to be the domain of a studio executive or chairman, but given the convergence and diversification of media industries, these decisions are increasingly made by committees consisting of representatives of different parts of the company. Especially for larger, big budget productions, the film or television programme is only one variable to consider next to (online) marketing, merchandising and licensing, and even toys and theme parks all play roles.

## THE ORGANIZATION OF MEDIA PRODUCTION: DIGITAL GAMES

Development studios and publishing companies are the two interacting institutional entities that make up the basic organizational structure of the game industry. In game development, the main jobs include design, production, art, programming, audio, and quality assurance, all of which are co-ordinated by a team lead (sometimes called producer or director). Designers (leads, associates, assistants) establish the basic game concept, characters and play mechanics. Before any work gets done, these gameworkers first write up a detailed design document – a blueprint outlining all aspects of the game – similar to a screenplay in film. Contrary to a film or television show, the design document of a game tends to be more of a dynamic document subject to continuous modification. Although game writers – those responsible for story structure, dialogue, plot and character development – are part of the design team, their work is often done by freelancers. Art directors, artists, modellers and animators develop characters, virtual worlds, animation and special effects. Sound engineers and designers are important in game development too, considering the introduction of surround-sound capabilities, as well as the crossmedia franchising of popular music. Indeed, a fair number of popular games today come with a separate soundtrack. That said, sound design is one of the specialisms that is often outsourced. Programmers develop game engines – the overall software that a game runs on – or modify existing ones to fit the design document of the project at hand, and design the important artificial intelligence for the game (that is, which AI has specific consequences for the level of difficulty and playability of the game). Finally, testers play the game to evaluate it for problems and playability.

At the end of a project, professionals in the industry have come to expect something called 'crunch time', as six- to seven-day workweeks and ten- to sixteen-hour workdays are to some extent considered normal in the industry (Prescott and Bogg, 2011). The caveat for this summary of the organization of gamework is that every game development project can be organized quite differently, with more specific similarities in the games produced by large corporations, and more diversity to be found among smaller and independent developers. Kerr (2006) notes how there are specific differences between companies in Japan and Europe, noting that, for example, British companies tend to concentrate all the necessary skills and specialties within the existing team (which means that people sometimes have nothing much to do), whereas Japanese firms are more likely to temporarily assign specialist groups of professionals to complete a particular task, after which these workers move on to another project.

Johns (2006) documents how since the early beginnings in the 1960s and 1970s the game industry has seen two major trends emerging in the organization and orientation of work. First, the digital games industry is and always has been highly dependent upon technological innovation, both from within and outside the industry. The second trend shows an industry that increasingly operates on a global scale, producing games in teams sometimes numbering in the hundreds of people who are dispersed across several studios around the world, each responsible for different elements of a game. These studios tend to be located in the US (California, Texas, Washington State), Canada (Vancouver, Montreal), Europe (notably France, the UK and Ireland), and Asia (primarily Japan and South Korea). Johns (2006: 177) considers this consolidation in 'supra-regions' of software production networks problematic in that '[a]s in many other cultural industries, the global domination of media conglomerates limits the ability of smaller firms to gain access to finance and distribution'. In recent years the industry has been moving further away from physical game production (for consoles and desktop computers), focusing more of its efforts on mobile and online games. New industries that have emerged in or next to games are those involved with eSports and mediated game streaming (Taylor, 2015).

What this review of the different ways in which media production is organized suggests is that the various media professions face similar challenges when it comes to the organization of production. Production tends to take place on a global scale, even though the dominant companies tend to be located in key urban centres in Europe, North America and Southeast Asia. Employment is often flexibly organized and contingent, even for those with permanent contracts, given the volatile and dynamic nature of these industries. The production process tends to be especially precarious in the ideation and pre-production phase, as financing and payment takes place after the moment of conception via systems such as copyright enforcement, project-based reimbursement and freelance compensation. Most major institutions earn revenue increasingly not from the production of material goods – such as music, films, television shows, newspapers, or games for consoles and personal computers – but from services, distribution deals, merchandising, and so on. This complicates the overall production process, as more departments, stakeholders and interests participate in decision-making processes. Production processes tend to be fairly strictly organized along hierarchical (and sometimes heterarchical) lines in order to accommodate increasingly complex productions involving different media and different skillsets and working against tight deadlines.

## MODELS OF DECISION-MAKING

In a review of the mechanisms according to which culture is produced in the commercial-industrial world of mass media, Ryan and Peterson (1982) describe five main frameworks for explaining how decisions are made. Their first model is that of the assembly line, which compares the media production process to the factory, with all skills and decisions built into the machinery and with clear procedural rules. Because media-cultural products, unlike material goods, have to be marginally different from each other, the result is overproduction at each stage.

The second model is that of craft and entrepreneurship, in which powerful figures, with established reputations for judging talent, raising finance and putting things together, manage all the creative inputs of artists, musicians, engineers, and the like, in innovative ways. This model applies especially to the film business, but can also hold for publications in which editors may play the role of personally charismatic and powerful figures with a supposed flair for picking winners. Increasingly, these individuals operate in teams or committees, given the complexity and what is at stake in contemporary media work.

The third model is that of convention and formula, in which members of a relevant 'art world' agree on a 'recipe', a set of widely held principles that tell workers how to combine elements to produce works in the particular genre. Fourthly, there is the model of audience image and conflict, which sees the creative production process as a matter of fitting production to an image of what the audience will like. Here decisions about the latter are central, and powerful competing entrepreneurs come into conflict over them.

The final model is that of the product image. Its essence is summarized in Box 11.3.

## 11.3
### The product image

Having a product image is to shape a piece of work so that it is most likely to be accepted by decision makers at the next link in the chain. The most common way of doing this is to produce works that are much like the products that have most recently passed through all the links in the decision chain to become successful.
(Ryan and Peterson, 1982: 25)

This model does not assume there to be a consensus among all involved. It is a model which seems closest to the notion of 'professionalism' or 'editorial' logic (see Chapter 10), defined as the special knowledge of what is a good piece of media production, in contrast to 'market' logic involving a prediction of what will succeed commercially.

Most studies of media production seem to confirm the strong feeling held by established professionals that they know how best to combine all the available factors of production within the inevitable constraints. This may be achieved at the cost of not actually communicating with or listening to the audience, but it does secure the integrity of the product on their terms.

## 11.4
### Five models of media decision-making

- The assembly line
- Craft and entrepreneurship
- Convention and formula
- Audience image and conflict
- Product image

Ryan and Peterson's typology is especially useful in stressing the diversity of frameworks within which a degree of regularity and predictability can be achieved in the production of cultural goods (including news). There are different ways of handling uncertainty, responding to outside pressures, and reconciling the need for continuous

MCQUAIL'S MEDIA AND MASS COMMUNICATION THEORY
ORGANIZATIONS

production with artistic originality, professional autonomy or creative freedom. The concepts of factory-like manufacturing or routine bureaucracy, often invoked to apply to media production, should be used with caution.

# MEDIA PARTICIPATION AND CONVERGENCE CULTURE

Although we will consider the roles audiences play in the media in Chapters 14 and 15, it is important to recognize the role audience participation plays in media production. Throughout history, audiences have played an important role – in doing the 'work' of consumption and thereby enabling media companies to sell their attention to advertisers. Some genres emerged that invited (or required) audiences to engage with the media, for example by opening 'Letters to the Editor' sections in newspapers or in the 'talk radio' and other call-in formats in broadcasting. However, consumers were not really expected to participate in the creative process. The interactive nature of the Internet contributed greatly to change this.

In an early assessment of the potential for two-way spontaneous interaction between journalists and citizens, Bucy and Gregson (2001) consider the type of participation that is possible online – active and direct versus passive/indirect modes of participation offered through 'old' media such as television, radio, newspapers and magazines. Both authors still considered audience participation in all types of media a largely symbolic type of empowerment. Reviewing the early history of online media and audience participation, Domingo and colleagues (2008) place newly interactive media and communication principles in the context of a global shift of small-scale, local communities to complex societies requiring expert systems – such as journalism – where professional observers and communicators access, select and filter, produce and edit news, to be distributed via mass media to mass audiences. As a 'network society' emerges (see Chapter 4), relationships between sender and receivers of news gradually become more reciprocal under influences of globalization, newly interactive technologies, and changing cultural and economic conditions of newswork. Dividing the news production process into five phases – access and observation, selection and filtering, processing and editing, distribution, consumption and interpretation – and testing the extent of audience participation in each phase at online news sites in nine countries, the researchers find such options generally limited to enabling users to act upon journalistic content, such as by ranking or commenting on it. Subsequent work reiterates this tension between professional control and audience participation in media work (Lewis, 2012).

Much of the work on participation of audiences in media production takes the perspective of the professional mass communicator 'sharing' the stage with the public. Loosen and Schmidt (2012) offer a corrective, considering audience inclusion in media work as 'a reciprocal co-orientation and interaction' with two general dimensions:

inclusion performance and inclusion expectations (see Figure 11.3). Inclusion performance covers features indicators and aspects of practices that involve some kind of participatory relationship in the media production process. Inclusion expectations are the sum of cognitive patterns guiding the practices of media professionals, and the audience, respectively (ibid.: 875).

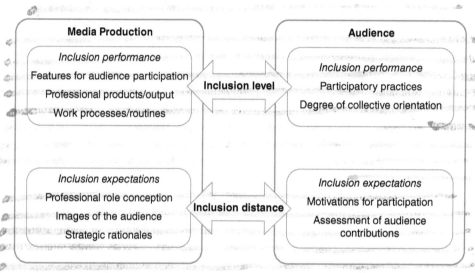

Figure 11.3 Heuristic model of audience inclusion in media production (Loosen and Schmidt, 2012: 874)

Two important caveats have to be made about audience participation in media production from the perspective of the industry. First, one has to take into account a general 'obduracy' among media professionals in general, and journalists in particular, as numerous studies document a resistance to change produced by 'routines, practices, and values, developed over time' (Borger, van Hoof, Costera Meijer and Sanders, 2013: 50). Regarding the audience role in the creative process, such resistance is amplified by references to professional autonomy and quality control. A second caveat is what Quandt (2019) evocatively labels 'dark participation', characterized by negative, selfish or sinister contributions such as cyberbullying, 'trolling' (deliberately making unsolicited and often controversial comments online with the intent to provoke an emotional response), 'doxxing' (discovering and revealing the real identity of a specific Internet user with the purpose of targeting them for malicious attacks), strategic 'piggy-backing' on the reputation of media professionals in order to spread disinformation, hate campaigns, or propaganda as widely as possible. To Quandt these acts are not reason to abandon the once hopeful analyses of audience participation in the media, but add a necessary caution to overly optimistic readings of collaboration and co-creation.

MCQUAIL'S MEDIA AND MASS COMMUNICATION THEORY
ORGANIZATIONS

The most influential and widely recognized of such hopeful accounts of media partici-pation has been coined by Jenkins as '**convergence culture**' (2004). The concept refers to a range of related phenomena that follow on from and seem to be caused by technological convergence, industry convergence and role convergence (Jenkins and Deuze, 2008). Primarily, they comprise the following: the participation of audiences in production, the blurring of the line between professional and amateur, and the breakdown of the line between producer and consumer – all within the context of converging and integrat-ing media industries. The convergence of producers and consumers has led to new terms such as 'prosumer' and 'produser' (Bruns, 2008). In his subsequent work on the concept, Jenkins (2006; Jenkins and Deuze, 2008; Jenkins et al., 2013, 2016) expands notions of convergence culture to argue for media to be 'spreadable' in order to accommodate active media users, and to acknowledge the role co-creating media plays for young people in particular to tell and share stories about issues that matter to them. This work is taken up among those involved with media literacy, embracing the notion that making media is argu-ably one of the best ways for children and youths to learn crucial skills when using media, and to develop a critical attitude towards media (Livingstone and Sefton-Green, 2016).

## CONCLUSION

The ground covered by this chapter has dealt mainly with the structure and elements of the production process within formal media organizations, as ideas and images are trans-formed into 'product' for distribution. The influences on this process are numerous and often conflicting. Despite certain recurring features and constants, media production still has a potential to be unpredictable and innovative, as it should be in a free society. The constraining economic, cultural and technological factors can also be facilitative, where there is enough money to buy freedom and cultural inventiveness and where technological innovation works to overcome obstacles.

We need to recall the dominant influence of the 'publicity' model compared with the 'transmission' or 'ritual' models of communication (as described in Chapter 3). The trans-mission model captures one image of the media organization – as a system for efficiently turning events into comprehensible information, or ideas into familiar cultural packages. The ritual model implies a private world in which routines are followed largely for the benefit of the participants and their clients. Both capture some element of the reality. The publicity model helps to remind us that mass communication is often primarily a business, and showbusiness at that. At the core of many media organizations, there are contrary ten-dencies that are often in tension, if not in open warfare, with each other, making illusory the search for any comprehensive theory of their work.

Fundamentally, the work that media professionals do matters, as do their intentions and decisions, as these 'have a great effect on cultural, economic and political processes'

(Hesmondhalgh, 2018: 466). If we are studying any element of the media and mass communication process – production, content or audience – we need a basic understanding of (and respect for) the other elements.

# FURTHER READING

Baym, N. (2018) *Playing to the Crowd: Musicians, Audiences, and the Intimate Work of Connection*. New York: New York University Press.

Fast, K., Örnebring, H. and Karlsson, M. (2016) 'Metaphors of free labor: a typology of unpaid work in the media sector', *Media, Culture & Society*, 38(7): 963–978.

Hesmondhalgh, D. (2018) *The Cultural Industries*, 4th edition. London: Sage.

Jenkins, H. (2006) *Convergence Culture: Where Old and New Media Collide*. New York: New York University Press.

Paterson, C., Lee, D., Saha, A. and Zoellner, A. (eds) (2016) *Advancing Media Production Research: Shifting Sites, Methods, and Politics*. London: Palgrave Macmillan.

Tuchman, G. (1978) *Making News: A Study in the Construction of Reality*. New York: Free Press.

# PART 5
## CONTENT

# 12

# MEDIA CONTENT: ISSUES, CONCEPTS, AND METHODS OF ANALYSIS

The most accessible evidence of how mass communication works is provided by its content. In a very literal sense, we can equate the media with the message, although it would be extremely misleading to do so. In this respect, the distinction between message and meaning is a significant one. The physical text of the message in print, sound or pictorial (still or moving) image is what we can directly observe and is in a sense 'fixed' – especially in a digital context where these 'texts' are not just occurring side-by-side, but also more or less constantly being acted upon – updated, edited and redacted, cut and pasted, remixed and shared. We cannot simply 'read off' the meanings that are somehow 'embedded' in the texts or transmitted to audiences. These meanings are not self-evident and certainly not fixed. They are also multiple and often ambiguous.

Theory and research concerning mass media content are fissured by this distinction between message and meaning, which largely parallels the choice between a 'transmission' and a 'ritual' (or cultural) view of communication (see p. 94). This remark exposes the difficulty in speaking about content at all with any certainty. Even so, we often encounter generalizations about the content of mass media as a whole, or a particular type of content, especially with reference to matters of media intention, 'bias' or expected effect. Our ability to generalize about these matters has been helped by the patterned and standardized forms that media content often takes.

The main purpose of this chapter is to review the various approaches to media content and the methods available. However, the choice of both approach and method depends on the purpose that we have in mind, of which there is some diversity. We mainly deal with three aspects of content analysis: content as information; content as meaning; and content as object of study within larger, multimethod approaches (involving communicators and/or audiences). The study of media content and the analysis of mediated messages has a long history, both in media and mass communication research and in many other scholarly disciplines – a history that tends to suffer somewhat from 'under-theorization' (Riffe, Lacy, Fico and Watson, 2019: 12), leading to many descriptive studies without much concern for the broader context within which media content functions. Consequently, we begin with the question of purpose.

# WHY STUDY MEDIA CONTENT?

The first reasons for studying media content in a systematic way stemmed either from an interest in the potential effects of mass communication, whether intended or unintended, or from a wish to understand the appeal of content for the audience. Both perspectives have a practical basis, from the point of view of mass communicators, but they have gradually been widened and supplemented to embrace a larger range of theoretical issues. Early studies of content reflected a concern about social problems with which the media were linked. Attention focused in particular on the portrayal of crime, violence and sex in popular entertainment, the use of media as propaganda and the performance of media in respect of racial or other kinds of prejudice. The range of purposes was gradually extended to cover news, information and much entertainment content.

Most early research was based on the assumption that content reflected the purposes and values of its originators, more or less directly; that 'meaning' could be discovered or inferred from messages; and that receivers would understand messages more or less as intended by producers. It was even thought that 'effects' could be discovered by inference from the seeming 'message' built into content. More plausibly, the content of mass media has often been regarded as more or less reliable evidence about the culture and society in which it is produced. All of these assumptions have been called into question, and the study of content has become correspondingly more complex and challenging. It may not be going too far to say that the most interesting aspects of media content are often not the overt messages, but the many more or less concealed and uncertain meanings that are present in media texts.

Despite these various complications, it is useful at this point to review the main motives that have guided the study of media content, as follows:

- *Describing and comparing media output.* For many purposes of analysis of mass communication (for instance, assessing change or making comparisons), we need to be able to characterize the content of particular media and channels.

- *Comparing media with 'social reality'.* A recurrent issue in media research has been the relation between media messages and 'reality'. The most basic question is whether media content does, or should, reflect the social reality, and if so, which or whose reality.

- *Media content as a reflection of social and cultural values and beliefs.* Historians, anthropologists and sociologists are interested in media content as evidence of values and beliefs of a particular time and place or social group.

- *Hypothesizing functions and effects of media.* We can interpret content in terms of its potential consequences, whether good or bad, intended or unintended. Although content on its own cannot be taken as evidence of effect, it is difficult to study effects without intelligent reference to content (as cause).

- *Considering content as a consequence of the process of production.* Content features can be seen as an outcome of conditions and influences under which mass-mediated messages came to be, including individual, social, economic and other contextual factors.

- *Evaluating media performance.* Krippendorf (2004) uses the term 'performance analysis' to refer to research designed to find answers about the quality of the media as judged by certain criteria (see Chapter 7 and pp. 379–381).

- *The study of media bias.* Much media content has either a clear direction of evaluation in relation to matters of dispute or is open to the perception of favouring one side over another, even if unintentionally or unconsciously.

- *Audience analysis.* Since audiences are always defined at least in part by media content, we cannot study audiences without studying content. Combinations of content analysis with survey data – so-called 'linkage studies' (De Vreese et al., 2017) – are particularly useful instruments in this context.
- *Tackling questions of genre, format, narrative and other formats.* In this context, the text itself is the object of study, with a view to understanding how it 'works' to produce effects desired by authors and readers.
- *Rating and classification of content.* Regulation or media responsibility often requires that certain kinds of content are classified according to potential harm or offence, especially in matters of violence, sex, discrimination, language, etc. The development of rating systems requires prior analysis of content.

# CRITICAL PERSPECTIVES ON CONTENT

The main grounds of criticism of mass media have already been introduced in earlier chapters. Here we look specifically at situations where the produced and transmitted content is the main focus of attention. At issue are possible failings, omissions and bad intentions, especially in the way social life is represented, with particular reference to groupings based on social class, ethnicity, gender or similar differentiating factors. Another set of concerns relates to potential harm from content that is perceived as violent or otherwise offensive or dangerous. The cultural quality of media is also sometimes at issue, for example in debates about mass culture or the matter of cultural and national identity.

## MARXIST APPROACHES

One main critical tradition has been based on a Marxist theory of ideology, which relates mainly to class inequality but can also deal with some other issues. Grossberg (1984) has pointed to several variations of Marxist cultural interpretation that deal with the 'politics of textuality'. He identifies three 'classical' Marxist approaches, of which the most relevant derive from the Frankfurt School and ideas concerning 'false consciousness' (see Chapter 5). Two later approaches distinguished by Grossberg are 'hermeneutic' (interpretative) and 'discursive' in character, and again there are several variants. Compared with classical approaches, however, the main differences are, first, that 'decoding' is recognized as problematic and, secondly, that texts are seen as not just 'mediating' reality but as actually constructing experience and shaping identity.

The Marxist tradition has paid most attention to news and actuality because of its capacity to define the social world and the world of events. Drawing on various sources, including Barthes and Althusser, Stuart Hall (1977) argued that the practice of signification through language establishes maps of cultural meaning that promote the dominance of a ruling-class ideology, especially by establishing a hegemonic view of the world, within which accounts of reality are framed. News contributes to this task in several ways. One is by 'masking' aspects of reality – especially by ignoring the exploitative nature of class society or by taking it for granted as 'natural'. Secondly, news produces a 'fragmentation' of interests (for example, by structuring content according to news 'beats' and parsing its audience into separate target groups and taste cultures), which undermines people's sense of solidarity. Thirdly, news imposes an 'imaginary unity or coherence' (for instance, by invoking concepts of community, nation, public opinion and consensus as well as by various forms of symbolic exclusion). Fuchs (2017: 40–41) notes how the Marxist tradition of thinking in terms of class structures and struggle – for example, as reproduced in mass media content – can provide a critical counter-narrative to analyses of society as a more or less neutral 'information' or 'network' society.

## CRITIQUE OF ADVERTISING AND COMMERCIALISM

There is a long tradition of critical attention to advertising that sometimes adopts the Marxist approach as described, but also derives from other cultural or humanistic values. Williamson (1978), in her study of advertising, applies the familiar concept of 'ideology', which is defined by Althusser (1971: 153) as representing 'the imaginary relationship of individuals to their real conditions of existence'. Althusser also says that 'All ideology has the function (which defines it) of "constituting" individuals as subjects'. For Williamson, the ideological work of advertising is accomplished (with the active co-operation of the 'reader' of the advertisement) by transferring significant meanings and ideas from experience (such as beauty, success, happiness) to commercial products and via that route to ourselves.

The commercial product becomes a way to achieve the desired social or cultural state and to be the kind of person we would like to be. We are 'reconstituted' by advertising but end up with an imaginary (and thus false) sense of our real selves and of our relation to the real conditions of our life. This has the same ideological tendency as that attributed to news in critical theory – masking real exploitation and fragmenting solidarity. A very similar process is described by Williamson (1978) in terms of 'commodification', based on earlier work by Adam Smith in 1776, referring to the way advertising converts the 'use value' or utility value of products into an 'exchange value' or its price on the market, allowing us (in our aspiration) to acquire (buy) happiness or other ideal states.

The ideological work of advertising is essentially achieved by constituting our environment for us and telling us who we are and what we really want (see Mills, 1951). In the critical perspective, all this is illusory and diversionary. What the effect of advertising might actually be is beyond the scope of any analysis of content, but it is possible to work back from content to intention, and the critical terminology of 'manipulation' and 'exploitation' is perhaps easier to justify than is the case with ideology in news. In a broad assessment of the 'mirror or moulder' effect of advertising and marketing on society, Lantos (1987: 122) concludes that the content of the majority of campaigns and advertisements mostly offers 'an imperfect and often lagged looking glass' of societal values and concerns rather than causing any particular attitudes or behaviours.

## VIOLENCE IN THE MASS MEDIA

In terms of sheer volume of words written and salience in the public mind, the foremost critical perspective on mass media would probably belong under this heading. Despite the difficulty of establishing direct causal connections, critics continually focus on the content of popular media – from magazines to radio, from television to popular music, and from there on to digital games and social media. It has always been much easier to demonstrate that media portray violence and aggression in news and fiction to a degree quite disproportionate to real-life experience than to show any effects. Many studies have produced seemingly shocking statistics of average exposure to mediated violence. The argument of critics has been not just that it might cause violence and crime, especially by the young, but that it is often intrinsically undesirable, producing emotional disturbance, fear, anxiety and deviant tastes.

Accepting that thrills and action are a staple part of popular entertainment that cannot simply be banned (although some degree of censorship has been widely legitimated in this matter), content research has often been devoted to understanding the more or less harmful ways in which violence can be depicted. The scope of criticism was widened to include not only the questions of socialization of children, but also the issue of (verbal and non-verbal) violent aggression directed at women. This occurs frequently, not just in pornographic content.

## INTERSECTIONAL CRITIQUE

There are several other varieties of critical perspective on media content. Initially, these were mainly concerned with issues of representation, particularly related to gender. Specific foci included stereotyping, neglect and the marginalization of women (see, for example, Tuchman, Daniels and Benet, 1978). As Rakow (1986) points out, media content can never be a true account of reality, and it is less important to change media representations (such as having more female characters) than to challenge the underlying sexist ideology of much media content. Gradually, concerns about gender came to include intersectional issues related to the representation of anyone who does not necessarily conform to the dominant social norm (in western countries) of having a professional, largely white, heterosexual and middle-class background. Murdock (1999: 13) suggests that concerns about representation in media – of gender, race, class, disability, sexuality, and so on – are:

first, questions about social delegation, about who is entitled to speak for and about others, and what responsibilities they owe to the constituencies whose views and hopes they claim to articulate … they are also questions about cultural forms and genres, about ways in which the raw materials of language and imagery are combined [and] how well these contribute to the resources of information, experience, interpretation and explanation required for the exercise of full citizenship.

Most central to intersectional critical analysis is a broader question beyond (but not excluding) representation of how texts 'position' the subject in narratives and textual interactions and in so doing contribute to a definition and construction of social identity (such as femininity or masculinity) in collaboration with the consumer. For the original feminist critique, two issues arise. The first is the extent to which media texts intended for the entertainment of women (such as soap operas or romances) can ever be liberating when they embody the realities of patriarchal society and family institutions (Radway, 1984; Ang, 1985). The second is the degree to which new kinds of mass media texts that challenge stereotyping and try to introduce positive role models – such as female, Asian and black superheroes in comic book-based media franchises – can have any 'empowering' effect (while remaining within the dominant commercial media system). Ultimately, the answers to these questions depend on how the texts are received by their audiences.

A variety of literary, discourse and psychoanalytic methods have been used in the critical study of content, and traditionally there has been a strong emphasis on interpretation rather than quantification. Exceptions exist, of course (see for example Verhoeven et al., 2019).

## ON THE QUESTION OF MEDIA CRITICISM AND QUALITY

Elitist and moralistic critiques of the mass media are never out of fashion, but generally fail to provide a clear definition of mass culture or offer subjective criteria for evaluating cultural quality. Even so, the issue is still a matter for public debate and even policy. The Marxist critique of mass (including social) media has enjoyed something of a revival given the increasingly pervasive and ubiquitous nature of the digital media environment and the dominant role media, ICT and telecommunications corporations play in it.

There have been a number of attempts to assess the quality of media in general, and television as well as social media in particular, in recent years and in different countries, especially in response to the expansion and privatization of media. One example is the Quality Assessment of Broadcasting project of the Japanese public broadcaster NHK (Ishikawa, 1996). Notable in this project is the attempt to evaluate quality of output from different perspectives, namely that of 'society', of the professional broadcasters and of the audience. Of most interest is the assessment made by programme makers themselves. We find a number of criteria being applied. These relate especially to degree and type of craft skill, resources and production values, originality, relevance and cultural authenticity, values expressed, integrity of purpose and audience appeal. There are other criteria and other ways of assessing quality because the range of content is so wide. Regarding social media, debates are continuing in the literature between those that warn against 'filter bubbles', 'echo chambers' and the rapid rise of disinformation (sometimes labelled with the misnomer 'fake news'), and media and mass communication scholars who document a general lack of empirical evidence to sustain such concerns, or point out that the benefits of an open Internet outweigh potential problems (Valkenburg and Piotrowksi, 2017; Bruns, 2019).

It has been suggested (Schrøder, 1992) that there are essentially three kinds of cultural standards to be applied to assessing the quality of media: the aesthetic (there are many dimensions), the ethical (questions of values, integrity, intended meaning, etc.) and the 'ecstatic' (measured by popularity, pleasure and performative value, essentially aspects of consumption). Costera Meijer (2001; Costera Meijer and Groot Kormelink, 2014) adds a notion of public quality, with criteria determined by the extent to which media products and services contribute to common experience and empowerment of the citizen. Furthermore, Hesmondhalgh and Baker (2011) raise the issue of quality from the perspective of production, in that media work should ideally lead to (and thus can partially be measured by) products and services that strive for excellence and contribute to the common good.

Developments in social and cultural theory have significantly extended the scope for estimating the quality of media output according to stated criteria. Even so, such assessments are bound to remain subjective, based on approximate criteria and varied perception. Intrinsic quality cannot be measured.

## MEDIA PERFORMANCE DISCOURSE

There is an extensive body of research into mass media content according to a number of normative criteria. Society expects a certain kind of quality or 'performance' from its media. Similarly, media professionals have, and to some extent share, a hopeful, sometimes even romantic set of ideals regarding the ways in which media should perform. The central difficulty is that 'the media' in a free society do not, for the most part, have any obligation to carry out many of the positively valued purposes that have been referred to and that are taken for granted. They are not run by the government, nor do they work on behalf of society. Their formal responsibilities are largely the same as those of other citizens and organizations within a society and thus are mainly defined in negative terms. They are required to do no harm. Beyond that, the media are free to choose, or avoid, various positive ends. They tend collectively to resent any attempt to prescribe their role in society, whether on the part of governments, special interests, individuals or even media theorists. Despite this, there is much in the history, constitution and conduct of the media institution which recognizes certain unwritten obligations that for various reasons are often respected in practice. There are also several sources of external pressure that cannot be ignored. Normative theory of media covers both internally chosen purposes and the claims from outside about how they should conduct themselves.

Among the sources of normative expectation, the most fundamental are probably those that stem from the historical context that has shaped the role of the media institution. In most democracies this has meant a close link between democratic political institutions and the role of the media as carrier of news and opinion, as well as the media as a 'carrier' of public values that can be quite specific to local contexts. Such links are not usually constitutionally established (although Germany is an exception) and often cannot be enforced, but neither is it really optional. In numerous countries around the world, the role of media in fact has become less free in recent years, within both dictatorial regimes and established democracies, in the context of growing concerns regarding the relatively unbridled dissemination of information and ideas online. Extensive reference to the expectations and obligations of the media – and specifically journalism – can be found in social and political theory. Related to this is the much broader orientation of journalism to the public life of the national society and international community. Other media industries, such as advertising, games and television, also face scrutiny, for example regarding the stereotypical depiction of women. All of this is also deeply embedded in custom and convention as well as in the expression of professional claims and aspirations.

Secondly, there are claims laid on the media as a whole by the general public and expressed either as public opinion or, more inescapably, by the public as an audience of a particular media publication. In this case, the view of the public about what the media ought to be doing, if it is clearly expressed, has a more binding character. This reflects the fact that media are tied into a nexus of market relations with their customers and clients, the latter (for example, as advertisers or sponsors) also having some influence on media conduct. There remain two other sources of influence, with variable power. One of these is the state and agents of government. Circumstances determine how independent media can be of the views of government, which always has some capacity to reward or punish. It is unusual to find large and well-established media that do not see some self-interest in respecting the legitimate wishes and interests of the state (for instance, in matters of public order or national emergency), even if the right to criticize is preserved.

The other source of influence is more diffuse but often effective. It stems from the many interests, especially economic but also cultural and social, that are affected by the mass media, particularly in respect of news and information. Powerful individuals and organizations can be hurt by the news and may also need it to further their ends. For this reason, they keep a close eye on media conduct for their own protection or seek to influence it. All in all, this adds up to an environment of expectation and scrutiny that has considerable cumulative influence on the production and assessment of media content. Box 12.1 provides a summary of the main sources of normative expectation on media conduct and performance.

MCQUAIL'S MEDIA AND MASS COMMUNICATION THEORY
CONTENT

Research on media content – its quality and performance – is usually based on some conception of the public interest (or good of society) that provides the point of reference and the relevant content criteria (McQuail, 1992). Although a given set of values provides the starting point for analysis of media, the procedures adopted are those of a neutral scientific observer, and the aim is to find independent evidence that will be relevant to public debate about the role of media in society (Stone, 1987; Lemert, 1989). The basic assumption of this tradition of work is that although quality cannot be intrinsically or directly measured, many relevant dimensions can be reliably assessed (Bogart, 2004). The NHK Quality Assessment project mentioned earlier (Ishikawa, 1996) is a good example of such work. The evidence sought should relate to particular media but needs also to have a general character.

It could be said that this particular discourse is about the politics of media content. It adjoins and occasionally overlaps with the critical tradition, but differs in that it stays within the boundaries of the system itself, accepting the goals of the media in society more or less on their own terms (or at least the more idealistic goals). What follows are some examples of the testable expectations about the quality of media provision which are implied in various performance principles: freedom and independence, content diversity, and objectivity.

## FREEDOM AND INDEPENDENCE

Perhaps the foremost expectation about media content (in societies operating under the various forms of liberal democracy) is that it should reflect or embody the spirit of free expression, despite the many institutional and organizational pressures. It is not easy to see how the quality of freedom (and here the reference is primarily to news, information and opinion functions of media) can be recognized in content. Several general aspects of content can, even so, be identified as indicating more or less freedom (from commercial, political or social pressure). For example, there is the general question of editorial 'vigour' or activity, which should be a sign of using freedom and shows itself in a number of ways. These include expressing opinions, especially on controversial issues; willingness to report conflict and controversy; following a 'proactive' policy in relation to sources (thus not relying on press handouts and public relations, or being too cosy with the powerful); and giving background and interpretation as well as facts.

The concept of 'editorial vigour' was coined by Thrift (1977) to refer to several related aspects of content, especially dealing with relevant and significant local matters, adopting an argumentative form and providing 'mobilizing information', which refers to information that helps people to act on their opinions (Lemert, 1989). Some critics and commentators also look for a measure of advocacy and of support for 'underdogs' as evidence of free media (Entman, 1989). Investigative reporting may also be regarded as a sign of news media using their freedom (see Ettema and Glasser, 1998).

In one way or another, most mass media content can be assessed in terms of the 'degree of freedom' exhibited. Outside the sphere of news, one would look for innovation and unexpectedness, non-conformity and experimentation in cultural matters. The freest media are also likely to deviate from conformity in matters of taste and be willing to be unpopular with audiences as well as with authorities. However, if so, they are not likely to remain mass media.

## CONTENT DIVERSITY

After freedom, probably the most frequently encountered term in the 'performance discourse' is diversity. It refers essentially to three main features of content:

- a wide range of choice for audiences, on all conceivable dimensions of interest and preference;
- many and different opportunities for access by voices and sources in society;
- a true or sufficient reflection in media of the varied reality of experience in society.

Each of these concepts is open to measurement (McQuail, 1992; Hellman, 2001; McDonald and Dimmick, 2003). In this context, we can really only speak of content diversity if we apply some external standard to media texts, whether of audience preference, social reality or (would-be) sources in society. Lack of diversity can be established only by identifying sources, references, events, types of content, and so on, that are missing or under-represented. In themselves, media texts cannot be said to be diverse in any absolute sense.

A more recent attempt by Katherine Champion (2015) to measure content diversity in the context of media companies increasingly pursuing a multi-platform strategy to recycle and reuse content showed how 'content bundles' consisting of stories produced for print and broadcast platforms tend to be partially repurposed online (on websites and mobile apps), supporting the claim that the emergence of multiple platforms for content distribution increases the volume of content being produced by media organizations (Doyle, 2010). However, the evidence concerning diversity was 'patchier', as Champion (2015: 50) notes, as organizations do not just copy and paste content across platforms, sometimes using long-term strategies to do so (requiring lengthy periods of content analysis), or specifically focus on social media – a platform not included in the original study design. Her findings 'confirms the need for a shift … towards a broader perspective of media diversity and plurality (beyond a sole focus on media ownership and concentration)' (ibid.: 51).

Essentially, diversity is another word for differentiation and is, in itself, rather empty of meaning, since everything we can distinguish is different, in some minimal sense of not being the very same thing, from everything else. The diversity value as applied to media content depends on some criteria of significant difference. These criteria are sometimes provided by the media themselves in the form of different formats, genres and types of culture. So, the same or different media channels can offer a changing supply of music, news, information, entertainment, comedy, drama, quiz shows, etc. External critics applying standards of social significance are usually more interested in differences of level and quality as well as format and genre. There are further criteria relating to the society in respect of representation of the whole range of social groupings, or providing for key minorities. The choice of criteria has to be made and justified by and according to the purpose at hand, and the possibilities are virtually unlimited. However, the purpose is usually decided by reference to one or another of the three points made above: the matter of audience choice and preference; the access given to social groups and voices; and the fair representation of social reality. Many questions about the effects of the media depend on being able to clearly articulate the concepts and means for measuring content diversity.

## OBJECTIVITY

The standard of news objectivity has given rise to much discussion of journalistic media content, under various headings, especially in relation to some form of bias, which is the reverse of objectivity. The ruling norms of most western media call for a certain practice of neutral, informative reporting of events, and it is against this positive expectation that much news has been found deficient. Journalists from all over the world tend to value some form of objectivity – as a neutral observer, a dispassionate witness, a mere recorder of events that are unfolding – even though how this ideal-typical value gets meaning in the prevailing news culture and everyday practice can be widely different from one news organization to the next. Objectivity is a relatively complex notion when one goes beyond the simple idea that news should reliably (and therefore honestly) report what is really going on in the world.

The simplest version of the idea that news tells us about the real world can be referred to as factuality. This refers to texts made up of distinct units of information that are necessary for understanding or acting upon a news 'event'. In journalistic terms it means at least providing dependable (correct) answers to the questions 'Who?', 'What?', 'Where?', 'When?', and maybe 'Why?', and going on from there. News can be more or less 'information rich' in terms of the number of (verified) facts offered.

In order to analyse the quality of news and the performance of a news organization, one needs more refined criteria. In particular, one asks whether the facts given are accurate and whether they are sufficient to constitute an adequate account, on the criterion of completeness. Accuracy itself can mean several things, since it cannot be directly 'read' or 'measured' from inspection of texts alone. One meaning of accuracy is conformity to independent records of events, whether in documents, other media or eyewitness accounts. Another meaning is more subjective: accuracy is conformity of reports to the perception of the source of the news or the subject of the news (object of reporting). Accuracy may also be a matter of internal consistency within news texts.

Completeness is equally difficult to pin down or measure since complete accounts of even simple events are not possible or necessary. Although one can always make assessments and comparisons of news in terms of more or less information, the question really turns on how much information is needed or can reasonably be expected, which is a subjective matter. We are quickly into another dimension of factuality – that of the relevance of the facts offered. Again, it is a simple notion that news information is relevant only if it is interesting and useful (and vice versa), but there are competing notions and criteria of what counts as relevant. One source of criteria is what theory says news ought to be like; another is what professional journalists decide is most relevant; and a third is what an audience actually finds interesting and useful. These three perspectives are unlikely to coincide on the same criteria or on the same assessment of content.

Theory tends to equate relevance with what is really significant in the longer perspective of history and what contributes to the working of society (for instance, informed democracy). From this point of view, a good deal of news, such as that about personalities, 'human interest', sport or entertainment, is not regarded as relevant. Journalists tend to apply professional criteria and a feel for news values that balance the longer-term significance with what they think their public is interested in.

The issue of what counts as impartiality in news seems relatively simple but can also be complex in practice, not least because there is little chance of achieving a value-free assessment of value freedom. Impartiality is appreciated mainly because many events

MCQUAIL'S MEDIA AND MASS COMMUNICATION THEORY
CONTENT

involve conflict and are open to alternative interpretations and evaluations (this is most obviously true of political news, but much the same can be said of sports). Most generally, the normal standard of impartiality calls for balance in the choice and use of sources, so as to reflect different points of view, and also the presentation of two (or more) sides where judgements or facts are contested.

Another aspect of impartiality is neutrality in the presentation of news: separating facts from opinion, avoiding value judgements or emotive language or pictures. The term 'sensationalism' has been used to refer to forms of presentation that depart from the objectivity ideal, and measures of news text sensationalism have been developed (for example, Tannenbaum and Lynch, 1960). Methods have also been tested for application to visual content in news (Grabe, Zhou, Lang and Boll, 2000; Grabe, Zhao and Barnett, 2001).

There is also evidence to show that the choice of words can reflect and imply value judgements in reporting on sensitive matters, for instance relating to patriotism (Glasgow Media Group, 1985) or race (Hartman and Husband, 1974; van Dijk, 1991). There are also indications that particular uses of visuals and camera shots can lead the viewer in certain evaluative directions (Tuchman, 1978; Kepplinger, 1983). Impartiality often comes down in the end simply to the absence of intentional or avoidable 'bias' and 'sensationalism'. Unfortunately, it is never that simple since bias is as much, if not more, a matter of perception as of measurable dimensions of content (D'Alessio and Allen, 2000; D'Alessio, 2003).

## REALITY REFLECTION OR DISTORTION: THE QUESTION OF BIAS

Bias or lack of balance in news content can refer, especially, to distorting reality, giving a negative picture of minority groups of many kinds, neglecting or misconstruing the role of women in society, or differentially favouring a particular political party or philosophy. There are many such kinds of news bias which stop short of lies, propaganda or ideology, but often overlap with and reinforce similar tendencies in fictional content. In general, this category can be classified as 'unwitting bias', arising from the context of production. A review of news bias studies indeed suggests that, while imbalance in news coverage sometimes occurs, this tends to be explained most forcefully by the way media routinely operate, rather than any particular political or otherwise biased belief system seeping through into media content (Hopmann, van Aelst and Legnante, 2012).

While the territory of media bias is now almost boundless and still extending, including bias produced by perceptions and pre-existing attitudes among audiences regardless of actual media content, we can summarize the most significant and best-documented generalizations in the following statements about news content, derived from numerous sources and examples:

- Media news over-represents the social 'top' and official voices in its sources.
- News attention is differentially bestowed on members of political and social elites.
- The social values which are most emphasized are consensual and supportive of the status quo.
- Foreign news concentrates on nearer, richer and more powerful nations.
- News has a nationalistic (patriotic) and ethnocentric bias in the choice of topics and opinions expressed and in the view of the world assumed or portrayed.
- More attention and more prominence are given to men than to women in the news.
- Ethnic minorities, migrants and refugees are differentially marginalized, stereotyped or stigmatized.
- News about crime over-represents violent and personal crime and neglects many of the realities of risk in society (such as 'white-collar' crimes: identity theft, embezzlement and tax evasion).
- Health news gives most attention to the most feared medical conditions and to new cures rather than prevention.
- Business leaders and employers receive more favoured treatment than unions and workers.
- The poor and those on welfare are neglected and/or stigmatized.
- War news typically avoids images of death or personal injury, sanitizing the reality.
- Well-resourced and well-organized news sources have more chance of defining news on their own terms.

Content analysis of fiction and drama has shown up similar systematic tendencies to allocate attention and esteem to the same groups who benefit from prominence in the news. Correlatively, the same minorities and outgroups tend to be stereotyped and stigmatized. Similar tendencies to give an unrealistic representation of crime, health and other risks and rewards are to be found. The evidence has normally been derived by applying methods of quantitative analysis to the overt content of texts, on the assumption that relative frequency of references will be taken as reflecting the 'real world'.

## A CRITIQUE OF THE REALITY REFLECTION NORM

It is striking how much the evaluation of media content comes down to the question of relation to reality, as if media ought to reflect more or less proportionately some empirical reality and ought always to be 'fair' as between the advantaged and the disadvantaged. This is referred to by Kepplinger and Habermeier (1995) as the 'correspondence assumption', which is often attributed to the audience. The assumption that media ought to reflect reality in some direct and proportional way has been the basis for much criticism of media performance, and has often been a key ingredient in research on media effects, but is itself open to question. According to Schulz (1988), it derives from an antiquated 'mechanistic' view of the relationship between media and society, more or less akin to the 'transportation model' of communication effects. It fails to recognize the essential specificity, arbitrariness and, sometimes, autonomy of media texts and neglects the active participation of the audience in the making of meaning. Perhaps most telling is the absence of evidence that the audience does actually assume any statistical correspondence between media content and reality. On the other hand, the expectation of reality reflection can also be about a hope (among groups and certain audiences) of not being stereotyped and marginalized in news coverage. Here, correspondence is not so much about facts, but about feelings, and an assumption of multi-perspectival news and a pluriform media system.

Apart from fundamental doubts about the expectation of proportional reality reflection, there are several reasons why media content should not normally be expected to 'reflect' reality in any literal (statistically representative) way. Functionalist theory of media as agents of social control, for instance, would lead us to expect that media content would over-represent the dominant social and economic values of the society. We would also expect social elites and authorities to have more visibility and access. Indeed, the media do reflect the social reality of inequality when they tip the scales of attention towards the powerful in society and towards powerful nations in the world. The complaint is really that in so doing they may reinforce it.

The analysis of media organizations has shown how unlikely it is that news will match some 'average' of reality. The need for authoritative news sources, the production on deadline (which in an online environment becomes a 24/7 'rolling' deadline) and the requirements of 'news values' are obvious sources of possible distortion. Drama, celebrity, novelty, crime and conflict are, by definition, abnormal. In addition, fictional media often deliberately seek to attract an audience by over-populating their stories with characters who lead more exciting lives and are richer, younger, more fashionable and more beautiful than the typical audience member (Martel and McCall, 1964). The study of 'key events' and 'framing' of news makes it both clear and understandable that 'reality' cannot be treated as if all happenings were of equal significance, even within the same category.

The simple fact that mass media are generally oriented to the interests of their audiences as 'consumers' of information and entertainment can easily account for most of the evidence of reality distortion summarized above. It is clear that audiences like many things that are inconsistent with reality reflection, especially fiction, fantasy, the unusual and bizarre, myths, nostalgia and amusement, even though such interests and preferences are not necessarily the same as an appreciation of quality. The media are often sought out precisely as a temporary alternative to and an escape from reality. When people look for models to follow or for objects of identification, they are as likely to seek an idealized as a realistic object or model. From this point of view, the reality 'distortions' observed in content are not in themselves surprising or necessarily regrettable. However, a significant determinant is also that of the efforts of interested agents to shape their own image and dominate the flow of communication.

In what follows we briefly review the main ways of thinking and doing media content analyses as a way of engaging questions regarding media quality and performance theoretically and empirically within the field of media and mass communication research.

## STRUCTURALISM, SEMIOTICS AND DISCOURSE ANALYSIS

One influential way of thinking about media content has origins in the general study of language. Basically, structuralism refers to the way meaning is constructed in texts, the term applying to certain 'structures of language', consisting of signs, narrative or myths. Generally, languages have been said to work because of inbuilt structures. The term 'structure' implies a constant and ordered relation of elements, although this may not be apparent on the surface and requires decoding. It has been assumed that such structures are located in and governed by particular cultures – much wider systems of meaning, reference and signification. Semiology and semiotics are more specific versions of the general structuralist approach. There are several classic explications of the structuralist approach to media content (for example, Barthes, 1967, 1977; Eco, 1977; see also Fiske, 1982).

Structuralism is a development of the linguistics and philosophy of de Saussure (1915/1960) and Peirce (1931–1935), and combines with it some principles from structural anthropology. It differs from linguistics in two main ways. First, it is concerned not only with conventional verbal languages, but also with any sign system that has language-like properties, including audiovisuals. Secondly, it directs attention less to the sign system itself than to chosen texts and the meaning of texts in the light of the 'host' culture. It is thus concerned with the elucidation of cultural as well as linguistic meaning, an activity for which a knowledge of the sign system is instrumental but insufficient on its own. Although semiology and semiotics have declined in popularity as a method, the underlying principles are still very relevant to other varieties of content analysis that looks not just for the occurrence of certain textual markers – specific words, particular sounds and images – but is also interested in finding out what this could mean.

## TOWARDS A SCIENCE OF SIGNS

North American (Peirce, 1931–35) and British (Ogden and Richards, 1923) scholars subsequently worked towards the goal of establishing a 'general science of signs' (semiology and semiotics). This field was to encompass structuralism and other things besides, and thus all things to do with signification (the giving of meaning by means of language), however loosely structured, diverse and fragmentary. The concepts of 'sign system' and 'signification' common to linguistics, structuralism, semiotics and semiology derive mainly from de Saussure. The same basic concepts were used in somewhat different ways by the three theorists mentioned, but the following are the essentials.

A sign is the basic physical vehicle of meaning in a language; it is any utterance that we can hear or see and that usually refers to some object or aspect of reality about which we wish to communicate, which is known as the referent. In human communication, we use signs to convey meanings about objects in the world of experience to others, who interpret the signs we use on the basis of sharing the same language or knowledge of the sign system we are using (for instance, **non-verbal communication**). According to de Saussure, the process of signification is accomplished by two elements of the sign. He called the physical element (word, image, sound) the signifier and used the term signified to refer to the mental concept invoked by a physical sign in a given language code (Figure 12.1). Semiology can be seen as a language-specific approach within semiotics, which is an overall science of signs and sign process. Interestingly, according to some semioticians, every cultural phenomenon can be studied as communication.

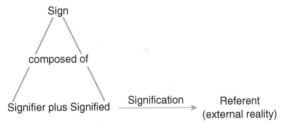

Figure 12.1 Elements of semiology. Signs in meaning systems have two elements: physical plus associated meanings in the culture and in use

Normally in (western) language systems, the connection between a physical signifier (such as a word) and a particular referent is arbitrary, but the relation between signifier and signified (meaning or concept conveyed) is governed by the rules of culture and has to be learned by the particular '**interpretative community**' and is generally dependent on context. In principle, anything that can make a sense impression can act as a sign, and this sense impression has no necessary correspondence with the sense impression made by the thing signified (for instance, the word 'tree' does not look at all like a representation of an actual tree). What matters is the sign system or 'referent system' that governs and interrelates the whole process of signification.

Generally, the separate signs gain their meaning from the systematic differences, contrasts and choices that are regulated in the linguistic or sign-system code and from the values (positive or negative valence) that are given by the rules of the culture and the sign system. Semiology has sought to explore the nature of sign systems that go beyond the rules of grammar and syntax and regulate complex, latent and culturally dependent meanings of texts that can only be understood by reference to the culture in which they are embedded and the precise context in which they appear.

## CONNOTATION AND DENOTATION

This has led to a concern with connotative as well as denotative meaning – the associations and images invoked and expressed by certain usages and combinations of signs. **Denotation** has been described as the 'first order of signification' (Barthes, 1967) because it describes the relationship within a sign between the signifier (physical aspect) and the signified (mental concept). The obvious straightforward meaning of a sign is its denotation. Williamson (1978) gives an example of an advertisement in which a photo of the film star Catherine Deneuve is used to advertise a French brand of perfume. The photo denotes Catherine Deneuve.

Connotation relates to a second order of signification, referring to the associated meaning that may be conjured up by the object signified. In the example of the advertisement, Catherine Deneuve is generally associated by members of the relevant language (and cultural) community with French 'chicness'. The relevance of this to advertisers is that the connotation of the chosen model (here a film star) is transferred by association to a perfume that she uses or recommends.

A seminal demonstration of this approach to text analysis was provided by Barthes (1977) in his analysis of a magazine advertisement for Panzani foods. This showed an image of a shopping bag containing groceries (the physical signifier), but these in turn were expected to invoke positive images of freshness and domesticity (the level of connotation). In addition, the red, white and green colours also signified 'Italianness' and could invoke a myth of culinary tradition and excellence. Thus, signification commonly works at two levels (or orders) of meaning: the surface level of literal meaning, and the second level of associated or connoted meaning. The activation of the second level requires some deeper knowledge of or familiarity with the culture on the part of the reader.

Barthes extended this basic idea by introducing the concept of a myth. Often the thing signified by a sign will have a place in a larger discrete system of meaning, which is also available to the member of a particular culture. Myths are pre-existing and value-laden sets of ideas derived from the culture and transmitted by communication. For instance, there are likely to be myths about national character or national greatness, or concerning science or nature (its purity and goodness), that can be invoked for communicative purposes (as they often are in advertising).

Denotative meaning has the characteristics of universality (the same fixed meaning for all) and objectivity (references are true and do not imply evaluation), while connotation involves both variable meaning according to the culture of the recipient and elements of evaluation (positive or negative direction). The main critique this approach has is its claim to universality, as some would argue that the meaning of both signifier and signified are not fixed. The relevance of all this for the study of media and mass communication lies primarily in the fact that structuralist approaches (and their post-structuralist criticisms) make us aware of both the structures embedded in any and all media content, and their particular meanings to specific (groups of) people in particular contexts. Media content consists of a large number of 'texts' (in the physical sense, from news stories to mobile games, from music videos to updates on someone's social media profile), often of a standardized and repetitive kind, that are composed on the basis of certain stylized conventions and codes. These often draw on familiar or latent myths and images present in the culture of the makers and receivers of texts (Barthes, 1972). The formulas and conventions underlying media production are therefore not just the result of the patterned ways in which mass communicators go about their work, but can also be seen as necessary in order for audiences to 'get' or understand the mediated message in the way intended.

## VISUAL LANGUAGE

For a long time, media and mass communication researchers largely ignored visual language. The visual image was considered to have no equivalent of the system of rules of a natural written language which enable us to interpret word signs more or less accurately. As Evans (1999: 12) argued, a still image, such as a photograph of a woman, is 'less the equivalent of "woman" than it is a series of disconnected descriptions: "an older woman, seen in the distance wearing a green coat, watching the traffic, as she crosses the road"'. She also suggested that pictures have no tense, and thus no clear location in time. For these and other reasons, Barthes once described the photograph as a 'picture without a code'. It presents us, wrote Evans, with an object as a *fait accompli*. This situation has changed, although most studies of media content still tend to privilege the written word, dialogue and scripts over systematic analyses of visual language.

Visual images are, like all forms of communication, inevitably ambiguous and polysemic, but they also have certain advantages over words. One is their greater denotative power when used deliberately and effectively. Another is their capacity to become **icons** – directly representing some concept with clarity, impact and wide recognition. An example of the power of visual language is provided by the case of the photographs of torture and abuse at Abu Ghraib prison that were published worldwide in May 2004. Anden-Papadopolous (2008) describes these as iconic images that had the power to shape both news and public perceptions, beyond the power of the authorities to counter or control. They have also been transformed into sites of protest and opposition to the deeds they represent. Visual images, still or moving, infographic or photographic (or videographic), can acquire a range of known meanings within the conventions and traditions of an art form (such as cinema or portrait painting) or a particular genre (such as television news).

This gives them considerable potential for skilful communication in certain contexts. Advertising is a primary example, as well as election campaigning.

In their work on the visual representation and framing of political candidates, journalists and elections, Bucy and Grabe (2007) outline a comprehensive argument for the rigorous study of visuals, building on the work of Doris Graber (2001). First, they argue that visual experience remains the most dominant mode of learning. Second, with reference to evolutionary history, they explain why it is so much easier for humans to process visuals rather than verbal or written communication. They show how visual language contains a great deal of important social information, and remind us that audiences are much more likely to remember images seen than the verbal narration (on television) or accompanying text (in print and online). Grabe and Bucy (2009) subsequently developed an instrument to do a content analysis of television news using the industry's genre conventions and production routines as a starting point, showing, for example, that the claim of 'liberal' bias against US media does not hold when it comes to television news, as Republicans receive consistently more favourable visual treatment than Democrats.

Given all that has happened by way of change in mass media, there is a pressing need to develop better concepts and methods for the analysis of many new formats and forms of expression, especially those that mix and innovate media forms, codes and formats. In a time where media are converging and new storytelling formats are emerging (for instance, multimedia, crossmedia and transmedia; see Chapter 13) with dominant visual components, comprehensive systematic analyses of such media content contribute significantly to the body of knowledge in our field (Grabe, Bas and van Driel, 2015; Grabe and Myrick, 2016).

Overall, the main tenets of structuralist and semiotic approaches are summarized in Box 12.2.

---

**12.2**

**Structuralism and semiotics: main tenets**

- Texts have meanings built in by way of language
- Meanings depend on a wider cultural and linguistic frame of reference
- Texts represent processes of signification
- Sign systems can be 'decoded' on the basis of knowledge of culture and sign systems
- Meanings of texts are connotative, denotative or mythical
- Visual language is processed more easily than verbal and written language
- Research including multiple media and forms of language is important in a digital, converged context

---

MCQUAIL'S MEDIA AND MASS COMMUNICATION THEORY
CONTENT

# DISCOURSE ANALYSIS

The general term 'discourse analysis' has gradually become preferred to the expression 'qualitative content analysis', although there is not much specific meaning to the term that differentiates it, and Hijmans (1996) considers discourse analysis a subset of qualitative content analysis – next to rhetorical, narrative, structuralist and semiotic analysis. Content analysis has traditionally been closely identified with the content of mass media, while the term 'discourse' has a broader connotation and covers all 'texts', in whatever form or language they are encoded, and also specifically implies that a text is constructed by those who read and decipher it as much as those who formulate it. Scheufele (2008) names four features shared by all discourses, as meant in the present context. First, discourses refer to *political or social issues* that are relevant for society, or at least for a major grouping of people. For instance, we can speak of a 'nuclear energy discourse' or a 'drug discourse'. Secondly, the elements of a discourse are called speech acts, emphasizing that they are *a form of social interaction* and wider patterns of social behaviour. Thirdly, discourse can be analysed by studying *bodies of text of all kinds*, including documents, transcripts of debates and media content. Fourthly, discourses are processes of *collectively construct-ing social reality*, often in the form of frames and schemata, which allow generalization. As to the purposes of discourse analysis, Scheufele reminds us that the primary aim is to uncover the substance or quality of a particular discourse, rather than to quantify the occurrence of different discourses.

According to Smith and Bell (2007), it is hard to give a precise definition of discourse analysis, but they say it is more common to find it referred to as 'critical discourse anal-ysis' because of its attention to the role of power. This is in line with Scheufele's point about it usually being connected with some current significant social issue, and Hijman's analysis that what underlies the logic of different types of qualitative content analysis is the search for a latent or 'deeper' meaning of the message.

Wodak and Meyer (2001: 2–3) define critical discourse analysis as being 'fundamen-tally concerned with analyzing opaque as well as transparent structural relationships of dominance, discrimination, power and control as manifested in language'. This definition sounds as if it would cover, if not the theory, at least many of the applications of earlier and more formal structuralism and semiology, as described above. Fundamentally, (critical) discourse analysis applies specifically to the study of written texts, where it is concerned with identifying the structures of text and talk from a perspective (van Dijk, 1985) – a method specifically applied to the study of news stories (van Dijk, 1983). As van Dijk (2011) argues, the approach to media content (and specifically the news) as a form of discourse with its own structures and properties suggests that media content should be studied as a 'communicative event' on its own with a particular social context, next to approaches that link content either to influences on media production or to the uses and effects of media. In discourse analysis, as in structuralist and semiotic analyses, key steps in the research process are summarized in Box 12.3 (based on van Zoonen, 1999: 84). Taken together, these steps aim to uncover how texts produce certain meanings for both producers and consumers of media.

---

**12.3**

**Key steps in structuralist, semiotic and discourse analysis**

- Identifying the structural building blocks (i.e. propositions) in a text
- Mapping how these propositions are combined
- Categorizing the grammatical, sequencing, word choice and other 'micro choices' made in the text
- Identifying the various rhetorical manoeuvres in the text

---

## QUESTIONS OF RESEARCH METHOD

The various frameworks and perspectives for theorizing about media content that have been discussed often imply sharp divergences of methods of research. The full range of alternatives cannot be discussed here since there are many different methods for different purposes (several have already been introduced). Methods range from simple and extensive classifications of types of content for organizational or descriptive purposes to deeply interpretative enquiries into specific examples of content, designed to uncover subtle and hidden potential meanings. Fundamentally, this entails a division between what George Gerbner in 1958 called 'micro' analysis of communication content – which would be 'interested in gathering information about persons and making predictions about their behavior' – and 'macro' analyses, searching for the 'hidden dynamics' and 'social determinants' of 'both personal and institutional dynamics reflected in cultural products' (Gerbner, 1958: 87).

Following the line of theoretical demarcation introduced in Chapter 3, we can broadly distinguish between quantitative and descriptive enquiry into overt meaning on the one hand, and more qualitative and interpretative enquiry into deeper meaning on the other. There are also enquiries directed at understanding the very nature of the various 'media languages' and how they work, especially in relation to visual imagery and sounds. Another demarcation line can be drawn between content analysis as a way to consider influences of media production (cf. 'content-as-consequence' approaches) and as part of a research project on the uses and effects of media (cf. 'content-and-effects' approaches).

Methodologically, both such lines of enquiry can follow either a qualitative or a quantitative approach, as outlined in Figure 12.2. Onto this model the most widely used approaches in content analysis can be plotted, with perhaps the exception of approaches within (critical) discourse analysis, which would consider content as its own communicative event.

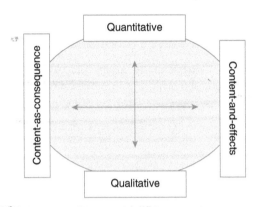

Figure 12.2   Approaches to media content analysis

## WHERE IS MEANING?

Theory has been perennially preoccupied with the question of the 'location' of meaning. Does meaning coincide with the intention of the sender, or is it embedded in the (audiovisual, verbal and written) language, or is it primarily a matter of the receiver's interpretation (Jensen, 1991)? As we have seen from the previous chapters, mass communicated information and culture are produced by complex organizations whose purposes are usually not very specific and yet often predominate over the aims of individual communicators. This makes it hard to know what the 'sender's' intention really is: who can say, for instance, what the purpose of news is, or whose purpose it is? The option of concentrating on the message itself as the source of meaning has been the most attractive one, partly for reasons of practicality. The physical texts themselves are always available for direct analysis, and they have the advantage (compared with human respondents) of being 'non-reactive' to the investigator. They do not decay with time, although their context does decay and with it the possibility of really knowing what they originally meant to senders or to receivers. The digital context adds a complication to this statement of affairs, as online material can often be more fluid than fixed, as Internet-based content can be edited, updated, remixed, aggregated and redistributed on a continuous basis.

It is impossible to 'extract' meaning from media content texts without also making assumptions which themselves shape the meaning extracted – for instance, the assumption that the amount or frequency of attention to something is a reliable guide to message meaning, intention and effect. The findings of content analysis generally do not 'speak for themselves' (unless put in a wider social context). In addition, the 'languages' of media are far from simple and are still only partially understood, especially where they involve music and visual images (both still and moving) in many combinations, drawing on numerous and varied codes and conventions.

## DOMINANT VERSUS ALTERNATIVE PARADIGMS AGAIN

The choices of research method generally follow the division between a dominant empirically oriented paradigm and a more qualitative (and often critical) variant (see Chapter 3). The former is mainly represented by traditional content analysis, which was defined by Berelson (1952: 18) as 'a research technique for the objective, systematic and quantitative description of the manifest content of communication' (see pp. 398–399). This assumes that the surface meaning of a text is fairly unambiguous and can be read by the investigator and expressed in quantitative terms. In fact, it is assumed that the numerical balance of elements in the text (such as the number of words or the space/time allocated to a set of topics) is a reliable guide to the overall meaning. Several relatively sophisticated forms of quantitative content analysis have been developed that go well beyond the simple counting and classifying of units of content that were characteristic of early research. There remains, even so, a fundamental assumption that media content is encoded according to the same language as the reality to which it refers.

The alternative approach is based on precisely the reverse assumption – that the concealed or latent meanings are the most significant, and these cannot be directly read from the numerical data. In particular, we have to take account not just of relative frequency but of links and relationships between elements in the text, and also to take note of what is missing or taken for granted. We need to identify and understand the particular discourse in which a text is encoded. In general, we need to be aware of the conventions and codes of any genre that we study since these indicate at a higher level what is going on in the text (Jensen and Jankowski, 1991). In contrast, content analysis may permit the conflation of several different kinds of media text, ignoring discursive variety.

Both varieties of analysis can claim some measure of scientific reliability. They deploy methods that can, in principle, be replicated by different people as well as by software, as substantial progress on automated and computerized (quantitative as well as qualitative) content analysis is made, and the 'findings' should be open to challenge according to the canons of scientific procedure. Secondly, they are both designed to deal with regularity and recurrence in cultural artefacts rather than with the unique and non-reproducible. They are thus more appropriate for application to the symbolic products of the culture industries than to those of the 'cultural elite' (such as 'works of art'). Thirdly, they avoid judgements of moral or aesthetic value (another sense of being objective). Fourthly, all such methods are, in principle, instrumental means to other ends. They can be used to answer questions about the links between content, creators, social context and receivers (Barker, 2003).

# QUANTITATIVE CONTENT ANALYSIS

## BASICS

Quantitative or 'traditional' content analysis, following Berelson's (1952) definition, is the earliest, most central and still most widely practised method of research. Its use goes back to the early decades of the century (see Kingsbury and Hart, 1937). The basic sequence in applying the technique is set out as follows:

- Choose a universe or sample of content.
- Establish a category frame of external referents relevant to the purpose of the enquiry (such as a set of political parties or countries which may be referred to in content).
- Choose a 'unit of analysis' from the content (this could be a word, a sentence, an item, a whole news story, a picture, a sequence, etc.).
- Seek to match the content to the category frame by counting the frequency of the references to relevant items in the category frame, per chosen unit of content.
- Determine the validity of the results through a matching procedure involving multiple coders, establishing intercoder reliability.
- Express the results as an overall distribution of the complete universe or chosen content sample in terms of the frequency of occurrence of the sought-for referents.

The procedure is based on two main assumptions. The first is that the link between the external object of reference and the reference to it in the text will be reasonably clear and unambiguous. The second is that the frequency of occurrence of chosen references will validly express the predominant 'meaning' of the text in an objective way. The approach is, in principle, no different from that adopted in surveys of people. One chooses a population (here a media type or subset), draws a sample of respondents from it that is representative of the whole (the units of analysis), collects data about individuals according to variables and assigns values to these variables. As with the survey, content analysis is held to be reliable (reproducible) and not unique to the investigator (which gets established through intercoder reliability). The method produces a statistical summary of a much larger media reality. It has been used for many purposes, but especially for comparing media content with a known frequency distribution in 'social reality'.

## LIMITS TO CONTENT ANALYSIS

The traditional approach has many limitations and pitfalls, which are of some theoretical interest as well as practical relevance. The usual practice of constructing a category system before applying it involves the risk of an investigator imposing a meaning system rather than discovering it in the content. Even when care is taken to avoid this, any such category system must be selective and potentially distorting. The outcome of content analysis is itself a new text, the meaning of which may, or even must, diverge from the original source material. This result is also based on a form of 'reading' of content that no actual 'reader' would ever, under natural circumstances, undertake. The new 'meaning' is neither that of the original sender, nor that of the text itself, nor that of the audience, but is a fourth construct, one particular interpretation. Account cannot easily be taken of the context of a reference within a text or of the text as a whole. Internal relationships between references in texts may also be neglected in the process of abstraction. There is an assumption that 'coders' can be trained to make reliable judgements about categories and meanings.

The boundaries of the kind of content analysis described are, in fact, rather elastic, and many variants can be accommodated within the same basic framework. The more one relaxes requirements of reliability, the easier it is to introduce categories and variables that will be useful for interpretation but 'low' in 'objectivity' and somewhat ambiguous. This is especially true of attempts to capture references to values, themes, settings, style and interpretative frameworks. Content analyses often display a wide range of reliability because of attempts to include some more subjective indicators of meaning.

The extensive digitization of current and past media content (especially print media such as newspapers) has opened up many new possibilities for computer-assisted quantitative analysis of very large quantities of material. It has become an important method for analysing large datasets of digitized content. However, there are serious concerns, as Deacon (2007) has pointed out. Aside from defects in particular databases (for example, gaps or duplications in the archives) that are unintended but also often unknown, there are several intrinsic obstacles that are not easy to overcome. For instance, it is not easy to capture complex thematic issues by way of key words. Large bodies of text have to be divided up for counting purposes, but the choice of unit is not fixed. Visuals are often not included in analyses, or the inclusion of non-written content does not follow a systematic framework. The specific context of references in the data cannot easily be recovered. All in all, Deacon concludes that content should wherever possible be studied in its original form. Stemler (2015) similarly cautions that the availability of massive amounts of digitally archived textual, visual and auditory data should not distract from 'the need for a guiding theory'. Reflecting on their high-volume automated comparative content analyses of almost 900,000 news articles,

Christian Baden and Keren Tenenboim-Weinblatt (2018) consider their approach as potentially rewarding for revealing general patterns, as well as labour-intensive and complex due to the numerous stages of collecting, grouping, disambiguating and collating concepts in the content sample. They also indicate the difficulty in using indicators to operationalize patterns in the data, as the automated approach requires only explicit references to be measured accurately.

## QUANTITATIVE AND QUALITATIVE ANALYSIS COMPARED

The contrast between traditional content analysis and interpretative approaches can now be summarized. Some differences are self-evident. First, structuralism and semiotics (as discussed earlier in this chapter) do not involve quantification, and there is even an antipathy towards counting as a way of arriving at significance, since meaning derives from textual relationships, oppositions and context rather than from number and balance of references. Secondly, attention is directed to latent rather than manifest content, and latent (thus deeper) meaning is regarded as actually more essential. Thirdly, structuralism is systematic in a different way from content analysis, giving no weight to procedures of sampling and rejecting the notion that all 'units' of content should be treated equally.

Fourthly, structuralism does not allow the assumption that the world of social and cultural 'reality', the message and the receiver all involve the same basic system of meanings. Social reality consists of numerous more or less discrete universes of meaning, each requiring separate elucidation. The 'audience' also divides up into 'interpretative communities', each possessing some unique possibilities for attributing meaning. Media content, as we have seen, is also composed on the basis of more than one code, language or sign system. All this makes it impossible, even absurd, to assume that any category system of references can be constructed in which a given element is likely to mean precisely the same in the 'reality', in the content, to the audience member and to the media analyst. That said, both approaches call for contextual analysis on top of (or integrated with) content analysis, and especially in the fast-growing world of automated content analysis, a qualitative (cf. discourse) analytical phase is essential in order to disambiguate the concepts and patterns measured in the data.

## MIXED METHODS

This comparison does not indicate the superiority of one approach over the other, since, despite the claim at the outset that these methods have something in common, they are essentially good for different purposes. Qualitative content analysis has traditionally been less than explicit when it comes to codifying its analytical steps and making its method concrete (Hijmans, 1996). It is not accountable in its results, according to standards of reliability used in analyses with the aim of reproducibility. Neither is it easy to generalize from the results to other texts, except perhaps in relation to form (for instance, comparing one genre with another), and with reference to deeper structures of meaning unearthed through rhetorical, narrative and discourse analysis.

For some purposes, it may be permissible and necessary to depart from the pure form of either 'Berelsonian' or 'Barthian' analysis, and a number of studies have used combinations of both approaches, despite their divergent assumptions. An example of such a hybrid approach is the work on British television news by the Glasgow Media Group (1976, 1980, 1985), which combined rigorous and detailed quantitative analysis of industrial news with an attempt to 'unpack' the deeper cultural meaning of specific news stories. The school of 'cultural indicators', as represented by Gerbner and colleagues, has also sought to arrive at the 'meaning structure' of dominant forms of television output by way of systematic quantitative analysis of overt elements of television representation.

There are methods that do not easily belong to either of the main approaches described. One is the psychoanalytic approach favoured at an early stage of content study. This focuses on the motivation of 'characters' and the underlying meaning of dominant themes in the popular (or less so) culture of a given society or period (for instance, Wolfenstein and Leites, 1947; McGranahan and Wayne, 1948; Kracauer, 1949). It was also taken up for studying gender issues and the meaning and influence of advertising (for example, Williamson, 1978).

Other variants of analysis method have already been noted – for instance, the analysis of narrative structure (Radway, 1984) or the study of content functions. In the past decade or so, automated and algorithmic content analyses have been developed, and there is a notable rise of so-called 'linkage' studies (combining content analysis with audience surveys). Fascinating challenges await in the analysis of content online and particularly on social media using digital methods (Rogers, 2013, 2019), and of multi-platform media content (Champion, 2015).

Such possibilities are a reminder of the relative character of most analysis of content, in that there always has to be some outside point of reference or purpose according to which one chooses one form of classification rather than another. Theory must guide the collection and analysis of data. Even semiotics can supply interpretation only in terms of a much larger system of social contexts, cultural meanings and sensemaking practices. The main differences between essentially quantitative and qualitative approaches are given in Box 12.4. Whether these differences are advantages or not depends on the purpose.

## 12.4
### Types of media content analysis compared

| Message content analysis | Structural analysis of texts |
| --- | --- |
| Quantitative | Qualitative |
| Fragmentary | Holistic |
| Systematic | Selective |
| Generalizing, extensive | Illustrative, specific |
| Manifest meaning | Latent meaning |
| Objective | Relative to audience |

One recurrent problem with all methods and approaches is the gap that often exists between the outcome of content analysis and the perceptions of the creators or the audience. The creators tend to think of what is unique and distinctive in what they do, while the audience is inclined to think of content in terms of a mixture of conventional genre or type labels and a set of satisfactions that have been experienced or are expected. The version extracted by the content analyst is thus not very recognizable to the two main sets of participants in the mass communication enterprise (producers and receivers) and often remains a scientific or literary abstraction. Again, the work of the Glasgow Media Group is a good example of a type of 'public sociology' as the scholars over time collaborated with journalists and audiences (Eldridge, 2000).

## CONCLUSION

The future of content analysis, one way or another, has to lie in relating 'content' as sent to the wider structures of meaning and social contexts in a society. This path can probably best be followed by way of discourse analysis, which takes account of other meaning systems in the originating culture, or by way of linkage studies combining content with audience reception analysis, which takes seriously the notion that media users also make meanings. Both are necessary in some degree for an adequate study of media.

The various frameworks and perspectives for theorizing about media content that have been introduced often imply sharp divergences of methods of research as well as differences of purpose. The quality and performance of the mass media matter, and systematic, theory-driven qualitative and quantitative content analysis is still our best instrument to tackle this crucial issue. Faced with industry convergence and multi-platform strategies, the digitization of massive textual and audiovisual archives, and the rapid development of digital and automated methods, there are exciting opportunities for research, although at times a lack of explicit theoretical and methodological underpinnings of published work is cause for concern.

## FURTHER READING

Baden, C. and Tenenboim-Weinblatt, K. (2018) 'The search for common ground in conflict news research: comparing the coverage of six current conflicts in domestic and international media over time', *Media, War & Conflict*, 11(1): 22–45.

De Vreese, C.H., Boukes, M., Schuck, A.R.T., Vliegenthart, R., Bos L. and Lelkes, Y. (2017) 'Linking survey and media content data: opportunities, considerations, and pitfalls', *Communication Methods and Measures*, 11(4): 221–244.

Grabe, M.E. and Bucy, E.P. (2009) *Image Bite Politics: News and the Visual Framing of Elections*. New York: Oxford University Press.

Hijmans, E. (1996) 'The logic of qualitative media content analysis: a typology', *Communications*, 21(1): 93–108.

Krippendorf, K. and Bock, A. (eds) (2009) *The Content Analysis Reader*. Thousand Oaks, CA: Sage.

Rogers, R. (2019) *Doing Digital Methods*. Boston, MA: MIT Press.

# 13

## MEDIA GENRES, FORMATS AND TEXTS

The aim of this chapter is to look more closely at some examples of typical media content as revealed by applying some of the approaches and the methods outlined in Chapter 12. It also introduces some of the concepts that are used to classify the output of mass media. In particular, we explore the concepts of media genre and format within the context of emerging approaches of storytelling within and outside the media industries to accommodate the contemporary media environment.

---

# QUESTIONS OF GENRE

In general use, the term 'genre' simply means a kind or type of text, and it is often loosely applied to any distinctive category of cultural product. In film theory, where it was first applied within media and mass communication research (after being imported from rhetoric), the term has been controversial because of the tension between individual creative authorship and location in a genre (Andrew, 1984). An emphasis on the genre tends to credit the value of a work to a cultural tradition rather than to an individual artist, who simply follows the rules laid down by the particular school of production. Fiske (1987) sees genre as a means of constructing the audience, in that appeal to or within a certain genre or mix of genre elements produces a certain type of audience with specific expectations and preferences. A film that, for example, combines elements of 'science fiction' with 'superheroes' constructs a target market for itself. Work by Negus (1998: 376) on genres in music similarly reveals their existence as industry constructs – a product of 'corporate strategies which utilize the technique of portfolio management as a way of allocating staff, artists and investment'. Negus notes the irony of how music develops and innovates primarily when different musicians and musical traditions meet and mix their approaches, while the industry tends to builds walls around specific genres and traditions as a way to profit from them.

Genres are not just defined and classified by industries. Audiences tend to have their own conception of genres as well (and tend to select products and services accordingly). Both of these constructs may or may not align with that of the scholar or critic of film, television, games or news. Furthermore, it is difficult to make clear-cut distinctions between one genre and another: genres overlap, and there are plenty of 'mixed genres' and crossovers. Mittell (2011: 7) advocates a nuanced approach that would 'locate genres within the complex interrelations among texts, industries, audiences, and historical contexts'.

In the digital context, genres are commonly defined by algorithms such as the recommendation software developed by companies like Amazon and Netflix that classify products on the basis of data-driven matches between a particular customer profile (what people consume, when they consume it, what they do before and after they consume it, what have they consumed historically), the availability and curation of products in the company catalogue, and so on. The results of such algorithmic construction of product categories then get labelled, resulting in 'hyperspecific' micro genres that can be particular to individual users of the platform.

Although it must be clear that the classification of genres is not a neutral procedure, and that genres are 'ultimately an abstract conception rather than something that exists empirically in the world' (Feuer, 1992: 144), the concept of genre is useful to the study of mass media content. For our purpose, genre can refer to any *category* of content that has the following characteristics:

- Its collective identity is recognized more or less equally by its producers (media professionals, organizations and industries) and its consumers (media audiences).
- This identity (or definition) relates to purposes (such as information, entertainment or subvariants) and form (length, pace, structure, language, etc.).
- The identity has been established over time and observes familiar conventions; cultural forms are preserved, although these can also change and develop within the framework of the original genre.
- A particular genre will follow an expected structure of narrative or sequence of action, draw on a predictable stock of images and have a repertoire of variants of basic themes.

It is important to note that every text belongs to or references one or more genres. Genres and elements thereof are highly useful and can help (or hinder) comprehension. According to Andrew (1984: 110), genres (of film):

> are specific networks of formulas that deliver a certified product to a waiting customer. They ensure the production of meaning by regulating the viewers' relation to the image and narrative construction for him or her. In fact, genres construct the proper spectators for their own consumption. They build the desires and then represent the satisfaction of what they have triggered.

This view overrates the extent to which the media can determine the response of an audience, but it is at least consistent with the aspirations of media themselves to control the environments in which they operate. In fact, there is a good deal of evidence of audience recognition and use of genre categories in discourse about media. Hoijer (2000), for instance, applied a reception analysis to the interpretation of different television genres and found that each genre generated certain expectations. Popular fiction in the realistic mode is expected to provide a valid reflection of everyday reality. Ideas of this kind were used by the audience as standards of criticism. Distinctions are made according to text characteristics of specific genre examples. Altman (1996) notes three different roles that the notion of genre plays in media production, content and reception (see Box 13.1)

From this notion of roles and functions of genres in the media, an important consideration follows, based on the work of Carolyn Miller (1984) on genre as a form of social action: genres produce meaning. By formatting a text (whether written, photographic, videographic or infographic) in a certain way, a creator increases the likelihood that a certain audience will understand it – although not necessarily agree with it. This compels us to understand media products as inherently relational as well as contextual, and the use of genre – what Schmidt (1987) calls 'media-action-schemata' – produces a certain action as much as it is a reflection of a particular communicator practice. In a reflection on the impact of her work, Miller (2015) notes that the Internet complicated concerns about genre, as so many new forms of media are produced continuously by a multitude of participants, including, but not limited to, media professionals, policymakers, academics, co-creating consumers and everyday users. This makes media genres much more dynamic and open-ended than they perhaps already were, although genre still provides an important 'mediating function' between intention and exigence, and between form and substance (ibid.: 67).

The genre may be considered as a practical device for helping any mass medium to produce consistently and efficiently and to relate its production to the expectations of its audience. Since it helps individual media users to plan their choices, it can also be considered as a mechanism for ordering the relations between producers and consumers.

## GENRE EXAMPLES

The origin of genre analysis can be credited to Stuart Kaminsky (1974: 3), who wrote that:

> genre study of the film is based in the realization that certain popular narrative forms have both cultural and universal roots, that the Western of today is related to archetypes of the past 200 years in the United States and to the folk tale and the myth.

Stuart Hall (1974/1980) also applied the genre idea to the 'B-movie western'. In his analysis, genre depends on the use of a particular 'code' or meaning system, which can draw on some consensus about meaning among users of the code (whether encoders or decoders) in a given culture. According to Hall, we can speak of a genre where coding and decoding are very close and where meaning is consequently relatively unambiguous, in the sense of being received much as it is sent.

The classic western movie, then, is said to derive from a particular myth concerning the conquest of the American West and involving such elements as displays of masculine prowess and womanly courage, the working out of destiny in the wide-open spaces and the struggle of good versus evil. The particular strength of the western genre is that it can generate many variant forms that can also be readily understood in relation to the original basic form. For instance, we have seen the psychological western, the parody western, the spaghetti western, the comedy western and the soap opera western. The meaning of the variant forms often depends on the reversal of elements in the original code. Altman (1984) uses the western to develop a theoretical approach to film genres based on a distinction between *semantic* and *syntactic* elements. Semantic approaches to genre focus on analysing a list of building blocks: common traits, attitudes, characters, shots, locations, sets, and so on, while a syntactic approach considers the relationships linking lexical elements. The western from a syntactic point of view is determined by the relationships between culture and nature, between individualism and community, between civilization and the frontier (ibid.: 10–11).

Many familiar examples of media content can be subjected to a genre analysis designed to uncover their essential recurring features or formulas, as Radway (1984) has done for the romance story, by exposing the typical 'narrative logic'. It is also possible to classify the different variants of the same genre, as Berger (1992) does for the detective mystery. According to Berger, the 'formula' is a subcategory or genre and involves the conventions of that genre, with particular reference to time, place, plots, costumes, types of hero, heroine and villain, and so on. A western, for instance, has a certain range of possibilities for the formulaic elements that will be known to experienced audience members. This knowledge enables the content to be read correctly when certain signs appear: for instance, white hats identifying good guys, and the music that heralds the approaching cavalry.

Mills (2004: 78), through an analysis of the situation comedy or 'sitcom' television genre, shows that even such a relatively stable genre is continually evolving and thus 'offers a site for subtle, yet powerful, critiques of television media'. The generic soap opera (starting in Australia, the USA and the UK) and telenovela (throughout Latin America) are typical examples of a serial form of narrative with global popular recognition and appeal. The great interest in the serial *Dallas* during the 1980s (Ang, 1985; Liebes and Katz, 1990), for somewhat different reasons, also drew attention to the soap opera as a genre. That particular example also stretched the meaning of the term to include a media product that was very different from the early radio or television daytime serial.

Even so, the wide and long currency of the term 'soap opera' as applied to different kinds of drama confirms, in some measure, the validity and utility of the concepts of genre and soap opera.

Developments in media-cultural studies have given prominence to several familiar television genres as well as emerging online and multi-platform storytelling genres, and provided the boundaries for new fields of enquiry (Liebes and Livingstone, 1998; Jenkins, 2004). Given the contemporary context of media convergence, new modes of multi-platform storytelling are emerging that combine, mix and remix genre elements across multiple platforms and channels. There are three basic multi-platform storytelling types:

- *Multimedia*: a single story has many forms, distributed via a single media channel. In journalism the most famous example is a Pulitzer prize-winning multimedia feature for *The New York Times* by John Branch about an avalanche, published on 20 December 2012. The story was published on the newspaper's website containing a six-part story interwoven with photo galleries, short video reports and interviews, interactive graphics and animated simulations. This approach to 'digital longform' even led to a new verb within the (global) news industry: whether to 'snowfall' a certain story (Dowling and Vogan, 2015).

- *Crossmedia*: one story is told across more than one media channel, designed to meet the requirements of each medium separately. The archetypical case of crossmedia would be the original iterations of the *Star Wars* franchise, as the integrity of the storyline was maintained across its various properties. When Disney took over the franchise (in 2012), the company and its creators took it into a transmedia direction, following fan-fiction and realizing audience appeal.

- *Transmedia*: instead of one story, elements of a story develop across multiple media platforms to constitute a larger 'story world' (Jenkins, 2006). In the music industry, an early example was the release of the Nine Inch Nails concept album 'Year Zero' in 2007. The album was conceived to be a story within a larger narrative of a dystopian future set in the United States of 2022. The release included a remix album, an alternate reality game whereby fans participated by finding clues via pre-recorded phone messages, and on t-shirts, websites and USB sticks left at the band's concerts (during one of these concerts a raid by the police was staged as part of the overall narrative). All these elements helped the fans as 'players' to make progress and make sense of the project.

Henry Jenkins is one of the few media scholars to have a receptive (as well as critical) audience within both the media industry and the academy. He can be seen as one of the key theorists of transmedia as a genre in the contemporary mass media, his definition of which is reproduced in Box 13.2.

As a genre, transmedia is an emerging area for both storytelling and research, and some conceptual confusion is to be expected. In a recent overview of the history of transmedia storytelling, Hassler-Forest and Guynes (2018), for example, take the *Star Wars* franchise as a fundamental example of transmedia, considering its contemporary iteration as a 'story world' coming from the first film's blockbuster success in 1977, which 'instantly launched an uncontrolled wave of merchandising and cross-media spin-offs that were incrementally developed into an elaborate storyworld with its own mythology, its own aesthetic, and its own fan culture' (ibid.: 1). Hassler-Forest and Guynes show how the success of *Star Wars* as a transmedia genre was not so much the consequence of cultural economic power or the creative genius of George Lucas, but results more from a rather unpredictable, precarious and dynamic process involving many stakeholders – including the audience.

In a semiotic analysis of the transmedia genre, Scolari (2009) identifies its 'consumer-nested structure' as a key building block, showing how a transmedia narrative creates multiple entry points for consumers (through the production of stories via multiple channels via a more or less pre-planned release schedule). Several types of story can be produced, marking four specific strategies for expanding the fictional world:

- *Creation of interstitial 'microstories'*: short narratives (for example, comics and games to fill the gaps between different seasons of a television series) with a close connection to the overall 'macrostory'.

- *Creation of parallel stories*: other stories that unfold at the same time as the 'macrostory' that can evolve and transform into spin-offs.

- *Creation of peripheral stories*: other stories that take place within the 'macrostory' that usually involve other characters or contain elements of 'origin' narratives.

- *Creation and/or support of user-generated content platforms*: environments that can be considered more or less open-source (depending on the level of copyright control) story-creation platforms that allows users to contribute to the fictional world (ibid.: 598).

In an innovative take on the transmedia genre, Hancox (2017) shows how a transmedia approach can also be used as a research method, using it to dissolve the hierarchical relationship between researchers and the researched, recognizing how all participants contribute materials and stories in their own way, and designing a project based on people participating in research both in and through the media.

One of the strengths of the genre idea is its capacity to adapt and extend to cope with dynamic developments. This is, for example, represented in the rise of the 'talk show' genre, which began as entertainment interviews with celebrities and as a 'breakfast television' format and has expanded luxuriantly throughout the world in manifestations that range from the sensationalist knockabout to very serious occasions for political participation. The common elements holding the genre together are not easy to identify, apart from the centrality of talk and the presence of a key anchor personality. But they often include some audience presence or participation, some conflict or drama, some degree or illusion of actuality, a strong dose of personalization and an illusion of intimacy (see Munson, 1993). The genre of reality television similarly moved from modest beginnings in which real-life scenes from a variety of sources were repackaged thematically (for example, police, accidents, weather, crime, pets, etc.) as entertainment and then into new forms in which volunteers were subjected to a variety of controlled contest or stress situations to produce a voyeuristic and engaging 'live' experience for the audience, which could also intervene in some way.

In a review of genre-based research, Miller, Devitt and Gallagher (2018) offer an outline of affordances of genre analysis that can be applicable to media and mass communication research. These key propositions are summarized in Box 13.3.

## 13.3

### Four theses about genre analysis

- Genre is multimodal, providing an analytical and explanatory framework across semiotic modes and media and thus across communication technologies.
- Genre is multidisciplinary, of interest across traditions of rhetoric, film and television studies, information sciences and many other disciplines.
- Genre is multidimensional, incorporating many perspectives on situated, mediated and motivated communicative interaction.
- Genre is multimethodological, yielding to multiple empirical and interpretative approaches.

## A TYPOLOGY OF GENRES

So far it has seemed that genre analysis can only be applied to discrete categories of content, each with certain key dimensions. An early attempt has been made at more of a meta-analysis by Berger (1992), who suggests that all television output can be classified according to four basic types, produced by two dimensions: degree of emotionality and degree of objectivity. The typology is shown in Figure 13.1.

|  |  | Objectivity | |
| --- | --- | --- | --- |
|  |  | High | Low |
| Emotionality | Strong | **Contests** | **Dramas** |
|  | Weak | **Actualities** | **Persuasions** |

Figure 13.1   The structure of television genres: a typology (Berger, 1992: 7)

The explanation of the terms is as follows:

- *Contests* are programmes with competition involving real players, including game shows, quizzes and sports. They are both real and emotionally involving (in intention).

- *Actualities* include all news, documentary and reality programming. They are objective and unemotional in principle.

- *Persuasions* are low on both dimensions and reflect an intention by the sender to persuade, especially by advertising or some form of advocacy or propaganda.

- *Dramas* cover almost all fictional storytelling and a wide range of genres.

As Berger notes, the application of this scheme is complicated by the fact that new and mixed genres are continually being created that do not belong to a unique category. Familiar examples are those of 'docudrama' and other kinds of 'infotainment'. But this is also a feature of individual genres and can be helpful in tracking and analysing what is happening. The category of 'reality television' in any given instance (for example, *Big Brother*) does not easily fit into one unique category, although there is an important element of contest in the format. This indicates a limitation in the typology, as it suggests that genre hybridization is possibly more common than genre 'purity', especially in a contemporary converged media context.

A more comprehensive typology of the key properties of a genre is summarized by Chandler (1997) based on a review of film and television genre scholarship. Adapted from Chandler, we can distinguish the following:

- *Narrative*: similar (sometimes formulaic) plots and structures, predictable situations, sequences, episodes, obstacles, conflicts and resolutions.
- *Characterization*: similar types of character (sometimes stereotypes), roles, personal qualities, motivations, goals, behaviour.
- *Patterns*: basic and recurring themes, topics, subject matter, propositions and values.
- *Settings*: geographical and historical.
- *Iconography*: a familiar stock of images or motifs, the connotations of which have become fixed; primarily but not necessarily visual, including décor, costume and objects, familiar patterns of dialogue, characteristic music and sounds.
- *Techniques*: stylistic or formal conventions of (in film and television) camera work, lighting, sound-recording, use of colour, editing, etc.
- *Tone, mood* and *mode of address*: elements that involve inbuilt assumptions about the audience.
- *Audience relationships*: specific genres come with expectations about audience involvement.

As we have aimed to show in this brief review, genre can be a useful concept for finding one's way in the luxuriant abundance of media output and for helping to describe and categorize content. The distinction between one genre and another is not easy to ascertain objectively, and the correspondence of recognition and understanding by producers and audience, named above as a characteristic of a genre, is not easy to demonstrate.

## PRINCIPLES OF GENRE ANALYSIS

Although genre analysis is wide-ranging and can be applied to multiple media texts, at the heart of the approach is a focus on the ways in which texts are organized, and how this organization makes sense to both producers and consumers of the text. Genre analysis, in other words, shows how a given text (which includes written, verbal, audio and video) 'communicates' to its environment. The approach thereby serves as an operationalization of the assumption that media content only exists through (the practices of) their production and reception. Genre analysis can be seen as a form of discourse analysis, as it is generally quite explicit about the cultural and cognitive context within which media texts operate. As Mittell (2011: 16) argues, 'genre definitions are always partial and contingent, emerging out of specific cultural relations, rather than abstract textual ideals. We need to examine how genres operate as conceptual frameworks, situating media texts within larger contexts of understanding'. In Box 13.4 Mittell offers five principles of cultural genre analysis that are particular to the study of media.

## MEDIA FORMAT

The genre concept has been useful for analysing media formats. Altheide and Snow (1979), for instance, developed a mode of analysis of media content, employing the terms *media logic* and *media format*. The first refers essentially to a set of implicit rules and norms that govern how content should be processed and presented in order to take most advantage of the characteristics of a given medium. This includes fitting the needs of the media organization (including the media's perception of the needs of the audience). Altheide sees content as tailored to fit media formats, and formats as tailored to fit listener/viewer preferences and assumed capacities. Formats are essentially sub-routines for dealing with specific themes within a genre. For instance, Altheide (1985) describes a 'format for crisis' in television news, which transcends the particularities of events and gives a common shape to the handling of different news stories. The main conditions necessary for the news handling of a crisis on a continuing basis are accessibility (to information or to the site of the crisis), visual quality (of film or any other footage), drama and action, relevance to the audience and thematic unity.

Graber (1981) has made notable contributions to the study of political languages in general and its television versions in particular. She confirms the points made by Altheide in her observations, suggesting that television journalists have certain repertoires, frames, logics and formats of highly stereotyped cues for many specific situations in politics. She argues that the encoding and decoding of audiovisual languages is essentially *different* from that of verbal languages in being more associational, connotative and unstructured and less logical, clearly defined and delimited.

Before leaving the subject of genres, formats and related concepts, it is worth emphasizing that they can, in principle, cut across the conventional content categories of media output, including the divide between fiction and non-fiction. Fiske (1987) underlines the essential *intertextuality* of genres. Intertextuality used to be a largely theoretical concept alerting the researcher to how media texts tend to reference each other and build on earlier work, but in an age of digital convergence and multi-platform storytelling, intertextuality has become a more or less deliberate media strategy to develop and promote properties (such as storylines, certain characters and brands) across different media channels.

Although media formats are fundamentally ways that media organizations and professionals translate stories and genre conventions into a more or less 'readymade' framework for production, formats also operate to make it easier for audiences to understand certain media. Audience research among children as well as adults suggests that people are quick to recognize and name specific formats, especially in film and television, and less so online and in print, which media tend to require more cognitive resources to process (see Yang and Grabe, 2011; Grabe et al., 2015).

When studying media formats, it is possible to take technical features of the medium into consideration. Bucy and Newhagen (1999), for example, include the use of close-ups as well as panoramic establishing shots, varied camera angles, editing techniques as well as 'image graphication' techniques (cf. digital video effects such as split screens, lines, borders, infographics and lettering) in their analysis of how viewers process various political communication formats. In order to document the 'image bites' of politicans – versus the much more common measurement of 'sound bites' – in television election campaign news, Bucy and Grabe (2007: 662) included in their content analysis various format conventions of 'shown and heard, shown but not heard, and heard but not shown' shots. Their work is an example of using media format as a gateway to content analysis.

# FRAMING ANALYSIS AND THE NEWS

News is arguably the most systematically researched category of media content. One general conclusion from the many content studies on this genre is that news exhibits a rather stable and predictable overall pattern when measured according to conventional categories of subject matter. Many of the reasons for this have already been discussed in relation to media production generally, and news in particular (see Chapters 10 and 11).

In the context of news as a specific media format, much attention has been paid to the question of how news information is typically presented or 'framed'. Tuchman (1978) cites Goffman (1974) as the originator of the idea that a frame is needed in order to organize otherwise fragmentary items of experience or information. The idea of a 'frame' in relation to news has been widely and loosely used in place of terms such as 'frame of reference', 'context', 'theme', or even 'news angle'. In a journalistic context, stories are given meaning by reference to some particular 'news value' that connects one event with other similar ones. While it is a common-sense notion, it is also necessary to use the term with some precision, especially when the aim is to study the possible effects of the framing of news. In that case, the content frame has to be compared with the frame of reference in the mind of an audience member. According to Entman (1993: 52), 'Framing involves *selection* and *salience*'. He summarizes the main aspects of framing by saying that frames define problems, diagnose causes, make moral judgements and suggest remedies. It is clear that a very large number of textual devices can be used to perform these activities. They include using certain words or phrases, making certain contextual references, choosing certain pictures or film, giving examples as typical, referring to certain sources, and so on. The possible effects of all this are discussed in Chapter 17, but generally speaking, 'framing studies have demonstrated effects on the evaluative direction of thoughts, issue interpretations, attitudes, perceptions of an issue, and levels of policy support and political behavior' (Schuck and Feinholdt, 2015: 3).

Framing is a way of giving some overall interpretation to isolated items of fact. Frames are more than just a headline, a particular camera angle, or the use of a specific hashtag in social media. Frames are consistent constructions of an issue as established through the use of selection, salience or emphasis, exclusion and/or elaboration (Chong and Druckman, 2007). Frames are useful tools for journalists to put (verified) facts in a meaningful context, as they can be helpful to audiences making sense of the news. At the same time, frames can exclude certain aspects and voices from the news, while privileging others. An awareness of particular frames or framing efforts on the part of journalists can make audiences wary and distrustful. It is almost unavoidable for journalists to do this, and in so doing to depart from pure 'objectivity' and to introduce some (unintended) bias. When information is supplied to news media by sources (as much often is), then it arrives with a built-in frame that suits the purpose of the source and is unlikely to be neutral in its perspective. Entman (2007) distinguishes between deliberate falsification or omission, 'content bias', where the reality of the news seems to favour one side over another in a conflict situation, and 'decision-making' bias, where the motivation and mindset of journalists are unintentionally influential. It is in the second instance that framing comes into play. There are numerous examples of framing in the literature on content analysis.

Race relations issues, for instance, have often been presented in the media as problematic for society rather than for immigrant minorities (Horsti, 2003; Downing and Husband, 2005). Van Gorp's (2005) account of Belgian press coverage of asylum seekers showed a division between a frame of 'victim' that invited sympathy and a frame of 'intruder' that raised public fears and opposition – a framing pattern found in much subsequent analyses of news coverage involving migrants and refugees. Almost all news about the Soviet Union and Eastern Europe was for decades reported in terms of the Cold War and the Soviet 'enemy' (McNair, 1988). Much the same was true for China, until it became too important to offend.

Inevitably, framing reflects both the sources that are chosen and the national context in which news is produced, thus also the foreign policies of the countries concerned. The Iraq war produced much evidence of the alignment of national media systems with their government and public opinion (for example, Tumber and Palmer, 2004; Aday, Slivington and Herbert, 2005; Ravi, 2005). Similar patterns were found in online news by Dimitrova, Kaid, Williams and Trammell (2005). Bird and Dardenne (2009) contrast US and British reporting of the 'shock and awe' bombing of Baghdad, which was described by the former in admiring terms as a demonstration of power and by the latter as catastrophic, destructive and outrageous. It must be clear that journalists can cover a story in many different ways, even when the 'facts' of the story are the same.

The analysis of texts according to framing theory often produces clear and interesting results, in a transparent and communicative way, even if we are left at the end without a clear measure of the strength and extent of the 'frames' uncovered. There are many cues to draw on, presumably the same ones that are available to the audience that give rise to supposed effects. These include visuals, language usage, labels, similes and metaphors, familiar narrative structures, and so on.

Framing also undergoes changes that reflect the goals of sources as well as changing realities. Schwalber, Silcode and Keith (2008) analysed visuals in US media over the early weeks of the invasion of Iraq and observed a shift from a master narrative of patriotic endeavour to a more fragmented and ambivalent view as the war dragged on. Framing analysis offers an apparently convincing impression of underlying meanings and assumptions, but Kitzinger (2007) reminds us that the most powerful frame may well be invisible or so transparently obvious that it is taken for granted. For instance, an issue that is treated as problematic in the news may lead to the alternative framing of narratives and solutions, while the framing of an issue in itself as a problem is unquestioned. She gives the example of homosexuality in the past, but there are plenty of contemporary examples, including climate change and global warming, migration and the refugee crisis, and so on.

As with genre analysis, framing analysis is not just the study of a particular piece of media content; it is a (qualitative or quantitative) systematic consideration of the interaction between journalists and news organizations, political elites, and the public jointly influencing how a frame takes shape (Hänggli and Kriesi, 2012).

# THE FORMAT OF THE NEWS REPORT

The strength of the news genre is attested to by the extent to which certain basic features are found across the different media of print, radio and television, online and mobile, despite the very different possibilities and limitations of each. Some of these features of regularity are found to be much the same in different countries (Rositi, 1976; Heinderyckx, 1993). What is striking is the extent to which a presumably unpredictable universe of events seems open to incorporation, day after day, into much the same temporal, spatial and topical frame. It is true that deviations occur, at times of crisis or exceptional events, but the news form is posited on the normality and predictability of the world of events. The audience is 'at work' here too, as experimental research on (print, broadcast and online) news shows that 'formal features have an influence on the meaning viewers derive from news content' (Grabe, Lang and Zhao, 2003: 387).

The news format provides indications of the relative significance of events and of types of content. Significance is mainly indicated by the sequencing of content and by the relative amount of space or time allocated. According to what the Glasgow Media Group (1980) called 'viewers' maxims', it will be understood that first-appearing items in television news are most 'important' and that, generally, items receiving more time are also more important. Television news bulletins are also generally constructed with a view to arousing initial interest by highlighting some event, maintaining interest through diversity and human interest, holding back some vital information to the end (sports results and weather forecast), then sending the viewer away at the close with a light touch. The Glasgow Media Group argued that the hidden purpose or effect of this is to reinforce a 'primary framework' of normality and control and a view of the world that is essentially ideological. The world is 'naturalized' (see also Tuchman, 1978). A similar structure is at work in most print and online news formats, using an 'inverted pyramid' style to bring the most salient facts of the news story first. As with television, the material context of the medium is an important influence on the development of the news format: in the old typesetting days of newspapers, an editor had to be able to sometimes cut off the bottom end of a news report in order to place it on a page, hence the pressure on reporters to include the most important parts of the news in the beginning and at the top of their stories. In television, the limited broadcast time and specific schedule of a news programme co-determines the length and sequence of stories.

The regularities described characterize the dominant western news form, and it is possible that media operating under different conditions will exert different kinds of regularity. There are almost certainly significant and systematic differences between mobile, online and television news-giving in different societies, although these are more likely to follow cultural and institutional lines of demarcation, which are different from national and language frontiers. An early comparison of US and Italian television news, for instance, led to the conclusion that each system's news gives a significantly different conception of what politics is about (Hallin and Mancini, 1984). The main differences were attributed to the much larger space occupied by a public sphere, other than the state, in the case of Italy. As a result, journalists in the USA have a much larger role as representatives of the public than they adopt, or are credited with, in Italy.

## NEWS AS NARRATIVE

Text as narrative has long been an object of study, and the narrative concept has proved useful in understanding a variety of media contents. Basic narrative forms span a wide range of types, including advertisements and news 'stories' as well as the more obvious candidates of drama and fiction. In one way or another, most media content tells stories, which take rather patterned and predictable forms. The main function of narrative is to help make sense of reports of experience. It does this in two main ways: by linking actions and events in a logical, sequential or causal way; and by providing the elements of people and places that have a fixed and recognizable (realistic) character. Narrative helps to provide the logic of human motive that makes sense of fragmentary observations, whether fictional or realistic. When news is considered as narrative, we can appreciate the way in which it draws on and retells the recurrent and dominant myths of a society, inevitably with some 'ideological' loading (Bird and Dardenne, 2009).

Darnton (1975) argues that our conception of news results from 'ancient ways of telling stories'. News accounts are typically cast in narrative form, with principal and minor actors, connected sequences, heroes and villains, a beginning, a middle and an end, a signalling of dramatic turns and a reliance on familiar plots. The analysis of news narrative structure has been formalized in the discourse analysis tradition, especially by van Dijk (1983, 1985), who developed an empirically based framework for the analysis of news based on the concept of 'news schemata', which provide a syntax of news stories. Bell (1991) reminds us that news cannot follow a normal narrative, because news structure requires an abstract of the story at the start and also a sequence that reflects the varying news values of actors and events. Fragments of information are reassembled by journalists in newsworthy rather than chronological order.

## THE CULTURAL TEXT AND ITS MEANINGS

Genre analysis and framing analysis are different approaches in research with a common goal: to provide a systematic way of analysing media content in its cultural context, helping us to find out how both media makers and users find and attribute meaning to any given text. Text, in this context, can refer to any type of symbolic language in written, audio, photographic, video or infographic form. Textual analysis can be considered a more general approach to analysing media content, whereas genre (mainly in film and television and emerging ways of storytelling online) and framing analysis (predominantly in news, to some extent also in advertising) look for particular structures. Textual analysis is a methodology that involves understanding texts to understand how people make sense of and communicate in the world. Such analyses can be descriptive, or seek to connect the text with larger social structures and power relationships. A convincing effort has been made by Fiske (1987) to bring much disparate theory on textual analysis together with specific reference to media, especially for the purposes of analysing and understanding popular (television) culture. New definitions of the media text have been introduced along with ways of identifying some key features.

## THE CONCEPT OF TEXT

The term 'text' has been mainly used in two basic senses. One refers very generally to the physical message itself – the printed document, film, television programme, digital game or musical score, as noted above. An alternative usage, recommended by Fiske, is to reserve the term 'text' for the meaningful outcome of the encounter between content and reader. For instance, a television programme 'becomes a text at the moment of reading, that is, when its interaction with one of its many audiences activates some of the meanings/pleasures that it is capable of provoking' (Fiske, 1987: 14). It follows from this definition that the same television programme can produce many different texts in the sense of accomplished meanings. Summing up this point, Fiske tells us that 'a programme is produced by the industry, a text by its readers' (ibid.: 14). It is important, from this perspective, to see that the word 'production' applies to the activities of both the 'mass communicators' and the audiences.

This is a central point in what is essentially a theory of media content looked at from the point of view of its reception (and to some extent its production) or intrinsic meaning. Other essential elements in this approach are to emphasize that the media text has many potential alternative meanings that can result in different readings. Mass media content is thus in principle *polysemic*, having multiple potential meanings for its 'readers' (in the generic sense of audience members, media consumers or users). Fiske argues that polysemy is a necessary feature of a truly popular media culture since the more potential meanings there are, the greater the chance of appeal to different audiences and to different social categories within the total audience. Polysemy can also be problematic for those who intend to convey a very specific kind of meaning with their work, such as journalists (or the politicians and businesspeople acting as news sources). For media professionals, genres, formats and frames can therefore be considered to be ways in which to reduce the inherently polysemic nature of text.

Multiplicity of textual meaning has an additional dimension, as Newcomb (1991) reminds us. Texts are constituted of many different languages and systems of meaning. These include codes of dress, physical appearance, class and occupation, religion, ethnicity, region, social circles and many more. Any words in a spoken language or interactions in a drama can have different meanings in relation to any or several of these other languages.

## DIFFERENTIAL ENCODING AND DECODING AGAIN

Despite this polysemic character, the discourses of particular examples of media content are often designed or inclined to control, confine or direct the taking of meaning – in part through the conventions and shared narratives of recognizable genres, formats and frames – which may in turn be resisted by the reader. This discussion relates to Hall's (1974/1980) model of *encoding/decoding* (discussed in Chapter 3), according to which there is usually a *preferred reading* encoded in a text – the meaning that the message producer would like the receiver to take. On the whole, it is the 'preferred readings' that are identified by analysis of overt content – the literal or surface meaning plus the ideology. One aspect of this relates to the notion of the '**inscribed reader**' (Sparks and Campbell, 1987). Particular media content can be said, in line with the theory of Bourdieu (1986), to 'construct' a reader, a construction that can to some extent be 'read back' by an analyst on the basis of the set of concerns in the text as written. The 'inscribed reader' is also the kind of reader who is primarily *addressed* by a message. A similar concept is that of the 'implied audience' (Deming, 1991) of media content.

The process by which this works has also been called *interpellation* or appellation, and usually refers back to the ideology theories of Althusser (1971). According to Fiske (1987: 53), 'interpellation refers to the way any use of discourse "hails" the addressee. In responding … we implicitly accept the discourse's definition of "us", or … we adopt the subject position proposed for us by the discourse'. This feature of discourse is widely exploited in advertising (Williamson, 1978), where advertisements commonly construct and project their image of a model consumer of the product in question. They then invite 'readers' to recognize themselves in these images. Such images normally associate certain desirable qualities (such as chicness, cleverness, youth or beauty) with using the product, and generally this is flattering to the consumer as well as to the product.

## INTERTEXTUALITY

As Fiske (1987) also reminds us, the text as produced by the reader is not confined in its meaning by the boundaries that are set on the production side between programmes or between content categories. A 'reader' of media texts can easily combine, for instance, the experience of a programme with that of advertisements inserted in it, or with adjoining programmes.

This is one aspect of the intertextuality of media, and it applies also to crossing boundaries between media (such as film, books and social media). Intertextuality is not only an accomplishment of the reader, but also a feature of media themselves, which are continually cross-referencing from one medium to another, and the same 'message', story or character can be found in very different media forms and genres. The expansion of marketing based on media images has extended the range of intertextuality from media content 'texts' to all kinds of consumption articles. Television, according to Fiske (1987), gives rise to a 'third level of intertextuality' – referring to the texts that viewers make themselves and reproduce in conversation or in writing about the media experience. Ethnographic researchers into media audiences draw on such 'third-level' texts when they listen in on conversations or organize group discussions to hear about how the media are experienced (for example, Radway, 1984; Ang, 1985; Liebes and Katz, 1986).

*Codes* are systems of meaning whose rules and conventions are shared by members of a culture or by what has been called an 'interpretative community' (for instance, a set of fans of the same media franchise, author or performer). Codes help to provide the links between media producers and media audiences by laying the foundations for interpretation. We make sense of the world by drawing on our understanding of communicative codes and conventions. Particular gestures, expressions, forms of dress and images, for example, carry more or less unambiguous meanings within particular cultures that have been established by usage and familiarity. An example of a film code (Monaco, 1981) is an image combining a weeping woman, a pillow and money, to symbolize shame.

## OPEN VERSUS CLOSED TEXTS

In the particular discourse about media content under discussion, the content may be considered to be more or less 'open' or 'closed' in its meanings. According to Eco (1979), an open text is one whose discourse does not try to constrain the reader to one particular meaning or interpretation. Different kinds and actual examples of media text can be differentiated according to their degree of openness. For instance, in general, news reports are intended not to be open but to lead to a uniform informational end, while serials and soap operas are often loosely articulated and lend themselves to varied 'readings'. This differentiation is not always consistent between genres, and there can be large variations within genres in the degree of textual openness. In the case of commercial advertisements, while they are intended to achieve a long-term goal benefiting the product advertised, the form of advertisement can range from the playful and ambiguous to the one-dimensional 'hard sell' or simple announcement. It has also been argued that television in general has a more open and ambiguous text than cinema film (Ellis, 1982). When studying online communication, websites and apps, the degree of openness versus closedness is further complicated by the level and kind of interactivity afforded by the platform, design and interface (Deuze, 2003), and the extent to which the professional creator allows for a direct, indirect or sustained 'reciprocal' relationship with audiences (Lewis et al., 2014).

The distinction between open and closed texts has a potential ideological significance. In their discussion of the television portrayal of terrorism, for instance, Schlesinger, Murdock and Elliott (1983) argued that a more open portrayal also leads to alternative viewpoints, while a closed portrayal tends to reinforce the dominant or consensual view. They make another distinction between a 'tight' or a 'loose' storyline, reinforcing the tendency of the closed versus open choice. They conclude that television news is in general both closed and tight, while documentary and fiction are more variable. They observe that, in the case of fiction, the larger the (expected) audience, the more closed and tighter the representation of terrorism, thus converging on the 'official' picture of reality as portrayed on the news. This suggests some form of ideological control (probably self-censorship), with risks not being taken with a mass audience. A similar observation can be made regarding the extent to which media professionals co-create with their audiences, for example in 'participatory journalism' genres in the news industry (Singer et al., 2011), 'upstream marketing' processes in advertising and marketing communication, or simply when musicians solicit engagement from their fans (Baym, 2018). These are all instances where media professionals relinquish some control over the creative process, which tends to be a sensitive issue among makers, and a source of both excitement and frustration among audiences. The newer media environment has made choices about open versus closed types of creativity, storytelling and narrative more fluid and dynamic. It is as yet unclear whether all of this in fact enhances the potential for ideological control on the part of media industries, or whether this may contribute to more 'collective intelligence' among professionals and what Jay Rosen (2006) describes as 'The People Formerly Known as the Audience'.

## SERIALITY

There is a continuing interest in narrative theory (Oltean, 1993), originally as a result of the great attention given to television drama, serials and series in media studies (for example, Seiter, Borchers and Warth, 1989), in a contemporary context because of developments in multi-platform storytelling and 'world building' efforts by media corporations in order to keep a franchise going and to sustain audience interest. The topic of seriality occupies a central place in narrative theory when it comes to media, focusing on the gradual unfolding and 'serially repetitive forms' of a story across novels, films, seasons of a television show, and across multiple media properties in a crossmedia/transmedia production or franchise.

Narrative theory itself owes much to the work of Propp (1968), who uncovered the basic similarity of narrative structure in Russian folktales. Modern popular media fiction also testifies to the high degree of constancy and similarity of a basic plot. For instance, Radway (1984) described the basic narrative logic of mass-produced romance stories for women in terms of a series of stages (see Figure 13.2). It starts with a disturbance for the heroine, through an antagonistic encounter with an aristocratic male, by way of a separation, to a reconciliation and a sexual union, concluding with a restoration of identity for the heroine.

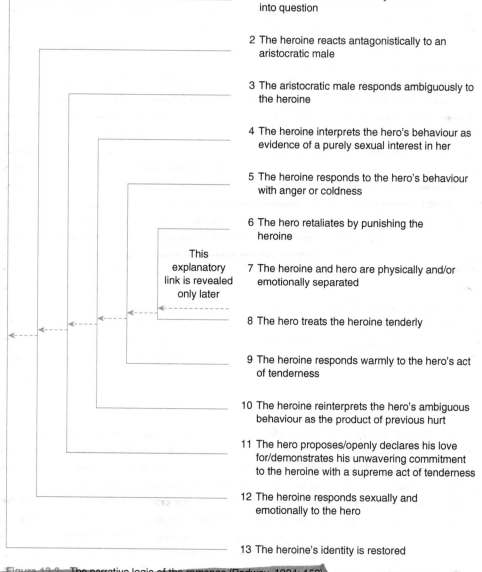

1 The heroine's social identity is thrown into question

2 The heroine reacts antagonistically to an aristocratic male

3 The aristocratic male responds ambiguously to the heroine

4 The heroine interprets the hero's behaviour as evidence of a purely sexual interest in her

5 The heroine responds to the hero's behaviour with anger or coldness

6 The hero retaliates by punishing the heroine

This explanatory link is revealed only later

7 The heroine and hero are physically and/or emotionally separated

8 The hero treats the heroine tenderly

9 The heroine responds warmly to the hero's act of tenderness

10 The heroine reinterprets the hero's ambiguous behaviour as the product of previous hurt

11 The hero proposes/openly declares his love for/demonstrates his unwavering commitment to the heroine with a supreme act of tenderness

12 The heroine responds sexually and emotionally to the hero

13 The heroine's identity is restored

Figure 13.2   The narrative logic of the romance (Radway, 1984: 150)

While basic plots can be found in many different genres, with a range of established but familiar variations, there are other narrative differences to note. Television *series* can, for instance, be clearly differentiated from *serials*, using narrative theory. The series consists of a set of discrete stories that are terminated in each episode. In the case of serials, the story continues without end from one episode to the next. In both cases,

MCQUAIL'S MEDIA AND MASS COMMUNICATION THEORY
CONTENT

there is continuity, primarily achieved by retaining the same principal characters. However, there is a difference. In series, the heroes and heroines (subjects) remain constant, while the villains (objects) differ from one episode to another. The same characters go through different narrative sequences in the same settings. In between episodes, as Oltean (1993) remarks, 'the marionettes stay put in a cabin placed outside the fictional reality'. By contrast, with serials (such as normal soap operas, which in their original form were broadcast daily) the same cast of characters appears each time, and an illusion is fostered that they continue their life actively between episodes. They 'remain fictively active'.

Another aspect of narrative underlined by Oltean is the difference between 'linear' and 'parallel' processing. In serials, there is a transition from one storyline to the next, while in series there is a 'meta-story' (concerning the permanent characters), with several different storylines as they encounter their new adventures week by week. The series organizes stories according to a principle of linearity, while serials (such as soap operas) prefer parallel processing with a network of concurrent storylines involving different subgroups of the permanent cast of characters interacting and interweaving on varying time scales.

As corporations invest heavily in media franchises, seriality in today's media environment sometimes gets a distinct intertextual character, where, for example, the same actress plays key roles in multiple franchises, when a game character appears in different games (often made by different studios), or when a certain piece of music can be a song on an album, a tune associated with a brand and a significant part of what makes a film memorable. Furthermore, seriality does not just occur within a franchise or when a character migrates across multiple media texts. It can also be identified when the dramatic strategies of one genre – for example, the soap opera – are used to build and sustain narrative development in another format – such as a police procedural (Mittell, 2006). Traditionally, seriality is investigated using insights from literature and television analysis. More recently, new elements of seriality have been documented in the ways people tell and share stories on social media (Page, 2013), and how digital games are serialized in terms of both production process and narrative building blocks (Denson and Jahn-Sudmann, 2013). As Page (2013: 50) notes, perceptions of seriality are not determined by the properties of a text, and depend on context in order to be recognized as such, suggesting that 'the experience of seriality is rooted in wider cultural concerns'.

## REALISM

Narrative often depends on assumptions about realism and helps to reinforce a sense of reality, by invoking the logic, normality and predictability of human behaviour. The conventions of realistic fiction were established by the early forms of the novel, although they were preceded by realism in other arts. On the one hand, realism of media depends on a certain attitude – that what is portrayed is 'true to life', if not literally true in the sense of having actually occurred. Realistic fiction depends on the belief that it *could* occur or might have done so. Even fantastic stories can be made realistic if they use actual settings and social backgrounds and gain verisimilitude from applying plausible logics of action. In fact, realism is not a simple concept. Research by Hall (2003), based on an exploration of audience evaluations, indicates that there are a number of dimensions. She identifies six of these under the following headings: plausibility, perceptual persuasiveness, typicality, factuality, emotional involvement and narrative consistency. She concludes that different genres require different concepts of realism.

There are techniques of writing and filming that emphasize realism. In the former case, accurate documentary-like descriptions and concrete, logical and sequential story-telling achieve this result. In filming, aside from representing real places, a continuous flow of action serves to create a realistic illusion. Sometimes black and white film stock is inserted (for instance, in flashbacks) to indicate that scenes have a real or documentary character. There are also classic realistic stylistic devices (Monaco, 1981). One of these is the 'shot, reverse shot', which moves the camera from one speaker to a partner in a dialogue to create the illusion for the spectator of involvement in the ongoing conversation (Fiske, 1987).

Film and television can also employ in fiction the 'documentary' mode or style, which is established on the basis of learned conventions. In general, documentary style relies on real places and social settings to create the illusion of actuality. According to Fiske (1987), media realism leads in a 'reactionary' (rather than a radical) direction because it 'naturalizes' the status quo, making it seem normal and therefore inevitable. In the terms used above, realism goes in the direction of 'closure', since the more real the portrayal seems, the more difficult it is for the reader, who is likely to take the reality of the world for granted, to establish any alternative meanings. This relates back to Schlesinger et al.'s (1983) evidence about differing degrees of openness and closure in news and fiction.

In media-saturated societies, the issue of realism has become one of what Gunn Enli (2015) calls 'mediated authenticity': the idea that our understanding of society is based on mediated representations of reality. Being authentic in media is not necessarily about being truthful, but becomes much more of a performance, using rhetorical strategies such as predictability, immediacy, (staged) spontaneity, confessions, ordinariness, ambivalence and imperfection (or amateurism). Enli argues that mediated authenticity is established through negotiations between producers and audiences, and that solving 'authenticity puzzles' – separating the fake from the real – has become an inherent practice in the context of the contemporary media environment. It is not that media until the advent of online, mobile and social media were more realistic, according to Enli, but that the 'authenticity contract' between audiences and the media generally remained more or less intact.

# GENDERED MEDIA TEXTS

The concept of an inscribed (written into) or interpellated reader can be used to analyse the audience image sought by particular media, in terms of class, cultural taste, age or lifestyle. Many kinds of media content, following the same line of argument, are differentially gendered. They have a built-in bias towards the supposed characteristics of one or other gender, presumably for reasons of appealing to a chosen audience, or simply because many language codes are innately gendered. Gender is but one way in which texts are constructed in particular ways to appeal or uniquely make sense to specific groups, and today's online media system makes it possible to micro-target messages to an almost individual level.

A number of writers (for example, Geraghty, 1991) have argued that the soap opera as a genre is intrinsically 'gendered' as female narrative, by way of its characterizations, settings and dialogue, and the positioning of male and female roles. Modleski (1982) suggested that the loose structure of the typical soap opera matches the fragmented pattern of the housewife's daily work. By contrast, television action serials and superhero media franchises can often be said to be gendered in a masculine way (Johnson, 2011). Some of the differences (as with advertising) are certainly caused by simply planning to appeal to different audience groups, following conventional and often stereotyped ideas about male–female differences. Mass-produced romances of the kind described by Radway (1984) are clearly 'gendered' from the start and are mostly written by women as well as being openly for women. However, this is not likely to be the whole explanation, and 'gendering' can take subtle and not always intended forms, which makes the pursuit of the topic worthwhile.

For example, a study of female and male film directors by Patsy Winsor, reported by Real (1989), showed a number of significant differences in the content of popular films made by men and women. Female film directors were noticeably less inclined to include acts of physical aggression or to associate them so strongly with men. They showed women in more active roles, and in several different and less predictable ways produced distinctive texts. The study concluded that, notwithstanding the constraints of popular filmmaking, there was some evidence of the emergence of a 'women's aesthetic'. There is other evidence that the gender of producers can affect the outcome, although there are more powerful organizational factors at work. For instance, Lanzen, Dozier and Horan (2008) analysed a sample of US prime-time network shows and found the usual tendency to gender stereotyping, but those with one or more female writers/creators were more likely to include male characters in interpersonal roles compared to all-male production teams. A recent pattern analysis of over 80,000 news items on the Israeli–Palestinian conflict and the conflict in the Democratic Republic of the Congo shows how women journalists emphasize slightly different styles than their male counterparts (Baden and Tenenboim-Weinblatt, 2018). While women were found to emphasize precision and professional distance, men tended to focus more on certitude and providing orientation – an overall subtle difference most likely the result of gendered reporting styles and professional socialization.

The approach to content, which has been reviewed under the heading of 'cultural text', has seemed suited to the study of popular mass entertainment, especially fictional and dramatic forms, which seek to involve the reader in fantasy but usually in realistic settings. The aim of such media content is not to convey any specific meaning but simply to provide 'entertainment', taking people out of themselves and into other worlds of the imagination, caught up in dramatic actions and emotions. The texts employed for this purpose tend to be relatively 'open' and do not have to work hard at the cognitive level. As television and film production becomes more complex, both in terms of global production networks and narrative development, and audiences more diffuse, media content becomes more richly layered with meaning. Research in this area continues to shed light on the tension between the postulate of *polysemy* and the view that texts are structured in certain ways to achieve their audience and their intended effect.

---

**13.5**

**The cultural text approach**

- Texts are jointly produced with their readers
- Texts are differentially encoded
- Texts are 'polysemic', i.e. have many potential meanings
- Texts are related to other texts (intertextuality)
- Texts employ different narrative forms
- Texts are gendered

---

## CONCLUSION

Generalization about the content of mass media has become progressively more difficult as the media have expanded and diversified and multimedia forms have come to predominate. Established genres have multiplied and mutated. Our capacity to analyse and understand how texts work is constantly trying to keep in pace with the variety of output of even conventional media, let alone of online, mobile and social media. We still have to live with the challenge that has always faced us, of where 'meaning' can be found, as well as with new challenges regarding the 'authenticity puzzle' (Enli, 2015) of the media.

Despite challenges and complexities, it is still possible and rewarding to analyse content if we have a clearly defined purpose in mind, a viable method and an awareness of pitfalls and opportunities. At the heart of the approaches outlined here is the notion that content always communicates: about (and to) the intentions of producers, the perceptions of receivers, and about the text itself (in relation to other, similar or different, texts). Media content tells us something about media context, and the deeper meanings and structures found through the analyses of genre, frames, format and text help us to understand how meaning gets made – possibly more so than what that meaning is.

## FURTHER READING

Enli, G. (2015) *Mediated Authenticity: How the Media Constructs Reality.* New York: Peter Lang.

Hancox, D. (2017) 'From subject to collaborator: transmedia storytelling and social research', *Convergence*, 23(1): 49–60.

Jenkins, H. (2006) *Convergence Culture: Where Old and New Media Collide.* New York: New York University Press.

Mittell, J. (2011) 'A cultural approach to TV genre theory', *Cinema Journal*, 40(3): 3–24.

Page, R. (2013) 'Seriality and storytelling in social media', *Storyworlds: A Journal of Narrative Studies*, 5: 31–54.

Radway, J. (1984) *Reading the Romance.* Chapel Hill, NC: University of North Carolina Press.

# PART 6
## AUDIENCES

# 14

---

# AUDIENCE THEORY AND RESEARCH TRADITIONS

What is an audience? It seems such a straightforward question, but disputes about the audience run across the field of media and mass communication research. The audience is first and foremost an industry construct – considering how media organizations and professionals engage in 'audiencemaking' (Ettema and Whitney, 1994) in order to regulate and streamline the division of consumers into markets to be targeted and sold to advertisers, sponsors and other clients. On the other hand, in today's media-saturated context we are all 'audiencing' (Fiske, 1992), as paying attention to and making sense of media 'has become a vital mode of engaging with the world' (Livingstone, 2013: 22). In industry-focused research, the audience has a crucial status, as in the dual product market for the media audiences are both customer and product. In studies focused on media effects and the various ways in which people give meaning to the media they use, audiences are a significant element of the mass communication process involving production, content and reception of mediated messages. And, interestingly, audiences have also all but disappeared from the literature, in part because audiences are theorized as powerless vis-à-vis the multinational corporations that supply the majority of news, information, advertising and entertainment on the planet (Turow and Draper, 2014), or because audiences are seen as 'active', 'participatory' (Carpentier, 2016) and increasingly 'reflexive' (Sender, 2015) to the extent that their meaning-making processes can be understood as almost completely autonomous from the media they consume.

It must be clear, then, that audiences are both an essential and a contested part of media and mass communication research. In this chapter, we will unpack this rich history and debate in light of contemporary developments in the field, while acknowledging the argument that the 'field' of audience theory and research has become almost impossible to locate and define given the multi-sited, fragmented and networked ways in which people engage with media today (Cavalcante, Press and Sender, 2017: 7). The chapter begins with a discussion of the origins of the audience concept, which has a number of different meanings and manifestations. Different types of audience are identified. The main issues that have guided audience theory are explained and the purposes of audience research outlined. A typology of audiences is proposed as a framework of analysis. The question of relations between media communicators and their audiences, actual or imagined, is addressed. The chapter continues with a discussion of various measures of media reach and concludes with an assessment of ideas about audience selectivity and different types and degrees of activity.

## THE AUDIENCE CONCEPT

The word 'audience' is very familiar as the collective term for the 'receivers' in the simple sequential model of the mass communication process (source, channel, message, receiver, effect) that was deployed by pioneers in the field of media research (for example, see Schramm, 1955). The audience generally tends to be considered at the end of Lasswell's

(1948) linear process of communication, expressed as 'who says what through which channel to whom with what effect?'. That said, the concept of the audience is enjoying renewed interest, inspired by research consistently showing the empirical fallacy of many assumptions about what audience are, how they behave, and the 'effects' mass media have on audiences. The audience concept is also undergoing new scrutiny because of the persistence of such assumptions about how people are potentially (and massively) duped by 'fake news' and other types of disinformation.

The audience is a term that is understood by media practitioners as well as theorists and is recognized by media users as an unambiguous description of themselves. Nevertheless, beyond common-sense usage, there is much room for differences of meaning and theoretical disputes. These stem mainly from the fact that a single word is being applied to a diverse and complex reality, open to alternative and competing formulations. It has been suggested that 'what is occurring is the breakdown of the *referent* for the word audience in communication research from both the humanities and the social sciences' (Biocca, 1988a: 103). In other words, we keep the familiar word, but the thing itself is disappearing.

To start with, the audience concept implies an attentive, receptive but relatively passive set of listeners or spectators assembled in a more or less public setting. The actual reception of mass media is a varied and messy experience with little regularity and does not match this version. This is especially so in a time of mobility, individualization and multiplicity of media usage. Secondly, the rise of new media has introduced entirely new forms of behaviour, involving interactivity and searching rather than watching or listening. Thirdly, the line between the producers and audiences has become blurred under conditions of convergence culture (Jenkins, 2006; see Chapter 11).

Audiences are both a product of social, cultural and geographical context (which leads to shared language, narratives, interests, understandings and information needs) and a response to a particular pattern of media provision (Taneja and Webster, 2016: 178). Often they are both at the same time, as when a medium sets out to appeal to the members of a social category or the residents of a certain place. Media use also reflects broader patterns of time use, availability, lifestyle and everyday routines.

An audience can thus be defined in different and overlapping ways: by *place* (as in the case of local media, or when people are part of 'audience networks' defined by geographical proximity); by *people* (as when a medium is characterized by an appeal to a certain age group, gender, political belief or income category); by the particular type of *medium* or *channel* involved (technology and organization combined); by the *content* of its messages (genres, subject matter, styles); and by *time* (as when one speaks of the 'daytime' or 'primetime' audience, or an audience that is fleeting and short-term compared with one that endures).

There are other ways of characterizing the different kinds of audience that have emerged with changing media and changing times. Nightingale (2003) offers a typology that captures key features of the diversity, proposing four types as follows:

- *Audience as 'the people assembled'.* Essentially the aggregate measured as paying attention to a given media presentation or product at a given time. These are the known 'spectators'.
- *Audience as 'the people addressed'.* Referring to the group of people imagined by the communicator and for whom content is shaped. This is otherwise known as the 'inscribed' or 'interpellated' audience.
- *Audience as 'happening'.* The experience of reception alone or with others as an interactive event in daily life, contextualized by place and other features.
- *Audience as 'hearing' or 'audition'.* Essentially refers to the participatory audience experience, when the audience is embedded in a show or is enabled to participate by remote means or to provide a response at the same time.

There are other possibilities for defining a distinctive kind of audience, depending on the medium concerned, the activity under investigation, and the perspective adopted. Online and mobile media provide for a variety of communicative relations that do not always neatly fit the typologies created for mass communication. Among the key challenges of contemporary audience theories and definitions are the ubiquity of media (leading to a 'high choice' media environment), the multi-sited and global spread of media options, and audiences becoming increasingly media-literate, critical and reflexive. Audiences are increasingly drawn into the production process of media industries too, which further complicates their existence as more or less 'passive' readers, viewers, listener or users. Correspondingly, as Napoli (2011, 2012) notes, relatively straightforward measuring and valuing audiences merely on the basis of their exposure to media content is making way for more complex ways of measuring and valuing audiences on the basis of their 'engagement' with the content.

A fundamental debate regarding the notion of 'audience' concerns on the one hand its existence as (a group, network or community of) individuals using, responding and giving meaning to mediated messages, and on the other hand the engagement of people interacting with an open text (incorporating any kind of medium or channel). The first perspective warrants research into media effects, while the second emphasizes various processes of interpretation, struggle and resistance.

## THE ORIGINAL AUDIENCE

The early origins of today's media industry conceptualization of a more or less 'engaged' audience lie in public theatrical and musical performances as well as in the games and spectacles of ancient times. Our earliest notions of audience are of a physical gathering in a certain place. A Greek or Roman city, for example, would have a theatre or arena, and it was no doubt preceded by less formal gatherings for similar events and for religious or state occasions. The original audience had many features that are familiar today in other areas of public performance, including those listed in Box 14.1.

## 14.1

### Characteristics of the original audience

- Planning and *organization* of viewing and listening as well as of the performances themselves
- Events with a *public* and 'popular' character (with no formal initiation necessary)
- *Secular* (thus not religious) content of performance — for entertainment, education and vicarious emotional experience
- *Voluntary*, individual acts of choice and attention
- *Specialization of roles* of authors, performers and spectators
- Physical *locatedness* of performance and spectator experience

The audience as a set of spectators for public events of a secular kind was thus already institutionalized more than 2000 years ago, across all continents. It had its own customs, rules and expectations about the time, place and content of performances, conditions for admission, and so forth. It was typically an urban phenomenon, often with a commercial basis, and content varied according to social class and status. Because of its public character, audience behaviour was subject to surveillance and social control.

The modern mass media audience shares some of these features but is also very different in some obvious ways. The audiences for mass media are much more diverse, in terms of the content available and the social behaviour involved. There is generally no element of public assembly, although one could argue that the mass use of smartphones to record and share the experience of attending public events such as weddings and concerts is a form of public assembly uniquely tied to mobile media use. The audience remains in a state of continuous existence, as well as re-forming occasionally for specific performances (consider, for example, the simultaneous release of all episodes of a season of a television serial). The mass media audience attracts a supply of content to keep it satisfied instead of re-forming in response to some periodic performance of interest – with the exception of live sports, which therefore command the highest costs to secure for broadcast organizations. In several linguistic cultures other than English, the term 'public' is conventionally used rather than 'audience', but this too has a number of similar limitations, including the fact that much media use is not at all public in the primary meaning of this term.

# FROM MASS TO MARKET

Although many observers commented on the amazing new possibilities for reaching so many disparate people so quickly by the press, film or radio, the first theoretical formulation of the media audience concept stemmed from a wider consideration of the changing nature of social life in modern society. Herbert Blumer (1939) first provided an explicit framework in which the audience could be exemplified as a new form of collectivity made possible by the conditions of modern societies. He called this phenomenon a 'mass' and differentiated it from older social forms – especially the group, the crowd and the public (see Chapter 3).

The mass audience was large, heterogeneous and widely dispersed, and its members did not and could not know each other. This view of the mass audience is less a description of reality than an accentuation of features typical of conditions of mass production and distribution of news and entertainment. When used by early commentators, the term generally had a pejorative connotation, reflecting a negative view of popular taste and mass culture.

## REDISCOVERY OF THE AUDIENCE AS A GROUP

The inadequacy of this concept of audience has long been apparent. The reality of people's experience of mass print and film was always very diverse. While impersonality, anonymity and vastness of scale might describe the phenomenon in general, much actual audience experience is personal, small-scale and integrated into social life and familiar ways. Many media operate in local environments and are embedded in local cultures. Since most people make their own media choices freely, they do not typically feel manipulated by remote powers. The social interaction that develops around media use helps people to incorporate it into everyday life as a friendly rather than an alienating presence.

At an early point in the history of media research, actual audiences were shown to consist of many overlapping networks of social relations based on locality and common interests, and the 'mass' media were incorporated into these networks in different ways (Delia, 1987). The communal and social group character of audiences was restored to conceptual prominence (for example, Merton, 1949; Janowitz, 1952; Katz and Lazarsfeld, 1955). Critical thinkers (for instance, Gitlin, 1978) objected that this supposed protection of the individual from manipulation was in itself an ideological move to obscure the much more typical vulnerability of the individual in the mass, and to allay fears of mass society. The notion of audiences as 'collectivities' next to others – such as the nation, or related to various aspects of social identity – is important, Livingstone (2013: 27) notes, as collectivities 'are planned for, designed into, regulated and anticipated by sociotechnical environments. Thus, they have a particular if often unpredictable power'.

## AUDIENCE AS MARKET

The press and film were already established as very profitable businesses when broadcasting made its uncertain appearance on the scene in the 1920s. The radio and television audience rapidly developed into an important consumer market for hardware and software. At first sight, the widely used expression 'media market' seems to offer a more objective alternative to other, more value-laden terms to describe the audience phenomenon. As the media have become bigger business, the term 'market' has gained in currency. It can designate regions served by media, social-demographic categories, or the actual or potential consumers of particular media services or products. It may be defined as an aggregate of consumers of media services and products, with a known socio-economic profile, and in the current data-driven digital economy can even be scrutinized on an almost individual level.

While the market concept is a pragmatic and necessary one for media industries and for analysing media management and economics, it is also problematic and not exactly value-free. It treats an audience as a set of consumers rather than as a group or public. It links sender and receiver in a 'calculative' rather than normative or social relationship, as a cash transaction between producer and consumer rather than a communication relationship. It ignores the internal social relations between individuals since these are of little interest to service providers. It privileges socio-economic criteria and focuses on media *consumption* rather than reception.

The significance of audience experience for the wider public sphere tends to be de-emphasized in market thinking. Originally, the quality of the audience experience did not really factor into much market thinking. The view of audience as market is inevitably the view 'from the media' (especially of their owners and managers), and within the terms of the media industries' discourse. People in audiences do not normally have any awareness of themselves as belonging to markets, and the market discourse in relation to the audience is implicitly manipulative.

In an innovative and sophisticated move, Dallas Smythe (1977) gave birth to the theory that audiences actually *work* for advertisers (thus, for their ultimate oppressors). They do so by giving their free time to watch media, with this labour then packaged and sold by the media to advertisers as a new kind of 'commodity'. The whole system of commercial television and the press rests on this extraction of surplus value from an economically exploited audience. The same audience has to pay yet again for its media, by way of the extra cost added to the advertised goods. It was an ingenious and convincing piece of theorizing which revealed the mass audience phenomenon in quite a new light (see Jhally and Livant, 1986). It is plausible to suppose that the media need their audiences more than audiences need their media, and there is also reason to view audience research as primarily a tool for the close control and management (call it manipulation) of media audiences.

Audiences are providing free labour for media corporations (and advertisers) is a theory that has gained much currency in the newer media environment, especially in the context of the media's use of 'user-generated content' and the many variations of reality television since the late 1990s and early 2000s (such as *Survivor*, *Big Brother* and *Idols*; see Andrejevic, 2002). With specific reference to online social media, Terranova (2004) considers how the free labour of the audience is both enjoyed and exploited. Audiences are not without agency in this context, even though their voluntary work contributes to corporate profits. This line of argument is, in some respects, particularly applicable to the Internet-based media that are almost entirely financed by advertising and also (perhaps for that reason) require a good deal more 'work' from their users than simply attending to advertisements. A new political-economic interpretation along these lines has been provided by Fuchs (2009). However, Dallas Smythe's argument has also been questioned by Bermejo (2009), mainly on the grounds that it is not very clear just what is being produced and sold. It is not the attention and time of an audience in a conventional sense. Essentially, this had first to be converted into 'ratings', based on time spent. However, the same time-based ratings system does not apply to the Internet, and media companies as well as advertisers are increasingly more interested in 'engagement' rather than (or next to) time spent.

With respect to television, the media industry transforms the actual television audience into a piece of commercial information called 'ratings' (Ang, 1991). Ratings are described as forming 'the basis for the agreed-upon standard by which advertisers and networks buy and sell the audience commodity' (ibid.: 54). Ang reminds us that 'watching television is an ongoing, day-to-day cultural practice engaged in by millions of people' and that the 'ratings discourse' serves to 'capture and encompass the viewing practice of all these people in a singular, objectified, streamlined construct of "television audience"' (ibid.). These comments essentially label the industry view of the audience as intrinsically dehumanizing and exploitative. Again, it reflects the view that commercial mass media are served by their audiences rather than vice versa.

Ang (1991) argued that media institutions have no real interest in *knowing* their audiences, only in being able to prove they exist by way of systems and techniques of measurement (generally based on a limited sample of people statistically representing the target audience) which convince their clients but which can never begin to capture the true essence of 'audiencehood'. Much the same critique applies to the Internet, where ratings are also pursued assiduously as clicks and hits (referring to the keyboard actions of users), albeit in new and even more detailed terms. We should not over-emphasize the supposed effectiveness of audience measurement in a digital context; as Press and Livingstone (2006: 186) write, 'filling in a survey to record an evening's viewing is tricky, but by no means as tricky as recording and interpreting an evening's surfing or chat'.

The main theoretical features of the audience as market are reviewed in Box 14.2.

## 14.2
## The audience as a market: main theoretical features

- Audiences are aggregates of many potential or actual consumers
- Members are unrelated to each other and have no shared identity of their own
- Boundaries assigned to audiences are based mainly on socio-economic criteria
- Audiences are objects of management and control by media providers
- The formation is temporary
- Public significance is subordinate
- Relations of audience with media are mutually calculative, not moral

## GOALS OF AUDIENCE RESEARCH

Since the audience has always been a contested category, it is not surprising that the purposes of doing research into audiences are varied and often inconsistent. Reviewing the history of audience research – or the lack thereof – Sonia Livingstone (2015: 440) remarks how audiences in research tend to be implied rather than actively studied, as they are lurking 'behind a host of homogenizing nouns (market, public, users, citizens, and people) and nominalized verbs (diffusion, adoption, culture, practice, mediation, identity, and change) that mask their agency, diversity, life contexts, and interests at stake'. Livingstone further notes, along with Parameswaran (2013), a pressing need to consider audiences transnationally, multiculturally and historically contingent with a specific place and time.

Audience research from both social scientific and humanist perspectives shares the general characteristic that it helps to 'construct', 'locate' or 'identify' an otherwise amorphous, shifting or unknowable social entity (Allor, 1988). But the methods used, the constructions of the audience arrived at, and the uses to which they are put all diverge considerably. Leaving aside the purpose of theory building, we can classify research goals in terms of the main uses to which information about the audience can be put. These are shown in Box 14.3.

Perhaps the most fundamental division of purpose is that between media industry goals and those that take the perspective and 'side' of the audience. Research can, as it were, represent the voice of the audience, or speak on its behalf. Although it is not at all certain that audience research can ever truly serve the audience alone, we can provisionally view the different purposes of research as extending along a dimension ranging from audience control to audience autonomy. This division approximates to that shown in Box 14.3. Eastman (1998) has sketched the history of audience research as a permanent tug-of-war between the media industry seeking to manage audience behaviour and people seeking to satisfy their media needs.

By far the greatest quantity of audience research belongs at the control end of the spectrum, since this is what the industry wants and pays for (Beniger, 1986; Eastman, 1998). Few of the results of industry research appear in the public domain, and they are consequently neglected in academic accounts of the audience.

Curiously enough scholarly research on the audience historically has made little or no impact on the media industry. Despite this overall imbalance and general disconnection of research effort, the clearest line of development in audience theory has been a move away from the perspective of the media communicator and towards that of the receiver. It seems as if the media industry has also accepted this as a pragmatic trend as a result of the steadily increasing competition for audience attention, and considering its own shifting needs towards engaging (and thereby necessitating understanding) audiences. Accounts of audience research have increasingly tended to emphasize the 'rediscovery' of people and user agency, in the sense of recognizing that the initiative for choice, interpretation, participation and response lies primarily much more with receivers than with senders, and with the notion of an active and obstinate audience in the face of attempted direction or outright manipulation. The preferences of audiences are still the driving forces of media use; and studies of media reception in general, and news use in particular, are increasingly based on industry–researcher partnerships (for example, see Costera Meijer and Groot Kormelink, 2014).

## MAIN TRADITIONS OF RESEARCH

For the present purposes, it is convenient to identify three main traditions of research, under the headings 'structural', 'behavioural' and 'social-cultural'.

### THE STRUCTURAL TRADITION OF AUDIENCE MEASUREMENT

The needs of media industries gave rise to the earliest and simplest kinds of research, which were designed to obtain reliable estimates of what were otherwise unknown quantities in a 'low-choice' media environment. These were especially the size and reach of radio audiences and the 'reach' of print publications (the number of potential readers as opposed to the circulation or print run). These data were essential to management, especially for gaining paid advertising. In addition to size, it was important to know about the social composition of audiences in basic terms – the who and where of the audience. These elementary needs gave rise to an immense industry interconnected with that of advertising and market research. There is generally little or no attention paid in this tradition of research to the (im-)possibility of 'knowing' the audience, or to the critique among media scholars regarding the lack of knowledge among media professionals about their audience (Schlesinger, 1978).

### THE BEHAVIOURAL TRADITION: MEDIA EFFECTS AND MEDIA USE

Early mass communication research was mainly preoccupied with media effects, especially on children and young people and with an emphasis on potential harm. Nearly every serious effects study has also been an audience study, in which the audience is conceptualized as 'exposed' to influence or impact, whether of a persuasive, learning or behavioural kind (see Chapter 16). The typical effects model was a one-way process in which the audience was conceived as an unwitting target or a passive recipient of media stimuli. The second main type of 'behavioural' audience research was in many ways a departure from the model of direct effects. Media *use* was now central, and the audience was viewed as a more or less active and motivated set of media users/consumers, who were 'in charge' of their media experience, rather than passive 'victims'. Research focused on the origin, nature and degree of motives for choice of media and media content. Audiences were also permitted to provide the definitions of their own behaviour (see Blumler and Katz, 1974). The 'uses and gratifications' approach is not strictly 'behavioural' since its main emphasis is on the social origins of media gratification and on the wider social functions of media, for instance in facilitating social contact and interaction or in reducing tension and anxiety.

An emerging area of scholarly interest is a 'biological' and neuroscientific approach to media use and effects, based on psychophysiological measurement and interpretation of brain activity during specific kinds of media use (Potter and Bolls, 2012). Grounded in a critique of the limits of the strictly behaviouralist approach and based on an appreciation of the human mind and cognition as embodied, media psychophysiology attempts to understand the cognitive processes as individuals take in, process and respond to media and mediated messages. Research in this area covers two domains of measurement: nervous system activity such as skin conductance, heart rate, facial muscle responses, cortical activity and brain imaging, for example, electroencephalogram (EEG) and functional magnetic resonance imaging (fMRI); and the psychological domain consisting of mental processes (Bolls, Weber, Lang and Potter, 2019).

## THE SOCIAL-CULTURAL TRADITION AND RECEPTION ANALYSIS

The cultural studies tradition occupies a borderland between social science and the humanities. It was originally almost exclusively concerned with works of popular culture, in contrast to an early literary tradition. Especially with regards to people's online behaviour and meaning-making practices, cultural studies have provided an important corrective to audience research based on hits and clicks. The approach emphasizes media use as a reflection of a particular social-cultural context and as a process of giving meaning to cultural products and experiences in everyday life. This school of research rejects both the stimulus–response model of effects and the notion of an all-powerful text or message. It involves a view of media use as in itself a significant aspect of 'everyday life'. Media reception research emphasized the deep study of audiences as 'interpretative communities' (Lindlof, 1988). Drotner (2000) characterizes audience ethnography by three main features: it looks at a group of people rather than the media or content; it follows the group in different locations; and it stays long enough to avoid preconceptions. Reception analysis is effectively the audience research arm of modern cultural studies, rather than an independent tradition.

The main features of the culturalist (reception) tradition of audience research can be summarized as follows (though not all are exclusive to this approach):

- The media text has to be 'read' through the perceptions of its audience, which constructs meanings and pleasures from the media texts offered (and these are never fixed or predictable).
- The very process of media use and the way in which it unfolds in a particular context are central objects of interest.
- Media use is typically situation-specific and oriented to social tasks that evolve out of participation in 'interpretative communities' (Lindlof, 1988).
- Audiences for particular media genres often comprise separate 'interpretative communities' which share much the same forms of discourse and frameworks for making sense of media.
- Audiences are never passive, nor are all their members equal, since some will be more experienced or more active fans than others.
- Methods have to be 'qualitative' and deep, often ethnographic, taking account of content, act of reception and context together.

The three traditions are summarily compared in Table 14.1.

Table 14.1 Three audience research traditions compared

|  | Structural | Behavioural | Cultural |
|---|---|---|---|
| **Main aims** | Describe composition, enumerate, relate to society | Explain and predict choices, reactions, effects | Understand meaning of content received and of use in context |
| **Main data** | Social-demographic, media and time use | Motives, acts of choice, reactions | Perceptions of meaning regarding social and cultural context |
| **Main methods** | Survey and statistical analysis | Survey, experiment, mental and psychophysiological measurement | Ethnographic, qualitative, creative |

There are indications of increasing convergence in research approaches (Schrøder, 1987; Curran, 1990), especially in the combination of quantitative and qualitative methods. Large differences in underlying philosophy and conceptualization remain between the different schools, yet integrated and otherwise 'mixed method' approaches are increasingly called for, particularly in audience research, even though publications combining

MCQUAIL'S MEDIA AND MASS COMMUNICATION THEORY
AUDIENCES

different research methods and traditions are still quite rare in media and mass communication scholarship (Walter, Cody and Ball-Rokeach, 2018).

What is interesting is a growing recognition in both the social sciences – particularly in media psychophysiological research – and the humanities – considering the 'affective turn' in media and communication studies – of the human body as playing a key role in the way people use, feel about (and subsequently) make sense of and respond to media and mass communication. The assumption is that such approaches 'can potentially overcome existing dichotomies between culture and nature, between cognition and emotion, between inside and outside, and between the psychological and the social' (Lünenborg and Maier, 2018: 2).

## AUDIENCE ISSUES OF PUBLIC CONCERN

This brief review of different research approaches helps us to identify the main issues and problems that have shaped thinking and research about mass media audiences, aside from the obvious practical need to have basic information about the audience. As we will see, the transformation of a straight question about the audience into an 'issue' or a social problem normally requires the injection of some value judgements, as described in the following paragraphs.

### MEDIA USE AS ADDICTION

'Excessive' media use has often been viewed as harmful and unhealthy (especially for children), leading to addiction, dissociation from reality, reduced social contacts, diversion from education and displacement of more worthwhile activities. Television has traditionally been the most usual suspect, and before that films and comics were regarded similarly, while digital games, the Internet and social media have become the latest perpetrators. Specific media genres, such as sex and violence, are similarly singled out for concerns about addiction (see Chapter 17). Generally, media and mass communication scholarship does not offer empirical evidence to support claims about addiction – for the most part, positive effects are considered to outweigh negative ones – while acknowledging that addictive behaviours can occur for specific people in particular circumstances, within certain contexts.

### THE MASS AUDIENCE AND SOCIAL ATOMIZATION

The more an audience is viewed as an aggregate of isolated individuals rather than a social group, the more it can be considered as a mass with the associated negative features of irrationality, lack of normative self-control and vulnerability to manipulation. In a curious reversal of this fear of the mass, it has been argued that the contemporary fragmentation of the audience poses a new threat of loss of national cohesion, following the decline of central broadcasting institutions and a corresponding concern about the rise of social polarization in online communication. Approaches informed by deindividuation theory in media and mass communication research show that such fears about groups tend to be unfounded, as people in a 'mass' do not lack morality or ignore reason, but are more likely to conform to group norms and behaviours that are not necessarily 'bad' (Reicher, Spears, Postmes and Kende, 2016). Likewise, the evidence found in numerous studies regarding the existence of filter bubbles and similar issues attributed to the algorithmic underpinnings of the Internet in general, and in social media in particular, 'is scant and riddled with methodological challenges' (Moeller and Helberger, 2018: 24), and the continuing focus on 'echo chambers' in the media may be more harmful than the underlying phenomenon of (the populist politicization of) social polarization (Bruns, 2019: 117).

## AUDIENCE BEHAVIOUR AS ACTIVE OR PASSIVE

In general, active is regarded as good and passive as bad, whether for children or adults. The media are criticized for offering mindless and soporific entertainment instead of original and stimulating content. The results are found, for instance, in escapism and diversion from social participation. Alternatively, the audience is criticized for choosing the easy path. While media use is by definition somewhat inactive, it can show signs of activity by way of selectivity, motivated attention and critical response. Much has been made (especially in advertising industry) of the transition from 'lean back' to 'lean forward' media, especially in a digital and mobile context, where 'lean back' media use – as in the case of television and radio – is considered to be 'passive' compared to presumably more engaging media, such as computers, mobile devices and the Internet. Most scholarship on the matter concurs that the 'active' versus 'passive' distinction is a false dichotomy, and that the concepts do not relate to more or fewer media effects (Livingstone, 2015).

## MANIPULATION OR RESISTANCE

Early formulations of the audience viewed it as readily available as an object of manipulation and control, open to suggestion and foolish in its adulation of media celebrity. The idea of an 'obstinate' audience was an early development in audience theory. Later, reception research emphasized the fact that audiences often have social and cultural roots and supports that protect them against unwanted influence and make for autonomy in choice and response to what they receive. This does not necessarily mean that audiences always resist the information and interpretation in the mediated messages they receive; in audience research, an important nuance is to stay open to ways in which audiences can surprise, resist or contradict expectations of mass media creators and scholars alike (Livingstone, 2013: 27).

## MINORITY AUDIENCE RIGHTS

Inevitably, mass communication tends to work against the interests of small and minority audiences. An audience research project that is independent and people-centred should pay attention to the needs and interests of minorities by way of recognition and finding ways to promote their viability. In this context, minority covers a potentially wide range of factors, including gender, political dissent, locality, taste, age, ethnicity and much besides.

## TYPES OF AUDIENCE

Audiences originate both in society and in media and their contents: either people stimulate an appropriate supply of content or the media attract people to the content they offer. If we take the first view, we can consider media as responding to the needs of a national society, local community, pre-existing social group or some category of individuals that the media choose as a 'target group'. Alternatively, if we consider audiences as primarily implied, imagined and created by the media, we can see that they are often brought into being by some new technology, as with the invention of film, radio or television, or they are attracted by some additional 'channel', such as a new magazine, radio station, music or video streaming service. In this case, the audience is defined by the media source (for example, the 'television audience' or the 'users of platform X') rather than by their shared characteristics.

The media are continuously seeking to develop and hold new audiences, and in doing so they anticipate what might otherwise be a spontaneous demand, or identify potential needs and interests that have not yet surfaced. In the continual flux of media audience formation and change, the sharp distinction made at the outset is not easy to demonstrate. Over time, media provision to pre-existing social groups has become hard to distinguish from media recruitment of social categories to the content offered. Media-created needs have also become indistinguishable from 'spontaneous' needs, or both have fused inextricably. Nevertheless, the theoretical distinction between receiver- and sender-created demand is a useful one for mapping out different versions of audience that have been introduced. The distinction is set out in Figure 14.1, first of all between society- and media-created needs and secondly between the different levels at which the process operates, namely macro or micro.

The four main types that are identified in Figure 14.1 are further described in the following sections.

| | | Source | |
|---|---|---|---|
| | | Society | Media |
| Level { | Macro | Social group or public | Medium audience |
| | Micro | Gratification set | Channel or content audience |

Figure    A typology of mass media audience formation

# THE AUDIENCE AS A GROUP OR PUBLIC

Today, the most common example of a media audience, which is also in some sense a social group, is probably the readership of a local newspaper or the listener group of a community radio station. Here the audience shares at least one significant social-cultural identifying characteristic – that of shared space and membership of a residential community. Local media can contribute significantly to local awareness and sense of belonging, and while such media are in decline in some cities and communities, community media are a particularly important part of civic life around the world (Janowitz, 1952; Stamm, 1985; Howley, 2009). Local residence defines and maintains a wide range of media-relevant interests (for example, leisure, environmental, work-related, social networks, etc.) and local media advertising serves local retail trade and labour markets as well as residents of the area. Social and economic forces together reinforce the integrative role of local media. Even if a local medium goes out of business, the local community that forms its audience will persist.

Beyond the case of local media, there are other circumstances where shared characteristics, relative homogeneity and stability of composition indicate the existence of some independent and group-like qualities in the audience. Newspapers are often characterized by readerships of varying political leaning, and readers express their political identity by their choice of paper as well as finding reinforcement for their beliefs. Newspapers and magazines may respond by shaping their contents and expressing opinions accordingly.

The conditions of society that militate against the formation of audiences as groups and publics include especially totalitarian government and very high levels of commercially monopolized media. In the first case there is no autonomy for social groups; and in the second, audience members are treated as customers and consumers, but with little power in the media market to realize their diverse wants. There are some other relevant examples of audience groups and special publics. For example, the broad term 'radical' media (Downing, 2000) embraces a wide range of more or less oppositional media channels that can be considered to carry on the tradition of the early radical and party press, especially in developing countries. Many such media are 'micro-media', operating at grass-roots level, discontinuous, non-professional, sometimes persecuted or just illegal. The *samizdat* publications forbidden under communism, the opposition press in Pinochet's Chile, or the underground press of occupied Europe during the Second World War are well-known examples. The publics for such media are often small, but they are likely to be intensely committed. They usually have clear social and political goals. Less unusual and more enduring examples are provided by the many minority ethnic and linguistic publications and channels that have grown up in numerous countries to serve immigrant groups.

Newer media have opened up new opportunities for the formation of very small audiences based on many different aims and identities and with the advantage of being able to serve very dispersed groups. An important element of the online environment is that of so-called 'hyperlocal' media, defined by Metzgar, Kurpius and Rowley (2011: 774) as media operations that 'are geographically-based, community-oriented, original-news-reporting organizations indigenous to the web and intended to fill perceived gaps in coverage of an issue or region and to promote civic engagement'. These examples of audiences as more or less distinct groups suggest that the 'audience' as an overall category is far from disappearing.

## THE GRATIFICATION SET AS AUDIENCE

The term 'gratification set' is chosen to refer to multiple possibilities for audiences to form and re-form on the basis of some media-related interest, need or preference. The use of the word 'set' implies that such audiences are typically aggregates of dispersed individuals, without mutual ties. While the audience as 'public' often has a wide range of media needs and interests, and derives its unity from shared social characteristics, the 'gratification set' is identified by a particular need or type of need (which may, nevertheless, derive from social experience). To a certain degree, this type of audience has gradually supplanted the older kind of public, the result of differentiation of media production and supply to meet distinctive consumer demands. Instead of each public (whether based on place, social class, religion or party) having its own dedicated medium, many self-perceived needs have stimulated their own corresponding supply.

Temporary assemblages of audiences have gained new theoretical currency in the context of newer media, as people come together around particular issues or events online, propelled into an audience form due to the potentially rapid global spread of news and information via social media. Coinciding with a rise of 'networked individualist' communities worldwide (Quan-Haase et al., 2018; see Chapter 9), online mass audiences can form and dissipate rather quickly. Several social theorists lament this kind of temporary and seemingly non-committal collectivity, and it certainly poses interesting challenges for audience research: is a million 'likes' in the course of a few hours online an example of a mass audience? If so, what can be said about such an audience, what kind of 'audiencehood' does it entail and perform, and how do people within such an audience feel about their experience?

The 'gratification set' is not new since popular newspapers, as well as gossip, fashion and 'family' magazines, have long catered for a diverse range of specific but overlapping audience interests. More recently, the range of interests covered has widened, with each type of medium (film, book, magazine, radio, phonogram, digital games, Internet sites and platforms, streaming services, mobile applications) packaging its potential audience appeal in a variety of ways. The sets of readers/viewers/listeners/users that result from a highly differentiated and 'customized' supply are unlikely to have any sense of collective identity, despite some shared characteristics. Integrated media choice theory that considers the roles of individual predispositions as well as structures in shaping media use offers some interesting insights here, suggesting that a shared language and geographic similarities tend to draw people to specific online media (Taneja and Webster, 2016).

Of relevance here is the concept of '**taste culture**', which was coined by Herbert Gans (1979) to describe something like the audience brought into being by the media based on a convergence of interests, rather than on shared locality or social background. He defined it as 'an aggregate of similar content chosen by the same people' (in Lewis, 1981: 204). Taste cultures are less sets of people than sets of similar media products – an outcome of form, style of presentation and genre that are intended to match the lifestyle of a segment of the audience. The more this happens, the more there is likely to be a distinctive social-demographic profile of a taste culture. It is important to note that Gans' take on taste 'effectively reversed half a century of theorizing on mass culture' (Binkley, 2000: 132), as he purposefully did away with hierarchical distinctions between 'high' and 'low' culture. In media, audiences coalesce around a variety of genres and products, escaping easy classifications.

Research in the tradition of 'media uses and gratifications' has shed light on the nature of the underlying audience demands and on the way in which they are structured. The motivations expressed for choice of media content and the ways in which this content is interpreted and evaluated by the audience point to the existence of a fairly stable and consistent structure of demand. These points are taken up in Chapter 15.

## THE MEDIUM AUDIENCE

The third version of the audience concept (Figure 14.1) is the one that identifies it by the choice of a particular type of medium – as in the 'television audience' or the 'cinemagoing public'. The earliest such usage was in the expression the 'reading public' – the small minority who could and did read books when literacy was not very common (which was a period leading well into the early twentieth century). The reference is usually to those whose behaviour or self-perception identifies them as regular and attracted 'users' of the medium concerned. Perhaps until recently, this was a relatively unproblematic audience category; however, in light of the ongoing convergence and digitalization of media, the definition of what we mean by 'medium' has become rather complicated.

'Communication studies developed around the media without ever feeling the need to define them', Miconi and Serra (2019: 3444) argue. They indicate that the concern about a contemporary definition of 'medium' is far from academic, as when 'we read the newspaper on our smartphones or watch television on computer screens, we witness not only the transformation of the very nature of these media but also the emergence of a series of new problems that span from business strategies to the language of contemporary media' (ibid.: 3445). In their survey of editorial board members of prominent scholarly media and communication journals, Miconi and Serra did not find consensus on what a 'medium' is. Most respondents indicated a preference for an understanding of medium as channel or platform, opting for a 'weak' conception of media as more or less neutral instruments in the communication process, seen as mere channels that transport information (ibid.: 3457). Media theory suggests otherwise, considering the rather powerful role a medium plays in structuring relationships between senders, content and receivers in the communication process. A medium audience based on a more neutral definition of 'medium' can be considered to be nothing more than a group identified on the basis of the channel or platform of use (see the next category, 'audience as defined by channel'). One that is approached from a more theoretically binding conception of 'medium' is seen as structured and shaped in a much more fundamental way by the technological affordances and cultural contexts of particular media, which has implications for the kind of research carried out and the kind of conclusions to be drawn.

Throughout history, each medium has had to establish a new set of consumers or devotees. It is not especially problematic to locate relevant sets of people in this way, but the further characterization of these audiences is often crude and imprecise, based on broad social-demographic categories. This type of audience is close to the idea of a 'mass audience', as described above (p. 439), since it is often very large, dispersed and heterogeneous, with no internal organization or structure. It also corresponds to the general notion of a 'market' for a particular kind of consumer service. By now, most such audiences are so overlapping that there is little differentiation involved, except in terms of subjective affinity and relative frequency or intensity of use. The audience for any one mass medium is often identical to the audience for another.

The audience continues to distinguish between media according to their particular social uses and functions and according to their perceived advantages and disadvantages. Media used to have fairly distinctive images (Perse and Courtright, 1992). Research has shown that some media are substitutable for each other for certain purposes, while others have distinctive uses (Katz, Gurevitch and Haas, 1973). In a contemporary context, medium differences are less clear-cut, and distinctions are more easily established on the basis of a medium's affordances rather than its unique or exclusive characteristics. While users tend to have clear notions of what their favourite 'media' are, in practice definitions of different digital (and digitalized) media from the perspective of audiences can overlap and even differ from one person to the next, further complicating research.

Competition between different media for audience and advertising income is intense, especially online where platform companies such as Facebook and Google dominate the global market for advertising revenue. The 'medium audience' is an important concept for those who want to use the media for purposes of advertising and other campaigns, despite the lack of exclusivity. A key decision in advertising is often that concerning the 'media mix' – the division of an advertising budget between the alternatives, taking into account the characteristics of each medium, the audience it reaches and the conditions of reception. In a digital context, audiences are generally framed as much more unpredictable and autonomous than before. It is questionable whether this newfound independence translates to more power for the contemporary medium audience. Pointing to the power of media buyers in advertising to construct and trade audiences, Turow and Draper (2014: 650) argue that in such industry definitions 'the hub of power in the emerging digital environment is still not interconnected individuals but interconnected corporations that often exercise their clout by encouraging people to think they are shaping the media'.

In media economics, the issue of media *substitutability* continues to be important and often turns on the extent to which distinctive medium audiences persist (Picard, 1989). Several considerations come into play, aside from the questions of audience size and demographics. Some messages are best delivered in a domestic or family context, indicating a choice of television, while others may be individual and more *risqué*, indicating posters or magazines. Some may be appropriate in an informational context, others against a background of relaxation and entertainment. Some work best in a mobile environment, others cater to sedentary media consumption. From this perspective, the medium audience as target is chosen not only on the basis of socio-economic characteristics, but with reference to typical content carried, specific technological affordances, as well as the social-cultural associations and context of the media behaviours concerned.

## AUDIENCE AS DEFINED BY CHANNEL OR CONTENT

The identification of an audience as the readers, viewers, listeners, players or users of a *particular* book, author, film, newspaper title, television channel and programme, game, website or mobile application is relatively straightforward. It is the usage with which audience research in the 'book-keeping' tradition is most comfortable, and it seems to pose few problems of empirical measurement. There are no hidden dimensions of group relations or

MCQUAIL'S MEDIA AND MASS COMMUNICATION THEORY
AUDIENCES

consciousness to take account of, no psychological variables of motivation that need to be measured. It is the audience in this very concrete sense on which the business of the media turns most of all. For this reason, specific content or channel has usually been privileged as a basis for defining audiences, especially in industry-related research.

This 'weak' conceptualization of media and audience is also consistent with market thinking, according to which audiences are sets of consumers for particular media products. The audience consists either of paying customers or of the heads and pockets delivered to advertisers per unit of media product and charged for accordingly. It is expressed as the 'ratings' and 'engagements', the 'numbers', which are central to the media business. It provides the main criteria of success in any arena of media politics, even where profit is not involved. It is the dominant meaning of the term 'audience', the only one with immediate practical significance and clear market value. It also involves a view of the audience as a *product* of the media – the first and most apparent *effect* of any medium.

This sense of audience is a valid one, but we cannot be limited to it. There are, for instance, audiences in the sense of 'followers' or fans of television or radio serials and series, which cannot be unambiguously measured. There are also audiences for particular films, books, games, songs and also for stars, characters, writers and performers, which only accumulate over time to a significant number or proportionate reach. In addition, content is often identified by audience according to genres, usually within the boundaries of a given medium. All of these are relevant aspects of the audience experience, although they usually evade any but the most approximate measurement.

This brings us to the yet more complex question of fans and **fandom**. The term can refer to any set of extremely devoted followers of a media star or performer, performance or text (Lewis, 1992). They are usually identified by great, even obsessive attachment to their object of attraction. Often, they show a strong sense of awareness and fellow-feeling with other fans. Being a fan also involves a pattern of supplementary behaviour, in dress, speech, other media use, consumption, and so on. Fans are highly sought after by media franchises, such as Pokémon, *Star Wars*, Mario, and the Marvel Cinematic Universe, not just as loyal customers, but also as participants (in publicizing and promoting activities) and sometimes even co-creators in maintaining a profitable value chain. As fans migrate within a franchise across multiple media properties, and franchises are increasingly created in ways as to entice such migration, metrics for the multi-channel audience become an important property of media business decision-making. In media and mass communication research, studies of 'audience networks' (Taneja and Webster, 2016; Mukerjee, Majó-Vázquez and González-Bailón, 2018) address this issue, tracking audience duplication across multiple media channels. Using insights from network analysis, Ksiazek (2011) suggests an approach to such research where media outlets are considered as nodes, and the extent to which audiences migrate across these media are represented by ties, allowing audiences to be measured as they cluster around (groups of) media channels.

# QUESTIONS OF AUDIENCE REACH

The most straightforward version of the audience concept is that which underlies the 'ratings' in their various forms, yet in a digital context this concept of the audience has become increasingly complex to measure. Media providers need to know a great deal about the extent of media reach (which is at the same time a measure of audience attention), for reasons of finance or policy or for organization and planning. These concerns create a strong vested interest in the 'canonical audience' referred to by Biocca (1988b: 127). This concept derives from the theatre and cinema and refers to a physical body of identifiable and attentive 'spectators'. A belief in the existence of such an audience is essential to the routine operation of media and provides a shared goal for the media organization (Tunstall, 1971). The fact of having an audience, and the right one as well, is a necessary condition of media organizational survival and it has to be continually demonstrated.

However, this requirement is less easy to meet than it seems because of the differences between media, the different ways of defining the 'reach' of a given medium or message, and the convergence of media in the digital age. Leaving intermedia differences aside, there are at least six relevant concepts of audience reach. All of these are industry constructions of audiences that reflect 'institutional realities' (Turow and Draper, 2014: 646) as much as these concepts refer to people actually using media in specific and measurable ways:

- the *available* (or potential) audience: all with the basic skills (for example, literacy) and/or reception capability;
- the *paying* audience: those who actually pay for a media product;
- the *attentive* audience: those who actually read, watch, listen, game, or otherwise engage with content;
- the *internal* audience: those who pay attention to particular sections, types or single items of content;
- the *cumulative* audience: the overall proportion of the potential audience that is reached over a particular period of time;
- the *target* audience: that section of a potential audience singled out for reach by a particular source (for example, an advertiser).

There is also the question of listening or viewing as a primary or secondary activity, since both can and do accompany other activities, radio more so than television. Increasingly, audience reach also involves those who engage with social media while consuming content. Concurrent media consumption on multiple screens is called 'second screen' usage in industry parlance (De Meulenaere, Bleumers and Van den Broeck, 2015). Conceptually, this is perhaps not crucial, but it matters greatly for measurement. Other less conventional audiences can also be distinguished, for instance for outdoor billboards and video screens, direct mail, telephone selling campaigns, and so on. The content and uses of old media also change. The terms and definitions presented here are not fixed. However, the principles of classification remain much the same and we can adapt these to new circumstances.

The basic features of audience reach, as viewed by the would-be communicator, are shown in Figure 14.2, derived from the work of Roger Clausse (1968). Although this model was developed for the case of broadcasting, it can apply, in principle, to all mass media to cover most of the distinctions made above. The outer band represents the almost unlimited potential for the reception of broadcast messages. In effect, it equates audience with a near-universal distribution system. The second band indicates the realistic maximum limits which apply to reception. These delineate the *potential* media public, which is defined by residence in a geographical area of reception, and by possession of the necessary apparatus to receive or the means to purchase or borrow publications, phonograms, video recordings, and the like. It is also determined by the degree of literacy and possession of other necessary skills.

The third band identifies another level of media public – the *actual* audience reached by a radio or television channel or programme or any other medium. This is what is usually measured by sales, admission and subscription figures, reading surveys and audience ratings (often expressed as a percentage of the potential audience), and so on. The fourth and the central band relate to the *quality* of attention, degree of impact and potential effect, some of which are empirically measurable. In practice, only a small fragment of the total *actual* audience behaviour can ever be measured and the rest is extrapolation, estimate or guesswork.

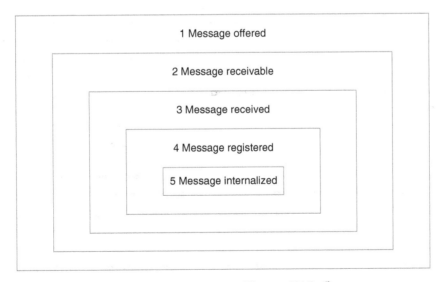

Figure 14.2   A schema of differential audience reach (Clausse, 1968)

From the point of view of the communicator, Figure 14.2 shows that there is a high degree of 'wastage' in mass communication, although this may not carry much extra cost. The question of differential reach and impact of mass media is of more than theoretical interest since it has to be taken into account in planning communication, especially in campaigns for commercial, political or informational ends. Most campaigns operate with a notion of a 'target group' (of voters, consumers, and the like) that becomes the audience a campaign tries to reach. In the newer media environment, campaigns and promotions also involve strategies whereby such a target group is not an audience, but rather a smaller subset of prominent media users or 'influencers' (operating on social media and video-sharing platforms) who are expected to pass on and publicize the product or service being brought to market.

# ACTIVITY AND SELECTIVITY

Research into audience selectivity was originally stimulated by fears about the effects of mass communication. Critics of mass culture feared that a large and *passive* audience would be exploited and culturally harmed and that passive and unselective attention, especially by children, should be discouraged. In addition, the media, especially television, were thought to encourage passivity in children and adults alike (for example, Himmelweit, Vince and Oppenheim, 1958; Schramm, Lyle and Parker, 1961). Similar concerns were voiced before about children and radio (Eisenberg, 1936), as well as book reading before that.

A distinction has been made between 'ritualized' and 'instrumental' patterns of use (Rubin, 1984). The former refers to habitual and frequent viewing by people with a strong affinity with the medium. Instrumental use is purposeful and selective, and thus more likely to qualify as active. Use of other media, especially radio, music and newspapers, can be similarly patterned. This version of the activity concept seems to imply that more active users are more sparing with their time.

The whole issue has also been defined in a normative way, with passivity as harmful, and active use of media as good. There are significant industry interests at stake, since too much audience activity can be interpreted as trouble for those who seek to control the audience by manipulation of programming and by exploiting the routine character of much media use (Eastman, 1998). As elaborated earlier, all-too-easy distinctions between 'active' and 'passive' media use do not hold, particularly in light of theoretical developments on people's cognitive processing of mediated information and the myriad ways of giving meaning to their media use. Contemporary empirical work on audience activities considers our 'audiencing' as a 'movement, flow, and process' (Markham, 2013: 438) rather than a relatively static object of study, and sees any particular media use as resisting simple categorization.

MCQUAIL'S MEDIA AND MASS COMMUNICATION THEORY
AUDIENCES

Biocca (1988a) has reviewed the different meanings and concepts of *audience activity*, proposing five different versions that are to be found in the literature, as follows:

- *Selectivity*. The extent to which choice and discrimination are exercised in relation to media and content within media. This is mainly likely to show up in evidence of planning of media use and in consistent patterns of choice (including buying, renting or borrowing films or books).
- *Utilitarianism*. Here the audience is the 'embodiment of the self-interested consumer'. Media consumption represents the satisfaction of some more or less conscious need, such as those postulated in the 'uses and gratifications' approach.
- *Intentionality*. A more deliberately engaged audience is one that can be found in rituals such as 'binge-watching' entire television series on streaming websites, taking out subscriptions to particular media products and services, or using micro-payment systems to purchase a particular story, episode, film, song or in-game element.
- *Resistance to influence*. Following the lines of the 'obstinate audience' concept (Bauer, 1964), the activity concept here emphasizes the limits set by members of the audience to unwanted influence or learning. The reader, viewer, listener or user remains more or less 'in control' and relatively unaffected, except as determined by personal choice.
- *Involvement*. In general, the more an audience member is 'caught up' or 'engrossed' in the ongoing media experience, the more we can speak of involvement. This can also be called 'affective arousal'. Involvement may also be indicated by such signs as 'talking back' to the television, shouting at developments in a game, or even lying to your laptop (Nass and Yen, 2010).

These different versions of the audience activity concept do not all relate to the same moment in the sequence of media exposure. As Levy and Windahl (1985) point out, they may relate to *advance* expectations and choice, or to activity *during* the experience, or to the *post-exposure* situation, for instance the transfer of satisfaction gained from the media to personal and social life (for example, in conversation about media or based upon media-derived topics).

There are some other aspects of active media use that may be missed by the five variants outlined. For instance, audience activity can take the form of a direct response by letter, telephone or mobile messaging system, whether or not encouraged by the media. Local or community media, whether print, broadcast or online, may generally have more involved audiences, or have more opportunity to develop and encourage such involvement.

Critical reflection on media experience, whether openly expressed in 'feedback' or not, is another example of audience activity, as is conscious membership of a fan group or club.

In the case of television, audience appreciation ratings that are either unusually high or low often indicate the presence within a programme audience of a set of active viewers who respond very positively or very negatively. The act of recording and replaying from radio or television is another indication of above-average engagement. Considering emerging deeply immersive media forms (such as elaborate multi-platform media franchises and complex digital open-world games), the concept of involvement seems somehow to be failing to capture the full extent of immersion. Finally, we can note the view, examined later in more detail, that audiences often participate in the media experience by giving meaning to it, thus actively *producing* the eventual media 'text' (Fiske, 1987, 1992).

The general notion of 'audience activity' is evidently an unsatisfactory concept. It is open to diverse definitions, its indicators are very mixed and ambiguous, and it means different things with different media. It is sometimes manifested in behaviour, but sometimes it is only a mentalistic construct (an attitude or feeling). According to Biocca (1988a: 59), it is almost empty of meaning in general because it is *unfalsifiable*: 'It is, by definition, nearly impossible for the audience *not* to be active'. This is as true of analogue media as it is of today's digital media environment.

## CONCLUSION

As we have seen, the apparently simple idea of an audience turns out to be quite complicated. The very concept is understood differently from quite different perspectives. For most of the media industry it is more or less the equivalent of an imagined and constructed market for media services, and is categorized accordingly. From the point of view of the audience, or those who take the audience perspective, this view of an audience is peripheral or unrecognized. The audience experience as a social event or a cultural event takes precedence. Being in an audience is often the outcome of quite varied motives. Yet other possibilities arise when the view of the sender or communicator is taken into consideration in terms not of selling services but of trying to communicate meaning. Audiences may be thought of by communicators in terms of their tastes, interests, capacities or their social composition and their location.

Overall, the paradox we have to contend with is that we are all 'audiencing' in a pervasive and ubiquitous media environment, and in this context we also, to some extent, disappear as a distinct audience. We participate, engage and immerse ourselves in a complex, interconnected, multi-platform media context, and the organizations and corporations operating in this space increasingly count on us to participate, whether voluntarily as fans and influencers, or involuntarily as those who supply the industry with 'free labour' – most often expressed in the sharing of detailed personal data online. Audience and reception research are traditionally positioned perfectly to help us make sense of this situation, and its relatively recent recognition of the body as playing an important part in the way we understand and experience our media and mass communication environment holds real promise for further exploration.

# FURTHER READING

Alasuutari, P. (ed.) (1999) *Rethinking the Media Audience*. London: Sage.

Carpentier, N. (2016) 'Beyond the ladder of participation: an analytical toolkit for the critical analysis of participatory media processes', *Javnost – The Public*, 23(1): 70–88.

LaRose, R. and Estin, M.S. (2004) 'A social cognitive theory of internet uses and gratifications: towards a new model of media attendance', *Journal of Broadcasting and Electronic Media*, 48(3): 358–377.

Markham, A.N. (2013) 'Fieldwork in social media', *Departures in Critical Qualitative Research*, 2(4): 434–446.

Potter, R.F. and Bolls, P. (2012) *Psychophysiological Measurement and Meaning: Cognitive and Emotional Processing of Media*. New York: Routledge.

Taneja, H. and Webster, J.G. (2016) 'How do global audiences take shape? The role of institutions and culture in patterns of web use', *Journal of Communication*, 66: 161–182.

# 15

---

# AUDIENCE FORMATION AND EXPERIENCE

This chapter looks at the reasons why audiences form in the first place – essentially the motives for attending to mass media and the satisfactions expected or derived. There are different theories about this, since being in the audience not only is the result of personal choice, but also depends on what is available to choose from, our social milieu or lifestyle, and the circumstances of the moment. The chapter is also concerned with other aspects of the audience experience, including its relationship to the social and cultural context. Media use is a social and often sociable activity and is governed to some extent by expectations and norms that vary from place to place and the type of media involved. Finally, the chapter looks at the implications of changing media for the audience, especially the question of the decline of the mass audience.

## THE 'WHY' OF MEDIA USE

In line with earlier remarks, we can approach the question of accounting for media use either from the 'side' of the audience, asking what influences individual choices and behaviours, or from the side of the media, asking what factors of industrial relations and circumstances, content, presentation and circumstance help to draw and keep audience attention, and what kinds of incentives keep audiences engaged. There is no sharp division between the two since questions of personal motivation cannot be answered without some reference to media products and contents. This mutually shaping 'circuit of culture' was theorized by Hall (1974/1980), Johnson (1986) and Du Gay (1997) to raise awareness of how media production, representation, identity, consumption and regulation are all inter-dependent, as well as to highlight the power – or lack thereof – of various stakeholders in the mass communication process (see Chapter 17).

We can also choose to follow one or more of the audience research schools described in Chapter 14, each of which suggests a somewhat different kind of explanation for media use behaviour. The 'structural' tradition emphasizes the media system and the social system as primary determinants; the behavioural approach takes individual needs, motives and circumstances as the starting point; while the social-cultural approach emphasizes the particular context in which an audience member is located (including language and proximity), and the way in which media alternatives are valued and given meaning. As we have seen, each approach has different theoretical foundations and entails different kinds of research strategy and methods. Given theoretical developments across media and mass communication research traditions, the 'why' of media use is generally considered to be a product of both individual preferences and social and technical structures (Taneja and Webster, 2016), requiring integrated research approaches.

A good deal is known about the general factors shaping audience behaviour, which has been remarkably stable and predictable (see, for example, Bryant and Zillman, 1986), although not unchanging. Broad patterns of attention to media alter only slowly and usually for obvious reasons, such as a change in media structure (for example, the rise of a new medium) or because of some wider social change (such as the development of a youth culture or the transition from communism to capitalism). For instance, the long dominance of American television by three big networks lasted forty or so years, family-owned near-monopolies dominated the Latin American media landscape for the longest time, and in Europe, similarly, viewing was monopolized by two or three channels before the audience broke up at the turn of the century. There are always random influences and chance combinations of factors, but audience research can often be a matter of routine recording of predictable outcomes. Such mystery as there is relates to questions of detailed choice within a media sector, how audiences move between and across channels or products, or concerns the success or failure of some specific innovation or item of content. If there were no mystery, the media business would not be as risky as it is and every film, song, game, book or show could be a hit.

These remarks are a reminder that there has always been a disjunction between the *general* pattern of mass media use and what happens on a day-to-day basis. In one respect this can be understood as the difference between a long-term average, based on much data, and the observation of a single case, where the latter might be one day's pattern or one person's habitual media use. As individuals, we usually have a fairly stable pattern of media preferences, choices and time use (although one 'pattern' may be of instability), but each day's media experience is unique and affected by varying and unpredictable circumstances.

In the following sections we look at some alternative theoretical models for accounting for the recruitment and composition of media audiences.

## A STRUCTURAL APPROACH TO AUDIENCE FORMATION

The basic premise, as indicated already, is that media use is largely shaped by certain relatively constant elements of individual traits, social structure and media structure. Individual traits include personality, attitudes, tastes, gratifications sought, medium and genre preferences. Social structure refers to 'social facts', such as those of education, income, gender, place of residence, position in the lifecycle, and so on, which have a strong determining influence on general outlook and social behaviour. Media structure refers to the relatively constant array of channels, choices and content that is available in a given place and time. The media system responds to pressures and to feedback from audiences, so as to maintain a stable self-regulating balance between supply and demand. At the same time, the industry pushes the boundaries of audience tastes and preferences, seeking to differentiate and innovate as much as it is interested in consolidating markets and sources of revenue.

The processes at work are sketched in the model shown in Figure 15.1, slightly adapted from Weibull (1985), which depicts the relationship between that habitual

MCQUAIL'S MEDIA AND MASS COMMUNICATION THEORY
AUDIENCES

pattern of media use behaviour and the particular choices, for instance on a given day. In the figure, the upper section shows an individual's habitual pattern of media use as an outcome of two main factors which themselves reflect the overall social structure. One is the more or less fixed *social situation* in which a person is located along with the associated media-related *needs* (for instance, for certain information, relaxation, social contact, and the like). The second factor (shown as 'mass media structure') consists of the available media possibilities in the particular place, given a person's economic and educational circumstances. Between them, these two factors lead not only to a regular pattern of *behaviour*, but also to a fairly constant disposition, tendency or 'set', which is called a person's *media orientation*. This is a joint outcome of social background and past media experience and takes the form of an affinity for certain media, specific preferences and interests, habits of use, expectations of what the media are good for, and so on (see McLeod and McDonald, 1985; McDonald, 1990; Ferguson and Perse, 2000). This provides the connection to what is contained in the lower part of the figure. Here we find the particular daily situation in which specific choices of media and content are made. These are likely to be influenced by three main variables:

- the specific daily menu of content on offer and the form of presentation (shown as 'media content');
- the circumstances of the moment, for instance amount of free time, availability to attend, range of alternative activities available (labelled as 'individual's circumstances');
- the social context of choice and use, for example the influence of family and friends.

Up to a point, what happens on a day-to-day basis is predictable from a person's 'media orientation', but the specifics are contingent on many unpredictable circumstances.

Weibull (1985: 145) has tested this model with newspaper reading and concluded that 'when an individual is highly motivated to obtain specific gratifications (for instance, a particular item of sports news) he or she is less affected by media structure. . . . Individuals with less interest in the media seem to be more influenced by specific contents or by content composition'. This finding corresponds with more recent work by Kim (2016), comparing 'media orientation' with someone's 'media repertoire' – measuring the extent to which a person follows similar content across different media platforms – showing that content preference outweighs media orientation during the media choice process, particularly when it comes to news. This is a reminder of the high degree of freedom we all have, in principle, to deviate from the general patterns arising from social and media structure. It also helps to explain why evidence about general tastes and preferences does not have a great short-term or individual predictive value.

While many features of daily media use can be traced back to their origins in social and media structure, this kind of model is no more than a preliminary orientation to the question of actual audience formation, which is based on many personal choices. It does have

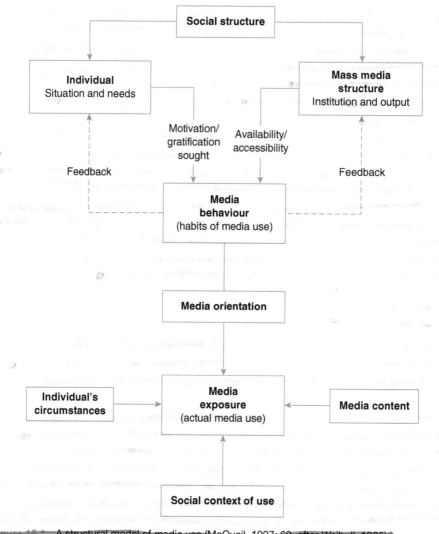

Figure 15.1 A structural model of media use (McQuail, 1997: 69, after Weibull, 1985)

the advantage, however, of showing the connection between a media system (or structure) and an individual audience member's social position. The media system reflects the given facts of a society (for example, economic, cultural and geographical conditions) and also responds to audience demands, which are partly determined by social background factors and partly by those that are idiosyncratic and contingent. This is even the case when globally operating corporations, such as News Corp, Verizon, Netflix and Facebook, move into specific national markets, adapting their offerings, settings and schedules to accommodate particular interests and sensitivities as well as media regulations.

# THE USES AND GRATIFICATIONS APPROACH

The idea that media use depends on the perceived satisfactions, needs, wishes or motives of the prospective audience member is almost as old as media research itself. As noted in Chapter 14, audiences are often formed on the basis of similarities of individual need, interest and taste. Many of these appear to have a social or psychological origin. Typical of such 'needs' are those for information, relaxation, companionship, diversion or 'escape'. Audiences for particular media and kinds of media content can often be typified according to such broad motivational types. The approach has also been applied to studying the appeal of newer media that tend to be more interactive in nature (Ruggiero, 2000) and even to uses of the telephone (Dimmick and Rothenbuhler, 1984). Relative affinity with different media is associated with differences of expectation and gratifications sought.

This way of thinking belongs to a research school which became known as the 'uses and gratifications approach', the origins of which lie in the search for explanations of the great appeal of certain staple media contents. The central question posed is: *why* do people use media, and what do they use them for? Functionalist sociology (see Wright, 1974) viewed the media as serving the various needs of the society – for example, for cohesion, cultural continuity, social control and a large circulation of public information of all kinds. This, in turn, presupposes that individuals also use media for related purposes, such as personal guidance, relaxation, adjustment, information and identity formation.

The first such research dates from the early 1940s and focused on the reasons for the popular appeal of different radio programmes, and also looked at daily newspaper reading (Lazarsfeld and Stanton, 1944, 1949). These studies led to some unexpected findings, for instance that daytime radio soap operas, although often dismissed as superficial and mindless stories to fill time, were also found significant by their (women) listeners. They provided a source of advice and support, a role model of housewife and mother, or an occasion for emotional release through laughter or tears (Herzog, 1944; Warner and Henry, 1948). From talking to newspaper readers, it was also discovered that these were more than just sources of useful information, but also important for giving readers a sense of security, shared topics of conversation and a structure to the daily routine (Berelson, 1949).

# USES AND GRATIFICATIONS REDISCOVERED

The basic assumptions of the approach when it was rediscovered and elaborated twenty years later (in the 1960s and 1970s) were as follows:

- Media and content choice are generally rational and directed towards certain specific goals and satisfactions (thus the audience is active and audience formation can be logically explained).

- Audience members are conscious of the media-related needs that arise in personal (individual) and social (shared) circumstances and can voice these in terms of motivations.
- Broadly speaking, cultural and aesthetic features of content play a much smaller part in attracting audiences than the satisfaction of various personal and social needs (for example, for relaxation, shared experience, passing time, etc.).
- All or most of the relevant factors for audience formation (motives, perceived or obtained satisfactions, media choices, background variables) can, in principle, be measured.

In line with these assumptions, the process of media selection was described by Katz, Blumler and Gurevitch (1974: 20) as being concerned with:

(1) the social and psychological origins of (2) needs which generate (3) expectations of (4) the mass media or other sources which lead to (5) differential exposure (or engaging in other activities), resulting in (6) need gratification and (7) other consequences.

A longer-term aim of the research school was to reach some general theoretical framework within which to place the many particular findings about audience motivations. McQuail, Blumler and Brown (1972), after studying a number of different radio and TV programmes in Britain, proposed a scheme of 'media–person interactions' (a term that reflects the dual origin of the media gratification concept) that capture the most important media satisfactions. This is shown in Box 15.1.

## 15.1
## A typology of media–person interactions (McQuail et al., 1972)

- *Diversion:* escape from routine or problems, emotional release
- *Personal relationships:* companionship, social utility
- *Personal identity:* self-reference, reality exploration, value reinforcement
- *Surveillance* (forms of information seeking)

A more psychological version of the theory of audience motivation was suggested by McGuire (1974), based on the general theory of human needs. He distinguished first between cognitive and affective needs, then added three further dimensions: 'active'

MCQUAIL'S MEDIA AND MASS COMMUNICATION THEORY
AUDIENCES

versus 'passive' initiation; 'external' versus 'internal' goal orientation; and orientation to 'growth' or to 'stability'. When interrelated, these factors yield sixteen different types of motivation that apply to media use. For instance, the motivation to read newspapers in order to attain cognitive consistency (meaning essentially to bring one's opinions into line with those of like-minded others and other relevant information) belongs to the category of active, externally directed behaviour that is oriented to maintaining stability. An example of an effective type of motive would be watching television drama 'in order to find models of personal behaviour'. This type of motive is also active, but internal to the person and oriented to growth and change rather than stability. In the nature of psychological theory of this kind, the media user is unlikely to be conscious of the underlying causes of motivations, expressed in these terms. Even so, there has been some research that shows a relationship between the McGuire factors and different motivational patterns of television use (Conway and Rubin, 1991).

There have been a number of other attempts to write a model of the uses and gratifications process. Renckstorf (1996) has outlined a 'social action' model of audience choice, based on symbolic interactionism and phenomenology. Essentially, he sees media use as a form of social action, shaped by a personal definition of the situation and oriented towards solving some newly perceived 'problem' in the social environment, or as an everyday routine designed to deal with unproblematic situations.

## COMMENT ON USES AND GRATIFICATIONS THEORY

This general approach was criticized in its own time as being too behaviourist and functionalist. It also failed to provide much successful prediction or causal explanation of media choice and use (McQuail, 1984). The reasons for poor prediction may lie partly in the difficulties of the measurement of motives and partly in the fact that much media use is actually very circumstantial and weakly motivated. The approach seems to work best in relation to specific types of content where motivation might be present, for example in relation to political content (Blumler and McQuail, 1968), news (Levy, 1977, 1978) or erotica (Perse, 1994). In fact, the connection between attitude to the media and media use behaviour is actually quite weak and the direction of the relationship is often uncertain. Typologies of 'motives' often fail to match patterns of actual selection or use, and it is hard to find a logical, consistent and sequential relation between the three factors of *liking/ preference*, actual *choosing* and subsequent *evaluation*.

The extent to which audience behaviour is guided by specific and conscious motives has always been in dispute. Babrow (1988) proposed that we think more in terms of 'interpretative frameworks', based on experience. Thus, some audience choice is meaningful in terms of such frameworks, while other exposure is based only on habit and reflex and may be considered unmotivated (Rubin, 1984). These ideas are in line with the concept of 'media orientation' introduced earlier in this chapter and the idea of a general preference set included in Figure 15.3 (see p. 475). A third element of media use is beyond deliberate choice, as people are increasingly concurrently exposed to multiple media in their environment (for example, television screen, smartphone or tablet, a magazine), some or even all of which are not chosen or activated with much deliberation.

In discussing the status of 'uses and gratifications' theory, Blumler (1985) made a distinction, based on extensive evidence, between 'social origins' and ongoing social experiences. The former seem to go with predictable constraints on the range of choice as well as with compensatory, adjustment-oriented, media expectations and uses. The latter – ongoing experience and current social situation – are much less predictable in their effects. They often go with 'facilitatory' media uses – with positive choice, and application, of media for personally chosen ends. This means that media use is an outcome of forces in society, of the personal biography of the individual and also of immediate circumstances. The *causes* of audience formation are located in the past as well as in the very immediate present and at points in between. It is not surprising that attempts at a general *explanation* of actual audience realities have had so little success.

The steady diversification of the media environment has made it even more difficult to find any single explanatory framework of audience patterns. It is likely that an increasing amount of media use can only be explained by reference to 'media side factors' (see Figure 15.3 on p. 475), especially specific content and publicity. Given the shift in the media industries from measuring audience choice, which tends to be largely focused on demographics, to engagement (Kosterich and Napoli, 2016), assessing when and how people form into an audience becomes even more complicated. Particularly in the advertising and marketing industry, a notion of 'customer engagement' is expected to lead to enhanced consumer loyalty and commitment, trust, self-brand connections and emotional attachment (Brodie et al., 2011). Such engagement is intrinsically interactive and context-dependent, and comprises cognitive, emotional and behavioural dimensions, none of which are easy to establish through traditional audience metrics. This in turn pushes industries to pursue more detailed data on (potential) consumers, collecting vast amounts of personal information online (that is, 'big data') as well as investing in ethnographic research (that is, 'thick data').

## EXPECTANCY-VALUE THEORY

Essential to most theory concerning personal motivations for media use is the idea that the media offer rewards which are expected (thus predicted) by potential members of an audience on the basis of relevant past experience. These rewards can be thought of as psychological effects which are valued by individuals (they are sometimes called media 'gratifications'). Such rewards can be derived from media use as such (for example, 'gaming') or from certain favourite genres (for instance, detective stories) or actual items of content (a particular film), and they provide guidance (or feedback) for subsequent choices, adding to the stock of media-relevant information. A funny take on this comes from the history of the popular term 'Netflix and chill', originally (when it emerged around 2009) denoting gratification sought or experienced from bingewatching series and films on the video-streaming platform, later on (from about 2014) also globally recognized as an euphemism for sexual activity – without a screen.

A model of the process involved has been proposed by Palmgreen and Rayburn (1985), based on the principle that attitudes (towards media) are an outcome of empirically located beliefs and also of values (and personal preferences). The resulting 'expectancy-value' model is depicted in Figure 15.2. Expectancy-value theory (EVT) was originally developed in the 1950s to link performance, persistence and choice directly to an individual's expectancy-related and task-value beliefs. Contemporary applications of the model are less common in the media and mass communication literature, although the basic assumptions about considering the interaction between a variety of internal and external forces as influencing expectancies, values and consequent behaviour forms the basis of most theory and research about media use.

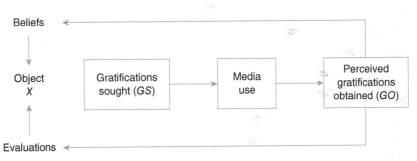

Figure 15.2  An expectancy-value model of media gratifications sought and obtained (Palmgreen and Rayburn, 1985)

In general, the model expresses the proposition that media use is accounted for by a combination of *perception* of benefits offered by the medium and the differential *value* of these benefits for the individual audience member. This helps to cover the fact that media use is shaped by *avoidance* as well as by varying degrees of positive choice among the potential gratifications expected from the media. The model distinguishes between expectation (gratifications sought) and satisfaction (gratifications obtained) and identifies an *increment* over time from media use behaviour. Thus, where the gratifications obtained are noticeably higher than any gratifications sought, we are likely to be dealing with situations of high audience satisfaction and high ratings of appreciation, attention and engagement. The reverse pattern can also occur, providing clues to falling circulation, sales or ratings, and channel switching in the case of television. This theoretical refinement has not altered the fact that audience motivational theory is not easy to translate into a sharp empirical tool.

An overview of the main gratifications from media use that have been identified is given in Box 15.2.

## 15.2

## Media gratifications sought or obtained

- Information and education
- Guidance and advice
- Diversion and relaxation
- Social contact
- Value reinforcement
- Cultural satisfaction
- Emotional release
- Identity formation and confirmation
- Lifestyle expression
- Security
- Sexual arousal
- Filling time
- Community and belonging
- Acceptance and support

## AN INTEGRATED MODEL OF AUDIENCE CHOICE

We can combine a number of the influences on media choice into a single heuristic model, which provides a guide to understanding the sequential process of audience formation. The main entries in the model (Figure 15.3) operate either on the 'audience side' of the media–person interaction or on the 'media side'. While described separately, the two sets of factors are not independent of each other but are the result of a continuing process of mutual orientation and adjustment. The form of the model as presented here was influenced initially by the work of Webster and Wakshlag (1983), who sought to explain television viewer choice in a similar way. The version shown here is intended, in principle, to apply to all mass media and not just television. First, the main explanatory factors can be introduced.

Audience side

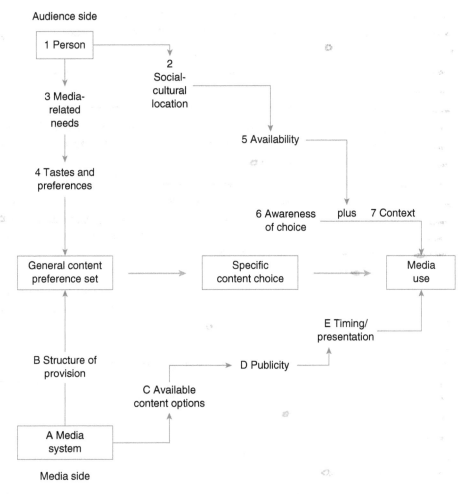

Figure 15.3    An integrated model of the process of media choice

## 'AUDIENCE SIDE' FACTORS

1.  *Personal attributes* of age, gender, family position, study and work situation, level of income, also 'lifestyle', if relevant. Personality differences also play a part (see Finn, 1997), particularly in the newer, more interactive media. To this one should add education, media literacy and digital skillset in terms of one's ability to navigate the complex contemporary media environment.

2.  *Social background and milieu*, especially as reflected in social class, education, religious, cultural, political and family environment and region or locality of residence.

We can also refer here to what Bourdieu (1986) calls 'cultural capital' – learnt cultural skills and tastes, often transmitted intergenerationally by way of family, education and the class system.

3. *Media-related needs*, of the kind discussed above, for such personal benefits as company, distraction, information, and so on. These needs are widely experienced, but the particular balance between them depends on personal background and circumstances.

4. *Personal tastes and preferences* for certain genres, formats or specific items of content. This includes people's emotional responses to and affective relationships with specific media (Papacharissi, 2014).

5. *General habits of leisure time media use and availability* to be in the audience at a particular time. Since media are used in space as well as time, availability also refers to being in the appropriate places to receive media (for example, at home, on trains, while driving, etc.). Availability also refers to the economic potential to be in an audience (for instance, being able and willing to pay the price of a cinema ticket or of a music recording).

6. *Awareness of the choices* available and the amount and kind of information possessed also play a part in audience formation. More engaged audience members can be expected to plan their media use accordingly.

7. *Specific contexts of use*. This varies according to the medium but generally refers to sociability and location of use. Most relevant is whether one is alone or in company (friends, family, others). Where media are used (such as at home, at work, while travelling, in a cinema, etc.) can also influence the character of the experience as well as the process of choice-making.

8. *Chance*, which occurs anywhere and everywhere in this model, often plays a part in media exposure, and its intervention reduces the ability to really *explain* choice or audience composition.

## 'MEDIA-SIDE' FACTORS

A. *The media system*. Preferences and choices are influenced by the makeup of the (national) media system (number, reach and type of media available) and by the specific characteristics of different media outlets. Following the tenets of media theory, we should add to this factor the (individual-level) characteristics and technological affordances of different media devices and interfaces.

B. *Structure of media provision*. This refers to the general pattern of what the media provide in a given society, which exerts a long-term influence on audience expectations.

C. *Available content options*. These are the specific devices, level of connectivity, media formats and genres that are on offer to the potential audience at particular times and places.

D. *Media publicity*. This includes advertising and image-making by the media on their own behalf as well as intensive marketing of some media products.

E. *Timing and presentation*. Media selection and use are likely to be influenced by specific strategies of timing, scheduling, placement, content and design of the media message according to competitive audience-gaining strategies. This factor is less influential due to time-shifting possibilities (such as the streaming of entire seasons of television serials), but remains valid.

Figure 15.3 represents the general process of choice-making, in which influences of different kinds (from the individual, society and from media) are shown sequentially according to their relative 'distance' from the moment of choice or attention (*media use*). Most distant (and more or less fixed) are social and cultural background and (for most adults at least) general sets of tastes and preferences, likes and interests. Thus, our social background (including cultural proximity and language) has a strongly orienting and dispositional influence on our choice behaviour (Taneja and Webster, 2016). The other, almost equally distant (but less constant) factor is the general makeup of different media and the mix of genres, of which we have accumulated knowledge and experience. There are affective, cognitive and evaluative aspects to our dispositions (see also the expectancy-value model above).

Personal knowledge of this kind and the related attitudes shape our tastes and preferences. The combination of the two (perception and evaluation) leads to a *general content preference set*. This is a hypothetical construct, but it shows up in consistent and thus predictable patterns of choice-making and also in more or less coherent patterns and types of media usage (these are close to what are sometimes called 'taste cultures'). We can think of it in terms of the 'repertoire' of available sources and content types with which we are familiar and from which we make actual choices (see Heeter, 1988). It is also very close to Weibull's 'media orientation' in the structural model (see Figure 15.1) and includes affinity for media as well as for types of content. Patterns of choice-making are always adapted according to changes in circumstances and experience with the media. There is a continuous process of response, feedback, learning and evaluation. Throughout it all runs the notion of affinity and emotional connection, as people's relationships with media tend to be deeply personal and often intimate. In media studies, this crucial aspect of media choice and use has been taken up by the study of affect – to the extent that some speak of an 'affective' turn in scholarship (Gregg, 2009) – whereas social scientific approaches in this context fall under the umbrella of studies on embodied cognition (Bradley, 2007). In both instances, scholars regard the body as an integral part of the way people process, respond to and make decisions about media. Approaches in human–computer interaction research – particularly in the field of 'experience centred design'– are at the forefront of integrating insights from materiality (for example, media theory), affect and media choice theory (Blythe, Wright, McCarthy and Bertelsen, 2006).

At a point much closer in time or place to media use, the circumstances of the potential audience member and the availability of the media coincide, resulting in actual audiences. These are never fully predictable, although the broad shape in aggregate terms is, as noted above, rather constant. It is the internal composition that is always shifting, since individual choice behaviour is affected by context and circumstances.

The complexity and multiplicity of audience formation preclude any simple descriptions or single theoretical explanation. We can certainly conclude that audiences are rarely what they seem from ratings alone. They are often shifting aggregates without clear boundaries. Motives, feelings and orientations are always mixed. Sometimes there are no motives. Even if motives were clearer and less mixed, they would not be 'readable' from the content alone, although in an efficient media market we may suppose that content and audience composition are well matched. There are enormous inbuilt uncertainties that cannot be eliminated. Nevertheless, within the complexity and seeming confusion there are some islands of stability and order – occasions where people and media meet to mutual satisfaction and stay with each other. However, this state is one that, by definition, is not easy to achieve by manipulation and publicity, but comes either from genuine social needs or from chance conjunctures of media creativity and public taste.

## PUBLIC AND PRIVATE SPHERES OF MEDIA USE

As noted, certain forms of media use have a distinctly public character, both in the sense of taking place outside the home (as with cinema or concerts, or mobile media while on the road) and in having a wider significance as a shared response to public performances and to public events. Saenz (1994: 576) refers to the continued significance of a 'widely shared, collectively appreciated performance, an immediate delivery … to a large and general audience'. He adds: 'The sense of performance and cultural currency in television programming constitutes an important dimension in viewers' appreciation of television drama as a prominent cultural event' (ibid.: 576). The term 'public' can have a reference to the type of content, the location of an event and also to the degree of shared, collective experience. Online such shared experience is amplified through 'second screen' viewing, as people engage with live media content on social media.

Mass media that are located in their use primarily in the home (especially television, streaming video, music and books, even though all such media are also consumed via mobile media) can be considered to bridge the gap between the private, domestic world and the concerns and activities of the wider society. Under some conditions, being a member of an audience has the meaning of sharing in the wider life of society, while in other circumstances it is a self-initiated experience that may be entirely personal or shared only by a small circle of fans, friends or family members.

It is not so much the physical location of the audience experience (for instance, cinema and theatre versus home) that matters as the definition of its meaning as more public or more private.

The public type of audiencehood is typified by occasions of consciously motivated attention to reports of events that are of wide social significance (such as election results, major disasters, world crises), or that involve the watching of major live sporting events or big entertainment events (for example, live concerts). Public audience experience normally involves some degree of identification with a wider social grouping – whether defined as fans, or citizens, or a local population, or a taste culture. It may also be an experience associated with some more or less public role, for instance citizen, voter or worker. Increasingly, this version of audiencehood involves a cross-over with the Internet, which serves to construct a network of loose contacts in response to mass media content.

In their study of 'media events', Dayan and Katz (1992) draw attention to a special category of occasions where the media (especially television) unite a population in a near-ritual manner to celebrate and join in some wider national or global experience. Such media events are always special and constitute interruptions of routine. Aside from their significance, they are typically pre-planned, remote and live. Rothenbuhler (1998) developed the concept of ritual communication to apply to participation by way of the media in the rites and ceremonies of public life. To be in the (media) audience for such events is to participate more fully in the public life of the nation or another significant membership group. This research reminds us again of the collective character of 'audiencehood'.

The private type of audience experience is constructed according to personal mood and circumstance and does not involve any reference to society or even to other people. When not purely introspective, it is likely to be concerned with self-comparison and matching with a media model, role or personality in the search for an acceptable identity for public self-presentation. The difference between the public and private types of audience experience depends on a combination of factors: the type of medium and content and the frame of mind of (or definition supplied by) the audience member. Expansion and development of media seem to be opening up relatively more possibilities for private audiencehood, by bringing more of media experience within the control of the individual to choose at will (see Neuman, 1991). The fragmentation of audiences can be seen as reducing the public significance of audience experience. On the other hand, empirical studies show little or no evidence of the often-suggested phenomenon that online news audiences are more fragmented than offline audiences (Fletcher and Kleis Nielsen, 2017). As Fletcher and Kleis Nielsen (2017: 493) remind us, this does not mean we should not be concerned about the potential damage to debate, a shared public agenda and common culture, as these 'do not have to take the form of fragmentation in order to be realized in high-choice media environments'.

# SUBCULTURE AND AUDIENCE

Early critics of 'mass society' theory pointed to the high degree of social differentiation of the seemingly homogeneous 'mass' audience. As media industries have developed and sought newer and 'niche' audience markets, they have needed no persuasion on this point, and have entered the business of trying to define and create new social and cultural subgroups, based on genre, taste or lifestyle, with which potential media consumers might identify – up to and including micro-targeted individual users through automated data-mining practices. There is a continuous process of creating media-based styles or pseudo-identities that are intended to strike a responsive chord in an audience.

Nevertheless, media use is always likely to be shaped predominantly according to early experience, emotional ties and identifications forged in personal life or in line with the social context of the moment. After the particular social milieu of one's family comes the peer group of school classmates or neighbourhood friends, which influences taste and media consumption, especially in respect of music, games and video – the most popular media for the young. There are many layers of differentiation, aside from the sometimes fine age grading of youthful preferences (von Feilitzen, 1976; Livingstone, 2002) and the general separation out of a 'youth culture' as distinct from that of adults. Young adult experience is reshaped by social contacts at work and in leisure. Such general environmental influences are cross-cut by many other specific factors, not least that of gender.

There is much evidence that media use can play an important role in the expression and reinforcement of identity for subgroups of different kinds (Hebdige, 1978). This is not surprising, since media are part of 'culture', but there is a particular point in noting the strong connection between deviant, critical and otherwise diverse subcultures in modern society and the media system. The focus of resistance to dominant forces and values of society has often been music and dance forms that are appropriated by subcultures and become a symbol of resistance (Hall and Jefferson, 1975; Lull, 1992). Given the rise of multi-platform franchising – usually involving large, complex, multidivisional ('M-form') global media corporations (see Eisenmann and Bower, 2000) – subcultures cut across genres, formats and media and are no longer contained by music, lifestyle, film, television or games. An icon of rap music may also be a playable character in a digital game and a star in a television show. Beyond this, many musicians, actors and actresses, journalists and other media personalities operate one or more social media channels through which they 'extend the brand' and do 'relational labour' (Baym, 2018) by engaging with audiences and distributing news and information. This allows people to feel much more involved with stars as well as the associated messages, codes and rituals of particular subcultures, tribes or scenes (Hesmondhalgh, 2005).

# LIFESTYLE

The concept of lifestyle has often been used in describing and categorizing different patterns of media use, often as part of a constellation of other attitudes and behaviours (for example, Eastman, 1979; Frank and Greenberg, 1980; Donohew, Palmgreen and Rayburn, 1987; Vyncke, 2002). The pioneering work of the French sociologist Pierre Bourdieu (1986) represents a long tradition of enquiry relating various expressions of cultural taste to social and family background. In one respect, the lifestyle concept offers an escape from the presumption that media taste (unlike traditional aesthetic and artistic taste) is determined by social class and education, since lifestyles are, to some extent, self-chosen patterns of behaviour and media use choice.

In commercial marketing research, the lifestyle concept is helpful for classifying consumers into various types in ways that assist the targeting and design of advertising. For such purposes it is desirable to go beyond basic social-demographic categories and to make finer distinctions, especially with psychological dimensions. The combination of demographic and psychological characteristics has been referred to as 'psychographics'. Lifestyle research involves studying a wide range of social positional variables, behaviours (including media use and other leisure and consumption practices) and attitudes, tastes and values. There is in fact no limit to the potential scope of such research or, perhaps, to the number of media-relevant lifestyles that can be identified (see Finn, 1997). Vyncke (2002) has described the construction of a typology intended to indicate segmented lifestyles. He found that the inclusion of media use variables significantly increased the power of the typology to discriminate. This suggests that media use plays an important role in expressing and forming lifestyle identity.

Johansson and Miegel (1992) distinguish three levels of analysis: that of the whole society (for international comparisons), that of differences within societies and cultures, and that of the individual. One of the main problems with the concept is finding an appropriate level. The second level is the most commonly applied, often with rather confusing results. Of the third level, they say that 'lifestyles are expressions of individuals' ambitions to create their own specific, personal, social and cultural identities' (ibid.: 23). Hesmondhalgh (2005: 25) offers an important counterpoint to an uncritical view and use of 'lifestyle' as a concept, as it is generally implicitly tied to a celebration of consumerism, asking the question: 'what of the factors that might limit or constrain such choice: poverty, addiction, mental illness, social suffering, marginalization, disempowerment, unequal access to education, childcare and healthcare, and so on?'.

There are potentially as many lifestyles as there are individuals. Nevertheless, the concept is helpful in understanding the many different ways in which media are meaningfully interrelated with social and cultural experience, how different communities, subcultures, tribes and scenes form around the products of the media industries, and how they establish and maintain boundaries and cultural prestige. Although lifestyle may be a concept with too narrow a focus (and developed largely in the service of industry), it is helpful to use this and similar concepts (such as genre or scene) to theorize and understand the relationship between aspects of the media industries – such as music, film and games – and the social.

## GENDERED AND INTERSECTIONAL AUDIENCES

The idea that media use is notably and persistently 'gendered' has also been developed in reception research, under the influence of feminist theory (Seiter et al., 1989). The differentiation of media use according to sex has long been recognized, and certain types of media are specifically produced for female audiences, often by women, especially perhaps certain magazines (Ferguson, 1983) and types of fiction (for example, romance). Male audiences are also served by distinctive media types and genres. More recent is a greater curiosity about the meaning of these differences and a search for an understanding of how the social construction of gender – as well as processes of intersectionality whereby gender, ethnicity and class are conflated – also influences media choice and vice versa (Lünenborg and Fürsich, 2014).

Gendered audience experience is a complex outcome of a certain kind of media content, typical everyday routines and the wider structure of what may still be described as 'patriarchal society' – or a 'man's world' as far as power is concerned. A much-cited example is Radway's (1984) research into one set of devoted (that is, really addicted) women readers of mass-produced romance fiction. Radway set out to account for the compulsive appeal of romance fiction by accepting in the first instance the main explanations offered by women readers themselves. From this perspective, romances offer an escape specifically designed for women, first by way of the act of reading, which establishes a private 'space' and time protected from incursion by husbands and family duties, and secondly by providing versions, albeit in fantasy form, of the ideal romance, which can be emotionally nurturing.

The notion of gendered audience has also been invoked in relation to another genre that attracts a largely female audience – that of radio and television 'soap operas' (for example, Hobson, 1982, 1989; Allen, 1989; Geraghty, 1991). Studies have linked their narrative form (continuity, indeterminacy) to typical features of the housewife's daily routine, which is fragmented and distracted (preventing continuous attention) but also flexible. Soap operas in general are significantly preferred and more watched by women, even when they recognize the low status of the genre (for example, Alasuutari, 1992). Ethnographic research into female soap opera viewers indicates that the genre is widely appropriated as especially meant for women and often serves for conversation and reflection about viewers' own everyday experiences (Livingstone, 1988).

In respect of the audience for women's magazines, Hermes (1995) identified a set of interpretative 'repertoires' or structures of meaning in terms of which women readers account for their reading behaviour and their relative attraction to the different varieties of the genre (ranging from feminist to traditional publications). Repertoires refer, for instance, to the sense of duty to support the cause of women or the mild guilt at reading traditional women's magazines. These sets of ideas are often mutually inconsistent or in dialogue with each other, but contradictions are made easier to handle by the relative lack of significance attached to the magazine medium by even their most faithful readers.

The essence of a gendered audience is not the sex ratio of its composition, but the degree to which conscious membership of an audience (audiencehood) is given some distinct meaning in terms of specific female or male experience, and is actively constructed as such by media producers. There are numerous indications in research into media use that gendered differences are associated with different preferences and satisfactions. For instance, Anderson, Collins, Schmitt and Jacobwitz (1996) found that stressed women watched more game and variety shows, while stressed men watched more action and violent programming, thus accentuating differences that show up in the general audience. Despite gender difference, there is much evidence of shared purpose, behaviour and understanding across gender lines. Furthermore, the link between modern, stressful and in many ways uncertain life and a subsequent increase in the importance of culture and the media has been established by Fornäs (1995), noting how media provide endless new markers for identity formation in the relative absence of traditional meaning-giving stable institutions such as family, school, work and community.

Research on gender and digital games similarly finds a systematic over-representation of males, whites and adults and a systematic under-representation of females, ethnic minorities, children and the elderly (Williams, Martins, Consalvo and Ivory, 2009). Although the global games industry reports even gender numbers among gaming audiences, developers overwhelmingly program content with male (or masculinized) players in mind. Lisa Nakamura's work on race and ethnicity on the Internet confirms that similar processes of exclusion are at work in newer media broadly defined (Nakamura, 2002; see also Nakamura and Chow-White, 2012). Payal Arora (2019) critically highlights how 'new' Internet audiences in developing countries all over the world are constructed in particular stereotypical ways, ignoring their voices and information (and entertainment) needs in the process. This work warns us against overly optimistic readings of media in general, and newer media in particular, as either 'neutral' or necessarily democratizing.

## SOCIABILITY AND USES OF THE MEDIA

It did not escape early audience researchers that media use was shaped by circumstances of time and place, and by social and cultural habits. People joined audiences for various social reasons (for example, for conversation, or as part of an organizing daily routine) as much as for some communicative value or purpose (such as learning from the news). For instance, 'going to the movies' has nearly always been viewed more as a social activity than as an occasion for seeing particular films (Handel, 1950). Eliot Friedson (1953) emphasized the group character of much actual media experience (in contrast to what the theory of mass behaviour proposed), drawing on the then contemporary evidence of film and broadcast audiences. He wrote:

> Much audience behavior, then, takes place in a complex network of local social activity. Certain times of day, certain days, certain seasons are the appropriate times for engaging in particular activities connected with various mass media. The individual is frequently accompanied by others of his social group … [and] participates in an interpersonal grid of spectators who discuss the meaning of past experience with mass communication and the anticipated significance of future experience.

The media occasion had a significance beyond that of any 'message' communicated or any individual gratification obtained. Seeing a 'bad' movie could be just as satisfying as seeing a 'good' one. Much the same could be said of radio, phonograph listening and television viewing, although, unlike the cinema, these have nearly always taken a secondary place in complex patterns of family life. 'Watching television' is generally a more accurate description of what is going on than 'watching television programmes', but it too overstates the significance of the ubiquitous flickering screen.

Despite the above, mass media use was often associated with forms of social isolation (Maccoby, 1954; Bailyn, 1959), and there have been similar anxieties about digital games, mobile media, and the Internet more generally. There are obviously many individuals who are both socially isolated and also strongly addicted to media use behaviours that might reinforce their isolation. The term 'addiction' has been viewed as both too loaded a word and also too vague to be useful. Efforts have been made to make it more precise and relevant. For instance, Horvath (2004) proposed a new scale for measuring TV addiction, with the following main factors: (1) actual time spent; (2) evidence of withdrawal problems; (3) the degree to which TV use is unintended; (4) the displacement effects on other activities; (5) continuation despite the problems caused; and (6) repeated attempts to cut down. Similar efforts are underway for addictive behaviours related to gaming and smartphones (see Chapter 17 for additional discussion of media addiction research).

An understandable and recurring concern about addiction to media has diverted attention from the more typical meanings of media attractiveness. Most uses of the media have been effectively rendered sociable. Media use is itself a ubiquitous form of normal social behaviour and an acceptable substitute for some social interaction. It is also widely perceived as a significant 'agent of socialization' – an occasion for social learning and a means towards participation in the wider society. Furthermore, it can be argued that in media we find clues and articulations of identity and belonging that are otherwise harder to find and sustain as traditional communities and institutions become more fragile and precarious under social conditions related to globalization, individualization, climate change and (mass) migration.

The sociability of the audience experience is indicated by certain familiar (and well-attested) features of media use, apart from just sharing the activity. Mass media (for example, television, digital games or music) are often used to entertain people or to ease social interaction. Media use is often accompanied by talk about the ongoing experience, whether in person or online via 'second screen' audience behaviour. The content of media (news items, stories, performances) provides an object of shared attention for many as well as topics of conversation. Media-related talk is especially useful in providing a non-intrusive basis of contact with strangers. Media in the home are frequently a background to virtually every other kind of activity, without necessarily impeding or displacing these activities. Mobile media in general and (noise-cancelling) headphones in particular allow media users some control over their environment. Using such 'orphic' media (Hagood, 2019) inevitably combines some activity with that of media usage, although such technologies also shut out other people and experiences. As Hagood (2011: 573) observes, linking media use with the social, 'reviewers and users affirm that the headphones offer clearer audio from portable media in noisy environments, but the devices' marketing, reception, and history of development suggest that their primary function has more to do with conflicts of sound, space, and self in an increasingly mobile modernity'.

There is no clear evidence that the classic forms of interpersonal 'sociability', such as conversation and 'hanging out', have disappeared, although it is very likely that some domestic entertainments that are sociable, like card-playing, musical parties and family games, have declined (although for other reasons as well). The collectivities of the past – family, neighbourhood, place of worship – have made way for numerous networks that any individual can belong to. Much of the 'identity work' of these collectivities gets done using the products of the media industries. Of course, families, local communities and nation states persist – and, some would argue, become more important than ever for a growing group of people for whom the 'networked individualist' lifestyle is unavailable, risky or otherwise problematic.

Rosengren and Windahl (1989), in their overview of the findings of the long-term Swedish Media Panel research into child development, have found much evidence of varied and complex patterns linking media use with other social activities. They find 'on the whole positive relations between children's television viewing and their social interaction' (ibid.: 200). Age (grade in school), gender and social class all played a part in mediating the link (see Buckingham, 2002). In a meta-analysis of decades of scholarship on children, youths and media, Valkenburg and Piotrowski (2017: 270) argue that the generally small to moderate effects found in studies on media, children and the family need to be taken seriously, 'since they may indicate that a small group of children and adolescents are particularly susceptible to the effects of media'. They conclude that media preferences and media effects are highly dependent on every individual's development and life phase – a conclusion mirrored in studies on ageing and media use (Givskov and Deuze, 2018).

From numerous studies on family life past and present, such as research done in the United States by the University of California, Los Angeles' (UCLA) Center on Everyday Lives of Families (CELF), across Europe by the scholars involved in the European Media and Technology in Everyday Life (EMTEL) network, and around the world by the Global Kids Online project (globalkidsonline.net), media feature prominently as sites of struggle and negotiation of power and authority in the family home.

The central role of media in general and online, as well as mobile media, particularly in social trends towards greater individualization and global connectivity, leads Fortunati (2001) to describe media as 'charismatic' technologies, enabling and enticing their users to incorporate them progressively into more and more aspects of everyday life. Quandt and von Pape (2010: 332) take a 'biophilosophical' approach, linking media, family life and social transformation in their year-long study of the average present-day media home, considering these common everyday living arrangements as *mediatopes*: social, physical and technological living environments of media. Through interviews, observations and surveys, Quandt and von Pape show how media move through the household in flocks, how the identities of various devices change over time, how younger and older media fight for survival in the home environment, and how therefore all have distinct and dynamic lifecycles 'connected to the life of the users themselves' (ibid.: 339). This intimate interrelationship between the individual and family lives of people and their media 'paints a picture of an evolving, living media world within the domestic environment of the household' (ibid.: 343).

This work fits in a long lineage of media use studies inspired by 'media domestication theory', which was developed by Roger Silverstone and others to take into account how various technologies and media are incorporated by people into their everyday lives and routines (see Silverstone and Hirsch, 2003). In this line of research, four phases are generally distinguished. First, technologies are integrated into everyday life and adapted to daily practices. Secondly, the user and their environment change and adapt accordingly. Thirdly, these adaptations feed back into innovation processes in industry, shaping the next generation of technologies and services. Fourthly, the technologies adapt and reflect the cultures of a household, office or other social setting within which they are appropriated. Media in this context are seen as physical objects, texts as well as socio-spatial contexts – referred to as the 'triple articulation' of media (Hartmann, 2006; Courtois, Verdegem and De Marez, 2013).

Most media use can be as sociable or not as one chooses, depending on our real-life resources (in terms of money, mobility, available friends and social contacts). This is what Rosengren and Windahl (1972) termed 'interaction potential'. In providing a substitute for 'real-life' social contact, which might simply not be available, especially in modern urban living, the media often help to alleviate loneliness and stress caused by isolation.

Mass-mediated social contact can supplement and complement, amplify as well as displace real personal contacts with others. As a result, the potential for social interaction can just as easily be enlarged by mass media as reduced. In so far as there is a general empirical answer to the question of relationship between social interaction and media use, it seems that higher levels of 'real' social contact are often accompanied by above-average levels of contact with the media. This finding does not settle the issue, but the correlation can be understood as supporting the claim that being in an audience is most accurately defined as 'social' rather than 'non-social'. There is a variety of ways in which media use becomes intertwined with everyday life. James Lull (1982) suggested a typology of social uses of television, based on participant observation of families. Some of the points also apply to other media. The first type is referred to as *structural* and identifies the numerous ways in which the media provide a time frame for daily activities. This begins with an early news bulletin, an accompaniment to breakfast, and continues, according to the daily schedule, to mark breaks from work, mealtimes, the return from work, and evening relaxation with familiar and suitable programming on radio and television. This is what Mendelsohn (1964) referred to as the function of radio in 'bracketing the day'. A media-derived structure of this kind provides a sense of companionship and marks off phases of the day, helping to establish appropriate moods. A second type is called *relational* and covers the points made earlier about content as a conversational 'coin of exchange' and a way of easing social contacts of an informal but non-intimate kind.

The third category is summarized in terms of *affiliation* and *avoidance*, referring to the fluctuating dynamics of social relations in which people want to be, by turns, socially close to, or separate from, others with whom they share the same physical space. Different media offer different opportunities for one or the other option. Affiliation is expressed by joining in the same spectatorship (for example, a football match on TV) in varying degrees of participation. Avoidance takes more diverse forms. Some involve the use of particular media that are, by definition, solitary in use, like books, headphone music or mobile phones (sometimes). In public as well as private places, reading newspapers often expresses a wish to be left alone, as does the wearing of (noise-cancelling) headphones. Having separate television and radio receivers or wireless speakers able to play music customized to the people in a particular room in different parts of a house helps in the dispersal of members of a household. These social devices are usually understood and accepted as legitimate, thus avoiding offence to others. It is impossible to separate out the more 'legitimate' media use motives from the less acceptable aspect of self-isolation. In families, as children grow up, there is a fairly clear pattern of increasing dispersal of individual activities, which is closely related to the use of different media (von Feilitzen, 1976; Livingstone, 2002).

Of the remaining social uses named by Lull, one – *social learning* – covers a wide range of socializing aspects of media use (for example, adopting certain role models) and a fifth carries the label *competence/dominance*. This refers to the socially structured power to control media use in a household, ranging from a decision to choose a daily newspaper to the use of the TV remote control, and including decision-making over the acquisition of media hardware and software. It also refers to the uses made of media-derived information and expertise to play the role of **opinion leader** in social contacts with family and friends (Katz and Lazarsfeld, 1955). Ethnographic research in domestic settings makes it clear that media use is often governed by quite complex, usually unspoken, rules and understandings, which vary from one family to another (see Morley, 1986) and which are becoming more complex as 'charismatic' media become a more substantial part of every-day (family) life (Valkenburg and Piotrowksi, 2017). The main social uses of the media that have been uncovered are listed in Box 15.3.

---

**15.3**

**Social uses of the media**

- Managing relations with others
- Conversation and social exchange
- Social attachment and avoidance
- Social learning and identification with role models
- Having control of media choice
- Sharing activity
- Vicarious companionship
- Filling ('killing' or 'reviving dead') time
- Framing daily activity

---

## NORMATIVE FRAMING OF MEDIA USE

The preceding discussion is a reminder of the extent to which research into the media audience has taken place within a normative, even judgemental, framework (see Barwise and Ehrenberg, 1988: 138ff), itself a sign that media use has been thoroughly incorporated in the socialization process. Although, as we have seen, high media use does not in itself have to be viewed as harmful, the most basic norm applied to the media has been that you can have too much, even of a good thing (see Valkenburg and Piotrowksi, 2017: 273). The normative framing of media use seems at first to run counter to the view that media use is a voluntary, free-time, 'out-of-role' and generally pleasurable activity, more or less unrelated to any social obligation. Yet audience research continually uncovers the existence of value systems that informally serve to regulate media behaviour, and raises our awareness about the significance of personal development and social context within which media use takes place.

There is plenty of evidence that the media are widely regarded by their own audiences as potentially influential for good or ill and thus in need of direction and control by society. At the very least they should be supervised by parents. As Valkenburg and Piotrowksi (2017: 268) similarly note, 'the network society has resulted in unprecedented freedom for today's youth, and the personalized social media they enjoy requires more intense supervision and comprehensive judgment from parents than any earlier medium'.

While no doubt much of the normative concern about media stems from fears of unwanted influences, media use in itself can be regarded as morally dubious (as noted above). Steiner (1963) long ago found a tendency for viewers to show guilt over their own high levels of television use, which he attributed to a legacy from the Protestant ethic, which frowns on 'unproductive' uses of time. Among middle-class audiences especially, a sensitivity to this value persists. Radway (1984: 105) found similar kinds of guilt feelings among keen female readers of romantic fiction and for similar reasons: 'guilt is the understandable result of their socialization within a culture that continues to value work above leisure and play'.

Yee, Bailenson and Ducheneaut (2009) demonstrate how people can feel equally guilty when temporarily 'abandoning' their avatars in collaborative virtual environments (such as online games, discussion platforms, company intranets, etc.). They call people's adaption of their behaviour based on what they look like online a 'Proteus effect' — found, for example, in people who become friendlier towards others online when their avatar seems attractive. In these examples, guilt was more evidenced in words than in behaviour, reflecting the influence of social desirability. This is reflected in longitudinal survey research on people's media use, where in the past people tended to underestimate their time spent, for example, watching television or using the Internet, whereas in contemporary projects people overestimate their media use — partly as an expression of concern.

## AUDIENCE NORMS FOR CONTENT

Normative expectations relate not only to media use behaviour, but also to aspects of media content. People voice complaints about, as well as appreciation of, the media. Positive response usually outweighs criticism, but what is striking is the fact that the performance of the media is so widely regarded as a proper topic for the expression of public attitudes, judgements and opinion. Audiences expect media to conform to certain norms of truthfulness and factuality (particularly when it comes to journalism), good taste and morality (especially in reference to advertising and television), and sometimes also to other values, such as those of the local community, patriotism and democracy. Norms for what is appropriate in fiction and entertainment usually refer to bad language, violence, sex, and the models of behaviour offered by media. Here family life, the protection of children and the personal susceptibilities and moral standards of adults are the main point of reference.

Morals aside, it is notable also that audiences are sensitive to the quality of media on the grounds of political bias and fairness, often placing more emphasis on impartiality and reliability than on the media's own rights to freedom of expression (for example, Comstock, 1988; Gunter and Winstone, 1993; Fitzsimon and McGill, 1995; Golding and van Snippenburg, 1995; McMasters, 2000). Audiences can often seem intolerant of the public expression in the mainstream media of extreme or deviant political views. Questions about censorship tend to reveal unexpected variations in public attitudes, with respondents in surveys often expressing support for advance censorship and for punishment of new media for causing social unrest. The norms applied by the audience to media information commonly refer to completeness and accuracy, balance and diversity of opinion. News sources are often judged according to their relative credibility (Gaziano and McGrath, 1987). By various accounts, the media have been losing trust and, once lost, it is hard to regain, just as it is hard for new media (for instance, online news) to acquire trust in the first place.

Despite the evidence of critical public attitudes, relatively few people seem personally offended by the media, and actual use behaviour shows a state of relative normlessness. This paradox may reflect the existence of private norms based on personal taste and preferences, which, as with many aspects of behaviour, do not correspond with the public norm. It also suggests that evaluative attitudes expressed towards media are somewhat superficial and learnt as socially desirable rather than deeply internalized. This is not to say that personal preferences in choosing and responding to media content will not be influenced by an individual's own personal values. Rather, these value influences are often implicit and beneath the surface – except when it comes to the behaviour of so-called 'trolls' and others who publish aggressively critical content or hate speech online.

Other forms of critical distance include an objection to some aspects of content on moral or ideological grounds. In other words, it seems that 'experienced' audience members (these kinds of data came from regular and articulate viewers) have a fairly extensive repertoire of positions they can take up in respect of particular media contents. Box 15.4 summarizes the main norms applied to use of television and other media.

- Too much media use is bad, especially for children
- Children's media use should be protected and supervised
- Different genres and (especially social) media received different valuations
- Audiences expect accuracy and impartiality in news
- General audience content should not offend against dominant moral and social norms
- Media should not be free to damage national interest or security

## THE VIEW FROM THE AUDIENCE

As noted in Chapter 11, mass communicators solve the 'problem' of orientation to an essentially unknown audience in a variety of ways, depending on their particular role conception and type of medium or concept. Here we look briefly at the communicator–audience relationship from the other end. In general, the audience does not experience its relations with the media and media communicators as problematic on a day-to-day basis. Under conditions of freedom and diversity, audiences choose their own media sources according to personal likes and perceptions of what is relevant and interesting. Nevertheless, some effort is required on the part of the audience and some discomfort may be entailed. The first dimension to consider in audience–source relations is that of *affective direction*.

Although media are freely chosen by their audiences, actual people in audiences may not have personally chosen their media or the specific content to which they find themselves exposed. This applies where members of families, households or other groups are subject to the choices of others about what is available to read, view or listen to. Such media 'micro-gatekeepers' may be parents, partners, friends, and the like. It also applies where there are few or no real alternatives, for instance where there is only one local television channel or newspaper which is hard, in practice, to ignore.

There is usually a large flow of unrequested and often unwanted media messages by way of media advertising of all kinds, which gives rise to a similar situation. Even where we do choose our own media channel, source and content, we can easily be dissatisfied with some aspects of media performance and there is much scope for negative responses to the media. We are continually faced with the need to select and evaluate, and this includes making choices *against* what we dislike. The algorithmic solutions offered to this 'problem' by online social media intend to 'relieve' consumers of this curatorial work by recommending or automatically generating content based on their preferences (and those of others like them). Audiences tend to report both pleasurable and sometimes deeply ambivalent feelings regarding such affordances of the newer media environment.

Apart from the existence of positive or negative feelings towards source, medium or message, we need to consider the degree of audience *involvement*, engagement or *attachment*, which can vary from that of casual spectatorship to a high sense of personal commitment to a media device, person or performance. From the earliest days of radio, communicators sought to establish an illusion of personal contact and intimacy with the invisible audience by using familiar forms of address, by incorporating sound effects to simulate the presence of audiences or by encouraging audience participation. There has always been much pseudo-participation associated with radio and television, in the context of interactive media offerings online now more than ever, and it is not surprising that it evokes some response in the audience. In practice it is difficult to empirically distinguish 'real' attachment from 'artificial' attachment. But, as Hermes (1999: 74) points out: 'Seeing media figures as real and as part of our everyday cultural and emotional experience is part and parcel of how media texts come to have meaning.'

The concept of **parasocial interaction** was introduced by Horton and Wohl (1956) to describe the displacement of a human interlocutor by a media character or personality, treating it, by implication, as less satisfactory than real social interaction. However, it may be considered as better than nothing, or as a reaction to a lack of real social contact. Scales have been developed to measure the degree of parasocial interaction (PSI) (Austin, 1992), following a definition of PSI as 'the degree to which audience members feel they interact with their favourite TV news persona' (Rubin, Perse and Powell, 1990: 250). Given the media industry's switch towards the valuing of audience engagement next to audience reach (Kosterich and Napoli, 2016), more attention in recent years has been paid to the phenomenon of media fandom. Originally marginalized, ridiculed and stigmatized, today these particular kinds of 'engaged' audiences seem to represent the vanguard of new relationships with and within the media (Duits, Zwaan and Reijnders, 2014; see Chapter 11 on participation and convergence culture). As audiences become increasingly comfortable with participating in different ways throughout the 'mediatic' process (Krämer, 2015) – of imagining, sharing, creating, transmitting, promoting and responding to media – their orientation to media can be seen as changing, becoming perhaps more engaged, yet also less aware of distinct media devices, appearances and uses.

Different forms and degrees of personal orientation to media personalities and characters are given in Box 15.5.

# THE END OF THE AUDIENCE?

As we noted at the beginning of Chapter 14, the audience concept has always been more problematic than it seems, because it can be defined and constructed in so many ways and has no fixed existence. The problems are compounded the more we take the view of the audience itself rather than the media industry. New and different audiences can be constituted by people themselves based on some shared interest or identity. New technologies are bringing into question the clear distinction between sender and receiver which is crucial to the original idea of the media audience, as well as introducing new forms of use of media (see Chapter 6). Interactive and consultative uses of media take away the spectatorship that was so characteristic of the original mass audience. Aside from radically new communication technologies, there are many changes to the 'old technologies' and to media industries that have implications for the audience.

The effects of change are quite mixed, however. On the one hand, they increase the size of audiences for particular products and performers, as a result of concentration and monopoly forming and the exploitation of the same content across multiple media platforms and in many different markets. Internationalization is also a route towards much larger (cumulative) audiences for certain high-profile types of content and mass-mediated experiences. On the other hand, 'actual' audiences are being diversified as a result of channel multiplication and specialization. There are many more, but often smaller and more homogeneous, audiences, especially those formed on the basis of cultural proximity. Instead of audiences being recruited from a given geographical area or social class, they are based more on tastes, value systems and lifestyles. The term *segmentation* is used to refer to the process by which media supply is matched more precisely to a relevant set of media consumers, and the process is aided by the greater possibility of selection (and subsequent sharing of personal data) on the part of consumers themselves.

Another process, that of *fragmentation*, involves the dispersal of the same amount of audience attention over more and more media sources. Ultimately, nearly all choices can be individualized, spelling the end of the audience as a significant social collectivity. Media users will come to have no more in common with each other than owners of any other consumer article. Along with the fragmentation of audiences and the individualization of use comes a decline in the strength of ties that bind people to their chosen media source and a loss of any sense of identity as an audience.

We can summarize the audience trends discussed in terms of four succeeding stages, as shown in Figure 15.4. This applies especially to television, but it has a wider reference. In the early years of television (1950s and 1960s), the majority of viewers in most countries had a very limited choice of up to three national channels. The same media experience was widely shared by nearly everyone. This *unitary model* implies a single audience more or less co-extensive with the general public. As supply of content and channels increase, there is more diversity, and more distinctive options begin to emerge within the framework of a unitary model (for example, daytime and night-time television, and regional variations). This pattern of limited internal diversification can be called a *pluralism model*. The third stage, the *core–periphery model*, is one in which the multiplication of channels undermines the unity of the framework. It becomes possible, as a result of cable and satellite transmission, recording technology and streaming video, to enjoy a television diet that differs significantly from the majority or mainstream, and that is not necessarily dependent on a TV set anymore. The final stage envisaged in Figure 15.4 is that of the *breakup model*, where fragmentation accelerates and there is no longer any 'centre', just very many and very diverse sets of media users. This stage should not be mistaken for a lack of power of the media industries that license, franchise and distribute television (and other content).

As we have seen in Chapter 10, the industry's core response has been to push for (national and international) political deregulation enabling an acceleration of media concentration through acquisitions and mergers. This has spread the risk of producing diversified content for segmented and fragmented audiences in 'high choice' media environments. In a review of media concentration developments around the world, Noam (2018: 5) notes four key developments, all contributing to a complex field, where elements of all four stages of audience fragmentation are present:

MCQUAIL'S MEDIA AND MASS COMMUNICATION THEORY
AUDIENCES

- Mergers leading to large global media corporations have taken place in the context of a corresponding growth of a mass media and information sector.
- Because of digital convergence, many new businesses have entered the media sector, and media companies have crossed over to telecommunications and computer industries.
- Through internationalization, established media firms from some countries have gained market size and power in other countries, challenging domestic oligopolies.
- The Internet has vastly expanded distribution channels and content providers.

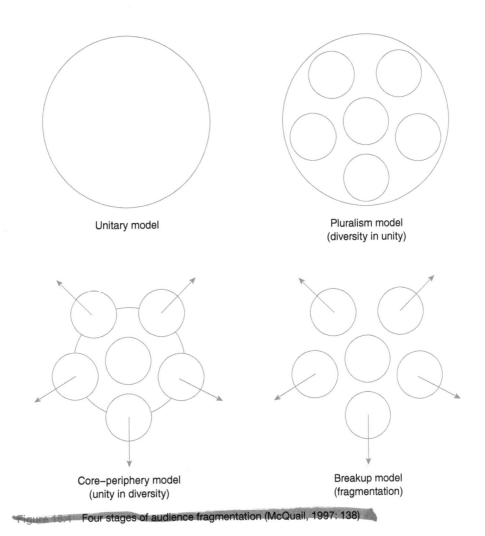

Unitary model

Pluralism model
(diversity in unity)

Core–periphery model
(unity in diversity)

Breakup model
(fragmentation)

Figure 18.1 Four stages of audience fragmentation (McQuail, 1997: 138)

# THE 'ESCAPE' OF THE AUDIENCE

The apparent changes in the general character of audiences can be assessed in different ways. The potential 'escape' of the audience from media industry management and control in the context of greatly increased choice seems to be an entry on the credit side in the balance of audience power, counterbalanced by the massive investments of these industries in audience-tracking practices and technologies.

When the Internet became a mass medium (in the early years of the twenty-first century) there was much optimism about a shift in favour of media consumers in the marketplace and even perhaps as individual citizens. Considering how there are more channels of relevant political and civic information and less likelihood of a mass audience being the object of semi-monopolistic propaganda or biased information, it was expected to be harder for would-be persuaders, whether political or commercial, to reach any large general public. The audience would also be less attentive to messages received than was the case in the early days of radio and television. The over-abundance of supply outstrips the capacity of people to notice or make use of it. Even when attention is given, the likelihood of influence is lower than it used to be. Neuman and Pool (1986) invoked the idea of an equilibrium model, according to which audience discomfort at overload is avoided by reducing the 'quality' of attention. The typical media user has less time and motivation and, according to comments made above, lacks the social or normative connection with a media source that would support influence. The quality as well as the quantity of potential influence has been diluted.

The increased 'power' of the audience should not be overstated since there are gains as well as losses. The more audiences become just another set of consumer markets, the more they lose collective social power. According to Cantor (1994: 168): 'Audiences as market segments rather than audiences as cultural politicians remain the most powerful influence on television content.' Aggregate market influence is far removed from that of public opinion or organized collective action. One of the continued advantages of public service television is that the audience has some collective rights as a body of citizens that still has formal control over media channels. Furthermore, the rise of Internet platform companies, through which a majority of people access media content and services online, has contributed to increasingly fine-grained, detailed information being shared about individual usage practices. The commodification of these personal data in turn has led to questionable uses thereof by companies and political parties alike to micro-target audiences with sometimes sophisticated, and often bluntly manipulated, news and information in order to influence elections and purchasing behaviours. Although the evidence of the actual 'effects' of such widespread attempts to influence behaviour is still lacking, there is a legitimate concern about such practices.

Changes affecting the audience as a concept and reality are summarized in Box 15.6.

---

**15.6**

## Media changes affecting the audience

- Multiplication of channels
- Conglomeration increasing some audience sizes
- Fragmentation of the mass audience
- Segmentation according to market characteristics
- Escape of the audience from management and measurement
- New types of audience emerge: interactive, participatory and consultative
- Recapture of audiences through online tracking and personal data sharing

---

# THE FUTURE OF THE AUDIENCE

At the present time, despite the trends discussed, we cannot conclude that the mass audience will fade away. It still exists, albeit in changing forms, and the mass media industries have shown a remarkable capacity to survive. Despite the multiplication of channels, the greater ease of entering the media market with new technology, the rise of a digital media system dominated by Internet platforms and mobile applications, and the increased capacity of individuals to exercise choice, the overall structure of media audiences has not yet changed fundamentally. Generally speaking, the industry is still driven by the search for successful formats that will reach the largest possible audiences at home and internationally.

It is still plausible to conclude, along with Neuman (1991), that there is a considerable inertial force that limits fundamental change in audience formation. One aspect of the resistance is attributable to 'the social psychology of media use', expressed in 'deeply ingrained habits of passive, half-attentive use' (ibid.: 42). The other pressure is the communications industry itself. According to Neuman (ibid.: 42): 'Economies of scale push in the direction of common-denominator, one-way mass communications, rather than promoting narrowcasting and two-way communications.' The rise of a 'long tail' economy consisting of many niche markets, products and audiences has not been as disruptive as perhaps expected, as a small subset of media products across all media still tend to dominate attention and sales worldwide (Elberse, 2008). It has perhaps become much riskier and more uncertain for the industry to produce games, films or any other type of content that can be predictably guaranteed 'top billing' (in film, 'tentpole' or 'blockbuster'; in digital games, 'triple A') status.

There are also powerful and varied social forces influencing media production and use that have deep roots and are resistant to the influence of technological change on its own. The shape of audiences reflects the structure, dynamics and needs of social formations, ranging from national societies to families. These forces do not all work in the same direction to support the mass audience, and some are likely to favour new uses of newer media and thus new audience realities.

# THE AUDIENCE CONCEPT AGAIN

Sufficient reasons have already been given to wonder whether the term 'audience' is still a useful one, especially as there are so many kinds of use of many different communications media. The term 'audience' cannot easily be divested of its strong connotation of 'spectatorship' – of rather passive watching and listening. It is also closely tied in meaning to the reception of some 'message', despite the fact that we know audience behaviour to involve several equally important motives or satisfactions – for instance, social togetherness and the pleasures of actual use of a medium, regardless of content. Despite this, there seems to be no viable alternative term, and we will go on using it to cover very diverse occasions. In its early manifestation as a mass audience for the 'industrial' media, it was always something of a caricature, ignoring the degree of sociability and negotiation involved in attending to media. At the heart of the concept remains our concern with audiences as collectivities that relate people to their social and cultural contexts.

By way of indicating and summarizing the diverse possibilities, Box 15.7 offers a list of the main dimensions of audience. Each variable shown can be used to describe and classify one or another of the many types of audience that exist, and each has a history in theory and research.

---

## 15.7

## The main dimensions of the audience

- Degree of activity or passivity
- Degree of interactivity and interchangeability
- Size and duration
- Locatedness in space and time

---

- Group character (social/cultural identity)
- Simultaneity of contact with source
- Heterogeneity of composition
- Social relations between sender and receiver
- Message versus social/behavioural definition of situation
- Degree of perceived 'social presence'
- Sociability of context of use

# CONCLUSION

This book is about media and mass communication, and it must be clear that the audience for these phenomena constitutes a foundational part for understanding, theorizing and explaining the 'circuit of culture' (see Chapter 17) in society. As we have seen, the concept of audience shades into other terms – such as user – to describe the use of a variety of converging communication technologies. There is common ground that straddles the boundary between media channels' communication forms, especially when we consider alternative ways of using spare time; various functions that can be met by different means; the fact of multiple dependencies on technology; the ownership and organization of mass and newer media; and some of the forms of content. As a result, we cannot make any certain predictions, even about the strength and direction of broad trends, other than that audience research has become both more important and fascinating than before, given profound concerns about a society's need for shared narratives and communal experience – not to be confused with social consensus.

# FURTHER READING

Courtois, C., Verdegem, P. and De Marez, L. (2013) 'The triple articulation of media technologies in audiovisual media consumption', *Television & New Media*, 14(5): 421–439.

Ettema, J.S. and Whitney, D.C. (eds) (1994) *Audiencemaking: How the Media Create the Audience*. Newbury Park, CA: Sage.

Fletcher, R. and Kleis Nielsen, R. (2017) 'Are news audiences increasingly fragmented? A cross-national comparative analysis of cross-platform news audience fragmentation and duplication', *Journal of Communication*, 67: 476–498.

Kim, S.J. (2016) 'A repertoire approach to cross-platform media use behavior', *New Media and Society*, 18(3): 353–372.

Papacharissi, Z. (2014) *Affective Publics: Sentiment, Technology, and Politics.* Oxford: Oxford University Press.

Quandt, T. and von Pape, T. (2010) 'Living in the mediatope', *The Information Society*, 26(5): 330–345.

# PART 7
## EFFECTS

# 16

## PROCESSES AND MODELS OF MEDIA EFFECTS

Media have effects – on people's feelings, thoughts, attitudes, beliefs and behaviours. Media use has consequences. This is a given in media and mass communication research. Yet what exactly constitutes a 'media effect', what the direction of such an effect is, what precisely explains an effect, and how one can effectively measure the effect are recurring topics of debate among scholars, students, policymakers, media professionals and the public alike. Both basic and elaborate theories on media effects and consequences have been formulated and tested going as far back as the 1920s. Clearly, the question of media effects is one of the foundational discussions of the field.

This chapter provides a general overview of theories and models of mass media effect. It begins with a paradox. There is a widespread belief, nearing on certainty, that the mass media are a powerful instrument of influence on opinion and of effects on behaviour. At the same time, there is great difficulty in predicting effects, engineering them by design or in proving that they have happened, after the event. Despite this difficulty, knowledge about the processes involved has gradually increased, and as a result we are in a better position to say when and which and for whom effects are more or less likely. The chapter charts the development of theory and explains the different kinds of effect that are involved and the various models according to which they occur.

## THE PREMISE OF MEDIA EFFECT

As noted above, the entire study of media and mass communication is based on the assumption that the media have significant effects on people's feelings, opinions, attitudes and behaviours, yet there is little agreement on the nature and extent of these assumed effects. This uncertainty is the more surprising since everyday experience provides countless, if minor, examples of influence. Media feature prominently in discussions among family and friends, triggered not least by the omnipresence of smartphones and other mobile devices in private encounters. We dress for the weather as forecast, buy something because of an advertisement, go to a film mentioned in social media, react in countless ways to news, to films, to streaming music, and so on. Good or bad economic news clearly affects business and consumer confidence. There are many cases of negative media publicity concerning, for instance, food contamination or adulteration, leading to significant changes in behaviour, sometimes with large economic impact. Public figures in all walks of life as well as firms and institutions are extremely sensitive about their image in the media – in what Thompson (2005) calls 'a new age of mediated visibility'. Acts of violence or suicide appear to be copied from, or stimulated by, media portrayals of such acts. Much policy and regulation is directed at preventing the media from causing harm, and encouraging the media to do some good.

Our minds are full of media-derived information and impressions. We live in a world saturated by media sounds and images, where politics, government and business operate on the assumption that we know what is going on in the wider world. Few of us cannot think of some personal instance of gaining significant information or of forming an opinion because of the media. Much money and effort are also spent on directing the media to achieve such effects, especially by way of advertising and public relations, and it is hard to believe that this would happen without a conviction that it works, more or less according to plan. Certainly, the media themselves seem confident of their capacity to achieve intended effects.

Media effects can be defined as 'the deliberative and non-deliberative short- and long-term within-person changes in cognitions, emotions, attitudes and behavior that result from media use' (Valkenburg and Peter, 2013a: 199). Despite such a clear and historically consistent focus of theory and research, considerable areas of uncertainty remain. We know that under some conditions – for instance, of consistency and consensus of message, prominence of news reports from trusted sources, coupled with large audiences – we can expect there to be certain effects on public knowledge and on opinions, but we cannot be sure of the degree of change that will occur, nor of which sectors of the audience will respond most, never mind the case of one individual. The media are rarely likely to be the only necessary or sufficient cause of an effect, and their relative contribution is hard to assess. There are many reasons for this uncertainty, and even common-sense wavers when faced with questions of media effect in the contested areas of morals, fears and deviant behaviour, which have attracted most public notice. On such matters the media are unlikely to be a primary or sufficient cause, and it would be extremely difficult to take full account of all the possible psychological, social and cultural factors involved. Furthermore, it makes little sense to speak of 'the media' as if they were one thing rather than the carriers of an enormously diverse set of messages, images and ideas that in turn are shaped by the affordances of particular technologies.

Most effect research has been initiated from outside rather than within the media, especially by social critics, politicians, interest groups, and so on. The underlying premise has usually been that mass media are some kind of 'problem' for the rest of society, and problematic aspects of media effects still tend to shape public debate on the media, including the Internet and social and mobile media. There remains a large gap between those who either claim great power for the media (usually for self-interested reasons) or are fearful of media power to cause harm, and those who dismiss the claims and fears as largely unproven. It is not going too far to say that there is a 'media power belief system' whose adherents do not need detailed proof of the kind demanded by sceptics. On the other hand, the rejection of all claims to media power on grounds of lack of empirical proof can lead to another kind of error. Many of the potential effects of mass media are either too complex, subtle or long-term to be captured by one-off studies, by often quite rudimentary forms of measurement, or by assuming unidirectional effects. However, this conflict of view can be fruitful. It is a reminder that we have to be careful not to accept the claims of the 'persuaders' or of the critics too readily, that we should not confuse particular messages with the medium as a whole, that we should discriminate carefully between different types of effect and different situations, and that we should be mindful of effects on individuals rather than on entire groups or populations. Most important, we should give due weight to the fact that the effects are determined at least as much by the receiver as by the sender.

## HISTORY OF MEDIA EFFECT RESEARCH AND THEORY

The development of thinking about media effects may be said to have a 'natural history', in the sense of it being strongly shaped by the circumstances of time and place. It has also been influenced by several 'environmental' factors, including the interests of governments and law-makers, changing technology, the events of history, the activities of pressure groups and propagandists, the ongoing concerns of public opinion, and even the findings and the fashions of media and mass communication scholarship. It is not surprising that no straight path of cumulative development of knowledge can be discerned.

The literature – including earlier iterations of this book – has tended to distinguish a number of phases in the history of the field. Although these stages are useful to map onto the history of media effects research, we cannot assume a neat, orderly progressive development, nor would we suggest that during these various phases research confirming other hypotheses and reporting conflicting results did not appear. Rather than phases, it is perhaps better to talk about different perceptions of media effects that have inspired – and continue to inspire – a variety of research and theory across disciplines. Such media effects perceptions are important to identify and study, if anything because such views explain why people recognize the media as important to their lives and to society, as 'people believe the media are important because they believe that the media have effects' (McLeod, Wise and Perryman, 2017: 52).

Overall, it can be argued that scholarship throughout history has consistently documented compelling evidence for media effects on what people talk about, on how we form and express opinions, and even on behaviour. However, across all these studies – over a period of about one hundred years of research involving several disciplines – generally only modest effects have been found. Reviewing sixty years (1956–2016) of communication scholarship, Rains, et al. (2018: 14) suggest that small effects are to be expected, and in fact are quite typical for research involving (the prediction of) human behaviour, concluding that the specific problem of communication is that it is multi-determined and highly contingent, as 'communication outcomes often depend on a vast number of situationally variable small causes rather than a small number of constantly powerful causes'. Lang (2013: 15) similarly summarizes her take on the field as follows: 'almost the only thing we have learned after 60 years of mass communication effects research is that the weight of exposure to almost any specific medium or content influences any given behavior, on average, very slightly',

Lang signals, as well as Valkenburg et al. (2016) do in their comprehensive assessment of the history of media effects theories and research, the somewhat frustrating notion of consistently finding only small to medium effects even though personal, first-hand experience and common sense certainly suggest otherwise. In his take on this history, Neuman (2016: 377) consequently admonishes the field that '[w]e can do better than simply and apologetically asserting after all these decades of scholarship that we now know that communication effects are "not so minimal"'.

These and many other reviews and meta-analyses of media effects research over the years showcase consistent efforts by generations of media and communication scholars to find more or less significant media 'effects'. Underpinning these efforts are a number of consistent assumptions about the influence of media on people and society. Four distinct ways of making sense of media effects can be found and traced as influential across media and mass communication scholarship: from 'all-powerful' to 'limited' via 'negotiated' to 'complex reciprocal' effects.

## ALL-POWERFUL MEDIA

It can be argued that scholarly interest in the media got its start by studying and assuming strong media effects, especially on young people. From the turn of the century until the 1930s the then new media of press, film and radio were credited with considerable power to shape opinion and belief, to change habits of life and to mould behaviour more or less according to the will of their controllers (Bauer and Bauer, 1960). This view was based not on scientific investigation, but on awe at the possibilities for mass persuasion that seemed to open up and on observation, of the enormous popularity of these media that intruded into many aspects of everyday life as well as public affairs.

In Europe, the use of media by advertisers, by First World War propagandists, by dictatorial states in the inter-war years and by the new revolutionary regime in Russia, all appeared to confirm what people were already inclined to believe – that the media could be immensely powerful. Against the background of such beliefs, systematic research using survey and experimental methods, and drawing heavily on social psychology, was begun during the 1920s and 1930s, although mainly limited to the United States. Many books were written about the power of propaganda in this period (for example, Lasswell, 1927; see also Jowett and O'Donnell, 1999).

Assumptions about powerful media have continued to surface throughout the history of media and communication research up to this day, whether informed by observations of media use and behavioural changes over longer periods of time – such as in the case of expectations of cultivation of people's worldviews through watching a lot of television (Gerbner and Gross, 1976) – or by considering the formidable power that the algorithms governing platforms like Facebook and Google have to become the 'new apostles of culture' (Striphas, 2015: 407).

Retrospective accounts of media effects research (for example, McGuire, 1973; Lang and Lang, 1981; McLeod, Kosicki and Pan, 1991; Valkenburg et al., 2016) shed considerable doubt on whether there ever was a watershed between a belief in media power and one in media impotence, instead showing considerable agreement about strong media effects in the context of many different interpretations and a wide variety of views on how best to study such effects. One particular problem plaguing much of the literature is a general and historically growing focus on short-term effects to the detriment of (more complex, iterative and expensive) longitudinal, theoretically rich research designs (Walter et al., 2018). This contributes to studies consistently finding small but significant media effects to the detriment of longitudinal designs focusing on direct as much as indirect effects.

The upsurge of critical theory in the 1960s made an important and lasting contribution by crediting the media with powerful legitimating and controlling effects in the interests of capitalist or bureaucratic states. Instead of devoting much time to empirically testing an assumption of effect, much critical and cultural scholarship of the media 'finds mass media effects to be self-evident' (Lang, 2013: 16). This has produced – and continues to produce – meticulously documented work unpacking the various ways dominant power-structures in society pervade the value systems of mass-mediated messages. Much of this work sees mass media operating – directly or indirectly – in the service of (reflecting and thereby) maintaining the established social order, which becomes empirically established primarily through analyses of content (see Chapter 12 on structuralism, semiotics and discourse analysis).

When media and mass communication scholarship got underway across Asia, Africa and particularly Latin America, it tended to be uniform in its assumption, as much as condemnation, of powerful media effects, primarily identified as western (or specifically American) influences on indigenous perspectives and cultures. Waisbord (2014: 5), for example, considers how the identity of Latin American communication/media studies has been 'grounded in a deliberate position against theoretical approaches identified with "Yankee/gringo" scholarship, government, and media industries'. Such 'American' approaches were seen as positivist and informed by the transmission model of mass communication, whereas a critical consciousness and resistant appropriations of media were preferred. In much of African communication research, effects have been consistently presumed in an overall scholarly trend of identifying opportunities for media to effect social betterment (Milton, 2017).

## LIMITED MEDIA POWER

The transition to empirical enquiry led to a second perspective of thinking about media effects. Its beginning is well exemplified in the research literature by the series of Payne Fund studies in the United States in the early 1930s (Blumer, 1933; Blumer and Hauser,

1933; Peterson and Thurstone, 1933). These studies were primarily concerned with the influence of films on children and young people. The results confirmed many ideas about the effects on the emotions, attitudes and behaviour of young people. This era of research into media effects continued until the early 1960s, with particular reference to the effects of television when it arrived in the post-war years (for example, Himmelweit et al., 1958). Many separate studies were carried out into the effects of different types of content and media, of particular films or programmes and of entire democratic election campaigns. Attention was mainly concentrated on the possibilities of using film and other media for planned persuasion or information.

In the immediate post-war era, research into media effects became much more sophisticated. More account was taken of the moderating effects of social and demographic variables, such as age, education and sex, and also of social psychological factors, such as predispositions and prior attitudes, personality type, persuadability, degree of interest and motivation, trust in the source, and so on. The influence of personal social contacts was also included in the range of potential variables as well as of the different motives for attending to media in the first place. The more variables that were added, the more difficult it became to pin down and quantify the precise contribution of the media to any change, and the suspicion grew that this might be typically quite small.

What now seems like the end of an era was marked by expressions of disillusion with the outcome of this kind of media effect research. One leading researcher, Berelson (1959), suggested that the field of mass communication research might be withering away. It was Berelson who summed up the achieved wisdom of research into media effects in a much-quoted conclusion (Box 16.1). This sounds like a confession of despair, but it also points to the key factors that need to be examined in any research into effects.

## 16.1
### Berelson on media effects

Some kinds of communication on some kinds of issues have brought to the attention of some kinds of people under some kinds of conditions have some kinds of effects. (Berelson, 1948: 172)

There were new statements of conventional wisdom which assigned a much more modest role to media in causing any planned or unintended effects. The still influential and useful summary of early research by Joseph Klapper, published in 1960 (though dating largely from 1949), appeared to set the seal on this research phase. It concluded that 'mass communication does not ordinarily serve as a necessary or sufficient cause of audience effects, but rather functions through a nexus of mediating factors' (1960: 8).

It was not that the media had been found to be without effects or influence; rather there was no direct or one-to-one link to be expected between media stimulus and audience response. Media were shown to operate within a pre-existing structure of social relationships and a particular social and cultural context. These factors took primacy in shaping the opinions, attitudes and behaviour under study and also in shaping media choice, attention and response on the part of audiences. It was also clear that information acquisition could occur without related attitude change, and attitude change without changes in behaviour (for example, Hovland, Lumsdaine and Sheffield, 1949; Trenaman and McQuail, 1961).

Such a sobriety of assessment was slow to modify opinion outside the scholarly community. It is particularly hard to accept for those who make a living from advertising, propaganda and misinformation campaigns online, and for those in the media who value the myth of their great potency. There was still room for varying assessments since the message of limited effect was heavily qualified and was itself a reaction against unrealistic claims. The failure of research to find powerful effects can generally be attributed to the complexity of the processes involved, as well as the inadequacy of research designs and methods.

The emergence of (critical) audience studies in the 1980s and 1990s, particularly in response to television, additionally contributed to insights into the various unexpected, resistant and 'active' ways in which readers, listeners and viewers give meaning to media (Ang, 1991). Furthermore, audiences were also seen as co-opting or 'poaching' (Jenkins, 1988) the stories and messages from the media into their own ways of making meaning – something that Jenkins (1988), referring to earlier work by De Certeau (1984), understood as acts of appropriating and reclaiming ownership of popular culture from corporate interests. Instead of an assumption of powerful (yet subtle) effects, audiences were seen as 'interpretative communities', and studies of fans and fandom in particular led the way to a reconsidered notion of agency 'to challenge the power of the culture industry to construct the common sense of a mass society' (Jenkins, 1988: 104).

Contemporary iterations of a limited effect perception ground assumptions in the changing nature of our contemporary digital media environment, which 'highlights the inadequacy of a set of theories premised on distinct communication constituents producing messages whose effects can be isolated, observed, and measured' (Singer, 2018: 9). In an 'immersive, interconnected, individualized, iterative, and instantaneous' (ibid.: 7) media environment, Singer (2018) argues that an appreciation of mediated effects should be based on understanding the relationships between people in the communication process, whereby their roles as senders and receivers are often interchangeable and constantly changing.

In most contemporary media theories, assessments of a pervasive and ubiquitous media environment, which would seem to presume profound media effects, go hand in hand with quite nuanced appreciations of the role and influence of media on people's lives. Madianou and Miller (2013), for example, conclude that people around the world, coming from a wide variety of social and economic backgrounds, increasingly live in a situation of '**polymedia**', exposed to a plurality of media that are at once omnipresent and seemingly effortlessly integrated into the social and emotional realm of everyday existence. They define polymedia as 'an emerging environment of communicative opportunities that functions as an "integrated structure" within which each individual medium is defined in relational terms in the context of all other media' (ibid.: 2). This ethnographic approach to the role and influence of media has become a thriving field of research, contributing to an understanding of the roles that media play at the micro-level of everyday life and the macro-level of society.

As with mediatization theory (see Chapter 4), this signals an important shift from seeing media as having powerful 'effects' on people and society to a dialectical consideration of media as being co-constitutive of any process governing social and societal affairs (Hepp et al., 2018). In this context, Couldry (2012: 67) illustrates 'the myth of the mediated centre', whereby researchers can at times contribute to naturalizing the central and privileged role that mass media claim in society. His argument fits in a broader 'non-media-centric' turn in the study of media influence and power (Krajina, Moores and Morley, 2014), which advocates a 'decentring' of media and communication research to take the categories of understanding of the majority population, as manifested in their everyday media-related activities, as the primary object of analysis (see also Tosoni and Ridell, 2016).

## NEGOTIATED MEDIA INFLUENCE

Beginning in the late 1970s, an approach to media effects emerged that can best be termed 'social constructivist' (Gamson and Modigliani, 1989). In essence, this involves a view of the media as having their most significant effects by constructing meanings. The media tend to offer a 'preferred' view of social reality (one that purports to be widely accepted and reliable, as determined by professional communicators and their sources). This includes both the information provided and the appropriate way of interpreting it, forming value judgements and opinions and reacting to it. These are the ready-made meanings that the media systematically offer to their audiences. It is up to the audience member to decide whether or not to adopt the views offered, although they are often the only material available for forming an opinion on distant matters. Alternative meanings and interpretations of sources could include influences from personal experience or from the social or cultural environment, which might even be a basis for active resistance to influence. Thus, there is no automatic or direct transfer of meaning but a negotiation between what is offered and what a receiver is inclined to accept. This view of the process is a break from the 'all-powerful media' paradigm and is also marked by a shift from quantitative and behaviourist methods towards qualitative and ethnographic methods.

Media influence tends to be seen as negotiated, and the origins of this perspective are diverse and lie quite deep in the past. The thinking has some points of similarity with early 'powerful media' theory, including, for example, the theory of ideology and false consciousness, Gerbner's cultivation theory (Signorielli and Morgan, 1990) and the ideas elaborated by Noelle-Neumann (1974) in her 'spiral of silence' theory. These are discussed in the next chapter of this book. At the same time, it recognizes people's agency *vis-à-vis* mediated messages in similar ways as a view that assumes limits to media power. This paradigm of effects has two main thrusts. First, media 'construct' social formations and even history itself by framing images of reality (in fiction as well as news) in predictable and patterned ways. Secondly, people in audiences construct for themselves their own view of social reality and their place in it, in interaction with the symbolic constructions offered by the media. The approach allows both for the power of media and for the power of people to choose, with a terrain of continuous negotiation (where people may choose to adopt, resist, or in other ways appropriate the information and meanings of media texts) in between, as it were.

The constructivist approach does not replace all earlier formulations of the effect process, for instance in matters of attention-gaining, direct stimulus to individual behaviour or emotional response. It is also consistent with a good deal of earlier theory, although it departs radically in terms of method and research design by calling for much deeper, broader and more qualitative kinds of evidence. It clearly owes more to the cultural than to the structural and behavioural traditions outlined earlier (Chapter 3). But it does not stand entirely apart from the latter, since investigation has to be located in a societal context and it assumes that eventual constructions are the outcome of numerous behaviours and cognitions by many participants in complex social events. The approach can be applied to a good many situations of presumed media influence, especially in relation to public opinion, social attitudes, political choice, ideology and many cognitions.

In contemporary accounts of the constructivist approach, changes in society and everyday life are considered to be inseparable from the structuring role media play (Couldry and Hepp, 2016). In this context, Mihelj and Stanyer (2019) advocate bridging the gap between approaches that consider media and mass communication as an *agent* of social change versus as an *environment* for social change – to move beyond powerful (or limited) effects – and instead embracing a processual perspective on the role of media (see also Chapter 3).

## COMPLEX RECIPROCAL MEDIA EFFECTS

The various perspectives informing and inspiring media effects research should not be understood as clear-cut. There is much overlap. First and foremost, we have to acknowledge that public and scholarly concern about effects of exposure to certain media – such as popular music, violent video games, or the seductions of smartphone applications – tends to follow the development and widespread (or 'mass') distribution of such a medium. Secondly, most researchers, regardless of their disciplinary background, methodological approach and overall view on the influence of media, have tended to be quite careful when interpreting data and drawing conclusions on the basis of their findings. A consistent theme in the various reports on media effects research over the decades has been that 'results were more complicated than the authors had expected' (Potter and Bolls, 2012: 18), prompting scholars to dig deeper and develop more sophisticated theories and methods.

In a content analysis of effects studies appearing between 1993 and 2005 in sixteen prominent scholarly journals in the field of media and mass communication research, Potter and Riddle (2007) identified mostly studies on the influence of television news, based on quantitative methods, grounded in 144 different theories. Their review paints a picture of the field as gradually coalescing around its own 'unique identity' and 'community of scholars' (2007: 100), featuring distinct research questions and methods, while at same time fragmenting across a wide variety of theories, especially regarding notions of media influence and effects. However, if we look beyond all the particular theories and methodologies, there is considerable agreement across the literature, no matter how 'stretched thin' the field at times appears. All in all, most scholarship today converges around nuanced notions of conditional, transactional and context-dependent effects and media influence. Contemporary theories tend to focus on the interaction between media factors (media use, media processing, technological affordances) and non-media factors (for example, disposition, social and cultural context). Scholarship in this area tends to diverge in either macro-level work on the ways in which the network society (Usher and Carlson, 2018), (deep) mediatization (Hepp, 2019), and notions of a 'media life' (Deuze, 2012) structure and shape societies and societal change, or gravitate towards increasingly specific, individual-level research on media use and influence.

Valkenburg and Peter (2013b) integrate existing high-profile media-effects theories into what they call the Differential Susceptibility to Media Effects Model (DSMM), with a focus on micro-level media effects, looking at the individual media user. Their model seems particularly useful to consider in more detail, as it is deliberately grounded in a historical appreciation and integration of media effects theories, and it includes (as much as it allows for) insights and assessments in a cross-disciplinary way.

The DSMM consists of an integrated set of four related propositions based on an appreciation of media effects as conditional, indirect and transactional. First, the authors make explicit the various ways in which media effects are conditional, based on dispositional, developmental and social context. *Dispositional susceptibility* to media influence refers to 'person dimensions' that predispose the selection of and responsiveness to media, including gender, temperament, personality, values, attitudes, beliefs and moods. *Developmental susceptibility* considers media use as determined by someone's media cognitive, emotional and social development, allowing for differences across the life span. *Social susceptibility* is defined as all social-context factors, including but not limited to one's interpersonal context (for example, family and friends), institutional context (such as school or work) and societal context, all of which restrict or enable particular media and uses thereof.

The second proposition of the DSMM is one of indirect media effects, operationalizing the various processes at work while people are using media. Valkenburg and

Peter (2013b: 227) distinguish three media response states: cognitive, emotional and excitative. These states are seen as mediating between media use and media effects rather than acting as moderators – the difference is determined by the extent to which someone always acts when using media (which can be generally controlled for), or how someone acts in a particular case and context (which would have to be measured specifically). Although the model investigates these response states separately, the researchers acknowledge that cognitions and emotions are not distinct 'forces' within the mind.

The third proposition follows from the second one, in that Valkenburg and Peter – in line with much qualitative research into media use – argue that the three differential-susceptibility variables they identified all have an influence on media response states. In other words, different people under different circumstances select, interpret and respond to media differently, and this should be taken into consideration when making claims about (and doing research on) media influence and effects.

The fourth and final proposition that Valkenburg and Peter (2013b) introduce is a notion of media effects as transactional, meaning that the outcomes of media influence can also cause media use. This is a stark departure from 'two-variable' research looking at unidirectional media effects (Chaffee, 1981). Whether someone likes to watch pornographic images and video or play violent digital games can be considered to be a result of their overly sexualized or aggressive personality as much as it is a consequence of using those kinds of media (see also Slater, 2007; Bandura, 2009). There is a reciprocal relationship between media use, influence, personality and behaviour at work here, suggesting a 'complimentary influence process' (Valkenburg and Peter, 2013a: 205).

It must be clear that media effects as seen from such a complex, reciprocal perspective require sophisticated, fine-tuned and often longitudinal research designs. Broadening the scope even further, Valkenburg et al. (2016) organize existing media effects theories into five global features that together provide a boundaried object of study grounded in a notion of complex reciprocal media effects (see Box 16.2).

## 16.2

### Boundary conditions of media effects (Valkenburg et al. 2016)

- Selectivity of media use
- Media properties are predictors
- Media effects are indirect
- Media effects are conditional
- Media effects are transactional

The four-stage account of the development of thinking about media effects is only one interpretation, and can best be seen as a review of different perspectives rather than a more or less linear historical trajectory of research and scholarship. In her overview of the field, Perse (2001) suggests that this and similar accounts of the development of effect theory are an oversimplification and may be misleading, especially by not recognizing the differences between various research areas. For instance, research on children and on political communication (see Chapter 17) have different histories. Instead, she proposes to deal with key differences in terms of alternative models of effect. The four models she names are:

- direct effects;
- conditional effects (varying according to social and psychological factors);
- cumulative effects (gradual and long-term);
- cognitive-transactional effects (with particular reference to **schema** and framing).

In fact, these models correspond quite closely to the four perspectives on media effects described above. Table 16.1 (from Perse, 2001) summarizes the main features of these models.

Table 16.1    Four models of media effects (Perse, 2001: 51)

| | Models of media effects | | |
| --- | --- | --- | --- |
| | Nature of effects | Media content variables | Audience variables |
| **Direct** | Immediate, uniform, observable<br>Short-term<br>Emphasis on change | Salience, arousal, realism | Not relevant |
| **Conditional** | Individualized reinforcement as well as change<br>Cognitive, affective and behavioural<br>Long- or short-term | Not relevant | Social categories<br>Social relationships<br>Individual differences |
| **Cumulative** | Based on cumulative exposure<br>Cognitive or affect<br>Rarely behavioural<br>Enduring | Consonant across channels<br>Repetition | Not relevant |
| **Cognitive-transactional** | Immediate and short-term<br>Based on one-shot exposure<br>Cognitive and affective, behavioural effects possible | Salience of visual cues | Schema make-up<br>Mood<br>Goals |

## MEDIA POWER CAN VARY WITH THE TIMES

Before leaving the historical aspect of research into media effects, it is worth reflecting on a suggestion by Carey (2009) that variations in belief in the power of mass communications may have a historical explanation. Carey contends that the shift in the argument about the effects from a powerful to a limited to a more powerful model has to be considered in the context of transformations of the social world over this period, and that expectations of media power and effects are uniquely tied to one's preferred theory of the mass society. Powerful effects were indeed signalled in a time of world upheaval around the two world wars, while the quieter 1950s and 1960s seemed more stable, until peace was again upset by social upheaval. In today's context of pervasive and ubiquitous media, the global domination of a handful of Internet platforms, and the enormous popularity of mobile media, concerns about powerful media have resurfaced. It does seem that whenever the stability of society is disturbed, by crime, war, economic malaise or some 'moral panic', the mass media are given some of the responsibility. This suggestion is confirmed by claims made that the media contributed to the banking and credit crisis of 2008–2009 by fuelling the earlier boom and failing to warn of impending bust. Some parts of the charge are convincing, but as usual the media are unlikely to have been more than a contributory factor.

We can only speculate about the reasons for such associations in time, but we cannot rule out the possibility that media are actually more influential in certain ways at times of crisis or heightened awareness. This might apply to the impact of the fall of communism in Europe or to international conflicts such as the Gulf and Balkan wars of the 1990s and the Afghanistan and Iraq wars that followed 9/11. Similar analyses can be made regarding the role of mass media (and PR strategies particularly) in fuelling fears as much as heightening awareness of global warming and climate change, including the remarkable role of Swedish teenager Greta Thunberg (from 2018 onwards) in mobilizing global action using the social media hashtag #ClimateStrike.

There are several reasons for this differential possibility of media power. People often know about the more significant historical events only through the media and may associate the message with the medium. In times of change and uncertainty, it is also highly probable that people are more dependent on media as a source of information and guidance (Ball-Rokeach and DeFleur, 1976; Ball-Rokeach, 1985, 1998). Media have also been shown to be more influential on matters outside immediate personal experience. Under conditions of tension and uncertainty, government, business and other elites and interests often try to use media to influence and control opinion. Perse (2001: 53–82) points out that media help to reduce uncertainty and fear by providing information and explanation. They also contribute to solidarity and mobilization in response to dangers and threats. The important point is that the media are not constant as a potential or actual influence, over time and between places.

# TYPES OF COMMUNICATIVE POWER

The concept of power in human affairs has proved difficult to pin down, and not only in relation to the media. Where it has been defined, two alternative paths have been followed. One takes a behavioural and causal line of reasoning that is consistent with stimulus–response thinking and in which power is equated with the probability of achieving some given outcome, intended or not. The other model is sociological and derives from Max Weber's definition of power as the 'chance of a man or number of men to realize their will in a communal action even against the resistance of others who are participating in the action' (1964: 152). In this view of power, a relationship is presumed to exist between the partners to action, and coercion is possible to achieve some aim. There are also winners and losers (a zero-sum situation).

While both models are relevant to the question of media effects, the second has proved to have more explanatory potential, even where effects are not intended, since the achievement of most effects requires the co-operation or compliance of the person to be influenced. However, when applied to mass communication, there may not be obvious partners to action and there is little chance of true coercion. Communicative or symbolic power is generally different from other kinds of power since it depends on non-material factors (trust, rationality, respect, affection, etc.). The point to underline here is also that there are different ways in which symbolic power can be used. The main types are as follows:

- by way of information;
- by stimulation to action;
- by directing attention differentially;
- by persuasion;
- by defining situations and framing 'reality'.

For a number of reasons (especially the lack of resistance and low threshold for an effect), more effects from media occur as a result of defining situations and framing reality, provision of information or the differential direction of attention (including the amplification of certain images and ideas) than for persuasion or stimulation to action. These points are largely indicated by and consistent with the 'negotiated influence' phase described above.

# LEVELS AND KINDS OF EFFECTS

Media 'effects' are simply the consequences of what the mass media do, whether intended or not. The expression 'media power', on the other hand, refers to a general potential on the part of the media to have effects, especially of a planned kind. 'Media effectiveness' is a statement about the potential of media in achieving a given aim and always implies intention or some planned communication goal. Such distinctions are important for precision, although it is hard to keep to a consistent usage. Even more essential for research and theory is to observe the distinction between 'levels' of occurrence, especially the levels of individual, group or organization, social institution, national society and culture. Each or all can be affected by mass communication, and effects at any one level (especially a 'higher' level) often imply some effects at other levels. Most media effect research has been carried out, methodologically, at the individual level, although often with the aim of drawing conclusions relating to collective or higher levels.

Perhaps the most confusing aspect of research on effects is the multiplicity and complexity of the phenomena involved. Broad distinctions are normally made between effects that are cognitive (to do with knowledge and opinion), effects that are affectual (relating to attitude and feelings) and effects on behaviour. This threefold distinction was treated in early research as following a logical order from the first to the third, and with an implied increase in significance (behaviour counting more than knowledge). In fact, it is no longer easy to sustain the distinction between the three concepts or to accept the unique logic of that particular order of occurrence.

There are several ways of differentiating between the types of media effect. Klapper (1960) distinguished between conversion, minor change and reinforcement, which are, respectively, change of opinion or belief according to the intention of the communicator; change in form or intensity of cognition, belief or behaviour; and confirmation by the receiver of an existing belief, opinion or behaviour pattern. This threefold distinction needs to be widened to include other possibilities, especially at levels above that of the individual (see Chapter 1). The main options are listed in Box 16.3. The two effect types that imply absence of any effect involve different conceptions of media processes. In the case of an individual, reinforcement is a probable consequence of selective and persistent attention on the part of the receiver to content that is congruent with his or her existing views.

---

**16.3**

## Main kinds of media-induced change

The media can:

- Cause intended change
- Cause unintended change
- Cause minor change (form or intensity)

*(Continued)*

PROCESSES AND MODELS OF MEDIA EFFECTS     519

- Facilitate change (intended or not)
- Reinforce what exists (no change)
- Prevent change

Any of these changes may occur at the level of the individual, society, institution, or culture.

The 'no change' effect from the media, of which we have so much evidence, requires very close attention because of its long-term implications. It is a somewhat misleading expression, since anything that alters the probability of opinion or belief distribution in the future is an intervention into social process and thus an effect (Neuman, 2018).

Lang and Lang (1981) pointed to yet other types of effect that have been observed, including 'reciprocal', 'boomerang' and 'third-party' effects. The first refers to the consequences for a person or even an institution of becoming the object of media coverage. A planned event, for instance, is often changed by the very fact of being televised. There is often an interaction between media and the objects of reporting. Gitlin (1980) showed, for example, how the US student movement in the 1960s was influenced by its own publicity. A 'boomerang' effect, causing change in the opposite direction to that intended, is a very familiar phenomenon (or risk) in campaigning. A 'third-party' effect refers to the belief, often encountered, that other people are likely to be influenced but not oneself. The term 'sleeper effect' has also been used to refer to effects that do not show up until much later.

In their discussion of dimensions of effects, McLeod et al. (1991) also point to the difference between effects that are diffuse or general (such as the supposed effects of television as a medium) and those that are content specific. In the latter case, a certain inbuilt structure or tendency (for instance, a political bias) is singled out as the potential cause of change.

## PROCESSES OF MEDIA EFFECT: A TYPOLOGY

In order to provide an outline of developments in theory and research, we begin by interrelating two of the distinctions already mentioned: between the intended and the unintended, and between the short term and the long term. This device was suggested by Golding (1981) to help distinguish different concepts of news and its effects. He argued that, in the case of news, intended short-term effects may be considered as 'bias'; unintended short-term effects fall under the heading of 'unwitting bias'; intended long-term effects indicate 'policy' (of the medium concerned); while unintended long-term effects of news are 'ideology'. Something of the same way of thinking helps us to map out, in terms of these two co-ordinates, the main kinds of media effect process which have been dealt with in the research literature. The result is given in Figure 16.1.

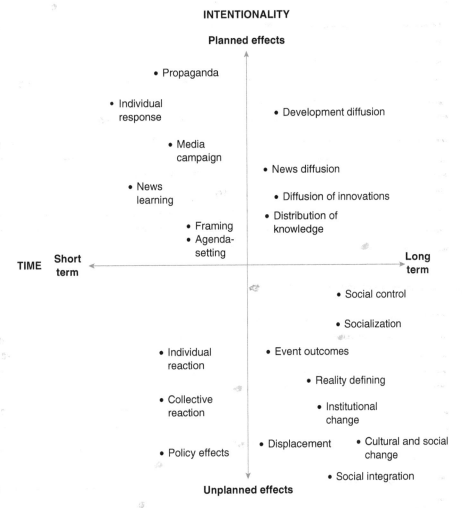

**INTENTIONALITY**

**Planned effects**

- Propaganda

- Individual
  response

                                    • Development diffusion

        • Media
          campaign

                                 • News diffusion

    • News
      learning                   • Diffusion of innovations

        • Framing               • Distribution of
        • Agenda-                 knowledge
          setting

**TIME** **Short**                                      **Long**
        **term** ←─────────────────────────────────→ **term**

                                    • Social control

                                    • Socialization

        • Individual              • Event outcomes
          reaction
                                     • Reality defining

        • Collective
          reaction                   • Institutional
                                       change

        • Policy effects     • Displacement    • Cultural and social
                                                 change

                                    • Social integration

**Unplanned effects**

Figure 16.1 A typology of news effects. Effects can be located on two dimensions: that of time span and that of intentionality

The main entries in Figure 16.1 can be briefly described, although their meaning will be made more explicit in the discussion of theory that follows.

## PLANNED AND SHORT TERM

- *Propaganda* (including political, commercial and health campaigns). Defined as 'the deliberate and systematic attempt to shape perceptions, manipulate cognitions, and direct behavior to achieve a response that furthers the desired intent of the propagandist' (Jowett and O'Donnell, 1999: 1). Propaganda can also be long term.

- *Individual response*. The process by which individuals change, or resist change, following exposure to messages designed to influence attitude, knowledge or behaviour.

- *Media campaign*. The situation in which a number of media are used in an organized way to achieve a persuasive or informational purpose with a chosen population.

- *News learning*. The short-term cognitive effect of exposure to mass media, as measured by tests of audience recall, recognition or comprehension.

- *Framing*. As a media effect, refers to the adoption by the audience of the same interpretative frameworks and 'spin' used to contextualize news reports and event accounts. An associated process is that of priming (where media foreground the criteria for assessing public events or figures).

- *Agenda-setting*. The process by which the relative attention given to items or issues in news coverage influences the rank order of public awareness of issues and attribution of significance.

## UNPLANNED AND SHORT TERM

- *Individual reaction*. Unplanned or unpredicted consequences of individual exposure to a media stimulus. This has mainly been noticed in the form of imitation and learning, especially of aggressive or deviant acts (including suicide). The term 'triggering' has also been used. Related types of effect include strong emotional responses, sexual arousal and reactions of fear or anxiety.

- *Collective reaction*. Here some of the same effects are experienced simultaneously by many people in a shared situation or context, leading to joint action, usually of an unregulated and non-institutional kind. Fear, anxiety and anger are the most potent reactions, which can lead to panic or civil disturbance.

- *Policy effects*. The unintended impact of news on government policy and action by the highlighting of some crisis, abuse, danger, and so on.

## PLANNED AND LONG TERM

- *Development diffusion*. The planned use of communication for purposes of long-term development, campaigns and other means of influence, especially the interpersonal network and authority structure of the community or society.

MCQUAIL'S MEDIA AND MASS COMMUNICATION THEORY
EFFECTS

- *Diffusion of news.* The spread of awareness of particular (news) events through a given population over time, with particular reference to the extent of penetration (proportion ultimately knowing) and the means by which information is received (personal versus media sources).
- *Diffusion of innovations.* The process of take-up of technological innovations within a given population, often on the basis of advertising or general publicity. It can be an unintended as well as an intended effect.
- *Distribution of knowledge.* The consequences of media news and information for the distribution of knowledge as between social groups. The main reference is to the closing or widening of '**knowledge gaps**'. A related phenomenon is the 'digital divide'.

## UNPLANNED AND LONG TERM

- *Social control.* Refers here to systematic tendencies to promote conformity to an established order or a pattern of behaviour. Depending on one's social theory, this can be considered as either a deliberate or an unintended extension of socialization.
- *Socialization.* The informal contribution of media to the learning and adoption of norms, values and expectations of behaviour in particular social roles and situations.
- *Event outcomes.* Referring to the part played by media in conjunction with institutional forces in the course and resolution of major 'critical' events (see Lang and Lang, 1981). Examples can include revolution, major domestic political upheavals and matters of war and peace. Less significant events, such as elections, can also figure here (Chaffee, 1975).
- *Reality defining and construction of meaning.* Effects on public cognitions and frames of interpretation. This kind of effect requires the more or less active participation of receivers in the process of constructing their own meaning.
- *Institutional change.* The adaptation by existing institutions to developments in the media, especially those affecting their own communication functions (see the notion of 'reciprocal effects').
- *Displacement.* The many possible consequences of allocation of time to media use away from other (mainly free-time) pursuits, including social participation.
- *Cultural and social change.* Shifts in the overall pattern of values, behaviours and symbolic forms characterizing a sector of society (such as youth), a whole society or a set of societies. The possible strengthening or weakening of cultural identity may also be an example of effect.
- *Social integration.* Integration (or its absence) may be observed at different levels, especially group, local community or nation, which also correspond with the distribution areas of media. Effects can also be short-term, as in response to a shared public disaster or emergency.

# INDIVIDUAL RESPONSE AND REACTION: THE STIMULUS–RESPONSE MODEL

The dimensions according to which types of effect have been classified in Figure 16.1 are not the only possibilities, and the resulting typology may not always seem completely logical. At the heart of the problem is the fact that any process of media effect on individuals must begin with attention, or 'exposure' to some media message. The results of this event extend through time and take different, often collective forms. The effects themselves, for instance acquiring knowledge of events by way of news, are not uniquely short or long term, but can be treated as both. Because the 'inputs' from media are so numerous, varied and interrelated, we cannot in practice separate them according to these or other dimensions, although we have to do so for purposes of analysis. However, the stimulus–response model is unambiguously short-term and individualistic. Two of the entries in Figure 16.1 – individual response and individual reaction – share this same underlying behavioural model. The model's main features can be simply represented as follows:

single message → individual receiver → reaction

This applies more or less equally to intended and unintended effects, although there is a significant difference between a response (implying some interaction with the receiver and also a learning process) and a reaction (which implies no choice or interaction on the part of the receiver and is essentially a behavioural reflex). A more extended version of the basic response and learning process as it occurs in persuasion and opinion formation is indicated by McGuire (1973) in the form of six stages in sequence: presentation, attention, comprehension, yielding, retention and overt behaviour.

This elaboration is sufficient to show why stimulus–response theory has had to be modified to take account of selective attention, interpretation, response and recall. The model, in whatever form, is highly pragmatic: it predicts, other things being equal, the occurrence of a response (a verbal or behavioural act) according to the presence or absence of an appropriate stimulus (message). It presumes a more or less direct behavioural effect in line with the intention of the initiator and consistent with some overt stimulus to act in a certain way that is built into the message. In discussions of media effect, this has sometimes been referred to as the 'bullet' or 'hypodermic' theory, terms that far exaggerate the probability of effect and the vulnerability of the receiver to influence. No adequate account can be taken of the many mediating effects that apply in natural settings of media influence (see the earlier discussion of the DSMM model). Nor can it take account of effects that occur over time, long after the moment of the 'stimulus'.

# MEDIATING CONDITIONS OF EFFECT

The revision of the stimulus–response model involved the identification of the conditions that predict, moderate or mediate effects. McGuire (1973) indicated the main kinds of variable as having to do with source, content, channel, receivers and destination. There is reason to believe that messages stemming from an authoritative and credible source will be relatively more effective, as will those from sources that are attractive or close (similar) to the receiver. As to content, effectiveness is associated with repetition, consistency and lack of alternatives (a monopoly situation). It is also more likely where the subject matter is unambiguous and concrete (Trenaman, 1967).

In general, effect as intended is also likely to be greater on topics that are distant from, or less important for, the receiver (lower degree of ego involvement or prior commitment). Variables of style (such as personalization), types of appeal (such as emotional versus rational) and order and balance of argument have been found to play a part, but too variably to sustain any general prediction. Channel (means of transmission: print, broadcast, online, mobile) factors have often been investigated, with mixed results, mainly because content and receiver factors dominate learning outcomes. Generally, research tends to struggle to establish clearly the relative value of different modes (audio, visual, and so on) in any consistent way, although images and video seem to take primacy according to measures of recall or comprehension (for example, Grabe and Bucy, 2009). However, this finding relates to cognitive learning from news information when averaged out. As we have seen, a number of obvious receiver variables can also be relevant to effect, requiring special notice to be given to individual, dispositional and contextual aspects of media use. The degree of motivation or 'engagement' has often been singled out as of particular importance in the influence process and in determining the sequence in which different kinds of effect occur, at the same time further complicating the isolation of particular effects in an otherwise interactive and at times 'participatory' digital media environment (Singer, 2018).

According to Ray (1973), the normal 'effect hierarchy' as found, for instance, in the work of Hovland et al. (1949) on wartime propaganda films, is a process leading from cognitive learning (the most common effect) to affective response (like or dislike, opinion, attitude) to 'conative' effect (behaviour or action). Ray argues, with some supporting evidence, that this model is normal only under conditions of high involvement (high interest and attention). With low involvement (common in many television viewing situations and especially with advertising) the sequence may go from cognition directly to behaviour, with affective adjustment occurring later to bring attitude in line with behaviour, or from affect to behaviour (without cognition), or from behaviour to affect (Van den Putte and Dhondt, 2005).

In itself, this formulation casts doubt on the logic and design of many persuasive communication campaigns that assume attitude to be an unambiguous correlate and predictor of behaviour. There is also a question mark against election or health communication campaign evaluations based on measures of attitude change alone. The question of consistency between the three elements is also at issue. According to Chaffee and Roser (1986), high involvement is also likely to be a necessary condition for consistency of effects, and thus for a stable and enduring influence. Their preferred model of media effect involves a repetitive sequence from low involvement, through perception of dissonance and then to learning, with cumulative results. In this view, shallow and easily forgotten information can develop into a reasoned set of ideas and into action, especially under conditions of repeated exposure (as in a systematic campaign).

In any natural (non-laboratory) media situation, individual receivers will choose which stimulus to attend to or to avoid, will interpret its meaning variably and will react or not behaviourally, according to choice (Bauer, 1964) and susceptibility (Valkenburg and Peter, 2013b). This seriously undermines the validity of the conditioning model, since the factors influencing selectivity are bound to be strongly related to the nature of the stimulus, working for or against the occurrence of an effect. Our attention should consequently be drawn away from the simple fact of experiencing a stimulus and towards the mediating conditions described above, especially in their totality and mutual interaction.

## SOURCE–RECEIVER RELATIONS AND EFFECT

As has been noted, trust in and respect for the source can be conducive to influence. There have been several attempts to develop theories of influence taking account of relationships between sender (or message sent) and receiver. Most of these theories refer to interpersonal relations. One framework has been suggested by French and Raven (1953), indicating five alternative forms of communication relationship in which social power may be exercised by a sender and influence accepted by a receiver. The underlying proposition is that influence through communication is a form of exercise of power that depends on certain assets or properties of the agent of influence (the communicator).

The first two types of power asset are classified as reward and coercion, respectively. The former depends on there being gratification for the recipient from a message (enjoyment, for instance, or useful advice); the latter depends on some negative consequence of non-compliance (uncommon in mass communication). A third type is described as referent power and refers to the attraction or prestige of the sender, such that the receiver identifies with the person and is willingly influenced, for affective reasons.

Fourthly, there is legitimate power, according to which influence is accepted on the assumption that a sender has a strong claim to expect to be followed or respected. This is not very common in mass communication but may occur where authoritative messages are transmitted from political sources or other relevant institutional leaders. This type of power presumes an established relationship between source and receiver that predates and survives any particular instance of mass communication. Finally, there is expert power, which operates where superior knowledge is attributed to the source or sender by the receiver. This situation is not uncommon in the spheres of media news and advertising, where experts are often brought in for explanation, comment or endorsement. Examples of exploitation of all five types of media power can be found in advertising and informational campaigns, and more than one of these power sources is likely to be operative on any given occasion.

In the contemporary context, source–receiver relations can be particularly salient given the interactive nature of digital media and the rise of mass self-communication activities online. As the lines dividing producers and consumers begin to disappear, influence and effects are most likely to be derived from the relations between various parties in the communication process, including the properties and technological affordances of the medium used. It is therefore perhaps unsurprising that current assessments of media effects include variables explicitly related to people's affect and *emotions* as well as the *materiality* of media channels in heuristic models and research designs.

## CHALLENGES FOR MEDIA EFFECTS RESEARCH

In a review of media effects research with the specific aim of increasing the explanatory power thereof, Valkenburg and Peter (2013a) identify five methodological and theoretical challenges for the future (see Box 16.4). Measuring the extent to which people in fact encounter specific media messages is key, even though consensus about how to operationalize this is absent from the literature. There is agreement, however, that global exposure does not add much to our ability to understand media influence when set against studies looking at specific content (such as a particular game, TV show or news genre). This is an area fertile for complex, mixed and creative methods (Buckingham, 2009). A second challenge has been mentioned before as it involves a recognition that media effects are conditional, based on someone's level of susceptibility to using and responding to certain media. One conclusion drawn by Potter and Riddle (2007), in their review of the media effects literature, concerned the both fragmentary and low level of theory use. They correspondingly advocated that communication scholars should consistently employ and test theories in their research. Valkenburg and Peter (2013a) similarly identify the need for more targeted, cumulative theory testing. Other challenges have been discussed earlier.

When it comes to media-uses-and-effects research in newer media environments, we can identify two specific ways in which scholars have responded. First, there are more calls for (and developments of) relations-based approaches, where effects are seen as mediated by producer–consumer relationships and role convergence, by the ensemblematic and networked nature of how people use and combine multiple media, and by the overall non-linear character of the contemporary media system.

A second response has been to develop new models and theories about media effects particular to the newer media environment. One such example is the Theory of Interactive Media Effects (TIME), developed by Sundar, Jia, Wadell and Huang (2015; Wang and Sundar, 2018). This approach considers the medium of communication more than a mere channel of conveying information between senders and receivers, instead focusing on the specific properties of interactive media, such as the smartphone, to understand and explain our fascination and sometimes obsessive use of such technologies. As Sundar et al. (2015: 48) argue, '[e]ach of these media have unique technological attributes which manifest themselves in terms of specific interface features and affordances that shape the nature of their communications, with consequent effects on their psychology'. Using TIME, researchers identify specific technological affordances of a medium (such as the particulars of the Facebook interface), measure how people use and respond to the medium, and control for mediating variables (such as engagement, self-determination and the user's sense of agency), leading to conclusions about how media users perceive and respond to technological affordances of interactive media, and what this use can do to their psychology, their media use and their communications with others (ibid.: 78). One consistent conclusion drawn from empirical work based on TIME is that the extent to which someone feels more or less in control and has fun in the process greatly determines their use and response to a particular medium.

Neuman (2018) adds a sixth challenge, arguing for a specific focus on 'miscommunication', such as all the different ways in which mediated messages fail to have intended effects, or have unintended and unanticipated consequences.

# CONCLUSION

This chapter has provided a general introduction to the question of media effects and their measurement. That media have influence and effects is not in doubt, although it is difficult to establish when and to what degree an effect has occurred or is likely to occur. This difficulty is not primarily due to methodological obstacles, although these do exist. It mainly arises from the very number and variety of possible effects and of the facts and conditions that relate to the occurrence of effects. Not least problematic is the fact that effects, when they do occur, involve not only the actions of communicators, but the orientations and actions of the audience, as well as the technological affordances of the medium involved. Most effects are in some degree interactions between senders, medium properties and receivers.

Historical developments highlight structural challenges in the rich field of media effects research, as well as the rapid emergence of immersive, interactive (and customizable) newer media environments that have prompted scholars towards developing more integrated models for theory testing, including both the emotional aspects of mediated message processing and the technological features of the medium. Most recently, research is called for that additionally includes 'machine agency' (Sundar et al., 2015: 65) as decisions about the production, distribution and formatting of content are increasingly made at the hardware and software levels of the mediatic process under the influence of algorithms and artificial intelligence.

# FURTHER READING

Bennett, W.L. and Iyengar, S. (2008) 'A new era of minimal effects? Changing foundations of political communication', *Journal of Communication*, 58(4): 707–731.

Graber, D. (1990) 'Seeing is remembering: how visuals contribute to TV news', *Journal of Communication*, 40(3): 134–155.

McLeod, D., Wise, D. and Perryman, M. (2017) 'Thinking about the media: a review of theory and research on media perceptions, media effects perceptions, and their consequences', *Review of Communication Research*, 5: 35–83.

Neuman, W.R. (2016) *The Digital Difference: Media Technology and the Theory of Communication Effects*. Cambridge, MA: Harvard University Press.

Striphas, T. (2015) 'Algorithmic culture', *European Journal of Cultural Studies*, 18(4–5): 395–412.

Valkenburg, P.M., Peter, J. and Walther, J.B. (2016) 'Media effects: theory and research', *Annual Review of Psychology*, 67(1): 315–338.

# A CANON OF MEDIA EFFECTS

This chapter first deals with examples of a wide range of media effects, including both short- and long-term processes, those that are collective as well as individual, and those that are considered as either negative or positive. To some extent these are effects not directly intended by the media, although they may be predictable. Intended informational and political effects are subsequently discussed, although there is no sharp division since unintended social effects also involve affect, learning and other emotional and cognitive processes. The effects dealt with often have a social problematic character, especially where they relate to children and young people and to anti-social tendencies generally. This is a bias that has shaped research into media and mass communication since its earliest days and should not be taken to mean that the actual effects of mass media are more negative than positive. For the most part, the basic theories and processes of effects have been outlined in Chapter 16. The main aim here is to assess briefly, with reference to the evidence, a number of hypotheses about the influence of the media within private and public domains of everyday life as addressed through key media effects theories throughout the twentieth and (early) twenty-first centuries.

The second goal of our chapter is to highlight the canonical foci of research on media influence and effects: the often-presumed and much-researched links among media and violence, sex, youth and children, as well as the role of media in public opinion formation and political communication. We conclude with a review of the literature on media addiction – a prominent theme in contemporary debates about the mass media, as the hardware and software we use to access and use them is becoming increasingly personal, intimate and customizable.

At the heart of this chapter is the issue of what media and mass communication (can) do in society and people's everyday lives.

---

# PROFILING MEDIA EFFECTS THEORIES

All of the key perspectives on the influence and effects of media on affect, emotion, cognition, attitude and behaviour – from 'all-powerful' to 'limited' via 'negotiated' to 'complex reciprocal' effects – are at work within the various theories scholars have deployed (and continue to use to this day) to structure their research. The most prominent theories we will highlight in this chapter focus on uncovering and measuring long-term, slowly-but-surely media effects – cultivation, the spiral of silence and cultural change – and those that emphasize short-term, almost immediate effects – agenda-setting, priming and framing. Of course, there are numerous other theories that can be exemplified here. In their reviews, Cacciatore, Scheufele and Iyengar (2016) as well as Valkenburg et al. (2016) highlight eleven much-cited theories of media effects, including the ones we selected here. As the purpose of this chapter is to showcase rather than to review, we opted for theories that have been adapted in promising ways to the newer media environment, necessitating a historical appreciation of their genealogies and the discussions and concerns of which they were part.

A second reason for inclusion is the powerful metaphors that these theories represent in public debate and discourse around 'the' media, signalling the 'double hermeneutics' of our field: we study cultural realities that already have been recognized, discussed and shaped as such by the people inhabiting them (Jensen, 2018: 177).

Concerns about media influence and effects tend to follow the generally evolutionary yet seemingly sudden rise to prominence of a particular medium, channel or format. However, the foci of real or perceived 'effects' often involve recurring themes: the consequences of media on infants, children and youths, the role of media in 'risky' behaviours related to aggression, violence, sex and sexuality, and the function of particularly news media in the democratic process. As our media converge, in the process becoming increasingly mobile and personal with people being 'always online', substantial attention and scholarship has been dedicated in recent decades to the question of media 'addiction', with Internet gaming disorder, for example, added to the authoritative *Diagnostic and Statistical Manual of Mental Disorders* (5th edition – DSM-5; a primary classification system for psychiatric disorders) in 2013 (American Psychiatric Association, 2013), and discussions abound on issues such as problematic Internet use, pornography addiction and smartphone addiction.

# CULTIVATION

Among theories of long-term media effect, the cultivation hypothesis of Gerbner (1973) remains probably the best documented and most investigated (see Signorielli and Morgan, 1990). It holds that television, among modern media, has acquired such a central place in daily life that it dominates our 'symbolic environment', substituting its (distorted) message about reality for personal experience and other means of knowing about the world. Television is also described as the 'cultural arm of the established industrial order [which] serves primarily to maintain, stabilize and reinforce rather than to alter, threaten or weaken conventional beliefs and behaviors' (Gross, 1977: 180). This statement brings the cultivation effect very close to that posited by the critical theorists of the Frankfurt School and not far from later Marxist analysis. According to Signorielli and Morgan (1990: 15):

> Cultivation analysis is the third component of a research paradigm called 'Cultural Indicators' that investigates (1) the institutional processes underlying the production of media content, (2) images in media content, and (3) relationships between exposure to television's message and audience beliefs and behaviors.

## THE THEORY

**Cultivation theory** is an example of a 'stalagmite' or 'drip-drip' theory about the role of media in society, presupposing that effects develop slowly (but surely) over time as people continue to immerse themselves in media. Such perspectives have been developed next to, and partly in response to, short-term effects theories. The original hypothesis of cultivation theory was that viewing television gradually leads to the adoption of beliefs about the nature of the social world that conform to the stereotyped, distorted and very selective view of reality as portrayed in a systematic way in television fiction and news. Cultivation is said to differ from a direct stimulus–response effect process mainly because of its gradual and cumulative character. It involves first learning and secondly the construction of a view of social reality dependent on personal circumstances and experience (such as of poverty, race or gender) and also on reference-group membership. It is also seen as an interactive, multiple-way shaping process between media industry practices, mass-mediated messages and audiences (as assembled for advertisers).

In this theory of media effect, television provides many people with a consistent and near-total symbolic environment that supplies norms for conduct and beliefs about a wide range of real-life situations. It is not a window on or a reflection of the world, but a world in itself. Of particular concern herein is the dominance of commercial motives in producing and shaping such a world. The resulting research has two main thrusts: one directed at testing the assumption about the consistency (and distortion) of the television 'message system'; the other designed to test, by way of survey analysis, a variety of public beliefs about social reality, especially those that can be tested against empirical indicators. The core of the ensuing analysis is the comparison between beliefs about reality and actual reality, taking account of varying degrees of habitual exposure to television. There is some basic similarity to the ideas underlying the 'agenda-setting' hypothesis (explored later in this chapter).

Although there can be some dispute over what exactly counts as 'television' in today's media environment, cultivation theory (or parts thereof) can be carried over to the various ways in which people today watch even more television than ever before, as programmes and shows migrate across many screens that viewers have access to. As contemporary cultivation researchers argue, 'it still makes sense to think about the relationships of large groups of people to story systems, and of course everything is still produced within the confines of commercial intent' (Morgan, Shanahan and Signorielli, 2015: 695).

## TESTING THE THEORY

Those who watch increasing amounts of television – whether at home in front of a 'box', while on some kind of personal computer, or through a mobile media device – are predicted to show increasing divergence of perceptions of reality away from the known picture of the social world and towards the 'television' picture of the world. A major focus of the research has always been on questions concerning violence and crime, with cultivation research paying attention to its television portrayal, its actual incidence and its differential risks on the one hand, and to public awareness of and attitudes towards crime on the other. Early cultivation research findings (Gerbner and Gross, 1976) showed that the more television people viewed, the more likely they were to exaggerate the incidence of crime in the real world and the personal risks they run. This relationship seems to hold (Romer, Jamieson and Ady, 2003; Jamieson and Romer, 2014), at least in the USA. Other topics of political and social concern have also been studied, including the media production of political consensus. Gerbner, Gross, Morgan and Signorielli (1984) applied their concept of 'mainstreaming' to the political sphere and found evidence that exposure to television shifted opinion in the direction of 'moderate' opinion.

Cultivation theory holds that the more time a person spends watching television (of all kinds), the more he or she will adopt the predominant outlook of the world that is expressed on the medium. This should also apply to politics since it is (or was) the main source of political information for most people. The study summarized here is based on the assumption that television (under pressure from commercial broadcasters and advertisers) seeks to avoid extremes, staying safely in the 'nonideological middle ground that holds the largest possible audience' (ibid.: 285). This leads to favouring 'moderate' or centrist political positions (or mainstreaming). The timing of the study (1981) was one of a shift to the right after a decade of upheaval in the USA. It was conducted using very large random sample surveys, with basic questions asked about the amount of viewing and the personal political outlook as either liberal, moderate or conservative. Controls for other variables were applied. The results confirmed the expectation. In the nine surveys (different years), heavy viewers were more likely than light viewers to choose the 'moderate' self-designation in all but one case. This relationship did not hold for other media. Newspaper readers were likely to be more conservative, and radio users more liberal. The authors warned that the meanings of the labels are not straightforward or stable. Specifically, they remarked that television is not genuinely a force for moderation (Gerbner et al., 1984).

In an extensive review of numerous studies of the television construction of reality, Hawkins and Pingree (1983) found many scattered indications of the expected relationships, but no conclusive proof of the *direction* of the relationship between television viewing and ideas about social reality. They say that television *can* teach about social reality and that the relationship between viewing and social reality may be reciprocal: television viewing causes a social reality to be constructed in a certain way, but this construction of social reality may also direct viewing behaviour. In a further overview of cultivation research, Morgan and Shanahan (1997) draw the conclusion that cultivation effects do occur but are on average quite small.

The television experience is now almost certainly more differentiated and non-cumulative than allowed for in the theory as production and supply increase. Hypotheses have to be much more specific about content and effects. For instance, a study of the cultivation effects of television on expectations about marriage (Segrin and Nabi, 2002) found that TV viewing of genre-specific 'romantic' content was associated with unrealistic expectations, but not general TV viewing. Sotirovic (2001) found negative images of welfare recipients among viewers of cable TV news and entertainment shows, as opposed to other sources. Rössler and Brosius (2001) also found limited cultivation effects in Germany from specific talk-show contents, but not from all TV or the genre as a whole. Active audience theory also challenges the assumption of the long-term cumulative effect of powerful 'message systems'. Several authors have raised doubts about the causal relationship posited between television use data and survey data concerning values and opinions (Hirsch, 1980, 1981; Hughes, 1980). The 'cultivation' effect was first identified in the United States, where (mainstream) television content was more commercial and initially less diverse.

The evidence from other countries is mixed, despite the amount of work that has been done. Rosengren and Windahl (1989) report a number of findings of longer-term changes in relation to the television experience of the young that can be taken as support for the cultivation hypothesis. One example appears in the 'mental maps' of the world that differ significantly according to the amount of television viewing. For high-viewing adolescent boys, the world outside Sweden consists of little apart from North America. Yay, Ranasubranuanian and Oliver (2008) found that consumption of American television content in South Korea and in India was associated with dissatisfaction with personal life (India) and dissatisfaction with society (in both countries). Cultivation effects from television on gender-role attitudes have also been found in Japan. According to Saito (2007), these effects were specific to certain subgroups. Thus, television decelerated social change by cultivating traditional attitudes among many viewers, although it also seemed to liberate the most conservative people. These findings are approximately in line with the 'mainstreaming' effects described above. In a more recent review of studies labelled as tests of the cultivation hypothesis, Potter (2014) finds partial support for the message system analysis, and overall weak support for cultivation analysis. Even when some evidence of cultivation is found, it tends to only affect a smaller part of the population. On the other hand, indicators of cultivation are consistently found across time, cultures and countries, and television still to this day is the dominant 'storyteller' in most people's media repertoires. Potter suggests that more work needs to be done to uncover the meanings of media messages (rather than just their overt patterns), and that the institutional practices that shape messages (see Chapter 12) need to be more explicitly integrated in cultivation research designs. In doing so, cultivation research would follow a trend among many other contemporary approaches in media and mass communication scholarship that call for integrated perspectives, mixed-method approaches and interdisciplinarity in research designs (see Chapter 18).

In more recent studies of television viewing and its relationship over time with changing attitudes, the evidence suggests that cultivation effects occur on very specific issues – for example, the exposure to a threatening news story about immigration that has been found to directly affect attitudes towards immigrants' human rights, but not broader feelings or attitudes towards immigration policy in general (Seate and Mastro, 2016).

This points towards a division in cultivation effects between first-order and second-order effects. First-order effects have to do with how significant people rate specific aspects of everyday life in relation to their media use, whereas second-order effects represent deeply held beliefs and worldviews, which are much less likely to be directly influenced or changed based on media use (Shrum, 1995). A similar conclusion has been drawn by Williams (2006), after applying cultivation theory to a study on the perceptions of real-world dangers among participants in an online game. Players did not become more fearful in general – just regarding the very precise situations they also faced when playing the game. As Williams (2006: 82) suggests, 'cultivation works as a precise phenomenon in online games, rather than being the broad gravitational system that Gerbner and colleagues' original theory would suggest'. Williams remains hopeful that the many games that reward prosocial and ethical behaviour can contribute to improving human relations – an important issue to consider given the worldwide prominence of digital games and gaming as a preferred leisure activity.

Cultivation has also been applied to the newer media environment, with specific reference to the rapid rise of personal, mobile media, online social networks and a corresponding proliferation of media offerings across many channels, offering much more diversity. Morgan et al. (2015: 678) suggest that cultivation stays relevant if we understand the core of the theory to be about the stories we tell (and are told) and how these stories – across platforms and channels, linking ideas and characters – 'have something to do with the way we think about the world'. As they argue, we may receive our stories differently than before, but important aspects of their content have perhaps not changed all that much. Particularly with reference to recurring themes, stereotypical formulations and common framing of issues regarding violence, victimization, gender, power, class, race and ethnicity, and so on, stories can be remarkably persistent. The content people create and share on social media can to some extent be seen as an aggregate of what we see and experience in other media, and therefore often perpetuates such stories and story elements.

Several studies have explored the ways in which cultivation theory contributes to our understanding of how migrants and refugees experience and give meaning to the cultural adaptation and acculturation process (Raman and Harwood, 2008; Tufekci, 2008; Croucher, 2011). When immigrants migrate to a new culture, the use of social networking sites is hypothesized to influence how they perceive the dominant culture, which cultivation effect may impact how they relate and adapt to their new environment as well as how they maintain ties with (often scattered) family members and their homeland(s).

However plausible the theory, it is almost impossible to deal convincingly with the complexity of posited relationships between symbolic structures, audience behaviour and audience views, given the many intervening variables. It is also hard to separate out any process of 'cultivation' from general socialization. Furthermore, evidence that cultivation is truly cumulative seems to be lacking, or suggests quite the opposite. Despite all this, it appears that the line of enquiry represented by cultural indicators and cultivation research is not a spent force and can lend itself to more specified and nuanced enquiries on particular topics and in particular contexts.

## SPIRAL OF SILENCE

The concept of the '**spiral of silence**' derives from a larger body of theory of public opinion that was developed and tested by Noelle-Neumann (1974, 1984, 1991) over a number of years. The relevant theory concerns the interplay between four elements: mass media, interpersonal communication and social relations, individual expressions of opinion, and the perceptions individuals have of the surrounding 'climate of opinion' in their own social environment. The main assumptions of the theory (Noelle-Neumann, 1991) are as follows:

- Society threatens deviant individuals with isolation.
- Individuals experience fear of isolation continuously.
- This fear of isolation causes individuals to try to assess the climate of opinion at all times.
- The results of this estimate affect their behaviour in public, especially their willingness or not to express opinions openly.

In brief, the theory proposes that, in order to avoid isolation on important public issues (such as political party support), many people are guided by what they think to be the dominant or declining opinions in their environment. People tend to conceal their views if they feel they are in a minority, and are more willing to express them if they think their position on a particular issue is consonant with how most people think about that issue. The result is that those views that are perceived to be dominant gain even more ground and alternatives retreat still further. This is the *spiralling* effect in the theory.

In the present context, the main point is that the mass media are the most readily accessible source for assessing the prevailing climate, and if a certain view predominates in the media it will tend to be magnified in the subsequent stages of personal opinion formation and expression. The theory was first formulated and tested to explain puzzling findings in German politics, where opinion poll indications were inconsistent with other data concerning expectations of who would win an election and signally failed to predict the result. The explanation put forward was that the media were offering a misleading view of the opinion consensus. They were said to be leaning in a leftist direction, against the underlying opinion of the (silent) majority. Subsequent studies in different parts of the world provided confirmation of an influence from the news media on public opinion about contentious issues (such as the situation in the Middle East) and on political opinion, which seemed to support the standpoint of Noelle-Neumann and other proponents of 'powerful mass media' and the spiral of silence.

The spiral of silence theory is a close neighbour of mass society theory and involves a similar, somewhat pessimistic, view of the quality of social relations (Taylor, 1982). According to Katz (1983), its validity will depend on the extent to which alternative reference groups are still alive and well in social life. The more that is the case, the less scope there is for the process described to operate, since there will be support for minority or deviant views. Moscovici (1991) also suggests that, in general, we should pay less attention to public opinion formation among silent majorities and more to 'loud minorities', which often play a larger part in opinion change. This seems a particularly apt suggestion for the opinion climate on social media.

The spiral of silence theory is much more than a theory of media effect and involves several dimensions that need to be investigated in conjunction. It is not surprising that it remains in a hypothetical form or that evidence is weak and inconsistent from one context to another. For instance, Glynn, Hayes and Shanahan (1997) concluded from a meta-analysis of survey studies that there was little evidence that perception of support or not for one's own opinion is related to willingness to speak out. Even so, there is supportive evidence (for example, Mutz and Soss, 1997; Gunther, 1998) for a simpler version of the theory that media coverage does shape individual perceptions of public sentiment on current issues (opinion about opinion). There is also continuing support for the view that 'fear of isolation' is a key factor in affecting willingness to speak out on a controversial issue (Moy, Domke and Stamm, 2001).

Research based on or inspired by the spiral of silence theory continues to this day, as the newer media environment provides a fascinating challenge to scholars: does the ongoing digital proliferation of devices, platforms and channels for media content make a thousand voices bloom, or are we overestimating the diversity of information and opinions available online? As found in cultivation research, there is much evidence to suggest that 'an expansion of the number of media outlets does not necessarily result in a diversification of positions and opinions' (Schulz and Roessler, 2012: 349). News organizations tend to follow each other's agenda (an approach attributed to the 'pack mentality' of reporters), a phenomenon variably labelled as 'interinstitutional news coherence' (Schudson, 2003: 109), 'media co-orientation' (Strömbäck and Esser, 2014: 380) and 'intermedia-agenda-setting' (McCombs and Funk, 2011). Beyond journalism, similar processes are at work in entertainment genres across different networks or franchises of different film and digital game studios mimicking each other in order to profit from a competitor's success formula – an outcome of the competitive pressure of product differentiation (versus market innovation; see Lampel, Lant and Shamsie, 2000: 226). As mass media increasingly reuse, recycle and repurpose content across multiple channels in the context of multimedia and crossmedia storytelling practices, a broader range of viewpoints and perspectives is not necessarily pursued in the process.

Schulz and Roessler (2012) theorize that engagement in terms of information-seeking behaviour and participation in exchanges and discussions online is based on a more or less balanced 'subjective-pluralistic' selection of sources. This assumption is confirmed by the lack of evidence for widespread 'filter bubbles' online (Bruns, 2019). Although this implies that the spiral of silence theory does not apply, Schulz and Roessler (2012: 360) suggest that '[p]ublic opinion changes that start online can be transferred to the offline world as soon as the traditional mass media start reporting on them'. This appreciation of the interaction between multiple media in opinion formation is key for contemporary media-effects theories.

Next to such an 'ensemblematic' recognition of media use and effect, current work emphasizes a reciprocal relationship between opinion formation and expression, mass media reporting, and online sharing and debate, necessitating a research design that takes measures of these various elements over time (Matthes, 2015). Studies applying the spiral of silence framework to social media broadly conceived (Hampton et al., 2014), and Facebook (Stoycheff, 2016) in particular, suggest that while people indicate that they are willing to have an in-person conversation about a contentious social issue, a majority would hesitate to share their opinions via such public platforms.

Related to the spiral of silence theory is the idea of **third-party effects** of media on public opinion, first proposed by Davison (1983). The key point is that many people seem to think (or say to pollsters) that other people are affected by various kinds of media content, but not they themselves. This perception goes with a tendency to support censorship (McLeod, Detember and Eveland, 2001). There is much empirical support for the tendency to attribute effects to others, which helps to explain the widespread belief in the power of the media, even where it is not supported by evidence (Hoffner et al., 2001). The overestimation of media effects is also associated with the equally widespread tendency to believe that the news media are biased against the point of view of those engaged by a particular issue (Gunther and Christen, 2002), also with little or no support in evidence. Asking people to estimate the influence of media on themselves is clearly not a way to uncover the direction and scale of actual effects. An interesting corollary to the hypothesis of third-party effect is that of the theory of 'second-person effect'. This refers to reactions of public actors to stories that enter into the news. Typically, they respond as if the fact of publication ensures that an entire public is paying attention (an unlikely circumstance). The result is to amplify and diffuse the original publication and set in train a new chain of events and interjections, with potential effects on public opinion. This process gives journalists (as part of their agenda-setting role) a degree of power that they would not otherwise have and which they may need to account for (Glasser, 2009).

What the spiral of silence theory, when applied to a contemporary media environment, helps us to do is to deliberately link a micro-level process – the way an individual makes up her mind about a certain issue – to macro-level phenomena – the interaction between social environment, mass media reporting and exchanges on social media (Poulakidakos, Veneti and Fangonikolopoulos, 2018: 374). It also provides a framework for considering (the interaction between) multiple media in the formation of an opinion climate.

# SOCIAL AND CULTURAL CHANGE

The theories of media and mass communication outlined in Chapters 4 and 5 all in some way posit a variety of significant social and cultural effects. The same is true of the effects of globalization, as discussed in Chapter 9. However, any such effects are likely to be gradual, long term and difficult to measure. There are also often divergent and even inconsistent possibilities. Mass media and the mass communication process has been considered to bring about new kinds of community and sociality, especially in the context of the Internet. Some suggest this brings about more social fragmentation and atomization. Other theorists have credited the media with (or accused them of) promoting homogeneity and social cohesion, sometimes to an excessive degree of conformity. The media have been blamed for declining cultural standards (and reducing content to the lowest common denominator) and also praised for disseminating both traditional and contemporary culture more widely. Despite the plausibility of these and other ideas about the influence of mass media on culture and society, there is little firm evidence of the general effects posited.

Central to the process by which the media contribute to social and cultural change is their capacity to define situations, provide frames of reference and disseminate images of social groups. They also tend to constitute the 'collective memory' of a given national society, in the absence of extensive historical knowledge. The media are not primary inventors or sources of any of these, but they put them together in more or less consistent and repetitive narratives that become the secondary sources for ideas and opinions that people have about their own society and their place in it. The media and their audiences have an insatiable appetite for novelty as well as continuity, and contribute to change by picking up on every new fashion, fear or significant fact that might become part of a larger story, whether in news or fiction. For the majority of people, the media for a long period of time were effectively the gatekeepers of change, especially when they seem to agree on the same selection and perception of what is going on. In an online context, such 'gatekeeping' efforts are to some extent better captured as 'way-finding' (Pearson and Kosicki, 2017) practices by individuals and media professionals alike, as we navigate to and from news and information via search engines, social media, influencers, within and across groups, networks and communities, traditional media titles and brands, as well as being directed by algorithms and automated recommendation systems (see also Barzilai-Nahon, 2008). At the same time, mass media organizations still play a fundamental role in the news and entertainment landscape, and continue to be the focus of much research into how media influence processes of social and cultural change.

In determining these and other questions, much depends on the perspective of the assessor and the initial assumptions made about the problem at issue. We should also keep in mind the fact that there is a continuous interaction between media, society, groups and individuals, albeit not one whereby every participant in this 'circuit of culture' (Du Gay et al., 1997) has the same power and agency. The media, whether as technology or as cultural content, do not have a simple one-way causal relation with cultural and social change. The outcomes of these interactions are very variable, unpredictable and different from one set of circumstances to another. As the media have developed, they have diverted time and attention from other activities (displacement effects), become a channel for reaching more people with more information than was available under 'pre-mass-media' conditions, and changed the way in which information and ideas circulate. These facts have implications for any social institution that needs to gain public attention and to communicate to the society at large. Other institutions are under pressure to adapt or respond in some way to the mass media, or to make their own use of mass media channels. In doing so, they are likely to change their own practices.

The influence of media is generally likely to be indirect. They work to change public expectations, the possibilities for meeting needs, and especially the way things are done in other social institutions. These have become more and more dependent on the media for their communicative links to their publics, and communication has adapted to what has been called a 'media logic' (see p. 365), which has profound effects on their conduct. As Altheide and Snow (1991: ix) have remarked, 'today all social institutions are media institutions'. The specific notion of mass media and society as mutually implicated – and therefore the phases of the mass communication process (production, content and reception) as reciprocal rather than unidirectional – was developed most explicitly in the field of media and cultural studies. The first step was Stuart Hall's (1974/1980) notion of the communication process as consisting of a 'totality' of encoding and decoding practices involving media makers and audiences in a continuous feedback loop (see Chapter 3). Hall developed this model as a critique of the assumption of 'perfect' communication governing the transmission model of communication. Media were still seen as having profound influence, but Hall's model opened up the question of 'effects' as a multiple-way process, all of which was governed by the 'field of meaning' that surrounds and distorts all media and communication.

Hall's work was followed by more detailed work on the influence of different elements and participants in the mass communication process, leading to the notion of culture as a circuit (Du Gay et al., 1997). The 'circuit of culture' in society offers a framework for analysis of how the different aspects of media and mass communication – specifically, production, identity, representations, regulations and consumption – are articulated (see Box 17.1). Articulation suggests interconnection and linking rather than any necessary or inevitable 'effect' flowing into one or other direction. It is possible to see this way of theorizing the influence of media and mass communication as more powerful than many, if not most, specific media-effects theories, as it assumes influence to potentially flow across all levels of analysis and from audiences to producers as much as the other way around. This circuit of culture approach has been applied to the study of various aspects of the mass communication process, from researching a particular film or game to the history of cell phones and mobile communication (see, for example, Goggin, 2006).

---

**17.1**

## The circuit of culture: five interconnected practices that give meaning to media

- *Production*: the process of making media (from conception to creation, marketing and distribution)
- *Identity*: who the people, groups and networks are (involved in the various elements of the circuit of culture)
- *Representations*: the form, format and genre of a media product (or message)
- *Regulations*: formal and informal rules and controls (including laws, cultural norms and expectations) and how these are enforced
- *Consumption*: all the different ways in which people consume and engage with media (text, product, service, message, channel)

---

Such contextual theorizing about the (long-term, multiple-way) impact of media on social and cultural change – where all the elements play a mutually shaping role and the direction of impact or effect of media is distributed across the circuit – seems particularly salient in our current context of pervasive and ubiquitous media, where people consume as well as produce more media than ever before, where the boundaries between public and private (that is, mass and interpersonal) communication are porous, and where a significant part of everyday life involves a more or less deliberate orientation towards the media around us. In an early assessment of this context, Altheide (1974) surmised how people, in the real or perceived presence of photo and video cameras, increasingly behaved in terms of what he labelled a 'media self', always aware of at least the possibility of being captured in media. According to Altheide, such a persona is deeply performative, and learns (or is forced to learn) to constantly adapt to changing mediated circumstances. Grossberg (1988: 389) similarly foresaw an emerging 'every-day world of media life'.

In the present context, the most central claim of theories on the influence of media on long-term social and cultural change (rather than on individuals or vulnerable populations, such as children) is that requirements of message and channel take precedence over the meaning of content. This introduces a requirement to make the material aspects of media part of our object of study. To this effect, the field has made what some call a 'material turn' in the social sciences and humanities (Miller, 1987; see also Casemajor, 2015), which in media and mass communication research can be conceived in terms of what Hayles (2004) calls 'media specific analysis' (MSA). This deliberately includes the object – device, artefact, hardware and software, technology – involved in the communication process as well as the specific material context of reception and use – in a movie theatre, while waiting for the bus, when drinking coffee at a café.

A major inspiration for MSA has been Actor-Network Theory (ANT), originally a particular approach within science and technology studies, which seeks to undo the distinction between biology and nature, or between 'humans' and 'non-humans' in academic scholarship (Latour, 1993). The assumption is that the material objects in people's lives have agency too, beyond what we may do with (or feel about) them. Although this approach has found particular adoption among humanities-based studies of media and mass communication, in the social sciences similarly-inspired work has been undertaken since the late twentieth century. Byron Reeves and Clifford Nass's (1996) 'media equation theory', for example, suggests that people treat media as real persons or places, which greatly shapes their response to such media. Reeves and Nass (ibid.: 5) argue that, '[i]ndividuals' interactions with computers, television, and new media are fundamentally social and natural, just like interactions in real life'. The notion that media are not simply tools or channels for transmitting messages, but are actual participants in our social world and that we respond to them as such, is at the heart of research based on the media equation. ANT takes this notion of 'non-human' participation one step further, suggesting that devices and technologies and material contexts have to 'do something' in order to make the communication process work, which in turn would suggest that these non-human actions have a distinct influence that is – in terms of ANT – 'symmetrical' to that of human actors (Law, 1992).

In recent years, ANT has found widespread application across media and mass communication research, in part informed by the basic observation that media are everywhere, and therefore needs to be taken into consideration in claims and hypotheses about media effects. A second reason for the emerging appreciation for this theoretical framework is that it postulates relationships of media influence and effect to always be both reciprocal and temporary – that is, effects flow both ways (to and from humans and non-humans), and are likely to change over time. ANT has proven to be quite useful in studies of the role and impact of (newer) technologies on established organizational practices, for example in journalism (Mitchelstein and Boczkowski, 2009; Plesner, 2009; Domingo, Masip and Costera Meijer, 2015). Across journalism studies, Lewis and Westlund (2015: 19) consider ANT as part of a 'socio-technical' emphasis in research, wherein they distinguish four elements: 'social *actors*, technological *actants*, work-practice *activities*, and different kinds of *audiences*' (italics in original) that are interlinked (see Box 17.2). The 'network' in ANT refers to the relations and interconnections between these various elements.

---

## 17.2

## Actor-Network Theory (adapted from Lewis and Westlund, 2015)

- *Actors*: three groups, consisting of those on the journalistic side, the information technology side and the business side
- *Actants*: technological objects (such as computers, a content management system, a programming interface and a social media platform) and material contexts (for example, the office environment, workplace, home)
- *Audiences*: individuals and groups seen as consumers of content, as statistically aggregated commodities for advertisers, and as active participants in cultural production
- *Activities*: editorial or non-editorial, manual or computational

---

Overall, the theories of long-term media influence and effects on people, groups and society show a gradual development over time towards more sophistication and complexity. In the process, we are reminded of the interplay between different media, between people and technologies, and between producers and users in determining the direction and extent of media effects. Although these elements in the mass communication process are not necessarily equal, these theories do account for power and agency to flow in multiple directions. The most recent interventions in this broad field of theory development include the role of affect, emotions and feelings in analyses of media and communication – a process dubbed as an 'affective turn' in cultural studies and social theory (Clough, 2008; Gregg and Seigworth, 2010), the 'emotional turn' in media studies (Wahl-Jorgensen, 2019), as much as recognition in more social scientifically oriented approaches of emotions as 'a powerful and relevant force' within the communication process (Lecheler, Schuck and De Vreese, 2013: 189). Affect is considered to be central to the overall process of 'mediation' that happens between the various elements of the communication process (Cefai, 2018), and emotions have been productively applied to studies of media production (Gregg, 2009; Beckett and Deuze, 2016; Siapera, 2019), content (Stolwijk, Schuck and De Vreese, 2017; Otto, Lecheler and Schuck, 2019), media channels and technologies (Karatzogianni and Kuntsman, 2012; work inspired by the 'media equation' theory comes to mind, see, for example, Brave, Nass and Hutchinson, 2005), and reception (Andrejevic, 2011; Papacharissi, 2014). In short, one can argue that affect can both mediate and moderate effects, as how we feel about certain issues can not only be a direct consequence of the way a certain story is told in media, but can also impact our exposure and response to specific media.

Other theoretical developments in media effects have been advanced with specific reference to micro-effects on people's opinions and behaviour, to which theories we turn next.

## AGENDA-SETTING, PRIMING AND FRAMING

The term '**agenda-setting**' was coined by McCombs and Shaw (1972, 1993) to describe a phenomenon that had long been noticed and studied in the context of election campaigns. The core idea is that the news media indicate to the public what the main issues of the day are and this is reflected in what the public perceives as the main issues. As Trenaman and McQuail (1961: 178) pointed out, 'The evidence strongly suggests that people think *about* what they are told but at no level do they think *what* they are told' (italics in original). The evidence collected at that time, and much since, consists of data showing a correspondence between the order of importance given in the media to 'issues' and the order of significance attached to the same issues by politicians and the public. A big difference in the contemporary media environment is perhaps that the type and number of media setting the agenda – for example, in online discussions on social media – are more diverse and to some extent more dynamic than in a time when certain newspapers and television stations were clearly dominant in the distribution and reach of news (Boynton and Richardson, 2016).

Dearing and Rogers (1996: 1–2) define the agenda-setting process as 'an ongoing competition among issue proponents to gain the attention of media professionals, the public and policy elites'. Lazarsfeld et al. (1944) referred to it as the power to 'structure issues'. Politicians seek to convince voters that the most important issues are those with which they are most closely identified. This is an essential part of advocacy and attempts at influencing public opinion. As a hypothesis, agenda-setting (set out in summary form below in Box 17.3) seems to have escaped the general conclusion that persuasive campaigns have small or no effects.

This is the essence of the agenda-setting hypothesis, but such evidence is insufficient to show a *causal* connection between the various issue 'agendas'. For that we need to know the content of party programmes, evidence of opinion change over time in a given section of the public (preferably with panel data), plus content analysis showing media attention to different issues in the relevant period. We also need some indication of relevant media use by the public concerned. Such data have rarely, if ever, been produced at the same time in support of the hypothesis of agenda-setting. The further one moves away from the general notion that media direct attention and shape cognitions and towards examining actual cases, the more uncertain it becomes whether such an effect actually occurs.

Davis and Robinson (1986) criticized previous agenda-setting research for neglecting possible effects on what people think concerning *who* is important, *where* important things happen, and *why* things are important. According to Rogers and Dearing (1987), we need to distinguish clearly between three different agendas: the priorities of the media, those of the public and those of policy. These interact in complex ways and may have effects in different directions. The same authors also note that media vary in their credibility, that personal experience and the media picture may diverge, and that the public may not share the same values about news events as the media. In addition, 'real-world' events may intervene in unexpected ways to upset previous agendas (Iyengar and Kinder, 1987). Reese (1991) has pointed out that much depends on the relative balance of power between media and sources, a factor that varies considerably from case to case. Agenda-setting effects are not unlike most other known effects in that they are also contingent on the right combination of factors in respect of the topic, the type of media and the larger context (Walgrave and van Aelst, 2006).

Each of these comments introduces new sources of variation. Despite the difficulties, agenda-setting has attracted mass communication researchers because it seems to offer an alternative to the search for directional media effects on individual attitudes and behaviour change. Most evidence (for example, Behr and Iyengar, 1985) is inconclusive, and assessments (among them by Kraus and Davis, 1976; Becker, 1982; Reese, 1991; Rogers, Dearing and Bergman, 1993) tend to leave agenda-setting with the status of a plausible but unproven idea.

The doubts stem not only from the strict methodological demands for proof of a causal connection, but also from theoretical ambiguities. The hypothesis presupposes a process of influence, from the priorities of political or other interest groups to the news priorities of media, in which news values and audience interests play a strong part, and from there to the opinions of the public. There are certainly alternative models of this relationship, of which the main one reverses the flow and states that underlying concerns of the public will shape issue definition by both political elites and the media. Such a process is fundamental to political theory and to the logic of free media. It is likely that the media do contribute to a *convergence* of the three 'agendas' mentioned above, but that is a different matter from setting any particular one of them. There are suggestions of a 'media logic' being at work, where politicians and journalists are primarily oriented towards each other, at times setting each other's agenda, loosely based on assumptions about the public agenda.

Furthermore, in a contemporary media context, the public's 'communication power' to introduce issues onto the news and political agenda by raising awareness via hashtags and (often intense and emotionally charged) discussions online – consider #MeToo, #ClimateStrike, and many other forms of mediated activism – must be taken into consideration. One common condition for agenda-setting is that different mass media tend to share the same set of news priorities. This condition is challenged by the availability of many new online news services, plus the greater chance for a 'news user' to seek and produce news according to personal preferences.

## PRIMING

When considering the consequences of agenda-setting for public opinion, reference is sometimes made (especially in political communication research) to 'media priming' effects, as a more specific aspect of agenda-setting (Weaver, 2007: 145). The idea of **priming** originated in social learning theory and the study of effects in aggression. It also has a long history in election campaign research in the attempts by politicians to be associated with the issues on which they have the strongest reputation. The authors of this idea (Iyengar and Kinder, 1987) show that the political issues that receive most attention (highest on the agenda) also figure more prominently in public assessments of the performance of political actors. The general assessment of a party or a politician thus depends on the perception of how they do on the most salient issues.

The priming 'effect' is essentially one of promoting certain evaluative criteria and it plays a part in attempts to manage news. For instance, the often-suspected attempts of national leaders to divert attention from domestic failure by some foreign policy success, real or perceived scandals, or even military adventure, is an extreme example of priming. Like agenda-setting, although it seems true to what is going on, it is difficult to prove in practice. In an attempt to specify the underlying theoretical construct of priming and thereby increase its effectiveness as a media-effects theory, Scheufele (2000) traces priming back to psychological theories of salience. Following this line of thinking, people would consider some issues (in the news) as being more salient than others if these issues are consistently covered (in specific ways) by the news media, which in turn increases the likelihood of people being affected in their subsequent thinking about such issues. Scheufele (ibid.: 300) argues that '[b]oth agenda-setting and priming are based on this assumption of attitude accessibility and, in particular, a memory-based model of information processing'. Cacciatore et al. (2016) argue that these effects are quite distinct from framing effects, even though these theories are often considered to be overlapping. Framing, they argue, is a much less general process among the public at large, as it relies on a match between the way news media cover certain issues and pre-existing cognitive notions or 'schema' and 'scripts'. In other words, agenda-setting and priming focus on how people access certain types of news and information, while framing considers how people attribute these issues to what they already know.

## FRAMING

The idea of framing is an attractive one and provides a strong hypothesis that an audience will be guided by journalistic frames in what it learns. It will also learn the frames themselves. However, it is not obvious how framing will work as an effect process. As Cappella and Jamieson (1997: 98) put it, 'The way the news is framed by journalists and how the audience frames news may be similar or different'. The same authors proposed a model of framing effects, with the central idea that news frames activate certain inferences, ideas, judgements and contrasts concerning issues, policies and politicians. Their particular concern was to assess whether consistent framing of political news as either 'strategic' (dealing with attempts to gain campaign advantage) or 'conflict oriented' (as opposed to objectively reporting substance) would contribute to greater public cynicism about politics. Their evidence supports the idea of a cumulative (spiralling) process of increased cynicism as a media effect.

Scheufele (1999) has suggested a process model of framing effects that recognizes them as outcomes of interaction between three different kinds of actor: interested sources and media organizations, journalists (media) and audiences. As he notes, we are dealing with two kinds of frame: media frames and individual (receiver) frames. Both kinds of frame can be either independent (a cause) or dependent (an effect). According to the model, there are four interrelated framing processes involving these actors. First, there is the construction and use of media frames by journalists and others working in news organizations under routine pressures, constantly dealing with sources and applying 'news values' and 'news angles' to event reports. Secondly, there is the transmission of 'framed' news reports (for example, a cynical view of politicians) to the audience. Thirdly, there is an acceptance of certain frames by members of the audience, with consequences for their attitudes, outlook (such as cynicism) and behaviour (for instance, non-participation).

The groundwork for much framing research was laid by Entman (1993), but there has been some criticism of his ambition to construct a single general paradigm of the framing process. Several scholars have noted the tendency of the rather loosely defined general theory of framing to produce such a wide variety of interpretations and examples of framing research that the field should abandon the term 'framing' as a catch-call phrase. Considering the many different approaches to framing, Schuck and Feinholdt (2015: 1) remark that 'upon closer inspection it becomes much less obvious and agreeable *what* a frame is and *how* and *under what conditions* frames have *what kind* of effect' (italics in original).

D'Angelo (2002) argues that the literature indicates the existence of at least three different framing paradigms. The first of these is a *cognitivist* model, according to which the texts of journalistic accounts become embodied in the thoughts and words of those affected. Secondly, there is a *constructionist* variant of the process, which sees journalists as providing 'interpretative packages' of the positions of sponsors (that is, sources) of news. Thirdly, there is a *critical* paradigm that sees frames as the outcome of news gathering routines and the values of elites. This attributes a hegemonic influence to framing. There has been some criticism of the general failure of framing research to pay much attention to power, although Entman (1993), in his founding presentation, did say that frames in news stories reveal the 'imprint of power'. Carragee and Roefs (2004) emphasized that frames are much more than story topics and do usually embody some direction of valuation.

Despite the complexities, there is sufficient evidence, especially from political communication research, to demonstrate the occurrence of effects on audiences that are in line with news frames. In contemporary applications of framing theory, attention has shifted somewhat from strictly cognitive effects to research on affective factors in mediating framing effects (Lecheler et al., 2013). Such work looks at the kinds of emotions that are triggered by political news frames, and to what extent, and under what conditions, framing impacts changes in attitudes and behaviours (Schuck and Feinholdt, 2015). In more qualitative approaches to framing research, work on affective news and affective publics by Papacharissi (2014, 2016) traces a similar path, emphasizing people's emotional engagement with certain issues, topics and stories, particularly in online contexts, as we do not just consume news but also comment, like, 'favourite', forward and share it in various ways based on personal preferences and emotional engagement with media (Costera Meijer and Groot Kormelink, 2014).

What this brief review of some key theories of short-term media effects suggests is again more sophistication as media and mass communication scholarship unfolds.

Such theoretical and methodological complexity manifests primarily in recognition of the 'multiple-way' influencing processes in today's interactive media environment, and of both the technological and emotional nature of the way people engage with media.

# CANONICAL FOCI OF MEDIA EFFECTS THEORY AND RESEARCH

Beyond specific enduring effects theories, certain foci of media influence and effects research can be considered to be canonical: the often-presumed and much-researched links between media and violence, youth and children, as well as the role of media in public opinion formation and political communication. As media become more personal, intimate, mobile and interconnected, there is a corresponding surge in theories about media addiction.

## THE MEDIA AND VIOLENCE

Much attention has focused on the potential of media to encourage, if not cause, crime, violence and aggressive, anti-social and even criminal behaviour. The reason for concern lies primarily in the repeated demonstration of the high level of portrayal of crime and violence in popular media of all kinds (see Prot et al., 2017). A secondary reason is the widespread perception, whether correct or not, that the social evils mentioned grew step by step with the rise of the mass media during the twentieth century. Each new popular medium has given rise to a new wave of alarm about its possible effects. Most recently, certain types of popular music, blockbuster films, and digital games have been linked to random acts of violence perpetrated by young people in particular. When aggression is more broadly conceived to include acts of 'relational' aggression such as bullying and gossiping with the intent to hurt someone, a meta-analysis of studies in the field suggests that media users indeed 'learn' from watching aggressive models in the media (Martins and Weaver, 2019).

Aside from the 'problem' posed by new media outside the control of society and parents, there has been a general change in media that has encouraged a fresh look at an old issue. There has been a proliferation of television channels and streaming platforms, a decline in regulation and a lowering of thresholds about what is acceptable, making it likely that children, infants and adults alike will have a much larger diet of televised violence across their lifetime than ever before.

The persistent belief that screen violence (especially) is a cause of actual violence and aggression has led to many thousands of research studies, but no great agreement on the degree of causal influence from the media. Nevertheless, the programme of research carried out for the US Surgeon General at the end of the 1960s resulted, according to Lowery and DeFleur (1995), in three main conclusions:

- Television content is heavily saturated with violence.
- Children are spending more and more time exposed to violent content.
- Overall, the evidence supports the hypothesis that the viewing of violent entertainment increases the likelihood of aggressive behaviour.

These conclusions still appear to stand in the contemporary context. As noted in a recent study among people in Australia, China, Croatia, Germany, Japan, Romania and the United States on the effects of screen media violence exposure (TV, films, digital games) on a composite measure of physical, verbal and relational aggression, 'First, violent media use was positively and significantly related to aggressive behavior in all countries. Second, these media violence effects were similar in magnitude across the seven countries' (Anderson et al., 2017: 994).

## THEORY

The main components of hypotheses about violent effects have remained fairly constant. Wartella, Olivarez and Jennings (1998: 58–59) outline three basic theoretical models for describing the process of learning and imitation of media violence. One is the 'social learning theory' of Albert Bandura, according to which children learn from media models what behaviour will be rewarded and what punished. Secondly, there are 'priming' effects (Berkowitz, 1984): when people view violence, it activates or 'primes' other related thoughts and evaluations, leading to a greater predisposition to use violence in interpersonal situations. Thirdly, Huesmann's (1986) script theory holds that social behaviour is controlled by 'scripts' that indicate how to respond to events. Violence on television (and in film and digital games) is encoded in such a way as to lead to violence, as a result of aggressive scripts.

Together these theories form the basis for a much-cited approach in media violence and aggression research: the General Aggression Model (GAM; DeWall, Anderson and Bushman, 2011). According to this theoretical perspective, exposure to a lot of violent or aggressive media content may result in both short- and long-term effects on attitudes and behaviours.

In addition to learning and modelling effects, there is a widespread belief that exposure to portrayals of violence leads to a general 'desensitization' that lowers inhibitions against, and increases tolerance of, violent behaviour. Viewing violent films and playing violent video games can lead to physiological desensitization to violence, decreased **empathy** for victims, and decreased helping (Bushman and Anderson, 2009; Greitemeyer and Mügge,

2014). Cultivation theory, as discussed earlier in this chapter, is also invoked at times in the literature as a possible explanation for influencing people's perceptions of danger, feelings of anger and fear, and support for aggressive public policies.

As with all such theories, there are many variables influencing the disposition of a person and several relating to the depiction of violence. The main contextual factors (in content) influencing audience reactions to media violence are summarized in Box 17.4. In addition to variables of personal disposition and content, there are also variables of the viewing situation that are important, especially being alone or being with parents or peers.

---

## 17.4

## Contextual factors in the portrayal of physical and relational aggression

- The nature and relative appeal of the perpetrator
- The nature and relative appeal of the victim
- The motivations for violence
- The verbal or non-verbal 'weapons' used
- The extensiveness and graphicness of the depiction
- Whether the aggressive behaviour is rewarded or punished (or remains without consequences)
- Whether the aggression is couched in humour (or other countering emotions)

---

Beyond explicit physical acts of violence, relational aggression is much more subtle and its effects are more clearly established. Across all media, relational aggression tends to be portrayed as 'normative, justified, consequence-free, and enacted by attractive perpetrators who are rewarded for their actions' (Martins and Weaver, 2019: 90).

## CONTENT

The main findings of the Surgeon General's report, as summarized above, have often been confirmed. There has continued to be a great deal of violence portrayed across all media, and it exerts a great attraction – not just for the young. Although most research on the amount and degree of violence in the media is conducted in the United States, the available evidence suggests that violence and aggression are dominant ingredients in media diets around the world. It is less easy to say whether the average degree of exposure has increased or not over time, but the potential to see screen violence has gradually extended to most parts of the world, along with the means of exposure. Groebel (1998), reporting on a global survey of violence on television on behalf of UNESCO, involving 5,000 children in twenty-three countries, commented on the universality of media violence and on the widespread fascination with aggressive media hero figures, especially among boys. With the rapid rise to global popularity of digital games, much concern has been voiced about the generally quite explicit nature of the violence portrayed (and played) in such games (Gunter, 2016). At the same time, some studies have not only found no evidence to suggest gaming was positively related to real-world violence, but have also reported a decrease in violent crime in response to violent video games (Markey, Markey and French, 2015). Other work in this field reports little or no effect from the actual violence in the game, but rather aggressive responses to the sometimes quite competitive nature of playing certain games (Dowsett and Jackson, 2019).

## EVIDENCE OF EFFECT

The effects of media violence on behaviour have always been controversial because of the industry and policy implications. It is not easy to be certain on this matter, and any general authoritative statement takes on a political character (Ball-Rokeach, 2001). Still, reviews and meta-analyses of the literature on the influence of media violence consistently find evidence of effects. It is just that, as with most media-effects theories, the effect sizes in such studies tend to be small to moderate, and often are based on single risk factors. In recent years, research has elaborated quite substantially, placing media violence in the context of a cumulative risk assessment including gender, abusive parenting, peer victim-ization or delinquency, and the prevalence of neighbourhood crime, finding that cumula-tive effects of multiple risk factors are more powerful than effects of single risk factors (Anderson et al., 2017: 993).

Media violence effects tend to be of small to moderate magnitude, and to be found in quite specific contexts. Because aggressive behaviour is influenced by a large number of risk factors (including genetic factors, cultural norms, parenting practices, per-sonality, social and cultural context), no single factor can explain more than a small proportion of individual differences in aggression. Even if there is general consensus in the literature that heavy consumers of media violence demonstrate increased accep-tance of aggressive attitudes and increased aggressive behaviour (Wartella et al., 1998), this falls short of causation and to call for censorship and other limitations on violent media content would be problematic (see also the discussion on game addiction later in this chapter).

Interestingly, Martins et al. (2013) have found that news coverage of media violence and aggression research since the start of the twenty-first century has increasingly down-played the strength of the link between media violence and aggression, despite the con-sistent patterns across the literature that exposure to media violence increases the risk of subsequent aggression. They offer three explanations for this apparent gap between the research and its coverage in the news (ibid.: 1081–1082):

- the journalistic value of objectivity and balance produces forced nuanced narrative;
- expert sources are available on both sides of the media effects debate, complicating clear-cut choices;
- news organizations may be attending to the need of audiences for 'good' news, and people perhaps do not want to hear that their favourite pastime has potentially problematic consequences.

Although most scholars are quite clear in their assessment of small but significant effects of media violence (particularly on undesirable opinions and attitudes regarding aggression), there is an active debate in the literature about the theoretical and methodological foundations of these conclusions, and even more so on the purported consequences of media violence. Ferguson and Kilburn (2009) in particular question the reliance of many scholars in this field on single risk factors, concluding that media violence cannot be seen as presenting a significant public health risk. Gauntlett (2005) also criticizes the research in this field as not bothering to study violence and the social problems associated with it, instead reducing a complex issue to that of a simple explanation for the potential behaviour of single individuals. This can be said to be a more contentious issue in the literature on media and mass communication theory in general, and media-effects research in particular: how to account for an individual's choices, opinions and behaviours in relation to the media while recognizing how every individual is simultaneously embedded in all kinds of social structures – such as family, friendship circle, peer groups, communities of practice, and so on – that provide such a person with a wide variety of meanings and other resources to handle whatever media they use.

The possibility that media portrayals of violence and aggression may have some positive effects by allowing a vicarious and harmless release of emotion and aggression has sometimes been advanced (see Perse, 2001: 220–221). The term 'catharsis', derived from Aristotle's theory of drama, has been applied to this process. Although it is clear that most aggression aroused by media portrayals is vicariously released without harm to others, there is little empirical support for a theory that sees a benefit in exposure to violence. Overall, it can be clear that concerns about media violence and aggression will not go away, and that the research in this field will most likely benefit from more interdisciplinary approaches.

# MEDIA, CHILDREN AND YOUNG PEOPLE

Expectations and fears (mostly the latter) abound in the general and research literature about the influence of media on children, aside from the issue of violence and delinquency. Much research has been carried out into children's use of and response to media from early to recent times (for example, Himmelweit et al., 1958; Schramm et al., 1961; Noble, 1975; Brown, 1976; Carlsson and von Feilitzen, 1998; Buckingham, 2002; Livingstone, 2002; Valkenburg and Piotrowski, 2017; see also globalkidsonline. net). Among all these studies, research on children's exposure to sex and violence in the media dominates. Among the ideas expressed and tested about undesirable effects are the following expectations from media:

- an increase in social isolation;
- reduction of time and attention to homework;
- increased passivity;
- reduced time for play and exercise (displacement);
- reduced time for reading (due to screens);
- undermining of parental authority;
- premature sexual knowledge and experience;
- unhealthy eating and obesity;
- promotion of anxiety about self-image, leading to anorexia;
- depressive tendencies;
- suffering from reputational damage committed by peers online;
- exposure to disturbing, violent or pornographic content (online).

Beneficial effects attributed to media include:

- provision of a basis for social interaction;
- learning about the wider world;
- learning of prosocial attitudes and behaviours;
- educational and learning effects;
- help in forming an identity;
- engaging in self-expression;
- having fun;
- developing the imagination.

Many of the above hypotheses can be supported as plausible according to social learning theory and a number have been investigated. No general conclusion is possible and none of these can be regarded as either fully proven or entirely ruled out. Experience of research reminds us to be cautious about the many other influences that contribute to any one of these 'effects'. Despite this, there still does seem to be a consensus among researchers that children are better off, on the whole, without high exposure to television, and without spending hours on end playing digital games. But as Seiter (2000) shows, adult attitudes to the dangers of different media vary according to social class, gender and other factors.

Hargrave and Livingstone (2006) provide a detailed review of evidence of harm and offence caused by media, with particular reference to young people. In line with earlier assessments, they find only modest effects, usually in combination with other factors. The most vulnerable are likely to be young males. The rise of a 'bedroom culture' has also been chronicled by Livingstone (2007) and will now be familiar to most parents. It means that children from an early age now determine their own media environment. This means at the very least a reduction in parental control and supervision, although it can also connect a child with a wider peer culture (and also be separating). One probable consequence is a higher level of consumption of media, as evidenced by numerous accounts signalling a doubling of hours spent using media by children and teenagers today versus only a decade or two ago. Beyond that it is hard to generalize.

In their most recent comprehensive review of scholarship on how media affect youth, Patti Valkenburg and Jessica Piotrowski (2017) remark on how (media and) cultural studies and media psychology are related fields that increasingly devote resources to the academic study of children and media, in part because of the rapid commercialization of the media environment around youth (including those younger than three years old) and the rise of social media (see Box 17.5).

---

## 17.5

## Media and youth (Valkenburg and Piotrowski, 2017: 3)

Research on youth and media requires an interdisciplinary approach integrating knowledge and theories from several disciplines. After all, to understand the effects of media on children and adolescents, we need to know theories about media in general as well as about cognitive and social-emotional development in youth, since it is this development that largely shapes their media use and its effects. We need to be familiar with theories about a child's social environment, such as family, friends, and the youth culture, since factors in these environments predict the nature of media effects to some or a great extent.

---

Valkenburg and Piotrowski identify four stages in thinking about children and childhood since the seventeenth century, starting with a view of children as 'miniature adults' until well into the eighteenth century. This was a time without dedicated media (or clothing) for children. During the industrial revolution up to the second half of the twentieth century, children became a vulnerable audience needing protection. Materials for children were created and existing books and stories were censored in order to protect the 'sweet and innocent' child. Under the influence of various emancipation movements of the 1960s, children began to be taken seriously, and 'formerly taboo subjects such as sexuality, death, and divorce once more became acceptable in media aimed at youth' (ibid.: 14). Several scholars, including those from the emerging discipline of communication studies, subsequently voiced concern about a potentially 'disappearing' childhood, and (originally inspired by the rapid spread of television, and later on by newer media such as the Internet) warned against exposing children to certain media content and experiences too soon. All in all, the evidence for all such changes in children over generations remains mixed, although Valkenburg and Piotrowski do suggest that today's children, on average, experience accelerated puberty, are more intelligent, have more self-awareness, self-esteem, and a higher degree of narcissism, as well as experiencing more psychosocial problems than previous generations.

When it comes to the impact of growing up in a pervasive and ubiquitous media environment, the literature allows several general observations to be made. First, it must be noted that, when it comes to children and youths, content matters (ibid.: 273). Scary, upsetting or highly sexualized content can lead to undesirable attitudes and behaviours. On the other hand, the upsides of, for example, gaming (enhanced cognitive skills) and social media (building self-esteem, enhancing peer relationships) tend to outweigh the downsides, even though for some children these media are clearly problematic, depending on dispositional and social factors.

Livingstone and Helsper (2010) note that more media use comes with more opportunities and risks for children, arguing for a focus on 'wellbeing' rather than on either 'good' or 'bad' media effects. In subsequent work, Livingstone and Third (2017: 662) introduce a rights-based approach to children's digital media practices, suggesting that what makes children exceptional in debates about media effects and society is that 'the child – as a cypher for our cultural anxieties and a focus of investment for our future desires – represents an important figure through which to (re)think the digital and human rights'. Livingstone and Third identify 'positive' rights (such as access, expression, privacy and participation) and 'negative' rights (as in protection from harms), showing that negative rights take priority in theory, policy and practice. This in turn makes children 'ever more spoken for rather than speaking subjects' (ibid.: 665), which is a conclusion that at times can also be drawn about media users as audiences in studies and reports about media effects more generally. This has prompted numerous scholars to advocate a 'return to basics' of some kind: studying what people actually do with media and what this means to them (Jensen, 2018: 182).

# MEDIA AND POLITICAL COMMUNICATION

A crucial focus of media effects research is the relationship between political elites (cf. parties, parliament and politicians), the public (as citizens and consumers) and the media. Political communication specifically considers how the content and flow of communication between these people and groups create and reflect power. There has always been an intimate connection between media and mass communication and the conduct of politics, in whatever kind of regime. In totalitarian or authoritarian societies, ruling elites use their control of the media to ensure conformity and compliance and to stifle dissent by one means or another. In democracies, the media have a complex relationship with sources of power and the political system. On the one hand, they usually find their *raison d'être* in their service to their audiences, to whom they provide information and views according to judgements of interest and need. In order to perform this service, they need to be independent of the state and of powerful interests. On the other hand, they also provide channels by which the state and powerful interests address the people, as well as platforms for the views of political parties and other interest groups. They also promote the circulation of news and opinion within the politically interested public.

This general view of the 'neutral' and mediating role of the media in politics has to be modified to take account of variant forms, especially one in which particular media choose to play a partisan role on behalf of a party or interest, or are closely allied with some powerful economic interest or ideological bloc. There is a third possibility where the state has considerable effective power over nominally free media and uses this power for its own advantage, including wielding its considerable assets to influence or manipulate the media. Such a situation appears to pertain in post-communist Russia, and other countries, such as Italy under Berlusconi, have approached a similar position. In global terms, the situation is not at all unusual.

Against this background we can identify and briefly characterize the main forms of political communication, which can be considered under the heading of 'effects'. First, there are periodic election *campaigns* in which the media are usually used intensively by competing candidates and parties. Secondly, there is the continuous flow of *news*, which carries messages about events that reflect positively or negatively on governments and other actors in the political arena. This provides many opportunities for news management and PR intervention. Thirdly, there are, in varying degrees, opportunities for political *advertising* by the same actors, independent of elections. Specific attempts are also sometimes made to influence opinion on particular issues on behalf of various lobbies and pressure groups, by various means. This process is defined in general terms by Strömbäck and Kiousis (2011: 8) as *political public relations*, 'a management process by which an organization or individual actor for political purposes, through purposeful communication and action, seeks to influence and to establish, build, and maintain beneficial relationships and reputations with its key publics to help support its mission and achieve its goals'.

The most studied communication form is that of the election campaign, with research going back at least to 1940, when Lazarsfeld et al. (1944) made a detailed enquiry into the presidential election of that year. Since then, thousands of democratic elections have been an object of research (see Semetko, 2004), with some consistency in broad findings about effects. Election campaigns are usually short and intensive and are not typically characterized by a great deal of net change from intention to vote. The media are intensively used by campaigners, but usually received with less interest by electors. It is rare to find clear support in evidence that media make a great deal of difference to the outcome of an election. They have little direct effect on voting (or not voting). Basic political attitudes are usually too deeply rooted to be susceptible to much change, although a growing detachment from firm allegiances, ongoing economic crises, and direct experience with the consequences of globalization have been shown to open the way for more influence, particularly within the realm of populist politics (Hameleers et al., 2018). Opinions on particular issues may be influenced by media and there is evidence of a potential for learning about issues and policy stands, especially by the relatively ignorant and disinterested, a phenomenon amplified and accelerated by micro-targeted political messaging online. To some extent this reflects the 'agenda-setting' process described above. Learning effects can be important when they lead to opinion change or, more likely, to perceptions of reality that favour one side or another.

Election campaigns attract widely varying degrees and kinds of motivated audience attention (and much inattention) and the effects they do have depend more on the dispositions and motives of voters than on the intentions of campaigners. Blumler and McQuail (1968) found that an intensive general election campaign had larger effects where it reached sectors of a more or less captive audience that was previously uninformed and without firm allegiances. Schoenbach and Lauf (2002) call this a 'trap' effect. A strong claim has been made that, as a result of audience fragmentation, we have entered a new era of minimal effects (Bennett and Iyengar, 2008). Yet in recent years, the pendulum seems to have swung back into the direction of potentially powerful effects, given the experiences with widespread disinformation and propaganda campaigns involving prominent politicians and parties – such as Bolsonaro in Brazil, Trump in the United States, and the Brexit campaign in the United Kingdom. Populism today is a truly global phenomenon, which can be treated as a communication phenomenon, as 'populist ideas must be communicated discursively to achieve the communicator's goals and the intended effects on the audience' (De Vreese et al., 2018: 425). An application of the taxonomy of political communication theory to the study of populism as a communication phenomenon is summarized in Box 17.6.

To address the question of media effect, a recent comparative experiment across sixteen European countries was conducted to test the effects of populist communication on political engagement (Hameleers et al., 2018). The study set out to investigate the effects of different combinations of populist messages within different countries to see whether exposure to such messages had specific behavioural outcomes. Effects on political engagement were operationalized as the willingness of the respondent to share the news article on **social network sites**, talk to a friend about the article, and sign an online petition to support the non-governmental organization (NGO) mentioned in the article (ibid.: 526). Populist politicians tend to combine appeals to certain 'pure' in-group characteristics with an identification of a 'credible scapegoat' for real or perceived problems experienced by members of the in-group. The researchers found that anti-elitist populism has a strong mobilizing effect, whereas anti-immigrant rhetoric in fact had an opposite, demobilizing effect, although overall effects were relatively modest. These media effects were moderated by national conditions such as the level of unemployment and the level of electoral success of the populist Left and Right.

The relative lack of decisive effects from media campaigns can be attributed to several factors aside from selective attention, variable motivation and the available political 'opportunity structures' within particular countries (such as the level of unemployment, distrust in politics, or experience with transnational migration). These include the lack of room for change on familiar issues, the cancelling effect of opposing messages, the part played by personal relations and social identity formation, and the ritual character of much campaigning that offers little that is new in any substantial way. In many western democracies, where the media are not co-opted by the political parties, the amount and quality of attention given to the main contenders tends to be very similar (Norris et al., 1999; D'Alessio and Allen, 2000; Noin, 2001). Campaigns tend to maintain the status quo, but we could expect large effects if one side failed to campaign, and sometimes a single incident can upset the equilibrium dramatically. Often election campaigns are aimed at maintaining the status quo rather than creating change. The newer media environment has upended much of the equilibrium in this area. Political campaigns have transitioned from the paradigm of mass media campaigning, primarily oriented towards mass persuasion via advertising and news coverage to what Stromer-Galley (2019) calls 'networked campaigning'. Efforts are increasingly directed towards identifying 'super-supporters' who can use their reputation and influence to mobilize potential voters. A second online campaign tactic is the automated micro-targeting of specific groups of voters, often shortly before election day, with tailor-made messages about particular issues they care about. As Stromer-Galley suggests, even though the interactive nature of the Internet seems to give citizens a more active role in the political communication process, these campaigns can be considered to be 'undemocratic affairs' as the ultimate goal remains to control and harness citizens as voters.

## THE MEDIATIZATION OF POLITICS

In an attempt to converge the traditional taxonomy of the political communication process – political actors, media and citizens – with the emerging multiple-way, interactive media environment, Brants and Voltmer (2011) suggest that changes in contemporary political communication can be understood as taking place in two dimensions (see Figure 17.1). They identify a horizontal dimension consisting of the relationships between political elites and journalists, and a vertical dimension denoting the interactions between these actors with citizens.

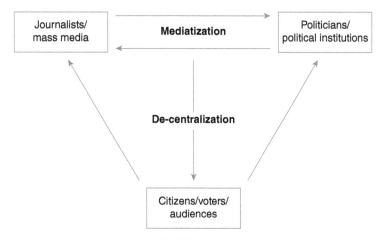

Figure 17.1   Changes in political communication (Brants and Voltmer, 2011: 4)

Based on an international comparative perspective, Brants and Voltmer signal two processes of transformation in political communication: the mediatization of politics–media relationships and a decentralization of relationships with citizens and audiences. Following the theory of mediatization (see Chapter 4), they suggest an increasing dependency of political actors on the media as having a logic that dictates how they can effectively communicate, and as a force that influences the process and institutional structure of politics: 'As a consequence, election campaigns – and political communications in general – have become more candidate-centred, image-driven, polarized and spectacular, and less organized around issues and ideologies' (Brants and Voltmer, 2011: 5). This in turn, the authors suggest, leads to a 'spiral of distrust' among politicians and journalists, as well as between citizens and the political system. With decentralization, Brants and Voltmer identify a common observation across the literature of the 'disappearing citizen', as people increasingly challenge the legitimacy and credibility of institutionalized politics as well as traditional media institutions. People are increasingly more likely to vote based on single issues (such as pensions, migration or health care), to take to the Internet to inform and express themselves, and to participate in all kinds of communities and social movements beyond the sphere of influence of mainstream media and politics. Archetti (2017a: 103) takes issue with the linear relations and transformations suggested by Brants and Voltmer, suggesting (based on fieldwork in Italy and the UK) that 'around every single individual there are overlapping clouds or constellations of relationships that exist at different levels and that constantly change over time. It is these relationships – their scope, the identity of the actors involved, their changing action – that shapes the impact that communication technologies have on political processes at any given time and location'.

The case of politics provides fairly clear evidence of the adaptation of a social institution to the rise of mass media. The challenge to politics from the growing centrality of the mass media and the rise of 'media logic' (whereby other institutions adapt to the rules and rituals governing the inner workings of the media industry) have taken several forms. These include:

- the diversion of time from political participation in a narrow sense (voting, party membership) to broader engagement through grass-roots-level organizing and (offline as well as online) social movements;
- the effects of 'political public relations' on voter trust and goodwill;
- the increasing negativity and polarizing perspectives in campaigning and campaign reporting;
- the rising costs, commercialization and bureaucratization of campaigning.

Suggestions about the influence of 'media logic' on political institutions and the mediatization of politics (Mazzoleni, 2014) include the diversion of attention from the local and regional to the national stage; the reliance on personality and image more than on substance and policy; the decline of face-to-face political campaigning; and the excessive reliance on and use of opinion polls. In addition to all this, 'trial by media' has become a fact of public life in most countries for any politician touched in any way by scandal (Thompson, 2000; Tumber and Waisbord, 2004). At the same time, these proposed 'effects' are questioned for their moralistic undertones, the assumption of a more or less gullible mass public, and the characterization of political actors as professional liars (Archetti, 2017a).

The view that modern political campaigning for national elections is counterproductive in respect of the aim to mobilize citizens to participate has not gone unchallenged. Norris (2000) reviewed much evidence showing that engagement with democratic politics is persistently associated with much attention to mass media. Pasek, Kensler, Romer and Jamieson (2006) concluded that media use, whether for information or entertainment, facilitates civic engagement and political awareness. Moy, Torres, Tanaka and McClusky (2005) found much the same. While the link between political learning (from the media) and political engagement is broadly assumed and established, cross-national comparative research suggests that the extent of such a relationship is highly variable across different geographical contexts (Fraile and Iyengar, 2014), with political learning and engagement, for example, strongly influenced by the degree of media freedom in any given country (Schoonvelde, 2014).

The true significance of voter cynicism has also been questioned. De Vreese (2006) found that strategic reporting was not conducive to cynicism, and in any case cynicism is not linked to non-voting *per se* since it is a quality of the politically more sophisticated. Results in a follow-up cross-national comparative study on the relationship between election news coverage and political cynicism in twenty-one countries found no overall direct effect of strategy news on political cynicism, except for some individuals in some circumstances (Schuck, Boomgaarden and De Vreese, 2013). It is arguable that the triumph of media logic and mediatization has been over-emphasized (Strömbäck and Esser, 2014). This is a reminder of how much always depends on time, place and context where communication is concerned.

## ELECTION CAMPAIGNS AND THE POLITICAL PROCESS IN CONTEXT

There is little doubt that election campaigns have been widely transformed into skilfully and professionally managed events more akin to advertising, public relations and marketing than to traditional politics (Blumler and Gurevitch, 1995). It is widely thought that the trends described originated in the USA and have been globally diffused (Swanson and Mancini, 1996; Bennett and Entman, 2001; Sussman and Galizio, 2003). The rise of the '**spin doctor**' has been interpreted as marking a new stage in the development of political communication, with journalism providing 'meta-communication' about media manipulation, defined as 'the news media's self-referential reflections on the nature of the interplay between PR and political journalism' (Esser, Reinemann and Fan, 2000).

As always, it is hard to separate out the effects of media change from broad changes in society working both on the media and on political institutions, and there is much room for dispute about the real cause of any given institutional effect. Cappella (2002) advises against treating the media as a 'cause'. Rather, media propagate and replicate a certain prevailing view. There is also a need for caution about the more sweeping complaints concerning the decay of political communication. There is no single condition and many of the traditional media supports for democracy still operate quite well.

The question of which medium is more effective in achieving results in campaigns was a central focus of attention in early research, especially with the arrival of television, but in a multimedia environment it is less salient and also harder to investigate. Rather than singling out any medium, the attention of contemporary political communication research to some extent shifts towards the role various contexts play in the political communication process. This is especially relevant given the continued dominance of the USA in political communication research (Boulianne, 2019), a general lack of making contextual characteristics of a particular study explicit (especially by scholars in dominant countries such as the USA and the UK; see Rojas and Valenzuela, 2019), and a continued over-emphasis on individual-level differences and effects (rather than integrating micro-, meso- and macro-level contexts; see Boomgaarden and Song, 2019: 547).

Political communication by way of general news reflects a continuous process of news management and competition to define events and issues. All significant actors employ professional news managers (spin doctors) to ensure access on favourable terms in normal daily news and to put the best gloss possible on a news story. Such influences are impossible to measure in terms of effectiveness, but there is reliable support, in theory, for the belief that the news provides a good environment for influential messages since it is usually characterized by independence of source, credibility and lack of propagandist associations. In practice, in most functioning democracies, more or less equal access to news is usually available to the main contenders for office, sufficient to prevent a single dominant shape being given to the news. Although mediatization theory suggests that the news media have become more powerful in shaping the political system and its agenda, a counter-trend would be that of 'disintermediation' (Katz, 1988), as people also bypass the news altogether either to avoid political information, to inform and express themselves online, or to follow politicians directly via social media. The effects of this are yet to be determined.

Political advertising, on the other hand, depends on having resources, but is also limited in its potential by its propagandist character. It may have unpredictable side-effects, and clear evidence of the value of political advertising is hard to come by (Goldstein and

Freedman, 2002), although it may work as intended by simple attrition and repetition. The same applies to all campaigns with a political objective. Advertising on television has tended to take negative forms, risking alienating voters (who tend to prefer more positive messages). Online, political advertising has taken on new forms as political actors in recent years have diverted much of their campaign budgets to purchasing micro-targeted advertising space on online social networks.

Ever since the famous Kennedy–Nixon televised debate in 1960, this campaign form has been advocated as a means of enlivening politics and providing a decisive test of leader competence and persuasiveness. It has been tried out in various forms (Kraus and Davis, 1976). The fear of disaster testifies to the potency attributed to such events. However, the findings of research (for example, Coleman, 2000) have reported little in the way of dramatic electoral consequences (true for the original debate), although they do lead to changed perceptions of candidates and some learning of policies. They seem to have reinforcement effects on voter choice. In fact, incumbent politicians have typically been very wary of debates, seeing no certain advantage and fearing uncontrolled effects.

It is tempting to suggest that the newer media environment, in conjunction with the suggested trends of mediatization and decentralization, has significantly altered the political communication process. However, claims that online campaigns are really all that successful in mobilizing new voters or changing the minds of existing ones have not found much evidence. Qualitative studies of the interactions of (and relations between) political actors, journalists and citizens paint quite a different picture, where the overall role of media is in fact less powerful than often suggested. In her comparative work on local councillors and members of parliament, Archetti (2017a) suggests that notions of 'mediatization' of politics only apply to a handful of top politicians, representing not the norm but an exception. This fits with earlier warnings in media and mass communication theory and research against 'fetishizing' large media organizations in production research, privileging the content of the most popular television series, or focusing only on high-profile actors in the communication process (Garnham, 2000: 86).

This brief overview of the effects of mass communication in election campaigns may seem inconsistent with the reality of contemporary political campaigning, in which communication strategies are planned in fine detail by myriad advisers and professional publicists and many ways are found to spend large sums of money, especially by those in (online) media advertising. The fact is that even though the chances of decisively influencing the outcome of an election by means of communication are usually quite small, it would be easy to lose an election by not campaigning or by campaigning badly. Mounting a glittering, clever and confident campaign is an essential part of the institutional ritual and the appeal for public support, and not to campaign to the utmost would mean not being taken seriously as a candidate.

# MEDIA ADDICTION

Considering the materiality of media, a growing area of media-effects scholarship focuses on the potential for media to lead to addictive behaviours. There is now an extensive literature on Internet addiction and problematic Internet use, digital game addiction, pornography and online porn addiction, smartphone addiction, and the potentially problematic consequences of social media use. Although such studies rarely make it into the journals and books of media and mass communication research, it is important to acknowledge this field of scholarship.

In the early 1990s, the first studies were conducted to assess the existence of television addiction, followed a few years later by the first concerns about 'netaholism' and 'Internet Addiction Disorder' (IAD) – satirically coined as such by an American psychiatrist who did not believe such a disease could exist (Wallis, 1997). These moments are considered the starting point for the field of media addiction research (Leung and Chen, 2018). After a relatively sporadic phase of limited growth, the literature on media addiction and disorders rapidly accelerated from 2011 onwards, largely inspired by the worldwide popularity of social media and mobile devices such as the smartphone.

Media addiction tends to be defined either as a psychiatric disorder or as part of a broader set of behavioural disorders involving excessive human–machine interactions. Such disorders differ in definition across the literature but generally contain two main components: compulsivity (the inability to control a certain type of media use) and impairment (how such media use harms or interferes with a person's life). In their review of the literature between 1991 and 2016, Leung and Chen (2018: 3) operationalize media addiction as 'the inability to control the use of media, which has adverse effects on the user's daily life'.

The literature tends to discern between addictions to a particular type of device (smartphone), platform (Facebook, YouTube, Twitter, Reddit), content (digital games, online gambling, cybersex and pornography) and behaviour. The majority of research in this area is based on self-reports using the survey method. Qualitative methods such as focus groups and interviews are quite rare. Surveys tend to be based on specific scales, indexes and diagnostic questionnaires developed to measure and classify specific behaviours as addictive. Interestingly, a significant theme across the various media addictions, as documented in the literature, is whether or not a particular addiction exists or whether it is a theoretical construct (ibid.: 11). Overall, there is much debate about the difference between addiction and 'high engagement' with media, and about the appropriateness of addiction criteria, the neglect of context, and a general lack of expert consensus on how to approach and measure disorders and addictions regarding media content and use (Kuss and Lopez-Fernandez, 2016).

All of this does not mean that various forms of media addictions do not occur. Clearly, addiction is a serious condition and should be treated with care. Beyond identifying addiction as a pathology, problematic media use is a salient issue given the affective and emotional nature of much of people's engagement with media. As Ferrara and Yang (2015: 2) report, based on a review of how emotions spread through online social networks, 'social media conversation affects the offline, physical world in tangible ways'. A salient example of this claim has come to be known as the 'Facebook emotional contagion experiment', conducted and published in 2012. Researchers working with a data team at Facebook manipulated the amount of emotional content in the News Feed of 689,003 users during one week. They found that '[w]hen positive expressions were reduced, people produced fewer positive posts and more negative posts; when negative expressions were reduced, the opposite pattern occurred. These results indicate that emotions expressed by others on Facebook influence our own emotions, constituting experimental evidence for massive-scale contagion via social networks' (Kramer, Guillory and Hancock, 2014: 8788). None of the users involved were aware that this happened. The researchers involved claimed to have found evidence that posts with emotional content are more engaging, and that emotionally charged content can spread throughout a network without direct interaction between people – although the reported effect sizes of the manipulations in the study were quite small. When the study was published, it garnered enormous media attention, including many scholars expressing grave concerns about the research ethics involved (see Jouhki et al., 2016; Selinger and Hartzog, 2016). The study's lead author responded in a Facebook post: 'Having written and designed this experiment myself, I can tell you that our goal was never to upset anyone. . . . In hindsight, the research benefits of the paper may not have justified all of this anxiety' (Kramer, 2012, quoted in Meyer, 2014). The experiment did highlight the extent to which emotions drive and influence people's participation in social media, and its fallout stresses the vulnerability and lack of control users of such media have.

What is particularly relevant for media and mass communication theory is the finding in much of the media addiction research literature, that many people – and the young in particular – report feeling that their media use has become excessive, that they experience a lack or loss of control and find it difficult to withdraw. These examples of problematic media use and emotional contagion throw theories and research findings about concurrent media exposure and media effects into sharp relief, and compel us to ask normative questions about not just the *quantity* but also the *quality* of media use.

## CONCLUSION

The influence and effects of media mass communication are difficult to assess for many reasons. There are some possibilities for observing short-term changes affecting individuals, which can then sometimes be generalized to larger aggregates and even to society as a whole. The methodological capacity to measure larger trends at higher levels of analysis with any reliability is increasingly sought by combining theoretical and methodological approaches, developing longitudinal research designs, and integrating micro-, meso- and macro-level contexts of media use. There is little doubt that media do have many effects and they probably do account for some general trends. However, media effects are often inconsistent and cancel each other out, and complex societies are often characterized by different lines of development at the same time. Still, the examples of theories and canonical foci in this chapter show that much of the field – and many colleagues in adjacent areas of investigation – are committed to finding answers to detailed questions about the role, influence and effects of media, all with the hope of improving people's lives.

In fact, overall one could argue that what sets media and mass communication studies apart from other disciplines is a fundamental assumption of the primacy of media in everyday life, in institutional processes, and in the functioning of societies, coupled with a shared conviction that media have effects that make a difference.

## FURTHER READING

Boomgaarden, H.G. and Song, H. (2019) 'Media use and its effects in cross-national perspective', *Kölner Zeitschrift für Soziologie und Sozialpsychologie*, 71(1): 545–571.

Cacciatore, M.A., Scheufele, D.A. and Iyengar, S. (2016) 'The end of framing as we know it … and the future of media effects', *Mass Communication and Society*, 19(1): 7–23.

Croucher, S.M. (2011) 'Social networking and cultural adaptation: a theoretical model', *Journal of International and Intercultural Communication*, 4(4): 259–264.

De Vreese, C.H., Esser, F., Aalberg, T., Reinemann, C. and Stanyer, J. (2018) 'Populism as an expression of political communication content and style: a new perspective', *The International Journal of Press/Politics*, 23(4): 423–438.

Karatzogianni, A. and Kuntsman, A. (2012) *Digital Cultures and the Politics of Emotion: Feelings, Affect and Technological Change*. Basingstoke: Palgrave Macmillan.

Leung, L. and Chen, C. (2018, August) 'A review of media addiction research from 1991 to 2016', *Social Science Computer Review*, 1–18, https://doi.org/10.1177/0894439318791770.

# PART 8
## EPILOGUE

# 18

## THE FUTURE

In this concluding chapter we make the case for a 'grand narrative' of media and mass communication theory in order to address the question of what the overall 'story' of the field is (or can be), based on the genealogy of theoretical traditions explored and outlined in this book.

After reviewing the origins, historical trajectory and contemporary debates around the mass communication idea, contemporary developments in media industries and production, content and audiences as well as the theories that have been developed to address these are considered as laying the groundwork for such a meta-narrative. In conclusion, possibilities for a more public role of media studies and communication scholarship are considered.

# ORIGINS OF THE MASS COMMUNICATION IDEA

The concept of mass communication was first coined during the 1920s or 1930s to apply to the new possibilities for public communication arising from the mass press, radio and film. These media enlarged the potential audience beyond the literate minority. The industrial style and scale of the organization of production and dissemination were also essentially new. Large populations of nation states could be reached more or less simultaneously with much the same content, often content that carried the stamp of approval of those with political and social power. The then new mass media of press, film and radio, along with recorded music, also gave rise to a new variant of 'popular culture', in which political and social ideologies were often embedded.

The context for those developments was one of rapid change in the world of newly industrialized and centralized nation states. It was a time of growth and concentration of population in large cities, of the mechanization and bureaucratization of all aspects of life, and of imperialist expansion by the great powers of the time, which were almost exclusively European or American. It was also a period of profound political change, large social movements, unrest within states, and catastrophic warfare between states. Populations were mobilized towards national achievement or survival and the new mass media played their part in these events as well as providing the masses with the means of relaxation and entertainment. Against this background it is easy to understand why the concept of mass communication was forged and why it rose to a dominant status.

The early meaning of 'mass communication', and one that still lingers, derived much more from the notion of people as a 'mass' and from the perceived characteristics of the mass media than from any idea of communication. As explained in earlier chapters, the 'mass' was perceived primarily in terms of its size, anonymity, general ignorance, lack of stability and rationality, and as a result was vulnerable to persuasion or suggestion. It was seen to be in need of control and guidance by the superior classes and leaders, and the mass media provided the means for achieving this.

As 'communication science' and 'media studies' developed, a more formal definition of the concept of mass communication emerged that was not based on untested impressions, the claims of publicists or social philosophy, but on objective characteristics of media that could be specified and put to the test. An abstract model of communication was developed with the following typical features:

- A centralized production of content by a few large channels, with a centre–peripheral network of dissemination that was typically hierarchical and one-directional.

- An organization of production and distribution operated according to the logic of the market or as a state-run institution of public communication.

- Message content in standardized forms open to all but also subject to normative and political supervision or control.

- A mass public of receivers made up of many dispersed, anonymous and disconnected individuals.

- The attribution of great power to persuade and inform, arising from the prestige or popularity of sources, the monopolistic control of channels, the near instantaneity of reception, the skill of practitioners, and the supposedly high impact and appeal of the means employed.

## THE END OF MASS COMMUNICATION?

The mass communication idea was a compelling one that has proved very resilient because it is based on much that seems observable and plausible. It has a broad appeal to those who seek to benefit from it as senders, as well as to audiences. It is a convenient formulation for those who study it and, for those who are highly critical, it provides a useful summary of what is essentially wrong with the phenomenon. It is not easy to redefine or replace, even when many of the conditions of its origin have changed and many of its inbuilt assumptions have been disputed. For much of the twentieth century, the concept in this form has exerted an excessive influence on both popular and expert ideas about the influence of mass media. It has also shaped the direction of media research, despite recurrent evidence that has undermined the foundations on which it was based and cast doubt on the hypothesized effects.

From one perspective, the general hypothesis of mass communication has played a fruitful role by the very fact of being comprehensively disputed and disproved. The research it generated led to a much firmer understanding of key principles underlying mediated communication and our sensemaking thereof, as recorded in this book. In this respect, we have been frequently reminded of a series of fundamental insights that hold up today as much as they have done throughout history, with updates and nuances added with the benefit of hindsight:

- Interpersonal communication is often a much more compelling or even competing form and source of influence, especially as this category coincides (and to some extent converges) with that of mass communication in the context of online, social and mobile media.

- The production of media follows an industrial logic, with subsequent highly structured and routinized processes, and simultaneously operates under a 'postindustrial' (Bell, 1973) logic, especially regarding the organization of work, the role of the consumer as producer, and an ongoing transformation of media formats, genres and texts.

- Media content typically has multiple (or no identifiable) purposes for its makers and transmitters, and no fixed meaning for its receivers, and thus is largely without predictable effects attached.

- The concept of an audience consisting of isolated individuals and additionally living inside their own media 'bubbles' (Sloterdijk, 2011) is largely an illusion, just as much as the view of the audience as a more or less amorphous and amoral 'mass' is.

- The conditions of effect (however conceptualized) depend on structural, social and individual contexts as well as media properties and technological affordances, and on variable features of reception rather than on the fact of transmission.

These and other lessons have been learned well enough and both challenge and confirm the media and mass communication thesis. There is, for example, no doubt that something like a predictable process of effect does occur in some circumstances. This applies especially to agenda-setting, news learning and opinion formation, in crisis situations and at times of heightened collective emotion (including 'moral panics' and recurring upheaval on social media) and celebration. These are not minor exceptions. There is also no doubt that the theory in general outline is still dear to the heart of advertisers and propagandists. Much critical theory directed at mass media still depends on the essential validity of the original mass communication thesis.

As argued in Chapter 2 of our book, notions of 'mass' media and 'mass' communication exist side by side with (inter-)personal communication and mass self-communication in today's digital, online and interconnected media environment, and these 'three forms of communication coexist, interact, and complement each other rather than substituting for one another' (Castells, 2009: 55). This map of conceivable communication patterns is a reminder of the possibly subsidiary status of 'mass communication' functions in the total spectrum of mediated communication. It is also a reminder that patterns of communication do not coincide very closely with particular media or even their dominant forms. Older types of mass media (even television) have developed consultation and conversational possibilities, and newer consultative online media are increasingly being used for different types of 'narrowcasting' and 'broadcasting'. The telephone, once predominantly a medium of conversation, has of course joined in this expansion of usage potential and technological affordance. These processes are part of the larger process of convergence made possible by – but in no circumstance determined by – digitalization. What is not in doubt is that in some respects, the traditional mass media are in decline *vis-à-vis* the role of new intermediaries such as Internet platform companies and the integration of the computing, information and telecommunications sectors, even if they are also being transformed, adapting and still expanding in some respects.

## THE EVOLUTION OF MASS COMMUNICATION

These and other circumstances reflect not the end of mass media or of mass communication, but rather a significant and ongoing shift in the ways that purposes of public communication can be achieved. The means consisted primarily of reaching an entire national public with a restricted range of content. Transmission would be direct, rapid and very cost-effective. This 'industrial' vision of both ends and means has given way to a different version of mass communication: more personal and private, more targeted and interactive, more diffuse and perhaps even more powerful than before in some instances.

The overall goal of public communication is still to be able to know and give shape to the mediated experience of a target population, although not by the monopoly imposition of a suitable limited range of ideas, information, motives and stimuli. Now the chosen means is to provide a highly differentiated range of content targeted towards innumerable subgroups and segments in the public, taking account of the interests, tastes and circumstances of the receivers. The purposes are more varied and more opaque than ever they were in the past. The whole process is held together not by a rigid and uniform structure of provision and a stable pattern of mass reception, but by the voluntary engagement of the public in its own immersion in a rich and varied world of mediated experience, to which it contributes both voluntarily (through mass self-communication) and involuntarily (through sharing detailed personal data with providers and platforms). The personal networks and ties that were said to provide a barrier to the influence of older mass media are now playing a positive role in reinforcing demand and consumption on an endlessly changing and kaleidoscopic journey.

The evolution of a condition or state of mass communication (as redefined), which can now scarcely be distinguished from other social processes, is primarily due to its high degree of functionality for key driving forces in society and its intimate connection with human aspirations. Many of the actors who benefit from the capacity to communicate to all in a measured and calculated way are visible and their motivations are transparent. They include big advertisers and global media firms (both bigger and more concentrated than ever before), the world financial system, rulers and national governments, states with imperial ambitions and concern for their image, and the list goes on. It is inconceivable that these and others could dispense with the results of even 'smarter' and more effective communication to any chosen public constituency. The emerging, revived and reinforced form of mass communication is highly consistent with underlying trends towards convergence and the globalization and mediatization of everything.

Alongside the forces and trends mentioned, there are other dynamics at work in changing the nature of media and mass communication. These stem from the potential of new media for open access and connectivity that is now widely becoming a reality. There are very many new voices making use of possibilities for open, interactive 'horizontal' communication. These individuals, movements and groups, with many different purposes, now have a much greater chance of being served by the means of communicating in and to the public, even if with no guarantee of being heard as intended. The wish to communicate does not stem only from political or economic necessity. People have always displayed an urge to combine, share and co-operate for personal and social ends that cannot be explained in material terms. This urge finds expression in the wish to share the pleasures and sorrows of life, to embody them in rituals and narratives of family, community, tribe or nation. In other words, there are strong, spontaneous tendencies that underlie the emergence of shared public culture. The success of the new 'social media', like the success of many forms of 'reality television' as well as the apparent drawing power of 'media events', are evidence enough of a deep attraction towards the wider sharing of interests, emotions and experiences.

At the same time, all this sharing and new forms of 'publicness' are part of what mass communication means.

## NEW MEDIA AND MASS COMMUNICATION THEORY

As explored in Chapter 6, we do not have evidence to support a deterministic role for new technologies and newer media in social, economic or political processes. That is not to say that these processes stay the same, or that mass communication flows more or less effectively across all the new channels. On the contrary, the emerging 'hybrid' media system has a logic of its own, with certain points of contrast to earlier media constellations. The newer media and mass communication systems and processes are multidirectional, not one-directional. They encourage, even require response. They have no scheduled 'audience', therefore no mass public. They are highly diverse in form and content, and of their essence multimedial and multimodal. They observe no clear line between private and public. They allow access to all and they seem to evade structures of state policy and control (with the exception of media systems directly owned by, or made to be responsible to, the state in less-than-democratic countries). They offer no coherent model of a system of public communication, only endless possibilities within the context of a generally untransparent system of corporate governance with little or no reference to public values.

These observations, all in varying degrees valid, have given rise to a rhetoric that is both optimistic and oppositional – as with all 'new' media throughout media history. The long-term consequences of digital media can be expressed in terms that both undermine and reinforce central elements of mass communication theory:

- The power of the communicator to persuade or inform selectively is much reduced by the inability to reach large, captive audiences and by the ready availability of alternative sources of ideas and knowledge.

- Individuals are no longer restricted by their immediate social group and environment or by the physical availability of a few media channels, controlled by authorities and other agencies. They can enter and belong to new groups and communities across space.

- There is no longer any unitary 'message system' to which people are routinely and consistently exposed, leading to stereotypes and the adoption of consensual values.

- Individuals can 'answer back' to figures of authority or remove themselves from contact. They can also participate actively in informational and opinion exchanges in the context of important social and political issues.

These and similar propositions have become the basis for a staggering amount of research and new theory, and the emergence of 'Internet research' as its own field. A careful balance needs to be maintained between hopeful accounts of the consequences of the newer media environment for alleviating human suffering (consider, for example, the role of smartphones and social media in the experiences of refugees), remedying social inequalities (addressing recurring issues related to digital divides in society), and cultivating critical work regarding increasingly automated aspects of our media and mass communication environment (for example, regarding crucial work on the inherent biases of algorithms and artificial intelligence systems).

The fact of a lack of regulation and even of self-regulation is at the root of some fears about the newer media environment, which seems to expose vulnerable groups and individuals to risks and exploitation. Even when used benignly, the Internet seems essentially individuating rather than participative, despite the promise of connectivity. Instead of a 'global village', we seem to have an endless number of tiny villages with constantly changing inhabitants, all governed by largely corporate entities with commercial motives that use public values to sell us their services, while refusing accountability based on such values.

With a more open media culture, in the context of individualization and globalization, there are persistent and insoluble problems of trust and reliability. The power of surveillance and registration of all communication uses and users greatly extends the central powers of the state and its agencies, without much chance of redress or possibility of

MCQUAIL'S MEDIA AND MASS COMMUNICATION THEORY
EPILOGUE

complaint. Since the 'labour' of surveillance is mostly done by ourselves, the corporations providing (generally free) access to their platforms and services greatly benefit from this unique version of capitalism. As more and more everyday and necessary communication transactions are happening online, whether wanted or not by the public, we are becoming in a very literal way dependent on access and appropriate skills. As a result, we are liable to new and serious forms of social exclusion if we cannot or will not conform. If we do conform, we become more vulnerable to unwanted persuasion and manipulation – happily exploited by micro social movements and politicians alike. Yet at the same time, these phenomena also make it possible to raise awareness of critical social issues that demand our attention. Consider the media activism (and underlying journalism and other 'traditional' processes) that brought us #BlackLivesMatter, #MeToo, #ClimateStrike and a host of other collective identities as expressed in both online groupings and offline political engagement (Gerbaudo and Treré, 2015), even though the effectiveness of such expressions of solidarity can be questioned (Miller, 2017).

As with mass communication in the past, we can choose a more optimistic or more pessimistic view of the consequences of 'new media'. We still lack clear support in evidence for either the benefits or harms of new communication, and it is unlikely that any such general balance can be struck, much as with our experience of the true mass media of the twentieth century. A framework of analysis that depends on simplified beliefs about society and speculation about the potential consequences of technology will not take us very far.

# MEDIA AND MASS COMMUNICATION THEORY: A GRAND NARRATIVE?

At the end of this book, let us return to its beginning. This book is, as it always has been, a story. A story about stories, really: the stories that the scholars in the field of media and mass communication tell themselves and each other about *what* they are doing, *how* they are doing it, and *why* they do what they do. It is therefore not just a story – it is, for all intents and purposes, a 'grand narrative' as conceptualized by Lyotard ([1979]1984): a meta-narrative offering a connection between an enormous variety of ideas and ideals, approaches and frameworks, disciplinary legacies and conceptual innovations, all in the context of permanent social and technological changes. This story does not only *explain* what we understand the role of media and mass communication to be in society, but also *legitimates* the work being done by all media and mass communication scholars, regardless of disciplinary background, theoretical lineage or methodological preference. There may be some who question the wisdom and the temerity of a 'grand narrative' for our field, as we continue to fragment as well as professionalize our work into more or less coherent strands of theory and research. Others may see in such an overarching story an attempt to colonize the field in the service of privileging certain WEIRD (western, educated, industrialized, rich and democratic) perspectives on media and mass communication (Henrich, Heine and Norenzayan, 2010). These concerns are certainly valid, and need to be consciously and critically reflected upon.

What is the 'grand narrative' of media and mass communication theory? Because it seems to us that we can, in fact, see a pattern of connections across the literature, especially now that developments in technologies, industries, production processes as well as audience behaviours are hybrid, complex and networked as much as they can be considered to be converging, pointing towards new directions for research and theory development.

We have seen that the industries of media and mass communication are converging, stretching their operations across multiple channels and platforms. That the content of mass mediated messages is similarly remixed, including various formats and genre conventions, as people continuously do 'transmedia work' (Fast and Jansson, 2019), both in the studios of large media conglomerates and in the comfort of our homes or while using the 'smart' mobile devices in our pockets. In our contemporary media system, audiences large and small congregate and dissipate in an instant, and are not always acting like audiences anymore – as media consumption can go hand in hand with media production. Underneath it all run vast social, economic and political transformations, not determined by but most certainly amplified and accelerated by rapid developments in new technologies and media – a process inspiring a 'materialist' turn in media and mass communication research (Fuchs and Qiu, 2018: 225), which warrants the deliberate inclusion of media theory in this book.

What seems to be the meta-narrative of media and mass communication since the last edition of this book is embodied in the big shift from more or less stable structures to highly fluid and flexible structures across both our field and object of study. Examples of the seemingly stable media and mass communication structures informing much of the research and theorizing, as documented in this book, are:

- media production taking place in newsrooms, in the film and television studio system, within large holding firms and multinational corporations, etc;
- media content based on more or less consensual, strategically ritualized and altogether formulaic industry formats and genre conventions;
- media audiences massively aggregated and programmed around schedules and more or less predictable media events.

These three key elements of the mass communication process are increasingly fluid or 'liquid' today, in that their constituent elements change faster than it takes new structures to sediment (paraphrasing Bauman, 2000):

- a trend towards multi-platform and multi-channel industry structures and value chains, with production increasingly organized through 'atypical' working arrangements (cf. as outsourced, subcontracted, freelanced and networked labour; as outlined in Chapters 8–11);
- the rapid development of a wide variety of multimedia, crossmedia and transmedia storytelling forms that strongly influence contemporary media production (see Chapters 12 and 13);
- concurrent media exposure, co-creation and ensemblematic media use as standard types of contemporary 'audiencing' (discussed in Chapters 14 and 15).

Across all these developments, the three types of communication – mass communication, interpersonal communication and mass self-communication – converge in a hybrid media environment that necessitates equally hybrid forms of scholarship. What all of this suggests is the need, now more than ever, to consider in conjunction the theories and theoretical traditions as narrativized in our book – indeed, to consider them as connections within a grand narrative that enables us to tackle the complexities of our media environment.

To talk about media influence and 'effects' in this context seems impossibly difficult, yet sophisticated theoretical frameworks are being developed across the humanities and social sciences that show great promise in tackling this discussion – including, but not limited to, work on (deep) mediatization and understanding media use as communicative figurations (Hepp et al., 2018), and emerging models and approaches to investigate complex reciprocal media effects (Valkenburg et al., 2016).

Across the literature, we see an emerging consensus around the need for cross-disciplinary theorizing, mixed-methods designs and other approaches that combine and remix the various strands and traditions of media and mass communication scholarship. As Valkenburg (2017: 11) remarks about the prospect of combining research on mass, interpersonal and computer-mediated communication, '[i]ntegrative research that crosses different communication subdisciplines is even more sorely needed than a few decades ago'. Likewise, Hartley (2012), in his assessment of the digital futures for media studies, passionately advocates research to go between disciplines, to translate across differences, and thereby to embrace a vitality in theory and research. While we acknowledge that investments in dewesternized, longitudinal, integrated and interdisciplinary research are costly (in every sense of the kind of resources required), we are hopeful that the current climate of increasing international collaborative networks may foster more of these transformative opportunities (Wasserman, 2020).

## CONCLUSION

We can now see quite clearly that the era of mass communication, as the concept is featured in this book, is best viewed as a transitional phase of industrial mass public communication. It followed an early stage of development in which public communication and society-wide communication depended largely on the medium of the channels of social organization and the medium of print. The main content of public communication then originated in governmental and ecclesiastical authorities or in professional and cultural elites and was directed primarily towards an urban and literate minority of subjects/citizens. The industrial model of mass communication that made its appearance early in the twentieth century represented a greatly expanded capacity for public communication, opening it also to a wider range of senders and varied new sources, and to new types of content. Its public was expanded to cover an entire population, reflecting more fundamental political and social changes rather than the capacity of the emerging media. By the end of the century this model had matured and was diffused globally. It has also gradually been changing, by way of supplementation and adaptation, into a new type whose form or forms are emerging as fast as they are being replaced with new ones, without necessarily transforming existing processes.

The continuity of mass communication as a society-wide process is established in new forms that are made up of a much finer and tightly woven network of lines and connections (online and offline) that has an organic character rather than being constructed and controlled by a few for their own ends. Mass communication in the original sense is still with us if we think of it in terms of single, central sources being received by large audiences and dedicated to maximum amplification and diffusion. It persists primarily because the organization of social life cannot dispense with roles, persons and institutions that are singled out as a focus of attention by a dispersed public, with an attribution of status, power, skill or other qualities. Similarly, key events, places, cultural works and a variety of objects of attention come inevitably to be ranked according to interest and significance and sought in varying degrees by, or brought to the attention of, a wider public. Online, we see such processes governed by powerful laws of distribution and network effects inherent to algorithmic culture, whereby a handful of sites and applications receive the majority of visitors and participants.

These features of social life were not created by mass media and will not go away even if mass media are replaced by less massive and centralized communication networks. There are some public functions that can only be served by dedicated professional and well-financed systems of communication. Apart from the needs of society for all things public – publication, public opinion, public order, shared norms and beliefs, public values, political organization, and so on – there are powerful economic and political forces that favour concentrations of (and control over) media for their own ends. In other words, institutionalization is inevitable and cannot be undone or escaped from. Digitalization in many respects has increased the effective deployment of mass communication, by refining reach, adding feedback and flexibility, and multiplying channels for transmission of the same messages. It has also provided alternative channels that operate in a parallel fashion. This does not change or replace all that goes before.

MCQUAIL'S MEDIA AND MASS COMMUNICATION THEORY
EPILOGUE

A rich vocabulary to talk about the implications of the developments of communication that are taking place is emerging – one that questions simplistic models and modes of doing research, one that takes technologies as much as affect into theoretical consideration, one that does justice to the multimedia nature of all aspects of the mass communication process. What is also remarkable is that media and mass communication scholarship is finding all kinds of more or less new ways to communicate about itself, truly doing justice to its role as a 'productive science' that 'considers not only what communication is, but what it could be' (Jensen, 2018: 182). Scholars take to social media, blogs and vlogs, and other forms of public expression – including the arts (for example, dance, poetry, and music) – to engage as practitioners, experts, advocates, activists and critics (Archetti, 2017b; Witschge, Deuze and Willemsen, 2019). In this context, Waisbord (2019) advocates a 'public scholarship' in our field and underscores its potential for contributing to the common good. Next to our books, journal articles, conference papers and presentations, the future of media and mass communication theory and research holds much promise.

As awareness across society is spreading of how central media are to our social, political and economic lives, media and mass communication scholarship is primed to be of significance to debates about media literacy, disinformation, influence and effects, digital ethics and sociality, and the future of algorithmic culture and artificial intelligence. These are the best of times and the worst of times, and it is our responsibility to respect both the historical tradition and normative promise of our field.

# GLOSSARY

Cross-references to other glossary entries are in italics.

**Access**    In a communication process or system, it can refer to the possibility either for a sender to reach a chosen audience or for an audience to receive certain messages or channels. In practice it mainly relates to the degree of openness of media channels to a wide range of voices, especially those with little power or limited resources. An example is a 'public access' channel provided in a cable system for community or non-profit purposes. As a general principle it is related to media *diversity*.

**Advertising**    Paid publicity in media for goods or services directed at consumers. It has various aims, including the creation of awareness, making brand images, forming positive associations and encouraging consumer behaviour. There are many different categories of advertising, which are linked to different media forms (classified, display, personal, etc.). For some major media, advertising provides the greater part of income. All advertising content shares the fact of being paid for by its source. Advertising has been controversial for several reasons, especially the following: it is not generally wanted by its receivers; it has a *propagandist* character and is suspected of deception and manipulation; it has a distorting effect on the relation between media and audience; its content is stereotyped and misleading; the presence of advertising influences other non-advertising content. The general effectiveness of advertising for its purposes is more or less accepted, but certain evidence of success or of reasons for success is hard to come by. Advertising is integrated into a very large industry of market research, *public relations* and marketing.

**Agenda-setting**    A process of media influence (intended or unintended) by which the relative importance of news events, issues or personages in the public mind are affected by the order of presentation (or relative salience) in news reports. It is assumed that the more the media attention given to a topic, the greater is the importance attributed to it by the news audience. The media influence is not on the direction of opinion but only on what people think about. The concept has been mainly applied to political communication and election campaigns especially. Despite the near certainty that the process does occur as hypothesized, it is not easy to prove, because media take their priorities from public opinion as well as from politicians. See also *framing*.

**Attitude**    An evaluative disposition of an individual towards an 'object' of whatever kind (person, idea, group, country, policy, etc.). For measurement purposes it is conceived as a mental set that can be elicited by verbal questioning about concepts related to the object of enquiry. Attitudes vary in direction (positive or negative) and in strength, and attitude scales have been developed to record these variations. In general, an attitude is considered as a relatively deep and underlying tendency, linked to personality and resistant to change by mass media. A single attitude is generally connected with other related attitudes in a consistent way.

**Audience**  All those who are actually reached by particular media content or media 'channels'. The audience can also exist as an imagined 'target' or intended group of receivers. It may coincide with a real social group or *public*. Audiences can be defined according to the relevant media and content or in terms of their social composition, location or time of day. Media audiences are not fixed entities and may only be known after the event as statistical abstractions (for example, 'the ratings'), with a known probability of recurrence. This is typically the view 'from the media', but there is an equally valid alternative perspective of the audience as a collective social-cultural entity.

**Bias**  Any tendency in a news report to deviate from an accurate, neutral, balanced and impartial representation of the 'reality' of events and social world according to stated criteria. A distinction is usually made between intended and unintended bias. The former stems mainly from partisanship, advocacy and the ideological standpoint of the medium or source. The latter is generally attributed to organizational and routine factors in the selection and processing of news. See also *objectivity*.

**Birmingham School**  Name used to denote a number of authors associated with the Centre for Contemporary Cultural Studies (CCCS) at the University of Birmingham, England, established in 1964 and (suddenly) closed by the university in 2002. The original founder was Richard Hoggart, in association with Stuart Hall. The work of the school was a major influence, first in the study of popular culture, and secondly in the development of critical cultural studies, including *reception analysis* and feminist media studies.

**Blogging**  The word 'blog' is a shortened version of weblog, which indicates its origin as a set of diary entries or related content posted on the Internet for a variety of reasons, originally mostly of a personal nature. Most interest centres on those blogs (or 'vlogs' when referring to video entries and channels) that are intended to play a public role of one kind of another, often a commentary on the news. The influence of blogs is much disputed, since few have a large *audience* of their own (and the ones that do tend to be sponsored through corporations while operating outside the regulations that govern most commercial media), but they represent a significant opening of public access and a challenge to institutional control of public information. The word 'blogosphere' has been coined to refer to the whole alternative public communication space occupied by non-institutionalized voices.

**Broadcasting**   The transmission of radio and television signals over air from fixed terrestrial transmitters and with limited range, before the advent of cable and satellite systems from the 1970s onwards. Broadcasting was intended for open reception by all within the transmission range and was mainly financed either by advertising or by receiver sets or household licences. It was and remains governed by legal and regulatory regimes designed to allocate licences and supervise performance. It is virtually the only major medium in public or government ownership in non-socialist societies. See *public service broadcasting*.

**Campaign**   The planned attempt to influence public opinion, behaviour, attitudes and knowledge on behalf of some cause, person, institution or topic, using different media over a specific period of time. The main types of campaign are advertising, political, public informational and fund-raising. Public campaigns are usually directed towards socially approved goals. They are often based on research and subject to evaluation of success.

**Catharsis**   A type of effect of tragic or violent fiction and drama that leaves the audience purged of emotion and released of any urge to be affected by the actions portrayed. Originally suggested by Aristotle and taken up by researchers into media violence to account for a seeming lack of harmful behavioural effects. Although theoretically plausible, it does not seem to have been specifically demonstrated or measured.

**Celebrity**   A quality of being extremely well known by the majority, often an object of adulation and *fandom*. In normal circumstances, high, continuing and positive media attention is a necessary condition of celebrity. Celebrity status can be based on recognition of distinction in different spheres, including sport, entertainment, the arts, science, politics and 'society'. Sometimes media prominence is a sufficient condition, as in the concept of 'being famous for being famous'. Persons who are celebrities are an object of *gossip* and their celebrity can be taken away as well as given by the media.

**Censorship**   Refers to the control by public authorities (usually church or state) of any form of publication or transmission, usually by some mechanism of examining all material before publication. Constitutional guarantees of press freedom typically outlaw advance or preventive censorship, although there may be legitimate grounds for suppression or even punishment of a publication after the event. The term is loosely applied to actions that impede expression, as in references to 'private censorship' by media editors or owners, and 'self-censorship' by, for example, journalists in order to prevent scrutiny or disfavour from political or corporate owners, clients and sources.

**Civil society**   The term has been widely used in recent social theory to refer to forms of social organization that offer alternatives to totalitarianism or excessive government control. The key aspect is the existence of an intermediate 'zone' between private life and the state, where independent voluntary collective associations and organizations can operate freely. A precondition for this is freedom of association and expression, including the necessary means, among which the media are very important. Free media can thus be regarded as an institution of civil society. See also *public sphere.*

Code    The most common meaning is of a set of laws, regulations or guidelines. When applied to mass media, it mainly refers to a set of standards applied in self-regulation of content and conduct, for instance in relation to *journalism.* Professional codes have been adopted by national and international associations of journalists. Codes have also been produced and applied in broadcasting and film exhibition, covering such matters as the display of violence, advertising, sexual matters, portrayal of crime, racism, blasphemy, etc. Another related meaning of code describes the precise instructions written into computer programs that can be used to limit freedom of use and open up content to surveillance (Lessig, 1999).

Cognitive dissonance    The term was coined by Leon Festinger (1957) to describe the situation of an individual faced with new *information* on a given topic that is inconsistent with existing information, attitudes and values. The underlying theory holds that an individual seeks balance and consistency of attitudes and values, and consequently avoids or misperceives incoming messages (for example, from mass media) that challenge settled opinions and beliefs. In so far as cognitive consistency dominates, it will limit change effects from communication and encourage reinforcement of existing views. However, compelling new information from trustworthy sources may overcome the barriers indicated and lead to change, but this will require a reassessment of outlook over a wide range. Although the theory is sound enough, there is quite a lot of evidence that in matters of *public opinion* that are not deeply held, people can tolerate quite high levels of apparent discrepancy.

Commercialization    A process by which media structures and content come to reflect the profit-seeking goals of media industries and are too much governed by market considerations. The main reference is usually to cultural consequences, and these always have a negative connotation. Commercialized media content is believed to be in varying degrees lacking in independence, 'inauthentic', standardized and stereotypical, given to sensationalism and personalization. It promotes materialism and consumerism. It is also thought to be less creative and trustworthy. Commercial media are suspected of lacking full independence from their owners and advertisers. See *advertising, tabloidization* and *commodification.*

Commodification    The word originates in Marxist theory, according to which all entities have a material cash value. In relation to media, three aspects stand out. One is the treatment of all media messages as 'product' to be bought or sold in the media market, without reference to other criteria of value. A second is that the audience can be treated as a commodity to be sold by media to advertisers at so much per head, according to ratings and other market criteria. A third is that in a precarious labour market for media professionals, their skills and personalities have to be constantly 'commodified' in order to attract clients and employers. See *Marxism*.

**Communication**  The term has many different meanings and definitions, but the central idea is of a process of increased commonality or sharing between participants, on the basis of sending and receiving 'messages'. Theoretical disagreement exists about whether we should count as communication the transmission or expression of some message, on its own, without evidence of reception or effect or completion of a sequence. The most important dimensions of communication concern two points: the degree of response or feedback (one-way versus interactive process); and the degree to which a communication relationship is also a social relationship. In general, modern technologies increase the possibility and likelihood of detaching communication (message transmission or exchange) from any social basis.

**Community**  An idealized form of human association in which the members share boundaries of space, identity and interaction. A community is typically a largish and enduring social group based on residence, but it can also be formed on the basis of some other significant identity. In its ideal form, community is characterized by a mutual liking and assistance and relative equality between members who put the common welfare ahead of individual wants.

**Computer-mediated communication (CMC)**  Any communicative transaction that takes place by way of a computer, whether online or offline, but especially the former. Characteristics include interactivity in situations where the participants are not physically together and the possibility for anonymity and concealment while communicating. CMC can transgress the social and physical boundaries that normally limit our potential for communicating with others. Not all CMC features are beneficial. We are more exposed to unwanted communication from others. Computer mediation reduces the personal character of the experience, and the commonality or community achieved in *cyberspace* may be illusory. Communication mediated by computers connected to networks is also more open to various forms of surveillance.

**Connectivity**  Essentially, the capacity of a network to link participants together in a common space of communication. As such, it is also an attribute of groups and communities that can vary according to the density of network links, the frequency of use and thus the strength and durability of ties. The Internet and other personal communication media can achieve much higher degrees of connectivity than traditional mass media. The term is also used as a function of media production, bringing together producers and consumers of media into a co-creative relationship (for example, in cases of citizen journalism, interactive advertising and upstream marketing).

Constructionism   An approach to the study of meaning and media effect that rests on the assumption that there is no uniquely correct and fixed version of the 'real world'. Reality can only be apprehended and communicated about by way of selectively perceived versions that are dependent on the attitudes, interests, knowledge and experience of the perceiver. The effects of communication about some aspect of 'reality' will depend on a negotiation of meaning between the participants in the circumstances of the moment. It makes no sense to search for direct effects in the sense of transfer of meaning from a source to a receiver.

Content analysis   A technique for the systematic, quantitative and objective description of media texts, that is useful for certain purposes of classifying output, looking for effects and making comparisons between media and over time or between content and 'reality'. Content analysis is not well suited to uncovering the underlying meaning of content, although it can provide certain indicators of 'quality' of media.

Convergence   The process of coming together or becoming more alike. It is usually applied to the convergence of media technologies as a result of digitalization (computerization). The distinctive physical characteristics of media cease to matter, at least for the purposes of production, processing and transmission. The contemporary trend of convergence has been used as an argument for media deregulation, since most regulatory regimes are linked to specific technologies (for example, printing, broadcasting, cable, projection, etc). Despite the potential at the reception 'end' for convergence on a single apparatus, diversification seems to increase.

Convergence culture   A concept introduced by Henry Jenkins to describe the cultural consequences of convergence between media industries as well as between the creative practices of both producers and consumers of media. In its broadest terms, it refers to the situation in which work, life and play are increasingly intermingled and overlapping, without separate compartments of time and space. Its most specific manifestation in relation to the mass media is the coming together of two trends: one is from the media to encourage engagement and participation of audiences and users in new interactive forms of communication; the other is the trend on the part of the public to become media producers and communicators, as enabled by the new technology. The most striking result is the appearance of forms of media in which production and consumption are blurred and the line between amateur and professional fades. The terms 'prosumer' and 'produser' have appeared to reflect a new role in the spectrum of media life. Wikipedia, the 'blogosphere',

Instagram and YouTube are primary sites where the new trends can be observed, but there are many others.

Copyright    Means essentially the recognition of the ownership rights of authors in their own published works. This was achieved long after the invention of printing. The issue of copyright (more broadly, intellectual property rights) has been much complicated by the extension of copyright claims to new categories of 'author' and new forms of media and publication and republication, especially in electronic form. The Internet changes the nature of publishing and has opened up an extensive and disputed territory.

Critical theory    A general term for late Marxist versions of the part played by the mass media in maintaining a dominant *ideology* or *hegemony*. The origins are usually found in the work of the *Frankfurt School*, but there are several variants, especially the cultural and the political-economic forms. The first of these has been associated with structuralist and semiological interpretations of texts (hermeneutics generally) and also with audience *reception analysis* and ethnography. The second has generally engaged with issues of structure and ownership and the control of the media. Critical theory is often regarded as an alternative to empirical, behaviourist or 'scientific' approaches to the study of mass media. It is by definition normative, involving notions of an alternative and better form of society and media system.

Cultivation theory    A term given to a particular type of media effect research, developed by George Gerbner. The underlying process is one of 'acculturation', meaning that people gradually come to accept the view of the world as portrayed on television (in particular) as a true representation of reality and adapt their hopes, fears and understandings accordingly. The main method of cultivation analysis is to chart the dominant 'television view of reality' in fiction and news and compare this with the views expressed by audience members, according to their degree of habitual exposure. The hypothesis is that the more people view television, the more their ideas correspond with the 'television view'.

Cultural imperialism    A general expression for the tendency of global media industry exporters (especially from the USA) to dominate the media consumption in other smaller and poorer countries and in so doing impose their own cultural and other values on audiences elsewhere. Not only content is exported, but also technology, production values, professional ideologies and ownership. The analogy is with historical imperialism where the means were military and economic power. Explicitly or implicitly, it is assumed that cultural imperialism leads to dependence, loss of autonomy and a decline in national or local cultures. Some latitude exists as to whether the process is deliberate and about the degree to which it is involuntary at the receiving end. The concept is a fairly crude one, but it has a strong resonance.

**Cultural studies**   A branch of theory and research that overlaps with the media and communication field but has a much wider reference to all forms of cultural experience and symbolic expression. It has been distinguished by a *critical* and humanistic orientation and also a strong focus on 'popular culture', especially of youth. It originated in Britain, but is international in scope, very diverse and largely independent of media and communication studies. See *Birmingham School*.

**Culture**   In the present context it has a primary reference to the symbolic artefacts produced by media industries as well as people online (for example, on social media), but it also has a wider reference to customs, practices and meanings associated with the mass communication process (production and reception). It is sometimes used to refer to the wider framework of beliefs, ideology, and so on, of society (the 'superstructure') that provides the context of media operation.

**Cyberspace**   This term is widely used to refer to the metaphorical space occupied by the World Wide Web and the Internet. It was first coined by William Gibson in 1984 to describe the world of cybernetics. It has no very precise meaning but, in contemporary usage, cyberspace is imagined by its inhabitants to be free from many of the constraints of real space, besides laws and regulations. The reality of cyberspace is turning out to be somewhat different from that dreamt of by its creators, has become deeply commodified, and is certainly not technically beyond the reach of regulation, as was once assumed.

**Decoding**   See *Encoding* and *decoding*.

**Denotation**   A term from *semiology*, referring to the direct literal signification of the meaning of some referent by linguistic or visual symbols. It is contrasted with connotation.

**Diffusion of innovations**   The process of spreading any kind of new technical device, idea or useful information. It generally follows an S-shaped pattern, with a slow start, an acceleration of adoption and a long tail. The 'early adopters' tend to be untypical in terms of social composition and communication behaviour. The mass media have been found to play a secondary role in influencing diffusion, with personal communication, example and known authority sources being primary. The media themselves provide examples of innovations that often fit the S-curve pattern of diffusion.

**Diffusion of news**   Process whereby awareness of 'events' is spread through a population either by mass media or via personal, word-of-mouth contact with or without media involvement. Key questions concern the degree and speed of public diffusion in relation to actual or types of events and also the relative weight of media and personal sources in achieving the outcome.

**Digital divide**   A term widely used to apply to the various inequalities opened up by the development of computer-based digital means of communication. The new inequalities derive from the relatively large cost of equipment, dependence on advanced infrastructure and the higher skills needed to communicate. These inequalities arise between persons, social groups and national societies, for the most part following (and thus reinforcing) familiar faultlines. See also *knowledge gap*.

**Discourse analysis**   Applies to all forms of language use and textual forms, but the essential idea is that communication occurs by way of forms of 'text and talk', adapted to particular social locations, topics and kinds of participant. These are sometimes known as 'interpretative communities'. 'Critical discourse analysis' investigates the dominance exerted and expressed through linguistic forms that are vehicles for carrying socially prevailing sentiments and ideologies.

**Diversity**   In simple terms, this is no more than the degree or range of difference on any chosen dimension: the more difference, the more diversity. When applied to mass media it can relate to structures of ownership and control, to content as produced and transmitted and to audience composition and content choices. Each of these can be empirically assessed in terms of diversity. Diversity is associated with access, freedom, choice, change and equality. It stands as a positive value in opposition to monopoly, uniformity, conformity and consensus.

**Effects of media**   The consequences or outcomes of the working of, or exposure to, mass media, whether or not intended. They can be sought at different levels of social analysis. There are many types of effect, but it is usual to distinguish at least between effects that are behavioural, attitudinal, affective and cognitive. Effects are distinct from 'effectiveness', which relates to the efficiency of achieving a given communicative objective.

**Empathy**   An attitude or orientation of sympathy and understanding towards others, especially with reference to casualties and victims of society and those who are stigmatized, marginalized and excluded. It is one of the informal roles adopted by the media, especially in *journalism*, documentary and realistic drama, to encourage public empathy. It can be achieved by reporting on its own, without conscious advocacy.

**Encoding and decoding**   Broad terms for the production and 'reading' of texts of all kinds. The reference is less to the use of specific language (verbal or visual) than to structures of meaning embedded in or extracted from texts. The terms were popularized by Stuart Hall and incorporated in a much-cited model of the relationship between media and audience. An important feature of the associated theory is that meaning is 'decoded' according to the social and cultural position of the receiver. Most texts 'as sent' are also held to carry some 'preferred reading', that is essentially ideological, but we can usually expect alternative readings. In the case of news, Stuart Hall suggested that interpretations could either take up the preferred 'hegemonic' meanings, follow some more distanced 'negotiated' variant, or reverse the intended meaning in an 'oppositional' reading. See also *ideology*.

Entertainment   Describes a main branch of media production and consumption, covering a range of formats that generally share the qualities of attracting, amusing, diverting and 'taking people out of themselves'. It also refers to the process of diversion itself, and in this sense it can also relate to the genres that are not usually regarded as entertaining, such as news, advertising or education. It is often perceived as problematic when addiction to entertainment excludes informational uses of media or when the 'entertainment' mode invades the sphere of reality content – especially news, information and politics, as it often does. The term 'infotainment' has been coined to describe the result.

Fandom   The phenomenon stimulated in response to much of mass media content, characters and *celebrities*, implying intense attachment to and involvement in the achievements and personal lives of star performers, especially in music, games, film and television. From early analyses that would consider such engagement problematic, it is increasingly considered to be a valuable asset for media industries, and a regular part of media usage (as most people are found to have some kind of deep emotional attachment to specific media).

First Amendment   The First Amendment to the Constitution of the United States was enacted in 1791 and it outlawed Congressional (that is, federal government) interference in or regulation of freedom of speech, religion and the press, etc. It has become a shorthand term to cover all matters of freedom of expression and opinion in the United States, often involving the mass media. Many other countries have equivalent constitutional provisions, although they are usually expressed in terms of the rights of citizens. The way the First Amendment is formulated has tended to identify government as the arch-enemy of freedom, strongly associating free media with the free market. See *freedom of the press*.

Folkcommunication   A theory developed by Brazilian researcher Luiz Beltrão (1971) to recognize, describe and explain the various ways in which interpersonal and group forms of cultural expression (mainly identified among marginalized groups and lower classes) develop independently (and are often critical) of those developed by mass and industrialized forms of communication.

Fourth Estate   A term attributed by the historian Thomas Carlyle to the eighteenth-century polemicist Edmund Burke and applicable to the press gallery of the British

House of Commons. Burke asserted that the power of the press was at least equal to that of the other three 'estates of the realm' – lords, commons and clergy. It became a conventional term for journalists in their role as reporters of and watchdogs on government.

**Fragmentation**   In respect of the media audience, fragmentation refers to the general decline of the mass audience for newspapers and dominant television channels, brought about by the multiplication of new media forms (including online platforms and streaming services) and television channels. There are many smaller and more temporary audiences. Fragmentation has been thought to reduce the power of mass media generally, although many smaller audiences does not necessarily mean greater diversity.

**Framing**   A term with two main meanings. One refers to the way in which news content is typically shaped and contextualized by journalists within some familiar frame of reference and according to some latent structure of meaning. A second, related meaning concerns the effect of framing on the public. The audience is thought to adopt the frames of reference offered by journalists and to see the world in a similar way. This process is related to *priming* and *agenda-setting*.

**Frankfurt School**   The name applied to the group of scholars who originally worked in the Frankfurt Institute of Social Research and emigrated to the USA after the Nazis came to power. The central project of the group was the critical analysis of modern culture and society in the Marxist tradition. The main figures included Theodor Adorno, Max Horkheimer, Herbert Marcuse and Leo Lowenthal. They were all very influential in the development of critical theory in North America and Europe after the Second World War and especially in media and cultural studies. Their pessimistic view of 'mass culture' was, paradoxically, one stimulus to a later revalidation of popular cultural forms.

**Freedom of expression**   Freedom of expression has a broad meaning that covers all aspects of public expression, communication and transmission of, and access to, all manner of content. It has been advanced as a human right that should be guaranteed internationally and not just within a society. In a narrow sense, it usually refers to public rights of access to information of public interest or relevance held by various kinds of authority or official agency.

**Freedom of the press**   A fundamental principle of individual, political and human rights that guarantees in law the right of all citizens to publish without advance *censorship* or permission by authority, or fear of reprisal. It has to be exercised within the limits of law and to respect the rights of others. In practice, freedom of the press is often limited by (economic) barriers of access to the means of publication. The right is usually regarded as fundamental to political democracy. It is related to, but distinct from, *freedom of expression*, opinion or belief as well as freedom of information and the *First Amendment*.

**Gatekeeping**   A general term for the role of the initial selection and later editorial processing of event reports in news organizations. News media have to decide what 'events' to admit through the 'gates' of the media on grounds of their 'newsworthiness' and other criteria. Key questions concern the criteria applied and the systematic *bias* that has been discerned in the exercise of the role.

**Genre**   Essentially just a word for any main type or category of media content. It can also apply to certain subcategories of theme or plot in fiction, film, drama, etc. It is useful for analysis because many genres embody certain 'rules of encoding' that can be manipulated by their producers and also certain 'rules for decoding' that allow audiences to develop appropriate expectations and 'read' texts as intended.

**Globalization**   The overall process whereby the location of production, transmission and reception of media content ceases to be geographically fixed, partly as a result of technology, but also through international media structure and organization. Many cultural consequences are predicted to follow, especially the delocalizing of content and undermining of local cultures. These may be regarded as positive when local cultures are enriched by new impulses and creative *hybridization* occurs. More often they are viewed as negative because of threats to cultural *identity*, autonomy and integrity. The new media are widely thought to be accelerating the process of globalization.

**Gossip**   A form of news characterized by its reference to personalities and its uncertain origin and reliability. Its main habitat is in personal conversation, but it provides the basis for a media genre found mainly in newspapers and magazines. Here the content focuses on *celebrities* (mainly the rich and famous). It differs from rumour, which often deals with highly significant news and travels faster and more completely in the relevant population. See also *human interest*.

**Governance**   A general term to cover all forms of control, regulation and guidance applied to some institutional process, involving multiple agencies, formal and informal, public and private. It has become common to use the term in relation to media structures that are typically organized in the form of networks open to many inputs and not fully hierarchical or autocratic, in keeping with the cultural and social roles fulfilled.

**Hegemony**   A term introduced by the early-twentieth-century Italian Marxist theorist Antonio Gramsci to describe a certain kind of power that arises from the all-embracing ideological tendencies of mass media to support the established power system and exclude opposition and competing values. In brief, it is a kind of dominant consensus that works in a concealed way without direct coercion.

**Human interest**   A type of news story or format that focuses on personal actions and consequences, employs dramatic, humorous or narrative styles, and usually deals with matters close to everyday emotions and experience. It is associated with *commercialization* and *tabloidization*, yet also with notions of 'public' quality.

**Hybridization**   The process whereby new cultural forms are forged out of disparate elements, especially a combination of alien or imported forms and indigenous, local or traditional cultures. Associated with *globalization*.

**Icon**   A type of sign that has a clear physical likeness to what it stands for. Different media can employ iconic signs, but usually they are depicted, reproduced or sculpted images of people, things or scenes. Early letter systems (hieroglyphs) made much use of icons. Photography has to rely almost entirely on icons to communicate meaning, since the first meaning of a photograph is the object photographed. More loosely, icon is sometimes used to refer to a person or piece of work so distinguished that it becomes the standard image.

**Identity**   Specific characterization of person, place, and so on by self or others, according to biographical, social, cultural or other features. Communication is a necessary condition for forming and maintaining identity. By the same token, it can weaken or undermine it. Mass communication is only one among several contributory factors. It can be argued that identity today is comprised of self-identity (how you see yourself), social identity (how others see you), and digital identity (how your contributions to the Internet – whether voluntary or not – make up who you are).

**Ideology**   Generally, this refers to some organized belief system or set of values that is disseminated or reinforced by communication. While mass media do not typically set out deliberately to propagate ideology, in practice most media content (of all kinds) does so implicitly by selectively emphasizing certain values and norms. This is referred to as a 'preferred reading' in the theory of *encoding and decoding*. Often these reflect the national culture that provides the context of the media system, but also the class position and the outlook of those who own, control and make media. A profession such as journalism can also be said to have its own occupational ideology, consisting of ideal-typical values that give meaning to the work.

**Information**   In a broad sense, the content (messages) of all meaningful communication is information. More narrowly (but still loosely), information usually refers to verifiable and thus reliable factual data about the 'real world'. This includes opinions as well as reports about the facts of the world. Even more narrowly and precisely, information may be equated with communicated 'data' that do (or can) enable discriminations to be made in some domain of reality and thus 'reduce uncertainty' for the receiver.

**Information society**   A term widely used to describe contemporary society in terms of what is thought to be its most central driving force or source of productive power, namely information of all kinds. The justification for this assumption derives from the seeming dependence of much of modern life, materially as well as culturally, on the production, handling and application of information and on the operation of complex networks of communication. The information and communication technology sector has become the chief source of wealth in more economically advanced societies.

**Infotainment**   A term coined to capture the intermingling of information and entertainment that characterized mass television in the later twentieth century. It seemed particularly applicable to the forms of news that were feared would result from the extensive privatization of broadcasting in Europe and increased competition for mass audiences. The term is generally used pejoratively, with the implication of 'dumbing-down' and the inevitable dilution and greater superficiality of news and information. It has analogies with the idea of *tabloidization* affecting newspapers.

**Inscribed reader**   Derives from the tendency of media communicators to shape their text according to an imagined or predefined audience, with certain characteristics of background, taste, interest, capacity, etc. To a certain extent the 'intended' audience can be read from the text. It is more typically a feature of mass communication than, say, artistic creation.

**Interactivity**   The capacity for reciprocal, two-way communication attributable to a communication medium or relationship. Interactivity allows for mutual adjustment, co-orientation, finer control and greater efficiency in most communication relationships and processes. The single most defining feature of 'new media' is their degree of interactivity, made increasingly possible by digitalization.

**Interpretative community**   A term originating in linguistics that describes the set of users of a given language or cultural code, among whom there will be shared understanding of texts and symbols. When applied to a media *audience*, it usually relates to a particular group of fans or devotees formed around some performance, performer or work, among whom similarly there is a large measure of shared values, interests and meanings. Such communities usually arise spontaneously and are not exclusive. They are also encouraged to form for the purposes of publicity.

**Intertextuality**    Refers to the tendency for different media texts to refer to each other at different levels and across genres, and also the process by which 'readers' make meaningful connections across formal boundaries of texts and genres. The connections extend from media texts to material objects of consumption by way of branding and merchandising. Advertising makes much deliberate use of intertextual connections. Conversational texts of media audiences extend the influence of the original texts into everyday life and language.

**Journalism**    Literally taken, this refers to the product or the work of professional 'news-workers'. As a product, it typically means informational (and verified) reports of recent or current events of interest to the public. In this sense, journalism is another word for 'news', with its many typical and familiar features, especially the aim of being up to date, relevant, credible and interesting to a chosen audience. As a work process, journalism has mixed connotations, reflecting uncertainty about the status of the profession. There are several styles, types and schools of journalism, differentiated by organizational form, purpose and audience, and also by local and national media cultures.

**Knowledge gap**    A term coined to refer to the structured differences in information levels between groups in society. The original promise of mass communication was that it would help to close the gaps between the 'information rich' and the 'information poor'. The concept has stimulated research to investigate how far this has happened and what types of media use and other conditions are associated with such an 'effect' (or its reversal). The dominant outcome has been that newspapers have been better at closing gaps than television. Current expectations are that new media are more likely to widen than to close gaps because of their differential availability to the already better informed.

**Lifestyle**    The idea has a long history in commercial market research and has affinities with theories of taste and family background developed by Pierre Bourdieu. It refers to patterns of personal consumption and tastes of all kinds that are generally self-chosen but also shared with some others. They can be relatively independent of social class and material circumstances although they are likely to be shaped by a number of external factors, among which income is certainly one, along with age, education, social milieu and outlook. A lifestyle may be a way of expressing an individual identity, but for media it can also be a way of constructing and managing consumer markets. See also *taste culture*.

**Marxism**    The theory of society based on the work of Karl Marx, according to whom human progress takes place on the basis of conflict between succeeding 'classes', whose dominant power depends on ownership of the current main factor of production (for example, land, raw material, capital or labour). The dominant class exploits other classes in order to maximize profit and output. The relevance for mass communication lies in the proposition that the media are an ideological asset that can be used to defend, or attack, a dominant class position. In Marx's own time and later, the mass media were owned and operated in the interests of the dominant class. This remains an issue to be determined.

**Mass**   The term describes a very large but amorphous set of individuals who engage in similar behaviour, under external influence, and are viewed by their would-be manipulators as having little or no separate identity, forms of organization or power, autonomy, integrity or self-determination. It represents one view of the media audience. It is used with the same negative connotations in a number of related expressions, including mass behaviour, mass opinion, mass consumption, *mass culture*, *mass society*, and so on, and of course 'mass communication' itself.

**Mass culture**   When current (approximately 1930–1970), this term described the 'culture of the masses', generally meaning 'lower' forms of entertainment and fiction appealing to the uneducated and 'uncultured' majority, as opposed to the 'high culture' of the minority. Cultural change and new perceptions of popular culture have changed the meaning of the term and made it largely redundant or undesirable. When current, it was more ideological (upholding elite cultural values) than empirically valid, since all but a small minority tended to participate in at least some aspects of 'mass culture'.

**Mass self-communication**   A concept introduced by Manuel Castells to capture the dominant use of the Internet: to share information about one's personal life online. Mass self-communication is a form of mass communication because it reaches potentially a global audience online, and it is simultaneously self-communication because, according to Castells, it is self-directed in the elaboration and sending of the message, self-selected in the reception of the message, and self-defined in terms of the formation of the communication space.

**Mass society**   A form of society theoretically identified as dominated by a small number of interconnected elites who control the conditions of life of the many, often by means of persuasion and manipulation. The term was first applied to the post-war United States by radical critics (especially C. Wright Mills) and also by political theorists to the European societies that fell under the spell of fascism and communism. Large-scale and centralized forms of social organization are typical, accompanied by feelings of anomie and powerlessness. The mass media are necessary instruments for achieving and maintaining mass society.

**Media accountability**   A composite term for the idea, and the associated processes for realizing it, that media can and should be held to account for the quality, means and consequences of their publishing activities to society in general and/or to other interests that may be affected. This brings accountability into potential conflict with freedom. The idea of media accountability is sometimes, though not necessarily, associated with ideas of *social responsibility*. It does presuppose some mutual relationship between media senders and receivers. It is also closely linked to the idea of there being *public interest* in the media.

**Media concentration**   The coming together of media organizations to form larger units by either vertical or horizontal integration of firms. The former refers to joining of various sequences in the media process (for example, paper production, printing, publishing and selling of books), the latter to conglomeration of firms at the same stage in the sequence. Both lead to greater monopoly and less *diversity*. Concentration can also take place within the same national market or transnationally. The usual main reference is to concentration of ownership, although it is possible for there to be varying levels of concentration of different work processes in a media conglomerate.

**Media ethics**   Principles of good conduct for media practitioners, bearing in mind the public role of the media in a given society, as well as the claims of individuals. The relevant conduct relates especially to the ways in which information is obtained and to decisions about what and how to publish, especially bearing in mind the consequences that might follow for all concerned. In non-informational content areas, there are also numerous ethical issues, although these are less likely to have been codified or play a part in decision-making. The claim of *journalism* to be a profession depends to some degree on the voluntary development and acceptance of ethical standards. See *media accountability*.

**Media event**   The specific idea was conceived by Dayan and Katz (1992), although the notion of 'pseudo-event' had already been used (Boorstin, 1961) to refer to events created by the media or minor events without substance that owed their apparent significance to media attention or 'hype'. Dayan and Katz's concept identifies a particular media genre, one they say is unique to television. For a televised occasion to count as a 'media event', certain conditions have to be met: unusual events of great symbolic or historic importance, such as coronations or state visits; live coverage; extramedia sponsorship; a high degree of preplanning; reverence and ceremony in presentation; an emphasis on national sharing and celebration; and having an appeal to very large (often international) audiences.

**Media logic**   Usually refers to a set of interrelated values that are believed by producers to constitute good (that is, successful) practice and professionalism for a given medium for given purposes, or believed by observers to be operating unconsciously. While different media (for example, radio, film, newspapers) may have different logics, there are a few central recurring components, especially personalization, sensationalism (appeal to senses and emotions), drama and action, conflict, spectacle and high tempo. These attributes are thought to widen appeal and increase attention and involvement. The term is usually used by critics with the implication that media logic exalts form over substance and conflicts with goals of being informative, or otherwise conveys deeper meaning or reflection. In relation to politics, it is held that media logic detracts from substance and conviction.

**Mediatization**   The process by which the mass media come to affect many other areas of society, especially institutions with a public role, such as politics, justice, health, education, religion. Observation suggests that many public activities are now undertaken with a high regard for how they can gain access to publicity on favourable terms and with maximum impact. The term implies that activity may often be distorted, with timing, priorities and meanings being adapted to the requirements of the media and to *media logic*.

**Medium theory**   The type of theory that attributes causal influence to the intrinsic character of a given medium of communication, distinctive by its technology and capability for carrying meaning. Although technological determinism along these lines is the most common form taken by medium theory, each medium has other attributes besides the technology which affect how it will be applied to communicative purpose and how it will be perceived and actually experienced. Media develop within particular institutional settings and cultural settings that have effects independent of technology. Medium theory is most commonly identified with the *Toronto School*, and is a subset of media theory, investigating the characteristics of the medium rather than its content, senders or receivers of messages.

**Moral panic**   The term was first applied by the criminologist Jock Young to sudden expressions of often irrational mass anxiety and alarm directed at 'crime waves' or other supposed evidence of disorder and social breakdown (including promiscuity and immigration). The media are implicated through their tendency to amplify such 'panics'. They are also sometimes objects of moral panics, when alarm at their harmful effects suddenly gains currency (for example, regarding the rise of populist political movements and disinformation campaigns online). Newer media, such as computer games and the Internet, tend to generate some degree of panic at alleged harm to their (young) users.

**Network**   Any interconnected set of points, which could be persons, places, organizations, machines, and so on. In communication, interest focuses on the flow of information through the 'lines' of a network, with particular reference to their carrying capacity and interactivity, and of course to whom or what one is connected more or less tightly and exclusively. Compared with other types of organized human association, networks are less hierarchical and more flexible and informal. The term 'network society' has been coined by theorists (for example, Castells and Van Dijk) as an alternative way of expressing the reality of the *information society*.

**News**   The main form in which current information about public events is carried by media of all kinds. There is a great diversity of types and formats as well as cross-cultural differences, but defining characteristics are generally held to be timeliness, relevance and reliability (truth value). See also *journalism*.

**News values**   The criteria applied by journalists and editors in news organizations to determine whether or not to carry particular items of *news*. In commercial media, the consensus 'value' is whether or not the item concerned is likely to interest a potential audience. However, there are other sources of value, including a judgement of intrinsic significance or the pull or pressure of influential interests other than the audience.

**Newspaper**   Traditionally, this has referred to a print media form appearing regularly (usually not less than once a week), containing (at least) reliable reports of recent or ongoing events of general interest and offered for public sale. Associated characteristics are usually independence or transparency of ownership and editing and a geographical range of coverage and circulation. Variant forms have emerged, including the 'free newspaper', paid for by advertising, and the 'digital first' newspaper, which is offered online (on a website and/or a dedicated mobile application) and lacks the limits of form, time, space and location of the traditional newspaper.

**Non-verbal communication**   The term refers primarily to non-verbal (vocal or non-vocal) communication between persons, rather than to media that use music or images, for instance. Non-verbal communication is sometimes called 'paralinguistic' or 'prelinguistic'. Non-verbal human communication often adds to or extends verbal communication. Although the lack of codification and rules for non-verbal communication makes it less than a language, there are often agreed meanings in a particular culture attaching to noises, gestures, postures, and the like that are characteristic of much non-verbal communication.

**Normative theory**   Refers to theory about how media ought to operate, rather than theory seeking to describe and explain how they actually operate or to predict outcomes of the way media operate (especially effects). The latter kind of theory might be described as objective or scientific theory. Normative theory applies primarily to the relationship between media and society and deals with claims on the part of the media, especially in respect of their freedom, and also claims on the part of society. See *freedom of the press* and *social responsibility*.

**Objectivity**   A theoretically contested term applied to *news*, although in 'common-sense' terms it sums up a number of the qualities that make for trust and reliability on the part of the news audience. These include factual accuracy, lack of *bias*, separation of fact from comment, transparency about sources, and not taking sides. The reasons for controversy about the term stem mainly from the view that true objectivity is unattainable and it is misleading to pretend otherwise. In brief, all news is said to be ideological, and objectivity is held by critics to be another ideology. The requirements of objectivity make it possible for sources to manipulate the news and only serve to conceal bias, whether this is intended or unintended.

Opinion leader   A term introduced by Elihu Katz and Paul Lazarsfeld (1955), in early research into the influence of mass media, to describe the social role of persons who influence the thinking or behaviour of others in informal social relationships. The identifying characteristics vary according to the 'topic' of influence and social setting, but the people concerned are generally better informed, make more use of mass media and other sources, are gregarious and are likely to be respected by those they influence. The failure of early research to find 'direct' effects from mass media was attributed in part to the variable and often invisible contribution of opinion leaders (known as 'personal influence').

Oramedia   Frank Okwu Ugboajah developed a theory of oramedia in the 1980s in an African context to acknowledge the use and development of various early forms of indigenous mass media, including opera, music, dance, drama, poetry and folktales. These can be considered as the first 'mass media', as a vehicle for disseminating culture and transmitting messages from a ruling elite to the people and vice versa.

Parasocial interaction   A term for the pseudo-interaction that can take place between individuals in audiences and fictional characters or media personalities. Some degree of loss of contact with reality is involved, and it may be the basis for influence on behaviour.

Platform logic   A dynamic set of relations governing the way platforms (such as Google and Facebook) work and make their money, consisting of how people express themselves, technological affordances, and the legal and regulatory environment within which platforms operate. Like portal websites before them, platforms become increasingly powerful online in determining access to (and attention for) any kind of information and services, while other institutions build or reorganize infrastructures to accommodate the logic of such platforms. The primary purpose of these platforms is attention, defined as 'time spent' using the platform interface.

Political economy   The original term for theoretical economics, but for some time used by critical theorists working in the neo-Marxist tradition to refer to a general view of media and society in which material (economic) factors play a determining role and in which politics is primarily about economic power.

Polymedia   A term devised by Madianou and Miller (2013), signalling the rather effortless, integrated structure that using multiple media offers to people in everyday life. Each medium gets meaning in terms of its relations to the other media in someone's media repertoire. Similar concepts, such as a the 'media ensemble', the 'communicative figurations' that media provide, and leading a 'media life', have been suggested in the literature (especially in recent years) to acknowledge our concurrent exposure to media.

Pornography   Used loosely to describe media content that involves description or display of explicit sexual themes and scenes that go beyond the normally accepted threshold for public acceptability with reference to offence or perceived harm (in particular to children or women, who are victimized in some forms of pornography). It is presumed that the main aim of media pornography (as shared with the audience) is sexual arousal. Publication of pornography is defined differently as an offence (or not) in different jurisdictions.

Portal   In the first decade of the World Wide Web, many websites aimed to become portals or gateways to the rest of the Web – a kind of access point into 'cyberspace' (as when seeking to connect) or from it (as when searching for some information). Their popularity and economic power (as in the ability to attract advertising) waned with the rise of social media and platforms. Portals are generally offered through a major media provider, such as Yahoo or AOL; a particular search engine; a *social network site* such as YouTube; a specific website for certain kinds of content; a community or network. The Internet portal is qualitatively different from the gateways provided by former mass media, since they enable a two-way flow.

Postmodernism   A widely current (cultural) theory that underwrites the view that the 'age of ideology' is over, along with the 'industrial society' and its massive forms of social organization and control and dedication to rationality. Instead we are living in an era of unstructured diversity, uncertainty, contradictions, open-ended creativity and individual freedom from imposed rules and social constraint. It has become fashionable to discern the exuberant growth of mass media forms as the essence of popular postmodern culture. Neither the material conditions of contemporary society nor forms of organization of mass media exhibit clear signs of postmodernism. Much as with earlier critical cultural theory, postmodern thinking can support divergent optimistic and pessimistic outlooks.

Power   A term that is open to many interpretations, but the basic idea is a reference to a capacity to gain the compliance of another, even against their will (as with police or military power). In this meaning it has no direct relevance for communication, since no effect can be compelled. However, we can speak of a probability of gaining compliance with some communicative purpose (in relation to information or opinion) and the term 'influence' is widely applicable to mass communication, with compliance gained by force of argument or certain psychological rewards.

**Prejudice**   A term applied either to attitudes on the part of the public, or to media publication that involves systematically negative views about or negative treatment of (usually) some social group or category. Frequent targets of prejudice have been ethnic minorities, or outgroups such as homosexuals, foreign immigrants, the mentally ill, etc. The media have been accused of fomenting prejudice, sometimes unintentionally, and also credited with some capacity to counter prejudice.

**Priming**   Refers to the activity of the media in proposing the values and standards by which objects of media attention can be judged. The origin of the term lies in social psychology (socialization theory) but it has latterly been more applied in political communication to the evaluation of political figures by public opinion. See also *framing* and *agenda-setting.*

**Profession**   Refers to particular occupations that maintain certain standards of technical performance and of ethics by means of self-regulatory procedures. Professions involve recognized training, and control of entry to the profession is maintained by the responsible body of the profession. There is much debate about the status of *journalism* in particular as a profession. On some, but not all, criteria it can claim professional status.

**Propaganda**   The process and product of deliberate attempts to influence collective behaviour and opinion by the use of multiple means of communication in ways that are systematic and one-sided. Propaganda is carried out in the interest of the source or sender, not the recipient. It is almost certain to be in some respects misleading or not fully truthful and can be entirely untrue, as with certain kinds of disinformation. It can also be psychologically aggressive and distorted in its representation of reality. Its effectiveness is variable, depending on the context and dispositions of the target audience more than on 'message' characteristics. See *advertising* and *campaign*. The term can also refer to the Propaganda Model, coined by Edward S. Herman and Noam Chomsky (1988), explaining how corporate mass media can be seen as systematically biased towards an 'undemocratic' maintenance of social order as defined by ruling elites in politics and business. See *political economy.*

**Public**   As a noun this refers to the general body of free citizens of a given society or some smaller geographical space. Its connotations are strongly influenced by democratic theory, since freedom and equality (of rights) are generally only available in a democracy. The members of a genuine public in a democracy are free to associate, converse, organize and express themselves on all subjects, and government is ultimately accountable to the will of the 'public as a whole' according to agreed procedures. This large notion of what constitutes the public is one reason why public communication has a certain claim to protection and to respect in a democracy, and why public values are seen as contradicting commercial and market values. See also *public opinion*, *public interest* and *public sphere.*

**Public interest (and public values)**  Expresses the idea that expectations from, and claims against, the mass media on grounds of the wider and longer-term good of society can be legitimately expressed and may lead to constraints on the structure or activity of media. The content of what is 'in the public interest' or 'of public value' takes various forms. Its most minimal interpretation is that media should meet the needs of their audiences, but ethical, ideological, political and legal considerations may also lead to much stronger definitions. The expression of public interest also takes place in many ways, including via *public opinion*, politicians, critics and many interest groups affected by public communication. See also *media accountability*.

**Public opinion**  The collective views of a significant part of any *public*. This part is sometimes taken to mean a numerical majority as measured by polling, but this far overstates the capacity of the measuring instruments and misses the essential point that opinion is always diverse, dynamic and variable in strength. Historically and in certain contexts, public opinion may be taken to refer to 'informed opinion', or the general view of the more educated and aware members of the society. No statement concerning public opinion is likely to be unambiguous or beyond dispute without some clear definition. See *spiral of silence*.

**Public relations**  Now a reference to all forms of influence carried out by professional, paid communicators on behalf of some 'client' and designed primarily to project a favourable image and to counter negative views that might exist. The means are various, ranging from direct communication to providing gifts and hospitality. Public relations is often a source of supply for news media or seeks to influence news in other ways. See also *advertising* and *propaganda*.

**Public service broadcasting (PSB)**  A system of broadcasting that is publicly funded and operated in a non-profit way in order to meet the various public communication needs of all citizens. These were originally virtually all needs (that is, inclusive of entertainment), and the justification for PSB lay in the 'natural monopoly' character of broadcasting distribution. This justification is no longer valid, and PSB survives on grounds of general *public interest* and because it can meet certain communication needs that tend to be neglected in commercial systems because they are unprofitable. These include universal service, special needs of certain minorities, certain kinds of educational provision, and services to the democratic political system by giving some degree of open and diverse access, supporting general informational aims and meeting the specific needs of politicians in the electoral and government process.

**Public sphere**  The conceptual 'space' that exists in a society outside the immediate circle of private life and the walls of enclosed institutions and organizations pursuing their own (albeit sometimes public) goals. In this space, the possibility exists for public association and debate leading to the formation of public opinion and political movements and parties that can hold private interests accountable. The media are the key institution of the public sphere, and its 'quality' will depend on the quality of media. Taken to extremes, certain structural tendencies of media, including concentration, commercialization and a general lack of transparency and accountability, are harmful to the public sphere.

**Publication**  The act of making public, thus crossing a line between private and public expression. Publication usually involves a clear decision to express ideas in a fixed or formal way via the press, public speech, poster, etc. Private expression is confined to a designated personal interlocutor or circle. The distinction has legal and practical significance, especially in connection with confidentiality, privacy, potential harm or offence. Newer media have blurred the distinction between what is actually and consciously public and what may be considered so because it can be accessed by others. Publication has also become much easier for individuals, if they choose it.

**Reception analysis**  An alternative to traditional audience research (concerned with counting and effect) that takes the perspective of the audience rather than the media sender and looks at the immediate contextual influences on media use and the interpretation and meaning of the whole experience as seen by the recipient. Ethnographic and qualitative methods are required.

**Rhetoric**  The art of public speaking with persuasive intention.

**Schema**  Refers to the preconceived frame or script that is typically available to journalists for reporting isolated cases or events. A schema is an aid to communication and understanding, because it provides some wider context and sensemaking. However, schemata also introduce some closure, by applying an existing frame of meaning. Audiences also have their own schemata for making sense of incoming news information. See *framing*.

**Segmentation**  The process of classifying a potential audience for purposes of production and delivering content according to relevant categories, usually either socio-demographic or psychographic (for example, by lifestyle and taste). It plays a key role in the planning and costing of advertising in all media. Although sometimes regarded as a trend running counter to mass communication, it can be considered as a better controlled and more effective form of mass communication. See also *fragmentation*.

**Semiology/semiotics**  The 'science of sign systems' or 'signification'. Originally founded on the study of general linguistics by Ferdinand de Saussure, it was developed into a method for the systematic analysis and interpretation of all symbolic texts. Systems of signs are organized within larger cultural and ideological systems that ultimately determine meaning. A key element of semiology is the dualist idea that any (meaningful) sign (of any kind) has a conceptual element that carries meaning (subjective) as well as a physical manifestation (word, image, etc.; objective). Semiotics, as developed by Charles Peirce, separates the categories of sign, object and mind (or understanding) in the text, introducing an additional layer of complexity for interpreting language.

**Soap opera (also telenovela)** A conventional term for a very wide range of radio and television drama in (long-running and frequent) serial form. The genre originated in early Latin American as well as US-based commercial radio, and later on gained prominence in Australian daytime television before becoming a global phenomenon. Despite the variations, some typical features of soap operas and telenovelas are contemporary realistic settings of the action; continuity of characters and plots, which link to issues of the moment; a focus on the intermixed personal relationships of the characters; a strong claim to audience identification and 'engagement'; and a particular appeal to women audiences in family settings.

**Social network sites** Generally known just as 'social media', these comprise a number of Internet websites that have been set up to enable and encourage users to create networks of acquaintances and also to share messages and audiovisual material, often available to a wider public and often evolving into platforms with a broader set of operations. Examples of very popular social media are Facebook, Instagam, Snapchat, Weibo, We Chat and LinkedIn. They have become valuable commercial properties, especially for related advertising, cross-media publicity and generating data from users. See *platform logic*.

**Social responsibility** Attributed to the mass media in certain normative theories of the press and based on propositions about the needs of (democratic) society. It involves the unwritten obligations towards society and its members that are implicit in freedom of publication as well, besides general moral principles relating to truth and justice.

**Socialization** The general process of social formation of the young under the influence of the so-called agencies of socialization – traditionally the family, neighbourhood, school and religion, and now mass media.

**Spin doctor** An industry term to refer to all those who have the job of managing (or massaging) the public presentation of information or ideas (especially on behalf of politicians, but also companies and brands operating in the public eye) to maximum advantage. Their work results in the manipulation of news and is related to *public relations* and *propaganda*.

**Spiral of silence**   Concept that describes one version of the 'third-party' effect in opinion formation: the tendency for people to be influenced in what they think (or say they do) or by what they think other people think. The term was first applied by Elizabeth Noelle-Neumann (1974) to refer to the tendency for those who think they hold a minority or deviant view to refrain from expressing it in public, thus accelerating the dominance of the supposed consensus (the spiraling effect). The hypothesis is based on a presumed 'fear of isolation'. The main thrust of the theory is to attribute to the (leftist) media a powerful effect, since they are the main source of what people think is the dominant opinion of the moment. Also related to the better-known 'bandwagon effect', whereby apparent front runners pick up support on this basis alone.

**Stereotyping**   The process of using stock images of social groups, situations, events, countries, etc., in fiction or factual mass communication. A stereotype is an early graphic form of facsimile reproduction. Since the early years of communication research, the idea of a stereotype has been applied to media content that encourages prejudice or to the expression of prejudice in opinion and attitude. There is an almost inevitable element of stereotyping mass media production for reasons of simplification and efficiency as well as ill-will or ignorance. The idea is related to that of *framing* and *schema*.

**Stimulus–response**   A psychological process by which an experimental subject learns to perform some action in response to a message stimulus that has become associated with the action in question. It underlies a large body of learning theory that was applied in early research into the effects of communication and media. It has not proved a very good guide to reality.

**Surveillance**   This term has three meanings in media studies. First, it refers to the 'function' of news media for the audience in providing a view on the events of the world. Secondly, it refers to the capacity built into new online media allowing third-party access (by service providers, platform companies and some authorities) to all communicative transactions. Use of these media is no longer guaranteed privacy. Thirdly, it refers to a broad field of surveillance studies and theories of surveillance, generally inspired by the work of Michel Foucault.

**Tabloidization**   A term derived from the common tabloid format for sensationalist (that is, gossip and scandal-mongering) newspapers to refer to the alleged process of 'dumbing down', or going 'down market', of the more serious press in many countries. The main believed cause was commercialization and intense competition for readers. The process has also affected television news and 'actuality' formats in general, especially in the United States, and caused alarm at the decline of journalistic standards, the rise in public ignorance and the risk of confusion between fiction and reality (for example, 'infotainment').

**Taste culture**   A more or less organized and semi-autonomous set of cultural preferences based on certain shared tastes, although independent of actual social organization. In this the concept differs from the earlier approaches to taste patterns, which were mainly explained in terms of social background, class or milieu. Related to *lifestyle*.

**Third-party effects**   The perceived effects on others that many people believe to occur, even though they think they are not affected themselves. See *spiral of silence*.

**Toronto School**   Describes a body of work mainly derived from the theories of Marshall McLuhan, and in turn derived from an earlier scholar at the University of Toronto, the economic historian Harold Innis. At the core is a form of communication technology determinism that attributes distinctive social and cultural effects to the dominant form and vehicle of communication, independent of the actual content.

**Transmedia**   Industry term referring to the practice of developing elements of a story (such as a book, game, film, music album or advertising campaign) into multiple media platforms to constitute a larger storyworld. Each medium makes its own unique contribution to the unfolding of the story, and often the audience is included in various ways in an interactive or co-creative role. It has also become a scholarly concept to denote research into multiple or mixed media use.

**Uses and gratifications approach**   A version of individualist functional theory and research that seeks to explain the uses of media and the satisfactions derived from them in terms of the motives and self-perceived needs of audience members. This is also one version of 'active audience' theory and has been applied in the study of media effects on the grounds that any effect has to be consistent with the needs of the audience.

**Virtual community**   Describes the group or close personal associations formed online by participants in Internet exchanges and discussions. A virtual community is thought to have many of the features of a real community, including identification, bonding, shared norms and outlook, even without any physical contact or real personal knowledge of other members. See *community*.

# REFERENCES

Aday, S., Slivington, M. and Herbert, M. (2005) 'Embedding the truth: a cross-cultural analysis of objectivity and TV coverage of the Iraq war', *Harvard International Journal of Press/Politics*, 10(1): 3–21.

Adorno, T. and Horkheimer, M. (1972) 'The culture industry: enlightenment as mass deception', in *The Dialectic of Enlightenment*. New York: Herder and Herder.

Alasuutari, P. (1992) '"I'm ashamed to admit it but I have watched *Dallas*": the moral hierarchy of television programmes', *Media, Culture & Society*, 14(1): 561–582.

Alasuutari, P. (ed.) (1999) *Rethinking the Media Audience*. London: Sage.

Albino, V., Berardi, U. and Dangelico, R.M. (2015) 'Smart cities: definitions, dimensions, performance, and initiatives', *Journal of Urban Technology*, 22(1): 3–21.

Alfter, B. (2019) *Cross-border Collaborative Journalism: A Step-by-Step Guide*. Abingdon: Routledge.

Allen, R.C. (1989) '"Soap opera", audiences and the limits of genre', in F. Seiter et al. (eds), *Remote Control*, pp. 4–55. Abingdon: Routledge.

Allor, M. (1988) 'Relocating the site of the audience', *Critical Studies in Mass Communication*, 5(3): 217–233.

Altheide, D.L. (1974) *Creating Reality*. Beverly Hills, CA: Sage.

Altheide, D.L. (1985) *Media Power*. Beverly Hills, CA: Sage.

Altheide, D.L. and Snow, R.P. (1979) *Media Logic*. Beverly Hills, CA: Sage.

Altheide, D.L. and Snow, R.P. (1991) *Media Worlds in the Postjournalism Era*. New York: Aldine de Gruyter.

Althusser, L. (1971) 'Ideology and ideological state apparatuses', in *Lenin and Philosophy and Other Essays*. London: New Left.

Altman, R. (1984) 'A semantic/syntactic approach to film genre', *Cinema Journal*, 23(3): 6–18.

Altman, R. (1996) *Film/Genre*. London: British Film Institute.

Altschull, J.H. (1984) *Agents of Power: The Role of the News Media in Human Affairs*. New York: Longman.

American Psychiatric Association (2013) *Diagnostic and Statistical Manual of Mental Disorders*, 5th edition (DSM-V). Washington, DC: APA.

Anden-Papadopolous, K. (2008) 'The Abu-Ghraib torture photographs: news frames, visual culture and the power of images', *Journalism*, 9(1): 5–30.

Anderson, C.A. et al. (2017) 'Media violence and other aggression risk factors in seven nations', *Personality and Social Psychology Bulletin*, 43(7): 986–998.

Anderson, C.W. (2011) 'Blowing up the newsroom: ethnography in an age of distributed journalism', in D. Domingo and C. Paterson (eds), *Making Online News*. New York: Peter Lang.

Anderson, J., Collins, P.A., Schmitt, R.S. and Jacobowitz, R.S. (1996) 'Stressful life events and television viewing', *Communication Research*, 23(2): 243–260.

Andersson, M. and Jansson, A. (1998) 'Media use and the progressive cultural lifestyle', *Nordicom Review*, 19(2): 63–77.

Andrejevic, M. (2002) 'The work of being watched: interactive media and the exploitation of self-disclosure', *Critical Studies in Media Communication*, 19(2): 230–248.

Andrejevic, M. (2011) 'The work that affective economics does', *Cultural Studies*, 25(4–5): 604–620.

Andrew, D. (1984) *Concepts in Film Theory*. New York: Oxford University Press.

Ang, I. (1985) *Watching 'Dallas': Soap Opera and the Melodramatic Imagination*. London: Methuen.

Ang, I. (1991) *Desperately Seeking the Audience*. Abingdon: Routledge.

Ang, I. (1998) 'The performance of the sponge: mass communication theory enters the postmodern world', in K. Brants, J. Hermes and L. van Zoonen (eds), *The Media in Question*, pp. 77–88. London: Sage.

Aouragh, M. and Chakravartty, P. (2016) 'Infrastructures of empire: towards a critical geopolitics of media and information studies', *Media, Culture & Society*, 38(4): 559–575.

Archetti, C. (2008) 'News coverage of 9/11 and the demise of the media flows, globalization and localization hypothesis', *International Communication Gazette*, 70(6): 463–485.

Archetti, C. (2017a) 'Image, self-presentation and political communication in the age of interconnection: an alternative understanding of the mediatization of politics', *Northern Lights*, 15: 89–109.

Archetti, C. (2017b) 'Journalism, Practice and ... Poetry', *Journalism Studies*, 18(9): 1106–1127.

Archetti, C. (2019) 'Mapping transnational journalism in the age of flows: or how I ditched "foreign correspondence" and the "immigrant press" and started to love *histoire croisée*', *Journalism Studies*, 20(15): 2150–2166.

Armbrust, W. (2012) 'A history of new media in the Arab Middle East', *Journal for Cultural Research*, 16(2–3): 155–174.

Aronowitz, A. and DiFazio, W. (1995) *The Jobless Future*. Minneapolis, MN: University of Minnesota Press.

Arora, P. (2019) *The Next Billion Users*. Cambridge, MA: Harvard University Press.

Arsenault, A.H. and Castells, M. (2008) 'The structure and dynamics of global multi-media business networks', *International Journal of Communication*, 1(2): 707–748.

Asp, K. (1990) 'Medialization, media logic and mediarchy', *Nordicom Review*, 11(2): 47–50.

Aufderheide, P. (1999) *Communications Policy and the Public Interest: The Telecommunications Act of 1996*. New York: Guilford Press.

Austin, P.J. (1992) 'Television that talks back: an experimental validation of a PSI scale', *Journal of Broadcasting and Electronic Media*, 36(1): 173–181.

Babrow, A.S. (1988) 'Theory and method in research on audience motives', *Journal of Broadcasting and Electronic Media*, 32(4): 471–487.

Baden, C. and Tenenboim-Weinblatt, K. (2018) 'The search for common ground in conflict news research: comparing the coverage of six current conflicts in domestic and international media over time', *Media, War & Conflict*, 11(1): 22–45.

Bagdikian, B. (1988) *The Media Monopoly*. Boston, MA: Beacon.

Bailyn, L. (1959) 'Mass media and children: a study of exposure habits and cognitive effects', *Psychological Monographs*, 73: 1–48.

Baker, C.E. (2007) *Media Concentraion and Democracy*. Cambridge: Cambridge University Press.

Bakker, P. (2002) 'Free daily newspapers – business models and strategies', *International Journal on Media Management*, 4(3): 180–187.

Ball-Rokeach, S.J. (1985) 'The origins of individual media-system dependency', *Communication Research*, 12(4): 485–510.

Ball-Rokeach, S.J. (1998) 'A theory of media power and a theory of media use: different stories, questions and ways of thinking', *Mass Communication and Society*, 1(2): 1–40.

Ball-Rokeach, S.J. (2001) 'The politics of studying media violence: reflections 30 years after the Violence Commission', *Mass Communication and Society*, 4(1): 3–18.

Ball-Rokeach, S.J. and DeFleur, M.L. (1976) 'A dependency model of mass media effects', *Communication Research*, 3: 3–21.

Baltruschat, D. (2010) *Global Media Ecologies: Networked Production in Film and Television*. Abingdon: Routledge.

Bandura A. (2009) 'Social cognitive theory of mass communication', in J. Bryant and M.B. Oliver (eds), *Media Effects: Advances in Theory and Research*, 3rd edition, pp. 94–124. New York: Routledge.

Banks, M., Lovatt, A., O'Connor, J. and Raffo, C. (2000) 'Risk and trust in the cultural industries', *Geoforum*, 31(4): 453–464.

Banks, M., Taylor, S. and Gill, R. (eds) (2013) *Theorizing Cultural Work*. Abingdon: Routledge.

Bantz, C.R. (1985) 'News organizations: conflict as crafted cultural norm', *Communication*, 8: 225–244.

Bantz, C.R., McCorkle, S. and Baade, R.C. (1980) 'The news factory', *Communication Research*, 7(1): 45–68.

Bar, F. and Sandvig, C. (2008) 'US communication policy after convergence', *Media, Culture & Society*, 30(4): 531–550.

Bar, F. with Simard, C. (2006) 'From hierarchies to network firms', in L. Lievrouw and S. Livingstone (eds), *Handbook of New Media: Social Shaping and Consequences of ICTs*, pp. 350–363. London: Sage.

Bardoel, J. and d'Haenens, L. (2008) 'Reinventing public service broadcasting: promise and problems', *Media, Culture & Society*, 30(3): 295–317.

Barker, M. (2003) 'Assessing the "quality" in qualitative research', *European Journal of Communication*, 18(3): 315–335.

Barthes, R. (1967) *Elements of Semiology*. London: Cape.

Barthes, R. (1972) *Mythologies*. London: Cape.

Barthes, R. (1977) *Image, Music, Text: Essays*, selected and translated by Stephen Heath. London: Fontana.

Barwise, T.P. and Ehrenberg, A.S.C. (1988) *Television and its Audience*. Newbury Park, CA: Sage.

Barzilai-Nahon, K. (2008) 'Toward a theory of network gatekeeping: a framework for exploring information control', *Journal of the American Society for Information Science and Technology*, 59: 1493–1512.

Bauer, R.A. (1958) 'The communicator and the audience', *Journal of Conflict Resolution*, 2(1): 67–77. Also in L.A. Dexter and D.M. White (eds), *People, Society and Mass Communication*, pp. 125–139. New York: Free Press.

Bauer, R.A. (1964) 'The obstinate audience', *American Psychologist*, 19: 319–328.

Bauer, R.A. and Bauer, A. (1960) 'America, mass society and mass media', *Journal of Social Issues*, 10(3): 366.

Bauerlein, M. (2008) *The Dumbest Generation*. New York: TarcherPerigee/Penguin.

Bauman, Z. (1972) 'A note on mass culture: on infrastructure', in D. McQuail (ed.), *Sociology of Mass Communication*, pp. 61–74. Harmondsworth: Penguin.

Bauman, Z. (2000) *Liquid Modernity*. Cambridge: Polity Press.

Bauman, Z. (2005) *Liquid Life*. Cambridge: Polity Press.

Bausinger, H. (1984) 'Media, technology and daily life', *Media, Culture & Society*, 6: 343–351.

Baym, N. (2015) *Personal Connections in the Digital Age*, 2nd edition. Cambridge: Polity Press.

Baym, N. (2018) *Playing to the Crowd: Musicians, Audiences, and the Intimate Work of Connection*. New York: New York University Press.

Baym, N., Campbell, S.W., Horst, H., Kalyanaraman, S., Oliver, M.B., Rothenbuhler, E., Weber, R. and Miller, K. (2012) 'Communication theory and research in the age of new media: a conversation from the CM Café', *Communication Monographs*, 79(2): 256–267.

Bean, A.M., Nielsen, R.K.L., van Rooij, A.J. and Ferguson, C.J. (2017) 'Video game addiction: the push to pathologize video games', *Professional Psychology: Research and Practice*, 48(5): 378–389.

Becker, L. (1982) 'The mass media and citizen assessment of issue importance', in D.C. Whitney et al. (eds), *Mass Communication Review Yearbook*, vol. 3, pp. 521–536. Beverly Hills, CA: Sage.

Beckett, C. and Deuze, M. (2016) 'On the role of emotion in the future of journalism', *Social Media + Society*, 2(3). Available at: http://journals.sagepub.com/doi/full/10.1177/2056305116662395.

Beckett, C. and Mansell, R. (2008) 'Crossing boundaries: new media and networked journalism', *Communication, Culture & Critique*, 1: 92–104.

Behr, R.L. and Iyengar, S. (1985) 'TV news, real world cues and changes in the public agenda', *Public Opinion Quarterly*, 49(1): 38–57.

Bell, A. (1991) *The Language of News Media*. Oxford: Blackwell.

Bell, D. (1973) *The Coming of Post-Industrial Society*. New York: Basic Books.

Beltrão, L. (1971) *Comunicação e folclore*. São Paulo: Melhoramentos.

Beniger, J.R. (1986) *The Control Revolution*. Cambridge, MA: Harvard University Press.

Benjamin, W. (1977) 'The work of art in an age of mechanical reproduction', in J. Curran et al. (eds), *Mass Communication and Society*, pp. 384–408. London: Edward Arnold.

Bennett, W.L. (1990) 'Towards a theory of press–state relations in the US', *Journal of Communication*, 40(2): 103–125.

Bennett, W.L. (2003) 'The burglar alarm that just keeps ringing: a response to Zaller', *Political Communication*, 20(2): 131–138.

Bennett, W.L. and Entman, R.M. (eds) (2001) *Mediated Politics*. Cambridge: Cambridge University Press.

Bennett, W.L. and Iyengar, S. (2008) 'A new era of minimal effects? Changing foundations of political communication', *Journal of Communication*, 58(4): 707–731.

Bennett, W.L., Lawrence, R.G. and Livingstone, S. (2007) *When the Press Fails*. Chicago, IL: University of Chicago Press.

Benson, R. (2019) 'How media ownership matters in the US: beyond the concentration debate', *Société Contemporaine*, 113: 71–83.

Benson, R. and Neveu, E. (2005) *Bourdieu and the Journalistic Field*. Cambridge: Polity Press.

Bentivegna, S. (2002) 'Politics and the new media', in L.A. Lievrouw and S. Livingstone (eds), *The Handbook of New Media*, pp. 50–61. London: Sage.

Berelson, B. (1948) 'Communication and public opinion', in W. Schramm (ed.), *Communications in Modern Society*. Urbana, IL: University of Illinois Press.

Berelson, B. (1949) 'What missing the newspaper means', in P.F. Lazarsfeld and F.M. Stanton (eds), *Communication Research 1948–9*, pp. 111–129. New York: Duell, Sloan and Pearce.

Berelson, B. (1952) *Content Analysis in Communication Research*. Glencoe, IL: Free Press.

Berelson, B. (1959) 'The state of communication research', *Public Opinion Quarterly*, 23(1): 16.

Berger, A.A. (1992) *Popular Genres*. Newbury Park, CA: Sage.

Berger, C.R. and Chaffee, S.H. (1987) 'The study of communication as a science', in C.R. Berger and S.H. Chaffee (eds), *Handbook of Communication Science*, pp. 15–19. Beverly Hills, CA: Sage.

Berger, P. and Luckmann, T. (1967) *The Social Construction of Reality*. Garden City, NJ: Anchor.

Berkowitz, L. (1984) 'Some effects of thoughts on anti- and prosocial influence of media events: a cognitive neoassociationistic analysis', *Psychological Bulletin*, 95(3): 410–427.

Bermejo, F. (2009) 'Audience manufacture in historical perspective: from broadcasting to Google', *New Media and Society*, 11(1/2): 133–154.

Bertrand, C.-J. (2003) *An Arsenal for Democracy: Media Accountancy Systems*. Creskill, NJ: Hampton Press.

Biltereyst, D. (1992) 'Language and culture as ultimate barriers?', *European Journal of Communication*, 7(4): 517–540.

Biltereyst, D. (1995) 'Qualitative audience research and transnational media effects: a new paradigm?', *European Journal of Communication*, 10(2): 245–270.

Bilton, C. (2007) *Management and Creativity: From Creative Industries to Creative Management*. Malden, MA: Blackwell.

Bilton, C. (2017) *The Disappearing Product: Marketing and Markets in the Creative Industries*. Cheltenham: Edward Elgar.

Binkley, S. (2000) 'Kitsch as a repetitive system: a problem for the theory of taste hierarchy', *Journal of Material Culture*, 5(2): 131–152.

Biocca, F.A. (1988a) 'The breakdown of the canonical audience', in J. Anderson (ed.), *Communication Yearbook 11*, pp. 127–132. Newbury Park, CA: Sage.

Biocca, F.A. (1988b) 'Opposing conceptions of the audience', in J. Anderson (ed.), *Communication Yearbook 11*, pp. 51–80. Newbury Park, CA: Sage.

Bird, S.E. (1998) 'An audience perspective on the tabloidisation of news', *The Public*, 5(3): 33–50.

Bird, S.E. and Dardenne, R.W. (2009) 'Rethinking news and myth as storytelling', in K. Wahl-Jorgensen and T. Hanitzsch (eds), *The Handbook of Journalism Studies*, pp. 205–217. Abingdon: Routledge.

Blair, H. (2003) 'Winning and losing in flexible labour markets: the formation and operation of networks of interdependence in the UK film industry', *Sociology*, 37(4): 677–694.

Blumer, H. (1933) *Movies and Conduct*. New York: Macmillan.

Blumer, H. (1939) 'The mass, the public and public opinion', in A.M. Lee (ed.), *New Outlines of the Principles of Sociology*. New York: Barnes and Noble.

Blumer, H. (1969) *Symbolic Interactionism*. New York: Prentice-Hall.

Blumer, H. and Hauser, P.M. (1933) *Movies, Delinquency and Crime*. New York: Macmillan.

Blumler, J.G. (1985) 'The social character of media gratifications', in K.E. Rosengren et al. (eds), *Media Gratification Research: Current Perspectives*, pp. 41–59. Beverly Hills, CA: Sage.

Blumler, J.G. and Gurevitch, M. (1995) *The Crisis of Public Communication*. Abingdon: Routledge.

Blumler, J.G. and Katz, E. (eds) (1974) *The Uses of Mass Communications*. Beverly Hills, CA: Sage.

Blumler, J.G. and McQuail, D. (1968) *Television in Politics: Its Uses and Influence*. London: Faber.

Blythe, M., Wright, P., McCarthy, J. and Bertelsen, O.W. (2006) 'Theory and method for experience centered design', in *CHI '06 Extended Abstracts on Human Factors in Computing Systems*, pp. 1691–1694. New York: ACM.

Boczkowski, P. and Mitchelstein, E. (2013) *The News Gap: When the Information Preferences of the Media and the Public Diverge*. Boston, MA: MIT Press.

Bogart, L. (1995) *Commercial Culture*. New York: Oxford University Press.

Bogart, L. (2004) 'Reflections on content quality in newspapers', *Newspaper Research Journal*, 25(1): 40–53.

Bolls, P.D., Weber, R., Lang, A. and Potter, R.F. (2019) 'Media psychophysiology and neuroscience: bringing brain science into media processes and effects research', in M.B. Oliver, A.A. Raney and J. Bryant (eds), *Media Effects: Advances in Theory and Research*, 4th edition. New York: Routledge.

Bolter, J.D. and Grusin, R. (1999) *Remediation: Understanding New Media*. Cambridge, MA: MIT Press.

Boomgaarden, H.G. and Song, H. (2019) 'Media use and its effects in cross-national perspective', *Kölner Zeitschrift für Soziologie und Sozialpsychologie*, 71(1): 545–571.

Boorstin, D. (1961) *The Image: A Guide to Pseudo-Events in America*. New York: Atheneum.

Bordewijk, J.L. and van Kaam, B. (1986) 'Towards a new classification of tele-information services', *Intermedia*, 14(1): 1621. Originally published in *Allocutie*. Baarn: Bosch and Keuning, 1982.

Borger, M., van Hoof, A., Costera Meijer, I. and Sanders, J. (2013) 'Constructing participatory journalism as a scholarly object', *Digital Journalism*, 1(1): 117–134.

Borgesius, F.Z., Trilling, D., Möller, J., Bodó, B., De Vreese, C.H. and Helberger, N. (2016) 'Should we worry about filter bubbles?', *Internet Policy Review*, 5(1): 1–16.

Boulianne, S. (2009) 'Does Internet use affect engagement? A meta-analysis of research', *Political Communication*, 26(2): 193–211.

Boulianne, S. (2019) 'US dominance of research on political communication: a meta-view', *Political Communication*, DOI: 10.1080/10584609.2019.1670899.

Bourdieu, P. (1986) *Distinction: A Social Critique of the Judgement of Taste*. Abingdon: Routledge.

boyd, d. (2010) 'Public by default, private when necessary', *Apophenia*, 25 January. Retrieved from: www.zephoria.org/thoughts/archives/2010/01/25/public_by_defau.html (18 November 2019).

Boyd-Barrett, O. (1980) *The International News Agencies*. London: Constable.

Boyd-Barrett, O. (2001) 'National and international news agencies', *International Communication Gazette*, 62(1): 5–18.

Boyd-Barrett, O. and Rantanen, T. (eds) (1998) *The Globalization of News*. London: Sage.

Boynton, G.R. and Richardson, G.W. (2016) 'Agenda setting in the 21st century', *New Media and Society*, 18(9): 1916–1934.

Bradley, S.D. (2007) 'Dynamic, embodied, limited-capacity attention and memory: modeling cognitive processing of mediated stimuli', *Media Psychology*, 9(1): 211–239.

Braman, S. (2004) 'Technology', in J.D.H. Downing, D. McQuail, P. Schlesinger and E. Wartella (eds), *The SAGE Handbook of Media Studies*, pp. 123–144. Thousand Oaks, CA: Sage.

Braman, S. and Roberts, S. (2003) 'Advantage ISP: terms of service as media law', *New Media and Society*, 5(4): 522–548.

Bramson, L. (1961) *The Political Context of Sociology*. Princeton, NJ: Princeton University Press.

Brannen, J. (2005) 'Mixing methods: the entry of qualitative and quantitative approaches into the research process', *International Journal of Social Research Methodology*, 8(3): 173–184.

Brants, K. (1998) 'Who's afraid of infotainment?', *European Journal of Communication*, 13(3): 315–336.

Brants, K. and Voltmer, I. (eds) (2011) *Political Communication in Postmodern Democracy: Challenging the Primacy of Politics*. New York and Basingstoke: Palgrave Macmillan.

Brave, S., Nass, C. and Hutchinson, K. (2005) 'Computers that care: investigating the effects of orientation of emotion exhibited by an embodied computer agent', *International Journal of Human-Computer Studies*, 62(2): 161–178.

Breed, W. (1955) 'Social control in the newsroom: a functional analysis', *Social Forces*, 33: 326–355.

Briggs, A. and Burke, P. (2010) *A Social History of the Media: From Gutenberg to the Internet*, 3rd edition. Oxford: Polity Press.

Bro, P. and Wallberg, F. (2015) 'Gatekeeping in a digital era', *Journalism Practice*, 9(1): 92–105.

Brodie, R.J., Hollebeek, L.D., Jurić, B. and Ilić, A. (2011) 'Customer engagement: conceptual domain, fundamental propositions, and implications for research', *Journal of Service Research*, 14(3): 252–271.

Brown, J.R. (ed.) (1976) *Children and Television*. London: Collier-Macmillan.

Bruns, A. (2008) *Blogs, Wikipedia, Second Life and Beyond*. New York: Peter Lang.

Bruns, A. (2019) *Are Filter Bubbles Real?* Cambridge: Polity Press.

Bryant, J. and Zillmann, D. (eds) (1986) *Perspectives on Media Effects*. Hillsdale, NJ: Erlbaum.

Buckingham, D. (2002) 'The electronic generation? Children and new media', in L. Lievrouw and S. Livingstone (eds), *The Handbook of New Media*, pp. 77–89. London: Sage.

Buckingham, D. (2009) '"Creative" visual methods in media research: possibilities, problems and proposals', *Media, Culture & Society*, 31(4): 633–652.

Bucy, E.P. and Grabe, M.E. (2007) 'Taking television seriously: a sound and image bite analysis of presidential campaign coverage, 1992–2004', *Journal of Communication*, 57: 652–675.

Bucy, E.P. and Gregson, K. (2001) 'Media participation: a legitimizing mechanism of mass democracy', *New Media and Society*, 3(3): 357–380.

Bucy, E.P. and Newhagen, J.E. (1999) 'The micro- and macrodrama of politics on television: effects of media format on candidate evaluations', *Journal of Broadcasting & Electronic Media*, 43(2): 193–210.

Burgess, J. and Green, J. (2018) *YouTube: Online Video and Participatory Culture*, 2nd edition. Cambridge: Polity Press.

Burnett, R. (1996) *The Global Jukebox*. Abingdon: Routledge.

Burns, T. (1969) 'Public service and private world', in P. Halmos (ed.), *The Sociology of Mass Media Communicators*, pp. 53–73. Keele: University of Keele.

Burns, T. (1977) *The BBC: Public Institution and Private World*. London: Macmillan.

Bushman, B.J. and Anderson, C.A. (2009) 'Comfortably numb: desensitizing effects of violent media on helping others', *Psychological Science*, 20(3): 273–277.

Cacciatore, M.A., Scheufele, D.A. and Iyengar, S. (2016) 'The end of framing as we know it … and the future of media effects', *Mass Communication and Society*, 19(1): 7–23.

Calhoun, C. (2011) 'Communication as social science (and more)', *International Journal of Communication*, 5: 1479–1496.

Cammaerts, B. and Mansell, R. (2020) 'Digital platform policy and regulation: Toward a radical democratic turn'. *International Journal of Communication*, 12: 135–154.

Canclini, N.G. (1995[1989]) *Hybrid Cultures*. Minneapolis, MN: University of Minnesota Press.

Cantor, M. (1971) *The Hollywood Television Producers*. New York: Basic Books.

Cantor, M. (1994) 'The role of the audience in the production of culture', in J.S. Ettema and D.C. Whitney (eds), *Audiencemaking: How the Media Create the Audience,* pp. 159–170. Thousand Oaks, CA: Sage.

Cappella, J.N. (2002) 'Cynicism and social trust in the new media environment', *Journal of Communication*, 52(1): 229–241.

Cappella, J.N. and Jamieson, K.H. (1997) *The Spiral of Cynicism: The Press and the Public Good*. New York: Oxford University Press.

Cardoso, G. (2008) 'From mass to networked communication: communicational models and the informational society', *International Journal of Communication*, 2: 587–630. Retrieved from: https://ijoc.org/index.php/ijoc/article/view/19

Carey, J.W. (1969) 'The communication revolution and the professional communicator', in P. Halmos (ed.), *The Sociology of Mass Media Communicators*, pp. 23–38. Keele: University of Keele.

Carey, J.W. (1975) 'A cultural approach to communication', *Communication*, 2: 1–22.

Carey, J.W. (1988) *Communication as Culture*. Boston, MA: Unwin Hyman.

Carey, J.W. (1998) 'Marshall McLuhan: genealogy and legacy', *Canadian Journal of Communication*, 23: 293–306.

Carey, J.W. (2003) 'New media and TV viewing behaviour', *NHK Broadcasting Studies*, 2: 45–63.

Carey, J.W. (2009) *Communication as Culture*, revised edition. New York: Routledge.

Carlson, M. (2015) 'The robotic reporter', *Digital Journalism*, 3(3): 416–431.

Carlsson, U. (2003) 'The rise and fall of NWICO', *Nordicom Review*, 24(2): 31–67.

Carlsson, U. and von Feilitzen, C. (eds) (1998) *Children, Media and Violence*. Paris: UNESCO.

Carney, N. (2016) 'All lives matter, but so does race: Black Lives Matter and the evolving role of social media', *Humanity & Society*, 40(2): 180–199.

Carpentier, N. (2016) 'Beyond the ladder of participation: an analytical toolkit for the critical analysis of participatory media processes', *Javnost – The Public*, 23(1): 70–88.

Carragee, K. and Roefs, W. (2004) 'The neglect of power in recent framing research', *Journal of Communication*, 54(2): 214–233.

Casemajor, N. (2015) 'Digital materialisms: frameworks for digital media studies', *Westminster Papers in Communication and Culture*, 10(1): 4–17.

Castello, E. (2007) 'The production of television fiction and nation-building', *European Journal of Communication*, 22(1): 49–64.

Castells, M. (1996) *The Information Age. Economy, Society, and Culture, Vol. I: The Rise of the Network Society*. Oxford: Blackwell.

Castells, M. (2001) *The Internet Galaxy*. Oxford: Oxford University Press.

Castells, M. (2007) 'Communication power and counter power in the network society', *International Journal of Communication*, 1: 238–266.

Castells, M. (2009) *Communication Power*. Oxford: Oxford University Press.

Castells, M. (2012) *Networks of Outrage and Hope: Social Movements in the Internet Age*. Cambridge: Polity Press.

Castronova, E. (2005) *Synthetic Worlds: The Business and Culture of Online Games*. Chicago, IL: University of Chicago Press.

Cavalcante, A., Press, A. and Sender, K. (2017) 'Feminist reception studies in a post-audience age: returning to audiences and everyday life', *Feminist Media Studies*, 17(1): 1–13.

Caves, R. (2000) *Creative Industries: Contracts between Art and Commerce*. Boston, MA: Harvard University Press.

Cefai, S. (2018) 'Introduction: mediating affect', *Cultural Studies*, 32(1): 1–17.

Chadha, K. and Kavoori, A. (2005) 'Globalization and national media systems: mapping interactions in policies, markets and formats', in J. Curran and M. Gurevitch (eds), *Mass Media and Society*, 4th edition, pp. 84–103. London: Hodder Arnold.

Chadwick, A. (2017) *The Hybrid Media System*, 2nd edition. Oxford: Oxford University Press.

Chaffee, S.H. (1975) 'The diffusion of political information', in S.H. Chaffee (ed.), *Political Communication*, pp. 85–128. Beverly Hills, CA: Sage.

Chaffee, S.H. (1981) 'Mass media effects: new research perspectives', in C.G. Wilhoit and H. de Back (eds), *Mass Communication Review Yearbook*, vol. 2, pp. 77–108. Beverly Hills, CA: Sage.

Chaffee, S.H. and Hochheimer, J.L. (1982) 'The beginnings of political communication research in the US: origins of the limited effects model', in E.M. Rogers and F. Balle (eds), *The Media Revolution in America and Europe*, pp. 263–283. Norwood, NJ: Ablex.

Chaffee, S.H. and Metzger, M.J. (2001) 'The End of Mass Communication?', *Mass Communication and Society*, 4(4): 365–379.

Chaffee, S.H. and Roser, C. (1986) 'Involvement and the consistency of knowledge, attitudes and behavior', *Communication Research*, 3: 373–399.

Chakravartty, P., Kuo, R., Grubbs, V. and McIlwain, C. (2018) '#CommunicationSoWhite', *Journal of Communication*, 68(2): 254–266.

Chalaby, J. (2001) 'New media, new freedoms, new threats', *International Communication Gazette*, 62(1): 19–29.

Chalaby, J. (2003) 'Television for a new global order', *International Communication Gazette*, 65(6): 457–472.

Champion, K. (2015) 'Measuring content diversity in a multi-platform context', *The Political Economy of Communication*, 3(1): 39–56.

Chan-Olmsted, S. and Chang, B.-H. (2003) 'Diversification strategy of global media conglomerates: examining its patterns and determinants', *Journal of Media Economics*, 16(4): 213–233.

Chan-Olmsted, S. and Wang, R. (2019) 'Shifts in consumer engagement and media business models', in M. Deuze and M. Prenger (eds), *Making Media: Production, Practices and Professions*, pp. 133–146. Amsterdam: Amsterdam University Press.

Chandler, D. (1997) *An Introduction to Genre Theory* [WWW document]. Retrieved from: www.aber.ac.uk/media/Documents/intgenre/chandler_genre_theory.pdf

Chang, T.-K., Himelboim, I. and Dong, D. (2009) 'Open global networks, closed international flows', *International Communication Gazette*, 71(3): 137–159.

Chong, D. and James N. Druckman (2007) 'Framing theory', *Annual Review of Political Science*, 10(1): 103–126.

Christopherson, S. and van Jaarsveld, D. (2005) 'New media after the Dot.com bust: the persistent influence of political institutions on work in cultural industries', *International Journal of Cultural Policy*, 11(1): 77–93.

Clark, T.N. (ed.) (1969) *On Communication and Social Influence: Collected Essays of Gabriel Tarde*. Chicago, IL: University of Chicago Press.

Clausse, R. (1968) 'The mass public at grips with mass communication', *International Social Science Journal*, 20(4): 625–643.

Clough, P. (2008) 'The affective turn: political economy, biomedia and bodies', *Theory, Culture & Society*, 25(1): 1–22.

Coe, N., Hess, M., Henry, Y.W., Dicken, P. and Henderson, J. (2004) '"Globalizing" regional development: a global production networks perspective', *Transactions of the Institute of British Geographers*, 29(4): 468–484.

Cohen, B. (1963) *The Press and Foreign Policy*. Princeton, NJ: Princeton University Press.

Coleman, S. (1999) 'The new media and democratic politics', *New Media and Society*, 1(1): 67–74.

Coleman, S. (ed.) (2000) *Televised Election Debates: International Perspectives*. New York: St Martin's Press.

Collins, P.H. (2000) 'Gender, black feminism, and black political economy', *The Annals of the American Academy of Political and Social Science*, 568(1): 41–53.

Collins, R. (2006) 'Internet governance in the UK', *Media, Culture & Society*, 28(3): 337–358.

Collins, R. (2008) 'Hierarchy or homeostasis? Hierarchy, markets and networks in UK media and communications governance', *Media, Culture & Society*, 30(3): 295–317.

Comstock, G. (ed.) (1988) *Public Communication and Behavior*. New York: Academic Press.

Connell, I. (1998) 'Mistaken identities: tabloid and broadsheet news discourses', *The Public*, 5(3): 11–31.

Conway, J.C. and Rubin, A.M. (1991) 'Psychological predictors of television viewing motivation', *Communication Research*, 18(4): 443–463.

Corner, J. (2018) '"Mediatization": media theory's word of the decade', *Media Theory*, 2(2): 79–90.

Costera Meijer, I. (2001) 'The public quality of popular journalism: developing a normative framework', *Journalism Studies*, 2(2): 189–205.

Costera Meijer, I. and Groot Kormelink, T. (2014) 'Checking, sharing, clicking and linking', *Digital Journalism*, 3(5): 664–679.

Cottle, S. (ed.) (2003) *Media Organization and Production*. London: Sage.

Cottle, S. (2007) 'Ethnography and news production: new(s) developments in the field', *Sociology Compass*, 1: 1–16.

Couldry, N. (2004) 'Theorising media as practice', *Social Semiotics*, 14(2): 115–132.

Couldry, N. (2012) *Media, Society, World: Social Theory and Digital Media Practice*. Cambridge: Polity Press.

Couldry, N. (2016) 'Life with the media manifold: between freedom and subjection', in L. Kramp et al. (eds), *Politics, Civil Society and Participation: Media and Communications in a Transforming Environment*, pp. 25–39. Bremen: Edition Lumière.

Couldry, N. and Hepp, A. (2016) *The Mediated Construction of Reality*. Cambridge: Polity Press.

Couldry, N., Rodriquez, C., Bolin, G., Cohen, J., Volkmer, I., Goggin, G., Kraidy, M., Iwabuchi, K. and Qiu, J.L. (2018) 'Media, communication and the struggle for social progress', *Global Media and Communication*, 14(2): 173–191.

Courtois, C., Verdegem, P. and De Marez, L. (2013) 'The triple articulation of media technologies in audiovisual media consumption', *Television & New Media*, 14(5): 421–439.

Craig, D. (2018) 'For a practical discipline', *Journal of Communication*, 68(2): 289–297.

Croucher, S.M. (2011) 'Social networking and cultural adaptation: a theoretical model', *Journal of International and Intercultural Communication*, 4(4): 259–264.

Curran, J. (1990) 'The new revisionism in mass communication research: a reappraisal', *European Journal of Communication*, 5(2/3): 135–164.

Curran, J. and Hesmondhalgh, D. (2019) *Media and Society*, 6th edition. London: Bloomsbury Academic.

Curran, J. and Seaton, J. (1997) *Power without Responsibility*, 5th edition. London: Fontana.

Curran, J., Iyengar, S., Lund, A.B. and Salovaara-Moring, I. (2009) 'Media system, public knowledge and democracy: a comparative study', *European Journal of Communication*, 24(1): 5–26.

Curran, J. and Park, M.-J. (2000) *De-Westernizing Media Studies*. Abingdon: Routledge.

D'Alessio, D. (2003) 'An experimental examination of readers' perceptions of media bias', *Journalism and Mass Communication Quarterly*, 80(2): 282–294.

D'Alessio, D. and Allen, M. (2000) 'Media bias in presidential elections: a meta-analysis', *Journal of Communication*, 50(1): 133–156.

D'Angelo, P. (2002) 'News framing as a multiparadigmatic research programme: a response to Entman', *Journal of Communication*, 52(4): 870–888.

Dahlberg, L. (2001) 'Democracy via cyberspace', *New Media and Society*, 3(2): 157–177.

Dahlberg, L. (2004) 'Cyber-publics and corporate control of online communication', *Javnost – The Public*, 11(2): 77–93.

Dahlen, M. and Rosengren, S. (2016) 'If advertising won't die, what will it be? Toward a working definition of advertising', *Journal of Advertising*, 45(3): 334–345.

Dahlgren, P. (1995) *Television and the Public Sphere*. London: Sage.

Dahlgren, P. (1996) 'Media logic in cyberspace: repositioning journalism and its publics', *Javnost – The Public*, 3(3): 59–72.

Dahlgren, P. (2005) 'The internet, public sphere and political communication', *Political Communication*, 22(2): 147–162.

Darnton, R. (1975) 'Writing news and telling stories', *Daedalus*, Spring: 175–194.

Davis, D.K. (1999) 'Media as public arena' in R.C. Vincent and K. Nordenstreng (eds), *Towards Equity in Global Communication*. Cresskill, NJ: Hampton Press.

Davis, D.K. and Robinson, J.P. (1986) 'News story attributes and comprehension', in J.P. Robinson and M. Levy (eds), *The Main Source*, pp. 179–210. Beverly Hills, CA: Sage.

Davison, W.P. (1983) 'The third person effect', *Public Opinion Quarterly*, 47(1): 1–15.

Dayan, D. and Katz, E. (1992) *Media Events*. Cambridge, MA: Harvard University Press.

De Certeau, M. (1984) *The Practice of Everyday Life*. Berkeley, CA: University of California Press.

De Meulenaere, J., Bleumers, L. and Van den Broeck, W. (2015) 'An audience perspective on the second screen phenomenon', *Journal of Media Innovations*, 2(2): 6–22.

de Ridder, J. (1984) *Persconcentratie in Nederland*. Amsterdam: Uitgeverij.

de Saussure, F. (1915/1960) *Course in General Linguistics* (English trans). London: Owen.

De Vreese, C. (2006) 'Media message flows and interpersonal communication', *Communication Research*, 33(1): 19–37.

De Vreese, C.H., Boukes, M., Schuck, A., Vliegenthart, R., Bos L. and Lelkes, Y. (2017) 'Linking survey and media content data: opportunities, considerations, and pitfalls', *Communication Methods and Measures*, 11(4): 221–244.

De Vreese, C.H., Esser, F., Aalberg, T., Reinemann, C. and Stanyer, J. (2018) 'Populism as an expression of political communication content and style: a new perspective', *The International Journal of Press/Politics*, 23(4): 423–438.

Deacon, D. (2007) 'Yesterday's papers and today's technology: digital newspaper archives and "push button" content analysis', *European Journal of Communication*, 22(1): 5–25.

Deacon, D. and Stanyer, J. (2014) 'Mediatization: key concept or conceptual bandwagon?', *Media, Culture & Society*, 36(7): 1032–1044.

Dearing, J.W. and Rogers, E.M. (1996) *Agenda-Setting*. Thousand Oaks, CA: Sage.

DeFleur, M.L. and Ball-Rokeach, S. (1989) *Theories of Mass Communication*, 5th edition. New York: Longman.

Delia, J.G. (1987) 'Communication research: a history', in S.H. Chaffee and C. Berger (eds), *Handbook of Communication Science*, pp. 20–98. Newbury Park, CA: Sage.

Deming, C.J. (1991) 'Hill Street Blues as narrative', in R. Avery and D. Eason (eds), *Critical Perspectives on Media and Society*, pp. 240–264. New York: Guilford Press.

Dennis, E., Gilmor, D. and Glasser, T. (eds) (1989) *Media Freedom and Accountability*. New York: Greenwood Press.

Denson, S. and Jahn-Sudmann, A. (2013) 'Digital seriality: on the serial aesthetics and practice of digital games', *Eludamos*, 7(1): 1–32.

Department for Digital, Culture, Media and Sport (2001) *Creative Industries Mapping Documents*. Available at: www.gov.uk/government/publications/creative-industries-mapping-documents-2001.

Deuze, M. (2003) 'The web and its journalisms', *New Media and Society*, 5(4): 203–230.

Deuze, M. (2005) 'Popular journalism and professional ideology: tabloid reporters and editors speak out', *Media, Culture & Society*, 27(6): 801–822.

Deuze, M. (2006) 'Participation, remediation, bricolage: considering principal components of a digital culture', *The Information Society*, 22(2): 63–75.

Deuze, M. (2007) *Media Work*. Cambridge: Polity Press.

Deuze, M. (2012) *Media Life*. Cambridge: Polity Press.

Deuze, M. (2015) 'Living as a zombie in media is the only way to survive', *Journal of the Fantastic in the Arts*, 26(1): 307–323.

Deuze, M. and Prenger, M. (eds) (2019) *Making Media: Production, Practices and Professions*. Amsterdam: Amsterdam University Press.

Deuze, M. and Witschge, T. (2020) *Beyond Journalism*. Cambridge: Polity Press.

DeWall, C.N., Anderson, C.A. and Bushman, B.J. (2011) 'The general aggression model: theoretical extensions to violence', *Psychology of Violence*, 1(3): 245–258.

Dimitrova, D.V., Kaid, L.L., Williams, A.P. and Trammell, K.D. (2005) 'War on the web: the immediate news framing of Gulf War II', *The Harvard International Journal of Press/Politics*, 10(1): 22–44.

Dimitrova, D.V. and Strömbäck, J. (2005) 'Mission accomplished? Framing of the Iraq war in the elite newspapers in Sweden and the United States', *International Communication Gazette*, 67(5): 399–417.

Dimmick, J. and Coit, P. (1982) 'Levels of analysis in mass media decision-making', *Communication Research*, 9(1): 3–32.

Dimmick, J. and Rothenbuhler, E. (1984) 'The theory of the niche: quantifying competition among media industries', *Journal of Communication*, 34(3): 103–119.

Domingo, D., Masip, P. and Costera Meijer, I. (2015) 'Tracing digital news networks', *Digital Journalism*, 3(1): 53–67.

Domingo, D., Quandt, T., Heinonen, A., Paulussen, S., Singer, J.B. and Vujnovic, M. (2008) 'Participatory journalism practices in the media and beyond', *Journalism Practice*, 2(3): 326–342.

Donath, J. (2007) 'Signals in social supernets', *Journal of Computer-Mediated Communication*, 13(1): article 12.

Donohew, L., Palmgreen, P. and Rayburn, J.D. (1987) 'Social and psychological origins of media use: a lifestyle analysis', *Journal of Broadcasting and Electronic Media*, 31(3): 255–278.

Dorfman, A. and Mattelart, A. (1975) *How to Read Donald Duck: Imperialist Ideology in the Disney Comic*. New York: International General.

Dourish, P. and Bell, G. (2011) *Divining a Digital Future*. Cambridge, MA: MIT Press.

Dowling, D. and Vogan, T. (2015) 'Can We "Snowfall" This?', *Digital Journalism*, 3(2): 209–224.

Downes, F.J. and McMillan, S.J. (2000) 'Defining interactivity: a qualitative identification of key dimensions', *New Media and Society*, 2(2): 157–179.

Downing, J. (2000) *Radical Media: Rebellious Communication and Social Movements*. Thousand Oaks, CA: Sage.

Downing, J.D. and Husband, C. (2005) *Ethnicity and Media*. London: Sage.

Dowsett, A. and Jackson, M. (2019) 'The effect of violence and competition within video games on aggression', *Computers in Human Behavior*, 99: 22–27.

Doyle, G. (2010) 'From television to multi-platform: less from more or more for less?', *Convergence*, 16(4): 431–449.

Doyle, G. (2013) *Understanding Media Economics*, 2nd edition. London: Sage.

Drotner, K. (1992) 'Modernity and media panics', in M. Skovmand and K. Schrøder (eds), *Media Cultures*, pp. 42–62. Abingdon: Routledge.

Drotner, K. (2000) 'Less is more: media ethnography and its limits', in I. Hagen and J. Wasko (eds), *Consuming Audiences?*, pp. 165–88. Cresskill, NJ: Hampton Press.

Du Gay, P. (ed.) (1997) *Production of Culture/Cultures of Production*. London/Milton Keynes: Sage/Open University.

Du Gay, P., Hall, S., Janes, L., Mackay, H. and Negus, K. (1997) *Doing Cultural Studies: The Story of the Sony Walkman*. London: Sage.

Duffy, B.E. (2017) *(Not) Getting Paid to Do What You Love*. New Haven, CT: Yale University Press.

Duits, L., Zwaan, K. and Reijnders, S. (eds) (2014) *The Ashgate Research Companion to Fan Cultures*. Farnham: Ashgate.

Dutton, W.H., Blumler, J.G. and Kraemar, K.L. (eds) (1986) *Wired Cities: Shaping the Future of Communications*. Boston, MA: Chapman Hall.

Dutton, W.H. and Fernandez, L. (2019) 'How susceptible are Internet users?', *Intermedia*, 46: 4. http://dx.doi.org/10.2139/ssrn.3316768.

Eastman, S.T. (1979) 'Uses of television and consumer lifestyles: a multivariate analysis', *Journal of Broadcasting*, 23(3): 491–500.

Eastman, S.T. (1998) 'Programming theory under strain: the active industry and the active audience', in M.E. Roloff and G.D. Paulson (eds), *Communication Yearbook 21*, pp. 323–377. Thousand Oaks, CA: Sage.

Eco, U. (1977) *A Theory of Semiotics*. London: Macmillan.

Eco, U. (1979) *The Role of the Reader*. Bloomington, IN: University of Indiana Press.

Eisenberg, A.L. (1936) *Children and Radio Programs*. New York: Columbia University Press.

Eisenmann, T.R. and Bower, J.L. (2000) 'The entrepreneurial M-form: strategic integration in global media firms', *Organization Science*, 11(3): 348–355.

Eisenstein, E. (1978) *The Printing Press as an Agent of Change*, 2 vols. New York: Cambridge University Press.

Ekdale, B., Tully, M., Harmsen, S. and Singer, J.B. (2015) 'Newswork within a culture of job insecurity', *Journalism Practice*, 9(3): 383–398.

Elberse, A. (2008) 'Should you invest in the long tail?', *HBS Centennial Issue Harvard Business Review*, 86(7/8): 88–96.

Eldridge, J. (2000) 'The contribution of the Glasgow Media Group to the study of television and print journalism', *Journalism Studies*, 1(1): 113–127.

Elliott, P. (1972) *The Making of a Television Series: A Case Study in the Production of Culture*. London: Constable.

Ellis, J. (1982) *Visible Fictions*. Abingdon: Routledge and Kegan Paul.

Engwall, L. (1978) *Newspapers as Organizations*. Farnborough: Saxon House.

Enli, G. (2008) 'Redefining public service broadcasting', *Convergence*, 14(1): 103–120.

Enli, G. (2015) *Mediated Authenticity: How the Media Constructs Reality*. New York: Peter Lang.

Entman, R.M. (1989) *Democracy without Citizens: Media and the Decay of American Politics*. New York: Oxford University Press.

Entman, R.M. (1993) 'Framing: towards clarification of a fractured paradigm', *Journal of Communication*, 43(4): 51–58.

Entman, R.M. (2005) 'Media and democracy without party competition', in J. Curran and M. Gurevitch (eds), *Mass Media and Society*, 4th edition, pp. 251–270. London: Hodder Arnold.

Entman, R.M. (2007) 'Framing bias: media in the distribution of power', *Journal of Communication*, 57(1): 163–173.

Esser, A., Smith, I.R. and Bernal-Merino, M.A. (2018) *Media across Borders: Localising TV, Film and Video Games*. London/Abingdon: CRC Press/Routledge.

Esser, F. (1999) '"Tabloidization" of news – a comparative analysis of Anglo-American and German press journalism', *European Journal of Communication*, 14(3): 291–324.

Esser, F., Reinemann, C. and Fan, D. (2000) 'Spin doctoring in British and German election campaigns', *European Journal of Communication*, 15(2): 209–240.

Ettema, J. and Glasser, T. (1998) *Custodians of Conscience: Investigative Journalism and Public Virtue*. New York: Columbia.

Ettema, J.S. and Whitney, D.C. (eds) (1994) *Audiencemaking: How the Media Create the Audience*. Newbury Park, CA: Sage.

Etzioni, A. (1961) *Complex Organizations*. Glencoe, IL: Free Press.

Evans, J. (1999) 'Cultures of the visual', in J. Evans and S. Hall (eds), *Visual Culture: A Reader*, pp. 11–19. London: Sage.

Fast, K. and Jansson, A. (2019) *Transmedia Work: Privilege and Precariousness in Digital Modernity*. London/Abingdon: CRC Press/Routledge.

Fast, K., Örnebring, H. and Karlsson, M. (2016) 'Metaphors of free labor: a typology of unpaid work in the media sector', *Media, Culture & Society*, 38(7): 963–978.

Faustino, P. and Noam, E. (2019) 'Media industries' management characteristics and challenges in a converging digital world', in M. Deuze and M. Prenger (eds), *Making Media: Production, Practices and Professions*, pp. 147–162. Amsterdam: Amsterdam University Press.

Febvre, L. and Martin, H.J. (1984) *The Coming of the Book*. London: Verso.

Feezell, J.T., Conroy, M. and Guerrero, M. (2016) 'Internet use and political participation: engaging citizenship norms through online activities', *Journal of Information Technology & Politics*, 13(2): 95–107.

Feintuck, M. (1999) *Media Regulation, Public Interest and the Law*. Edinburgh: University of Edinburgh Press.

Fengler, S. (2003) 'Holding the news media accountable: a study of media reporters and media criticism in the US', *Journalism and Mass Communication Quarterly*, 80(4): 818–832.

Fengler, S. and Russ-Mohl, S. (2008) 'Journalists and the information-attention markets: towards an economic theory of journalism', *Journalism*, 9(6): 667–690.

Ferguson, C.J. and Kilburn, J. (2009) 'The public health risks of media violence: a meta-analytic review', *Journal of Pediatrics*, 154(5): 759–763.

Ferguson, D.A. and Perse, E.M. (2000) 'The WWW as a functional alternative to television', *Journal of Broadcasting and Electronic Media*, 44(2): 155–175.

Ferguson, M. (1983) *Forever Feminine: Women's Magazines and the Cult of Femininity*. London: Heinemann.

Ferguson, M. (1986) 'The challenge of neo-technological determinism for communication systems of industry and culture', in M. Ferguson (ed.), *New Communication Technologies and the Public Interest*, pp. 52–70. London: Sage.

Ferguson, M. (ed.) (1992) 'The mythology about globalization', *European Journal of Communication*, 7: 69–93.

Ferguson, M. and Golding, P. (eds) (1997) *Cultural Studies in Question*. London: Sage.

Ferrara, E. and Yang, Z. (2015) 'Measuring emotional contagion in social media', *PLoS ONE*, 10(11): e0142390.

Festinger, L.A. (1957) *A Theory of Cognitive Dissonance*. New York: Row Peterson.

Feuer, J. (1992) 'Genre study and television', in R.C. Allen (ed.), *Channels of Discourse, Reassembled: Television and Contemporary Criticism*, pp. 138–159. Abingdon: Routledge.

Fidler, R. (1997) *Mediamorphosis: Understanding New Media*. Thousand Oaks, CA: Pine Forge Press.

Fink, E.J. and Gantz, W. (1996) 'A content analysis of three mass communication research traditions: social science, interpretive studies, and critical analysis', *Journalism and Mass Communication Quarterly*, 73(1): 114–134.

Finn, S. (1997) 'Origins of media exposure: linking personality traits to TV, radio, print and film use', *Communication Research*, 24(5): 507–529.

Fiske, J. (1982) *Introduction to Communication Studies*. London: Methuen.

Fiske, J. (1987) *Television Culture*. London: Methuen.

Fiske, J. (1992) 'The cultural economy of fandom', in L. Lewis (ed.), *The Adoring Audience*, pp. 30–49. Abingdon: Routledge.

Fitzsimon, M. and McGill, L.T. (1995) 'The citizen as media critic', *Media Studies Journal*, Spring: 91–102.

Flegel, R.C. and Chaffee, S.H. (1971) 'Influences of editors, readers and personal opinion on reporters', *Journalism Quarterly*, 48: 645–651.

Fletcher, R. and Nielsen, R.K. (2017) 'Are news audiences increasingly fragmented? A cross-national comparative analysis of cross-platform news audience fragmentation and duplication', *Journal of Communication*, 67: 476–498.

Flew, T. (2016) 'National media regulations in an age of convergent media: beyond globalisation, neo-liberalism and internet freedom theories', in T. Flew, P. Iosifidis and J. Steemers (eds), *Global Media and National Policies*, pp. 75–91. New York: Springer.

Flew, T. (2018) *Understanding Global Media*, 2nd edition. London: Palgrave Macmillan.

Flew, T., Martin, F. and Suzor, N. (2019) 'Internet regulation as media policy: rethinking the question of digital communication platform governance', *Journal of Digital Media & Policy*, 10(1): 33–50.

Fornäs, J. (1995) *Cultural Theory and Late Modernity*. London: Sage.

Fortunati, L. (2001) 'The mobile phone: an identity on the move', *Personal and Ubiquitous Computing*, 5: 85–98.

Fortunati, L. (2005a) 'Mediatizing the net and intermediatizing the media', *International Communication Gazette*, 67(6): 29–44.

Fortunati, L. (2005b) ''Is body-to-body communication still the prototype?, *The Information Society*, 21: 53–61.

Fraile, M. and Iyengar, S. (2014) 'Not all news sources are equally informative: a cross-national analysis of political knowledge in Europe', *The International Journal of Press/Politics*, 19(3): 275–294.

Frank, R.E. and Greenberg, B. (1980) *The Public's View of Television*. Beverly Hills, CA: Sage.

French, J.R.P. and Raven, B.H. (1953) 'The bases of social power', in D. Cartwright and A. Zander (eds), *Group Dynamics*, pp. 259–69. London: Tavistock.

Friedson, E. (1953) 'Communications research and the concept of the mass', *American Sociological Review*, 18(3): 313–317.

Frith, S. (1981) *Sound Effects*. New York: Pantheon.

Fuchs, C. (2009) 'Information and communication technologies and society: a contribution to the critique of the political economy of the internet', *European Journal of Communication*, 24(1): 69–87.

Fuchs, C. (2016) *Critical Theory of Communication*. London: University of Westminster Press.

Fuchs, C. (2017) 'From digital positivism and administrative big data analytics towards critical digital and social media research!', *European Journal of Communication*, 32(1): 37–49.

Fuchs, C. and Mosco, V. (eds) (2016) *Marx in the Age of Digital Capitalism*. Leiden: Brill.

Fuchs, C. and Qiu, J.L. (2018) 'Ferments in the field: introductory reflections on the past, present and future of communication studies', *Journal of Communication*, 68(2): 219–232.

Gallagher, M. (2003) 'Feminist media perspectives', in A.N. Valdivia (ed.), *A Companion to Media Studies*, pp. 19–39. Oxford: Blackwell.

Galtung, J. and Ruge, M. (1965) 'The structure of foreign news', *Journal of Peace Research*, 1: 64–90. Also in J. Tunstall (ed.), *Media Sociology*, pp. 259–298. London: Constable.

Gamble, A. and Watanabe, T. (2004) *A Public Betrayed*. Washington, DC: Regnery Publishing.

Gamson, W. and Modigliani, A. (1989) 'Media discourse and public opinion on nuclear power: a constructivist approach', *American Journal of Sociology*, 95: 1–37.

Gans, H.J. (1979) *Deciding What's News*. New York: Vintage.

Gans, H.J. (2011) 'Multiperspectival news revisited: journalism and representative democracy', *Journalism*, 12(1): 3–13.

Garnham, N. (2000) *Emancipation, the Media, and Modernity*. Oxford: Oxford University Press.

Gauntlett, D. (2005) *Moving Experiences: Media Effects and Beyond*, 2nd edition. London: John Libbey Publishing.

Gaziano, C. and McGrath, K. (1987) 'Newspaper credibility and relationships of newspaper journalists to communities', *Journalism Quarterly*, 64(2): 317–328.

Geraghty, C. (1991) *Women and Soap Operas*. Cambridge: Polity Press.

Gerbaudo, P. and Treré, E. (2015) 'In search of the "we" of social media activism', *Information, Communication & Society*, 18(8): 865–871.

Gerbner, G. (1958) 'On content analysis and critical research in mass communication', *Audiovisual Communication Review*, 6(3): 85–108.

Gerbner, G. (1969) 'Institutional pressures on mass communicators', in P. Halmos (ed.), *The Sociology of Mass Media Communicators*, pp. 205–248. Keele: University of Keele.

Gerbner, G. (1973) 'Cultural indicators: the third voice', in G. Gerbner, L. Gross and W. Melody (eds), *Communications Technology and Social Policy*, pp. 553–573. New York: Wiley.

Gerbner, G. and Gross, L. (1976) 'Living with television: the violence profile', *Journal of Communication*, 26(2): 173–199.

Gerbner, G., Gross, L., Morgan, M. and Signorielli, N. (1984) 'The political correlates of TV viewing', *Public Opinion Quarterly*, 48: 283–300.

Gerbner, G. and Marvanyi, G. (1977) 'The many worlds of the world's press', *Journal of Communication*, 27(1): 52–66.

Giddens, A. (1991) *Modernity and Self-Identity*. Oxford: Polity Press.

Giddens, A. (1999) *Runaway World: How Globalisation is Shaping Our Lives*. London: Profile Books.

Gieber, W. (1956) 'Across the desk: a study of 16 *Telegraph* editors', *Journalism Quarterly*, 33: 423–433.

Giffard, C.A. (1989) *UNESCO and the Media*. White Plains, NY: Longman.

Gitlin, T. (1978) 'Media sociology: the dominant paradigm', *Theory and Society*, 6: 205–253. Reprinted in G.C. Wilhoit and H. de Back (eds) (1981), *Mass Communication Review Yearbook*, vol. 2, pp. 73–122. Beverly Hills, CA: Sage.

Gitlin, T. (1980) *The Whole World is Watching: Mass Media in the Making and Unmaking of the New Left*. Berkeley, CA: University of California Press.

Gitlin, T. (1989) 'Postmodernism: roots and politics', in I. Angus and S. Jhally (eds), *Cultural Politics in Contemporary America*, pp. 347–360. New York: Routledge.

Gitlin, T. (1997) 'The anti-political populism of cultural studies', in M. Ferguson and P. Golding (eds), *Cultural Studies in Question*, pp. 25–38. London: Sage.

Givskov, C. and Deuze, M. (2018) 'Researching new media and social diversity in later life', *New Media & Society*, 20(1): 399–412.

Glas, R., Lammes, S., de Lange, M., Raessens, J. and de Vries, I. (eds) (2019) *The Playful Citizen: Power, Creativity, Knowledge*. Amsterdam: Amsterdam University Press.

Glasgow Media Group (1976) *Bad News*. Abingdon: Routledge and Kegan Paul.

Glasgow Media Group (1980) *More Bad News*. Abingdon: Routledge and Kegan Paul.

Glasgow Media Group (1985) *War and Peace News*. Milton Keynes: Open University Press.

Glasser, T.L. (1984) 'Competition among radio formats', *Journal of Broadcasting*, 28(2): 127–142.

Glasser, T.L. (2009) 'Journalism and the second-order effect', *Journalism*, 2: 326–328.

Glynn, C.J., Hayes, A.F. and Shanahan, J. (1997) 'Perceived support for one's opinion and willingness to speak out', *Public Opinion Quarterly*, 61(3): 452–463.

Goffman, E. (1974) *Frame Analysis: An Essay on the Organization of Experience*. New York: Harper & Row.

Goffman, E. (1976) *Gender Advertisements*. London: Macmillan.

Goggin, G. (2006) *Cell Phone Culture: Mobile Technology in Everyday Life*. New York: Routledge.

Golding, P. (1977) 'Media professionalism in the Third World: the transfer of an ideology', in J. Curran, M. Gurevitch and J. Woollacott (eds), *Mass Communication and Society*, pp. 291–308. London: Edward Arnold.

Golding, P. (1981) 'The missing dimensions: news media and the management of change', in E. Katz and T. Szecsk (eds), *Mass Media and Social Change*. London: Sage.

Golding, P. and Harris, P. (1998) *Beyond Cultural Imperialism*. London: Sage.

Golding, P. and Murdock, G. (1978) 'Theories of communication and theories of society', *Communication Research*, 5(3): 339–356.

Golding, P. and van Snippenburg, L. (1995) 'Government communications and the media', in *Beliefs in Government*, vol. 30. London: Oxford University Press.

Goldstein, K. and Freedman, P. (2002) 'Lessons learned: campaign advertising in the 2000 elections', *Political Communication*, 19(1): 5–28.

Gouldner, A. (1976) *The Dialectic of Ideology and Technology*. London: Macmillan.

Grabe, M.E. (1999) 'Television news magazines and functionalism', *Critical Studies in Mass Communication*, 16: 155–171.

Grabe, M.E., Bas, O. and van Driel, I.I. (2015) 'Defecting from the Gutenberg legacy: employing images to test knowledge gaps', *Journal of Communication*, 65: 300–319.

Grabe, M.E. and Bucy, E.P. (2009) *Image Bite Politics: News and the Visual Framing of Elections*. New York: Oxford University Press.

Grabe, M.E., Lang, A. and Zhao, X. (2003) 'News content and form: implications for memory and audience evaluations', *Communication Research*, 30(4): 387–413.

Grabe, M.E. and Myrick, J.G. (2016) 'Informed citizenship in a media-centric way of life', *Journal of Communication*, 66: 215–235.

Grabe, M.E., Zhao, S. and Barnett, B. (2001) 'Explicating sensationalism in TV news: content and the bells and whistles of form', *Journal of Broadcasting and Electronic Media*, 45(2): 635–655.

Grabe, M.E., Zhou, S., Lang, A. and Boll, P.D. (2000) 'Packaging TV news: the effects of tabloids on information processing and evaluative response', *Journal of Broadcasting and Electronic Media*, 44(4): 581–598.

Graber, D. (1981) 'Political language', in D.D. Nimmo and D. Sanders (eds), *Handbook of Political Communication*, pp. 195–224. Beverly Hills, CA: Sage.

Graber, D. (1984) *Processing the News*. New York: Longman.

Graber, D. (1990) 'Seeing is remembering: how visuals contribute to TV news', *Journal of Communication*, 40 (3): 134–155.

Graber, D.A. (2001) *Processing Politics: Learning from Television in the Internet Age*. Chicago, IL: University of Chicago Press.

Grabher, G. (2002) 'The project ecology of advertising: tasks, talents and teams', *Regional Studies*, 36(3): 245–262.

Gramsci, A. (1971) *Selections from the Prison Notebooks*. London: Lawrence and Wishart.

Grasland, C. (2019) 'International news flow theory revisited through a space–time interaction model', *International Communication Gazette*, https://doi.org/10.1177/1748048518825091

Green, A. (2003) 'The development of mass media in Asia-Pacific', *International Journal of Advertising*, 22(2): 1–29.

Gregg, M. (2009) 'Learning to (love) labour: production cultures and the affective turn', *Communication and Critical/Cultural Studies*, 6(2): 209–214.

Gregg, M. and Seigworth, G.J. (eds) (2010) *The Affect Theory Reader*. Durham, NC: Duke University Press.

Greitemeyer, T. and Mügge, D.O. (2014) 'Video games do affect social outcomes: a meta-analytic review of the effects of violent and prosocial video game play', *Personality and Social Psychology Bulletin*, 40(5): 578–589.

Gripsrud, J. (1989) 'High culture revisited', *Cultural Studies*, 3(2): 194–197.

Groebel, J. (1998) 'The UNESCO global study on media violence', in U. Carlsson and C. von Feilitzen (eds), *Children and Media Violence*, pp. 155–180. Göteborg: University of Göteborg.

Gross, L.P. (1977) 'Television as a Trojan horse', *School Media Quarterly*, Spring: 175–180.

Grossberg, L. (1984) 'Strategies of Marxist cultural interpretation', *Critical Studies in Mass Communication*, 1(4): 392–421.

Grossberg, L. (1986) 'On postmodernism and articulation: an interview with Stuart Hall', *Journal of Communication Inquiry*, 10(2): 45–60.

Grossberg, L. (1988) 'Wandering audiences, nomadic critics', *Cultural Studies*, 2(3): 377–391.

Grossberg, L. (1989) 'MTV: swinging on the (postmodern) star', in I. Angus and S. Jhally (eds), *Cultural Politics in Contemporary Politics*, pp. 254–268. New York: Routledge.

Grossberg, L., Wartella, E. and Whitney, D.C. (1998) *Media Making: Mass Media in a Popular Culture*. Thousand Oaks, CA: Sage.

Gumucio-Dagron, A. (2004) 'Alternative media', in J.D.H. Downing, D. McQuail, P. Schlesinger and E. Wartella (eds), *The SAGE Handbook of Media Studies*, pp. 41–64. Thousand Oaks, CA: Sage.

Gunaratne, S. (2010) 'De-westernizing communication/social science research: opportunities and limitations', *Media, Culture & Society*, 32(3): 473–500.

Gunter, B. (2016) *Does Playing Video Games Make Players More Violent?* Basingstoke: Palgrave Macmillan.

Gunter, B. and Winstone, P. (1993) *Public Attitudes to Television*. London: John Libbey Publishing.

Gunther, A.C. (1998) 'The persuasive press inference: effects of the media on perceived public opinion', *Communication Research*, 25(5): 486–504.

Gunther, A.C. and Christen, C.-T. (2002) 'Projection or persuasive press? Contrary effects of personal opinion and perceived news coverage on estimates of public opinion', *Journal of Communication*, 52(1): 177–195.

Gunther, A.C. and Mughan, R. (2000) *Democracy and the Media*. Cambridge: Cambridge University Press.

Gurevitch, M., Bennet, T., Curran, J. and Woollacott, J. (eds) (1982) *Culture, Society and the Media*. London: Methuen.

Guzman, A. L. and Lewis, S. C. (2019) 'Artificial intelligence and communication: a human–machine communication research agenda', *New Media and Society*, https://doi.org/10.1177/1461444819858691

Habermas, J. (1962/1989) *The Structural Transformation of the Public Sphere*. Cambridge, MA: MIT Press.

Habermas, J. (1997) 'Modernity: an unfinished project', in M. Passerin d'Entrèves and S. Benhabib (eds), *Habermas and the Unfinished Project of Modernity: Critical Essays on The Philosophical Discourse of Modernity*, pp. 38–55. Boston, MA: MIT Press.

Habuchi, I. (2005) 'Accelerating reflexivity', in M. Ito, D. Okabe and M. Matsuda (eds), *Personal, Portable, Pedestrian: Mobile Phones in Japanese Life*. Cambridge, MA: MIT Press.

Hackett, K., Ramsden, P., Sattar, D. and Guene, C. (2000) *Banking on Culture: New Financial Instruments for Expanding the Cultural Sector in Europe*. Available at: https://webarchive.nationalarchives.gov.uk/20160204124325 or www.artscouncil.org.uk/advice-and-guidance/browse-advice-and-guidance/banking-on-culture-new-financial-instruments-for-expanding-the-cultural-sector-in-europe.

Hackett, R.A. (1984) 'Decline of a paradigm? Bias and objectivity in news media studies', *Critical Studies in Mass Communication*, 1: 229–259.

Haddon, L. (2016) 'The domestication of complex media repertoires', in K. Sandvik, A.M. Thorhauge and B. Valtysson (eds), *The Media and the Mundane*, pp. 17–30. Göteborg: Nordicom.

Hagen, I. (1999) 'Slaves of the ratings tyranny? Media images of the audience', in P. Alasuutari (ed.), *Rethinking the Media Audience*, pp. 130–150. London: Sage.

Hagood, M. (2011) 'Quiet comfort: noise, otherness, and the mobile production of personal space', *American Quarterly*, 63(3): 573–589.

Hagood, M. (2019) *Hush: Media and Sonic Self-control*. Durham, NC: Duke University Press.

Halavais, A. (2000) 'National borders on the world wide web', *New Media and Society*, 2(1): 7–28.

Hall, A. (2003) 'Reading realism: audiences' evaluations of the reality of media texts', *Journal of Communication*, 53(4): 624–641.

Hall, S. (1974/1980) 'Coding and encoding in the television discourse', in S. Hall et al. (eds), *Culture, Media, Language*, pp. 197–208. London: Hutchinson.

Hall, S. (1977) 'Culture, the media and the ideological effect', in J. Curran et al. (eds), *Mass Communication and Society*, pp. 315–348. London: Edward Arnold.

Hall, S. and Jefferson, T. (eds) (1975) 'Resistance through rituals', *Working Papers in Cultural Studies*, no. 7/8. Birmingham: The Centre for Contemporary Cultural Studies, University of Birmingham.

Hallett, T. and Ventresca, M. (2006) 'Inhabited institutions', *Theory and Society*, 35(2): 213–236.

Hallin, D.C. and Mancini, P. (1984) 'Political structure and representational form in US and Italian TV news', *Theory and Society*, 13(40): 829–850.

Hallin, D.C. and Mancini, P. (2004) *Comparing Media Systems*. Cambridge: Cambridge University Press.

Hallin, D.C. and Mancini, P. (eds) (2012) *Comparing Media Systems beyond the Western World*. Cambridge: Cambridge University Press.

Hameleers, M. et al. (2018) 'Start spreading the news: a comparative experiment on the effects of populist communication on political engagement in sixteen European countries', *The International Journal of Press/Politics*, 23(4): 517–538.

Hamelink, C. (1983) *Cultural Autonomy in Global Communications*. Norwood, NJ: Ablex.

Hamelink, C. (1994) *The Politics of Global Communication*. London: Sage.

Hamelink, C. (1998) 'New realities in the politics of world communication', *The Public*, 5(4): 71–74.

Hamelink, C. (2000) *The Ethics of Cyberspace*. London: Sage.

Hampton, K.N., Rainie, L., Lu, W., Dwyer, M., Shin, I. and Purcell, K. (2014) *Social Media and the 'Spiral of Silence'*. Washington, DC: Pew Research Center. Available at: www.pewinternet.org/2014/08/26/social-media-and-the-spiral-of-silence.

Hancox, D. (2017) 'From subject to collaborator: transmedia storytelling and social research', *Convergence*, 23(1): 49–60.

Handel, L. (1950) *Hollywood Looks at its Audience*. Urbana, IL: University of Illinois Press.

Hänggli, R. and Kriesi, H. (2012) 'Frame construction and frame promotion', *American Behavioral Scientist*, 56(3): 260–278.

Hanitzsch, T., Hanusch, F., Ramaprasad, J. and De Beer, A.S. (eds) (2019) *Worlds of Journalism: Journalistic Cultures around the Globe*. New York: Columbia University Press.

Hannerz, U. (1980) *Exploring the City: Inquiries Toward an Urban Anthropology*. New York: Columbia University Press.

Harcup, T. and O'Neill, D. (2017) 'What is news?', *Journalism Studies*, 18(12): 1470–1488.

Hardt, H. (1979) *Social Theories of the Press: Early German and American Perspectives*. Beverly Hills, CA: Sage.

Hardt, H. (1991) *Critical Communication Studies*. Abingdon: Routledge.

Hardt, H. (2003) *Social Theories of the Press*, 2nd edition. Lanham, MD: Rowman and Littlefield.

Hargittai, E. (2004) 'Internet access and use in context', *New Media and Society*, 6(1): 115–121.

Hargrave, A.M. and Livingstone, S. (2006) *Harm and Offence in Media Content*. Bristol: Intellect.

Hartley, J. (1982) *Understanding News*. London: Methuen.

Hartley, J. (1992) *The Politics of Pictures*. Abingdon: Routledge.

Hartley, J. (ed.) (2005) *Creative Industries*. Malden, MA: Blackwell.

Hartley, J. (2012) *Digital Futures for Cultural and Media Studies*. New York: Wiley.

Hartman, P. and Husband, C. (1974) *Racism and Mass Media*. London: Davis Poynter.

Hartmann, M. (2006) 'The triple articulation of ICTs: media as technological objects, symbolic environments and individual texts', in T. Berker, M. Hartmann, Y. Punie and K. Ward (eds), *Domestication of Media and Technology*, pp. 80–102. Maidenhead: Open University Press.

Hartmann, M. (2009) 'The changing urban landscapes of media consumption and production', *European Journal of Communication*, 24(4): 421–436.

Harvey, D. (1989) *The Condition of Postmodernity*. Oxford: Blackwell.

Hassan, R. (2008) *The Information Society*. Cambridge: Polity Press.

Hassler-Forest, D. and Guynes, S. (eds) (2018) *Star Wars and the History of Transmedia Storytelling*. Amsterdam: Amsterdam University Press.

Hawkins, R.P. and Pingree, S. (1983) 'TV's influence on social reality', in E. Wartella et al. (eds), *Mass Communication Review Yearbook*, vol. 4, pp. 53–76. Beverly Hills, CA: Sage.

Hayles, K. (2012) *How We Think: Digital Media and Contemporary Technogenesis*. Chicago, IL: University of Chicago Press.

Hayles, N.K. (2004) 'Print is flat, code is deep: the importance of media-specific analysis', *Poetics Today*, 25(1): 67–90.

Hebdige, D. (1978) *Subculture: The Meaning of Style*. London: Methuen.

Heeter, C. (1988) 'The choice process model', in C. Heeter and B.S. Greenberg (eds), *Cable Viewing*, pp. 11–32. Norwood, NJ: Ablex.

Heinderyckx, F. (1993) 'TV news programmes in West Europe: a comparative study', *European Journal of Communication*, 8(4): 425–450.

Held, D. (2010) *Cosmopolitanism: Ideals and Realities*. Cambridge: Polity Press.

Held, V. (1970) *The Public Interest and Individual Interests*. New York: Basic Books.

Hellman, H. (2001) 'Diversity: an end in itself?', *European Journal of Communication Research*, 16(2): 281–308.

Helmond, A. (2015, September) 'The platformization of the web: making web data platform ready', *Social Media + Society*, https://doi.org/10.1177/2056305115603080

Helsper, E.J. (2012) 'A corresponding fields model for the links between social and digital exclusion', *Communication Theory*, 22: 403–426.

Hemánus, P. (1976) 'Objectivity in news transmission', *Journal of Communication*, 26: 102–107.

Henrich, J., Heine, S.J. and Norenzayan, A. (2010) 'The weirdest people in the world?', *Behavioral and Brain Sciences*, 33(2–3): 61–83.

Hepp, A. (2013) 'The communicative figurations of mediatized worlds: mediatization research in times of the "mediation of everything"', *European Journal of Communication*, 28(6): 615–629.

Hepp, A. (2019) *Deep Mediatization*. Abingdon: Routledge.

Hepp, A., Breiter, A. and Hasebrink, U. (eds) (2018) *Communicative Figurations: Transforming Communications in Times of Deep Mediatization*. Cham: Springer.

Hepp, A., Hjarvard, S. and Lundby, K. (2015) 'Mediatization: theorizing the interplay between media, culture and society', *Media, Culture & Society*, 37(2): 314–324.

Herman, E. and Chomsky, N. (1988) *Manufacturing Consent: The Political Economy of Mass Media*. New York: Pantheon.

Hermes, J. (1995) *Reading Women's Magazines*. Cambridge: Polity Press.

Hermes, J. (1997) 'Gender and media studies: no woman, no cry', in J. Corner, P. Schlesinger and R. Silverstone (eds), *International Media Research*, pp. 65–95. Abingdon: Routledge.

Hermes, J. (1999) 'Media figures in identity construction', in P. Alasuutari (ed.), *Rethinking the Media Audience*, pp. 69–85. London: Sage.

Hermes, J. (2005) *Re-reading Popular Culture: Rethinking Gender, Television, and Popular Media Audiences*. Malden, MA: Wiley-Blackwell.

Hermes, J. (2007) 'Media representations of social structure: gender', in E. Devereux (ed.), *Media Studies*, pp. 191–210. London: Sage.

Hermes, J., Kooijman, J., Littler, J. and Wood, H. (2017) 'On the move: twentieth anniversary editorial of the *European Journal of Cultural Studies*', *European Journal of Cultural Studies*, 20(6): 595–605.

Hermida, A. (2010) 'Twittering the news: the emergence of ambient journalism', *Journalism Practice*, 4(3): 297–308.

Herrero, L.C., Humprecht, E., Engesser, S., Brüggemann, M. and Büchel, F. (2017) 'Rethinking Hallin and Mancini beyond the West: an analysis of media systems in Central and Eastern Europe', *International Journal of Communication*, 11: 4797–4823.

Herzog, H. (1944) 'What do we really know about daytime serial listeners?', in P.F. Lazarsfeld (ed.), *Radio Research 1942–3*, pp. 2–23. New York: Duell, Sloan and Pearce.

Hesmondhalgh, D. (2005) 'Subcultures, scenes or tribes? None of the above', *Journal of Youth Studies*, 8(1): 21–40.

Hesmondhalgh, D. (2010) 'Media industry studies, media production studies', in J. Curran (ed.), *Media and Society*, p. 147. London: Bloomsbury Academic.

Hesmondhalgh, D. (2018) *The Cultural Industries*, 4th edition. London: Sage.

Hesmondhalgh, D. and Baker, S. (2011) *Creative Labour: Media Work in Three Cultural Industries*. Abingdon: Routledge.

Hesmondhalgh, D. and Baker, S. (2015) 'Sex, gender and work segregation in the cultural industries', *The Sociological Review*, 63: 23–36.

Hesmondhalgh, D. and Toynbee, J. (eds) (2008) *The Media and Social Theory*. Abingdon: Routledge.

Hetherington, A. (1985) *News, Newspapers and Television*. London: Macmillan.

Hijmans, E. (1996) 'The logic of qualitative media content analysis: a typology', *Communications*, 21(1): 93–108.

Hill, A. (2018) *Media Experiences*. Abingdon: Routledge.

Hills, J. (2002) *The Struggle for the Control of Global Communication*. Urbana, IL: University of Illinois Press.

Himmelweit, H.T., Vince, P. and Oppenheim, A.N. (1958) *Television and the Child*. London: Oxford University Press.

Hirsch, P.M. (1977) 'Occupational, organizational and institutional models in mass communication', in P.M. Hirsch et al. (eds), *Strategies for Communication Research*, pp. 13–42. Beverly Hills, CA: Sage.

Hirsch, P.M. (1980) 'The "scary world" of the non-viewer and other anomalies: a reanalysis of Gerbner et al.'s findings in cultivation analysis, Part 1', *Communication Research*, 7(4): 403–456.

Hirsch, P.M. (1981) 'On not learning from one's mistakes, Part II', *Communication Research*, 8(1): 3–38.

Hjarvard, S. (2008a) '"The mediatization of society": a study of media as agents of social and cultural change', *Nordicom Review*, 29(1): 105–134.

Hjarvard, S. (2008b) 'The mediatization of religion: a theory of the media as agents of religious change', *Northern Lights*, 6(1): 9–26.

Hobson, D. (1982) *Crossroads: The Drama of Soap Opera*. London: Methuen.

Hobson, D. (1989) 'Soap operas at work', in F. Seiter et al. (eds), *Remote Control*, pp. 130–149. Abingdon: Routledge.

Hodges, L. (1986) 'Defining press responsibility: a functional approach', in D. Elliot (ed.), *Responsible Journalism*, pp. 13–31. Beverly Hills, CA: Sage.

Hodges, L. (2004) 'Accountability in journalism', *Journal of Mass Media Ethics*, 19(3&4): 173–180.

Hoffmann-Riem, W. (1996) *Regulating Media*. New York: Guilford Press.

Hoffner, C.H., Plotkin, R.S. et al. (2001) 'The third-person effects in perceptions of the influence of TV violence', *Journal of Communication*, 51(2): 383–399.

Hoijer, B. (2000) 'Audiences' expectations and interpretations of different TV genres', in I. Hagen and J. Wasko (eds), *Consuming Audiences? Production and Reception in Media Research*, pp. 189–208. Cresskill, NJ: Hampton Press.

Holub, R. (1984) *Reception Theory*. London: Methuen.

Hopmann, D.N., van Aelst, P. and Legnante, G. (2012) 'Political balance in the news: a review of concepts, operationalizations and key findings', *Journalism*, 13(2): 240–257.

Horsti, K. (2003) 'Global mobility and the media: presenting asylum seekers as a threat', *Nordicom Review*, 24(1): 41–54.

Horton, D. and Wohl, R.R. (1956) 'Mass communication and parasocial interaction', *Psychiatry*, 19: 215–229.

Horvath, C.W. (2004) 'Measuring TV addiction', *Journal of Broadcasting and Electronic Media*, 48(3): 378–398.

Hoskins, C. and Mirus, R. (1988) 'Reasons for the US dominance of the international trade in television programmes', *Media, Culture & Society*, 10: 499–515.

Hovland, C.I., Lumsdaine, A.A. and Sheffield, F.D. (1949) *Experiments in Mass Communication*. Princeton, NJ: Princeton University Press.

Howley, K. (2009) *Community Media: People, Places, and Communication Technologies*. Cambridge: Cambridge University Press.

Hoyler, M. and Watson, A. (2013) 'Global media cities in transnational media networks', *Tijdschrift voor Economische en Sociale Geografie*, 104: 90–108.

Huaco, G.A. (1963) *The Sociology of Film Art*. New York: Basic Books.

Huesca, R. (2003) 'From modernization to participation: the past and future of development communication in media studies', in A.N. Valdivia (ed.), *A Companion to Media Studies*, pp. 50–71. Oxford: Blackwell.

Huesmann, L.R. (1986) 'Psychological processes prompting the relation between exposure to media violence and aggressive behavior by the viewer', *Journal of Social Issues*, 42(3): 125–139.

Hughes, H.M. (1940) *News and the Human Interest Story*. Chicago, IL: University of Chicago Press.

Hughes, M. (1980) 'The fruits of cultivation analysis: a re-examination of some effects of TV viewing', *Public Opinion Quarterly*, 44(3): 287–302.

Innis, H. (1950) *Empire and Communication*. Oxford: Clarendon Press.

Innis, H. (1951) *The Bias of Communication*. Toronto: University of Toronto Press.

Iosifides, P. (2002) 'Digital convergence: challenges for European regulation', *The Public*, 9(3): 27–48.

Ishikawa, S. (ed.) (1996) *Quality Assessment of Television*. Luton: Luton University Press.

Ito, M. (2005) 'Technologies of the childhood imagination: Yugioh, media mixes, and everyday cultural production', in J. Karaganis and N. Jeremijenko (eds), *Structures of Participation in Digital Culture*. Durham, NC: Duke University Press.

Ito, Y. (1981) 'The "Johoka Shakai" approach to the study of communication in Japan', in G.C. Wilhoit and H. de Bock (eds), *Mass Communication Review Yearbook*, vol. 2. Beverly Hills, CA: Sage.

Ito, Y. and Koshevar, I.J. (1983) 'Factors accounting for the flow of international communications', *Keio Communication Review*, 4: 13–38.

Iyengar, S. and Kinder, D.R. (1987) *News That Matters: Television and American Opinion*. Chicago, IL: University of Chicago Press.

Izushi, H. and Aoyama, Y. (2006) 'Industry evolution and cross-sectoral skill transfers: a comparative analysis of the video game industry in Japan, the United States, and the United Kingdom', *Environment and Planning A*, 38: 1843–1861.

Jacobs, K., Janssen, M. and Pasquinelli, M. (eds) (2007) *C'LICKME: A Netporn Studies Reader*. Amsterdam: Institute of Network Cultures.

Jakubovicz, K. (2007) 'The Eastern European/post communist media model countries', in G. Terzis (ed.), *European Media Governance*, pp. 303–314. Bristol: Intellect.

Jameson, F. (1984) 'Postmodernism: the cultural logic of late capitalism', *New Left Review*, 146(July–August): 53–92.

Jamieson, K.H. and Cappella, J.N. (2008) *Echo Chamber*. Oxford: Oxford University Press.

Jamieson, P.E. and Romer, D. (2014) 'Violence in popular U.S. prime time TV dramas and the cultivation of fear: a time series analysis', *Media and Communication*, 2(2): 31–41.

Jankowski, N. (2002) 'Creating community with media', in L. Lievrouw and S. Livingstone (eds), *The Handbook of New Media*, pp. 34–49. London: Sage.

Janowitz, M. (1952) *The Community Press in an Urban Setting*. Glencoe, IL: Free Press.

Janowitz, M. (1968) 'The study of mass communication', in *International Encyclopedia of the Social Sciences*, vol. 3, pp. 41–53. New York: Macmillan.

Janowitz, M. (1975) 'Professional models in journalism: the gatekeeper and advocate', *Journalism Quarterly*, 52(4): 618–626.

Jansen, S.C. (1988) *Censorship*. New York: Oxford University Press.

Jansson, A. and Falkheimer, J. (2006) *Geographies of Communication: The Spatial Turn in Media Studies*. Göteborg: Nordicom.

Jay, M. (1973) *The Dialectical Imagination*. London: Heinemann.

Jenkins, H. (1988) 'Star Trek rerun, reread, rewritten: fan writing as textual poaching', *Critical Studies in Mass Communication*, 5(2): 85–107.

Jenkins, H. (2004) 'The cultural logic of media convergence', *International Journal of Cultural Studies*, 7(1): 33–43.

Jenkins, H. (2006) *Convergence Culture: Where Old and New Media Collide*. New York: New York University Press.

Jenkins, H. (2007) 'Transmedia storytelling 101', *Confessions of an Aca-fan* weblog, 21 March. Available at: http://henryjenkins.org/blog/2007/03/transmedia_storytelling_101.html.

Jenkins, H. and Deuze, M. (2008) 'Convergence culture', *Convergence*, 14(1): 5–12.

Jenkins, H., Ford, S. and Green, J. (2013) *Spreadable Media*. New York: New York University Press.

Jenkins, H., Shresthova, S., Gamber-Thompson, L., Kligler-Vilenchik, N. and Zimmerman, A. (2016) *By Any Media Necessary: The New Youth Activism*. New York: New York University Press.

Jensen, K.B. (1991) 'When is meaning? Communication theory, pragmatism and mass media reception', in J. Anderson (ed.), *Communication Yearbook 14*, pp. 3–32. Newbury Park, CA: Sage.

Jensen, K.B. (2018) 'The double hermeneutics of communication research', *Javnost – The Public*, 25(1–2): 177–183.

Jensen, K.B. (2019) 'The double hermeneutics of audience research', *Television & New Media*, 20(2): 142–154.

Jensen, K.B. and Jankowski, N. (eds) (1991) *A Handbook of Qualitative Methodologies*. Abingdon: Routledge.

Jensen, K.B. and Rosengren, K.E. (1990) 'Five traditions in search of the audience', *European Journal of Communication*, 5(2/3): 207–238.

Jhally, S. and Livant, B. (1986) 'Watching as working: the valorization of audience consciousness', *Journal of Communication*, 36(2): 124–163.

Jia, W. (2017) 'Chinese communication studies: three paths converging', *Westminster Papers in Communication and Culture*, 12(1): 33–34.

Johansson, T. and Miegel, F. (1992) *Do the Right Thing*. Stockholm: Almqvist and Wiksell.

Johns, J. (2006) 'Video game production networks: value capture, power relations and embeddedness', *Journal of Economic Geography*, 6(2): 151–180.

Johnson, D. (2011) 'Devaluing and revaluing seriality: the gendered discourses of media franchising', *Media, Culture & Society*, 33(7): 1077–1093.

Johnson R. (1986) 'What is cultural studies anyway?', *Social Text*, 16: 36–80.

Johnstone, J.W.L., Slawski, E.J. and Bowman, W.W. (1976) *The News People*. Urbana, IL: University of Illinois Press.

Jones, S.G. (ed.) (1997) *Virtual Culture: Identity and Communication in Cybersociety*. London: Sage.

Jones, S.G. (ed.) (1998) *Cybersociety 2.0: Revisiting Computer-Mediated Communication and Community*. London: Sage.

Jouhki, J., Lauk, E., Penttinen, M., Sormanen, N. and Uskali, T. (2016) 'Facebook's emotional contagion experiment as a challenge to research ethics', *Media and Communication*, 4(4): 75–85.

Jowett, G. and Linton, J.M. (1980) *Movies as Mass Communication*. Beverly Hills, CA: Sage.

Jowett, G. and O'Donnell, V. (1999) *Propaganda and Persuasion*, 3rd edition. Beverly Hills, CA: Sage.

Joye, S., Heinrich, A. and Wöhlert, R. (2016) '50 years of Galtung and Ruge: reflections on their model of news values and its relevance for the study of journalism and communication today', *Communication and Media*, XI(36): 5–28.

Juul, J. (2005) *Half-Real: Video Games between Real Rules and Fictional Worlds*. Boston, MA: MIT Press.

Kaminsky, S.M. (1974) *American Film Genres*. Dayton, OH: Pflaum.

Kaplan, E.A. (1987) *Rocking around the Clock: Music Television, Postmodernism and Consumer Culture*. London: Methuen.

Kaplan, E.A. (1992) 'Feminist critiques and television', in R.C. Allen (ed.), *Channels of Discourse Reassembled*, pp. 247–283. Abingdon: Routledge.

Karatzogianni, A. (2015) *Firebrand Waves of Digital Activism 1994–2014*. New York: Springer.

Karatzogianni, A. and Kuntsman, A. (2012) *Digital Cultures and the Politics of Emotion: Feelings, Affect and Technological Change*. Basingstoke: Palgrave Macmillan.

Karppingen, K. (2007) 'Against naïve pluralism in media politics: on implications of radical-pluralist approach to the public sphere', *Media, Culture & Society*, 29(3): 495–508.

Katz, E. (1977) *Social Research and Broadcasting: Proposals for Further Development*. London: BBC.

Katz, E. (1983) 'Publicity and pluralistic ignorance: notes on the spiral of silence', in E. Wartella et al. (eds), *Mass Communication Review Yearbook*, vol. 4, pp. 89–99. Beverly Hills, CA: Sage.

Katz, E. (1988) 'Disintermediation: cutting out the middle man', *Intermedia*, 16(2): 30–31.

Katz, E., Blumler, J.G. and Gurevitch, M. (1974) 'Utilization of mass communication by the individual', in J.G. Blumler and E. Katz (eds), *The Uses of Mass Communication*, pp. 19–32. Beverly Hills, CA: Sage.

Katz, E., Gurevitch, M. and Haas, H. (1973) 'On the use of mass media for important things', *American Sociological Review*, 38: 164–181.

Katz, E. and Lazarsfeld, P.F. (1955) *Personal Influence*. Glencoe, IL: Free Press.

Kaun, A. and Uldam, J. (2018) 'Digital activism: after the hype', *New Media and Society*, 20(6): 2099–2106.

Kepplinger, H.M. (1983) 'Visual biases in TV campaign coverage', in E. Wartella et al. (eds), *Mass Communication Review Yearbook*, vol. 4, pp. 391–405. Beverly Hills, CA: Sage.

Kepplinger, H.M. and Habermeier, J. (1995) 'The impact of key events on the presentation of reality', *European Journal of Communication*, 10(3): 371–390.

Kepplinger, H.M. and Koecher, R. (1990) 'Professionalism in the media world?', *European Journal of Communication*, 5(2/3): 285–311.

Kerr, A. (2006) *The Business and Culture of Digital Games*. London: Sage.

Kerr, A. (2016) *Global Games: Production, Circulation and Policy in the Networked Era*. Abingdon: Routledge.

Kim, S.J. (2016) 'A repertoire approach to cross-platform media use behavior', *New Media and Society*, 18(3): 353–372.

Kingsbury, S.M. and Hart, M. (1937) *Newspapers and the News*. New York: Putnam.

Kiousis, S. (2002) 'Interactivity: a concept explication', *New Media and Society*, 4(3): 329–354.

Kitzinger, J. (2007) 'Framing and frame analysis', in E. Devereux (ed.), *Media Studies*, pp. 134–161. London: Sage.

Klapper, J. (1960) *The Effects of Mass Communication*. New York: Free Press.

Knee, J.A., Greenwald, B.C. and Seave, A. (2009) *The Curse of the Mogul*. New York: Penguin Random House.

Knight, A., Geuze, C. and Gerlis, A. (2008) 'Who is a journalist?', *Journalism Studies*, 9(1): 117–131.

Knobloch-Westerwick, S., Glynn, C.J. and Huge, M. (2013) 'The Matilda Effect in science communication: an experiment on gender bias in publication quality perceptions and collaboration interest', *Science Communication*, 35(5): 603–625.

Kosterich, A. and Napoli, P.M. (2016) 'Reconfiguring the audience commodity: the institutionalization of social TV analytics as market information regime', *Television & New Media*, 17(3): 254–271.

Kowert, R. and Quandt, T. (eds) (2015) *The Video Game Debate: Unravelling the Physical, Social, and Psychological Effects of Video Games*. Abingdon: Routledge.

Kracauer, S. (1949) 'National types as Hollywood represents them', *Public Opinion Quarterly*, 13: 53–72.

Kraidy, M. (2003) 'Glocalisation: an international communication framework?', *Journal of International Communication*, 9(2): 29–49.

Krajina, Z., Moores, S. and Morley, D. (2014) 'Non-media-centric media studies: a cross-generational conversation', *European Journal of Cultural Studies*, 17(6): 682–700.

Kramer, A.D., Guillory, J.E. and Hancock, J.T. (2014) 'Experimental evidence of massive-scale emotional contagion through social networks', *Proceedings of the National Academy of Sciences*, 111(24): 8788–8790.

Krämer, S. (2015) *Medium, Messenger, Transmission: An Approach to Media Philosophy*. Amsterdam: Amsterdam University Press.

Kraus, S. and Davis, D.K. (1976) *The Effects of Mass Communication on Political Behavior*. University Park, PA: Pennsylvania State University Press.

Krippendorf, K. (2004) *Content Analysis*, 2nd edition. Thousand Oaks, CA: Sage.

Krotz, F. (2007) 'The meta-process of "mediatization" as a conceptual frame', *Global Media and Communication*, 3(3): 256–260.

Kruikemeier, S., Gattermann, K. and Vliegenthart, R. (2018) 'Understanding the dynamics of politicians' visibility in traditional and social media', *The Information Society*, 34(4): 215–228.

Kruikemeier, S., Sezgin, M. and Boerman, S.C. (2016) 'Political microtargeting: relationship between personalized advertising on Facebook and voters' responses', *Cyberpsychology, Behavior and Social Networking*, 19(6): 367–372.

Ksiazek, T.B. (2011) 'A network analytic approach to understanding cross-platform audience behavior', *Journal of Media Economics*, 24(4): 237–251.

Küng, L. (2017) *Strategic Management in the Media*, 2nd edition. London: Sage.

Küng, L., Picard, R.G. and Towse, R. (eds) (2008) *The Internet and the Mass Media*. London: Sage.

Kuss, D.J. and Fernandez, O. (2016) 'Internet addiction and problematic Internet use: a systematic review of clinical research', *World Journal of Psychiatry*, 6(1): 143–176.

Lacy, S. and Martin, H.J. (2004) 'Competition, circulation and advertising', *Newspaper Research Journal*, 25(1): 18–39.

Lampel, J., Lant, T. and Jamal, S. (2000) 'Balancing act: learning from organizing practices in cultural industries', *Organization Science*, 11(3): 263–269.

Lang, A. (2013) 'Discipline in crisis? The shifting paradigm of mass communication research', *Communication Theory*, 23: 10–24.

Lang, G. and Lang, K. (1981) 'Mass communication and public opinion: strategies for research', in M. Rosenberg and R.H. Turner (eds), *Social Psychology: Sociological Perspectives*, pp. 653–682. New York: Basic Books.

Langer, J. (2003) 'Tabloid television and news culture', in S. Cottle (ed.), *News, Public Relations and Power*, pp. 135–52. London: Sage.

Lantos, G.P. (1987) 'Advertising: looking glass or molder of the masses?', *Journal of Public Policy & Marketing*, 6(1): 104–128.

Lanzen, M.M., Dozier, D.M. and Horan, N. (2008) 'Constructing gender stereotypes through social roles in prime-time TV', *Journal of Broadcasting and Electronic Media*, 52(2): 200–214.

LaRose, R. and Eastin, M.S. (2004) 'A social cognitive theory of internet uses and gratifications: towards a new model of media attendance', *Journal of Broadcasting and Electronic Media*, 48(3): 358–377.

Lash, S. (2002) *Critique of Information*. London: Sage.

Lasswell, H. (1927) *Propaganda Techniques in the First World War*. New York: Knopf.

Lasswell, H. (1948) 'The structure and function of communication in society', in L. Bryson (ed.), *The Communication of Ideas*, pp. 32–51. New York: Harper & Row.

Latour, B. (1993) *We Have Never Been Modern*. Cambridge, MA: Harvard University Press.

Law, J. (1992) *Notes on the Theory of the Actor Network: Ordering, Strategy and Heterogeneity*. Available at: www.lancs.ac.uk/fass/sociology/papers/law-notes-on-ant.pdf.

Lazarsfeld, P.F. (1941) 'Remarks on administrative and critical communication research studies', *Philosophy and Social Science*, IX(2).

Lazarsfeld, P.F. and Stanton, F. (1944) *Radio Research 1942–3*. New York: Duell, Sloan and Pearce.

Lazarsfeld, P.F. and Stanton, F. (1949) *Communication Research 1948–9*. New York: Harper & Row.

Leadbeater, C. and Oakley, K. (1999) *The New Independents*. London: Demos. Available at: www.demos.co.uk/publications/independents

Lecheler, S., Schuck, A.R.T. and De Vreese, C.H. (2013) 'Dealing with feelings: positive and negative discrete emotions as mediators of news framing effects', *Communications*, 38(2): 189–209.

Lee, F.L.F. and Chan, J. (2015) 'Digital media activities and mode of participation in a protest campaign: a study of the Umbrella Movement', *Information, Communication & Society*, 19: 4–22.

Lehman-Wilzig, S. and Cohen-Avigdor, N. (2004) 'The natural life cycle of new media evolution', *New Media and Society*, 6(6): 707–730.

Leiss, W. (1989) 'The myth of the information society', in I. Angus and S. Jhally (eds), *Cultural Politics in Contemporary America*, pp. 282–298. New York: Routledge.

Lemert, J.B. (1989) *Criticizing the Media*. Newbury Park, CA: Sage.

Lerner, D. (1958) *The Passing of Traditional Society*. New York: Free Press.

Lessig, L. (1999) *Code and Other Laws of Cyberspace*. New York: Basic Books.

Leung, L. and Chen, C. (2018, August) 'A review of media addiction research from 1991 to 2016', *Social Science Computer Review*, 1–18, https://doi.org/10.1177/0894439318791770.

Leurs, K. (2019) 'Transnational connectivity and the affective paradoxes of digital care labour: Exploring how young refugees technologically mediate co-presence', *European Journal of Communication*, 34(6): 641–649.

Levy, M.R. (1977) 'Experiencing television news', *Journal of Communication*, 27: 112–117.

Levy, M.R. (1978) 'The audience experience with television news', *Journalism Monographs*, 55.

Levy, M.R. and Windahl, S. (1985) 'The concept of audience activity', in K.E. Rosengren et al. (eds), *Media Gratification Research*, pp. 109–122. Beverly Hills, CA: Sage.

Lewis, G.H. (1981) 'Taste cultures and their composition: towards a new theoretical perspective', in E. Katz and T. Szecskö (eds), *Mass Media and Social Change*, pp. 201–217. Newbury Park, CA: Sage.

Lewis, G.H. (1992) 'Who do you love? The dimensions of musical taste', in J. Lull (ed.), *Popular Music and Communication*, 2nd edition, pp. 134–151. Newbury Park, CA: Sage.

Lewis, S.C. (2012) 'The tension between professional control and open participation', *Information, Communication & Society*, 15(6): 836–866.

Lewis, S.C., Holton, A.E. and Coddington, M. (2014) 'Reciprocal journalism', *Journalism Practice*, 8(2): 229–241.

Lewis, S.C. and Westlund, O. (2015) 'Actors, actants, audiences, and activities in cross-media news work', *Digital Journalism*, 3(1): 19–37.

Liebes, T. and Katz, E. (1986) 'Patterns of involvement in television fiction: a comparative analysis', *European Journal of Communication*, 1(2): 151–172.

Liebes, T. and Katz, E. (1990) *The Export of Meaning: Cross-Cultural Readings of 'Dallas'*. Oxford: Oxford University Press.

Liebes, T. and Livingstone, S. (1998) 'European soap operas', *European Journal of Communication*, 13(2): 147–180.

Lievrouw, L.A. (2004) 'What's changed about new media?', *New Media and Society*, 6(1): 9–15.

Lievrouw, L.A. and Livingstone, S. (eds) (2006) *The Handbook of New Media*, 2nd edition. London: Sage.

Lindlof, T.R. (1988) 'Media audiences as interpretive communities', in J. Anderson (ed.), *Communication Yearbook* 11, pp. 81–107. Newbury Park, CA: Sage.

Lindlof, T.R. and Schatzer, J. (1998) 'Media ethnography in virtual space: strategies, limits and possibilities', *Journal of Broadcasting and Electronic Media*, 42(2): 170–189.

Lippmann, W. (1922) *Public Opinion*. New York: Harcourt Brace.

Livingstone, S. (1988) 'Why people watch soap opera: an analysis of the explanations of British viewers', *European Journal of Communication*, 31(1): 55–80.

Livingstone, S. (1999) 'New media, new audiences?', *New Media and Society*, 1(1): 59–66.

Livingstone, S. (2002) *Young People and New Media*. London: Sage.

Livingstone, S. (2007) 'From family television to bedroom culture: young people's media at home', in E. Devereux (ed.), *Media Culture*, pp. 302–321. London: Sage.

Livingstone, S. (2009) 'On the mediation of everything', *Journal of Communication*, 59(1): 1–18.

Livingstone, S. (2011) 'If everything is mediated, what is distinctive about the field of communication?', *International Journal of Communication*, 5: 1472–1475.

Livingstone, S. (2013) 'The participation paradigm in audience research', *The Communication Review*, 16(1–2): 21–30.

Livingstone, S. (2015) 'Active audiences? The debate progresses but is far from resolved', *Communication Theory*, 25: 439–446.

Livingstone, S. and Helsper, E. (2010) 'Balancing opportunities and risks in teenagers' use of the internet: the role of online skills and internet self-efficacy', *New Media and Society*, 12(2): 309–329.

Livingstone, S. and Sefton-Green. J. (2016) *The Class: Living and Learning in the Digital Age*. New York: New York University Press.

Livingstone, S. and Third, A. (2017) 'Children and young people's rights in the digital age: an emerging agenda', *New Media and Society*, 19(5): 657–670.

Long, E. (1991) 'Feminism and cultural studies', in R. Avery and D. Eason (eds), *Cultural Perspectives on Media and Society*, pp. 114–125. New York: Guilford Press.

Loosen, W. and Schmidt, J.-H. (2012) '(Re-)discovering the audience', *Information, Communication & Society*, 15(6): 867–887.

Lowe, G.F. and Brown, C. (eds) (2016) *Managing Media Firms and Industries*. New York: Springer.

Lowery, S.A. and DeFleur, M.L. (eds) (1995) *Milestones in Mass Communication Research*, 3rd edition. New York: Longman.

Lüders, M. (2008) 'Conceptualizing personal media', *New Media and Society*, 10(5): 683–702.

Luhmann, N. (2000) *The Reality of the Mass Media*. Cambridge: Polity Press.

Lull, J. (1982) 'The social uses of television', in D.C. Whitney et al. (eds), *Mass Communication Review Yearbook*, vol. 3, pp. 397–409. Beverly Hills, CA: Sage.

Lull, J. (ed.) (1992) *Popular Music and Communication*. Newbury Park, CA: Sage.

Lull, J. and Wallis, R. (1992) 'The beat of Vietnam', in J. Lull (ed.), *Popular Music and Communication*, pp. 207–236. Newbury Park, CA: Sage.

Lünenborg, M. and Fürsich, E. (2014) 'Media and the intersectional other', *Feminist Media Studies*, 14(6): 959–975.

Lünenborg, M. and Maier, T. (2018) 'The turn to affect and emotion in media studies', *Media and Communication*, 6(3): 1–4.

Lunt, P. and Livingstone, S. (2016) 'Is "mediatization" the new paradigm for our field?', *Media, Culture & Society*, 38(3): 462–470.

Lynch, M. and Swink, E. (1967) 'Some effects of priming, incubation and creative aptitude on journalism performance', *Journal of Communication*, 17(4): 372–382.

Lynch, T., Tompkins, J.E., van Driel, I.I. and Fritz, N. (2016) 'Sexy, strong, and secondary: a content analysis of female characters in video games across 31 years', *Journal of Communication*, 66: 564–584.

Lyotard, J.-F. ([1979]1984) *The Postmodern Condition: A Report on Knowledge*. Manchester: Manchester University Press.

M'Bayo, R.T., Sunday, O. and Amobi, I. (2012) 'Intellectual property and theory building in African mass communication research', *Journal of African Media Studies*, 4(2): 139–155.

Maccoby, E. (1954) 'Why do children watch TV?', *Public Opinion Quarterly*, 18: 239–244.

Machill, M., Beiler, M. and Zenker, M. (2008) 'Search-engine research: a European–American overview and systematization of an interdisciplinary and international research field', *Media, Culture & Society*, 30(5): 591–608.

Machlup, F. (1962) *The Production and Distribution of Knowledge in the United States*. Princeton, NJ: Princeton University Press.

Madianou, M. and Miller, D. (2013) 'Polymedia: towards a new theory of digital media in interpersonal communication', *International Journal of Cultural Studies*, 16(2): 169–187.

Maisel, R. (1973) 'The decline of mass media', *Public Opinion Quarterly*, 37: 159–170.

Malmelin, N. and Virta, S. (2016) 'Managing creativity in change', *Journalism Practice*, 10(8): 1041–1054.

Mansell, R. (2004) 'Political economy, power and the new media', *New Media and Society*, 6(1): 96–105.

Mansell, R. and Raboy, M. (eds) (2011) *The Handbook of Global Media and Communication Policy*. Hoboken, NJ: Wiley-Blackwell.

Maras, S. (2014) 'Media accountability: double binds and responsibility gaps', *Global Media Journal: Australian Edition*, 8(2): 1–13.

March, J.G. (1991) 'Exploration and exploitation in organizational learning', *Organization Science*, 2: 71–87.

Marcuse, H. (1964) *One-Dimensional Man*. Abingdon: Routledge and Kegan Paul.

Marjoribanks, T. (2000) *News Corporation, Technology and the Workplace: Global Strategies, Local Change*. Cambridge: Cambridge University Press.

Marjoribanks, T. (2011) 'Understanding multinational media management', in M. Deuze (ed.), *Managing Media Work*, pp. 133–144. London: Sage.

Markey, P.M., Markey, C.N. and French, J.E. (2015) 'Violent video games and real-world violence: rhetoric versus data', *Psychology of Popular Media Culture*, 4(4): 277–295.

Markham, A.N. (2013) 'Fieldwork in social media', *Departures in Critical Qualitative Research*, 2(4): 434–446.

Martel, M.U. and McCall, G.J. (1964) 'Reality-orientation and the pleasure principle', in L.A. Dexter and D.M. White (eds), *People, Society and Mass Communication*, pp. 283–333. New York: Free Press.

Martín-Barbero, M. (1993) *Communication, Culture and Hegemony: From the Media to Mediations*. London: Sage.

Martins, N. and Weaver, A.J. (2019) 'The role of media exposure on relational aggression: a meta-analysis', *Aggression and Violent Behavior*, 47: 90–99.

Martins, N., Weaver, A.J., Yeshua-Katz, D., Lewis, N.H., Tyree, N.E. and Jensen, J.D. (2013) 'A content analysis of print news coverage of media violence and aggression research', *Journal of Communication*, 63: 1070–1087.

Massey, D. (2005) *For Space*. London: Sage.

Massey, D. (2007) *World City*. Cambridge: Polity Press.

Mattelart, A. (2003) *The Information Society*. London: Sage.

Matthes, J. (2015) 'Observing the "spiral" in the spiral of silence', *International Journal of Public Opinion Research*, 27(2): 155–176.

Maxwell, R. and Miller, T. (2012) *Greening the Media*. Oxford: Oxford University Press.

Mayer, V., Press, A., Verhoeven, D. and Sterne, J. (2017) 'How do we intervene in the stubborn persistence of patriarchy in communication research?', in D.T. Scott and A. Shaw (eds), *Interventions: Communication Theory and Practice*. New York: Peter Lang. Available at: www.peterlang.com/view/product/84180?rskey=7eP1r6&result=1.

Mazzoleni, G. (2014) 'Mediatization and political populism', in J. Strömbäck and F. Esser (eds), *Mediatization of Politics: Understanding the Transformation of Western Democracies*, pp. 42–56. New York and London: Palgrave Macmillan.

Mazzoleni, G. and Schulz, W. (1999) '"Mediatization" of politics: a challenge for democracy?', *Political Communication*, 16(3): 247–261.

McBride, S. et al. (1980) *Many Voices, One World*. Report by the International Commission for the Study of Communication Problems. Paris: UNESCO; London: Kogan Page.

McChesney, R. (2000) *Rich Media, Poor Democracy*. New York: New Press.

McCombs, M. and Funk, M. (2011) 'Shaping the agenda of local daily newspapers: a methodology merging the agenda setting and community structure perspectives', *Mass Communication and Society*, 14(6): 905–919.

McCombs, M.E. and Shaw, D.L. (1972) 'The agenda-setting function of the press', *Public Opinion Quarterly*, 36: 176–187.

McCombs, M.E. and Shaw, D.L. (1993) 'The evolution of agenda-setting theory: 25 years in the marketplace of ideas', *Journal of Communication*, 43(2): 58–66.

McCormack, T. (1961) 'Social theory and the mass media', *Canadian Journal of Economics and Political Science*, 4: 479–849.

McDonald, D.G. (1990) 'Media orientation and television news viewing', *Journalism Quarterly*, 67(1): 11–20.

McDonald, D.G. and Dimmick, J. (2003) 'The conceptualization and measurement of diversity', *Communication Research*, 30(1): 60–79.

McGranahan, D.V. and Wayne, L. (1948) 'German and American traits reflected in popular drama', *Human Relations*, 1(4): 429–455.

McGuigan, J. (1992) *Cultural Populism*. Abingdon: Routledge.

McGuire, W.J. (1973) 'Persuasion, resistance and attitude change', in I. de Sola Pool et al. (eds), *Handbook of Communication*, pp. 216–252. Chicago, IL: Rand McNally.

McGuire, W.J. (1974) 'Psychological motives and communication gratifications', in J.G. Blumler and E. Katz (eds), *The Uses of Mass Communications*, pp. 167–196. Beverly Hills, CA: Sage.

McLeod, D., Detember, B.H. and Eveland, W.P. (2001) 'Behind the third-person effect: differentiating perceptual process for self and other', *Journal of Communication*, 51(4): 678–696.

McLeod, D., Wise, D. and Perryman, M. (2017) 'Thinking about the media: a review of theory and research on media perceptions, media effects perceptions, and their consequences', *Review of Communication Research*, 5: 35–83.

McLeod, J.M., Kosicki, G.M. and Pan, Z. (1991) 'On understanding and not understanding media effects', in J. Curran and M. Gurevitch (eds), *Mass Media and Society*, pp. 235–266. London: Edward Arnold.

McLeod, J.M. and McDonald, D.G. (1985) 'Beyond simple exposure: media orientations and their impact on political processes', *Communication Research*, 12(1): 3–32.

McLuhan, M. (1962) *The Gutenberg Galaxy*. Toronto: Toronto University Press.

McLuhan, M. (1964) *Understanding Media*. Abingdon: Routledge and Kegan Paul.

McManus, J.H. (1994) *Market-driven Journalism: Let the Citizen Beware*. Thousand Oaks, CA: Sage.

McMasters, P.K. (2000) 'Unease with excess', *Media Studies Journal*, Fall: 108–112.

McNair, B. (1988) *Images of the Enemy*. Abingdon: Routledge.

McNair, B. (2017) 'After objectivity?', *Journalism Studies*, 18(10): 1318–1333.

McQuail, D. (1977) *Analysis of Newspaper Content*. Royal Commission on the Press, Research Series 4. London: HMSO.

McQuail, D. (1983) *Mass Communication Theory: An Introduction*. London: Sage.

McQuail, D. (1984) 'With the benefit of hindsight: reflections on uses and gratifications research', *Critical Studies in Mass Communication*, 1: 177–193.

McQuail, D. (1992) *Media Performance: Mass Communication and the Public Interest*. London: Sage.

McQuail, D. (1997) *Audience Analysis*. Thousand Oaks, CA: Sage.

McQuail, D. (2003a) *Media Accountability and Freedom of Publication*. Oxford: Oxford University Press.

McQuail, D. (2003b) 'Making progress in a trackless, weightless and intangible space: a response to Keith Roe', *Communications*, 27: 275–284.

McQuail, D. (2006) 'The mediatization of war', *International Communication Gazette*, 68(2): 107–118.

McQuail, D. (2009) 'Editorial: EJC Symposium Special Issue', *European Journal of Communication*, 24(4): 387–389.

McQuail, D., Blumler, J.G. and Brown, J. (1972) 'The television audience: a revised perspective', in D. McQuail (ed.), *Sociology of Mass Communication*, pp. 135–165. Harmondsworth: Penguin.

McQuail, D. and Siune, K. (1998) *Media Policy: Convergence, Concentration and Commerce*. London: Sage.

McQuail, D. and Windahl, S. (1993) *Communication Models for the Study of Mass Communication*, 2nd edition. London: Longman.

McRobbie, A. (1996) '*More!* New sexualities in girls' and women's magazines', in J. Curran, D. Morley and V. Walkerdine (eds), *Cultural Studies and Communications*, pp. 172–194. London: Edward Arnold.

McRobbie, A. (2016) *Be Creative: Making a Living in the New Culture Industries*. Cambridge: Polity Press.

Meehan, E. and Wasko, J. (2013) 'In defense of a political economy of the media', *Javnost – The Public*, 20(1): 39–53.

Mellado, C., Hellmueller, L. and Donsbach, W. (eds) (2017) *Journalistic Role Performance: Concepts, Contexts, and Methods*. New York: Routledge.

Mellado, C., Hellmueller, L., Márquez-Ramírez, M., Humanes, M.L., Sparks, C., Stepinska, A., Pasti, S., Schielicke, A., Tandoc, E. and Wang, H. (2017) 'The hybridization of journalistic cultures: a comparative study of journalistic role performance', *Journal of Communication*, 67: 944–967.

Melody, W.H. (1990) 'Communications policy in the global information economy', in M.F. Ferguson (ed.), *Public Communication: The New Imperatives*, pp. 16–39. London: Sage.

Mendelsohn, H. (1964) 'Listening to radio', in L.A. Dexter and D.M. White (eds), *People, Society and Mass Communication*, pp. 239–248. New York: Free Press.

Mendelsohn, H. (1966) *Mass Entertainment*. New Haven, CT: College and University Press.

Merton, R.K. (1949) 'Patterns of influence', in *Social Theory and Social Structure*, pp. 387–470. Glencoe, IL: Free Press.

Merton, R.K. (1957) *Social Theory and Social Structure*. Glencoe, IL: Free Press.

Metz, M., Kruikemeier, S. and Lecheler, S. (2019) 'Personalization of politics on Facebook: examining the content and effects of professional, emotional and private self-personalization', *Information, Communication & Society*, DOI: 10.1080/1369118X.2019.1581244

Metzgar, E.T., Kurpius, D.D. and Rowley, K.M. (2011) 'Defining hyperlocal media: proposing a framework for discussion', *New Media and Society*, 13(5): 772–787.

Meyer, P. (1987) *Ethical Journalism*. New York: Longman.

Meyer, R. (2014) 'Everything We Know About Facebook's secret mood manipulation experiment', *The Atlantic*, 28 June. Available at: www.theatlantic.com/technology/archive/2014/06/everything-we-know-about-facebooks-secret-mood-manipulation-experiment/373648.

Meyrowitz, J. (1985) *No Sense of Place*. New York: Oxford University Press.

Meyrowitz, J. (2008) 'Power, pleasure, patterns: intersecting narratives of media influence', *Journal of Communication*, 58(4): 641–663.

Miconi, A. and Serra, M. (2019) 'On the concept of medium: an empirical study', *International Journal of Communication*, 13: 3444–3461.

Miège, B. (1979) 'The cultural commodity', *Media, Culture & Society*, 1: 297–311.

Miège, B. (1989) *The Capitalization of Cultural Production*. New York/Bagnolet: International General.

Miège, B. (2019) 'Cultural and creative industries and the political economy of communication', in M. Deuze and M. Prenger (eds), *Making Media: Production, Practices and Professions*, pp. 73–83. Amsterdam: Amsterdam University Press.

Mihelj, S. and Stanyer, J. (2019) 'Theorizing media, communication and social change: towards a processual approach', *Media, Culture & Society*, 41(4): 482–501.

Miller, C.R. (1984) 'Genre as social action', *Quarterly Journal of Speech*, 70(2): 151–167.

Miller, C.R. (2015) '"Genre as social action" (1984), revisited 30 years later (2014)', *Letras & Letras*, 31(3): 56–72.

Miller, C.R., Devitt, A.J. and Gallagher, V.J. (2018) 'Genre: permanence and change', *Rhetoric Society Quarterly*, 48(3): 269–277.

Miller, D. (1987) *Material Culture and Mass Consumption*. Oxford: Basil Blackwell.

Miller, T. (2009) 'Media Studies 3.0', *Television & New Media*, 10(1): 5–6.

Miller, T., Govil, N., McMurria, J., Maxwell, R. and Wang, T. (2005) *Global Hollywood 2*. London: BFI Publishing.

Miller, T. and Kraidy, M.M. (2016) *Global Media Studies*. Cambridge: Polity Press.

Miller, T. and Leger, M.-C. (2001) 'Runaway production, runaway consumption, runaway citizenship: the new international division of cultural labor', *Emergences*, 11(1): 89–115.

Miller, V. (2008) 'New media, networking and phatic culture', *Convergence*, 14(4): 387–400.

Miller, V. (2017) 'Phatic culture and the status quo: reconsidering the purpose of social media activism', *Convergence*, 23(3): 251–269.

Mills, B. (2004) 'Comedy verite: contemporary sitcom form', *Screen*, 45(1): 63–78.

Mills, C.W. (1951) *White Collar*. New York: Oxford University Press.

Mills, C.W. (1956) *The Power Elite*. New York: Oxford University Press.

Milton, V. (2017) 'Difficult questions: trends in communication studies – a South African view', *Westminster Papers in Communication and Culture*, 12(1): 30–32.

Mitchelstein, E. and Boczkowski, P.J. (2009) 'Between tradition and change: a review of recent research on online news production', *Journalism*, 10(5): 562–586.

Mittell, J. (2006) 'Narrative complexity in contemporary American television', *The Velvet Light Trap*, 58: 29–40.

Mittell, J. (2011) 'A cultural approach to TV genre theory', *Cinema Journal*, 40(3): 3–24.

Modleski, T. (1982) *Loving with a Vengeance: Mass-produced Fantasies for Women*. London: Methuen.

Moeller, J. and Helberger, N. (2018) 'Beyond the filter bubble: concepts, myths, evidence and issues for future debates', *Dutch Media Regulator Report*. Amsterdam: University of Amsterdam.

Möller, J., Trilling, D., Helberger, N. and Van Es, B. (2018) 'Do not blame it on the algorithm: an empirical assessment of multiple recommender systems and their impact on content diversity', *Information, Communication & Society*, 21(7): 959–977.

Monaco, J. (1981) *How to Read a Film*. New York: Oxford University Press.

Moorti, S. (2003) 'Out of India: fashion culture and the marketing of ethnic style', in A.N. Valdivia (ed.), *A Companion to Media Studies*, pp. 293–310. Oxford: Blackwell.

Morgan, M. and Shanahan, J. (1997) 'Two decades of cultivation research: an appraisal and meta-analysis', *Communication Yearbook*, 20(1): 1–46.

Morgan, M., Shanahan, J. and Signorielli, N. (2015) 'Yesterday's new cultivation, tomorrow', *Mass Communication and Society*, 18(5): 674–699.

Morley, D. (1980) *The 'Nationwide' Audience: Structure and Decoding*. BFI TV Monographs no. 11. London: British Film Institute.

Morley, D. (1986) *Family Television*. London: Comedia.

Morley, D. (1992) *Television, Audiences and Cultural Studies*. Abingdon: Routledge.

Morley, D. (1996) 'Postmodernism: the rough guide', in J. Curran, D. Morley and V. Walkerdine (eds), *Cultural Studies and Communication*, pp. 50–65. London: Edward Arnold.

Morley, D. (2015) 'Cultural studies, common sense and communications', *Cultural Studies*, 29(1): 23–31.

Morris, M. and Ogan, C. (1996) 'The Internet as mass medium', *Journal of Communication*, 46(1): 39–50.

Mosco, V. (1996) *The Political Economy of Communication*. London: Sage.

Mosco, V. (2009) *The Political Economy of Communication*, 2nd edition. London: Sage.

Moscovici, S. (1991) 'Silent majorities and loud minorities', in J. Anderson (ed.), *Communication Yearbook 14*, pp. 298–308. Newbury Park, CA: Sage.

Mowlana, H. (1985) *International Flows of Information*. Paris: UNESCO.

Moy, P., Domke, D. and Stamm, K. (2001) 'The spiral of silence and public opinion on affirmative action', *Journalism and Mass Communication Quarterly*, 78(1): 7–25.

Moy, P., Torres, M., Tanaka, K. and McClusky, R. (2005) 'Knowledge or trust? Investigating linkages between media reliance and participation', *Communication Research*, 32(1): 59–86.

Mukerjee, S., Majó-Vázquez, S. and González-Bailón, S. (2018) 'Networks of audience overlap in the consumption of digital news', *Journal of Communication*, 68(1), February: 26–50.

Müller, L. (2014) *Comparing Mass Media in Established Democracies: Patterns of Media Performance*. Basingstoke: Palgrave Macmillan.

Muñoz-Torres, J.R. (2012) 'Truth and objectivity in journalism', *Journalism Studies*, 13(4): 566–582.

Munson, W. (1993) *All Talk: The Talkshow in Media Culture*. Philadelphia, PA: University of Temple Press.

Murdock, G. (1990) 'Redrawing the map of the communication industries', in M. Ferguson (ed.), *Public Communication*, pp. 1–15. London: Sage.

Murdock, G. (1999) 'Rights and representations: public discourse and cultural citizenship', in J. Gripsrud (ed.), *Television and Common Knowledge*, pp. 7–17. Abingdon: Routledge.

Murthy, C. (2016) 'Unbearable lightness? Maybe because of the irrelevance/incommensurability of Western theories? An enigma of Indian media research', *International Communication Gazette*, 78(7): 636–642.

Mutz, D.C. and Soss, J. (1997) 'Reading public opinion: the influence of news coverage on perceptions of public sentiment', *Public Opinion Quarterly*, 61(3): 431–451.

Nakamura, L. (2002) *Cybertypes: Race, Ethnicity, and Identity on the Internet*. New York: Routledge.

Nakamura, L. and Chow-White, P.A. (eds) (2012) *Race after the Internet*. New York: Routledge.

Napoli, P.M. (2001) *Foundations of Communication Policy*. Creskill, NJ: Hampton Press.

Napoli, P.M. (2011) *Audience Evolution: New Technologies and the Transformation of Media Audience*. New York: Columbia University Press.

Napoli, P.M. (2012) 'Audience evolution and the future of audience research', *International Journal on Media Management*, 14(2): 79–97.

Napoli, P.M. (2019) *Social Media and the Public Interest: Media Regulation in the Disinformation Age*. New York: Columbia University Press.

Nass, C. and Yen, C. (2010) *The Man Who Lied to His Laptop*. New York: Penguin Random House.

Negus, K. (1992) *Producing Pop*. London: Edward Arnold.

Negus, K. (1998) 'Cultural production and the corporation: musical genres and the strategic management of creativity in the US recording industry', *Media, Culture & Society*, 20(3): 359–379.

Neilson, B. and Rossiter, N. (2005) 'From precarity to precariousness and back again: labour, life and unstable networks', *Fibre Culture*, 5, http://journal.fibreculture.org/issue5.

Neuman, W.R. (1991) *The Future of the Mass Audience*. Cambridge: Cambridge University Press.

Neuman, W.R. (2016) *The Digital Difference: Media Technology and the Theory of Communication Effects*. Cambridge, MA: Harvard University Press.

Neuman, W.R. (2018) 'The paradox of the paradigm: an important gap in media effects research', *Journal of Communication*, 68(2): 369–379.

Neuman, W.R. and Pool, I. de Sola (1986) 'The flow of communication into the home', in S. Ball-Rokeach and M. Cantor (eds), *Media, Audience and Social Structure*, pp. 71–86. Newbury Park, CA: Sage.

Newcomb, H. (1991) 'On the dialogic aspects of mass communication', in R. Avery and D. Easton (eds), *Critical Perspectives on Media and Society*, pp. 69–87. New York: Guilford Press.

Nieborg, D., Poell, T. (2019) 'The platformization of making media', in M. Deuze and M. Prenger (eds), *Making Media: Production, Practices and Professions*, pp. 85–98. Amsterdam: Amsterdam University Press.

Nightingale, V. (2003) 'The cultural revolution in audience research', in A.N. Valdivia (ed.), *A Companion to Media Studies*, pp. 360–381. Oxford: Blackwell.

Nixon, S. (2011) 'From full-service agency to 3-D marketing consultants: "creativity" and organizational change in advertising', in M. Deuze (ed.), *Managing Media Work*, pp. 199–208. London: Sage.

Noam, E. (1991) *Television in Europe*. New York: Oxford University Press.

Noam, E. (2018) 'Beyond the mogul: from media conglomerates to portfolio media', *Journalism*, 19(8): 1096–1130.

Noam, E. and The International Media Concentration Collaboration (2016) *Who Owns the World's Media? Media Concentration and Ownership around the World*. Oxford: Oxford University Press.

Noble, G. (1975) *Children in Front of the Small Screen*. London: Constable.

Noelle-Neumann, E. (1974) 'The spiral of silence: a theory of public opinion', *Journal of Communication*, 24: 24–51.

Noelle-Neumann, E. (1984) *The Spiral of Silence*. Chicago, IL: University of Chicago Press.

Noelle-Neumann, E. (1991) 'The theory of public opinion: the concept of the spiral of silence', in J. Anderson (ed.), *Communication Yearbook 14*, pp. 256–287. Newbury Park, CA: Sage.

Noin, D. (2001) 'Bias in the news: partisanship and negativity in media coverage of Presidents G. Bush and Bill Clinton', *Harvard Journal of Press/Politics*, 6(3): 31–46.

Nordenstreng, K. (1974) *Informational Mass Communication*. Helsinki: Tammi.

Nordenstreng, K. (2010) 'Self-regulation: a contradiction in terms? Discussing constituents of journalistic responsibility', in H. Pöttker and C. Schwarzenegger (eds), *Europäische Öffentlichkeit und journalistische Verantvortung*, pp. 417–438. Cologne: Herbert von Halem Verlag.

Norris, P. (2000) *A Virtuous Circle*. New York: Cambridge University Press.

Norris, P. (2002) *Digital Divide*. New York: Cambridge University Press.

Norris, P., Curtice, J., Sanders, D., Scammell, M. and Semetko, H. (1999) *On Message: Communicating the Campaign*. Thousand Oaks, CA: Sage.

Ó Siochrú, S. and Girard, B., with Mahan, A. (2003) *Global Media Governance: A Beginner's Guide*. Lanham, MD: Rowman and Littlefield.

O'Donnell, P., Zion, L. and Sherwood, M. (2016) 'Where do journalists go after newsroom job cuts?', *Journalism Practice*, 10(1): 35–51.

O'Sullivan, P.B. and Carr, C.T. (2018) 'Masspersonal communication: a model bridging the mass-interpersonal divide', *New Media and Society*, 20(3): 1161–1180.

Ogden, C.K. and Richards, I.A. (1923) *The Meaning of Meaning* (reprinted 1985). Abingdon: Routledge and Kegan Paul.

Olen, J. (1988) *Ethics in Journalism*. Englewood Cliffs, NJ: Prentice-Hall.

Olson, S.R. (1999) *Hollywood Planet. Global Media: The Competitive Advantage of Narrative Transparency*. Mahwah, NJ: Erlbaum.

Oltean, O. (1993) 'Series and seriality in media culture', *European Journal of Communication*, 8(1): 5–31.

Ong, W. (1982) *Orality and Literacy*. Abingdon: Routledge.

Orben, A. and Przybylski, A.K. (2019) 'Screens, teens, and psychological well-being: evidence from three time-use-diary studies', *Psychological Science*, 30: 682–696.

Otto, L.B., Lecheler, S. and Schuck, A.R.T. (2019) 'Is context the key? The (non-) differential effects of mediated incivility in three European countries', *Political Communication*, DOI: 10.1080/10584609.2019.1663324.

Padioleau, J. (1985) *Le Monde et le Washington Post*. Paris: PUF.

Page, R. (2013) 'Seriality and storytelling in social media', *Storyworlds: A Journal of Narrative Studies*, 5: 31–54.

Paletz, D.L. and Entman, R. (1981) *Media, Power, Politics*. New York: Free Press.

Palfrey, J. and Gasser, U. (2008) *Born Digital*. New York: Basic Books.

Palmer, L. (2019) *The Fixers: Local News Workers and the Underground Labour of International Reporting*. Oxford: Oxford University Press.

Palmgreen, P. and Rayburn, J.D. (1985) 'An expectancy-value approach to media gratifications', in K.E. Rosengren et al. (eds), *Media Gratification Research*, pp. 61–72. Beverly Hills, CA: Sage.

Papacharissi, Z. (2010) *A Private Sphere: Democracy in a Digital Age*. Cambridge: Polity Press.

Papacharissi, Z. (2014) *Affective Publics: Sentiment, Technology, and Politics*. Oxford: Oxford University Press.

Papacharissi, Z. (2016) 'Affective publics and structures of storytelling: sentiment, events and mediality', *Information, Communication & Society*, 19(3): 304–327.

Papacharissi, Z. (ed.) (2018a) *A Networked Self: Birth, Life, Death*. Abingdon: Routledge.

Papacharissi, Z. (ed.) (2018b) *A Networked Self: Human Augmentics, Artificial Intelligence, Sentience*. Abingdon: Routledge.

Papacharissi, Z. (ed.) (2018c) *A Networked Self: Love*. Abingdon: Routledge.

Papacharissi, Z. (ed.) (2018d) *A Networked Self: Platforms, Stories, Connections*. Abingdon: Routledge.

Parameswaran, R. (ed.) (2013) 'Audience and interpretation in media studies', in *International Encyclopedia of Media Studies*, vol. 4. Malden, MA: Wiley-Blackwell.

Pariser, E. (2012) *The Filter Bubble*. London: Viking/Penguin.

Parks, L. (2018) *Rethinking Media Coverage: Vertical Mediation and the War on Terror*. Abingdon: Routledge.

Pasek, J., Kensler, K., Romer, D. and Jamieson, K.H. (2006) 'America's media use and community engagement', *Communication Research*, 33(3): 115–135.

Paterson, C., Lee, D., Saha, A. and Zoellner, A. (eds) (2016) *Advancing Media Production Research: Shifting Sites, Methods and Politics*. London: Palgrave Macmillan.

Paz Aléncar, A., Kondova, K. and Ribbens, W. (2018) 'The smartphone as a lifeline', *Media, Culture & Society*, 41(6): 828–844.

Peacock, A. (1986) *Report of the Committee on Financing the BBC*. Cmnd 9824. London: HMSO.

Pearson, G.D.H. and Kosicki, G.M. (2017) 'How way-finding is challenging gatekeeping in the digital age', *Journalism Studies*, 18(9): 1087–1105.

Peirce, C.S. (1931–1935) *Collected Papers*, edited by C. Harteshorne and P. Weiss, vols II and V. Cambridge, MA: Harvard University Press.

Pekurny, R. (1982) 'Coping with television production', in J.S. Ettema and D.C. Whitney (eds), *Individuals in Mass Media Organizations*, pp. 131–143. Beverly Hills, CA: Sage.

Perse, E.M. (1994) 'Uses of erotica', *Communication Research*, 20(4): 488–515.

Perse, E.M. (2001) *Media Effects and Society*. Mahwah, NJ: Erlbaum.

Perse, E.M. and Courtright, J.A. (1992) 'Normative images of communication media: mass and interpersonal channels in the new media environment', *Human Communication Research*, 19: 485–503.

Peters, A.K. and Cantor, M.G. (1982) 'Screen acting as work', in J.S. Ettema and D.C. Whitney (eds), *Individuals in Mass Media Organizations*, pp. 53–68. Beverly Hills, CA: Sage.

Peters, J.D. (1994) 'The gap of which communication is made', *Critical Studies in Mass Communication*, 11(2): 117–140.

Peters, J.D. (2016) *The Marvelous Clouds*. Chicago, IL: University of Chicago Press.

Peterson, R. and Anand, N. (2004) 'The production of culture perspective', *Annual Review of Sociology*, 30: 311–334.

Peterson, R.C. and Thurstone, L.L. (1933) *Motion Pictures and Social Attitudes*. New York: Macmillan.

Picard, R.G. (1989) *Media Economics*. Newbury Park, CA: Sage.

Picard, R.G. (2004) 'Commercialism and newspaper quality', *Newspaper Research Journal*, 25(1): 54–65.

Picard, R.G., McCombs, M., Winter, J.P. and Lacy, S. (eds) (1988) *Press Concentration and Monopoly*. Norwood, NJ: Ablex.

Plantin, J.-C., Lagoze, C., Edwards, P. N. and Sandvig, C. (2018) 'Infrastructure studies meet platform studies in the age of Google and Facebook', *New Media and Society*, 20(1): 293–310.

Plesner, U. (2009) 'An actor-network perspective on changing work practices: communication technologies as actants in newswork', *Journalism*, 10(5): 604–626.

Podkalicka, A. and Rennie, E. (2018) *Using Media for Social Innovation*. Bristol: Intellect.

Pool, I. de Sola (1974) *Direct Broadcasting and the Integrity of National Cultures*. New York: Aspen Institute.

Pool, I. de Sola (1983) *Technologies of Freedom*. Cambridge, MA: Belknap.

Pool, I. de Sola and Shulman, I. (1959) 'Newsmen's fantasies, audiences and newswriting', *Public Opinion Quarterly*, 23(2): 145–158.

Porat, M. (1977) *The Information Economy: Definitions and Measurement*. Washington, DC: Department of Commerce.

Porto, M.P. (2007) 'Frame diversity and citizen competence: towards a critical approach to news quality', *Critical Studies in Mass Communication*, 24(4): 303–321.

Poster, M. (1999) 'Underdetermination', *New Media and Society*, 1(1): 12–17.

Poster, M. (2006) 'Culture and new media: a historical view', in L.A. Lievrow and S. Livingstone (eds), *The Handbook of New Media*, pp. 134–140. London: Sage.

Postman, N. (1993) *Technopoly: The Surrender of Culture to Technology*. New York: Vintage.

Postmes, T., Spears, R. and Lea, M. (1998) 'Breaching or building social boundaries? Side-effects of computer mediated communication', *Communication Research*, 25(6): 689–715.

Potter, J. and Riddle, K. (2007) 'A content analysis of the media effects literature', *Journalism & Mass Communication Quarterly*, 84(1): 90–104.

Potter, R.F. and Bolls, P. (2012) *Psychophysiological Measurement and Meaning: Cognitive and Emotional Processing of Media*. New York: Routledge.

Potter, W.J. (2014) 'A critical analysis of cultivation theory', *Journal of Communication*, 64: 1015–1036.

Potter, W.J., Cooper, R. and Dupagne, M. (1993) 'The three paradigms of mass media research in mass communication journals', *Communication Theory*, 3: 317–335.

Poulakidakos, S., Veneti, A. and Fangonikolopoulos, C. (2018) 'Post-truth, propaganda and the transformation of the spiral of silence', *International Journal of Media & Cultural Politics*, 14(3): 367–382.

Prescott, J. and Bogg, J. (2011) 'Career attitudes of men and women working in the computer games industry', *Eludamos: Journal for Computer Game Culture*, 5(1): 7–28.

Press, A. and Livingstone, S. (2006) 'Taking audience research into the age of new media: old problems and new challenges', in M. White and J. Schwoch (eds), *The Question of Method in Cultural Studies*, pp. 175–200. Oxford: Blackwell.

Price, M. and Thompson, M. (2002) *Forging Peace*. Edinburgh: Edinburgh University Press.

Pritchard, D. (2000) *Holding the Media Accountable*. Bloomington, IN: University of Indiana Press.

Propp, V. (1968) *The Morphology of Folk Tales*. Austin, TX: University of Texas Press.

Prot, S., Anderson, C.A., Barlett, C.P., Coyne, S.M. and Saleem, M. (2017) 'Content effects: violence in the media', in P. Roessler, C.A. Hoffner and L. van Zoonen (eds), *International Encyclopedia of Media Effects*. Malden, MA: Wiley-Blackwell. DOI: 10.1002/9781118783764.wbieme0121.

Putnam, D. (2000) *Bowling Alone*. New York: Simon & Schuster.

Quan-Haase, A., Wang, H., Wellman, B. and Zhang, R. (2018) 'Weaving family connections on and offline: the turn to networked individualism', in B.B. Neves and C. Casimiro (eds), *Connecting Families? Information and Communication Technologies in a Life Course Perspective*. Bristol: Policy Press.

Quandt, T. (2019) 'Dark participation', *Media and Communication*, 6(4): 36–48.

Quandt, T. and von Pape, T. (2010) 'Living in the mediatope', *The Information Society*, 26(5): 330–345.

Radway, J. (1984) *Reading the Romance*. Chapel Hill, NC: University of North Carolina Press.

Raessens, J. and Goldstein, J. (eds) (2011) *Handbook of Computer Game Studies*. Boston, MA: MIT Press.

Rains, S.A., Levine, T.R. and Weber, R. (2018) 'Sixty years of quantitative communication research summarized: lessons from 149 meta-analyses', *Annals of the International Communication Association*, 42(2): 105–124.

Rakow, L. (1986) 'Rethinking gender research in communication', *Journal of Communication*, 36(1): 11–26.

Raman, P. and Harwood, J.T. (2008) 'Acculturation of Asian Indian sojourners in America: application of the cultivation framework', *Southern Communication Journal*, 73(4): 295–311.

Rantanen, T. (2001) 'The old and the new: communications technology and globalization in Russia', *New Media and Society*, 3(1): 85–105.

Rasmussen, T. (2000) *Social Theory and Communication Technology*. Aldershot: Ashgate.

Ravi, N. (2005) 'Looking beyond flawed journalism', *Harvard International Journal of Press/Politics*, 10(1): 45–62.

Ray, M.L. (1973) 'Marketing communication and the hierarchy of effects', in P. Clarke (ed.), *New Models for Communication Research*, pp. 147–176. Beverly Hills, CA: Sage.

Raymond, J. (ed.) (1999) *News, Newspapers and Society in Early Modern Britain*. London: Cass.

Real, M. (1989) *Supermedia*. Newbury Park, CA: Sage.

Reardon, K.K. and Rogers, E.M. (1988) 'Interpersonal versus mass media communication a false dichotomy', *Human Communication Research*, 15: 284–303.

Redmond, J. and Trager, R. (2004) *Balancing on the Wire: The Art of Managing Media*. Boulder, CO: Coursewise.

Reese, S.D. (1991) 'Setting the media's agenda: a power balance perspective', in J. Anderson (ed.), *Communication Yearbook 14*, pp. 309–340. Newbury Park, CA: Sage.

Reese, S.D. and Ballinger, J. (2001) 'The roots of a sociology of news: remembering Mr. Gates and social control in the newsroom', *Journalism and Mass Communication Quarterly*, 78(4): 641–658.

Reese, S.D. and Shoemaker, P.J. (2016) 'A media sociology for the networked public sphere: the hierarchy of influences model', *Mass Communication and Society*, 19(4): 389–410.

Reeves, B. and Nass, C. (1996) *The Media Equation: How People Treat Computers, Television, and New Media Like Real People and Places*. Cambridge: Cambridge University Press.

Reicher, S.D., Spears, R., Postmes, T. and Kende, A. (2016) 'Disputing deindividuation: why negative group behaviours derive from group norms, not group immersion', *Behavioral and Brain Sciences*, 39: e161, https://doi.org/10.1017/S0140525X15001491.

Reinardy, S. (2011) 'Newspaper journalism in crisis: burnout on the rise, eroding young journalists' career commitment', *Journalism*, 12(1): 33–50.

Renckstorf, K. (1996) 'Media use as social action: a theoretical perspective', in K. Renckstorf, D. McQuail and N. Janknowski (eds), *Media Use as Social Action*, pp. 18–31. London: John Libbey Publishing.

Rheingold, H. (1994) *The Virtual Community*. London: Secker and Warburg.

Rice, R.E. (1999) 'Artifacts and paradoxes in new media', *New Media and Society*, 1(1): 24–32.

Rice, R.E. et al. (1983) *The New Media*. Beverly Hills, CA: Sage.

Riffe, D., Lacy, S., Fico, F. and Watson, B. (2019) *Analyzing Media Messages: Using Quantitative Content Analysis in Research*, 4th edition. New York: Routledge.

Robillard, S. (1995) *Television in Europe: Regulatory Bodies*. European Institute for the Media. London: John Libbey Publishing.

Robinson, L., Cotten, S.R., Ono, H., Quan-Haase, A., Mesch, G., Chen, W., Schulz, J., Hale, T.M. and Stern, M.J. (2015) 'Digital inequalities and why they matter', *Information, Communication & Society*, 18(5): 569–582.

Robinson, S. (2017) *Networked News, Racial Divides*. Cambridge: Cambridge University Press.

Roe, K. and de Meyer, G. (2000) 'MTV: one music – many languages', in J. Wieten, G. Murdock and P. Dahlgren (eds), *Television Across Europe*, pp. 141–157. London: Sage.

Rogers, E.M. (1986) *Communication Technology*. New York: Free Press.

Rogers, E.M. (1993) 'Looking back, looking forward: a century of communication research', in P. Gaunt (ed.), *Beyond Agendas: New Directions in Communication Research*, pp. 19–40. New Haven, CT: Greenwood Press.

Rogers, E.M. and Dearing, J.W. (1987) 'Agenda-setting research: Where has it been? Where is it going?', in J. Anderson (ed.), *Communication Yearbook 11*, pp. 555–594. Newbury Park, CA: Sage.

Rogers, E.M., Dearing, J.W. and Bergman, D. (1993) 'The anatomy of agenda-setting research', *Journal of Communication*, 43(2): 68–84.

Rogers, E.M. and Shoemaker, F. (1973) *Communication of Innovations*. New York: Free Press.

Rogers, R. (2013) *Digital Methods*. Boston, MA: MIT Press.

Rogers, R. (2019) *Doing Digital Methods*. Boston, MA: MIT Press.

Rojas, H. and Valenzuela, S. (2019) 'A call to contextualize public opinion-based research in political communication', *Political Communication*, DOI: 10.1080/10584609.2019.1670897.

Romer, D., Jamieson, K.H. and Ady, S. (2003) 'TV news and the cultivation of fear of crime', *Journal of Communication*, 53(1): 88–104.

Rosen, J. (2006) *The People Formerly Known as the Audience*. PressThink blog: http://archive.pressthink.org/2006/06/27/ppl_frmr.html.

Rosenberg, B. and White, D.M. (eds) (1957) *Mass Culture*. New York: Free Press.

Rosengren, K.E. (1974) 'International news: methods, data, theory', *Journal of Peace Research*, II: 45–56.

Rosengren, K.E. (1981) 'Mass media and social change: some current approaches', in E. Katz and T. Szecskö (eds), *Mass Media and Social Change*, pp. 247–263. Beverly Hills, CA: Sage.

Rosengren, K.E. (2000) *Communication: An Introduction*. London: Sage.

Rosengren, K.E. and Windahl, S. (1972) 'Mass media consumption as a functional alternative', in D. McQuail (ed.), *Sociology of Mass Communications*, pp. 166–194. Harmondsworth: Penguin.

Rosengren, K.E. and Windahl, S. (1989) *Media Matter*. Norwood, NJ: Ablex.

Rosengren, S. (2019) 'Redefining advertising in a changing media landscape', in M. Deuze and M. Prenger (eds), *Making Media: Production, Practices and Professions*, pp. 389–398. Amsterdam: Amsterdam University Press.

Rositi, F. (1976) 'The television news programme: fragmentation and recomposition of our image of society', in *News and Current Events on TV*. Rome: RAI.

Ross, K. (ed.) (2012) *The Handbook of Gender, Sex and Media*. Malden, MA: Wiley-Blackwell.

Rossiter, N. (2006) *Organized Networks: Media Theory, Creative Labour, New Institutions*. Rotterdam: Nai Publishers.

Rössler, P. (2001) 'Between online heaven and cyberhell: the framing of "the internet" by traditional media coverage in Germany', *New Media and Society*, 3(1): 49–66.

Rössler, P. and Brosius, H.-B. (2001) 'Talk show viewing in Germany', *Journal of Communication*, 51(1): 143–163.

Rosten, L.C. (1937) *The Washington Correspondents*. New York: Harcourt Brace.

Rosten, L.C. (1941) *Hollywood: The Movie Colony, the Movie Makers*. New York: Harcourt Brace.

Rothenbuhler, E.W. (1998) *Ritual Communication*. Thousand Oaks, CA: Sage.

Roudikova, N. (2008) 'Media political clientilism – a lesson from anthropology', *Media, Culture & Society*, 30(1): 41–59.

Rowland, A.L. and Simonson, P. (2014) 'The founding mothers of communication research: toward a history of a gendered assemblage', *Critical Studies in Media Communication*, 31(1): 3–26.

Royal Commission on the Press (1977) *Report*. Cmnd 6810. London: HMSO.

Rubin, A.M. (1984) 'Ritualized and instrumental television viewing', *Journal of Communication*, 34(3): 67–77.

Rubin, A.M., Perse, E.M. and Powell, E. (1990) 'Loneliness, parasocial interaction and local TV news viewing', *Communication Research*, 14(2): 246–268.

Ruggiero, T.E. (2000) 'Uses and gratifications theory in the 21st century', *Mass Communication and Society*, 3(1): 3–37.

Ryan, J. and Peterson, R.A. (1982) 'The product image: the fate of creativity in country music song writing', in J.S. Ettema and D.C. Whitney (eds), *Individuals in Mass Media Organizations*, pp. 11–32. Beverly Hills, CA: Sage.

Ryan, M. (2001) 'Journalistic ethics, objectivity, existential journalism, standpoint epistemology, and public journalism', *Journal of Mass Media Ethics*, 16(1): 3–22.

Saenz, M.K. (1994) 'Television viewing and cultural practice', in H. Newcomb (ed.), *Television: The Critical View*, 5th edition, pp. 573–586. New York: Oxford University Press.

Saito, S. (2007) 'Television and the cultivation of gender-role attitudes in Japan: Does television contribute to the maintenance of the status quo?', *Journal of Communication*, 57(3), September: 511–531.

Sardar, Z. (1999) *Postmodernism and the Other: New Imperialism of Western Culture*. London: Pluto Press.

Scannell, P. (2014) *Television and the Meaning of Live*. Cambridge: Polity Press.

Scannell, P. (2017) 'The academic study of media has always been the study of new media', *Westminster Papers in Communication and Culture*, 12(1), 5–6.

Schauster, E.E., Ferrucci, P. and Neill, M.S. (2016) 'Native advertising is the new journalism: how deception affects social responsibility', *American Behavioral Scientist*, 60(12): 1408–1424.

Schement, J. and Curtis, T. (1995) *Tendencies and Tensions of the Information Age*. New Brunswick, NJ: Transaction.

Scheufele, B. (2008) 'Discourse analysis', in W. Donsbach (ed.), *The International Encyclopedia of Communication*. Oxford: Blackwell.

Scheufele, D.A. (1999) 'Framing as a theory of media effects', *Journal of Communication*, 49(1): 103–122.

Scheufele, D.A. (2000) 'Agenda-setting, priming, and framing revisited: another look at cognitive effects of political communication', *Mass Communication & Society*, 3(2–3): 297–316.

Scheufele, D.A. and Nisbet, M.C. (2002) 'Being a citizen online: new opportunities and dead ends', *Harvard Journal of Press/Politics*, 7(3): 55–75.

Schiller, H. (1969) *Mass Communication and American Empire*. New York: Kelly.

Schlesinger, P. (1978) *Putting 'Reality' Together: BBC News*. London: Constable.

Schlesinger, P. (1987) 'On national identity', *Social Science Information*, 25(2): 219–264.

Schlesinger, P., Murdock, G. and Elliott, P. (1983) *Televising Terrorism*. London: Comedia.

Schmidt, S.J. (1987) 'Towards a constructivist theory of media genre', *Poetics*, 16(5): 371–395.

Schoenbach, K. and Lauf, E. (2002) 'The "trap" effect of television and its competitors', *Communication Research*, 29(6): 564–583.

Schoonvelde, M. (2014) 'Media freedom and the institutional underpinnings of political knowledge', *Political Science Research and Methods*, 2(2): 163–178.

Schramm, W. (1955) 'Information theory and mass communication', *Journalism Quarterly*, 32: 131–146.

Schramm, W., Lyle, J. and Parker, E. (1961) *Television in the Lives of Our Children*. Stanford, CA: Stanford University Press.

Schrøder, K.C. (1987) 'Convergence of antagonistic traditions?', *European Journal of Communication*, 2(1): 7–31.

Schrøder, K.C. (1992) 'Cultural quality: search for a phantom?', in M. Skovmand and K.C. Schrøder (eds), *Media Cultures: Reappraising Transnational Media*, pp. 161–180. Abingdon: Routledge.

Schuck, A.R.T., Boomgaarden, H.G. and De Vreese, C.H. (2013) 'Cynics all around? The impact of election news on political cynicism in comparative perspective', *Journal of Communication*, 63: 287–311.

Schuck, A.R.T. and Feinholdt, A. (2015) 'News framing effects and emotions', in R. Scott and S. Kosslyn (eds), *Emerging Trends in the Social and Behavioral Sciences*, pp. 1–15. Wiley Online Library: DOI: 10.1002/9781118900772.

Schudson, M. (1978) *Discovering the News*. New York: Basic Books.

Schudson, M. (1991) 'The new validation of popular culture', in R.K. Avery and D. Eason (eds), *Critical Perspectives on Media and Society*, pp. 49–68. New York: Guilford Press.

Schudson, M. (2003) *The Sociology of News*. New York: Norton.

Schudson, M. (2005) 'The virtues of an unlovable press', *The Political Quarterly*, 76: 23–32.

Schultz, J. (1998) *Reviving the Fourth Estate*. Cambridge: Cambridge University Press.

Schulz, A. and Roessler, P. (2012) 'The spiral of silence and the Internet: selection of online content and the perception of the public opinion climate in computer-mediated communication environments', *International Journal of Public Opinion Research*, 24(3): 346–367.

Schulz, W. (1988) 'Media and reality'. Unpublished paper for Sommatie Conference, Veldhoven, The Netherlands.

Schulze, B., Thielmann, B., Sieprath, S. and Hess, T. (2005) 'The Bertelsmann AG: an exploratory case study on synergy management in a globally acting media organization', *International Journal on Media Management*, 7(3–4): 138–147.

Schutz, A. (1972) *The Phenomenology of the Social World*. London: Heinemann.

Schwalber, C.B., Silcode, B.W. and Keith, S. (2008) 'Visual framing of the early weeks of the US led invasion of Iraq', *Journal of Broadcasting and Electronic Media*, 52(3): 448–465.

Scolari, C.A. (2009) 'Mapping conversations about new media: the theoretical field of digital communication', *New Media and Society*, 11(6): 943–964.

Scott, A. (2000) *The Cultural Economy of Cities*. London: Sage.

Seate, A. and Mastro, D. (2016) 'Media's influence on immigration attitudes: an intergroup threat theory approach', *Communication Monographs*, 83(2): 194–213.

Segev, E. (2015) 'Visible and invisible countries: news flow theory revised', *Journalism*, 16(3): 412–428.

Segrin, C. and Nabi, R.L. (2002) 'Does TV viewing cultivate unrealistic expectations about marriage?', *Journal of Communication*, 52(2): 247–263.

Seiter, E. (2000) *Television and New Media Audiences*. New York: Oxford University Press.

Seiter, F., Borchers, H. and Warth, E.-M. (eds) (1989) *Remote Control*. Abingdon: Routledge.

Selinger, E. and Hartzog, W. (2016) 'Facebook's emotional contagion study and the ethical problem of co-opted identity in mediated environments where users lack control', *Research Ethics*, 12(1): 35–43.

Selwyn, N. (2004) 'Reconsidering political and popular understanding of the digital divide', *New Media and Society*, 6(3): 341–362.

Semetko, H.A. (2004) 'Political communication', in J.D.H. Downing, D. McQuail, P. Schlesinger and E. Wartella (eds), *The SAGE Handbook of Media Studies*, pp. 351–374. Thousand Oaks, CA: Sage.

Sender, K. (2015) 'Reconsidering reflexivity: audience research and reality television', *The Communication Review*, 18(1): 37–52.

Sepstrup, P. (1989) 'Research into international TV flows', *European Journal of Communication*, 4(4): 393–408.

Shannon, C. and Weaver, W. (eds) (1949) *The Mathematical Theory of Communication*. Urbana, IL: University of Illinois Press.

Shoemaker, P.J. (1984) 'Media treatment of deviant political groups', *Journalism Quarterly*, 61(1): 66–75, 82.

Shoemaker, P.J. (1991) *Gatekeeping*. Thousand Oaks, CA: Sage.

Shoemaker, P.J. and Reese, S.D. (1991) *Mediating the Message*. New York: Longman.

Shoemaker, P.J. and Reese, S.D. (2013) *Mediating the Message in the 21st Century*. New York: Routledge.

Shoemaker, P.J. et al. (2001) 'Individual and routine forces in gatekeeping', *Journalism and Mass Communication Quarterly*, 78(2): 233–246.

Shrum, L.J. (1995) 'Assessing the social influence of television: a social cognition perspective on cultivation effects', *Communication Research*, 22(4): 402–429.

Siapera, E. (2019) 'Affective labour and media work', in M. Deuze and M. Prenger (eds), *Making Media: Production, Practices and Professions*, pp. 275–286. Amsterdam: Amsterdam University Press.

Siebert, F., Peterson, T. and Schramm, W. (1956) *Four Theories of the Press*. Urbana, IL: University of Illinois Press.

Sigelman, L. (1973) 'Reporting the news: an organizational analysis', *American Journal of Sociology*, 79: 132–151.

Signorielli, N. and Morgan, M. (eds) (1990) *Cultivation Analysis*. Newbury Park, CA: Sage.

Silverstone, R. (1999) *Why Study the Media?* London: Sage.

Silverstone, R. (2007) *Media and Morality: On the Rise of the Mediapolis*. Cambridge: Polity Press.

Silverstone, R. and Hirsch, E. (eds) (2003) *Consuming Technologies: Media and Information in Domestic Spaces*. Abingdon and New York: Routledge.

Singer, J.B. (2018) 'Transmission creep', *Journalism Studies*, 19(2): 209–226.

Singer, J.B., Domingo, D., Heinonen, A., Hermida, A., Paulussen, S., Quandt, T., Reich, Z. and Vujnovic, M. (2011) *Participatory Journalism: Guarding Open Gates at Online Newspapers*. Malden, MA: Wiley-Blackwell.

Sklair, L. (2000) 'The transnational capitalist class and the discourse of globalisation', *Cambridge Review of International Affairs*, 14(1): 67–85.

Slater, D. and Tonkiss, F. (2001) *Market Society: Markets and Modern Social Theory*. Hoboken, NJ: Wiley-Blackwell.

Slater, M.D. (2007) 'Reinforcing spirals: the mutual influence of media selectivity and media effects and their impact on individual behavior and social identity', *Communication Theory*, 17: 281–303.

Slevin, J. (2000) *The Internet and Society*. Cambridge: Polity Press.

Sloterdijk, P. (2011) *Bubbles*. Boston, MA: MIT Press.

Smith, A. (1776) *The Wealth of Nations*. London: W. Strahan and T. Cadell.

Smith, P. and Bell, A. (2007) 'Unravelling the web of discourse analysis', in E. Devereux (ed.), *Media Studies*, pp. 78–100. London: Sage.

Smythe, D.W. (1977) 'Communications: blindspot of Western Marxism', *Canadian Journal of Political and Social Theory*, I: 120–127.

Sotirovic, M. (2001) 'Media use and perceptions of welfare', *Journal of Communication*, 51(4): 750–774.

Sparks, C. (1995) 'The media as a power for democracy', *Javnost – The Public*, 2(1): 45–61.

Sparks, C. (2011) 'Media and transition in Latin America', *Westminster Papers in Communication and Culture*, 8(2): 154–177.

Sparks, C. and Campbell, M. (1987) 'The inscribed reader of the British quality press', *European Journal of Communication*, 2(4): 455–472.

Spitzer, M. (2012) *Digitale Demenz*. München: Droemer.

Squires, J.D. (1992) 'Plundering the newsroom', *Washington Journalism Review*, 14(10): 18–24.

Sreberny-Mohammadi, A. (1996) 'The global and the local in international communication', in J. Curran and M. Gurevitch (eds), *Mass Media and Society*, pp. 177–203. London: Edward Arnold.

Stamm, K.R. (1985) *Newspaper Use and Community Ties: Towards a Dynamic Theory*. Norwood, NJ: Ablex.

Steemers, J. (2001) 'In search of a third way: balancing public purpose and commerce in German and British public service broadcasting', *Canadian Journal of Communication*, 26(1): 69–87.

Steiner, G. (1963) *The People Look at Television*. New York: Knopf.

Steiner, L. (2012) 'Failed theories: explaining gender difference in journalism', *Review of Communication*, 12(3): 201–223.

Stemler, S.E. (2015) 'Content analysis', in R.A. Scott and S.M. Kosslyn (eds), *Emerging Trends in the Social and Behavioral Sciences*, pp. 1–14. Wiley Online Library: https://doi.org/10.1002/9781118900772.etrds0053.

Stober, R. (2004) 'What media evolution is: a theoretical approach to the history of new media', *European Journal of Communication*, 19(4): 483–505.

Stolwijk, S.B., Schuck, A.R.T. and De Vreese, C.H. (2017) 'How anxiety and enthusiasm help explain the bandwagon effect', *International Journal of Public Opinion Research*, 29(4): 554–574.

Stone, G.C. (1987) *Examining Newspapers*. Beverly Hills, CA: Sage.

Stoycheff, E. (2016) 'Under surveillance: examining Facebook's spiral of silence effects in the wake of NSA Internet monitoring', *Journalism & Mass Communication Quarterly*, 93(2): 296–311.

Striphas, T. (2015) 'Algorithmic culture', *European Journal of Cultural Studies*, 18(4–5): 395–412.

Strömbäck, J. and Esser, F. (eds) (2014) *Mediatization of Politics: Understanding the Transformation of Western Democracies*. New York and London: Palgrave Macmillan.

Strömbäck, J. and Kiousis, S. (eds) (2011) *Political Public Relations: Principles and Applications*. New York: Routledge.

Stromer-Galley, J. (2019) *Presidential Campaigning in the Internet Age*, 2nd edition. Oxford: Oxford University Press.

Sundar, S.S., Jia, H., Waddell, T.F. and Huang, Y. (2015) 'Toward a Theory of Interactive Media Effects (TIME): four models for explaining how interface features affect user psychology', in S.S. Sundar (ed.), *The Handbook of the Psychology of Communication Technology*, pp. 47–86. Malden, MA: Wiley-Blackwell.

Sunstein, C. (2001) *republic.com*. Princeton, NJ: Princeton University Press.

Sunstein, C. (2006) *republic.com.2.0*. Princeton, NJ: Princeton University Press.

Sussman, G. (1997) *Communication, Technology and Politics in the Information Age*. Thousand Oaks, CA: Sage.

Sussman, G. and Galizio, L. (2003) 'The global reproduction of American politics', *Political Communication*, 20(3): 309–328.

Swanson, D. and Mancini, P. (eds) (1996) *Politics, Media and Modern Democracy*. Westport, CT: Praeger.

Taneja, H. and Webster, J.G. (2016) 'How do global audiences take shape? The role of institutions and culture in patterns of web use', *Journal of Communication*, 66: 161–182.

Tannenbaum, P.H. and Lynch, M.D. (1960) 'Sensationalism: the concept and its measurement', *Journalism Quarterly*, 30: 381–393.

Taylor, D.G. (1982) 'Pluralistic ignorance and the spiral of silence', *Public Opinion Quarterly*, 46: 311–355.

Taylor, T.L. (2015) *Raising the Stakes: E-Sports and the Professionalization of Computer Gaming*. Boston, MA: MIT Press.

Terranova, T. (2000) 'Free labour: producing culture for the digital economy', *Social Text*, 18(2): 33–57. Available at: http://web.mit.edu/schock/www/docs/18.2terranova.pdf.

Terras, M., Nyhan, J. and Vanhoutte, E. (eds) (2013) *Defining Digital Humanities: A Reader*. Farnham: Ashgate.

Tettey, W.J. (2006) 'The politics of media accountability in Africa: an examination of mechanisms and institutions', *International Communication Gazette*, 68(3): 229–248.

Thompson, J. (2000) *Political Scandals*. Cambridge: Polity Press.

Thompson, J.B. (1993) 'Social theory and the media', in D. Crowley and D. Mitchell (eds), *Communication Theory Today*, pp. 27–49. Cambridge: Polity Press.

Thompson, J.B. (1995) *The Media and Modernity*. Cambridge: Polity Press.

Thompson, J.B. (2005) 'The new visibility', *Theory, Culture & Society*, 22(6): 31–51.

Thrift, R.R. (1977) 'How chain ownership affects editorial vigor of newspapers', *Journalism Quarterly*, 54: 327–331.

Thussu, D.K. (2007) 'The "Murdochization" of news? The case of Star TV in India', *Media, Culture & Society*, 29(4): 593–611.

Thussu, D.K. (2009a) *The News as Entertainment: The Rise of Global Infotainment*. London: Sage.

Thussu, D.K. (2009b) *Internationalizing Media Studies*. Abingdon: Routledge.

Tomlinson, J. (1999) *The Globalisation of Culture*. Cambridge: Polity Press.

Tosoni, S. and Ridell, S. (2016) 'Decentering media studies, verbing the audience: methodological considerations concerning people's uses of media in urban space', *International Journal of Communication*, 10: 1277–1293.

Trenaman, J.S.M. (1967) *Communication and Comprehension*. London: Longman.

Trenaman, J.S.M. and McQuail, D. (1961) *Television and the Political Image*. London: Methuen.

Treré, E., Jeppesen, S. and Mattoni, A. (2017) 'Comparing digital protest media imaginaries: anti-austerity movements in Spain, Italy and Greece', *triple*, 15(2): 404–422.

Tuchman, G. (1971) 'Objectivity as strategic ritual: an examination of newsmen's notions of objectivity', *American Journal of Sociology*, 77(4): 660–679.

Tuchman, G. (1978) *Making News: A Study in the Construction of Reality*. New York: Free Press.

Tuchman, G., Daniels, A.K. and Benet, J. (eds) (1978) *Hearth and Home: Images of Women in Mass Media*. New York: Oxford University Press.

Tufekci, Z. (2008) 'Grooming, gossip, Facebook and Myspace', *Information, Communication & Society*, 11(4): 544–564.

Tulloch, J. and Middleweek, B. (2017) *Real Sex Films: The New Intimacy and Risk in Cinema*. Oxford: Oxford University Press.

Tumber, H. and Palmer, J. (2004) *Media at War: the Iraq Crisis*. London: Sage.

Tumber, H. and Waisbord, S. (2004) 'Political scandals and media across democracies', *American Behavioral Scientist*, 47(8): 1031–1039.

Tunstall, J. (1971) *Journalists at Work*. London: Constable.

Tunstall, J. (1977) *The Media Are American*. London: Constable.

Tunstall, J. (1991) 'A media industry perspective', in J. Anderson (ed.), *Communication Yearbook 14*, pp. 163–186. Newbury Park, CA: Sage.

Tunstall, J. (2007) *The Media Were American*. Oxford: Oxford University Press.

Tunstall, J. and Machin, D. (1999) *The Anglo-American Media Connection*. Oxford: Oxford University Press.

Tunstall, J. and Palmer, M. (eds) (1991) *Media Moguls*. Abingdon: Routledge.

Turkle, S. (2011) *Alone Together*. New York: Basic Books.

Turner, B. (2003) 'McDonaldization: linearity and liquidity in consumer cultures', *American Behavioral Scientist*, 47(2): 137–153.

Turow, J. (1994) 'Hidden conflicts and journalistic norms: the case of self-coverage', *Journal of Communication*, 44(2): 29–46.

Turow, J. (2005) 'Audience construction and culture production', *The Annals of the American Academy of Political and Social Sciences*, 597: 103–121.

Turow, J. (2009) *Media Today: An Introduction to Mass Communication*, 3rd edition. New York and Abingdon: Routledge.

Turow, J. and Draper, N. (2014) 'Industry conceptions of audience in the digital space', *Cultural Studies*, 28(4): 643–656.

Twenge, J. (2017) *iGen*. New York: Atria/Simon & Schuster.

Ugboajah, F. (1986) 'Communication as technology in African rural development', *Africa Media Review*, 1(1): 1–19.

UNESCO (1980) *Many Voices One World*. London: Kogan Page.

Usher, N. and Carlson, M. (2018) 'The midlife crisis of the network society', *Media and Communication*, 6(4): 107–110.

Vaccari, C. (2008a) 'Italian parties' websites in the 2006 election', *European Journal of Communication*, 23(1): 69–77.

Vaccari, C. (2008b) 'From the air to the ground: the internet in the 2004 US presidential election campaign', *New Media and Society*, 10(4): 647–665.

Valkenburg, P.M. (2017) 'Understanding self-effects in social media', *Human Communication Research*, 43: 477–490.

Valkenburg, P.M. and Peter, J. (2013a) 'Five challenges for the future of media-effects research', *International Journal of Communication*, 7: 197–215.

Valkenburg, P.M. and Peter, J. (2013b) 'The differential susceptibility to media effects model', *Journal of Communication*, 63: 221–243.

Valkenburg, P.M., Peter, J. and Walther, J.B. (2016) 'Media effects: theory and research', *Annual Review of Psychology*, 67(1): 315–338.

Valkenburg, P.M. and Piotrowksi, J. (2017) *Plugged In: How Media Attract and Affect Youth*. New Haven, CT: Yale University Press.

van Cuilenburg, J.J. (1987) 'The information society: some trends and implications', *European Journal of Communication*, 2(1): 105–121.

van Cuilenburg, J.J. and McQuail, D. (2003) 'Media policy paradigm shifts', *European Journal of Communication*, 18(2): 181–207.

Van den Putte, B. and Dhondt, G. (2005) 'Developing successful communication strategies: a test of an integrated framework for effective communication', *Journal of Applied Social Psychology*, 35: 2399–2420.

van der Wurf, R. (2004) 'Supplying and viewing diversity: the role of competition and viewer choice in Dutch broadcasting', *European Journal of Communication*, 19(2): 215–237.

Van Deursen, A. and Helsper, E. (2015) 'The third-level digital divide: who benefits most from being online?', in *Communication and Information Technologies Annual. Digital Distinctions and Inequalities: Studies in Media and Communications*, vol. 10, pp. 29–52. Bingley, UK: Emerald Group Publishing, https://doi.org/10.1108/S2050-206020150000010002.

Van Dijck, J. (2013) *The Culture of Connectivity: A Critical History of Social Media*. Oxford: Oxford University Press.

Van Dijck, J., Poell, T. and De Waal, M. (2018) *The Platform Society*. Oxford: Oxford University Press.

Van Dijk, J.A.G.M. (1992) *De Netwerk Maatschappij*. Houten, NL: Bohm Staffen von Loghum.

Van Dijk, J.A.G.M. (2005) *The Network Society: Social Aspects of New Media*, 2nd edition. London: Sage.

van Dijk, T. (1983) 'Discourse analysis: its development and application to the structure of news', *Journal of Communication*, 33(3): 20–43.

van Dijk, T. (1985) *Discourse and Communication*. Berlin: de Gruyter.

van Dijk, T. (1991) *Racism and the Press*. Abingdon: Routledge.

van Dijk, T. (2011) 'Discourse studies and hermeneutics', *Discourse Studies*, 13(5): 609–621.

Van Gorp, B. (2005) 'What is the frame? Victims and intruders in the Belgian press coverage of the asylum issue', *European Journal of Communication*, 20(4): 484–507.

van Zoonen, L. (1991) 'Feminist perspectives on the media', in J. Curran and M. Gurevitch (eds), *Mass Media and Society*, pp. 33–51. London: Arnold Edward.

van Zoonen, L. (1994) *Feminist Media Studies*. London: Sage.

van Zoonen, L. (1998) 'A professional, unreliable, heroic marionette (M/F): structure, agency and subjectivity in contemporary journalisms', *European Journal of Cultural Studies*, 1(1): 123–143.

van Zoonen, L. (1999) *Media, cultuur en burgerschap*. Amsterdam: Het Spinhuis.

Vartanova, E. (2002) 'The digital divide and the changing political/media environment of post-socialist Russia', *International Communication Gazette*, 64(5): 449–645.

Verhoeven, D., Coate, B. and Zemaityte, V. (2019) 'Re-distributing gender in the global film industry: beyond #MeToo and #MeThree', *Media Industries*, 6(1): 135–155.

Vincent, R. and Nordenstreng, K. (eds) (2016) *Towards Equity in Global Communication?*, 2nd edition. New York: Hampton Press.

Voltmer, K. (2000) 'Constructing political reality in Russia. *Izvestya* – between old and new journalistic practices', *European Journal of Communication*, 15(4): 469–500.

von Feilitzen, C. (1976) 'The functions served by the mass media', in J.W. Brown (ed.), *Children and Television*, pp. 90–115. London: Collier-Macmillan.

Vos, T.P. and Craft, S. (2017) 'The discursive construction of journalistic transparency', *Journalism Studies*, 18(12): 1505–1522.

Vyncke, P. (2002) 'Lifestyle segmentation', *European Journal of Communication*, 17(4): 445–464.

Wahl-Jorgensen, K. (2006) 'How not to found a field: new evidence on the origins of mass communication research' *Journal of Communication*, 54(3): 547–564.

Wahl-Jorgensen, K. (2009) 'News production, ethnography, and power: on the challenges of newsroom-centricity', in E. Bird (ed.), *Journalism and Antropology*, pp. 21–35. Bloomington, IN: Indiana University Press.

Wahl-Jorgensen, K. (2019) 'Questioning the ideal of the public sphere: the emotional turn', *Social Media + Society*, https://doi.org/10.1177/2056305119852175

Waisbord, S. (1998) 'When the cart of media is put before the horse of identity: a critique of technology-centered views on globalization', *Communication Research*, 25(4): 377–398.

Waisbord, S. (2000) *Watchdog Journalism in South America*. New York: Columbia University Press.

Waisbord, S. (2014) 'United and fragmented: communication and media studies in Latin America', *Journal of Latin American Communication Research*, 4(1): 1–23.

Waisbord, S. (2019) *The Communication Manifesto*. Cambridge: Polity Press.

Waisbord, S. and Mellado, C. (2014) 'De-westernizing communication studies: a reassessment', *Communication Theory*, 24: 361–372.

Waldfogel, J. (2012) 'Copyright protection, technological change, and the quality of new products: evidence from recorded music since Napster', *Journal of Law and Economics*, 55: 715–740.

Walgrave, S. and van Aelst, P. (2006) 'The contingency effect of the mass media's agenda setting', *Journal of Communication*, 56(1): 88–109.

Wallis, D. (1997) 'Just click no', *The New Yorker*, 13 January, p. 28.

Wallis, R. and Baran, S. (1990) *The World of Broadcast News*. Abingdon: Routledge.

Walter, N., Cody, M.J. and Ball-Rokeach, S.J. (2018) 'The ebb and flow of communication research: seven decades of publication trends and research priorities', *Journal of Communication*, 68(2): 424–440.

Walther, J.B. and Valkenburg, P. (2017) 'Merging mass and interpersonal communication via interactive communication technology', *Human Communication Research*, 43: 415–423.

Wang, R. and Sundar, S.S. (2018) 'How does parallax scrolling influence user experience? A test of TIME (Theory of Interactive Media Effects)', *International Journal of Human–Computer Interaction*, 34(6): 533–543.

Ward, S. (2005) *The Invention of Journalism Ethics: The Path to Objectivity and Beyond*. Montreal: McGill-Queen's University Press.

Warhurst, C., Thompson, P. and Lockyer, C. (2005) *From Conception to Consumption: Myopic Analysis of the Creative Industries*. Available at: www.hrm.strath.ac.uk/ILPC/2005/conf-papers/Warhurst-Thompson-Lockyer.pdf.

Warner, W.L. and Henry, W.E. (1948) 'The radio day-time serial: a symbolic analysis', *Psychological Monographs*, 37(1): 7–13, 55–64.

Wartella, E., Olivarez, A. and Jennings, N. (1998) 'Children and television violence in the United States', in U. Carlsson and C. von Feilitzen (eds), *Children and Media Violence*, pp. 55–62. Göteborg: University of Göteborg.

Wasko, J. (2004) 'The political economy of communication', in J.D.H. Downing, D. McQuail, P. Schlesinger and E. Wartella (eds), *The SAGE Handbook of Media Studies*, pp. 309–330. Thousand Oaks, CA: Sage.

Wasserman, H. (2010) 'Freedom's just another word? Perspectives on media freedom and responsibility in South Africa and Namibia', *International Communication Gazette*, 72(7): 567–588.

Wasserman, H. (2018) 'Power, meaning and geopolitics: ethics as an entry point for global communication studies', *Journal of Communication*, 68: 441–451.

Wasserman, H. (2020) 'Moving from diversity to transformation in communication scholarship', *Annals of the International Communication Association*, 44(1): 1–3.

Wasserman, H. and Rao, S. (2008) 'The glocalization of journalism ethics', *Journalism*, 9(2): 163–181.

Weaver, D. (ed.) (1998) *The Global Journalist*. Cresskill, NJ: Hampton Press.

Weaver, D. (2007) 'Thoughts on agenda setting, framing, and priming', *Journal of Communication*, 57: 142–147.

Weaver, D. and Wilhoit, C.G. (1986) *The American Journalist*. Bloomington, IN: University of Indiana Press.

Weaver, D. and Wilhoit, C.G. (1996) *The American Journalist in the 1990s: US News People at the End of an Era*. Mahwah, NJ: Erlbaum.

Weber, M. (1948) 'Politics as a vocation', in H. Gerth and C.W. Mills (eds), *Max Weber: Essays*. Abingdon: Routledge and Kegan Paul.

Weber, M. (1964) *Theory of Social and Economic Organization*. Ed. T. Parsons. New York: Free Press.

Webster, F. (1995) *Images of the Information Society*. Abingdon: Routledge.

Webster, F. (2002) 'The information society revisited', in L.A. Lievrouw and S. Livingstone (eds), *The Handbook of New Media*, pp. 22–33. London: Sage.

Webster, J.G. and Wakshlag, J.J. (1983) 'A theory of TV program choice', *Communication Research*, 10(4): 430–446.

Weibull, L. (1985) 'Structural factors in gratifications research', in K.E. Rosengren, P. Palmgreen and L. Wenner (eds), *Media Gratification Research: Current Perspectives*, pp. 123–47. Beverly Hills, CA: Sage.

Weimann, G., Weiss-Blatt, N., Mengistu, G., Mazor Tregerman, M. and Oren, R. (2014) 'Reevaluating "The End of Mass Communication?", *Mass Communication and Society*, 17(6): 803–829.

Weischenberg, S. (1992) *Journalistik: Theorie und Praxis aktueller Medienkommunikation. Vol. 1: Mediensysteme, Medienethik, Medieninstitutionen*. Opladen: Westdeutscher Verlag.

Wellman, B. (2002) 'Little boxes, glocalization, and networked individualism', in M. Tanabe, P. Van den Besselaar and T. Ishida (eds), *Digital Cities II*, pp. 10–25. Berlin: Springer.

Westerstahl, J. (1983) 'Objective news reporting', *Communication Research*, 10(3): 403–424.

Westley, B. and MacLean, M. (1957) 'A conceptual model for mass communication research', *Journalism Quarterly*, 34: 31–38.

Westlund, O. and Ekström, M. (2019) 'News organizations', in K. Wahl-Jorgensen and T. Hanitzsch (eds), *Handbook of Journalism Studies*, pp. 135–166. Abingdon: Routledge.

Wharton, A.S. (2009) 'The sociology of emotional labor', *Annual Review of Sociology*, 35(1): 147–165.

White, D.M. (1950) 'The gatekeeper: a case-study in the selection of news', *Journalism Quarterly*, 27: 383–390.

Wildman, S.S. (1991) 'Explaining trade in films and programs', *Journal of Communication*, 41: 190–192.

Wilensky, H. (1964) 'Mass society and mass culture: interdependence or independence?', *American Sociological Review*, 29(2): 173–197.

Wilke, J. (1995) 'Agenda-setting in a historical perspective: the coverage of the American revolution in the German press (1773–83)', *European Journal of Communication*, 10(1): 63–86.

Willems, W. (2014) 'Provincializing hegemonic histories of media and communication studies: toward a genealogy of epistemic resistance in Africa', *Communication Theory*, 24: 415–434.

Williams, D. (2006) 'Virtual cultivation: online worlds, offline perceptions', *Journal of Communication*, 56: 69–87.

Williams, D., Martins, N., Consalvo, M. and Ivory, J.D. (2009) 'The virtual census: representations of gender, race and age in video games', *New Media and Society*, 11(5): 815–834.

Williams, R. (1961) *Culture and Society*. Harmondsworth: Penguin.

Williams, R. (1975) *Television, Technology and Cultural Form*. London: Fontana.

Williamson, J. (1978) *Decoding Advertisements*. London: Boyars.

Willnat, L., Weaver, D.H. and Choi, J. (2013) 'The global journalist in the twenty-first century', *Journalism Practice*, 7(2): 163–183.

Windahl, S., Signitzer, B. and Olson, J. (2007) *Using Communication Theory*, 2nd edition. London: Sage.

Winseck, D. (2002) 'Wired cities and transnational communications', in L.A. Lievrouw and S. Livingstone (eds), *The Handbook of New Media*, pp. 393–409. London: Sage.

Winseck, D. (2016) 'Reconstructing the political economy of communication for the digital media age', *The Political Economy of Communication* 4(2): 73–114.

Winseck, D. (2019) 'Media concentration in the age of the internet and mobile phones', in M. Deuze and M. Prenger (eds), *Making Media: Production, Practices and Professions*, pp. 175–192. Amsterdam: Amsterdam University Press.

Winston, B. (1986) *Misunderstanding Media*. Cambridge, MA: Harvard University Press.

Witschge, T., Deuze, M. and Willemsen, S. (2019) 'Creativity in (digital) journalism studies: broadening our perspective on journalism practice', *Digital Journalism*, 7(7): 972–979.

Wittel, A. (2001) 'Toward a network sociality', *Theory, Culture & Society*, 18(6): 51–76.

Wodak, R. and Meyer, M. (eds) (2001) *Methods of Critical Discourse Analysis*. London: Sage.

Woitowicz, K.J. and Gadini, S.L. (2018) 'Folkcommunication and social group strategies: aspects of public opinion in the mass media society', *Sphera Publica*, 2(18): 117–131.

Wojdynski, B.W. and Evans, N.J. (2016) 'Going native: effects of disclosure position and language on the recognition and evaluation of online native advertising', *Journal of Advertising*, 45(2): 157–168.

Wolfenstein, M. and Leites, N. (1947) 'An analysis of themes and plots in motion pictures', *Annals of the American Academy of Political and Social Sciences*, 254: 41–48.

Womack, B. (1981) 'Attention maps of ten major newspapers', *Journalism Quarterly*, 58(2): 260–265.

Wright, C.R. (1960) 'Functional analysis and mass communication', *Public Opinion Quarterly*, 24: 606–620.

Wright, C.R. (1974) 'Functional analysis and mass communication revisited', in J.G. Blumler and E. Katz (eds), *The Uses of Mass Communications*, pp. 197–212. Beverly Hills, CA: Sage.

Wright, K. (2018) *Who's Reporting Africa Now? Non-Governmental Organizations, Journalists, and Multimedia*. New York: Peter Lang.

Wu, H.D. (2003) 'Homogeneity around the world? Comparing the systemic determinants of international news flow between developed and developing countries', *International Communication Gazette*, 65(1): 9–24.

Wu, H.D. (2007) 'A brave new world for international news? Exploring the determinants of foreign news on US websites', *International Communication Gazette*, 69(6): 539–552.

Yang, J. and Grabe, M.E. (2011) 'Knowledge acquisition gaps: a comparison of print versus online news sources', *New Media and Society*, 13(8): 1211–1227.

Yay, H., Ranasubranuanian, S. and Oliver, M.B. (2008) 'Cultivation effect on quality of life indicators', *Journal of Broadcasting and Electronic Media*, 52(2): 247–267.

Yee, N., Bailenson, J.N. and Ducheneaut, N. (2009) 'The Proteus effect: implications of transformed digital self-representation on online and offline behavior', *Communication Research*, 36(2): 285–312.

Yoon, Y. (2005) 'Legitimacy, public relations and media access', *Communication Research*, 32(6): 762–793.

Zaller, J.R. (1997) 'A model of communication effects at the outbreak of the Gulf War', in S. Iyengar and R. Reeves (eds), *Do the Media Govern?*, pp. 296–311. Thousand Oaks, CA: Sage.

Zayani, M. (2015) *Networked Publics and Digital Contention*. Oxford: Oxford University Press.

Zeno-Zencovich, V. (2008) *Freedom of Expression*. Abingdon: Routledge.

Zuboff, S. (2019) *The Age of Surveillance Capitalism*. London: Profile Books.

# AUTHOR INDEX

Quandt, T., 366, 486

Radway, J., 408, 423–4, 427, 482, 489
Rains, S.A., 507
Rakow, L., 377
Ranasubranuanian, S., 537
Rasmussen, T., 181–2
Raven, B.H., 526–7
Ray, M.L., 525
Rayburn, J.D., 473
Real, M., 427
Reese, S.D., 307–8, 309, 323, 548
Reeves, Byron, 545
Renckstorf, K., 471
Rice, R.E., 176, 183
Riddle, K., 514, 527
Robinson, J.P., 548
Roe, K., 291
Roefs, W., 551
Roessler, P., 541
Rogers, E.M., 87, 133, 547, 548
Rosen, Jay, 423
Rosengren, K.E., 105–6, 107–8, 485, 486–7, 537
Roser, C., 526
Rössler, P., 537
Rothenbuhler, E.W., 479
Rowley, K.M., 451
Ruge, M., 289, 350
Russ-Mohl, S., 319
Ryan, J., 328, 359–60, 363–5

Saenz, M.K., 478
Saito, S., 537
Sardar, Ziauddin, 166
Scannell, P., 171
Schement, J., 133
Scheufele, D.A., 179–80, 393, 533, 550–1
Schlesinger, P., 293, 326, 423, 426
Schmidt, J.-H., 365–6
Schmidt, S.J., 407
Schoenbach, K., 561
Schramm, W., 264
Schuck, A.R.T., 551
Schudson, M., 320, 321
Schultz, J., 326
Schulz, A., 541
Schulz, W., 387
Schutz, Alfred, 131
Schwalber, C.B., 417
Scolari, C.A., 410
Scott, A., 343
Seiter, E., 558

Selwyn, N., 195
Sepstrup, P., 285–6
Serra, M., 453
Sezgin, M., 355
Shanahan, J., 536, 538, 540
Shannon, C., 86
Shaw, D.L., 547
Shoemaker, P.J., 307–8, 309, 323, 348
Siebert, F., 264
Sigelman, L., 334
Signitzer, B., 320
Signorielli, N., 534, 536, 538
Silcode, B.W., 417
Silverstone, Roger, 486
Simard, C., 346
Singer, J.B., 511
Slawski, E.J., 331
Smith, Adam, 376
Smith, P., 393
Smythe, Dallas, 440, 441
Snow, R.P., 356, 414, 543
Sotirovic, M., 536–7
Sparks, Colin, 206
Spears, R., 174
Sreberny-Mohammadi, A., 290, 291
Stanyer, J., 108, 141, 513
Steiner, G., 489
Steiner, Linda, 332
Stemler, S.E., 398
Strömbäck, J., 560–1
Stromer-Galley, J., 563
Sundar, S.S., 528

Tarde, Gabriel, 107
Tenenboim-Weinblatt, K., 399
Terranova, T., 76, 441
Tettey, W.J., 227
Third, A., 559
Thompson, J.B., 110, 172, 505
Thrift, R.R., 382
Thussu, D.K., 293
Trenaman, J.S.M., 547
Tuchman, G., 416
Tunstall, J., 244, 275, 277, 291, 329
Turkle, Sherry, 192
Turner, B., 349
Turow, J., 328, 334

Uldam, J., 322

Vaccari, C., 180
Valkenburg, Patti, 28

# SUBJECT INDEX

books, 33–6, 55, 58–9, 71, 259, 271
boomerang effect, 520
boundary conditions, 515
Brexit, 561
broadcasting, 43–7, 55, 73, 80, 127, 174, 184, 244, 589
broadcasting councils, 228–9
broadcasting model, 258tab, 259–60
burglar alarm standard, 218

cable, 43, 55, 58, 59, 188, 190, 192, 212, 250, 260, 272, 494, 537
campaigns, 71, 589
canonical audience, 456
catharsis, 556, 589
causation, 9
celebrity, 96, 589
censorship, 32, 35, 39, 56, 192, 207, 259, 490, 541, 555, 589
Center on Everyday Lives of Families, 486
Centre for Contemporary Cultural Studies, 150–1
Chicago School, 71, 150
children, 556–9
China
    film as propaganda, 42
    Internet, 182
    national cyber-sovereignty, 254
    press ownership, 323–4
cinema, 42–3, 78, 163–4, 249, 259, 272, 422, 452, 456, 476
    *see also* film
circuit of culture, 543–4
civil society, 178, 251, 255, 260, 298, 589–90
clientelism, 265
ClimateStrike, 517, 549, 581
clustering, 343–4, 353, 357, 360
codes, 73, 422, 590
cognitive dissonance, 590
collective identity, 293
commercialization, 158–61, 166, 590
commodification, 127, 149, 159, 241, 590–1
common carrier model, 258tab, 260, 261
common-sense theory, 17–18
communication, 18–22, 145–8, 591
communication networks, 19–23
communication technology, 161–5
communication technology determinism, 133–6, 613
    *see also* technological determinism
communicative power, 188, 518
communism, 85, 121, 195, 275, 282, 451, 517
communitarianism, 124, 178
communities of interest, 190

community, 71, 189–92, 294, 591
competition, 127, 249, 254, 271, 275, 603
computer-mediated communication, 18, 187, 191, 192, 583, 591
concentration, 127, 248–55, 271, 275, 603
connectivity, 339, 340, 353–4, 486, 591–2
connotation, 390–1
constructionism, 592
consultation pattern, 187, 188, 189fig
consumer markets, 240
content *see* media content
content analysis, 91, 375, 386, 388, 393, 592
    *see also* qualitative content analysis; quantitative content analysis
content management systems, 345–6, 347
control, 55–7
control revolution, 194
convergence, 20, 54, 59, 62, 77, 80, 127, 135–6, 173–4, 176, 184, 192, 198, 237, 253, 254, 258, 259, 260, 263, 275, 339, 341, 345, 346–7, 367, 392, 578, 582, 592
convergence culture, 365, 367, 592–3
conversation pattern, 187, 188, 189fig
copyright, 35, 62, 164, 175, 253, 593
Copyright Directive (2019) (EU), 253
correspondence assumption, 386–7
cost structure, 244–6
creative industries, 310–11
crime, 71, 73, 130, 535–6, 552
critical cultural theory, 147, 149–51, 155, 607, 612
    *see also* cultural theory
critical dependency model, 282
critical discourse analysis *see* discourse analysis
critical theory, 13, 91, 97, 120, 132, 147, 149, 219, 282, 376, 509, 534, 577, 593, 612
    *see also* critical cultural theory
crossmedia, 409
crowd, 78, 439
cultivation theory, 513, 534, 554, 593
cultural approaches, 24, 446tab, 513
cultural capital, 83, 154, 476
cultural change, 542–7
cultural citizenship, 157–8
cultural imperialism, 107, 272, 281–2, 283, 284, 293, 593
cultural industries, 310–11
cultural order, 220–1
cultural studies, 81, 83, 90, 145, 154, 445–6, 594
cultural text, 419–20, 428
cultural theory, 16, 379
    *see also* critical cultural theory
culturalist perspective, 14, 15, 145, 156, 446

fragmentation, 118, 120, 181, 376, 479, 494–5, 597
framing, 522, 550–1, 597
framing analysis, 415–17
franchising, 238–9, 260, 480
Frankfurt School, 89, 148–9, 153, 375, 534, 597
free press model, 258–9
freedom of expression, 55–7, 116, 120, 178, 198, 204, 206–8, 221–2, 256, 257, 271, 296, 320, 381–2, 490, 597
freedom of the press, 35, 38, 80, 116, 206–9, 215, 222–3, 256, 259, 381–2, 597–8
free-flow model, 282, 288
full news standard, 218
functionalism, 86, 89, 128–31, 142, 219, 387, 469

games *see* digital games
gatekeeping, 111, 175, 287, 347–53, 542, 598
gender
    audience, 482–3
    mass media, 155–8
    media communicators, 331–3
    media content, 377–8
    media texts, 427–8
    stereotyping, 380
    texts, 427–8
General Aggression Model, 553
General Agreement on Tariffs and Trade (GATT), 253
General Data Protection Regulation (GDPR), 181, 296
genres
    definition, 598
    encoding, 98
    examples of, 407–11
    genre analysis, 406, 407, 411–12, 413–14, 417, 419
    involving audience participation, 365
    overview, 405–7
    types of, 239, 412–13
Global Kids Online, 486
globalization, 21, 42, 54, 82, 107, 140–1, 148, 164, 167, 194, 253, 254, 262, 271–4, 275, 277, 279–80, 282, 283–5, 292–6, 561, 579, 598
glocalization, 284, 341
Google, 53, 61, 96, 138, 231, 251, 253, 254, 325, 454, 508
gossip, 289, 598
governance, 10, 255–8, 261, 296–8, 598
gratification set, 451–2
GSM (Global System for Mobile communications) phones, 59

harm, 222, 224, 256, 257, 379, 558
hegemony, 86, 126, 376, 598–9
high culture, 81
hourglass effect, 247, 277, 312
human interest, 39–40, 160, 289, 599
hybridization, 148, 599
hyperlocal media, 451
hypersociality, 294

ICANN (International Corporation for Assigned Names and Numbers), 297
icons, 391–2, 599
identity, 10, 72, 105, 108, 148, 485, 599
ideology, 89, 90, 134, 148, 150–1, 376, 513, 521, 599
imperialism, 282, 283, 284, 285
income sources, 240–3, 244
indexation theory, 266–7
indigenous culture, 81–2
inequality, 85, 92, 114
    *see also* social inequality
information, 73, 214–18, 599–600
information economy, 127, 136, 138
information society, 136–9, 142, 171, 600
information theory, 86
infotainment, 160, 293, 412, 600
inscribed reader, 421, 600
Instagram, 138, 593
interaction potential, 486–7
interactivity, 59, 60, 111, 175, 184, 185–6, 187, 600
interest groups, 321–2
International Corporation for Assigned Names and Numbers (ICANN), 297
International Covenant on Civil and Political Rights, 221–2
International Panel on Social Progress, 121–2
International Telecommunication Union, 297
International Telegraph Union, 296
internationalization, 237, 263, 271, 272–3, 276–7, 284, 285, 293, 493
Internet
    audiences, 441
    China, 182
    control of, 56, 57
    dangers of, 74
    diversity of markets, 243–4
    globalization, 272–3
    governance, 261
    interactivity, 59
    as medium, 53–4
    as news source, 38
    novel features of, 174–5

Marxist critiques, 375–6, 378
media performance discourse, 379–88
mixed methods research, 399–401
objectivity, 383–5
overview, 373
qualitative content analysis, 393–5, 396, 399–401
quality, 378–9
quantitative content analysis, 394–5, 397–401
rationale for studying, 373–5
research methods, 393–401
semiology/semiotics, 388–92, 393, 394, 399
structuralism, 388, 389, 391, 392, 393, 394, 399
violence, 377
media domestication theory, 486
media effects
addiction, 534, 568–9
agenda-setting hypothesis, 547–9, 561
audience, 444, 446tab
boundary conditions, 515
children and young people, 556–9
communicative power, 518
cultivation theory, 513, 534, 554, 593
Differential Susceptibility to Media Effects
    Model, 514–15
four models, 516
framing, 550–1
levels and kinds of, 518–20
mediating conditions of, 525–6
overview, 505–7, 533
political communication, 560–7
priming, 549–50, 553
processes, 520–3
research and theory, 506, 507–17, 527–8, 533–4
social and cultural change, 542–7
source-receiver relations, 526–7
spiral of silence theory, 513, 539–42, 612
stimulus-response theory, 524–5
violence, 552–6
media equation theory, 545
media life, 100, 514, 607
media logic, 96, 113, 263, 356, 414, 543, 549,
    564–5, 603–4
media organizations
clustering, 353
cultural and creative industries, 310–11
gatekeeping, 347–53
goals of, 315–16
key issues, 307–10
media communicators, 330–3
relations with advertisers, 324–5
relations with audiences, 325–8
relations with owners, 322–4

relations with pressure and interest groups, 321–2
relations with society, 314–21
research on, 305–6
role conflicts, 333–4
role dilemmas, 334–5
and social forces, 313–14
structure, 311–12, 329
media orientation, 467, 468fig, 471, 477
media performance discourse, 379–88
media production
access, 353–5
advertising, 357–8
audience participation, 365–7
clustering, 343–4, 357, 360
decision-making, 363–5
digital games, 361–3
features of, 340–3
film and television, 360–1
journalism, 358–9
keys trends in, 343–7
management, 344–5
music and recording, 359–60
organisation of, 356–63
overview, 339–40
technology, 345–7
media specific analysis, 545
media studies, 18, 19, 69, 89, 140, 292, 296, 423,
    477, 509, 546, 575, 583
media-centred approaches, 133, 142
media-centric approaches, 14, 15, 15fig, 23, 24, 120,
    133, 142, 306, 322, 443
media-cultural theory, 145, 147–8
media-culturalist perspective, 15
media-materialist approach, 15
media-person interactions, 470
mediated authenticity, 426
mediating conditions, 525–6
mediation, 9–10, 108–13, 145
mediatization, 74, 80, 100, 139–41, 142, 184, 514,
    563–4, 565, 566, 567, 579, 604
mediatopes, 486
medium audience, 452–4
medium theory, 92, 162, 183–6, 604
MeToo, 332–3, 549, 581
Microsoft, 53, 61
micro-targeting, 355
middle-classification, 331
migrants, 72, 118, 191, 292, 386, 417, 451, 537,
    538, 562
Milano, Alyssa, 332
mixed methods research, 399–401, 446–7
modernism, 165

postmodernism, 153, 158, 165–7, 174, 607
power, 9, 53, 56, 69, 70–1, 90, 91, 92, 114–15, 124,
    134, 156, 180, 210, 281, 289, 465, 508–9, 513,
    517, 518, 526–7, 551, 607
predictive analytics, 177
preferred readings, 421
prejudice, 74, 608
presentism, 171
press, 80
press councils, 228–9
pressure groups, 321–2
prestige press, 39
priming, 549–50, 553, 608
print media, 31–2, 33–41, 134, 174, 259, 345
privacy, 164
privatization, 260, 262, 297
product placement, 242
production *see* media production
production logic, 356
produser, 367, 592
professionalism, 229–30
professions, 608
project ecologies, 357
propaganda, 41–2, 70, 132, 180, 257, 508, 511, 522,
    523, 561, 566, 608
prosumer, 367, 592
psychoanalytic perspectives, 24, 156, 378, 400
psychographics, 481
public interest, 58, 61, 193, 203–5, 223, 228, 236,
    248–9, 260, 261, 381, 609
public opinion, 70, 609
public ownership, 246, 248, 259
public relations, 71, 609
public responsibility, 228–9
public service broadcasting, 45, 73, 209, 215–16,
    244, 257, 259–60, 262–3, 609–10
public sphere, 110, 117, 124, 158, 178, 610
public values, 609
publication, 79, 609
publicity model, 95–6, 98–9, 101
publics, 8, 78, 439, 450–1, 478, 608
publishers, 175, 176

qualitative content analysis, 393–5, 396–7, 399–401
qualitative research, 90, 91, 515
quality, 154, 378–9
Quality Assessment of Broadcasting, 378–9, 381
quantitative content analysis, 394–5, 396, 397–401

radical media, 451
radio, 44, 46–7, 55, 57, 58, 73, 78, 134, 192, 259,
    272, 444, 469

ratings, 441, 456
rationalization, 165
reach, 456–8
real virtuality, 167
realism, 425–6
reality television, 160, 410, 412, 441, 579
reception analysis, 97, 406, 445–6, 610
reception model, 97–9
recorded music, 47–9
registration pattern, 187–8, 189fig
regulation, 194, 227, 237, 257, 258–62, 263
    broadcasting model, 258tab, 259–60
    common carrier model, 258tab, 260, 261
    free press model, 258–9
    international, 296
    Internet, 261–2
    new media, 580
    *see also* deregulation
relational aggression, 552, 553, 554
remediation, 162
research
    alternative paradigm, 88–92
    audience, 442–7
    dominant paradigm, 84–8, 91–2, 93, 101
    integrated model, 99–100
    Internet, 580
    media effects, 506, 527–8, 533–4
    media organizations, 305–6
    mixed methods, 399–401, 446–7
    qualitative content analysis, 393–5,
        396–7, 399–401
    quantitative content analysis, 394–5,
        396, 397–401
Reuters, 277
rhetoric, 610
ritual model, 94–5, 98–9, 100fig, 101, 145, 160, 189
romances, 423–4, 427, 482
Russia, 33, 38, 120, 150, 195, 265, 267, 272, 277,
    423, 508, 560

satellite television, 58, 59, 272, 273, 291–2
schemas, 610
script theory, 553, 610
search engines, 184, 607
Second World War, 70, 262, 271, 272, 277, 451
second-person effect, 541
segmentation, 161, 494, 610
self, media, 544–5
semiology/semiotics, 97, 152–3, 388–92, 393, 394,
    399, 410, 610–11
semiotic power, 153
seriality, 423–5

serials, 424–5
signification, 145, 375–6, 388, 389, 390
sleeper effect, 520
smart cities, 190–1
smartphones, 96, 110, 117, 133, 184, 438, 453, 484,
    505, 513, 528, 534, 568, 580
soap operas, 72, 98, 157, 408–9, 425, 427,
    469, 482, 611
    see also telenovelas
sociability, 483–8
social action model, 471
social atomization, 447–8
social capital, 117
social change, 120–2, 182, 542–7
social constructionism, 131–2, 140–1, 142
social constructivist perspective, 512–13
social documentaries, 41
social inequality, 195–7, 387
    see also inequality
social integration, 69, 71–2, 116–19, 130,
    181–2, 523
social interaction, 483–8
social isolation, 484, 487, 542, 557
social learning theory, 549, 553, 557
social media, 53, 54, 56, 58, 59, 71, 117, 121, 184,
    400, 538, 540, 541, 568, 569, 579, 580
social networking sites, 184, 611
social order, 218–20
social reality, 9
social responsibility, 611
social scientific theory, 16
social-culturalist perspective, 15
socialization, 126, 155, 523, 538, 611
social-materialist perspective, 15
society
    and culture relations, 105–7, 108
    definition, 105
    and media, 112–14
society-centric approaches, 306
socio-centric approaches, 14, 15, 23, 142, 322
software, 147
solidarity, 219fig, 220
source-receiver relations, 526–7
space, 122–3, 134, 182
spatial turn, 122
speculative work, 357–8
spin, 97, 99
spin doctors, 566, 611
spiral of silence theory, 513, 539–42, 612
Star Wars, 409, 410, 455
statistical analysis, 86
stereotyping, 84, 155, 378, 380, 386, 427, 612

stimulus-response theory, 87, 518, 524–5, 612
streaming services, 43, 45, 46, 47, 48, 58,
    273, 360
structural approaches, 23–4, 401, 446tab, 466–8,
    487, 513
structuralism, 388, 389, 391, 392, 393, 394, 399
subcultures, 480
subscription-based models, 243
substitutability, 454
superstructure, 149, 150
surveillance, 125, 129, 180, 181, 188, 193,
    194, 580–1
surveillance capitalism, 160, 194
Swedish Media Panel, 485
symbolic cannibalism, 292
symbolic interactionism, 90, 131, 471
symmetrical mediated interaction, 172–3
synergy, 252

tabloidization, 40, 160, 244, 612
talk show, 410
taste culture, 452, 613
technogenesis, 135
technological determinism, 120, 135, 136,
    183, 194, 330, 604
    see also communication technology
        determinism
technology, 345–7
telecommunications, 20, 26, 55, 181, 188, 237, 253,
    261, 263, 274
Telegram, 184
telenovelas, 33–41, 72, 408, 611
    see also soap operas
television, 42, 44–6, 55, 56, 57, 58, 72,
    73, 134, 163–4, 192, 259, 272, 273–4,
    285–6, 287–8, 354–5, 360–1, 409, 412,
    441, 466, 534–7
Tencent, 53, 61, 239, 251, 254, 275
terrorism, 10, 74, 86, 92, 130, 423
    see also war on terror
texts, 391, 393, 394
    concept of, 420–1
    encoding and decoding, 421
    gender, 427–8
    intertextuality, 421–2
    open versus closed, 422–3
    realism, 425–6
    seriality, 423–5
    textual analysis, 419–20
theory, 16–18, 25–6
Theory of Interactive Media Effects (TIME), 528
Third World, 85, 90, 121, 197, 275, 296

third-party effects, 541, 613
Thunberg, Greta, 517
time, 8, 122, 123, 134, 182–3
Tinder, 138, 184
Toronto School, 133–4, 162, 183, 613
trade, 290–2
transculturation, 284
transmedia genre, 409–11
transmedia properties, 239, 613
transmedia work, 582
transmission model, 86, 87, 88–9, 93–4, 95,
    97, 98, 99, 100fig, 101, 156, 160, 188,
    189, 367, 509, 543
transnationalization, 165, 285–7, 323
transparency, 216, 222
transportation model, 284
treaties, 296–7
trolling, 366
Trump, Donald, 180, 561
trustee model, 228
truth, 214, 215
Twitter, 121, 134, 138, 180, 332,
    351, 568

Uber, 138, 184
UNESCO, 288, 296, 297, 323, 555
unitarian position, 204
United National Charter, 259

United Nations, 196, 259, 296, 297, 298
United States, 48, 50, 70, 71, 85, 210, 261, 266, 272,
    274, 275, 279, 596, 602
usage, 445, 446tab, 483–8
user-generated content, 175, 315, 410, 441
uses and gratifications approach, 130, 613

violence, 377, 552–6
virtual communities, 191–2, 613
    see also online communities
virtual space, 123
visual language, 391–2

war on terror, 42, 70, 194, 266, 284, 517
    see also terrorism
WeChat, 53
westernization, 85, 281, 282
WhatsApp, 180, 184
wired community, 190
women's magazines, 482–3
World Intellectual Property Organization, 297
World Trade Organization (WTO), 253, 297
World Wide Web, 59, 279, 287, 297, 594

young people, 556–9
YouTube, 110, 127, 134, 166, 214, 251, 568

zombies, 84

CPSIA information can be obtained
at www.ICGtesting.com
Printed in the USA
FSHW020612291121
86303FS